THE EARLY WORKS OF ORESTES A. BROWNSON

VOLUME IV: THE TRANSCENDENTALIST YEARS, 1838–39

Edited by
Patrick W. Carey

MARQUETTE UNIVERSITY PRESS
2003

MARQUETTE STUDIES IN THEOLOGY NO. 34
Andrew Tallon, Series Editor

Library of Congress Cataloguing in Publication Data

Brownson, Orestes Augustus, 1803-1876.
[Selections. 2003]
The early works of Orestes A. Brownson: Volume IV: The Transcendentalist Years, 1838-39 / edited by Patrick W. Carey.
p. cm. — (Marquette studies in theology ; no. 34)
Includes indexes.
ISBN **0-87462-686-2** (v. 4: pbk. : alk. paper)
1. Philosophy. 2. Theology. I. Carey, Patrick W., 1940- II. Title.
III. Marquette studies in theology ; #34.
B908 .B612 2000
191—dc21

99-050779

Member, THE ASSOCIATION OF AMERICAN UNIVERSITY PRESSES

MARQUETTE UNIVERSITY PRESS
MILWAUKEE

The Association of Jesuit University Presses

MARQUETTE UNIVERSITY PRESS
MILWAUKEE WISCONSIN USA
2003

TABLE OF CONTENTS

ACKNOWLEDGMENTS

I am indebted to a number of persons and institutions who assisted me in the preparation and completion of this volume. As with the previous volumes, this one has been served well by excellent graduate research assistants for whose aid I am deeply grateful. I also want to thank Marquette University and the chair of my department, Philip Rossi, S.J., who has been gracious in assigning them to the project. Jeffrey Barbeau spent two years on this and previous volumes while he was my graduate research assistant. He helped format the texts and located a number of quotations. Constance Nielsen, another graduate assistant, however, was primarily responsible for guiding this volume to its completion. She identified all the biblical texts and a good number of the classical, philosophical and theological citations, proofread the text, and gave sagacious advice on the introduction. During the fall semester of 2002, when I was making final preparations for this volume, I taught at the University of Dayton. Thanks to professor Terrence Tilley, chair of the Department of Religious Studies, I had the good services of Matthew Shadle, a graduate assistant in the department, to help me proofread the gallies and prepare the indexes. Those who have done projects like this know the value of good graduate assistants.

I also am grateful to Francis Paul Prucha, S.J., professor emeritus in Màrquette University's Department of History, who not only read and provided judicious comments on chapter 15, "Our Indian Policy," but helped me identify the government sources that Brownson used in writing that essay.

During the past twenty years or so I have been collecting sources for these volumes and therefore owe thanks to a number of libraries and their staffs for multiple kindnesses and general helpfulness. I am particularly grateful to the staffs of the Archives of the University of Notre Dame, where the Brownson papers are located; Harvard University; the American Antiquarian Society (Worcester, Mass.), the Boston Public Library, and the New York Historical Society. As ever, I am most appreciative of the good cheer and responsiveness I have always received from Joan Sommers and the Reference and Interlibrary Loan staffs of Memorial Library at Marquette University. Numerous and almost constant requests over the past number of years have been met with competent and generous responses.

As in the previous volumes so also in this one, Dr. Andrew Tallon, director of Marquette University Press, has provided encouragement. His associate Joan Skocir once again has with patience accepted my numerous requests for changes in the "final" copy, and has provided competent technical assistance in preparing the manuscript for publication.

INTRODUCTION

This volume covers Brownson's writings from August of 1838 to the end of 1839, i.e., from his initial reactions to Emerson's "Divinity School Address" to the hotly-contested presidential political campaign between the Whigs and the Democrats that was just beginning to get off the ground at the end of 1839. During these years Brownson addressed four subject areas he had outlined when he introduced his *Boston Quarterly Review* in January of 1838: religion, philosophy, politics, and literature. Although he considered himself a member of the so-called "movement party"—the party of Transcendentalists, change, freedom, and progress—he was beginning to separate himself from what he considered the more radical elements within the movement party. He became much more sympathetic, too, with the values of the "stationary party"—the respect for the past achievements of church and state, the emphasis on order in society, and the value placed on continuity with tradition.

Brownson was, as he himself admitted here and there, becoming more conservative in his participation in the movement party. More than in the immediate past, he detached himself ideologically, for example, from the anti-traditionalism of some Transcendentalists like Emerson and Amos Bronson Alcott, and from the immediatism of radical abolitionists like William Lloyd Garrison. He supported, furthermore, a cool gradualism with respect to the elimination of Negro slavery and the cultural advancement of Native Americans, but with respect to the material and cultural progress of the working class he passionately called for immediate reforms in the mentality of politicians and churchmen.

On the other hand, Brownson fought tooth and nail along side the Transcendentalists in their war on Lockean epistemology and their battles with Andrews Norton's "materialist" and evidentiary approach to religion and Christianity. He battled, moreover, against the rising individualism he saw in both new school Transcendentalism and the old school British empirical tradition, and emphasized together with French social thinkers an incipient Christian socialism for church and society. Although he had repeatedly asserted that he was a no party man in politics, he became forcefully identified with the Democratic party in the campaign against the Whigs who were parading as Democrats in the hotly contested presidential election that was getting off the ground at the end of 1839. He was no literary critic, but he did articulate a Jacksonian philosophy of literature that emphasized the socially redemptive value of good literature for all American people, not just the educated elite. As editor of one of the leading intellectual journals of the day, the *Boston Quarterly Review*, he saw his role in American society primarily as that of a critic and an intellectual *provocateur*, stirring up thought in the areas of religion, philosophy, politics, and literature. But, there were unresolved tensions in his thought as he tried to work out the relationship between the self and God, subject and object, the individual and society, internal inspiration and external revelation, the present and past.

During these years, Brownson continued to be Steward of the Marine Hospital of Chelsea, a position that he obtained from George Bancroft and the Democratic patronage system. Brownson's superintendency of the Hospital gave him the financial security and indeed the freedom to manage, edit, and do most of the writing for his journal. It also gave him the kind of resources he needed to support his young family. The Brownsons had four young sons (Orestes Augustus, Jr., age 10; John Healy, age 9; William Ignatius, age 4; and Henry Francis, age 3) and on 7 June 1839 they gave birth to their only daughter, Sarah Nicolena. The five children must have been a handful for a busy thirty-five year old father. Most of the child rearing, however, more than likely belonged to Sally Healy Brownson, Orestes' thirty-four year old wife. We learn very little from Brownson's writings about the household, his wife, the children, or his relationships with any of them. He also wrote nothing in general during these years about marriage, children, and family in American society, which might have thrown some light on his own experience.

Brownson's philosophy of religion and Christianity developed during these years in the crucible of Unitarian conflicts, the most important of which revolved around Emerson's so-called Harvard "Divinity School Address" of July 1838. That Address brought the battle over Transcendentalism into full public view for the first time. The paper warfare over that address and the issues that surrounded it for the next two years helped Brownson define more clearly than previously his own views of religion and Christianity's role in a new democratic society. Since at least 1836, Brownson had supported Transcendentalism because of its spiritual dimension and its hostility to Lockean "materialist" philosophy. He began to become much more critical of the direction of the Transcendental movement after he read Emerson's address. In two essays—one published anonymously in the *Boston Post* and one published later in the *Boston Quarterly Review*—he upheld Emerson's freedom to speak his mind, but clearly separated himself from the antinomian and subjective philosophical implications of Emerson's address, and from the ahistorical direction of his view of Christianity. To some extent his reactions to Emerson's address became a defining moment in his intellectual development, as it was a critical moment in the history of American Transcendentalism.

Emerson's address to the senior class of Harvard's Divinity School was a new American call for a converted ministry, but a conversion that focused on the potentialities of divinity that resided within all human persons, not on the supernatural redemptive grace of Christ. Emerson intended to awaken the new ministerial candidates to their responsibilities to speak out of the fullness of their hearts in a language that would evoke a spiritual response from their people. In the course of the address he called for the new ministers to emancipate themselves from a spirituality that was borrowed from or imitative of that found in biblical revelation or the tradition of the church. To thine own self be true, Emerson said, and such authenticity would resonate with the hidden dimensions of divinity within the people. Emerson's address was a declaration of independence from the ecclesiastical establishment, and was read as such by many of the leading Unitarian Harvard professors of divinity.[1]

The "Address" created a newspaper, journal, and pamphlet war within the Unitarian community and beyond.[2] On 27 August 1838 Andrews Norton, professor of biblical studies at Harvard's Divinity School, published an anonymous vitriolic attack on Emerson's talk and on Transcendentalism in the *Boston Daily Advertiser*. The "Socinian Pope, " as Thomas Carlyle had characterized him,[3] interpreted Emerson's Address as "disastrous and alarming" because it rejected "all belief in Christianity as a revelation." Resorting to a public newspaper indicated that Norton believed the threat would be widespread unless the denizens of Unitarian Orthodoxy stood up against this "Latest Form of Infidelity," as he would tag Emerson's speech in his own Divinity School address of 1839. He identified the new school of thought that Emerson represented as "Transcenden-

[1] For a copy of the address, see "The Divinity School Address," in *The Collected Works of Ralph Waldo Emerson*, general editor, Alfred R. Ferguson, 5 vols. (Cambridge, Massachusetts: The Belknap Press of Harvard University Press, 1971-1994), 1:76-93.

[2] Emerson reported to Thomas Carlyle, 17 October 1838, that there was "an outcry in our leading local newspapers against my 'infidelity,' 'pantheism,' & 'atheism'" and that Carlyle himself had been implicated in the universal assault. On this see, *The Correspondence of Emerson and Carlyle*, edited by Joseph Slater (New York: Columbia University Press, 1964), 196.

[3] Carlyle to Emerson, 8 February 1839, in ibid., 214.

talism," including in that group the followers of Kant, the post-Kantian German idealist philosophies, Thomas Carlyle (1795-1881), the French philosopher Victor Cousin (1792-1876), and the "pantheist" theologian Friedrich Schlieremacher (1768-1834).[4] Brownson responded to Norton's attack in the August 31 *Boston Morning Post.* He sustained Emerson, but wanted to make it clear that there were at least two very different philosophical schools within what Norton had designated "Transcendentalism." This was not Brownson's first attempt to make the distinction he makes here, nor would it be his last.[5]

The *Boston Morning Post* article was unsigned. Brownson's authorship was determined by external as well as internal evidence. Andrews Norton attributed the article to George Thomas Davis,[6] but Theodore Parker attributed it to Brownson.[7] Parker's attribution seems most accurate to me because of the internal evidence. The arguments, rhetorical style, and even the language used here are Brownson's and these same arguments and language are used in an article Brownson published in his *Boston Quarterly Review* ("Philosophy and Common Sense," January, 1838) prior to this essay, and in his more substantial and extensive review of Emerson's "Address" in the *Boston Quarterly Review* (October, 1838). The *Morning Post,* moreover, like Brownson, supported the Jacksonian Democratic party and the political positions of Martin Van Buren. Brownson agreed, furthermore, with the Jacksonian decision to remove the Cherokee Indians from Georgia and asserted that Emerson's previous opposition to such a decision was wrong-headed, just as Brownson later justified the Jacksonian decision in "Our Indian Policy" and opined that many gifted orators "manifested a zeal in their opposition to the project, worthy of a better cause."[8]

[4] "The New School in Literature and Religion," *Boston Daily Advertiser* (August 27, 1838), 2. See also Perry Miller, ed., *The Transcendentalists: An Anthology* (Cambridge, Massachusetts: Harvard University Press, 1950), 193-96, quotations on 195. Miller opines, p. 193, that Norton's essay "could have been inspired by nothing less than pure rage."

[5] Brownson did a much more extensive review of "Mr. Emerson's Address," *Boston Quarterly Review* 1 (October, 1838): 500-14. See also chapter 6 in this volume.

[6] On this, see William R. Hutchison, *The Transcendentalist Ministers: Church Reform in the New England Renaissance* (New Haven: Yale University Press, 1958), 71-72.

[7] On this, see John McAleer, *Ralph Waldo Emerson: Days of Encounter* (Boston: Little, Brown and Company, 1984), 687-88, n.35.

[8] *Boston Quarterly Review* 2 (April, 1839): 229-59, especially 357. See also Chapter 15 in this volume, p. 331.

The *Post* article praised Emerson's "free and independent spirit" and made it clear to Emerson's religious opponents that if they did not give young men a sense of the free spirit of the age, as Emerson had done, young men would follow Emerson and not his insensitive opponents. But, Emerson's own sensibility and his conscious reflection of the freedom-loving spirit of the age did not, in Brownson's view, hide the inherent philosophical and religious weaknesses of the address. Brownson wanted to make it clear, too, that there were two new schools of thought in the United States and not one "Transcendentalism" as Andrews Norton had asserted, grouping together Emerson, Thomas Carlyle, German Transcendentalists like Immanuel Kant, and the French philosopher Victor Cousin. Brownson instead distinguished between two wings of the new school of literature and religion: the Emerson-Carlyle wing, influenced by the German idealists and Transcendentalists, and the Cousinian school to which Brownson himself belonged. A year later, in a letter to Cousin, Brownson made the same distinction within the new school when he tried to explain the current tendencies and orientations in American philosophy.[9]

Cousin, Brownson maintained, was a philosopher and a metaphysician who wrote with forceful logical arguments. Carlyle was no philosopher or metaphysician but a poet who had genius, like Emerson, a judgment very similar to one made by Leslie Stephen at the beginning of the twentieth century.[10] The Transcendentalists of the Emerson-Carlyle brand were not to be confused with those who followed Cousin. Brownson clearly wanted to separate himself from the philosophical and religious implications of the Divinity School Address and he did it by detailing the differences between these two groups. Emerson's opponents had nothing to fear from his address because it was too misty and dreamy for hardy Americans to latch unto. It was true that both schools valued instinct, intuition, and spontaneity, but the key difference between the two schools was that the Emerson-Carlyle crowd took instinct to be the sole guide in life without any effort to legitimate it. They rejected reflection, argumentation, and all philosophic reasoning, while the Cousinians or Eclectics refused to obey intuition until it had been legitimated by

[9] Brownson to Cousin, 6 September 1839, in Brownson Papers, microfilm roll #1 of the *Microfilm Edition of the Orestes Augustus Brownson Papers*, edited by Thomas T. McAvoy and Lawrence J. Bradley (Notre Dame, Indiana: University of Notre Dame Archives, 1966). Hereafter only the roll number is cited.

[10] See *The English Utilitarians*, vol. 3 (London: Duckworth and Co., 1900), 464.

the understanding or reflective reason. In a word, the "mystical" Transcendentalists depreciated the value of rigorous philosophy—primarily because they were poets and not philosophers. As poets, though, they provided a very useful service by emancipating the people from dead custom and the conventionalisms of the day.

Brownson's review was an attempt to support Emerson in his trials with his vigorous opponents, but at the same time it distanced Brownson and the Cousinian Eclectics from the philosophical subjectivism of the Emersonians. Carlyle, too, had praised the address, but he told Emerson that he thought the address lacked concreteness; "some concrete thing" was necessary to give it life,[11] a criticism very different from Brownson's. Brownson was not concerned with the same kind of literary concreteness Carlyle had in mind; he was more interested in the philosophical concreteness that was verifiable by the understanding. Nonetheless, at this point in his life Brownson did not believe the Carlyle-Emerson tendency would "do any harm," as his letter to Cousin asserted, because Americans in general had little inclination to mysticism.

In the Brownson papers there is another review of the "Divinity School Address" that was apparently sent to Brownson to be published in the *Boston Quarterly Review*.[12] Brownson did not publish the review. This review was highly laudatory of Emerson's "Address," entirely unaware of the philosophical orientation of the piece. The author of the review saw that Emerson was trying to awaken young men to the nature of true devotion as the "spontaneous out breaking" of the "intuitive moral sentiment in the soul of man." The author interpreted the speech within the context of biblical injunctions, indicating that, "Verily it seemed to us that a voice from the mountain-side of Palestine had come thru space & time to our [indecipherable] and slumbering spirit." Emerson's speech sought "the good of the individual, not the interest & honor of a non-entity, named church, state, or society." Such uncritical praise was not to Brownson's liking, and so the review never saw the light of day in his journal.

One month after his first brief review of Emerson's "Address," Brownson published a second, more extensive, essay on it for the

[11] Carlyle to Emerson, 8 February 1839, in *Correspondence of Emerson and Carlyle*, 215.

[12] In the Brownson papers, located at the Archives of the University of Notre Dame, is an essay a contributor wrote on "An Address Delivered before the Senior Class, Divinity College, Cambridge. Sunday, 15 July 1838. By Ralph Waldo Emerson." On this, see also microfilm roll #19, "Manuscripts of Contributors."

Boston Quarterly Review. He praised Emerson's poetic abilities but criticized the unarticulated philosophical presuppositions. From his own Cousinian perspective, Brownson charged that the central doctrine of the speech, i.e., the divine laws of the soul (or moral sentiment) as the sole guide to life, was not "psychologically true." Emerson's dictum, "obey thyself," moreover, supplied no fundamental motivation or reason for self-perfection—i.e., no philosophical grounds for moral obligation. The address was excessively individualistic and anti-social in philosophical orientation. Emerson, furthermore, confounded religious with moral sentiment and therefore could not provide an adequate understanding of either religion or morality. God, for Brownson, was not the soul's conception of God. Brownson, too, criticized Emerson's ahistorical view of Christianity, one of the first times Brownson himself began to see that a totally spiritualized view of Christianity (one like he had himself articulated earlier in his career) was not justified by the facts of history. Human beings because they were concrete beings in history, moreover, needed the historical Christ, not just a gnostic Christ, or an ahistorical and ideal Christ; they required a mediator with the divine; the soul alone could not provide immediate access to the divine. Brownson's review was sowing seeds for the future evolution of his thought. No criticism he made in this essay was fully developed, but the criticisms themselves indicated that something was radically wrong with the application of the Emerson-Carlyle philosophical principles and he was beginning to become very uneasy with that direction. Emerson, however, was not to be suspected of a "conscious hostility to religion and morality," as some charged. Such a charge was not true to Emerson's character nor was it his intent; for Brownson, though, religion and morality were undermined by the logical consequence or trajectory of Emerson's premises. Nevertheless, Brownson could not accept the Lockean criticisms of Emerson that emanated from the minds of the Harvard divines.

Brownson sent his review article to one of his close friends and a frequent correspondent, Isaac B. Pierce, pastor of a Unitarian Church in Trenton, New York. Pierce knew Brownson's mind fairly well. He told Brownson that he had read Emerson's address at least six times trying to figure out what Emerson meant. He also read Henry Ware Jr.'s criticism in the *Personality of the Deity* (1839) and a few critical articles in the *Christian Register*, but, he told Brownson, "nobody seems to understand" Emerson's views. In Brownson's review essay, moreover, Pierce detected a "constant forebearance" in Brownson's assessment of Emerson's views. Pierce had a sense that Brownson was reticent to criticize Emerson and asked him, "Do tell me openly, or confidentially what are his real views of God, and Christ, and the soul!"[13] We have no record of Brownson's response, but Pierce saw clearly that Brownson's criticisms ran deeper than he had articulated in the review article. Perhaps they were deeper than Brownson was able to articulate at the time.

In July of 1839, after almost a year of constant and severe criticisms of Emerson's "'infidelity,' 'pantheism,' & 'atheism,'"[14] in the newspaper and pamphlet warfare, Brownson "heartily repent[ed] of having appeared among his [Emerson's] opponents." He regretted that his attacks were part of the general onslaught against Emerson who had the boldness "to speak from his own convictions, from his own free soul!" Brownson liked Emerson's spirit, but not the substance of his thought. He never took back his substantive criticisms; he simply re-asserted Emerson's right to speak his own mind, whatever that word might be. Emerson could be a "servant of the true God, even though it be a left-handed one."[15] Since his early twenties he had advocated the right of free inquiry and free expression of the truth. When he saw Emerson being unjustly hammered, he spoke out again against what he considered the public pressure to suppress free speech, something he deemed inconsistent with the liberal Christianity to which he and Emerson's critics belonged. In historical fact, it must be acknowledged, there was no effective attempt to repress free speech. Diametrically opposed positions were expressed fully and freely from all quarters of the religious community.

Brownson's criticisms of the Carlyle-Emersonian wing of Transcendentalism continued in his assessment of the educational theories of Amos Bronson Alcott (1799-1888), a distant relative. Alcott had been a pedlar in the South during his early years and then became a teacher in Connecticut, Philadelphia, and Boston. In 1834 with the encouragement and support of William Ellery Channing he opened a "School for Human Culture" in Boston and hired Elizabeth Palmer Peabody (1804-94), another American Transcendentalist, as his assistant. The school was established in the Masonic Temple and was therefore called the Temple school. At the school he worked out innovative educational methods that he had been developing since the late 1820s.

[13] Isaac B. Pierce to Brownson, 2 April 1839, Brownson Papers, microfilm roll # 1.

[14] Emerson to Carlyle, October 17, 1838, in *Correspondence*, 196.

[15] Brownson published these remarks in his review of "Bulwer's Novels," *Boston Quarterly Review* 2 (July, 1839): 272. See also Chapter 16 in this volume, p. 344.

Brownson and Alcott had early on developed a close relationship. Brownson had roomed with the Alcotts in 1835 and 1836 before moving to Chelsea, Massachusetts. Alcott had joined Brownson's "Society for Christian Union and Progress" and had listened to a number of Brownson's sermons and lectures during the summer and fall of 1836. Both were charter members of the Transcendentalist Club in 1836. Gradually, however, as the two began to know more clearly the other's mind and as they expressed their deepening ideological divide, their friendship deteriorated and then ceased altogether. At Brownson's death in 1876, Alcott asserted that their friendship ended because of Brownson's "dogmatic temperament."[16] Brownson's sharp pen, of course, alienated many of those he disagreed with, but the ideological differences were themselves the fundamental reason for the alienation and those later differences colored all assessments of their earlier relationships.

Alcott applied his own transcendental philosophy to teaching, developing in the process a transcendental theory of education. In 1836, he published a pamphlet, *The Doctrine and Discipline of Human Culture*,[17] which became the theoretical justification for what he was doing at the Temple School in Boston. The fundamental aim of all education was the development of human culture. Such an aim was achieved primarily by evoking the divinity that resided within the souls of children. For Alcott, children were the true embodiment of divinity, or, as he said, the child was "a type of Divinity."[18] Human culture was for Alcott "the art of revealing to a man the true idea of his being, his endowments, his possessions and of fitting him to use these for the growth, renewal, and perfection of his spirit. It is the art of completing a man."[19] The role of the sensitive and inspiring teacher, then, was to evoke the divinity within the child to bring it to completion in the individual's life with the hope that through such individual self-development society itself might be renewed and reformed. Educational instruction, therefore, became much more a matter of inspiration and evocation than communication of information. The models for this approach to education were Socrates, Jesus, and the

[16] On this, see Frederick C. Dahlstrand, *Amos Bronson Alcott: An Intellectual Biography* (Rutherford, New Jersey: Fairleigh Dickinson University Press, 1982), 321.

[17] (Boston: James Munroe and Co., 1836).

[18] Quotations from Alcott's *Doctrine and Discipline* are taken from a reprint in George Hochfield's edition of the *Selected Writings of the American Transcendentalists* (New York: The New American Library, 1966), 142.

[19] Ibid., 131.

Gospels. Jesus especially was the "harmonious unfolding of spirit into the image of a perfect man—as a worthy symbol of the Divinity, wherein human nature is revealed in its fullness."[20] The Gospels were, then, the "history of spirit accomplishing its mission on the earth."[21] Jesus' conversational method of instruction, as illustrated in the Gospels, was for Alcott the model of the right method of education.

Alcott used an inductive method to develop his own theories of education, observing the way his own children learned and experimenting in class with evocative methods of instructing children entrusted to his care. Although he fostered self-discipline in the school and trained children to avoid dissipation, he refused to use corporal punishment in the classroom (an innovation for the times). In 1835 he began a series of conversations on the Gospels with the children he was teaching, keeping extensive notations on their responses to questions he posed to them. He used the life of Jesus as the external symbol of the spirit, and his own questions and conversational style to evoke from children "a revelation of Divinity in the soul of childhood."[22] For Alcott the ultimate aim of education was to help children realize their oneness with God. "Men," he wrote, "shall be one with God, as was the Man of Nazareth."[23]

Alcott's school had enrolled about forty children of the Boston elite. His methods of education, however, were not widely known until he published a two-volume report on them in *Conversations with Children on the Gospels* (1836, 1837),[24] texts Alcott hoped would spread his ideas about education and increase enrollment in his school. Those volumes, however, disturbed a number of people because of their explicit references to and conversations on birth, circumcision, and other physiological facts. After reading *Conversations*, Boston critics unloaded their guns upon Alcott and his school began to decline, forcing him to close it in 1838.

The major Boston secular as well as religious newspapers raised a storm of protests against *Conversations*. Alcott's view of the innocence of human nature in children horrified some, others were dis-

[20] Ibid., 133.

[21] Ibid., 132.

[22] Amos Bronson Alcott, *Conversations with Children on the Gospels*, 2 vols. (Boston: James Munroe and Co., 1836, 1837), 1:xiv.

[23] Ibid., 1:liii.

[24] Prior to this Elizabeth Peabody had published her *Record of a School* (1835, rev. edition, 1836) that had outlined something of the methods Alcott used in the school. In August of 1836, however, she left the school because of what she considered Alcott's excessive use of introspection and his frank and open discussion of physiology with the children.

turbed by his Socratic method of treating the Gospels, and still others believed his identification of human nature and the divinity was pantheistic. The *Boston Daily Advertiser*'s proprietor, Nathan Hale, thought Alcott's approach to the Scripture was unsuitable for immature minds. Joseph H. Buckingham wrote in the *Boston Courier* that the book was "one third absurd, one third blasphemous, and one third obscene."[25] Alcott's work on education, like Emerson's "Divinity School Address" in 1838, discredited Transcendentalism in a large segment of the Boston public press. Alcott's close Transcendentalist friends—Emerson, James Freeman Clarke, Elizabeth Peabody, Convers Francis, and others—came to Alcott's defense,[26] but the damage had been done.

Brownson's review of Alcott's work was neither as negative as those in the public press nor as positive as that of Alcott's Transcendentalist friends. Although Brownson backed Alcott and his good intentions as a reformer and member of the new school, he focused primarily upon the philosophical presuppositions of Alcott's epistemological and metaphysical system. As an Eclectic, Brownson perceived in Alcott an epistemology that denied the fundamental importance of the senses. For Alcott, according to Brownson, the real was always the invisible and the real could be apprehended only by reason or instinct. The external world was thus a purely phenomenal world for Alcott, and the senses, whose proper object was the phenomenal world, could not attain to the real behind the phenomenal. To know the truth, therefore, as Alcott's educational theory proclaimed, one must study one's instincts. Education must draw out of the soul, not put into it. Such a system Brownson did not accept, though he did not want to criticize it.

But Brownson did take issue with what he perceived to be Alcott's tendency to pantheism. "We do not admit that identity between man and God, and God and nature, which he does. God is in his works; but he is also separate from them. Creation does not exhaust the Creator. Without Him his works are nothing; but He nevertheless *is*, and *all* He is, without them."[27] His criticism of Alcott, like that of Emerson, was not fully developed, but it demonstrated that he was not buying into the subjective idealism that he would later identify as the crux of the problem with Emerson and Alcott.

[25] On these criticisms, see Frederick C. Dahlstrand, 141, 159 n.34.

[26] On the defense, see ibid., 142.

[27] "Alcott on Human Culture," *Boston Quarterly Review* 1 (October, 1838), 431. See also Chapter 2 in this volume, pp. 63-64.

Although he had separated himself from what he considered the excessive subjectivism and the tendency to pantheism that he saw in both Emerson and Alcott, he continued to fight on behalf of the new school in opposition to the Harvard dons of Unitarianism who in his mind represented an eighteenth century religious rationalism that was deadening for the human religious spirit. He was still looking for the new church of the future (one that he had announced in 1836) that would bring into synthesis matter and spirit, but he could not find it in the uninspiring defenses of the Henry Ware Jrs. and the Andrew Nortons of old school Unitarianism.

In 1837 Andrews Norton, retired professor of biblical literature at Harvard, published *Evidences of the Genuineness of the Gospels*, a study that he had begun in 1819. The book was intended to be his magnum opus.[28] Norton set out to demonstrate two things: (1) that the Gospels remained essentially the same (though he admitted some spurious editorial additions) as they were originally composed; and (2) that they had been ascribed to their true authors.[29] Norton argued in the Preface and in the early chapters that his book was necessitated by eighteenth-century skeptical rationalist attacks upon the authenticity of the Gospels. He cited in particular Henry St. John, Viscount Bolingbroke (1678-1715), a British politician, philosopher, and historian, and the German biblical critic Johann Gottfried Eichhorn (1752-1827), both of whom Norton believed had undermined trust in the New Testament documents. Norton amassed huge amounts of historical evidence to support his position, arguing in particular against the early Christian gnostics who found little value in the public revealed record of Christianity.

The early gnostics were men of "more than common" learning and ability; they were distinguished from others "by the peculiar possession of a spiritual principle, implanted in their nature, which was a constant source of divine illumination"; they claimed superiority over the written record; and they were looked upon as adversaries and heretics by the majority of Christians.[30] The whole book was not just against the eighteenth century rationalists, but, closer to home, an attack upon the American Transcendentalists, the modern-day gnostics in Norton's mind. The gnostics were very much like the

[28] Originally Norton intended the project to be a four volume work; only three volumes, however, were actually published. The second and third volumes were published in 1844.

[29] *The Evidences of the Genuineness of the Gospels*, vol. 1 (Boston: American Stationers' Co., John B. Russell, 1837), 18.

[30] Ibid., 5, 6, 10.

"religionists of modern times, who, through reliance on their spiritual intuitions, reject the belief of Revelation." These latter-day gnostics maintained that "the objects of faith may be felt, or may be discerned, by each individual mind, without the aid of Revelation, the belief in which they consequently reject." But, the early gnostics, unlike the contemporary ones, acknowledged the "miraculous interposition" and supernatural character of Christianity.[31] Like many in the early American Unitarian movement, Norton placed a great deal of confidence in reason's capacity to establish the credibility of the supernatural revealed tradition by investigating the historical record. This book, published as it was before Emerson's Divinity School Address, anticipated many of the arguments that would be used against that address.

Brownson reviewed the book in January of 1839, after Emerson had published his "Address." And, it would be with that address in mind that he examined Norton's book, demonstrating that, though he had criticized Emerson, he was still with him on some important religious issues. Although, Brownson wrote, Norton was a respected and erudite scholar, his methodology was false and if followed through in its logical trajectory it would end up in the same atheistic position of Abner Kneeland and Frances Wright, both of whom had followed Locke's rational skepticism to its logical conclusion. Norton may argue with the eighteenth century rationalists, but he accepted their confidence in reason, and his own skepticism was just a matter of degree and not of kind. Arguing on the basis of historical and rational probabilities was a weak foundation for faith (an argument Brownson would use in the future against John Henry Newman and other Tractarian developmentalists). Besides that, Norton's appeal to historical evidence to ground a supernatural faith was really an innovation in American Christianity. American Christianity was primarily an experiential and experimental religion. Norton's approach was contrary to the approach of Jonathan Edwards and the other fathers of the New England theology. The American Transcendentalists, in Brownson's opinion, were closer to this tradition because they emphasized the inner light that was absolutely essential to comprehend the meaning of the miracles, external evidence, and revelation.

Brownson highlighted the question of miracles in Christianity. The so-called miracles controversy had its origins in 1836.[32] In his review of Norton's work Brownson sided somewhat with Emerson, George Ripley, and other Transcendentalists. Brownson, Ripley, and

[31] Ibid., 181, 182.

[32] On Brownson's participation in the 1836 miracles controversy, see EW 3: 13.

a number of other Christian Transcendentalists (though not Emerson) assumed the authenticity of the biblical miracles. What they did not accept was Norton's contention that the miracles provided historical evidence for the infallible truth and authenticity of revelation. According to Norton the biblical miracles proved that Jesus was a true witness to and teacher of the truth of God. Brownson asked quite simply: how does one logically get from the fact of a miracle worker to the infallibility of the truth he asserts? How, moreover, could one recognize a miracle as a divine communication? What were the conditions for such an assumption? The problem with historical criticism was that there was no real criterion for determining true and false miracles (and Norton supplied none). If one placed the truth of Christianity upon the external evidence of the Gospels, one had not sufficient grounds for justifying Christian truths. The Transcendentalist move toward a more subjective understanding of religion and religious authority arose in part, Brownson implied, from its attempt to escape the problems posed by critical reason. There had to be some *a priori* condition that would allow one to see a miracle as a divine communication, and that condition was the inner light, as the Quakers, Jonathan Edwards, and a host of other American Christians had previously argued. The rational supernaturalism of Norton was shaky ground upon which to build a solid religious faith.

Brownson was not done with Norton. A year after Emerson's "Address," Norton gave a commencement address to the Harvard divinity student body to set the record straight and to provide a counter to Emerson. Published as the *Latest Form of Infidelity*, Norton's address made his differences with Emerson and the Transcendentalists very clear. For him the latest form of infidelity "strikes directly at the root of faith in Christianity, and indirectly at all religion, by denying the miracles attesting the divine mission of Christ."[33] Against the Transcendentalists he asserted that what constituted the internal evidence of Christianity, was not some inner light, but the fact that Jesus spoke with the authority of God, attested to by his power of miracles. The Transcendentalists were dreamers who lived outside the realm of the historical concrete. "There can be no intuition, no direct perception, of the truth of Christianity, no metaphysical certainty."[34] One could deal only with probabilities. Religious feelings

[33] *A Discourse on the Latest Form of Infidelity; delivered at the Request of the "Association of the Alumni of the Cambridge Theological School," on the 19th of July, 1839* (Cambridge, Mass.: John Owen, 1839; rpt. Port Washington, New York: Kennikat Press, 1971), 11.

[34] Ibid., 32.

and intuitions must ultimately be founded on religious beliefs, and "all rational belief must be founded on reason."[35] Here was a summation of all his arguments against the dangerous tendencies of the new school of De Wette, Schleiermacher, David Strauss, and the Transcendentalists. What was at stake was the historical reliability of Christianity and an emphasis on the verifiability and authenticity of one's religious inspirations. In the end, though, one had to trust the intellectual elites to discover the rational grounding of faith because they have made the sifting of evidence their particular study.[36] Norton had made his case.

Norton had made some of the same criticisms of Emerson's "Address" as had Brownson, but when Norton made them, Brownson came to "our friend"[37] Emerson's defense in his essay on "Democracy and Reform."[38] The thesis of that essay was that all true reformers should sustain the Democratic party. The essay was a piece of political propaganda in which Brownson digressed for a few pages on Norton's *Latest Form of Infidelity*. Brownson traced Norton's intellectual pedigree and principles back to Locke and the Whigs, and tried to demonstrate how in principle everything Norton held in his essay associated him with an anti-democratic elitism that was sharply contrasted with a Transcendental Democratic egalitarianism. Religious principles had political and social implications and Brownson tried to show that Norton's principles were Whiggish. Such principles championed the privileged few whether in religion or in politics. The position was as undemocratic as it was unchristian.[39]

Norton was the most important though not the only Unitarian to publish against Emerson. Henry Ware, Jr. (1794-1843), Emerson's former fellow pastor at Boston's Second Church and since 1830 a professor of Pulpit Eloquence and Pastoral Care at Harvard Divinity School, did not like much of Emerson's "Address" and preached against it, although not in the same vein as Norton. The sermon was published in September of 1838 as the *Personality of the Deity*. Ware made no explicit reference to the "Address" but maintained that he was

[35] Ibid., 50.

[36] Ibid., 58-59.

[37] See "Bulwer's Novels," 272, where Brownson regretted having criticized Emerson's "Divinity School Address" and referred to "our friend Emerson." See also Chapter 16 in this volume, p. 344.

[38] On the essay, see *Boston Quarterly Review* 2 (October, 1839): 478-517. See also chapter 20 in this volume.

[39] Ibid., 501-02. See also Chapter 20 in this volume, pp. 610-15.

taking issue with those in the community who presented God as an impersonal abstraction. Such a view of God undercut, he believed, the foundations and sanctions for all morality.[40] Brownson read the address, but dismissed it as a feeble, though well-meant, performance.[41]

In the midst of the Divinity School controversy, Brownson developed more than in the past his own religious views in two other articles, "The Kingdom of God" and "Unitarianism and Trinitarianism." The two articles demonstrate a religious idealism akin to his Cousinian philosophical idealism. The two articles, moreover, must be interpreted within the context of the Divinity School Address and the second stage of the Unitarian controversy over miracles. Distinctions he made in these two addresses would remain with him for the next year or so until he read the French ex-Saint-Simonian and utopian socialist Pierre Leroux (1797-1871) and began to call these distinctions into question. For him the "Kingdom of God" (July 1839) was the ideal that Jesus came to proclaim, the divine ideal of truth, of justice, of goodness. The biblical kingdom, therefore, was no special society, visible corporation, no church creed, as some in the past had maintained. The New Testament kingdom ideal that Jesus preached was the living revelation of God seeking realization in time and space. The kingdom was not the church, but the church was an objective means for realizing the ideal. Unlike Emerson, Brownson affirmed a positive role for biblical revelation and the historical church. The ideal was not entirely within the soul. Still, there was a radical separation between the kingdom, or what Brownson also called the Christianity of Christ, and the Christianity of the church. The Christianity of Christ was seeking realization in and through the church, but it was a reality separate from the church, which was a mere arbitrary form of the ideal kingdom. This ecclesial idealism, or what might be called a Nestorian ecclesiology,[42] would be at the heart of his 1840 essay on "The Laboring Classes."

To some extent Brownson was reminding his readers that he was still searching for the ideal church (i.e., the new church he had announced in his 1836 *New Views*), or the fullest manifestation of the

[40] Henry Ware, Jr., *Personality of the Deity. A Sermon, preached in the Chapel of Harvard University, September 23, 1838* (Boston: J. Munroe and Co., 1838).

[41] "Bulwer's Novels," 272. See also Chapter 16 in this volume, p. 344.

[42] I am using the term "Nestorian" freely to indicate a moral, rather than an ontological or real, union or relation between Christ's kingdom ideal and the church. The ideal was to be realized in the "will" of the church.

ideal kingdom within space and time. That search became even clearer in his article on "Unitarianism and Trinitarianism" (July 1839). Here he used his Cousinian eclecticism as a method of discernment for distinguishing between truth and error in two different religious systems, the Unitarian and the Trinitarian. He asserted, as he had been doing since at least 1836, that Unitarianism as a denomination was "virtually, if not literally dead." Its death was to be expected because it was from its beginnings a "negative system." It had protested against real abuses in the older Trinitarian system but it had not provided for contemporary spiritual and intellectual wants. It had not provided substance.

The older Calvinist Trinitarian system, on the other hand, had some substantial truths but those truths were buried beneath outmoded forms so that Trinitarianism was as dead as Unitarianism. What was needed in the present was a reconciliation of the Unitarian and Trinitarian systems of religion—a real synthesis of the truths of Calvinism and the truths of Arminian Unitarianism. Such a "wise Eclecticism" would create, in fact was creating, the new liberal party emerging out of Unitarianism. Such a view accepted neither the radicalism of Emerson, nor the criticisms of the Unitarian dons, nor the postulations of the orthodox Trinitarians. Brownson was looking for some new combination that respected the insights of the past and the inspirations of the present. The human race progresses, and what he saw in the present was a process of development, the end of which was not at all clear. In light of the Divinity School Address, these articles appear to be a conservative statement of the direction of the movement party. The task for the present, according to Brownson, was reinterpretation of the old symbols which contained the ideals. The doctrine of the Trinity, for example, needed to be reinterpreted so that moderns could comprehend the truth the doctrine intended to teach. That truth and love were one with God and that they needed to become flesh in the world was at the heart of the old trinitarian symbol. The preservation of such a truth was the task of the church and the responsibility of those who were in the forefront of reinterpreting the orthodox Christian symbols. Thus did Brownson reduce the doctrine of the Trinity to transcendental ideals of truth and love and their identity with God. The Incarnation, then, became the manifestation or historical realization of truth and love.

Behind much of Brownson's religious philosophy, as is evident in the above paragraphs, was a quasi-Hegelian view of history and an objective idealism that he had appropriated from Victor Cousin, the French philosopher and historian of philosophy. In the midst of the religious controversies, the Transcendentalists' opponents had associated Cousin's name with Emerson, Kant, Carlyle, and other "dreamy" Transcendentalists.

In two essays on Cousin's philosophy,[43] Brownson tried to place Cousin within the pantheon of contemporary philosophical gods. He argued that although Cousin's philosophy appropriated much of the idealism of Kant and the other German idealists like Johann Gottlieb Fichte (1762-1814) and Friedrich Wilhelm Joseph Schelling (1775-1854), it could not be identified with them. Likewise, although Cousin used the empirical method of Thomas Reid (1710-96) and other Scottish Common Sense philosophers, he could not be coupled with them. Cousin had his own unique branch of philosophy that synthesized idealism and empiricism. With these essays Brownson hoped to demonstrate that Cousin and his followers could not be linked with American Transcendentalism, as that term was being defined by its opponents. He was also showing that there were at least two major philosophical schools within the American movement party. By defending Cousin Brownson was trying to show precisely where the philosophical divide was between the Emersonians who were descendants of Kant by way of Coleridge and Carlyle and the followers of Cousin.

Brownson declared that Cousin was not a Transcendentalist, as that term was understood by its opponents. The term "Transcendentalism," as used by its opponents, appeared to mean that in philosophizing one "disregards experience and builds on principles obtained not by experience, but by reasoning *a priori*."[44] In this sense, Brownson contended, neither Cousin nor Kant were Transcendentalists. Cousin was not a subjective idealist or rationalist who put no reliance upon experience and the objective world outside the self. In fact, both Cousin and Kant placed experience at the foundation of all knowledge, but they did not limit experience, as did the Lockeans, to the senses or make the senses the conduit of all knowledge. Kant and Cousin were preoccupied with establishing the *a priori* conditions in which experience itself was possible. But Cousin could not go all the way with Kant who placed the conditions of knowledge within the categories which he located within the self, leading, Cousin objected, to subjectivism. What saved Cousin from the Kantian subjectivism

[43] "The Eclectic Philosophy" and "Eclecticism—Ontology," *Boston Quarterly Review* 2 (January and April, 1839): 27-53, 169-87. See also chapter 8 in this volume.

[44] Ibid., 29. See also Chapter 8 in this volume, p. 155.

was his reliance upon the experimental method he had obtained from Scottish Common Sense philosophers like Thomas Reid, and his understanding of reason as spontaneous and impersonal.

Using the empirical method of observation became a barrier against Kantian subjectivism because it placed greater reliance upon the empirical than did Kant. But the Scots did not go far enough in the Kantian direction because they did not apply the method of observation to the facts of consciousness; if they had done so, they would have discovered, with Kant, the *a priori* conditions of experience and knowledge. Brownson was trying to show, as indeed Cousin himself did, that Cousin's philosophy was half-way between Kant and the Scots. Cousin did not go as far as Kant in the direction of subjectivism but Cousin went further than the Scots in using the empirical method of observation to discover the foundations of knowledge. Cousin's philosophy was a synthesis of German idealism and Scottish empiricism.

Brownson argued that Cousin used an experimental method to demonstrate the non-sensual origins of transcendental ideas like cause, the infinite, and space. Observation of consciousness revealed the primitive facts of consciousness (i.e., those abstract, universal, and necessary ideas like cause, the infinite, and space). Such observation, however, was not done by the senses, but by an interior light called consciousness.[45] Such ideas or facts of consciousness were the conditions of all human experience. Such an empirical or experimental method demonstrated that "there are facts of consciousness which have a rational origin, and not, as some pretend, that all our ideas have an exclusively empirical origin."[46] The empirical method, which Cousin and Brownson used, was not itself the source of those necessary ideas; but it provided a means for discovering them. Cousin's philosophy was grounded in experience, broadly conceived, relied on observable evidence, and was not a visionary enterprise devoid of any objective referent.

Those ideas had a rational origin; they were "intuitions of the reason."[47] By reason here Cousin meant spontaneous reason, i.e., an impersonal or objective reason, the universal reason that was within the ME but not identified with the ME. Reason in this sense revealed laws and realities outside of the self. Spontaneous reason was

[45] Ibid., 36. See also Chapter 8 in this volume, p. 161.
[46] Ibid., 51. See also Chapter 8 in this volume, p. 173.
[47] Ibid., 52. See also Chapter 8 in this volume, p. 173.

independent of personality, self, and will or activity (i.e., the essential characteristic of personality for Cousin). By defining reason as spontaneous or impersonal Cousin hoped to escape the subjectivism of Kant, who placed the *a priori* categories and forms within the subject—and even that of Reid, who placed first principles of common sense in the constitution of human nature, i.e., in the self. Cousin, therefore, was not an unrealistic idealist, but an empirically grounded and spiritually sensitive idealist. He was called an Eclectic because he chose to unite the best elements of idealism and empiricism while avoiding their worst components.

Cousin's philosophical method and his definition of spontaneous reason saved him from the charge of subjectivism. Cousin's impersonal reason combined the elements of necessity that he found in Kant and Reid with the elements of freedom that he found in Fichte and Marie François Pierre Gontier de Biran (called Maine de Biran, 1766-1824). Reason in this sense was both objective and subjective. Objective in the sense that its revelations came from outside the self, and subjective in the sense that it was one of the constitutive elements of the ME (the other two being sensibility or feeling, and activity or will).

Cousin could be called an objective idealist because the transcendental ideals came to the self from a revelation, universal reason, outside the self. Brownson's acceptance of Cousin's philosophy separated him fundamentally from the subjective idealism he perceived in Emerson and Alcott, among others. Such a view of the different philosophical schools of thought has been overlooked by some scholars of the history of Transcendentalism and American philosophy. Brownson represented an intellectual tradition that has not been given sufficient attention in American historical scholarship.

Brownson focused most of his attention upon Cousin's empirical or scientific (in a Baconian sense) method of demonstrating the facts of consciousness because the Lockean opponents had charged that his system of philosophy, like that of Kant and other German idealist, was unverifiable. But he was aware that such an emphasis did not respond to the ontological question: i.e., did the notions or facts of consciousness correspond to anything independent of one's consciousness. What objective validity did the facts possess? Did they refer to anything real outside of the self? Or, how did one get philosophically from the psychological realm to the ontological order? Brownson responded to this question by asserting the objective and impersonal nature of reason itself, but, it was clear in his second article, that he had difficulty trying to justify or demonstrate the assertion. His attempt to do so was not a very convincing philosophical performance. But, Brownson had demonstrated to his own satisfaction that Cousin was not a Transcendentalist, as that term was being defined by its opponents, and that Cousin's idealism had an objectivity to it that separated him from those among American Transcendentalists who placed little value on philosophical demonstration and were excessively preoccupied with the ideals within the self and not concerned with the question of their objective validity. Cousin was an idealist, but an objective idealist. That separated him philosophically from the subjective idealism of the Emersonians. That was the point of Brownson's essays.

Brownson's religious and philosophical idealism had implications for all facets of life; it penetrated his notions of society, politics, labor, education, science, the arts and literature—to name those areas of life he generally addressed. From his very earliest Universalist days, Brownson had emphasized the fact that Christianity was an idea or ideal that had multiple social implications. Christ came not just to save a people for some heaven beyond the grave, but to liberate human life within history. Thus, he called upon the clergy in particular to separate themselves from the powerful classes and the powers of oppression so that they might lead their people into the liberty and equality that God intended them to have. In the late 1820s and early 1830s he associated himself with the workingmen hoping to legitimate their cause with the power of the gospel. In the midst of that struggle he discovered the French Saint-Simonians whom he saw as fellow travelers in social Christianity. By the middle of the 1830s he was also reading the French Catholic priest Félicité Robert de Lamennais whose publications of the early 1830s and whose separation from the Catholic Church had attracted considerable attention in Boston.[48] Brownson saw in Lamennais another sign that the Christian world was awakening to the transformative social power of the Christian gospel and he was drawn to Lamennais' vision of a Christian future where democracy and liberty were identified with Christianity, and where the clergy separated themselves from all forms of absolutism and assisted the people in winning their rightful liberties, social as well as political. The situation of Christianity in the United States, of course, was not the same as it was in Europe where the

[48] Two of Lamennais' works, *Paroles d'un croyant* (1834) and *Le Livre du peuple* (1837), had been translated into English and others were available in French to Bostonians: *The Words of a Believer* (New York: DeBehr, 1834), and *The People's Own Book*, trans. by Nathaniel Greene (Boston: Charles C. Little and James Brown, 1839).

clergy and the church had been aligned with political absolutism, but there was, in Brownson's mind, an analogous situation in the United States where the clergy and the church were identified with the prestige of the rich and socially powerful. As in Europe, so in the United States, the church and clergy had to take a stand on the side of liberty, social equity, democracy—in a word, on the side of the people. The church needed to be democratized, and democracy needed to be Christianized. To some extent, both Lamennais and Brownson were calling clergy and people to return to what they considered the authentic Christian covenant with God.

In September of 1836, as editor of the *Boston Reformer*, Brownson translated and published Lamennais' "Absolutisme et liberté," an essay that was attached to the seventh edition of *Paroles d'un croyant* (1834).[49] In other essays—namely, "The Education of the People" (May 1836) and *Babylon is Falling* (May 1837)—[50] Brownson also referred to Lamennais' works and his significance for the world-wide movement party. In "Democracy of Christianity" (October 1838) he argued that the "natural association of the clergy and of Christians generally is also with democracy." Over forty percent of that essay was a direct quotation from Lamennais' "Absolutism and Liberty."

Such talk of democracy and Christianity was as revolutionary in Boston as it was in Paris and in Rome. Brownson was not talking about political democracy as much as he was about social democracy, and that sounded very much like socialism and an equality of goods in the ears of the Bostonian gentry. John Quincy Adams thought of Brownson as a Marat democrat,[51] and others considered him a radical agrarian. Brownson was neither. He was preoccupied during these years with drawing out the "social and political character" of Christianity, as he wrote in "Democracy of Christianity."

A number of interpreters of Transcendentalist thought, especially those in the history of American literature, have missed the impact of Brownson's connection with the French intellectual and social tradition in the early nineteenth century. He was not only associated with

[49] See "Absolutism and Liberty," *Boston Reformer* 3 (September 13, 1836): 2.

[50] On these see EW, 3, chapters 1 and 10.

[51] Jean Paul Marat (1743-93) was a Jacobin French political revolutionary. Adams made the comment to his diary on August 2, 1840, after Brownson's "Laboring Classes" essay was published. "Garrison and the non-resistant abolitionists, Brownson and the Marat democrats, phrenology and animal magnetism, all come in, furnishing each some plausible rascality as an ingredient for the bubbling cauldron of religion and politics." See *Memoirs of John Quincy Adams, comprising portions of his diary from 1795 to 1848*, ed. Charles Francis Adams, 12 vols. (rpt. Freeport, New York: Books for Libraries Press, 1969), 10:345.

the philosophical idealism of Cousin, but also with the social Christians in France. But, it was not to borrow from a foreign source that Brownson went to France. He discovered in the French thinkers something that resonated with his own prior interpretation of the American experience. French thought reinforced and in some cases gave him a language for describing his own view of the future.

The focus on the Christian content of democracy, liberty, and equality was central to Brownson's essays during 1838, 1839 and 1840, and especially during the presidential campaign of 1839 and 1840. For him, democracy was "nothing but the political application of Christianity." And those in society who called for social and political reforms were no longer infidels (as in the days of Robert Dale Owen and Fanny Wright), but those who had reconciled Christian principles and social reform.[52] It was very difficult to distinguish between Brownson the priest and Brownson the politician, but, of course, that was the point. In his mind there was no separation, and, it must be said, very little distinction.

During these years, Brownson was highly involved in the Massachusetts Democratic party and in party politics. We learn very little, however, about his notions of society and government from his published essays. They are primarily concerned with the political advancement of the democratic principle and the Democratic party on the state and federal levels. Despite his earlier abhorrence for party politics, he was in the thick of it during the late 1830s and his journal was considered by many an organ of the radical wing of the Democratic party in Massachusetts. What little there was of Brownson's own theories of the origin and nature of society and government was evident in his review of Francis Lieber's (1800-72) *Political Ethics* and in his essay on "Democracy and Reform." The primitive and rather unsystematic notions set forth in these two essays, included in this volume, were the basis of further reflections on the origin of society and state that develop in his later career.

Brownson was quick to point out that he did not accept Jean Jacques Rousseau's or John Locke's contractual notion of society and state. Brownson wrote that Lieber was right to reject the notion that there existed "a state of individual independence anterior to the existence of society." For Brownson society itself was the "original condition" of humanity. He agreed with Cicero that human beings were social by nature and that the aim of all society was the common

[52] "Democracy and Reform," 479-80. See also Chapter 20 in this volume, pp. 425-26.

good. Human beings were born into society and, as Charles de Secondat, baron de Montesquieu (1689-1755) asserted, the family itself was the origin of society. Human beings were, then, led to it both by instinct and reflection. Although these ideas of the priority of society over individuals were undeveloped, they provided the grounds for his assaults upon individualism, political as well as religious.

Individuals live and move and have their being within society. They were not isolated automatons or laws unto themselves. Their labor and the fruits of their labor, moreover, were not just the products of individual effort. The fruits of any individual's work represented "first, his [the individual's] own labor . . . and, secondly, the labor of society and his family, which has been employed upon him, and, as it were, accumulated in his person." The person reflected the community, and this was true in all individual effort, whether in labor, literature, politics, or religion. It followed as a corollary, therefore, that society itself, through the state or government, had a right to distribute the fruits of an individual's labor. The "supposed right of property in the individual to the fruits of his labor" was a very misguided idea (an idea behind much of the Whig view of society, according to Brownson). Brownson's incipient doctrine of society placed a more powerful emphasis upon the role of government and law than was entertained by some in the Transcendentalist movement. For him, "Society is, in short, a great joint-stock concern, possessing of right, and exercising in fact, under all forms of government, the power of disposing, at discretion, of the products of the labor of all its members."[53]

The power, or authority, or sovereignty of the state or government, as the representative of society, was derived "from the power which created society in the first place."[54] The Christian doctrine (Brownson was here thinking of Rom 13:1) was that "government is of divine origin and rests for its legitimacy on the authority of God."[55] Such a view not only legitimated the authority of government, it was consistent with "the most perfect freedom." Divine sovereignty made all other sovereignties relative; it made kings as well as people, therefore, subject to the same God. Such a view, moreover, was a hedge

[53] For these notions, see "Lieber's Political Ethics," *Boston Quarterly Review* 2 (January, 1839): 120. See also Chapter 10 in this volume, p. 221.

[54] Ibid., 210-11. See also Chapter 10 in this volume, p. 223.

[55] "Democracy and Reform," 494. See also Chapter 20 in this volume, p. 437.

against both tyranny and anarchy. The divine origin of government, Brownson asserted, was the "only ground on which freedom can be safely rested; for freedom consists not in the absence of restraint, but in being subjected to no restraint but the will of God."[56] For Brownson this was the true Democratic and Christian understanding of government.

The best form of government, in his mind, was that of the United States, a form which he called representative democracy, not pure democracy. Such a form of government was, in François René Chateaubriand's (1768-1848) terminology "the most brilliant scientific discovery of modern times." In this form of government, the people, through their elected representatives, have the power to make binding laws. "Eternal justice ruling through the people" was an apt definition for democracy; it was a definition Brownson repeatedly borrowed from his Democratic colleague, George Bancroft.[57] The laws of the state, grounded in eternal justice, bind the individuals but also limit the powers of the state. That is what was meant by "representative democracy." Such a form of government limited the authority of the state, protected the freedom and rights of individuals, and promoted the common good. No other form of government united so perfectly liberty and power.[58]

Brownson's philosophical idealism showed through in his understanding of partisan party politics as well as in his understanding of the form of government. Modern political parties, the Whigs and the Democrats in particular, represented and were the outward realization of basic ideas. And, the parties and their ideas were stronger than individuals who belonged to the parties. Originally, in the seventeenth and eighteenth centuries, the Whigs, under the philosophy of Locke and others, were the mercantile class party of reform, change, progress, and property. But once the party won out over the previous feudal system and its ideals became incarnated in the structures of society it became the party of conservation, the status quo, and the vested economic interests of the mercantile class. The Democratic party rose up in the nineteenth century to realize in new ways and under new circumstances the ideas of equality and freedom and progress and reform. The Democratic party was becoming the movement party in society, emphasizing a new role for all the people, not

[56] Ibid., 496. See also Chapter 20 in this volume, p. 439.

[57] Ibid., 510. See also Chapter 20 in this volume, p. 450.

[58] The discussion on Representative Democracy is taken from Brownson's second review of Lieber's work. See "Lieber's Political Ethics," *Boston Quarterly Review* 3 (April, 1840): 187-93. See also Chapter 10 in this volume, pp. 229-32.

just the propertied classes. Brownson saw the battles of the late 1830s in these idealistic terms. It was a fundamental battle for the realization of a set of transcendental ideals in American society. For him the "mission of the Democratic party is to unfold the great idea of justice and reduce it to practice in all man's social and political relations."[59]

Much of Brownson's theory of government was hidden behind his preoccupation with partisan politics in the heady days of 1838 and 1839 in the Massachusetts Democratic party. If one was a left wing Democrat (i.e., the Democrats most opposed to the National Bank and paper money), as Brownson was, one had a right to feel some cautious optimism. In the aftermath of the financial depression of 1837 and its prolonged effects the radical Democrats were beginning to gain some political ground.[60] In January of 1838 Brownson's friend Bancroft had become the leader of the Massachusetts Democratic party, and in 1839 the left wing was able to elect Marcus Morton (1784-1864) governor of Massachusetts. That wing had made some significant advances in Massachusetts but they had lost ground in New York. And, from Brownson's perspective, there was a bit of confusion in the current political scene because some conservative Democrats had supported Whig ideas while some Whigs were toting democratic slogans. In the current climate he hoped to draw out for the nation the true issues in the contest between what he called the stationary party and the movement party. That was going to be difficult, however, if the members of the parties were not identified with the ideas that gave their parties life and a reason for existence.

In "Prospects of Democracy"[61] he outlined the eternal principles that were at war in society: the principle of conservation and that of progress and liberty. The current Whigs were representatives of the

[59] "Democracy and Reform," 512. See also Chapter 20 in this volume, p. 453. This entire essay can be seen as a form of political idealism.

[60] One indication of a shift in mood was John C. Calhoun's return to the Democratic party after the crisis of 1837. Like Brownson and some other hard-money Democrats in the North he saw at least four major issues that the nation needed to face in the future: (1) a more equitable distribution of wealth; (2) the growing frustration of the masses and the workers with the capitalists; (3) the conservative business party's attempts to increase the power of the central government at the expense of states rights; (4) the movements of northern radical reformers whose principles threatened to undermine the stability and order of society. Calhoun would be a powerful voice for such issues. On this, see Arthur M. Schlesinger, Jr., *The Age of Jackson* (Boston: Little, Brown and Co., 1945), 242-49.

[61] *Boston Quarterly Review* 2 (January, 1839): 123-36. See also Chapter 11 in this volume.

first, and the true Democrats the representative of the second. Men—like Henry Clay, Daniel Webster, Martin Van Buren, and John C. Calhoun—were popular statesmen in American society not just because of their own gifts and abilities but because they represented universal ideas and values within the community. Very much like Calhoun, Brownson believed that politics was primarily a matter of principles not men, and the battle should be over ideas. The current political contest, he asserted, was between the Whigs as representatives of privilege and power (i.e., those who wanted to preserve their vested stakes in society) and Democrats as representatives of reform and equality of opportunity in the country. The battle was joined, but the outcome he could not predict because of the confusion of the identities of both parties in the climate of the late 1830s. And by the end of 1839, the political situation would only get more confusing as the Whigs chose as their presidential candidate the old general, Henry Harrison, a false but intended imitation of Andrew Jackson. They were going to out do the Democrats in upholding democracy. Could the Democrats make the people believe that the Whigs were in fact the party of privilege and vested interests? The answer would not be a matter of political ideology, and it would not come until the elections of 1840.

In the midst of articulating his idealist philosophy of American politics, Brownson also addressed three specific controversial issues that had a new vitality and excitement in the national debate: abolitionism, the government's Indian policy, and the education of the people. Brownson had always opposed slavery, and in this he was very much unlike Calhoun, but he was becoming increasingly concerned about the radical philosophical and political tendencies of those abolitionists who were demanding immediate abolition, calling for resistance to established laws, and providing no realistic alternative for the slaves who would be emancipated in the future. In reacting against the "revolutionary tendencies" of the immediatist abolitionists he manifested a conservative streak in his thought that would continue in subsequent years. To some extent, though, it was consistent with his reactions to the subjectivism he saw in Emerson and Alcott.

In October of 1838 Brownson formally announced his "painful" separation from the abolitionist movement, which he in fact had never formally joined.[62] Although he continued to oppose slavery he

[62] "Abolition Proceedings," *Boston Quarterly Review* 1 (October, 1838): 473-500. See also chapter 5 in this volume.

was becoming alarmed by some radical abolitionist tactics and proceedings. Earlier, in April and May of 1838, Brownson had had a run-in with William Lloyd Garrison and had been slashed by Garrison's sharp tongue. His own split from the movement, therefore, was personal as well as ideological. His own separation, moreover, took place within the context of great internal tensions within the movement. From July of 1837 to the spring of 1839, abolitionists in Boston split into separate movements because some of the more radical Garrisonian immediatists had identified themselves with other social issues (e.g., women's rights) that the more conservative members of the movement could not accept. The Boston Female Anti-Slavery society was "rocked with factionalism" after 1837 and broke up into two different groups in 1838. In the spring of 1839 the male Massachusetts Anti-Slavery Society (MAS) for similar reasons also split, creating the Massachusetts Abolition Society, one that was in union with the American Anti-Slavery Society, which had also separated itself from Garrison and the MAS.[63]

Brownson saw the increasingly aggressive tactics used in the abolitionist movement as sufficient grounds for a separation. It was no longer simply a matter of discussing an issue in public; it was a matter of "agitation, the agitation of the community, inflaming its passions and directing by means of the ballot box the force they thus collect to bear directly on Southern institutions."[64] The real threat here, however, was antinomianism, a threat to the stability and order of society and a threat to the peace of the republic. The United States form of government was ultimately endangered by the alarming and revolutionary intentions of the abolitionist movement. Brownson declared his identification with the movement party in society but that did not mean he was a radical. Basically, he was a conservative with respect to the constitutional provisions of American government. He declared: "As a lover of our race, as the devoted friend of liberty, of the progress of mankind, we feel that we must, in this country, be conservative, not radical."[65] And that meant supporting reform "in accordance with our institutions" and particularly in conjunction with the provisions of the Constitution.

One could rightly appeal to a higher law of justice, as the abolitionists were doing, but one could not use the higher law as grounds

[63] On these splits, see Debra Gold Hansen, *Strained Sisterhood: Gender and Class in the Boston Female Anti-Slavery Society* (Amherst: University of Massachusetts Press, 1993), 6, 24-25.

[64] "Abolition Proceedings," 479. See also Chapter 5 in this volume, p. 104.

[65] Ibid., 494. See also Chapter 5 in this volume, p. 116.

for destroying the order and peace of the community. "If one class of the community may set the laws at defiance, why may not another."[66] The eternal principle of justice demanded indeed the abolition of slavery, but a morally righteous cause must take account of a morally just application of fundamental principles and abstract rights. Undoubtedly there was an intuitive sense of justice in regard to the abolition of slavery, but that intuition had to be applied to concrete circumstances; it had to be judged by experience, and it needed to be clarified on the basis of the understanding. Brownson reacted to the abolitionists as he had to Emerson and Alcott—they had not brought the higher law into communion with the understanding in the concrete circumstances of human living.

Central to his opposition to the abolitionists tactics, moreover, was his Calhoun-like understanding of the doctrine of states rights. He saw the non-slaveholding states' abolitionists' actions on behalf of immediate emancipation of the slaves as a violation of slaveholding states rights. No matter how morally wrong slavery was, abolitionists had no legal right in those states to abolish slavery. Slavery was a matter of a state's jurisdiction. Abolitionists, therefore, violated the right relations between the states, as those rights were outlined in the Constitution. And, by violating the Constitution they endangered the freedoms (all the freedoms) the Constitution aimed to protect. Brownson's argument in effect protected the social institution of slavery and made it impossible for reformers to abolish any form of injustice outside of their own states. The states alone had the legal or constitutional right to abolish slavery, or, on his principle, any other form of injustice.

Despite his implicit support of the social institution of slavery, Brownson rejected slavery and asserted that it would definitely be abolished in time. Slavery was opposed to the American genius of liberty, which was embedded in the Constitution and other institutions of the country. It would be abolished, he asserted, with the "gradual unfolding" of the American spirit of liberty. Those in the non-slaveholding states could work for that eventuality by focusing upon "a steady development and realization of democratic freedom" within their own states, and by devoting themselves to the doctrine of equal rights for the "free white laborer."[67] This would be a doctrine Brownson would reiterate for over twenty years before he came to call the doctrine of states rights into question at the beginning of the Civil War.

[66] Ibid., 480. See also Chapter 5 in this volume, p. 105.

[67] Ibid., 499. See also Chapter 5 in this volume, p. 120.

But, he would never again side with the abolitionists and that for the simple reason that he rejected almost all reforming associations. He saw the proliferation of voluntary reform societies as a curse upon the body politic. These organizations, he asserted, "are fast swallowing up individual freedom, and making the individual man but a mere appendage to a huge social machine, with neither mind nor will of his own."[68] Although he abhorred rugged individualism, he admired an independent, non-conformist spirit, that he thought essential to American life. He hated what a later generation would call the herd mentality or organization man.

Increasingly Brownson began to perceive and to call himself a conservative. The more radical direction of thought and action, in Emerson and Garrison for example, helped him to measure his own self-understanding. His philosophical reactions to Emerson and Garrison were similar; both in his estimate were subjective idealists, and he believed such a position was a threat to truth and social order. But, calling Brownson a conservative at this point in his career does not seem to square with the so-called radical tendencies of his 1840 "Laboring Classes" essay, which shall be examined in the next volume. At this point it is enough to say two things about this conservative trajectory and the "Laboring Classes" essay. First, Brownson was always much more passionately concerned with the plight of the laboring classes than with that of the Negro slaves, or, as shall be seen, with the American Indians. And, as was evident in the previous paragraph, he saw the reform and improvement of the working classes as a fundamental condition for the realization of social democracy in American society. Emancipated slaves and Indians would not have a chance for true freedom and equity in a society that was unjust to workers. Second, being a conservative did not mean that he had divorced himself from the movement party. He still considered himself part of the new school and continued to call for change, reform, equality and liberty in society as long as such reforms "preserved our institutions" and did not overthrow the social order. Although it had some radical social and economic provisions, the "Laboring Classes" essay, I will argue in the next volume, fit into Brownson's conservative ideological trajectory.

Another of the major social-political issues of the 1830s was the federal government's policy on the removal of eastern Indian tribes to territory west of the Mississippi River. In the mid and late 1820s a number of southeastern Indian tribes had been removed to the west,

[68] Ibid., 498. See also Chapter 5 in this volume, pp. 118-19.

but the most celebrated of cases was the removal of the Cherokees from Georgia to what is now Oklahoma. The removal policy, which had been set in place in the 1820s, was fostered and promoted by President Andrew Jackson.[69] On 28 May 1830 Congress passed an act calling for the removal of the Cherokees. Motives for removal were mixed, as Francis Paul Prucha has argued.[70] Some wanted the Cherokees removed from Georgia simply because of the desire for more land. Others supported the removal on the basis of the states rights doctrine. Still others sought removal because of humanitarian concerns for the preservation of the tribes themselves. In many perhaps there was a mixture of these motives.

From 1829 to 1839 and beyond there arose a major battle over the justice and humanity of the government's policy. The battle was motivated to a considerable extent by "strong party feeling."[71] On one side were Jacksonian Democrats like Brownson who interpreted the policy as a most humanitarian way to protect the Indian from the corruptions of American society and the inevitable clashes and violence of close interaction between two totally different races. In their own territory west of the Mississippi, so the argument went, the Indians could be gradually "civilized" and made ready for American society within the confines of their own communities where they could preserve their own values and mores. On the other side were many Whigs, other anti-Jacksonians, and Christian philanthropists who saw the removal policy as a fundamental violation of the Indians' rights to their lands, secured to them by numerous treaties. Towns and other bodies in Massachusetts, as in a number of other northern states, sent numerous petitions to Congress protesting the barbarism of the government's policy, siding with those Cherokee Indians who protested against the territorial incursions of the State of Georgia upon Indian lands within the state, and upon the government's acquiescence to Georgia's demands for the Indian removal from Georgia and restoration of Indian lands to the state.

The one person almost solely responsible for publicizing the plight of the Cherokees and organizing national opposition to the government's removal policies was Jeremiah Evarts (1781-1831), a lawyer and in the late 1820s and early 1830s secretary of the Ameri-

[69] For historical background and analysis of governmental removal policies and relations with the Indian tribes, see the magisterial work of Francis Paul Prucha, *The Great Father: The United States Government and the American Indian*, 2 vols. (Lincoln, Nebraska: University of Nebraska Press, 1984), 1: 179-270.

[70] Ibid., 197-98.

[71] Ibid., 205.

can Board of Commissioners for Foreign Missions.[72] From 1829 until his death in 1831, he was indefatigable in informing the nation and the national congressional leaders, especially the Whigs, about the Indians' legal and humanitarian rights to their lands, and the Christian responsibility of the nation to live up to its covenants with the Indians. No doubt much of the information about the Indians' legal and social conditions came from Evarts' pen, and much of the national campaign against the removal policy was initiated by him. After his death, Whig leaders like Daniel Webster and Chancellor James Kent sided with the Indians' cause in highly publicized and celebrated Supreme Court cases. National and local newspapers buzzed with news about the Indians and arguments for and against removal.

Brownson entered the national debate in April of 1839 with "Our Indian Policy."[73] He sided with the Jacksonians, interpreting the removal policy as a humane way of protecting the Indians from the white population and providing them an opportunity, far removed from American society, for gradual improvement in religious instruction, education, and civilization.

Brownson wanted to provide a very "prejudiced" public with the facts of a removal that had already been accomplished by the time he wrote. His article was clearly an attempt to support the legality of the removal policy, citing as it did numerous Supreme Court decisions and treaties that supplied legal justification.

Brownson shared with many in his society a paternalistic attitude toward the Indian. The Indians were "uncivilized and improvident" and needed the government's protection so they could gradually become acculturated into American society. At the present time, however, the two races, Indian and white, could not live together. The white race was "cultivated, laborious, and highly progressive; the other ignorant, idle, and stationary."[74] And since Providence had ordained that the progressive and superior race would subdue the earth, it was not possible for the two races to live side by side without constant mutual wrongs and strife. The removal, therefore, would be best for both races. Gradual and progressive improvement of the Indian race would in the distant future make coexistence possible. "We

[72] On Evarts' campaign, see *Cherokee Removal: The "William Penn" Essays and Other Writings. By Jeremiah Evarts*, edited and introduced by Francis Paul Prucha (Knoxville: University of Tennessee Press, 1981).

[73] *Boston Quarterly Review* 2 (April, 1839): 229-59. See also chapter 15 in this volume.

[74] Ibid., 234. See also Chapter 15 in this volume, p. 315.

would make him [the Indian] a new being. We would mold him a new destiny."[75]

Brownson's humanitarian paternalism and Jacksonian partisan politics separated him from many of the Whigs, Unitarians, Transcendentalists, and evangelical Christians in Massachusetts who were clearly against the removal policies.

The issue of public or common school education also loomed large in Massachusetts during the late 1830s and Brownson weighed in on it. The chief advocate of universal education, the reform of educational systems, and preparatory programs for teachers at the time was Horace Mann (1796-1859), the father of the American public school system.[76] Mann came to prominence after Massachusetts enacted a law creating the Massachusetts Board of Education on 20 April 1837, and the governor selected Mann to act as its first secretary. The Board had little power, but Mann used it and its annual reports to the state to raise consciousness about the needs of education in the state. In the late 1830s Mann and the Board of Education promoted better organization of the schools, the establishment of teacher training programs, and the improvement of methods of education. Besides providing basic skills and instruction the common schools, in Mann's view, were to emphasize non-sectarian moral and religious values, preparing students for their participation in and contribution to a free republic.

Massachusetts had a strong tradition of the education of children at the local levels and had established a number of local private and common schools prior to the organization of the Board. Under Mann's leadership the Board and its annual reports to the state, written by Mann, publicized the need for universal education and tried to create a state-wide consensus for improving educational systems and methods. Mann's annual reports between 1837 and 1848 articulated the grounds for universal education and the need for effective institutionalization of the state's educational mission and responsibilities.[77] Public support (in the form of a consensus on the need for

[75] Ibid., 233-34. See also Chapter 15 in this volume, p.314.

[76] For Mann's role in the development of a republican philosophy of education and in initiating state-wide supervision of public education, see Lawrence A. Cremin, *American Education: The National Experience, 1783-1876* (New York: Harper and Row, 1980), 133-42, 154-57.

[77] For the significance of the reports and substantive selections from them, see *The Republic and the School: The Education of Free Men*, edited by Lawrence A. Cremin (New York: Teachers College, Columbia University, 1957).

universal education, and in the form of public taxation) and public control (in the form of state-supported acquisition and distribution of resources and information for the improvement and institutionalization of reform efforts) were the two major keys to Mann's efforts at educational reform.

Mann saw public education as the key to the preservation of American democracy and a republican form of government. Like Jefferson and a large segment of American society he believed that the people could not long remain free if ignorant. For him education, to be the servant of freedom and democracy, had to be universal, moral, and religious. But, how could a common or public education be religious in a society that was divided into vastly different religious sects. Mann, a Unitarian, provided a specifically Unitarian solution to the problem of religious diversity in American society by calling for a non-denominational approach to education that would emphasize the commonly agreed upon religious principles found in natural religion and in the Bible. Commonly accepted religious principles would provide fundamental support for the moral development and improvement of all children, a form of self-culture that would make students sensitive to and zealous for the common good.

Brownson found much to admire in the attempts to improve and reform common school education, but also much to criticize in Mann's approach.[78] Since his early days with the Workingmen's party in upstate New York Brownson had promoted universal education and considered it a central issue for the nation.[79] In 1839, Brownson reacted to some of Mann's views of the common school, but also put the whole issue of education in a much broader context than the common school—emphasizing the total, life-long education of the people not only through schools but also through three of the many other means of education: i.e., the clergy, the lyceums, and the press.[80] Brownson agreed with most in Massachusetts that popular education was a matter of right and that it was the foundation of free

[78] Mann was not unprepared for Brownson's criticisms. It was known in some Boston circles that Brownson had planned to take issue with the Board of Education. Mann told Samuel G. Howe that Brownson would "attack them because they are Whigs & me for the same reason." And, Mann was right, but partisan politics was not the only reason. On the controversy, see Arthur E. Bestor, "Horace Mann, Elizabeth P. Peabody, and Orestes A. Brownson," *Proceedings of the Middle States Association of History and Social Science Teachers* 38 (1940-41): 47-53, quotation on 49.

[79] On his early views, see the Introduction to EW, 2.

[80] "Education of the People," *Boston Quarterly Review* 2 (October, 1839): 393-434. See also chapter 19 in this volume.

government. But, he wanted to address questions that he thought the first Massachusetts Board of Education and its secretary had neglected in its second annual report on education. The board had not addressed what Brownson considered the fundamental question—namely the ultimate ends and means of the education of human beings as individuals and as social beings. Such questions were inherently religious and political questions, and therefore for him all education, in its very nature, was religious and political because it had to deal with the ultimate destiny of individuals and societies. In this respect he criticized the report of 1839 because it had no leading idea in it on the ends of education and no clear examination of the appropriate means to those ends.

Brownson went on to criticize the idea that education could in fact be non-sectarian. It could be religious or Christian, but religion and Christianity did not exist in the abstract; it resided in concrete historical communities with creeds and beliefs that were shared. In fact, there was no common ground between the Christian sects, he observed, and to build education on such a presupposition was foolhardy and historically unrealistic. In fact, the differences between the sects were fundamental, extending to the nature of human destiny itself. In a non-sectarian common school, "Much," he maintained, "may be taught in general, but nothing in particular. No sect will be satisfied; all sects will be dissatisfied. For, it is not that my children are not educated in a belief contrary to my own; I would have them educated to believe what I hold to be important truth; and I always hold that to be important truth, wherein I differ from others."[81] It would be almost impossible, furthermore, to appoint non-sectarian teachers; such creatures did not exist in the real world. What he said about the religious ends of education he also said about the political. In the current political climate there were major and essential differences between a Whig and a Democratic understanding of the ends and means of our common destiny as a society.

Although Brownson recognized the importance of efforts to reform education he did not like the idea of a state-instituted board of education. It looked too much like government control of education. Such control was dangerous in a democratic society; it resembled the absolutist atmosphere of Prussia. Even more, he was concerned that the members appointed to the board, with a token exception,

[81] Ibid., 404. See also Chapter 19 in this volume, p. 399.

were Whigs.[82] Education would lose its necessary freedom if it were under the supervision of government-appointed guardians because those guardians would have to be safe and popular men. To be popular, for Brownson, meant to be dependent, dependent upon common values; such men could not be intellectually daring and innovative. Such kind of popular men, he opined, had filled the colleges and "Colleges, as a general rule, are the last place to which you should look for new ideas, or inspiration to devote one's self to the cause of spiritual and social progress."[83] Brownson's residual anti-elitism came out throughout the essay. What he wanted was not state dictation of education, but local parental participation and control. Government must not be installed, he ended, as the educator of the people.

Brownson did not look for any real reform from the Board of Education. That board would serve well the material and utilitarian educational needs of the community, but it would not promote genuine educational reform. The common schools, even under a Board of Education, would provide instruction in reading, writing, and the positive sciences, but such instruction was not real education. "The community can never be educated in schools, technically so called; they can be educated only by the free action of mind on mind."[84] There were many other institutions (e.g., the clergy, lyceums, press) and individuals in society that could provide real education, if only they lived out their potential and brought mind to act upon mind.

Another issue that received some widespread attention during the late 1830s was the relatively new science of phrenology. Phrenologists claimed to be able to identify a person's psychological and moral characteristics, as well as mental capacities and faculties by empirically examining the configuration of the skull. Phrenology had its origins in the thought of the Viennese physician Franz-Joseph Gall (1758-1828), was modified and carried forward into English-speaking countries by his assistant, the German physician Johann Kaspar Spurzheim (1776-1832), and the Scottish educational re-

[82] Whig Governor Edward Everett appointed himself and his Lieutenant-Governor George Hull as *ex officio* members of the Board, and the following other members: Jared Sparks, the president of Harvard; Edmund Dwight, a wealthy Boston businessman; Edward A. Newton, a Pittsfield merchant and banker; Emerson Davis and Thomas Robbins, prominent Congregational ministers; Mann; James G. Carter, state Senator; and the sole Democrat, Robert Rantoul, Jr. On the make-up of the Board, see Cremin, *American Education: The National Experience*, 136.

[83] "Education of the People," 411. See also Chapter 19 in this volume, p. 404.

[84] Ibid., 434. See also Chapter 19 in this volume, p. 423.

former George Combe (1788-1858). Spurzheim had come to the United States to spread the phrenological word, and in fact died in Boston on a lecture circuit. Combe had published a number of texts which were read in the United States, and in 1837 and 1838 he lectured in Boston and elsewhere in the United States. Brownson had read some of Combe's works and had attended his Boston lectures on phrenology.

Gall had proposed that the skull's configuration was a good indicator of individual character traits, and intellectual and moral capacities. Such traits and qualities were located in definite areas of the brain and the size of each area indicated the degree or quality of the individual traits. Gall named twenty-seven traits (e.g., attentiveness, amity, benevolence, violence) and powers, which were innate but could be identified empirically. Spurzheim identified thirty-five traits and altered Gall's system by trying to demonstrate that phrenology was capable of ameliorating most of the social ills of the day. Combe used the system to further educational reform and popularized it with his many publications which were republished in the United States.

Combe emphasized the perfectibility of human beings and the innate qualities of the intellectual and moral powers of the soul. He also held up individual responsibility by stressing the individual's and society's responsibility to investigate physiology and the corresponding temperaments, and to control and regulate those innate human traits and characteristics. The so-called science of phrenology has been thoroughly discredited in the twentieth century, but it had large popular fascination in the nineteenth century, even though a few nineteenth century critics considered it a crackpot science.

Combe's phrenology appealed in particular to Horace Mann and many Transcendentalists.[85] Mann saw in the new science a scientific or empirical justification for his non-sectarian approach to moral and religious education. Phrenology had demonstrated for him that religious and moral characteristics were not the products of culture or history or tradition, but were inherent and that with proper methods of education those inherent qualities could be developed and perfected. Transcendentalists, too, were initially attracted to the new science because its psychology reinforced their own intuitionism and belief in human perfectibility. Some, like Brownson, even thought that it had some empirical merit, but that it went beyond the natural

[85] See, e.g., *The Republic and the School*, 13-14; John B. Wilson, "Phrenology and the Transcendentalists," *American Literature* 28 (May, 1956): 220-25.

boundaries of empiricism when it made philosophical assertions about human nature and destiny (i.e., areas empirical science was incapable of discerning).

In April of 1839, after listening to Combe's Boston lectures and reading his *A System of Phrenology* (1835), Brownson published an essay on the "Pretensions of Phrenology" from his own Transcendentalist philosophical perspective.[86] The pretension Brownson referred to was the claim that a philosophy of the mind could be created on the basis of empirical science. He asserted his impatience with the "arrogant pretensions" of scientists who transcended the boundaries of their methods and drew conclusions which were philosophical (and not scientific) in their nature.[87]

Brownson accepted the facts of phrenology, i.e., he accepted its legitimate sphere of "a physiological account of the brain."[88] Phrenology did enable human beings to explain the causes of the differences one observed in individual characters. But he refused to "erect it into a complete system of mental philosophy."[89] He asserted, furthermore, that the phrenologists did not in fact rely on empiricism for their philosophy of mind because their philosophy was prior to their empiricism and indeed directed or conditioned their empiricism. Behind Brownson's entire essay was a distinction between the methodologies of empirical science and that of philosophy, a distinction that would only increase in his mind over time.

One of Brownson's major criticisms of phrenology was that it promoted a certain kind of empirical determinism because phrenologists identified desire and will, and therefore they had no place for personality (or a personal will that was essentially free). Desire, in Brownson's understanding, was essentially involuntary, a matter of necessity arising from nature; will was essentially a matter of personal free determination. Here again Brownson's criticism stemmed from his acceptance of Cousin's view of personality, which Cousin had learned from Maine de Biran. Phrenologists had no place in their psychology for the human free will which was the distinguishing characteristic and faculty of human personality. Willing was not desiring, and was not intellect. Brownson asserted that Combe had confused these powers in the human psyche. Because they lacked these essential distinctions the phrenologists could not give an ad-

[86] *Boston Quarterly Review* 2 (April, 1839): 205-29. See also chapter 14 in this volume.

[87] Ibid., 227. See also Chapter 14 in this volume, p. 309.

[88] Ibid., 226. See also Chapter 14 in this volume, p. 308.

[89] Ibid., 206. See also Chapter 14 in this volume, p. 294.

equate philosophical explanation of human accountability. Like the subjective idealists George Berkeley and Johann Gottlieb Fichte, moreover, they were unable to account for an objective world, a world outside and independent of the self. And, although they claimed that their system harmonized with Christianity, they could provide no sound reasons for the existence of God, nor could they provide grounds for determining whether religion was a truth or an illusion—because they defined religion almost exclusively as an internal sentiment. Nor, finally, were they able to explicate an intelligible basis for morality or the immortality of the soul.

Although Brownson demonstrated a certain openness to the new science of phrenology and other new reform movements, he was becoming increasingly impatient with a reforming attitude that showed no respect for the past. Again, as with the abolitionists, Brownson indicated that he distrusted a person "who can see nothing to venerate in his forefathers, and who bows not before the wisdom of antiquity."[90] This generalized conservative respect for the past was a minor motif in Brownson's writings during the heyday of high reform in Boston intellectual and social circles, but it indicated a mentality that would only increase over the next few years when he saw the reforming mentality as a manifestation of philosophical individualism and subjectivism that was a fundamental threat to social order if carried to its logical conclusions.

Brownson focused most of his attention on religion, philosophy, politics and social reform, but in all of these interests philosophy was his primary concern. This was true, too, with his approach to literature. Almost every issue of the *Boston Quarterly Review* devoted at least one article to what could loosely be called literary criticism. When Brownson reviewed either prose or poetry, he criticized and evaluated it by the standards of his own philosophy of art, focusing almost entirely upon the ends of literature because he interpreted literature primarily as a means to an end, not an end in itself. His "Introductory Statement" for the January 1840 issue of the *Quarterly* summed up nicely his fundamental approach to literature in general: "Of literature proper, I have not much to say, I place no value on literature for its own sake, and never make it an end to be sought. It deserves our attention only as a means of individual and social growth. The literary aim of this journal will be to breathe into our literature a free and elevated spirit, and to give it a democratic cast, a truly American direction. I would enlist literature on the side

[90] Ibid., 228. See also Chapter 14 in this volume, p. 310.

of the people, and secure all its influence to the cause of democracy."[91] Brownson was, as Charles Carroll Hollis correctly pointed out, a Jacksonian literary critic who was primarily interested in the socially and democratically redemptive value of art and literature.[92]

Brownson did not write every review in the *Quarterly*, and one needs to be aware of this when examining his philosophy of literature because attributing some articles to him would make him appear to be more inconsistent and self-contradictory than he actually was. What is said about Carlyle in "Carlyle's French Revolution," for example, contradicts what Brownson says about Carlyle in a number of other essays in the *Quarterly*. "Carlyle's French Revolution" was in fact written by William Henry Channing.[93]

Brownson's own approach to art and literature must be seen within the wider currents of developing American literary sensitivities.[94] Emerson had uttered the clarion call for the development of a new literature in his "The American Scholar" address of 1837, an address that William Henry Channing reviewed in the *Quarterly*.[95] Since the War of 1812 there had been repeated calls for a literary emancipation especially from England, and a corresponding advocacy for the development of a distinctively American literature.[96] Emerson's "American Scholars" oration echoed that concern, but with a forcefulness

[91] 3 (January, 1840): 19.

[92] The most comprehensive examination of Brownson's literary criticism is in Charles Carroll Hollis' "The Literary Criticism of Orestes Brownson," Ph.D. dissertation, University of Michigan, 1954. I follow Hollis in much of what follows here. One flaw in the dissertation is in attributing to Brownson reviews that he did not write. Hollis, for example, attributes "Bacon's Poems" and "Carlyle's French Revolution" to Brownson, but those articles were written by John Sullivan Dwight and William Henry Channing. The mistake is easy to make, and I have in the past made it, because many of the persons who wrote for the *Quarterly* shared common ideas. See the following note for correct attribution of authorship.

[93] Marginal notes in Theodore Parker's copy of the *Quarterly* indicate that Channing was the author. Parker's copy is in the Boston Public Library. I am indebted to Clarence L. F. Gohdes, *The Periodicals of American Transcendentalism* (Durham: Duke University Press, 1931), 48-49, for this information.

[94] Brownson's views of the emergence of an American literature, and his understanding of the nature and function of art and literature were not clearly articulated in any single essay; they must be pieced together from various essays where he indicated the criteria he used to evaluate literature.

[95] See *The Collected Works of Ralph Waldo Emerson*, 1:52-70; and for the review, "Emerson's Phi Beta Kappa Oration," *Boston Quarterly Review* 1 (January, 1838): 106-20.

[96] One early, and relatively unknown, representative of this trend in American letters was the Philadelphian Robert Walsh (1784-1859), an English teacher at the University of Pennsylvania (1823-33).

and clarity that drew significant attention to the problem and created a new American mission to develop a specifically American literary tradition. Of course, there was a prior receptivity to such an address because of the Romantic and idealistic notions of language and art that had been developing in Transcendentalist circles here and there in American society. James Marsh's 1833 translation of Johann Gottfried Herder's (1744-1803) *The Spirit of Hebrew Poetry*[97] and George Ripley's critical examination of Marsh's translation in the *Christian Examiner* of 1835,[98] too, indicated something of a new mentality relative to understanding language and its functions within a society and within literature itself.

The American Transcendentalists were trying to break the chains of the Lockean hold on words and language and to forge a new understanding of language itself. In his third book of the *Essay Concerning Human Understanding*, which many Unitarians had accepted as a blueprint for understanding the meaning of words and language, Locke had articulated his nominalist, empiricist, and conventionalist view of words. For him, words were conventionally agreed upon signs for the ideas in the mind of him who used them or of the community who agreed upon their meaning. Words, in effect, therefore, were arbitrary signs indicating nothing universal. They were artificial constructs that rested upon a societal agreed upon meaning. Such a view of language came out clearly in the Unitarian-Trinitarian struggles over biblical interpretation in the early nineteenth century, and came to the fore again in the Unitarian battle with the emerging American Transcendentalism in the mid to late 1830s. From their own Romantic and idealist perspectives, the Transcendentalists developed a new "symbolist theory of language," challenging the Lockean perspective.[99] The new theory was somewhat evident in Emerson's *Nature* (1836), *The American Scholar* (1837), and *The Divinity School Address* (1838).

There were numerous sources for a new theory of language: Kant, Herder, Coleridge, Carlyle, and Cousin, to name but a few. Lan-

[97] (Burlington, Maine: Smith, 1833).

[98] "Professor Marsh's Translation of Herder," *Christian Examiner* 18 (May, 1835): 167-221.

[99] On the origins of a new "symbolist theory of language," as articulated here, I am indebted to Philip F. Gura's "The Transcendentalists and Language: The Unitarian Exegetical Background," in Philip F. Gura and Joel Myerson, ed. *Critical Essays on American Transcendentalism* (Boston: G. K. Hall, 1982), 611-12, and Gura's *The Wisdom of Words: Language, Theology, and Literature in the New England Renaissance* (Middletown, Conn.: Wesleyan University Press, 1981).

guage for the Transcendentalists symbolized the universal truth that was at the heart of all inspiration and revelation; language could not fully captured in any didactic or comprehensive way the full reality of the universal truth that was at the bottom of all revelatory and ecstatic experiences. Spirit corresponded to matter, but matter could never fully comprehend or body forth spirit. Language, as an expression of spirit, became the vehicle of concealing as well as revealing the inner reality to which it pointed. Such a view of language, however, did not completely escape the didacticism of the past because for the Transcendentalists language was useful for the expression and development of moral character. But, unlike the Lockean perspective, it was the concretization of universal inspiration. Its primary function was to evoke, not declare, the universal truth, goodness, and beauty that was available to all through inspiration.

To some extent the Transcendentalist ministers had been experimenting with a new theory of language in their own sermons and conversations. As Lawrence Buell has indicated, the sermon for many Transcendentalist ministers was an "inspirational oration" rather than a didactic enterprise that had been almost stock and trade for many of the old school ministers. These sermons, and Emerson's are a good example, made much more of "imagination and creativity" than had been the case among so many Unitarian as well as orthodox Puritan ministers.[100]

Brownson had very little to say about a new symbolist theory of language, and even less to say about literary techniques or style, but he was interested in the development of a new American literature that was democratic in appeal and orientation, reflective of issues of social justice and particularly of the problems of economic equity in society, and intentionally focused on motivating readers to regenerate society. Brownson shared the new generation's desire for a literary renaissance that would emancipate American letters from its excessive dependence upon England. But, Brownson separated himself from what he perceived to be an excessively egotistical view of literature—that is, Emerson's view that the solitary scholar should create literature from the depths of his own soul and should rise above the mediocrity of society. According to Brownson, Emerson believed that "the creation of a literature is a thing entirely dependent on the individual will." Brownson, on the other hand, believed that literature "is the expression and embodiment of the national life. The time and manner of its creation are determined by as necessary and invariable

[100] On this, see Lawrence Buell, *Literary Transcendentalism: Style and Vision in the American Renaissance* (Ithaca, New York: Cornell University Press, 1973), 105.

laws, as the motions of the sun, the revolutions of the earth, the growth of a tree, or the blowing of a flower."[101] Brownson thought Emerson's view of "Man Thinking" reflected literary elitism that was inconsistent with democracy. That view represented too much the "act out thyself" philosophy of Goethe and Carlyle. Literature, instead, was a product of the society in which it appeared, and the true author was the one who could identify with the national genius of the people and their social aspirations, and show the masses the way to the realization of their God-given spirit. Like many of the Romantics, Brownson accepted the idea that each nation had its own particular spirit and genius, and that its literature ought to reflect a "development to some one element of universal truth, which is given to no other nation."[102] He believed that there was a literature in the American soul that was just waiting to burst forth into print. It could not develop, however, without the time and leisure necessary for its creation, and indeed for its reception because literature had to be received and read by the people before it could be considered truly great literature. In order to create and to receive good literature, therefore, the country needed to augment and distribute the wealth of the country. Such a distribution would provide the conditions of time and leisure that were necessary for creation and reception. Scholars should be about the business of making the whole nation a "fit audience" for literary genius. Literature in the United States needed to reflect the democratic aspirations of the country, the genius of its freedom, the universal equality of rights and opportunities, and a concern for the social and material welfare of all the people. Literature was an expression of social, not just individual liberation and emancipation.

From various essays one can piece together Brownson's transcendental and democratic philosophy of art and literature. Any work of art should appeal, Brownson insisted following Cousin, to the whole of human nature: to intelligibility (knowing), sensibility (feeling), activity (willing), and indeed to the moral sense. Good art had lofty purposes. It should provide evidence that the artist had "communed with a beauty, a worth, not of this world." Truly great artists tended "to enlarge our ideals, to give us glimpses of something purer and more elevated than has yet been attained, to exalt our sentiments, to

[101] "American Literature," *Boston Quarterly Review* 2 (January, 1839): 19. See also Chapter 7 in this volume, pp. 146-47.

[102] On this see Brownson's review of Ripley's "Specimens of Foreign Literature," *Boston Quarterly Review* 1 (October, 1838): 433. See also Chapter 3 in this volume, p. 65.

purify our affections, to create in us inexpressible longings for what we have not, and to make us consecrate ourselves to the glorious work of regenerating the world."[103] Genuine art could serve such elevated purposes because it was the expression of what Cousin called spontaneous reason, that impersonal and universal inspiration that was present in all human beings. Such spontaneous reason was not the creation of a personal will. Good art, therefore, reflected and evoked a fundamental experience of the divinity within, and, as Cousin argued, that experience could be expressed "only in language of the same character."[104]

For Cousin, as for Herder and a whole host of Romantics and Transcendentalists, poetry was that language. "The necessary form, the language of inspiration, is poetry; and the first oration, is a hymn. We do not commence with prose, but with poetry; for we do not commence with reflection, but with intuition and absolute affirmation."[105] In his review of "Wordsworth's Poems," Brownson followed Cousin in seeing poetry as the highest literary form, superior to all forms of prose in expressing universal revelation.[106] Poetry was "inspiration, clothing itself with words."[107] Not everything that claimed to be poetry, however, served its exalted purposes. There was true poetry "only where spontaneity so utters itself as to move the sensibility."[108] When it was genuine, poetry produced the spiritual state one generally called enthusiasm. That is why poetry was so close to religious sentiment and devotion. In fact, poetry was itself religious devotion when it considered the absolute it experienced and expressed as God, as Father, and as sovereign. Any poetry that did not elevate the reader to a level of ecstacy, therefore, was not authentic. All human beings had spontaneous reason, but not all were true poets. Inspiration moved the sensibility and produced enthusiasm only in the true poets. Such poets were able to choose a language that evoked fire from the listener, that made the audience burn as the poet burned with delight in the divine that the poet experienced. Thus, poetry, for Brownson, was truer than philosophy, which was a form of prose. Poetry was closer to the font of inspiration. God spoke in poetry,

[103] "Bulwer's Novels," 271. See also Chapter 16 in this volume, p. 343.

[104] *Introduction to the History of Philosophy*, trans. Henning Gotfried Linberg (Boston: Hilliard, Gray, Little, and Wilkins, 1832), 166-67.

[105] Ibid.

[106] *Boston Quarterly Review* 2 (April, 1839): 137-49. See also chapter 12 in this volume.

[107] Ibid., 144. See also Chapter 12 in this volume, p. 252.

[108] Ibid., 140. See also Chapter 12 in this volume, p. 249.

only the human being spoke in philosophy. Such a view coming from Brownson the philosopher indicates the high regard he had for poetry, even though, as he admitted several times, he was not an artist and was incompetent to judge "the niceties of art,"[109] meaning the forms and technicalities of artistic expression. He did claim, nevertheless, that he knew good literature, whether prose or poetry, when he experienced it because it transported him to its noble ends.

Good literature, whether prose or poetry, uplifted not only the individual, but the masses because its mission was to reflect the universal reason which was the word of God for all human beings. Literature and all good art had a social responsibility because it was called upon to image divine care for the entire human race. Literature had to possess, therefore, a social conscience, not just in the sense of sympathizing with the poor and oppressed of society, but in the sense of inspiring people to do something about economic and social systems that brought about poverty and oppression in the first place. Good literature had to express a heart that burned to better the conditions of the human race, but especially of those who were on the fringes of society. Any literature that did not fulfill these social, democratic and moral goals did not receive Brownson's blessing.

Good literature had to be moral, but to be genuine art, it could not be didactic. Brownson hated those sentimental or dogmatic religious novels that were created to express "some special dogma" or "some special moral lesson." Good art was not propaganda, was not didactic. Didactic novels and poetry abandoned freedom, genius, and inspiration for the sake of a lesson. The authentic artist created with a moral purpose, with reference to a moral effect, but without being preachy, moralistic, or magisterial.[110]

In 1838 and 1839, in the midst of political campaigns in the United States, Brownson's reviews of literature focused particularly on the democratic and social standards he was articulating in his reviews of specific works. Although he had high praise for Emerson, Goethe, Carlyle, and Wordsworth as artists and as representatives of the new school, he found them less than good artists on the score of democracy, concern for social justice, and the uplift of the masses. On the other hand, although he believed that the novelist Edward George Earle Bulwer-Lytton (1803-73) did not fulfill all the designs of good art, he praised his novels highly because Bulwer was listed on the side of humanity. His novels, moreover, demonstrated a keen

[109] "Bulwer's Novels," 267. See also Chapter 16 in this volume, p. 340.
[110] Ibid., 268. See also Chapter 16 in this volume, p. 340.

social sense because he was able to show that "many of the depravities of individual character are due to the depravities of that social state in which the character is formed." Like William Godwin (1756-1836), the British novelist and political writer whom Brownson had read as a young man, Bulwer was aware that individuals were many times "victims of an imperfect, a corrupt social state." Novels that depict such conditions should inspire one to labor for the "regeneration of society."[111] Bulwer's novels evoked that great truth "that individuals are not alone responsible for their acts, that society shares the responsibility for them." Such a truth, in Brownson's view, "has not received that place in our moral and criminal codes which its importance demands."[112] Bulwer, too, was able to demonstrate that even corrupted individuals have within their being powers and instincts of their better natures.[113] In anticipation of a presidential democratic campaign Brownson had high praise for Bulwer who is "for the people" and against the aristocratic few; he had joined the revolution on the right side, on the side of democracy.[114] Later in his life Brownson criticized Bulwer's novels as a manifestation of a quasi-environmental determinism that Brownson himself had partially accepted in his early years.[115] During the late 1830s, however, Brownson saw Bulwer as another bulwark for the Democratic party and its campaign to retain the presidency, a campaign whose failure in 1840 was a great disappointment to Brownson.

The editorial principles and procedures followed in this volume are the same as those in volume one of *The Early Works of Orestes A. Brownson,*[116] which is referred to in the footnotes in this and subsequent volumes as EW.

[111] Ibid., 277-78. See also Chapter 16 in this volume, p. 349. Brownson was here referring to Bulwer's novel *Paul Clifford.*

[112] Ibid., 292. See also Chapter 16 in this volume, p. 360.

[113] Ibid., 286, 288. See also Chapter 16 in this volume, pp. 357-80.

[114] Ibid., 297. See also Chapter 16 in this volume, p. 364.

[115] For one example of that criticism, see "Education and the Republic" (January, 1874) in *The Works of Orestes A. Brownson,* ed. Henry F. Brownson, 20 vols. (Detroit: Thorndike Nourse, 1882-87), 13:447.

[116] See, *The Universalist Years, 1826-29* (Milwaukee, Wis.: Marquette University Press, 2000), 30-34.

I.

EMERSON'S DIVINITY SCHOOL ADDRESS[1]

Boston Morning Post 204 (August 31, 1838): 1

We notice this address, not on account of its intrinsic merits, nor because we sympathize with the peculiar views of the author; but because it has created some little excitement in certain circles and called forth censures, which, without a word or two of explanation, may affect the characters of some who are very far from entertaining views similar to those which Mr. Emerson is in the habit of putting forth.

We are not likely to be thought peculiarly partial to Mr. Emerson. We shall not soon forget his ill-advised letter to Mr. Van Buren concerning the Cherokees.[2] Nevertheless, we respect Mr. Emerson, as an accomplished scholar, an agreeable and entertaining lecturer, a high-minded and honorable man, a free and independent spirit, willing to utter himself, and be himself, and not another. We reverence his honesty, his independence, his boldness. In this respect we shall always be ready to enroll ourselves among his friends, and to the best of [3] our ability defend his character.

But when it concerns Mr. Emerson's peculiar religious and philosophical views, it is quite another affair. We are not always sure that we understand him, and when we feel confident that we do catch his

[1] [Ed. The editor has supplied the title for Brownson's review of Ralph Waldo Emerson's *An Address, Delivered before the Senior Class, in Divinity College, Cambridge, Sunday evening, 15 July, 1838* (Boston: J. Munroe and Co., 1838).]

[2] [Ed. Reference is to Emerson's "Letter to Martin Van Buren, President of the United States," 23 April 1838, published, among other places, in the *Daily National Intelligencer* (Washington, D.C.), May 14, 1838. The letter was written one day after a town meeting in Concord, Massachusetts, that protested the removal of the Cherokees "to a wilderness at a vast distance beyond the Mississippi." Emerson's letter represented the protests of the people of Concord against the shameful "so-called " treaty of 1835 that provided the legal basis for such a savage act of injustice. One version of this letter is republished in James Elliot Cabot, *A Memoir of Ralph Waldo Emerson*, 2 vols. (Boston: Houghton, Mifflin and Co., 1885, 1887), 2:697-702. On Brownson's later view of Emerson's wrong-headed opposition to the removal of the Cherokees from Georgia, see "Our Indian Policy," chapter 15 in this volume.]

[3] [Ed. The original had "to the of best our ability defend his character."]

meaning, we do not always, by any means, approve it. But his views are his own; he has a right to entertain them and to do his best to propagate them. All we have to do with them is to examine them if we deem them worth examining, and to reject them, so far as they seem to us to be false or unsound. For ourselves, we have no fears that the cause of truth can be essentially injured or retarded by the promulgation of error. Error has always a tendency to destroy itself.

There is one thing, however, we wish to notice, and concerning which we think it desirable the public should be set in the right. There has been for sometime manifested in certain quarters a disposition to throw into the same category men who have very little in common, and who entertain opinions in philosophical and religious matters widely different. This disposition was strikingly displayed by a writer in the Daily Advertiser of Monday last.[4] That writer speaks of a "New School in Literature and Religion," as having lately sprung up amongst us; and he gives it, for its chiefs, the distinguished French philosopher, Victor Cousin; and the somewhat distinguished, but eccentric, Germanized-English scholar, Thomas Carlyle.[5] He also adroitly seizes upon this address of Mr. Emerson as a sort of exposition of the doctrines of this new school. Now in all this there is much misconception or great disingenuousness.

There are, undoubtedly, certain movements, tendencies, amongst us, which may in time lead to the creation of a new school in litera-

[4] [Ed. Reference is to Andrews Norton's (1786-1853) assault on Emerson in "The New School in Literature and Religion," *Boston Daily Advertiser* (August 27, 1838); reprinted in Perry Miller, ed., *The Transcendentalists*, 193-96. Norton was a biblical scholar and professor at Harvard, primarily known for his vigorous defense of Unitarianism and his vitriolic attacks on American Transcendentalism. For an analysis of Norton's response, see William R. Hutchison, *The Transcendentalist Ministers: Church Reform in the New England Renaissance* (New Haven: Yale University Press, 1959), 69-70.]

[5] [Ed. Cousin (1792-1867) was the founder of French Eclecticism. He tried to synthesize the Scottish Common Sense tradition with German idealism. Brownson began reading Cousin in 1833 and became a primary promoter of his philosophy until 1841 when he began to criticize Eclecticism. On the influence of Cousin on Brownson and other Unitarians and Transcendentalists, see the introductions to *The Early Works of Orestes A. Brownson*, Volume 2, *The Free Thought and Unitarian Years, 1830-1835*, and Volume 3, *The Transcendentalist Years, 1836-1838*. Thomas Carlyle (1795-1881) was a Scottish intellectual who was influenced considerably by German writers, particularly Immanuel Kant (1724-1804) and Johann Wolfgang von Goethe (1749-1832). Hostile to Lockean philosophy and extremely critical of historical Christianity and organized religion, Carlyle had an enormous influence upon a large number of American Transcendentalists who were primarily drawn to his emphasis upon duty and the moral will.]

ture. A new school is certainly needed, from which may come forth a literature in perfect harmony with the higher nature of man and the democratic spirit of the institutions of this country. There are many warm hearts here craving such a school, and many noble spirits at work in earnest to create it. Nevertheless, it is hardly true to say that a new school has as yet been created.

As it concerns the movements, the tendencies, to which the writer in question alludes, it is certain that they have been much influenced by the publications of Cousin and Carlyle. But there is manifest injustice in classing the friends and admirers of the one with those of the other. It is impossible to conceive two men more unlike than Victor Cousin and Thomas Carlyle. Cousin is a philosopher, a metaphysician, remarkable for his good taste, good sense, uncommon logical powers, and the clearness and elegance of his style. He is a rigorous logician, one of the severest reasoners that can be found. With him no proposition can be admitted till it has given an account of itself, and fully verified its claims to the understanding. Carlyle, on the other hand, is no philosopher, no metaphysician. He laughs at metaphysics, at all attempts to account to ourselves for ourselves, to account for any of the phenomena of man or of nature, or to form any system of philosophy, politics, theology, or ethics. He is a poet, a seer, who has frequent and glorious glimpses of truth, and of sublime and far-reaching truth, too; but one who never verifies what he sets forth as truth, who never asks how he knows what he sees is truth or shows us how we may know that it is truth. He has genius; in many respects he is a remarkable man; and, notwithstanding his eccentric, and very objectionable style, he may be read with pleasure and with profit.[6]

Now the difference there is between these two men is still more striking between their friends in this country. The admirers of Mr. Carlyle, at the head of whom may be placed the author of the address before us, are termed, properly or improperly, Transcendentalists, and are, perhaps, in the main, correctly enough described by the correspondent of the Advertiser. But the friends of M. Cousin, ranked by the same correspondent with them, choose to be called Eclectics. They are a very different class of men, men of very different literary tendencies and philosophical views. The Transcendentalists, so called, are by no means philosophers; they are either dreamers, or mere speculatists, condemning logic, and holding the understanding in

[6] [Ed. Brownson's characterization of Carlyle reflects his current understanding of Emerson.]

light esteem. The Eclectics aim to be a very sober and a very rational sort of people. They are not materialists; they do not believe John Locke finished philosophy; nevertheless, they profess to follow the experimental method of philosophizing. They differ from the Scotch school of Reid and Stewart,[7] only in going a little further in the same route. They do not believe, indeed, that all our ideas originate in the senses; they believe that the reason furnishes from its own stores certain elements of every fact of consciousness; but at the same time they believe, with the German philosopher, Kant "that all our knowledge begins with experience" and that the ideas or elements furnished by the reason, are developed only on the occasion of experience. As philosophers, their aim is, by analysis, to separate, in the case of all the facts of consciousness, the rational elements from the sensible elements, and, by tracing each to their source, to determine the origin and validity of our ideas, to fix the criterion of truth, and to account for, and legitimate the universal beliefs of mankind. With the Transcendentalists, they admit spontaneity or instinct, the fact of primitive intuition; but they differ from the Transcendentalists in this important particular, that whereas the Transcendentalists tell us that instinct is to be taken as our guide without any effort to legitimate it, thereby rejecting reflection, reasoning, all philosophic thought properly so called; the Eclectics summon instinct, intuition itself to the bar of reason and refuse to obey it till it has legitimated to the understanding its right to command.

To all who are competent to judge of the matter, here is surely a wide difference, and one which no man can be pardoned for overlooking. They whom we have designated as Transcendentalists are not in the habit of speaking respectfully of Cousin.[8] They do not

[7] [Ed. Thomas Reid (1710-96), philosopher of Aberdeen and later of Glasgow University, was the founder and leading light of the Scottish Common Sense tradition. Dugald Stewart (1753-1828), Reid's disciple, was a philosopher at Edinburgh University. Stewart was a more systematic philosopher than Reid and popularized the Scottish tradition. Stewart's texts were widely used in American colleges after about 1820, replacing in particular John Locke's *Essay Concerning Human Understanding*, which had reigned as a textbook during much of the eighteenth and the first part of the nineteenth centuries.]

[8] [Ed. Cousin had been widely read by American Transcendentalists, but some, like Emerson, who were influenced by Cousin during the early 1830s began by the mid and late 1830s to criticize his "superficial " eclecticism. Emerson's *Literary Ethics—An Oration Delivered before the Literary Societies of Dartmouth College, July 24, 1838*, in *The Complete Works of Ralph Waldo Emerson*, Ed. by Edward Waldo Emerson, 12 vols. (Boston: Houghton Mifflin, 1903-04), 1:171, indicates his reactions to Cousin's eclecticism.]

study him, and we may venture to assert, that they are ignorant of both the method and spirit of his philosophy. It is wrong, altogether wrong, therefore, to represent them as the followers of Cousin. It is a wrong to them; and a still greater wrong to those individuals among us who do really study and take an interest in Cousin's system of philosophy. Honor to whom honor is due is a good maxim; and give to every one his due is a precept that no advocate for religion and morality has any right on any occasion whatever to neglect.

We have made these remarks for the sole purpose of pointing out and requiring the public to notice an obvious, and as we regard it, a very essential difference between the two classes ranked in the same category by the correspondent of the Advertiser. For ourselves, we are not disposed to make war on either class. We say, let all opinions, all doctrines, have an "open field and fair play." We cannot, however, believe that the peculiar views set forth with so much confidence and fascination by Mr. Emerson, are likely to take a very deep root in the American heart. They are too dreamy, too misty, too vague, to have much effect except on young misses just from the boarding school or young lads who begin to fancy themselves in love. The Americans are a sturdy race; they are a reasoning people, and they will not long follow anyone who cannot give to the understanding a reason for the hope that is in him.

The popularity Mr. Emerson has acquired for the moment, and which seems to have alarmed some of the grave doctors at Cambridge, is easily accounted for without supposing any especial regard for his peculiar notions. Something is due to his personal manners, much to the peculiar characteristics of his style as a writer and as a lecturer; but still more to his independence, to the homage he pays to the spirit of freedom. Our young men have grown weary of leading strings. They are dissatisfied with the tyranny which custom, conventionalism, has exercised over them. They have felt the old formulas too straitened for them, and the air of their prison-houses too compressed, and too oppressive, and they have wished to break away, to roam at large over the green fields, and to breathe the fresh air of heaven. The state of mind here described, and which we may term a craving after freedom, exists in our community to a very great extent. To this craving Mr. Emerson has spoken; this craving he has done something to satisfy; therefore, his popularity. It is as the advocate of the rights of the mind, as the defender of personal independence in the spiritual world, not as the idealist, the pantheist, or the atheist, that he is run after, and all but worshiped by many young, ardent and yet noble minds. In this we see an omen of good and not of evil.

It is a proof that the spirit of liberty is yet living and active in our community; that the American institutions are doing their work, and embodying their sublime Idea in literature, art, and religion. For this we are thankful, and in it we rejoice.

The Cambridge professors who denounce Mr. Emerson, are very unwise, and seem to be verifying the old maxim, "whom the Gods will to destroy they first deprive of reason."[9] Their own insensibility to the free spirit of the age and country is the cause which leads the young men committed to their care to seek inspiration and instruction elsewhere. And elsewhere they will be sure to continue to go, unless their regular professors prove themselves capable of meeting the wants of their souls. They want freedom and life, and they will go where freedom and life are to be found. Let the professors be assured of this, and govern themselves accordingly. They must show that freedom and life can be found elsewhere than in connection with the speculations of Ralph Waldo Emerson, or to Ralph Waldo Emerson they may rest assured their pupils will resort.

[9] [Ed. The quotation could have any number of different sources (starting with Euripides, "Those whom God wishes to destroy, he first makes mad"), but it might be a paraphrase of John Dryden's (1631-1700) *The Hind and the Panther* (1687), 3, line 1093: "For those whom God to ruin has designed, he fits for fate, and first destroys their mind."]

2.

ALCOTT *ON HUMAN CULTURE*[1]

Boston Quarterly Review 1 (October, 1838): 417-32

This is a difficult book for reviewers. It is not easy to say what it is, or what it is not. It is hardly safe to assume it as an index to the views and opinions of its editor, or to the character and worth of the school in which these Conversations were held. The Conversations published are incomplete; they comprise only one year of what was intended to be a four years' course. The very nature of such conversations precludes the possibility of recording them with perfect accuracy, though these were recorded with great fidelity; and then, they constituted the exercise of the scholars for only a part of one half day in a week, the rest of the time being taken up with the studies common in other schools. As it regards Mr. Alcott, these Conversations very imperfectly reveal him, or his system of instruction. One is in constant danger of misapprehending him, and of ascribing to him views and opinions which belong solely to the children. Even his own questions, if we are not on our guard, may mislead us; for they were frequently suggested by the remarks of the scholars, and designed merely to induce them to carry out their own thought.

Mr. Alcott has received much reproach and we fear been made to suffer in the prosperity of his school on account of this book. He has been treated with great illiberality, and made to undergo as severe a persecution as the times allow. As a man he is singularly evangelical, pure minded, in love with all that is beautiful and good, and devoted soul and body to what he deems truth, and the regeneration of mankind. He is conscious of being sent into this world on a high and important mission, and his great study is to discharge that mis-

[1] [Ed. Review of Amos Bronson Alcott's *Conversations with Children on the Gospels*, 2 vols. (Boston: James Munroe and Co., 1836, 1837). Alcott (1799-1888) was a lay school teacher who experimented with a "conversational " teaching method to evoke from children their intuitive knowledge of religion and morality. With the help of William Ellery Channing and some wealthy Boston merchants he established the Temple School in Boston in 1834 to help children cultivate their human potential. Shortly after the publication of his first volume of *Conversations* in 1836 a number of parents and patrons objected to his radical methods and withdrew their children from the school, which ceased to exist in 1838.]

sion to the acceptance of him that sent him. Yet no man among us has been spoken of in severer tones, or been more seriously injured, for the moment, by the misapprehension and ill nature, the misrepresentation and abuse, he has had to endure from those who affect to lead public opinion.[2] It is painful to record this fact. For there is no man in our country who so well understands the art of education, and who is capable or desirous of doing more for establishing a system of human culture, in consonance with our faith as Christians and as republicans. And there is no fault, nor even shadow of a fault to be found with him; save that he will be true to the deepest and holiest convictions of his own mind; and will never sacrifice what he holds as truth, virtue, manhood, independence, to popular opinion, to a sickly taste, or a heartless conventionalism. It is not much to our credit that we condemn him for this.

Mr. Alcott may not be sound in his philosophy, he may not be correct in all his views, and he may carry, and we believe he does carry, some of his favorite notions to extremes; but he deserves profound reverence for his determination to be a man; to be true to human nature; for his fearless assertion of his own convictions, and for his deep and living faith in God and humanity. He aims to be himself and not another; to think his own thoughts and not another's; and having done this, he will not lock up his thoughts in his own bosom, and seem to acquiesce in reigning dogmas; but he will utter them, regardless of the reproach or injury he may sustain by so doing. Such a man in these times, when there are so few who feel that they are men and have a part of their own to act, is not to be cast aside, to be trampled on, without great detriment to our social and moral progress. Did we know what is for our good, we should seek out such men, and honor them as prophets sent from God to foretell and to usher in a more glorious future.

Still we are not at all surprised that Mr. Alcott and his publications are so little appreciated, and so greatly misapprehended. Mr. Alcott is a reformer. He does not believe that the past has realized the highest worth man may aspire to; he does not believe that the methods of teaching usually adopted, or the systems of education contended for by our teachers and professors generally, are at all adapted

[2] [Ed. Nathan Hale of the *Boston Daily Advertiser* and Joseph H. Buckingham of the *Boston Courier*, among a host of other newspaper and periodical writers, attacked the volumes as "indecent," "obscene," and "absurd." On the opposition, see Frederick C. Dahlstrand, *Amos Bronson Alcott: An Intellectual Biography* (London and Toronto: Associated University Presses, 1982), 141-42.]

to the purpose of rearing up MEN, and of making them walk as becomes moral and intellectual beings, made in the image of God and possessing a Divine nature; he thinks that the aim of our systems of education, whether private, public, domestic, or social, is too low, and that the methods adopted are destitute of science, above all of vitality, that they are too mechanical, and make of our schools only commendable "treadmills." Now to think and say all this is to reflect no great credit on our thousands of school teachers and learned professors and their friends, nor upon those who boast the efforts we have made and are making in the cause of education. This is as much as to tell his disciples, that unless their righteousness, in this respect, exceed that of the Scribes and Pharisees, the chief priests and elders in the teaching art, they shall in no wise be qualified for undertaking to rear up men and women, fit to be the citizens of a free and Christian republic. Can the chief priests and elders, the Scribes and Pharisees, be made to believe this; or to regard him who utters it in any other light than that of a reviler, a blasphemer? Reformers are never understood and appreciated, till the reforms for which they contend are to a good degree realized.

Then again, Mr. Alcott is a peculiar man. He has observed more than he has read, and reflected more than he has observed. He is a man, though eminently social in his feelings and tastes, who has lived mostly in communion with himself, with children, and with nature. His system is one which he has thought out for himself and by himself. It has therefore almost necessarily taken the hues of his own mind, and become somewhat difficult to communicate to minds not constructed like his own. The terms he has made use of in his solitary reflections to express his thoughts to himself have a special meaning, a special value in his use of them, of which those with whom he converses are ignorant, and of which it is often extremely difficult for them to conceive. In consequence of his solitary reflections, of his little intercourse with the world at large, and his limited acquaintance with books, he has framed to himself a peculiar language, which, though formed of the choicest English, is almost, if not quite wholly unintelligible to all who have not become extensively acquainted with his mode of thinking. He very easily translates the thoughts of others into his language, but it is with great difficulty that he translates his thoughts into their language. People generally in hearing him converse form no conception of his real meaning; and if they attach any meaning to what he says, it will in nine cases out of ten be a false one. This, however, though it accounts for the misapprehension of people, in regard to him, is not altogether his fault. People may misapprehend him because they do not understand themselves. There are not many men who have thoroughly analyzed their own minds, become masters of their own ideas, and so familiar with them that they can recognize them when clothed in a new dress. We are familiar with certain words, which we suppose we use as signs of ideas, but which we use very often as substitutes for ideas. When we find these words defined, or hear them used indeed as signs of ideas, and as signs of the very ideas for which we should have used them, had we used them for any, we are at fault; we find ourselves introduced to entire strangers with whom we can hold no conversation. We know not our own ideas; and very likely are frightened at them, and run away from them as though they were the Evil One himself.

But due allowance made for men's own ignorance as it regards the ideas they really express, if any, by the words they use, it is still extremely difficult to understand Mr. Alcott's system in all its parts. In the work before us it is but partially developed, and nowhere has he to our knowledge given us a complete development of it. But as we believe he really has a system, and one which is truly his own, and withal one for which he is willing to labor and suffer reproach, privation, and perhaps death itself, were it necessary, we shall—availing ourselves of all our means of arriving at a just comprehension of it—endeavor to lay it before our readers, as faithfully and as fully as we can, within the very narrow limits to which we are necessarily restricted.

Mr. Alcott is known mainly as a schoolmaster, but as a schoolmaster, as we usually think of schoolmasters, he must not be viewed. Unblessed with an abundance of this world's goods, he has often been obliged to confine himself to the drudgery of mere schoolmaster duties; but he is an original thinker, and he aspires to be an educator, not of children only, but of mankind. His system of human culture is designed for the human race, and is valued by him as true in itself, and as the means of raising all men to the stature of perfect men in Christ Jesus. He professes to have a whole system of theology, morality—a philosophy of man, of nature, of God. His method of teaching is but the means by which men are to be led ideally and actually to the Absolute. His philosophy he regards as the philosophy of the Absolute. It is as the theologian, the philosopher, the moralist, and the philanthropist, rather than as a schoolmaster, that he is to be regarded. But we proceed to develop his system.

Suppose a man who has no means of knowledge but his five senses. Such a man can take cognizance, of only material objects, of sensible qualities. Color, form, extension, solidity, sound, odor, taste, comprise all the objects of knowledge he can consistently admit. In a word, external nature is all he knows. External nature is to him what it appears. It is real, not symbolical. It indicates nothing which it is not, nothing on which it depends and of which it may be regarded as the sign or apparition. It is what it appears, and when seen it is known, and when known that is the end of knowledge. Nothing more is to be known.

In nature everything, as known by this man of five senses, and of five senses only, is concrete. Nothing is abstract. There are particulars but no generals. Mankind is merely a collective name, and has no meaning beyond the number of individual men and women it designates. A tree is a tree and nothing more. Truth and virtue are abstract nouns, invented for the convenience of conversation, but void of meaning. There may be true stories, true views, but not truth, conformity to which makes the individual story or view a true one. There may be virtuous men and women, but no virtue, conformity to which makes one virtuous.

But is this true? Are all things what they appear? And does all that is appear? Is the appearance the thing? Or is the thing that appears always back of the appearance? Is it the thing that we recognize with our senses, or is it only the sign, symbol, or shadow of the thing? In man, is it the man that is apparent to the senses? The senses perceive the body, but is the body anything more than the symbol of the man? Take all the phenomena with regard to a man, presented us by the senses, and do they constitute the man? The man is evidently a collection of forces, moral, intellectual, and physical. We observe in him moral affections; we know that he performs the act of thinking; we see that such things as growth, decay, digestion, nutrition, and the like, are constantly going on in him. Now is there not back of these something that produces them? Is it the feet that walk, or is it the man that walks? Does the brain think, or is it the man that thinks? The stomach, does it digest, or is it the man that digests? The heart, does it love, or is it the man that loves? Back then of the sense-phenomena lies the real man, the thing, the reality, of which what is apparent to the senses is the mere symbol, or sign. The appearance, the apparition is not the man, but a mere index to point us to where the man is and to what he does.

Take a plant. The senses show us a certain number of phenomena. But in that plant are there not things which the senses do not show us, of which they can take no cognizance? Back of this sense-plant is there not the spirit-plant, that is, the real plant of which the senses show us only the appearance or symbol? The real plant is the law that is manifesting itself; the force which pushes itself out in what we call growth, in the bud, the blossom, the fruit; and which makes it precisely what it is, and not something else. It is not meant by this that the senses deceive us; it is only meant that they do not show us the thing, but its sign; not the reality, but the phenomenon, as a word is not the idea, but its sign or symbol.

We do not give these examples as demonstrations, but merely as illustrations to make our meaning obvious. Now apply the remarks we have made of man and of the plant to all nature, and you have Mr. Alcott's doctrine of nature, or more properly of the external world. The external world is merely the world of the senses; it is not a real but an apparent world, not substantial, but phenomenal. He does not distrust the senses as do the Idealists, but he denies their power to attain to realities. They stop short of the thing, and merely give us its sign. They show us where the thing is, but leave it for the spirit to see what it is.

Pursuing the path in which we have started we may go much further. The real is always the invisible. But the invisible world which we have found lying immediately back of the sensible or apparent world, is it the ultimate world? Is there not another world which the soul may discover back of that? All effects are included in their causes, and we have not attained to the thing till we have attained to the ultimate cause. Absolute reality of all things can then be found only in the absolute cause of all things. A cause in order to be a cause must be free, self-sufficing, and self-acting. If absolute then it must be one, for more absolute causes than one is an absurdity which the reason rejects. The world of the senses must then be resolved into the invisible world of the reason, which may for distinction's sake be called the *intelligible* world; and the intelligible world must then be resolved into the absolute world, the world of unity, which, if we understand Mr. Alcott in his terminology, may be called the world of faith. In man he recognizes sense, understanding, or reason, and faith or instinct; each of these has a world of its own. The absolute world, that is, Absolute reality is found only by faith or instinct, and is the world of absolute unity.

Now, absolute unity, in the bosom of which all things exist, is God. In the last analysis all reality resolves itself into God. God is the sum total of all that is; the only substance, the only absolute being, the only absolute reality. God is the universe, and the universe is God; not the sensible universe, nor the intelligible, but the instinctive; not the universe seen by the eye of sense, nor that seen by the eye of reason or understanding, but that seen by the inner eye of the soul, by faith or instinct.

Now the universe of the senses and that of the understanding are both manifestations of God. The sensible universe is God as he appears to the senses; the intelligible universe is God as he unfolds himself to the intellect; the universe beheld by faith or instinct, that is, by the highest in man, is God in his absoluteness; as he is in himself, the real, not the manifested God. We take our stand now on the revelations of instinct; that is, in God himself, and from his point of view examine and interpret all phenomenal worlds and beings. In descending from him through the intelligible world and the sensible, we perceive that all laws, all forces, all things, so far forth as they have any real being, are identical with God. God is not the plant as it exists to the understanding, or the senses; nevertheless, he is all the reality, all the absolute being there is in the plant; God is not man, and man is not God, as he exists to the senses, or to the understanding; nevertheless all the real being there is in man, all that is not phenomenal, appearance merely, is God, "in whom we live, and move, and have our *being* "[Acts 17:28].

By a psychological examination of man, we find that he takes cognizance of the three worlds or universes we have enumerated. Man must have then three orders of faculties, corresponding to these three worlds. He is not then merely endowed with five senses, as we supposed in the beginning; he has, above his five senses, reason or understanding; and above this, as that which attains to the absolute, faith or instinct; which, so far as we can perceive, is very nearly identical with what M. Cousin calls spontaneity or the spontaneous reason. Now in the business of education, we should have reference to these three worlds, or these three orders of faculties, and according to their relative importance. The education which has been and is most common has reference almost exclusively to the world of the senses; some few philosophers and teachers are laboring to make it conform to the world of the understanding; few or none labor to make it conform to the world of instinct, to the absolute truth and reality of things. This last is Mr. Alcott's work. To call attention to this work, to show by his instructions what it is, and by his example how it may be and is to be done, is what he regards as his mission. As a partial experiment, as an intimation of what may under more favorable circumstances be accomplished, he had these Conversations recorded as they occurred, and has finally published them to the world.

Having thus far glanced at what may be called Mr. Alcott's metaphysical system, we may now proceed without much difficulty to seize his theory of education, and to a general comprehension of his views of childhood and of religion. These views have struck many minds as absurd, but the absurdity, we think we find in the views of others, is often an absurdity for which we alone are responsible. We assign to others very frequently the absurd views which originate with ourselves; and it is a good rule for us to observe, that so long as a man's views appear to us to be wholly absurd, if he be a man of but tolerable understanding, we should judge ourselves ignorant of his real meaning.

Instinct, which must be carefully distinguished from impulse, is according to Mr. Alcott's theory the Divine in man. It is the Incarnate God. Our instincts are all divine and holy, and being the immediate actings, or promptings of the Divinity, they constitute the criterion of truth and duty. They are what there is in man the most real and absolute. They are then the most Godlike, the most Divine, partake the most of God; they are then to be regarded as the highest in man, to which all else in him is to be subordinated. The instincts are to be followed as the supreme law of the soul.

The instincts, inasmuch as they are the Divine in man, the Incarnate God, contain all the truth, goodness, reality there is in man. The Divine in man, or the God Incarnate, is one with the universal, the absolute God. There is nothing in the sensible universe, nor in the intelligible universe, that is not in the absolute God. All things are in God, and God is in man. In our instincts then are included, in their law, their reality, both the world of sense and the world of the understanding. To know these worlds then we must look within, not abroad. To become acquainted with God and his manifestations we must study the instincts. Knowledge, truth, goodness, all that can deserve to be called by either name, must be drawn out of the soul, not poured into it. Human culture, therefore, as the word *education* (from *e* and *duco*) literally implies, is merely drawing forth what exists, though enveloped, in the soul from the beginning.

As the child is born with all the instincts and with them more active and pure than they are in after life, it follows that the child is born in possession of all truth, goodness, worth, human nature can aspire to. Therefore said Jesus, "Suffer little children to come unto me, for of such is the kingdom of heaven " [Matt. 10:14]. Childhood is therefore to be reverenced. The wise men from the East do always hail with joy the star of the new-born babe, and haste to the cradle to present their offerings and to worship. The educator must sit down with reverence and awe at the feet of the child, and listen. Till this be done, little progress can be expected in human culture.

The child is pure and holy. It obeys freely and without reserve its Divine instincts. It smiles, loves, acts, as God commands. The true end, or one of the great ends of human culture must be to preserve the child in the grown up man. Most people at a very early day lose the child, and go through life bewailing their lost childhood. The whole family of man may be represented as the distracted mother, who wept with loud lamentation for her children because they were not. The only exception to this is that they too often lose their childhood without being conscious of their loss. Childhood is lost; the innocency, the freedom, the light of the instincts are obscured, and all but annihilated, by the false modes of life which are adopted; by the wrong state of society which prevails; by intemperance, in eating, drinking, sleeping, and the like; and by the mistaken education which men have unwisely encouraged—an education which tends perpetually to raise sense and understanding above Divine instinct, and to subject us to shadows and illusions, rather than to truth and reality. Hence, the necessity of strict temperance in all the habits of the body, and of early attention to the instincts, so that they may be called forth and strengthened before the senses and the understanding have established their dominion over us.

The body in its true state is to the soul what the outward universe is to God—its veil or covering, or more properly, its symbol which marks to the senses the place where it is. What are called bodily appetites and inclinations come from the soul not from the body; proceeding from the soul, they should be regarded in themselves as of like purity and divinity, as any of the instincts of our nature. The exercise of them all, and in all cases, should be regarded as a religious exercise, and should be performed with all the feelings of awe and responsibleness, with which we accompany the most solemn act of religious worship. All the functions of the body, as we call them, but which are really functions of the soul, are holy, and should be early surrounded with holy and purifying associations. Hence the conversations in the volumes before us with the children, on the mysterious phenomena attending the production and birth of a new member to the human family, or what Mr. Alcott calls the Incarnation of Spirit, conversations which have caused him much reproach, and done him, for the moment, we fear no little injury. His motives were pure and praiseworthy, and his theory seemed to require him to take the course he did, and he should not be censured; but for ourselves, we regard as one of the most certain instincts of our nature, that one which leads us to throw a veil over the mysterious phenomena by which the human race is preserved and its members multiplied. Mr. Alcott's theory requires him to respect all the instincts, and why this less than others? In attempting to eradicate it, he appears to us to be inconsistent with himself, and likely to encourage more prurient fancies than he will be able to suppress. Nature in this has provided better, in our judgment, for the preservation of chastity in thought and in deed, than man can do by any system of culture he can devise.

Pursuing the rules implied in these general principles, the educator aims to call forth into full glory and activity the grace and truth with which man is endowed. He labors to train up the human being committed to his care, in obedience to the Highest, to see, and respect, and love all things in the light, not of the senses, not of the intellect even, but of faith, of instinct, of the Spirit of God—the "true light, which enlighteneth every man that cometh into the world " [John 1:9]. If he succeeds in realizing his aim, the result is a perfect man, "armed at all points, to use the body, nature, and life for his growth and renewal, and to hold dominion over the fluctuating things of the outward."[3] Realize this in the case of every child born into the world, and you have reformed the world—made earth a heaven, and men the sons of God in very deed. This is the end Mr. Alcott contemplates; this end he believes can be attained by his method of viewing and disciplining the soul, and by no other. Hence the magnitude of the work he is engaged in—the importance of his doctrine, and his method of culture to the human race.

If now for the word *God,* we substitute the word *Spirit,* and call spirit absolute being, and the absolute, the real universe, which lies back of the sensible universe and the intelligible, also spirit, and therefore regard all power, force, cause, reality, as spirit, and spirit everywhere as identical, we may, with the expositions we have made, attain to a proximate notion of Mr. Alcott's theory of God, man, and nature, as well as of human culture. He sees spirit everywhere, and in everything he seeks spirit. Spirit regarded as the cause and law of organization is God; spirit organized is the universe; spirit incarnated is man. An identity therefore runs through God, man, and nature; they are all one in the fulness of universal and everlasting spirit.

Spirit, though incarnate in the case of every human being, attains rarely to anything like a perfect manifestation. A perfect manifestation, however, is not to be expected because there are no bounds to the growth of spirit. Many bright specimens of the worth men may attain to have been exhibited at distant intervals in the world's history; among which Moses, Socrates, and Jesus are the worthiest. Of these three Jesus stands first.

[3] [Ed. *Conversations,* 1:xxx.]

With this estimate of the character of Jesus, the records[4] of his life must of course be regarded as the most suitable text book for the educator. They give the children for their study the model nearest to perfection that can as yet be found. Besides all this, the identity of spirit, and therefore of human nature in all ages and countries of the world, implies an identity between Jesus, or the instincts of Jesus and the instincts of the child. The coincidence, which we may discover between the manifestations of the pure instincts of childhood and those recorded of Jesus, becomes therefore a proof of the accuracy of the record. If we can reproduce in children, as yet unspoiled, the phenomena recorded of Jesus, then we have a new proof, and a strong proof, that the record is a faithful one. These Conversations on the Gospels, therefore, so far as the answers of the children may be regarded as a reproduction of Jesus, the doctrines or precepts ascribed to Jesus, constitute a class of evidence for Christianity, which the Christian theologian will find not without value.

These are, rudely and imperfectly sketched, the chief outlines of Mr. Alcott's system, so far as we have ourselves been able to comprehend it. Of the two volumes before us we will not attempt to form an estimate. Different minds will estimate them differently. That they do in part accomplish the end for which they were designed we think no one can reasonably deny. They may be read with profit by all students of the New Testament; and to minds of some quickness of apprehension they will open up, in that often read but poorly comprehended volume, many views of rich and varied beauty on which the soul may feast with delight. Parents and Sunday School teachers will find them a valuable help in their work of instructing their children, and in conversing with children on religious subjects; and to them we conscientiously commend these volumes, not for the doctrines they may be supposed to teach, but for the suggestions they contain, and for the method of approaching the young mind they in part unfold.

As it regards Mr. Alcott's religious and metaphysical system, we have not much to offer. We have aimed to state it, not to criticize it. It strikes us as neither absurd nor alarming. We see much truth in it, and we recognize in it the marks of a mind earnestly in love with truth and willing to labor to gain it. The system, though original with Mr. Alcott, is by no means new or peculiar. As a whole we do not embrace it. We differ from him in several essential particulars. We do not admit that identity between man and God, and God and

[4] [Ed. Brownson refers here to the Scriptures, or more directly to the Gospels.]

nature, which he does.[5] God is in his works; but he is also separate from them. Creation does not exhaust the Creator. Without Him his works are nothing; but He nevertheless *is,* and *all* He is, without them. I am in my intention, but my intention makes up no part of me. I am in the word I utter; and yet I am the same without the word that I am with it. In uttering it I have put forth a creative energy, but I nevertheless retain, after uttering it and independently of it, all the creative energy I had before. So of God. The universe is his intention, his word, and we may find him in it; but he remains independent of it, and is no more identical with it, than my resolution is identical with the power I have of forming resolutions, or than my word is identical with the power that utters it. Mr. Alcott appears to us not to distinguish with sufficient accuracy between the creation and the Creator. The relation of the universe to God, according to him, is the relation of a word to the idea it stands for, whereas we regard it as the relation of an effect to its cause. It would be hard for us to entertain his views, without becoming more pantheistic than we believe truth and piety warrant.

But notwithstanding this, Mr. Alcott's views of education, as he reduces them to practice, are unexceptionable. If he runs into an extreme in some cases, if he dwells too much in the inward, and insists too much on spontaneity, he probably goes not farther than is necessary to counteract the strong tendency in an opposite direction, which is the most striking characteristic of our schools as they are. What we regard as erroneous in his theory, can in the actual state of things amongst us have no bad effect. We have overlooked the inward; we have lost our faith in the spiritual; and it is well that a man comes amongst us, who persists in directing our attention to the voice of God that speaks to us, is ever speaking to us in the soul of man. The instincts, as Mr. Alcott calls them, are no doubt from God; they deserve to be studied and reverenced; we must, however, be on our guard that we do not become exclusively devoted to them, for if we do we shall become mystics.

[5] [Ed. Brownson had since 1836 consistently argued against Emerson's and Alcott's theoretical pantheism, and he would continue to do so throughout his life. By "theoretical pantheism " I mean that their theories of the relation of God to nature were pantheistic in Brownson's view, even though they may not have been pure pantheists and may have believed in a God distinct from the created order.]

3.

SPECIMENS OF FOREIGN LITERATURE[1]

Boston Quarterly Review 1 (October, 1838): 433-44

These two volumes are the first of a series of translations Mr. Ripley proposes to bring out from time to time under the general title of Specimens of Foreign Standard Literature. The works he proposes to translate, or to cause to be translated are the works in highest repute in France and Germany, the best works of the ablest scholars and most distinguished authors of the two nations in the departments of philosophy, theology, history, and general literature. He will be assisted in this undertaking by some of our first scholars and most eminent literary men, and will, if he realizes his plan, give us not only specimens of foreign standard literature, but also specimens of correct and elegant translation.

Mr. Ripley's undertaking is a noble one and one in which our whole country is deeply interested. The importance of reproducing in our own language the standard literature of other nations cannot easily be overrated. Every nation has its peculiar idea, its special manner of viewing things in general, and gives a prominence, a development to some one element of universal truth, which is given by no other nation. The literature of one nation has therefore always something peculiar to itself; something of value, which can be found in the literature of no other. The study of the literatures of different nations will necessarily tend, therefore, to liberalize our minds, to enlarge our ideas, and augment our sum of truth. Very few among us have the leisure or the opportunity to make ourselves sufficiently acquainted with foreign languages to be able to relish the works of foreigners save in translations. It is always on translations that the great mass of the people must depend for all the direct benefit they are to receive from the labors and researches of foreign scholars; and it is the direct benefit of the great mass of the people that the American scholar is bound always to consult.

[1] [Ed. Review of George Ripley's edition and translation of *Philosophical Miscellanies, Translated from the French of Cousin, Jouffroy, and Benjamin Constant*, 2 vols. (Boston: Hilliard, Gray, and Co., 1838).]

If translations are to be made at all, they ought to be well made, and to be of the best works, the standard works of the languages from which they are made. We have many translations from the French and German, but in a majority of cases, perhaps, we may say of works that were hardly worth the translating. This may be said especially in reference to the German. The American public study Germany not in the mature productions of her ripest scholars. Second and third rate authors, and second and third rate performances, at best, are those most generally translated. This is a grievous wrong to Germany for it compels us to judge her for altogether less than she is; it is also a grievous wrong to ourselves for it deprives us of a good we might receive, and which we need. Translations too are in general miserably executed by persons who are in no sense whatever qualified to be translators. This perhaps is more especially the case in England than in this country. They are made too often by literary hacks, who must make them or starve, and who have no adequate knowledge of either the foreign language or their own, and not the faintest conception of the thought they undertake to reproduce. In consequence of want of taste and judgment in selecting the works to be translated, and of proper qualifications on the part of translators, translations in general, unless of purely scientific works, serve little other end than to encumber our bookshelves, corrupt the language, and overload it with foreign idioms and barbarous words and phrases. Both these evils are sought to be avoided by Mr. Ripley's plan, and will be, if his plan be realized, as we doubt not it must. His plan ensures us a French or German classic reproduced in English, and constituting ever after an English classic, whereby the intellectual and literary treasures within reach of the mere English student will be greatly augmented, the language itself enriched and perfected, the national taste refined and purified, and the national character elevated.

We are also much in want of the works Mr. Ripley proposes to reproduce. We have much to learn in the departments of philosophy, theology, and history, from the literatures of France and Germany. We are comparatively a young people. We have had a savage world to subdue, primitive forests to clear away, material interests to provide for. Our hands have necessarily and rightly been employed, and our thoughts busy, in procuring the means of subsistence and in preparing the theater of our future glory; and we have not had the leisure to pore over the records of the past, to push our inquiries into surrounding nature, to sit down and patiently watch the fleeting phenomena which rapidly pass and repass over the field of consciousness, or to engage with spirit and ardor in high and extensive literary pursuits. It is not our fault, then, if we are in some respects behind the cultivated nations of the Old World. We shall not be behind them long. There is a literature in the American soul, waiting but a favorable moment to burst forth, before which the most admired literatures of the Old World will shrink into insignificance, and be forgotten. This nation is destined to excel in every department of human activity. It now takes the lead in commercial and industrial activity; it will take the lead in the sciences and the arts. From us is, one day, light to radiate, as from the central sun, to illumine the moral and intellectual universe. To us shall come, from all lands, the statesman, the philosopher, the artist, to gain instruction and inspiration, as from the God-appointed prophets of humanity. We need not blush, then, to avail ourselves for the moment of foreign resources. The capital we borrow from abroad we shall profitably invest, and be able soon to repay, and with usury too.

This is not all. We are now the literary vassals of England and continue to do homage to the mother country. Our literature is tame and servile, wanting in freshness, freedom, and originality. We write as Englishmen, not as Americans. We are afraid to think our own thoughts, to speak our own words, or to give utterance to the rich and gushing sentiments of our own hearts. And so must it be so long as we rely on England's literature as exclusively as we have hitherto done. Not indeed so much because that literature is not a good one. English literature, so long as it boasts a Shakespeare and a Milton, cannot suffer in comparison with the literature of any other nation. For ourselves we reverence it, and would on no account speak lightly of it. But it cramps our national genius, and exercises a tyrannical sway over the American mind. We cannot become independent and original, till we have in some degree weakened its empire. This will be best done by the study of the fresher and in some respects superior literatures of continental Europe. We must bring in France and Germany to combat or neutralize England, so that our national spirit may gain the freedom to manifest itself.

Moreover, excellent as is the English literature, it is not exactly the literature for young republicans. England is the most aristocratic country in the world. Its literature is, with some noble exceptions, aristocratic. It is deficient in true reverence for man as man, wholly unconscious of the fact that man is everywhere equal to man. It is full of reverence for that mass of incongruities, the British Constitution, which contains more of the character of the institutions of the Middle Age than any other constitution or form of government to be found in Europe. It bristles from beginning to end with Dukes and

Duchesses, Lords and Ladies, and overflows with servility to the great, and with contempt, or what is worse, condescension for the little. The constant and exclusive study of a literature like this cannot fail to be deeply prejudicial to republican simplicity of thought and taste, to create a sort of disgust for republican manners and institutions, and to make us sigh to reproduce, on American soil, the aristocratic manners and institutions of England. Things seen at a distance are always more enchanting than when seen close by. Did we live in England we should spurn her institutions; but seeing them only at a distance and through the idealizing medium of poetry and works of fiction, they appear unto us beautiful and exceedingly desirable. We think it would be a fine thing to be Dukes and Duchesses, Lords and Ladies, to wear titles, ribbons, stars, and coronets, and to be elevated above the vulgar herd. We grow aweary of our democratic institutions, submit to them with an ill grace, and do what in us lies to hinder their free and beneficial working. It does not occur to us that those of us, who sigh to reproduce English institutions, might, were the thing done, possibly be at the foot instead of the summit of the new social hierarchy; nor do we reflect that a nobility is elevated to its height only by making the immense majority of the people serve as its pedestal. It may be pleasant to be one of the nobility, to stand with one's head far above one's fellows; but it is not very pleasant to be the pedestal on which another stands. We wish no brother man to appear tall because his feet stand on our head; and rather than be obliged to run the risk of having some vain, fat, ignorant, proud, titled mortal stand on our head, we choose to forego the pleasure of standing on another man's head.

The corrupting tendency of English literature in this respect on our young men and young women, too, is easy to be seen, and threatens to be disastrous. Patriotism dies out; love for democracy becomes extinct; and our own government, in proportion to its fidelity to American principles, becomes the object of the severest censure, the most uncompromising hostility, or the most withering ridicule. Our own writers cannot arrest the tendency; because a considerable portion of them, formed by the study of English literature, are themselves carried away by it; and because the remainder are too few in number, and their voices, though clear and strong, are lost in the universal din of English voices, which we are continually importing. In other words, English works reprinted and circulated here are so much more numerous, and owing to the fact that they can be furnished much cheaper, are so much more extensively circulated than the works of native authors, that they overpower them, and almost wholly counteract their influence.

Now in this situation nothing can be more suitable or more succoring for us than large importations of French and German literature. France and Germany are monarchical, it is true, but not aristocratic. Monarchy has been in Europe in general popular rather than aristocratic in its tendency. The people have in most countries less to dread from the monarch than from the noble. Monarchy raises one man indeed above, far above the people, but in doing this, it lessens or neutralizes to some extent the distinctions which obtain below it. The writings of French or even German scholars breathe altogether more of a democratic spirit than do those of the English. Those of the French are altogether more democratic than the writings of American scholars themselves. Then, again, we have in this country not much to fear from the monarchical tendency. There is nothing monarchical in the genius or temper of the American people. We remember yet the struggles our fathers had with the king, and that we are the descendants of those who dethroned Mary Stuart, and brought Charles Stuart to the scaffold.[2] Then we have no powerful families as yet that could make interest for a throne, no individual influential enough, universally popular enough, or far enough elevated above his brethren, to be thought of in connection with a crown. We have too long been accustomed to govern ourselves, too large a portion of our citizens have taken a direct share in the affairs of government, and may always hope to take a direct share in them, to think of abandoning them to any one man. We can arrive at monarchy in this country only through aristocracy. We do not apprehend that this will ever be the case. The aristocratic tendency is the only tendency we have to apprehend serious danger from; but even this tendency will, we trust, be arrested before it shall have done any lasting injury to our institutions. The study of French and German literature will arrest this tendency. It will break the dominion of England; and, without excluding English literature, will furnish us new elements, and a broader and more democratic basis for our own.

We are also anxious that French and German literature should be cultivated among us, because it will correct in some measure the

[2] [Ed. Mary (1542-87) Stewart queen of Scots (1542-67), a Catholic and mother of the future James VI, was dethroned after her supposed complicity in the murder of her husband Darnley. She was eventually executed by order of queen Elizabeth of England. Charles I (1600-49) king of England, Scotland, and Ireland, son of James VI, was executed by the 'rump' Parliament after a series of violent outbreaks of civil war in England.]

faults of our own democracy. One extreme always begets another. The tendency on the one hand to adore England, and approach English manners and institutions, begets on the other hand a tendency to a rabid radicalism, from which danger may be apprehended, but from which good is not to be looked for. If the wealthy, the cultivated, and literary, as is and has been too much the case, approach England, the democracy of the country becomes to a great degree deprived of the helps of refinement, cultivation, literature, and the conservative element which always goes with them. True democracy has always a conservative element and is no less wedded to order than to liberty. It unites the two; and is always normal in its proceedings. It is broad enough to take in all humanity, and free enough to allow all the elements of human nature to develop themselves fully and harmoniously. Now in English literature this is never the case. The element of order and its adherents are separated from the element of liberty and its adherents. The exclusive study of that literature has to a considerable extent produced the same result here. Hence our democracy becomes in some measure partial, exclusive, and able to enlist on its side only at best a small majority of the nation. This is a serious evil and it is that from which we have more to dread than from anything else whatever. Democracy so long as it is broad and comprehensive, so long as it is true to itself, and to all the elements of human nature, is invincible, and able to go forth "conquering and to conquer" [Rev 6:2].

Now in the masterpieces of French and German literature we shall find the two great elements of which we have spoken always united and working in harmony. There is nothing rash, nothing violent, destructive. Progress, the perfectibility of man and society is admitted and contended for, at the same time peaceable and orderly means by which to effect it are pointed out. The tree has its natural growth, and by natural growth attains its height. It is not made higher by being plucked up by the roots, and held up by artificial means. Erudition, science, philosophy, religion, art, refinement, are all combined with the spirit of progress, and made subservient to the elevation of the people. The cultivation of French and German literature must have a similar effect here, and this is what we want, and what, if Mr. Ripley's plan succeeds, we shall have.

This too is the country in which the noble ideas of man and society, which French and German scholars strike out in their speculations, are to be first applied to practice, realized in institutions. There the scholar may study; there the philosopher may investigate man; there the politician may explore the city, and ascertain how the state should be organized; and there they all may deposit the result of their speculations, their researches, their inspirations in books; but, alas, in books only; for to them is wanting the theater on which to act them out, the practical world in which to realize them. They have old institutions to combat; old prejudices to overcome; old castles and old churches to clear away; an old people to re-youth, before they can proceed to embody their ideas, or to reduce them to practice. More than all this, they want the freedom to do it. Authority is against them, and armed soldiery are ready to repulse them. But here is a virgin soil, an open field, a new people, full of the future, with unbounded faith in ideas, and the most ample freedom. Here, if anywhere on earth, may the philosopher experiment on human nature, and demonstrate what man has it in him to be when and where he has the freedom and the means to be himself. Let Germany then explore the mines, and bring out the ore, let France smelt it, extract the pure metal, determine its weight and fineness, and we will work it up into vessels of ornament or utility, apply it to the practical purposes of life.

In passing from the proposed series of translations and the importance of the undertaking to the volumes before us, we would remark that, viewed simply as translations, they must possess in the estimation of every scholar a high worth. We doubt whether better specimens of translation are to be found in the language—better specimens certainly *we* have never met. Familiar as we are with the originals, we read these translations with pleasure. They do not seem to be translations. They have all the freedom and freshness of original compositions. Yet they are faithful and literal even, altogether more so than translations in general. They are true reproductions, and could have been made only by a man who comprehended their subject-matter hardly less thoroughly than did their original authors. Mr. Ripley deserves high praise for the example he has set to all future translators. He has not only reproduced his authors, but he has done it in pure classic English, in which the most fastidious critic will be troubled to find a single idiom, word, or phrase at which to take offence. In doing this he has done much. He has proved that translations may be made without corrupting the language. He has also rendered an important service, in these volumes, to the philosophical student, by doing much to fix our philosophical language, and to free it from that vagueness and uncertainty, which have heretofore so grievously afflicted all who have attempted to write or read on philosophical subjects.

The several pieces which make up these volumes are selected with great judgment and taste. They are, of their shorter productions, the most important productions of their authors, and are superior to anything else of the kind that we know of in any language. They are so selected and arranged as to form, with the Introductory and Critical Notices by the translator, very nearly a continuous whole, and to constitute something like a regular treatise on the object, method, and history of philosophy, the philosophy of history, morals, and religion, and the destiny of man and society. The Notices are in part original, and in part selected or translated. They are of great value, and were other proof wanting, would prove the translator an acute critic, an accomplished scholar, an able philosopher, and a true and warm-hearted friend of his race.

As to the general merits of the authors of these Miscellanies, we refer our readers to the introductory notices by the translator. They are three authors, who are an honor to France, and to mankind. Benjamin Constant was long known throughout Europe as an ardent lover of liberty, as the devoted advocate of constitutional government, and as a distinguished literary and political writer. His great work, *De la religion considerée dans sa source, ses formes, et ses developpements,* exhibits much erudition, philosophic insight, and religious and philanthropic sentiment.[3] We are glad to find that it is to be included in Mr. Ripley's series. It is just the work needed in the present state of religious doubt, indifference, and fanaticism in this country, and its study would do much to reconcile faith and reason, and to restore us to a pure, rational, and living faith in Christianity. Jouffroy is a profound psychologist, a clear and eloquent writer, and one of the ablest and safest moral philosophers it has ever been our good fortune to meet. He was a pupil of Cousin, is a professor of philosophy in the Faculty of Letters at Paris, and one of the principal disciples of the new French school. Cousin is well known as the chief of the new French philosophy, and he is unquestionably, if not the first, one of the first philosophers of the age.

The subject matter of these volumes is worthy of the most serious attention. The time has gone by in this country when it could be accounted a mark of good taste or of superior wisdom to sneer at metaphysical studies. The public mind has been awakened, and mental and moral science is henceforth one of our most cherished studies. Men have outgrown tradition, and they begin to find themselves unable to legitimate their beliefs. They begin to be troubled with the problem of human destiny. They ask themselves, wherefore they are here; what is the solution of the enigma of human existence; what

[3] [Ed. For Brownson's view of this text, see EW, 2, chapter 36.]

man knows, and wherefore he can know that he knows. They find themselves forced by the state of their spiritual affairs to give an account to themselves of themselves, of their knowledge and their belief, their hopes, fears, and doubts. They are compelled therefore to philosophize. And they must continue to philosophize, for the problem once raised, it will not down till it is solved. Every work therefore that treats on this problem which torments the soul, every work which proposes to aid us to meet this inward questioning, of which we have become conscious, and which we indulge more and more every day, must be hailed with joy, and sought after with avidity. We have lost the early faith of childhood, we have arraigned the catechism, and we must now wear out a life of painful doubt, or attain to a rational conviction.

These Miscellanies will aid us. They state with great clearness and distinctness the principal problems which have tormented the soul in all ages; and if they do not solve them, they at least give us the law of their solution. If they do not give us a philosophy which is perfectly satisfactory, which exhausts human nature, they do give us the true method of philosophizing, of legitimating scientifically the universal beliefs of mankind. More appropriate to the present state of the public mind they could not be. The scholar will read them with delight; the divine, the moralist, the statesman will find them invaluable in directing them in the discharge of their several functions, and in solving the theological, moral, and political doubts they everywhere meet, and which seem almost to paralyze the spiritual powers of man. They are full of masculine thought. They breathe a liberal tone, assert with earnestness and power the rights and the worth of man, as man, and show a profound reverence for truth, beauty, goodness—God. They are just the volumes for us young Americans, to quicken within us a sense of the dignity and reach of our mission, to kindle our faith in ourselves and in Providence, and to enable us to elaborate the glorious future which awaits mankind.

4.

DEMOCRACY OF CHRISTIANITY[1]

Boston Quarterly Review 1 (October, 1838): 444-73

It is not our intention in this article to review at length the works, the titles of which we have quoted, though we desist from doing it not without much self-denial. We have introduced these works together because they have something kindred in their spirit and object, and because they show us men, reared in widely different communions and countries, coming to virtually the same general conclusions.[2] Dr. Tuckerman's work needs no commendation from us in this community.[3] His own character and the ministry with which he has inseparably connected his name speak for him as no reviewer can. The works of the Abbé de la Mennais,[4] here introduced, are not his greatest works, but the most in consonance with our present purpose of any we have seen. They possess a high value and should be in

[1] [Ed. Review of Joseph Tuckerman's *Principles and Results of the Ministry at Large in Boston* (Boston: James Munroe & Co., 1838); Félicité de Lamennais's *Affaires de Rome. Mémoires adressés au pape; Des maux de l'Eglise et de la societé, et des moyens d'y remédier* (Bruxelles: J. P. Meline, 1837); idem, *Paroles d'un croyant.* Septieme Edition, *Augmentee de De l'absolutisme et de la liberté* (Paris: Eugene Renduel, 1834).]

[2] [Ed. The association of American Unitarian concerns for social issues with that of liberal French Catholics was unique in the United States in the 1830s. Brownson's long-standing interests in the social and moral dimension of Christianity was echoed in French socialist-leaning literature, and such an association would eventually turn Brownson's mind toward Catholicism, a move that radically differed from some French socialists who were moving away from Catholicism and organized religion.]

[3] [Ed. On Joseph Tuckerman (1786-1840), a leading Unitarian minister and social reformer in Boston, see Daniel T. McColgan, *Joseph Tuckerman: Pioneer in American Social Work* (Washington, D.C.: The Catholic University of America Press, 1940).]

[4] [Ed. Lamennais (1782-1854) was a French Catholic priest and editor of *L'Avenir*, a liberal Catholic paper that argued the compatibility of Catholicism with modern liberties. His ideas were condemned by Pope Gregory XVI in *Mirari vos* in 1832. Lamennais responded with *Paroles* (1834), a book that evoked much excitement throughout Europe. The book was condemned in Gregory XVI's *Singular nos* (1834), after which Lamennais left the church, continuing to write on religion, politics and social reform. Brownson considered Lamennais one of the members of the world-wide movement party in religion and politics.]

the hands of every one who believes Christianity has yet a mission to fulfil.

In a foregoing article we have endeavored to prove that the natural association of men of letters is with the democracy; we design in what follows to present some considerations which may tend to show, that the natural association of the clergy and of Christians generally is also with the democracy.

In attempting to do this we shall enter into no discussion concerning theological dogmas; we shall take sides with no sect, and show a preference for no particular communion; we shall by no means approach the borders of another world, and attempt to determine the happiness or the misery that awaits us hereafter, or the means of gaining the one or avoiding the other. We propose to speak of Christianity merely in its social and political aspects, in its bearings upon man's earthly condition.

We regard the mission of Jesus as twofold. One of its objects, and perhaps its most important object, was to make an atonement for sin, and raise man to God and heaven in the world to come. Of this object—the more exclusively theological object—we have nothing to say in this journal. The other object of his mission was to found a new order of things on the earth, to establish a kingdom of righteousness and peace for men while yet in the flesh. In this sense Christianity has a social and political character.

In its social and political character, Christianity has been too seldom considered. The clergy have rarely presented it in any other character than that in which it relates to another world. They have dwelt on its power to create a heaven for the sanctified soul hereafter; but only incidentally have they touched upon its power to create a heaven for the human race on the earth. They have boasted its efficacy in preparing us to die; but rarely its efficacy in preparing us to live. To hear them, one would be led to suppose that the great object of our thoughts and efforts should be to get out of the world the easiest way we can, and that the great value of religion consists in its ability to aid us in accomplishing this laudable object. Yet who knows not to live knows not to die; and who studies not to create a paradise here, may, perhaps, doubt whether he shall find the gates of a paradise open to him hereafter.

We risk nothing in saying that the great object of Christianity is to raise us all up to "the stature of perfect men in Christ Jesus."[5] In order to accomplish this object, it must neglect no element of hu-

[5] [Ed. A paraphrase of Eph 4:13.]

man nature. Man's whole nature must be accepted, freely and harmoniously developed, or he cannot be perfected. Leave out of the account that part of his nature which connects him with the Unseen, the Eternal, and the Immutable, and bestow what care you will upon what remains, and he will be forever dwarfed in his growth. Nor different will be the result if you call forth into full activity his religious elements, but neglect those by which he is led to found the state and live in society. If then man is to be perfected by the aid of Christianity, Christianity must accept and develop his social and political nature as well as his religious nature.

This granted, it follows that Christianity has concern no less with politics than with theology, with earth than with heaven, with time than with eternity. Whatever relates to forms of government, to state policy, to the actual or possible condition of men, to the actual or possible influences which combine or may combine in the formation of character, it must concern itself with, as well as with what relates to theological dogmas, or religious rites and ceremonies. It must have instructions for us as statesmen and as citizens, as well as instructions for us as church members, dreaming only of saving our souls in a world to come.

And what in its social and political character does Christianity teach us? What cause does it espouse? Does it take sides with the people, or with the people's masters? Does it declare all men equal before God, and consequently equal among themselves; or does it show us the Father as instituting and approving the social distinctions which obtain in civilized communities, and thinking twice, as a French lady has it, before damning persons of a given quality? Does it teach us that the many were created to be used by the few? Was Jesus the prophet of kings, hierarchies, nobilities, the rich, the great, the powerful; or was he the prophet of the democracy, sent from God to preach glad tidings to the poor? In a word, is the natural position of Christians, so far forth as they are Christians, with the aristocracy, or with the democracy, with those who would govern the people, or with those who would clear the field for the people to govern themselves? We will let the Abbé de la Mennais speak for awhile. Perhaps we can gather the answer to these questions from what he shall tell us.

"Two doctrines, two systems dispute today the empire of the world—the doctrine of Liberty and the doctrine of Absolutism; the system which would found society on right and that which would yield it up to brute force. On the triumph of one or the other will depend the future destinies of the human race. If victory remain with brute force, men, bowed to the earth like beasts, dull, mute, panting, hastened by the whip of the master, will go through life moistening with their sweat and tears the rude furrows they must turn up, and without hope, save that of burying in the grave at last the grievous burden of their misery. But if right obtain the victory, the human race will pursue its course with its head erect, its brow serene, and its eye fixed on the future, the radiant sanctuary where Providence has deposited the rewards promised to its persevering efforts.

"The struggle between these two systems becomes every day more violent. On one side are the people, their patience exhausted, burning with desire and hope, stirred even to the bottom of their hearts by the long dormant but now awakened instinct of all that which constitutes the real dignity and grandeur of man, strong by their faith in justice, by their love of liberty, which rightly comprehended is true order, and by their unflinching resolution to conquer; on the other side, are the absolute governments, with their soldiers and agents of all sorts, their public resources, money, credit, and the innumerable advantages of an organization, all the parts of which hold together, are mutually interlinked, and afford one another a reciprocal support, whilst it isolates, restrains all outside of itself, and renders all movement impossible, except between the sabers of a couple of *gendarmes*, and all speech out of the question, except in the ears of a couple of spies.

"Nothing at first sight can seem more unequal than the respective forces of these two opposite camps. But let it be observed, on the one hand, that in proportion as the armies are more numerous, the more immediately are they from the people, and the more thoughts, wishes, and feelings must they have in common with the people; the people in fine themselves, having in the main, however it may be attempted to persuade them to the contrary, no interests but their own, cannot be made to submit for a great while to come to be mere passive instruments in the hands of their oppressors. Let it also be observed, on the other hand, that the excessive expenses which the maintenance of these armies exacts, involving sooner or later universal bankruptcy, which becomes every day more and more threatening to every European state, must hasten the moment when these huge masses of men [. . .][6] will be dissolved for the want of the means to keep them on foot. Besides, experience proves that in a contest between two forces, one material, the other moral, the last in the long run is always sure to triumph. Now moral force or power is

[6] [Ed. Brownson left out: "rassemblée dan le but d'étayer la tyrannie."]

wholly on the side of the people. To be convinced of this, we need but consider for a moment in themselves the system of liberty defended by the people, and the system of absolutism which the sovereigns have undertaken to make prevail for their own profit.

"Liberty, which has its root in the holiest and most imprescriptible laws of human nature, would represent perfect order, were it possible to realize perfect order on earth. But if this perfection be denied to man, by reason of the internal disease with which he is afflicted, it nevertheless should be regarded as the goal to which he should tend, the end towards which he should unceasingly direct all his efforts. Neither the people nor individuals can in this life be wholly delivered from their infirmities, which to a certain extent are inseparable from them; but it is the duty of both to be constantly advancing in the cure which begins here, to be completed elsewhere. Whence it follows, that society, progressive by its very nature, must involve continual changes, successive revolutions. We are frightened at this word revolution, and we well may be, if we understand by it the disorders produced by selfish interests and heated passions in the bosom of a nation, in which new ideas and new hopes are fermenting. But revolutions which mark an onward step taken in true civilization, and open thus a happier era, revolutions which spring from the development of the sense of justice, have assuredly in their result a character altogether different; and instead of being dreaded as curses, whatever the sufferings which accompany them, they ought to be hailed as blessings from God, and as striking proofs of the influence he exercises over the general destinies of humanity. They are, so to speak, God manifested to our senses in the world. For certainly these transformations which change the condition of mankind by elevating it, these sudden gales which drive us, albeit now and then athwart rocks or shoals, towards more fortunate shores, have in them some thing that is divine.

"The most radical revolution, taking it in all its bearings, which the human race has in fact ever undergone, was without any comparison the establishment of Christianity; and that which has been going on in Europe for the last fifty years is nothing but a continuation of it. Who sees not this is totally incapable of seeing anything, and more incapable yet of comprehending contemporaneous events. Eighteen hundred years of social labor have hardly sufficed to prepare these events. For what is now the question? Is it merely to modify some of the forms of power, to reform a few abuses, and introduce into the laws a few amendments which everybody judges to be necessary? Not at all. It is not this which so powerfully agitates and stirs up the people. With them it is a question of substituting, in relation to the very foundations of social order, one principle for another, the equality of nature for the inequality of blood, the liberty of all for the native and absolute dominion of a few. And what is this but Christianity diffusing itself outside of the purely religious society, and quickening with its puissant life the political world, after having perfected the moral and intellectual world, far beyond what the most sanguine formerly dared hope?

"Christianity lays down as the fundamental principle of its doctrine, under the point of view we are now considering it, the equality of men before God, or the equal rights of all the members of the human family. And on this subject we may remark, that this important doctrine has no historical and philosophical value, unless we admit the unity of the race, without which evidently one race might be naturally superior to another, as Aristotle among the ancients maintained.[7] The Christian doctrine, therefore, which in conformity with ancient traditions teaches that the human race springs from one and the same stock, is unquestionably the most favorable to humanity, and ought to be guarded with the greatest care, as the very foundation of all reciprocally equal justice, and of all equitable society. In this respect, science, which at times is quite too hardy in its physiological conjectures, has some important duties to fulfil.

"The principle of the equality of men before God necessarily brings forth another, which is only its development, or rather its application, namely, the equality of men among themselves, or social equality; for should there exist under this relation any essential and radical inequality relative to rights, this inequality would render them primarily unequal before God. Religious equality tends therefore to produce, as its consequence and complement, civil and political equality. Now civil and political equality has, for its form, liberty; for it excludes fundamentally all power of man over man, and obliges us to conceive, in the outset, society, the state, under the idea of a free association, the object of which is to guaranty to each of its members his rights, that is, his liberty, his native independence.

"These rights guarantied by the association are of two orders. First, spiritual rights of thought and of conscience, which are held from God only, whether he be considered as the author of the moral law, which binds all intelligent beings together, and to which they owe voluntary obedience, or as the primal source of all virtue and of all reason. Second, rights of a secondary order, so to speak, material,

[7] [Ed. Brownson may be referring to Aristotle, *Politics*, Book 1, Chapter 5, Lines 1254a17—1255a2.]

relative to the body, to organism, and which are reduced in their essence to the right of preserving life, that is, of organism itself and the external things necessary to its preservation. These external things are called property.

"It follows from this that, as the direct object of all true society is to guaranty right, it must, in order to realize this object, guaranty to each and all of its members, in the external order, liberty of thought and conscience, and [secondairement] the liberty of living and acting, or the liberty of person and property.

"Liberty of thought and of conscience, in union with the recognition of a moral spiritual law, that alone which makes man sociable, precedes the free association, or the institution of the state, and is its indispensable condition. This law, no more than the liberty which corresponds to it, namely, the civil liberty of thought and conscience, can therefore in any manner whatever be made to depend on the social compact, or a subject of the explicit or implicit preliminary deliberations which the formation of the social compact supposes; and consequently civil and political law, possessing no power to pass any statutes on this primitive right, which it can neither create nor destroy, and which it must protect against all acts that would impair it, respects it as superior to itself, prohibits and punishes as offences against society certain acts which are hostile to it; but it does not establish it by any of its prescriptions.

"Personal liberty, or the right to live and act freely, implies the absence of all will, of all authority that would impose arbitrary restrictions upon this liberty itself; that is, it implies the cooperation of each member of society in support of the fundamental law of society.

"The natural element of society, relative to human organism, or to the constitution of the state, is not the individual, but the family; because the element of society should be able like society to perpetuate itself; and because the individual dies, but family is immortal.

"Family is composed of the father, the principle of generation, of the wife, who is its medium, and of the child, which is its expression. These three together constitute the organic man, man reproductive, perpetuated—man that does not die.

"Hence it follows that marriage, without which there is no family, is in this respect the first basis of society.

"The second basis of society is property, for without property life is not possible. Now as life is not arrested in its transmission, property should not be; it should be hereditary like life, because it is inseparable from it. And since man cannot live without some property, permanent or transitory, it follows that he cannot be free and independent in his person, if his property be dependent, if he be not the sovereign master of his field, his house, his industry, his labor.

"Liberty of property and property itself may be attacked in three ways: first, by attributing to the state or its chief, a paramount right of domain, which would be at bottom only an indirect and arbitrary power of life and death over all the members of the state; second, by attributing to the state or its chief, the right to collect, under the title of impost or tax, some portion of the revenues of property, without the consent of its owners; for this right, to which it would be impossible to assign any fixed limits, would imply that of seizing the totality of the revenues of property, or pure and simple confiscation; the third is to attribute in any degree whatever to the state or to its chief, the right of administering the property of its members; for the right of administering one's own property is inherent in the very right of property itself, without which it would be purely fictitious.

"We can now comprehend how that the movement, which is everywhere remarked among Christian nations, is only the social action of Christianity itself, which continually tends to realize, in the political and civil order, the liberties, which the fundamental maxim of the equality of men before God contains in germ; and consequently, to free the spiritual man entirely from all human control, and property from all arbitrary dependence on government. Now this object can be obtained only by a social organization, the double character of which shall be the exclusion of all constraint in the spiritual order, and all intervention of government in the administration of property, or special interests, whether individual or collective. In this regard, government, the simple executor of the law made by all, or by the delegates of all, will merely take care that no one overstep the boundary of his own rights, or do violence to the rights or liberty of others.

"Spiritual liberty has for its expression liberty of religion or of worship, liberty of teaching, liberty of the press, and of association. When one of these, especially the last, is not complete, the others are but so many empty names. Ask not then under what form of society live the people thus deprived of their natural rights; ask rather under what tyranny they live.

"Liberty of person and of property has for its foundation election, combined with a system of free administrations within the limits we have determined. There is in fact no liberty, where the agents of power are not responsible, and where they are really responsible they cannot be hereditary. If the one be real, the other must be fictitious, and reciprocally.

"On the hypothesis of hereditary government no remedy for its abuses can be offered but the maxim supposed to be implied of the amissibility of power. But power may be amissible in two ways, one regular, the other violent; that is, by election and by insurrection. Who can hesitate between the two? And what is it to organize society, but precisely the same thing it is to establish a series of means which, as far as human foresight can go, shall render it unnecessary, in order to save invaded rights, to recur to the dangerous hazard of insurrection?

"Such are the principles the people are instinctively seeking to realize, and which they will realize sooner or later most assuredly; [. . .] for a right once known is a right conquered. Man never renounces a right which has once revealed itself to him as just. If he would do it, he could not. His nature would oppose him. And in this opposition is that very moral power, which is always sure to triumph in its struggles with material force.

"With the doctrines of liberty now compare the doctrines of absolutism. We will draw these from documents of unquestionable authority. The first two are catechisms, published by the express order of the Emperor of Russia and the Emperor of Austria.[8] The third is a semi-official writing, which produced, some years since, a very lively sensation in Italy, where the governments took great pains to circulate a large number of copies.[9] We will speak first of the catechisms.

"His Apostolic Majesty of Austria teaches the little children of his empire, that the persons as well as the goods of his subjects belong to him, that he is absolute master, and may dispose of them as seemeth to him good. This doctrine, if it find credence, has the advantage of simplifying, to a marvelous degree, the whole administration of government. Does the emperor need money or soldiers? He has but to say to one, Give me thy purse, and to another, Give me thy son. All is his, all without exception. This is his gospel, the *good news,* which he commands to be preached to the people in the name of Jesus Christ. And apparently for fear that, through mistake or evil intention, the purity of these maxims should be impaired in the Christian pulpit, he orders that the priests in certain places, in Milan for instance, be constrained to submit their sermons, before pronouncing them, to the superior lights of the police! The minds of the people and their hearts too, in the case of the Italians especially, must needs be very corrupt not to bless such an order of government! When

[8] [Ed. Unable to identify these two catechisms.]

[9] [Ed. Lamennais is referring to *Dialoghetti sulle materie correnti nell' anno 1831.*]

the people become so ungrateful to their sovereigns, what can they look for but the vengeance of heaven and the end of this guilty world?

"We have just seen that the Emperor of Austria has a very lofty idea of himself and his rights; but it is nothing by the side of the Czar Nicholas.[10] The head of a church foreign to Catholicism, he yet believes it—so does his zeal for the truth devour him—his duty to concern himself with the religious instructions of his Catholic subjects; and in a catechism, printed at Wilna, and taught officially in all the schools and churches, he teaches them how they are to *adore* the autocrat, and explains to them, with great unction, the religious *worship* they are bound in conscience to offer him. Is he not for them, in fact, not merely the image but a real incarnation of the Divinity? Down on your knees! His will is the sovereign order! His commandment the law! Goods, life, all must be lavished, all must be sacrificed at the first nod of the Tartar-God. His subjects must love him from the bottom of their hearts, obey him, whatever he ordains, and never suffer themselves to complain, even in secret; but follow the example of Jesus Christ, *who submitted without a murmur to the sentence of death pronounced against him by the legitimate authority.* The pen drops from my hand. It was reserved for this man to enlarge the borders of blasphemy."[11]

The other document referred to is entitled *Dialoghetti sulle materie correnti nell' anno 1831,* and from the account the Abbé de la Mennais gives of it (for we know it only through him) it must be a very interesting production. It gives us, he says, "under forms sometimes grossly burlesque, sometimes downright atrocious, the whole system of absolutism, with a frankness and a fidelity to be sought for in vain elsewhere. Here is no reticence, no hypocrisy; all is naked. One might call it a candid *proces-verbal* of the counsels of Pandemonium. The author, in more than one place appears to be very indignant that a timid policy, through prudential considerations, should sometimes judge it necessary to veil, modify, soften the doctrines which are at

[10] [Ed. Czar Nicholas I (Nikolai Pavlovich) (1796-1855) was emperor of Russia from 1825 to 1855. Nicholas demanded conformity in religious as in political matters. He would not tolerate disagreements. With state support of the Orthodox Church came governmental control, even over the internal operations of the Church.]

[11] [Ed. Brownson cites *Paroles d'un Croyant. De l'Absolutisme et de la Liberte,* 203-14. I could not locate the seventh edition of this text, but Brownson's translation of Lamennais' "Absolutism and Liberty" is verified in *De l'absolutisme et de la liberté* (Louvain: F. Michel, 1834), 5-16. Brownson had earlier published this translation in the *Boston Reformer* 3 (September 13, 1836): 1. This issue of the *Reformer* is in the Boston Public Library.]

bottom its invariable rule. As for us, who prefer above all things a language clear, precise, exempt from all falsehood, circumlocution, or equivocation, we are so far from blaming this fiery defender of despotism for his contempt of those wily and pusillanimous managements, that we really thank him for the brutal sincerity of his convictions and of his speech. The word which others retain upon their lips he utters in a loud and distinct voice. This is surely much the best."[12] But interesting as the document is in itself, and notwithstanding the light it throws on the system of absolutism, and the designs according to which the sovereigns of Europe regulate their conduct, we must pass it over with merely two or three extracts. The system it unveils must strike every citizen of this country, at all imbued with the spirit of our institutions, as absolutely atrocious. This system is as simple as it is revolting. "God has given the people to the kings. The people belong to the king in like manner as your flocks and herds belong to you; they are their property, their *patrimony.* This is all. Conditions, compacts, charters—such things must not be dreamed of, that is clear."[13] The doctrine of these Dialogues, we suppose, is contained in the letter which experience is represented as addressing to the European sovereigns. We extract a few paragraphs.

"When, in order to restrain the wicked, it is not sufficient to raise the voice, you must raise the hand and punish, and let the punishment be both certain and severe. Those who meditate the overturning of the world have taken their measures from afar, and prepared impunity for themselves and adherents by *preaching humanity and the moderation of penalties.*

"For some time you have allowed yourselves to be seduced by their nonsense, and in order to be gentle and merciful, you have ceased to be just. Thus has the way been opened for the introduction of all iniquity. The certainty of pardon has loosened the restraints imposed by fear, and for each criminal absolved, a hundred faithful subjects have become criminals. Retrace your steps; and if you would have few to condemn, be sure that you condemn inexorably. Forbearance has been tried, and proved to produce only evil; *make trial of blood,* and you will soon see that it will no longer be the fashion to profess oneself a rebel. Begin with small offences which lead to great ones, and be sure that the punishments you inflict be *severe and terrible.* The ferocious souls of base wretches are not to be frightened by infantile chastisements, advised by a silly philosophy. God, who is the father of mercies, has created a hell for the punishment of the

[12] [Ed. *De l'absolutisme et de la liberté*, 17.]

[13] [Ed. Ibid., 18.]

sinner, and the *creation of a hell serves in a marvelous manner to people heaven.* Would you spare innocent blood, be persuaded that HE IS THE BEST PRINCE WHO HAS A HANGMAN FOR HIS PRIME MINISTER."[14]

This is not precisely the language held by those who amongst us labor for the melioration of our criminal code, but it will no doubt be acceptable to those who still believe there is use in inflicting capital punishment. But here is an extract we commend to the grave consideration of the advocates of universal education.

"One great cause of the disorder, which now obtains in the world, is the too wide diffusion of literature, and that itching desire for reading which has penetrated the very bones of even fishermen and hostlers. Literary and scientific men are doubtless needed in the world, and so too are shoemakers, tailors, blacksmiths, ploughmen, and artisans of all sorts. It is always necessary to have a great mass of tranquil and honest folks, who can be contented to live on the faith of others, and who are satisfied to have the world guided by the intelligence of others, without aspiring to guide it by their own. *For all these folks reading is dangerous; because it stimulates minds which nature predestinated to a narrow sphere, gives rise to doubts which their limited information cannot solve, accustoms them to intellectual pleasures which render labor monotonous and wearisome, quickens desires out of all keeping with their humble condition, and by rendering them discontented with their lot, leads them to attempt to procure another.*

"This is wherefore instead of favoring unlimited instruction and civilization (*civilità*) you should, with prudence, set some bounds to them. Were there a master found who could in a single lesson make all men as learned and as scientific as Aristotle, and as polite as the Grand Chamberlain of the king of France, it would be necessary to knock him in head forthwith, so that society should not be destroyed. Reserve books and studies for the *higher classes* and for such extraordinary geniuses as may break through the obscurity of their condition; let the cobbler stick to his last, the peasant be contented with his mattock, without striving to spoil both heart and head by learning the alphabet. In consequence of a mistaken diffusion of literature, and disproportioned culture, an innumerable race of clowns and catch-pennies have turned society into chaos, by attempting in *spite of nature* to associate themselves with the higher classes, and you are compelled to skin one half of your people to make breeches for

[14] [Ed. Brownson cites *Paroles d'un Croyant. De l'Absolutisme et de la Liberte,* 224, 225. See also *De l'absolutisme et de la liberté,* 29-30.]

the other half; who, born to live by the axe and spade, demand places and pensions, and pretend to obtain the means of living, and of living well, by their pen. All these petty sages, without solid study or judgment, all these diminutive lords, with patrimony insufficient to boil a pot, have naturally in their hearts discontent and envy, and are combustible materials ever ready to be kindled into a revolution. The fatal propagation of letters has collected this inflammable mass; and by an adroit and discreet diminution of culture, you must stifle the flames of a self-styled philosophy, and remove the train from your thrones. . . .

"Above all, if you would keep the people quiet, secure your thrones, and cure the disorders of the world, you must bring back respect for religion, which, everywhere derided and rejected, finds no safe asylum, no not even in the temples. Ministers of the altar are become the scoff of the people, and their very name serves with the vulgar to designate all sorts of extravagance and baseness. . . . This hatred and this contempt of religion is the work of the revolution allied to impiety; and you cannot but be aware that the blows struck at religion have shaken your thrones and threatened to demolish them. And what have you done to reestablish in the hearts of the people religion, that protector of thrones? And where is the king whose zeal is ardent for the cause of God? Princes, you are yourselves good and religious, but are the goodness and religion of kings always the power which governs states? Does it never happen that religion may rule in the heart of kings, and yet become the tool of the interests and policy of cabinets? Lay your hands upon your breasts [. . .] and answer me truly, which one of your kingdoms is it, in which a volume of edicts and royal ordinances may not be collected in opposition to the canons of the church? Which of your palaces is it, in which there is no saloon[15] ornamented with the spoils of the sanctuary? Which one of your governments is it that has not compelled the pastor of the Vatican to weep? So long as religion, struck by kings, stands trembling before their thrones, how can it regain its dominion over the hearts of the people? And so long as the people do not respect the restraints of religion, how can they be expected to submit to the empire of kings? Princes, comprehend, ponder, and hope; league yourselves in good faith with the priesthood; and without placing yourselves under its feet, give it your hand; for though you are the first born, you are nevertheless children of the church. Accord with that wise, discreet,

[15] [Ed. Brownson has "saloon" in the original. He consistently uses the British "saloon" for "salon."]

and pious mother, employ speech, example, address, clemency, and severity to heal the wounds of religion. Raise again the stones of the altar, and its solidity shall give strength and permanency to your thrones. . . .

"What we have thus far read," says the Abbé in conclusion, "is then only the *secret* thought of those who now govern the world. And what in fact are they doing everywhere, but conforming to it in their practice? Thus we know their object and what they hope to accomplish. What most strikes us in this theory of despotism is its perfect consistency as a whole; attempt to modify it on any one point, and the whole system crumbles to pieces. Counsels in appearance the most exaggerated, maxims the most atrocious, are the legitimate consequences of the principle, the triumph of which is to be secured. There are no means of avoiding them. The inflexible logic of things, invincible necessity, leads to this result; and when I see everywhere princes or their agents carrying out these execrable principles into practice, I censure the men far less than the doctrines which rule them. Slaves of their own tyranny, they are compelled to forego every sentiment of justice, piety, fraternal love, to divest themselves of the human form, to be clothed with that of I know not what infernal phantom. Marked in the forehead with a fearful sign, God has decided that their aspect should shock the earth, so that the horror they inspire might begin for them here below the punishment of hell, to which they are doomed.

"But examine somewhat closely this system, which is presented as a perfect model of social organization. At the summit is placed the absolute prince who may do whatever he will; by his side stands the hangman; all else, men and property, are his *patrimony.* But there will at least be equality of servitude, equality of wretchedness? Alas, no. Below the prince are two distinct races, eternally separated; to the one wealth, instruction, information; to the other labor, ignorance, the bed of straw, and *polenta* (the food of the lazzaroni of Naples[16]), the entire and eternal deprivation of the *dangerous pleasures of the intellect,* hopeless poverty, and an irrevocable brutishness. This last race is properly compared to beasts of burden. *Nature has made it what it is,* and that it must remain. But beasts of burden have plenty of provender and fresh straw on which to rest. The plebeian merits not so much.

"In the society confided to the care of the hangman, the *galley-slave is more fortunate than the laborer, and the prison is sweeter than*

[16] [Ed. The parenthesis is Brownson's insertion identifying *polenta* as the food of Neapolitan beggars. *Polenta* is a pudding made from maize or chestnut flour.]

the domestic fireside. This is indeed an anomaly, but what shall we do to make it disappear? Meliorate the condition of the workingmen? Allow some rays of enjoyment to pierce the roof of the dark hovel of the poor? What say you? These are the *whimsies* of a silly philosophy. What then shall we do? Consult Experience? She will tell us that to restore the monarchical felicity of former times, and bring back order into all things, it is necessary to augment the horrors of the prison, and the tortures of the galley, in a word, to create a hell upon earth.

"We cannot believe that such a doctrine is destined to prevail henceforth in the world, that it can succeed in stilling the love of liberty, which is now rising into a flame in the hearts of the people. In vain you abuse force, imprison, torture, kill; neither cudgelings, nor fetters, nor musket balls can disannul the eternal laws of God and humanity. You may say, and cause to be said, that in struggling against your despotism, in claiming the political and civil enfranchisement of the people, in laboring to redress their wrongs, to solace their unutterable sufferings, to elevate their social condition, that we shake the foundation of all society, provoke disorder, and violate the precepts of Christianity; but, *it is too late;* these means are now used up. For in our turn, we may ask, what then for you is society, order, and Christianity? We may, we *will* ask you to show the act of cession, by which God and Christ have delivered over the human race to you, as your inheritance?"[17]

Here are the two doctrines, the two systems, which are now disputing the empire of the world. The cause of liberty is the cause of the people, the democratic cause. The cause of absolutism is the cause of the people's masters and oppressors. Which of these two causes does Christianity espouse? Christianity, says the Abbé, espouses the democratic cause, the cause of the people; for the liberty the people are seeking to realize, is nothing but the social and political application of Christianity. From this he draws the very natural inference that Christians, that the church, ought to espouse the popular cause, league with the people, and not with the sovereigns.

The governments throughout all Europe are in one sense distinct from the people, and have interests of their own in opposition to the people's interests. They everywhere oppose the system of liberty, and consequently the people who are laboring to realize it. They everywhere are seeking to reestablish, or to perpetuate a system of absolute rule, which reduces the millions to complete slavery in per-

[17] [Ed. Brownson cites *Paroles d'un Croyant. De l'Absolutisme et de la Liberte*, 230-37. See also *De l'absolutisme et de la liberté*, 36-40, 42-46.]

son and in property. And in this nefarious design the sovereigns have the hearty cooperation of the church in all its divisions and subdivisions. The church, throughout all Europe, leagues with the governments, clothes their arbitrary authority with the sacred character of legitimacy, and shelters them with its spiritual aegis from the arrows of popular indignation. Instead of speaking to the people in tones of sympathy and encouragement, instead of feeding the holy love of liberty burning in their hearts, firing them with the zeal, the energy, the indomitable will to be free, to rise from their thraldom, and to be men, and men in a condition to show forth the virtues and the bearing of men, it steps in between them and their tyrants, commands them in the name of the Father, of the Son, and of the Holy Ghost to desist; and assures them that another step forward is taken at the hazard of the vengeance of the sovereign, the curse of the church here, and the curse of God hereafter.

This is now the position of the church throughout the old world. And its position, allowance made for the difference of political institutions, is very much the same here. Here the government is founded on right, and is with the people. Our government is an attempt to realize the doctrine of liberty. Here therefore the church, to favor the cause of liberty, is not called upon to side with the people against the government. We have no war between the people and the government, for the government is but the simple executor of the popular will. The true position of the church here, if it would be the friend of liberty, is to side with the government, or rather with the cause the government in theory represents; and its duty in this case would be to explain to its members and, by all the legitimate authority it possesses, induce them to cherish the principles on which our political institutions are founded. Does it do this? Not at all. It is here an opponent of the government, and of course an opponent of the people, inasmuch as it opposes the government of the people's choice. It is as faithful to the doctrine of absolutism, as it can be in a democratic country. It is here a disturbing force, and anti-popular in its influence. The people find it here, as elsewhere, a let and a hindrance. Its ministers, with comparatively few exceptions, have no sympathies with the democracy. They have been educated in schools into which the utmost care is taken to prevent the spirit of the age from penetrating; and they are educated to look for the golden age in the past, not in the future. They read old books, or old books reproduced, form their minds in the study of the aristocratic literature of England, treasure up old maxims, and sympathize almost entirely with their European brethren. They have no confidence in the people, of whom they know but little, no just conceptions of the rights and the worth of man, no dream that they are set apart to the holy work of realizing a kingdom of freedom, righteousness, and peace on the earth. They are ill-informed, thoughtless, or apparently thoughtless, as to the destiny of man in this life; sometimes, indeed, they are zealous in some partial reform, which they endanger by their indiscreet zeal; at other times so prudent as to be useless, except to serve as drawbacks upon the democracy, and to give the alarm when the prophet from God speaks, or to cry out "blasphemy," when a brother pleads for the rights of man, and calls upon the people to take possession of their rights.

We know very well that the clergy will not admit our statement to its full extent, because they probably are in some sense like those who crucified Jesus, doing they know not what. We charge them with no evil intention. We are not their judges. They seem to us to be entirely ignorant of their true position and of their real duty. Not many of them, perhaps none of them, would maintain, in general thesis, the doctrine of absolutism, and most of them, we are inclined to believe, regard themselves as friendly to liberty. Nevertheless they are not truly democratic.

The doctrine of liberty in the main is realized politically in this country; but not yet socially. The form of government is free, but the people are not all of them as yet imbued with the true spirit of freedom. A large party in the country are laboring to secure the adoption of measures which may render even our political freedom insecure. But be this as it may; there is a wide discrepancy in American society between the theory we have avowed in our institutions, and the principles according to which we regulate our practice. If we have realized political equality, we have not yet realized social equality. We have here, in this blessed land of equality, vast multitudes who are yet far below the rank to which man is entitled. The doctrine of liberty here leads us to labor for the realization of social equality. In Europe the doctrine must be applied politically, to the forms of the government, to the constitution of the state; but here its application requires us to labor for the abolition of all artificial distinctions, of all inequalities of ranks or classes, and of all differences in the social position of members of the same community, not growing out of differences founded in nature, or in moral worth. It requires us to labor to make every man a man, neither more nor less than man.

Well, do the clergy understand this? Do they exert themselves to do this? Do they in their conversation, their sermons, their publications, countenance an equality of the kind we have stated? Do they teach that men are equal, have equal rights, and that it is impossible for them to enjoy equal rights in a social state, where great inequality of conditions obtains? Do they make the poor conscious of their rights, feel that they are men, and were not born to be used by their more fortunate neighbors? We fear they do not. They preach that all the distinctions which obtain in society are the appointment, the express appointment of God; and that he who attempts to do them away is not only visionary but impious. They preach to the poor, to the down-trodden, we admit; but they preach submission, and quiet. Keep quiet, they say to those they regard as the lower class, submit to the order of things you find established. God has wisely ordered distinctions in society, made some to be great and others to be small, some to be rich and others to be poor. It is necessary for the beauty and harmony of society, that some should be at the base of society, as well as some at its summit. Do not be envious of those above you. Do not complain of the rich and prosperous. You cannot all be rich and distinguished. They who are above you have cares and anxieties you know not of. The tallest oaks feel most the fury of the blast. The humble reed is sheltered at their feet, and soon recovers its erect position, if perchance a passing wind bend it to the ground. The distinctions you complain of are the sources of your greatest happiness, and of some of the noblest virtues of which human nature is capable. Were all equal, where would be gratitude for benefits received, where were the protection and kindness which the favored show the unfortunate? If there were no rich men, who would give you employment, and how would you find bread for your wives and little ones? Be satisfied then with your lot. God has assigned you the place which best befits you; submit. Do your duty where you are, and hope that ere long God will take you to himself, and permit you to live in a world, where there are no high or low, no rich or poor, no bond or free, but where all are brothers and like the angels of God!

We are sorry to send this report of our clergy to the old world. It will not, we apprehend, exalt our national character, nor do much to commend American institutions, or to encourage the friends of humanity struggling there and dying in the cause of liberty. Nevertheless we have no right to send a different report. If the clergy knowingly and intentionally side with despotism, as far as they can in this country, we suppose they are willing it should be known; if they do it ignorantly, our report may be of some service to them, by enabling them to see themselves, as the friends of freedom see them.

In a civil and political sense, we cannot discover that the church regards Christianity in any other light than that of a curb, a bit, a restraint, a means by which the people may be kept in order and in submission to their masters. The clergy, under this point of view, are a sort of constabulatory force at the service of the police, and meeting-houses a substitute for police offices, houses of correction, and penitentiaries. Far be it from us to deny the great worth of Christianity in this respect. We acknowledge the virtues of the church, as an agent of the police; but we hope we may be allowed to believe that Christianity requires the church to possess other and far higher virtues. It should not merely keep the people in subjection to an order of things which is, but fire them with the spirit and the energy to create a social order, to which it shall need no constabulatory force, lay or clerical, to make the millions submissive.

But if the church, both here and in Europe, does not desert the cause of absolutism, and make common cause with the people, its doom is sealed. Its union with the cause of liberty is the only thing which can save it. The party of the people, the democracy throughout the civilized world, is every day increasing in numbers and in power. It is already too strong to be defeated. Popes may issue their bulls against it; bishops may denounce it; priests may slander its apostles, as they did and do Jefferson, and appeal to the superstition of the multitude; kings and nobilities may collect their forces and bribe or dragoon; but in vain; IT IS TOO LATE. Democracy has become a power, and sweeps on resistless as one of the great agents of nature. Absolute monarchs must be swept away before it. They will fail in their mad attempt to arrest the progress of the people, and to roll back the tide of civilization. They will be prostrated in the dust, and rise no more forever. Whoever or whatever leagues with them must take their fate. If the altar be supported on the throne, and the church joined to the palace, both must fall together. Would the church could see this in time to avert the sad catastrophe. It is a melancholy thing to reflect on the ruin of that majestic temple which has stood so long, over which so many ages have passed, on which so many storms have beaten, and in which so many human hearts have found shelter, solace, and heaven. It is melancholy to reflect on the condition of the people deprived of all forms of worship, and with no altar on which to offer the heart's incense to God the Father. Yet assuredly churchless, altar less, with no form or shadow of worship will the people be, if the church continue its league with absolutism. The people have sworn deep in their hearts that they will be free. They pursue freedom as a divinity, and freedom they will have—with the church if it may be, without the church if it must be. God grant that they who profess to be his especial servants may be cured of their madness in season to save the altar!

The people almost universally identify Christianity with the church. They cannot reject the church without seeming to themselves to be rejecting Christianity, and therefore not without regarding themselves as infidels. Will the clergy consent to drive the people into infidelity? Can they not discern the signs of the times? Will they persist in maintaining social doctrines, more abhorrent to the awakening instincts of the people than atheism itself? A people, regarding itself as infidel, is in the worst plight possible to pursue the work of social regeneration. It is then deprived of the hallowed and hallowing influence and guidance of the religious sentiment; and it can hardly fail to become disorderly in the pursuit of order, and to find license instead of liberty, and anarchy instead of a popular government. For its own sake then, and for the sake of liberty also, the church should break its league with the despots and join with the people, and give them its purifying and ennobling influence.

The church must do this or die. Already is it losing its hold on the hearts of the people. Everywhere is their complaint of men's want of interest in religion; everywhere is there need of most extraordinary efforts, and various and powerful machinery to bring people into the church, and few are brought in, save women and children. The pulpit has ceased to be a power. Its voice no longer charms or kindles. It finds no echo in the universal heart. Sermons are thought to be dull and vapid; and when they call forth applause, it is the preacher that wins it, not the cause he pleads. Are we at any loss to account for this? The old doctrines, the old maxims, the old exhortations, the old topics of discussion, which the clergy judge it their duty to reproduce, are not those which now most interest the people. The dominant sentiment of the people is not what it was. Once it was thought that the earth was smitten with a curse from God, and happiness was no more to be looked for *on* it than *from* it. Then all thoughts turned to another world, and the chief inquiry was, how to secure it. To save the soul from hell hereafter was then the one thing needful; and the preacher, who could show how that was to be done and heaven secured, was sure to be listened to. It is different now. Men think less of escaping hell, have less fear of the devil, more faith in the possibility of improving their earthly condition, and are more in earnest to extinguish the fires of that hell which has been burning here ever since the Fall. The church must conform to the new state of things. She cannot bring back the past. Yesterday never returns. If she would have her voice responded to, she must speak in tones that shall harmonize with the dominant sentiment of the age. *She must preach democracy,* and then will she wake an echo in every heart, and call forth a response from the depths of the universal soul of humanity. She can speak with power only when she speaks to the dominant sentiment, and command love and obedience, only when she commands that which the people feel, for the time at least, to be the one thing needful.

In calling upon the church, by which term we mean especially the clergy of all communions, to associate with the democracy, and to labor for the realization of that equality towards which the people are everywhere tending, we seem to ourselves to be merely recalling the church to Christianity. We freely acknowledge the past services of the church. She has done much and done nobly. She has protected the friendless, fed the orphan, raised up the bowed down, and delivered him who was ready to perish. She has tamed the ruthless barbarian, infused into his heart the sentiment of chaste love, and warmed him with admiration for the generous and humane; she has made kings and potentates, who trample on their brethren without remorse, and lord it without scruple over God's heritage, feel that there is a power above them, and that thrones and diadem, scepter and dominion, shall avail them nought in presence of the King of kings, before whom they must one day stand and be judged, as well as the meanest of their slaves; she has done a thousand times over more good for the human race than we have space or ability to relate, and blessings on her memory! Eternal gratitude to God for that august assembly of saints, martyrs, and heroes, which she has nourished in her bosom, and sent forth to teach the world by their lives, the divinity there is in man, one day to be awakened and called forth in its infinite beauty and omnipotent energy!

But while we say this, we feel that the church now, in both its Catholic and Protestant divisions, is unconscious of its mission, and has become false to its great founder. Jesus was, under a political and social aspect, the prophet of the democracy. He came to the poor and afflicted, to the wronged and the outraged, to the masses, the downtrodden millions, and he spoke to them as a brother, in the tones of an infinite love, an infinite compassion, while he thundered the rebukes of heaven against their oppressors. "Ye serpents, ye generation of vipers," says he to the people's masters, "how can ye escape the damnation of hell" [Matt 23:33]! His word was with power. Ay, was it, because he spoke to the common soul, because he spoke out for outraged humanity, and because he did not fear to speak to the great, the renowned, the rich, the boastingly religious, in terms of terrible plainness and severity. Before his piercing glance earth-born distinctions vanish, and kings and princes, Scribes and Pharisees, chief priests and elders sink down below the meanest fishermen, or the vilest slave, and seem to be less worthy to enter the kingdom of heaven than publicans and harlots. Their robes and widened phylacteries, their loud pretensions, their wealth, rank, refinement, influence, do not deceive him. He sees the hollow heart within them, the whited sepulchers they are, full of dead men's bones and all manner of uncleanness, vessels merely washed on the outside, all filthy within, and he denounces them in woes too terrible to be repeated. Here was the secret of his power. The great, the honored, the respectable, the aristocracy, social or religious, beheld in him a fearful denouncer of their oppressions, a ruthless unveiler of their hidden deformity, while the poor, the "common people," saw in him a friend, an advocate, a protector, ay, an avenger.

Jesus declared that the spirit of the Lord was upon him because he was anointed to preach the gospel to the poor; and he gave, when asked by the disciples of John, the fact that the gospel was preached to the poor as one of the principal proofs of his messiahship. He chose his disciples from the lowest ranks of his countrymen; and they were the common people who heard him gladly. Was he not a prophet from God to the masses? Was he a prophet to them merely because he prepared the way for their salvation hereafter? Say it not. The earth he came to bless; on the earth he came to establish a kingdom; and it was said of him that he should not fail nor be discouraged till he had set judgment—justice—in the earth and the isles waited for his law. He was to bring forth victory unto truth. In his days the earth was to be blest; under his reign all the nations were to be at peace; the sword was to be beaten into the ploughshare and the spear into the pruning hook; and war was to be no more. The wolf and the lamb were to lie down together, and they were not to hurt or destroy in all the holy mountain of the Lord. The wilderness was to rejoice and blossom as the rose, and the solitary place was to be glad. Every man was to sit under his *own* vine and fig tree, with none to molest or to make afraid. On the earth was he to found a new order of things, to bring round the blissful ages, and to give to renovated man a foretaste of heaven. It was here then the millions were to be blessed with a heaven, as well as hereafter.

This is the great truth that should arrest the attention of the church. The time has now come for this truth to be distinctly proclaimed and cordially accepted by every professed follower of Jesus. In saying this we cast no reproach on the Christian world for not having proclaimed it heretofore; for there is a time for all things, and nothing can come before its time. The time for the direct application of the social and political doctrines of Christianity was not until now. Nor in asking for a more prominent place for the social and political doctrines of Christianity, do we ask that men's attention be drawn off from the world to come. All worlds have their places and their claims, and no truth or aspect of truth should be neglected. We ask not that men should strive less to save their souls and secure a heaven hereafter; we merely ask that they strive more, and more systematically and more religiously, to create a heaven here; we ask that the clergy bring out the great democratic principles of the gospel; that they study and point out, and induce others to study and comprehend, their application to men's social and political relations; that they speak the language of encouragement to all who hunger and thirst after freedom; and inspire faith in the possibility of an essential improvement of man's earthly condition; that they preach ever the kindling doctrine of the fraternity of the human race, the natural equality of man with man, the equal rights of all men, and remind their congregations that all social conditions, social practices, and governmental measures, which strike against the doctrine of equal rights, are as repugnant to Christianity, as they are to democratic liberty and the true interests of mankind. We ask them to do more than to preach honesty and fidelity in the discharge of the duties belonging to the respective positions occupied by their hearers. There may be honesty and fidelity among thieves, and the thief may discharge, with the utmost promptness and fidelity, the duties that belong to his profession as a thief. Yet is he not the less a thief for that. We ask more than this of the clergy. We ask that they preach against all false positions, and take it upon them to point out what is the true social position of a man, as well as what are the proper duties of the position a man may hold.

In this we are far from asking the clergy to amuse us with visionary theories, or to send us on a wild goose chase after a social perfection which can never be realized, and which perhaps it is not desirable to realize. Our own views of the social progress to be effected are by no means extravagant. We believe in the indefinite perfectibility of man and society, but we have struggled too long for progress, seen and encountered and suffered too much, to look for any rapid advancement in either. But we do ask the clergy, and we do it not in our own name, but in the name of the Father, and of the Son, and of the Holy Ghost, and of humanity, to preach social progress, to teach that society, as well as the individual, may advance, and that it is a *Christian* duty to seek to perfect society no less than it is to perfect the individual.

It is by no means our intention to underrate the importance of seeking to perfect the individual man. Society is for man, not man for society. The growth and perfection of the individual man is, no doubt, the end always to be consulted in our social labors. Yet is the perfection of society, viewed in itself, of vastly more importance than the perfection of any one generation of individuals. In laboring to perfect the social state we are laboring for all coming time, for the countless millions of individuals to come after us; whereas in laboring to perfect the individual we are laboring for but an insignificant unit of an innumerable multitude, and for a being, so far as this world is concerned, that is today and tomorrow is not. But let this pass. Give to individual perfection all the prominence the clergy have ever claimed for it, still the perfection of the social state is a means to attain it. Man can never perfect himself so long as he makes his own perfection the end of his exertions. He who labors merely to perfect his own soul, although he may make the doing of good to others his means, is no less selfish than he, who labors merely to gratify his senses, or to promote his own worldly interests; and we need not at this late day undertake to prove that no selfish man, no man, all of whose acts terminate in himself, is or can be perfect. All that is noble and praiseworthy in man is disinterested and self-sacrificing. To perfect ourselves we must, as it were, forget ourselves, even the perfecting of ourselves, the saving of our own souls, and bind ourselves to a good which is not specially ours, and seek a perfection which is out of us and independent on us, as well as in us. A truth we utter here, which the clergy themselves have taught in that maxim so offensive to some, yet veiling the profoundest philosophy, that "a man must be willing to be damned before he can be saved."[18] Jesus was not concerned with himself. He did not seek his own perfection; he did not labor, suffer, and die to save his own soul, but to redeem the human race, and establish the kingdom of God on the earth. He is our pattern. Let the clergy insist upon it, that we follow his example. Let them proclaim from the heights of their pulpits, with all the authority of their sacred profession, that wherever social evils can be found, there is the Christian's place, there the Christian's work; and that so long as social evils exist, no man is a true Christian who has not done

[18] [Ed. Brownson refers to the doctrine of Samuel Hopkins (1721-1803), a Congregationalist Puritan pastor and theologian who stressed the doctrine of Predestination to such an extent that he was popularly identified with this phrase. The Hopkinsian doctrine was repeatedly assaulted by early nineteenth century anti-Calvinists.]

his best to remove them; that no man is or can be a true Christian, in the full significance of the term, who has not done all that, with the force and light he possesses, he can do, to place every brother man in a condition to enjoy all his rights as a man and a citizen, and to unfold all the moral beauty and intellectual energy which God hath wrapped up in his soul.

Once more: We ask the clergy to refrain from checking the courage, and damping the enthusiasm of the warm-hearted champions of liberty, that ever and anon spring up in all communities, and demand a social advance. Let them refrain from taking counsel with Herod to destroy the "young child's life" [Matt 2:20]. Let them be ever, like the Wise Men from the East, able to recognize the star of him born to be king, and ready to fall down before the babe in the manger, and present their offerings of gold, frankincense, and myrrh. Let them be ever on the side of the people; let them use all their efforts to cause every question, which comes up, to be decided in a sense favorable to the millions; let them not court the wealthy and the respectable, and shape their doctrines to the interests and tastes of "the better sort"; but let them speak to the common mind; let them catch the inspirations of the masses, and be the organs through which the common soul of humanity may give utterance to the divine thoughts and emotions which struggle within her. Let them do this, and they shall entwine themselves with the holiest and strongest affections of the age, resuscitate a love for religion, reverence for the church, and obedience to her commands; let them do this, and they shall again become a power sacred and legitimate, they shall realize the teachings of their Master in the sense in which those teachings are specially applicable to our times and the present wants of Christendom, make democracy an honor and not an accusation, give the people the powerful and hallowing support of the religious sentiment, baptize liberty in the font of holiness, and send her forth with a benediction to "make the tour of the globe."

5.

ABOLITION PROCEEDINGS[1]

Boston Quarterly Review 1 (October, 1838): 473-500

Mr. Treadwell has attempted in this book to settle definitively the whole question as to the right of the abolitionists to labor for the emancipation of the slaves. He takes up and professes to answer some forty popular objections to the proceedings of the abolitionists. He has done the thing admirably, no doubt, and to the entire satisfaction of his friends. But we are sorry to find that he has mistaken entirely the real question at issue, and paid not the least attention to what we regard as the really weighty objections which may be urged against abolition proceedings.

Mr. Treadwell proceeds through his whole book, at least so far as we have read it, on the ground that the real question at issue is, have the Northern abolitionists a right to *discuss* the abstract question of slavery? Now this is a great mistake, and this way of putting the question is altogether unpardonable. We have a right, as men and as citizens of an independent state, to discuss any question and all questions which concern any portion of the human race, and to discuss them freely and unreservedly. There is no limitation to this right, except as to the manner of exercising it. In discussing any question whatever we are bound to show that respect for the opinions and characters of others, we exact from others for our own. Nobody objects to the mere discussion of slavery; and anybody may advocate, in the freest and ablest manner he can, the inalienable right of every man, whether black or white, to be a freeman.

We insist on this point. The abolitionists make no small outcry about the right of free discussion; they represent themselves as the champions of free discussion; and they take unwearied pains to make it believed that the whole cause of free discussion is involved in the

[1] [Ed. Review of Seymour Boughton Treadwell's (1795-1867) *American Liberties and American Slavery, Morally and Politically Illustrated* (New York: John S. Taylor; Boston: Weeks, Jordan, and Co., 1838). Treadwell was a temperance and anti-slavery political advocate who lived in Rochester, New York, at the time he published this tract. In 1839 he moved to Jackson, Michigan, where he edited the *Michigan Freeman*, an anti-slavery paper, and where he became involved in Michigan politics as commissioner of the state land office.]

abolition question. Nothing is or can be more disingenuous than this. Abolitionists are in no sense whatever, either in principle or in practice, the champions of free discussion. Their conceptions of free discussion, so far as we can gather them from their publications, are exceedingly narrow and crude. In their estimation free discussion is to denounce slavery and slave holders; and opposition to free discussion is the free expression of one's honest convictions against abolition proceedings. A man who supports them defends the rights of the mind; he who opposes them attacks the rights of the mind. Now this sort of free discussion is altogether too one-sided to suit our taste. It is very much like our pilgrim fathers' respect for the freedom of conscience. Our pilgrim fathers loved freedom of conscience so much that they took it into their own especial keeping and spurned the idea of sharing its custody with others.

Moreover, the abolitionists do not, properly speaking, discuss the subject of slavery. Nay, it is not their object to discuss it. Their object is not to enlighten the community on the subject, but to agitate it. Discussion is a calm exercise of the reasoning powers, not the ebullition of passion, nor the ravings of a maddened zeal. To discuss an important question we need not the aid of women and children,[2] but of wise and sober men, men of strong intellects and well-informed minds. Discussion is also best carried on in one's closet, at least where one can keep cool; not in a crowd, where people of all ages and both sexes are brought together, and by the strong appeals of impassioned orators thrown into a state of excitement bordering upon insanity. When men have made up their minds, when the epoch for deliberation has gone by, and that for action has come; when their object is less to convince than it is to rouse, to quicken, to inflame; then proceedings like those of the abolitionists are very appropriate, and it is only then that they are ever adopted. It is perfect folly therefore for the abolitionists to talk about discussion. Any man, with his eyes half open, may see clearly that all this is mere pretence. Action, not discussion, is what they demand. Deeds, not words, are what they contemplate. To agitate the whole community, to inflame all hearts, to collect the whole population into one vast body, and to roll it down on the South to force the planters to emancipate their

[2] [Ed. Brownson's reference here may be to Amos Bronson Alcott's conversational method with school children on the meaning of the Gospels, and to Lydia Marie Child and other abolitionist women of the Boston Female Anti-Slavery Society. On women involved in the Boston abolitionist movement, see Debra Gold Hansen, *Strained Sisterhood: Gender and Class in the Boston Female Anti-Slavery Society* (Amherst: University of Massachusetts Press, 1993).]

slaves, this is what they are striving to do. It is the *abolition* of slavery, not its *discussion,* they band together for, and it is idle for them to pretend to the contrary.

If any proof of this were wanted it might be found in their treatment of every man who adopts conclusions different from their own. Do they reason with him? Not they. They denounce him. They rush upon him with the fury of cannibals, and, as far as it depends on them, destroy his character, and make it impossible for him to hold up his head in the community. Do they answer the arguments urged against them? They? Mr. Garrison,[3] we have it on good authority, stated in a public meeting in this city, that the arguments adduced against the abolitionists had never been answered, and he did not wish to have them answered. Discussion do you call this? Discussion! They know better than to stop to discuss the matter. We are right, say they. God and man are with us. We have a holy cause. Wo, wo, to whomsoever opposes us; mark him, friends of freedom; mark him, friends of the slave; he is a robber, a man-stealer, a murderer, and it requires "a pencil dipped in the midnight blackness of hell"[4] to paint in appropriate colors the foulness of his heart. This is discussion, is it? The rights of free discussion are invaded, are they, because opposition to this method of treating our brethren is sometimes shown?

Abolitionists are merely discussing the question of slavery, are they? What mean then these thousands of petitions to Congress, with their seven hundred thousand signers, a large portion of whom are women and children? What kind of arguments are these? What new light do they throw on the question of slavery? What understanding do they convince? What conscience do they persuade? They are merely discussing the subject of slavery, are they? What mean then these political movements they are preparing, these interrogatories they are addressing to candidates for office? Take the following from their official publications.

"The candidates presented to your choice will, of course, be nominated either by the Whigs or Democrats. The most prominent individual of the Whig party, and probably their next candidate for the presidency, is a slaveholder, president of that stupendous imposture, the Colonization Society, author of the fatal Missouri 'compromise,' and of the slavish resolutions against the abolitionists, lately passed

[3] [Ed. William Lloyd Garrison (1805-79), editor of *The Liberator*, was the foremost abolitionist in the United States after 1830. Brownson had a bumpy relationship with him. On this, see EW, 3, Introduction and Chapters 18 and 19.]

[4] [Ed. Unable to identify quotation.]

by the Senate of the United States.[5] On the other hand, the leader of the Democratic party, 'the northern president with southern principles,' has deeply insulted this nation, by avowing his determination to veto any bill for the abolition of slavery in the District of Columbia, which may be passed by a majority of the people in opposition to the wishes of the slave states.[6]

"No consistent abolitionist can vote for either of those individuals. It does not however follow that he cannot vote for candidates for state offices, or for Congress, who may be their friends and supporters. If the candidate before you be honest, capable, and true to your principles, we think you may fairly vote for him, without considering too curiously, whether his success might not have an indirect bearing on the interests of Mr. Clay, or Mr. Van Buren. It is a golden maxim, 'Do the duty that lies nearest thee.' Vote for each man by himself, and on his own merits. If you attempt to make your rule more complicated, so as to include distant contingencies and consequences, it will be found perplexing and impracticable.

"The independent course in politics, which we have recommended, supposes great prudence, disinterestedness, energy of purpose, and self-control, in those who are to adopt it. May you justify our confidence in you. Do your duty. Come out, in your strength, to the polls. Refuse to support any public man who trims, or equivocates, or conceals his opinions. Beware of half-way abolitionists; and of men, who are abolitionists but once a year. Prove that you do not require the machinery of party discipline, to vote strictly according to your professed principles. Do this, and you will rapidly acquire a deserved influence. 'Such a party,' as Mr. Webster[7] justly said in speaking of the abolitionists, 'will assuredly cause itself to be respected.'[8]

[5] [Ed. Reference here is to Henry Clay (1777-1852), who at the time was United States senator from Kentucky (1831-42). In December of 1839 the Whigs chose William Henry Harrison rather than Clay as Whig candidate for the presidency. Harrison won the election.]

[6] [Ed. Reference is to the Democrat Martin Van Buren (1782-1862), president of the United States (1837-41). He lost the presidential election of 1840 to William Henry Harrison.]

[7] [Ed. Daniel Webster (1782-1852), orator and statesman, was at the time this was written a United States Senator from Massachusetts who opposed slavery and state rights nullification.]

[8] [Ed. Part of the quotation is from a speech given by Daniel Webster at a reception in New York. He does not actually mention the abolitionists by name or as a party. Speaking of anti-slavery in general Webster stated, "He is a rash man, indeed, and little conversant with human nature, and especially has he a very erroneous estimate of the character of the people of this country, who supposes that a feeling of this kind is to be trifled with or despised. It will assuredly cause itself to

Within the next two years, the friends of freedom might hold the balance of power in every free state in the Union; and no man could ascend the presidential seat against their will."[9]

So say the Board of Managers of the Massachusetts Anti-Slavery Society in their Address to Abolitionists, an address, by the way, the least exceptionable and the best written of any abolition document we have seen. But does this look like *discussing* the subject of slavery? Take also the following from the "Human Rights," published by the American Anti-Slavery Society.

"*There is but one remedy.* Men must be sent to Congress, made of sterner stuff—men who, like Senator Morris of Ohio,[10] are not ashamed to advocate the *rights* of their constituents. Dough-faces have had their day. Let us keep them at home—their proper vocation is to head our Northern pro-slavery squadrons, armed with brick-bats and stale eggs. State offices, too, and County and Town offices must be filled with men who will at least show as much zeal for the great objects which the 'Union' was intended to secure, as for the 'Union' itself—men who will not esteem it their duty to choke discussion and encourage mobs to please the slaveholders. We need not debate this point. Every man's conscience will show him his duty.

"What we beg is, that duty may be done *in season.* Don't wait till candidates are before the people, and the elections are at the door, and the lines of party are drawn—and its wire work all fixed. Let your voice be heard at once. Let your determination be known, not to support any man who will not unequivocally pledge himself to *free discussion, free petition, and abolition where Congress has the power.* Let the political parties have this to reflect on before they select their candidates. No candidate ought to expect the vote of an abolitionist, who is not prepared to answer the following questions in the affirmative.

"1. Are you in favor of abolishing slavery in the District of Columbia—for the honor and welfare of the nation?

"2. Are you in favor of so regulating commerce among the several states that human beings shall not be made subjects of such trade?

be respected." See, "Reception at New York, March 15th, 1837," in *The Papers of Daniel Webster: Speeches and Formal Writings*, vol. 2 1834-1852, ed. Charles M. Wiltese (Hanover, London: University Press of New England, 1988), 131.]

[9] [Ed. Massachusetts Anti-Slavery Society. Board of Managers, *An Address to the Abolitionists of Massachusetts on the Subject of Political Action* (Boston, 1838), 15-16.]

[10] [Ed. Arthur Schlesinger, Jr., *The Age of Jackson*, 426, has called the Van Buren Democratic Senator Thomas Morris (1776-1844) from Ohio the "first real antislavery" Senator.]

"3. Are you opposed to the annexation of Texas to this Union, under any circumstances, so long as slaves are held therein?

"4. Are you in favor of acknowledging the independence of Hayti, and of establishing commercial relations with that nation on the same terms with the most favored nations?

"But they *will* expect votes unless abolitionists bestir themselves in time. Crafty politicians always calculate on humanity's '*dying away*.' By our 'fathers' ashes 'let them be disappointed henceforth and forever. Let the abolitionists meet in their societies, resolve on energetic and up-to-the-mark political action, and *publish* their resolution in the *county* as well as the abolition papers. Such demonstrations, in good time, will not be without their effect. Above all things, let the action when begun, like the good cause itself, '*die away*' *bigger and bigger*."[11]

The abolitionists are merely *discussing* the subject of slavery, are they? What have the respective merits of candidates for office, state or federal, to do with the merits of slavery? What has the recognition of the independence of Hayti to do with the merits of slavery? If abolitionists are merely discussing slavery, we ask, what they have to do, *as abolitionists,* with questions like those here introduced? But we need dwell no longer upon this point. Abolitionists may say and believe what they will, but it is perfectly idle for them to dream of convincing any intelligent observer that they are merely discussing the question of slavery. As we have said, their object is to abolish it, not to discuss it, and their means for abolishing it are not calm and rational discussion, but agitation, the agitation of the community, inflaming its passions and directing by means of the ballot box the force they thus collect to bear directly on Southern institutions.

We say again, then, that Mr. Treadwell has not stated the real question at issue, and his book is therefore worthless. The real question at issue is, Have the citizens of the non-slaveholding states the right to set on foot a series of measures—no matter what measures—intentionally and avowedly for the purpose of emancipating the slaves? This is the question. Have we the right to commence a series of operations for the accomplishment of an object, and to prosecute them with strict and sole reference to the accomplishment of an object, over which we have no rightful jurisdiction?

[11] [Ed. "Political Action," *Human Rights* 4 (August 1838): 3.]

Why is it that the abolitionists shrink from this question? Why is it that—so far as our knowledge extends—they have never in a single instance met this question, or even alluded to it? Shall we say, because they are conscious that they cannot meet it, without being forced to acknowledge that they are wrong in their proceedings, and ought forthwith to disband their associations?

Doubtless somebody must have the jurisdiction of the slave question. Who is it? Who has the legal right to abolish slavery? The states in which it exists, and the sole right to do it, says the constitution of the American Anti-Slavery Society.[12] If this be so, it is certain that the abolitionists, as citizens of non-slaveholding states, have not the right to abolish slavery. In laboring to abolish it then, they are laboring to do that which they have no legal right to do, even according to their own official confession. They then, so far as they labor to abolish it, are acting against law, are transgressors of the law, and obnoxious to its penalties. There is no gainsaying this.

This being so, on what ground will the abolitionists justify their proceedings? Will they take their stand above law, appeal from law to their individual conceptions of right, to the paramount law of humanity—of God? We presume so. We believe this is their appeal, this the ground on which they attempt to legitimate their proceedings. Be it so. In taking this ground they set the law at defiance, and are either a mob or a band of insurrectionists. In taking this ground they justify all the lawless violence against which they have so vehemently declaimed. If one class of the community may set the laws at defiance, why may not another? If the abolitionists may set at nought the international law, which gives the slaveholding states the exclusive jurisdiction of the slave question, why may not other citizens say they have a right by mob-law to prevent them, if they can, from doing it? It were not difficult to convict the abolitionists of preaching the very doctrines the mobocrats attempt to reduce to practice. They ought not therefore to think it strange that they have been in but too many instances the victims of lawless violence. When a portion of the community take it into their heads that they are wiser than the law, and commence the performance of acts in contravention of law, they ought to be aware that they open the door to every species of lawless violence, unchain the tiger, and must be answerable for the consequences.

[12] [Ed. See *The Constitution of the American Anti-Slavery Society: with the declaration of the national anti-slavery convention of Philadelphia, December, 1833; and, The Address to the public, issued by the executive committee of the society, in September, 1835* (New York: American Anti-Slavery Society, 1838), 10.]

Nevertheless we cheerfully admit, that, in saying the abolitionists appeal from law as it is to what they consider it ought to be, to the paramount law of humanity, we do not necessarily condemn them, nor even cast a shadow of a reproach upon them. There may be cases in which men shall be justified in doing this; nay, when it shall be their duty to do this. But this cannot be done without rebellion. They who do it declare the bonds of society broken, and society itself reduced to its original elements. It cannot be done in accordance with any existing social order; it therefore can be justified only in such cases as do justify rebellion, revolution. Revolutions are sometimes justifiable, and we as a nation hold to the sacred right of insurrection. If the abolitionists take the ground we suppose they do, they are in fact insurrectionists, they are revolutionists. This is their character. Now in order to justify themselves they must make out a clear case, that the present circumstances of our Republic are such as to warrant a revolution.

No doubt justice, the paramount law of humanity, demands the abolition of slavery. But of whom does it demand it? And on what conditions does it demand it? Does humanity command us to abolish it in contravention of law? Is humanity, all things considered, more interested in declaring the Negroes free, than in maintaining those laws which the abolitionists violate in laboring to bring about the declaration? We say *declaring* the slaves free, and we do so designedly; for this is as far as the efforts of the abolitionists, if successful, can go. They cannot make the slaves free. The slave is never converted into a freeman by a stroke of the pen. Freedom cannot be conferred; it must be conquered. The slave must grow into freedom and be able to maintain his freedom, or he is a slave still, whatever he may be called. If then the abolitionists cannot make out clearly and beyond the possibility of cavil that humanity is more interested in declaring the slaves free than she is in maintaining the laws, the citizens of non-slaveholding states must violate, before they can cause them to be declared free, they cannot make out a case that justifies revolution, nor a case that justifies their proceedings even admitting their own premises.

Slavery ought to be abolished, says the abolitionist, and what ought to be done it is right to do. It is right then to abolish slavery. This is enough for me. Ask me not to stop and consider what may be found in statute laws and paper constitutions. The tyrant's foot is on the neck of my brother; don't tell me to stop and ask whether, all things considered, it be my duty to run to his rescue. It may not be expedient to do it. But what of that? Let me alone. I will hurl the tyrant to the dust, and deliver my brother. We understand this feeling very well, and by dwelling upon it could work ourselves up, as we often have done, into a glorious passion, and become quite heroic. Still we believe harm seldom comes from stopping to consider.

We eschew expediency as a rule of action as heartily as do our friends the abolitionists. We are not among those who sneer at abstract right, and say we are not to regard it in practical life. Abstract right, as we view it, is absolute right, which is simply right, neither more nor less. Now we hold that every one is bound to consult the right and the right only, and having found it, to do it, let who or what will oppose. But we believe it is, before acting, very proper to determine what is right, not only in a general case, but in the particular case in which it is proposed to act. In determining what is right in any given case, it is necessary to take into consideration all the circumstances and bearings of that case. Right, it is true, never varies, but the action varies according to the circumstances under which it is performed. An action with certain general characteristics, performed under certain circumstances, shall be right, but performed under other circumstances shall be wrong; because in the latter case it is in fact a different action from what it is in the former. A given action viewed in one of its relations may be right, yet viewed in all its relations it shall be improper to be done. It is therefore always necessary, in order to determine whether a particular action should be done or not, to survey it in all its relations, and to examine as far as we can all its bearings. The consequences of the action are by no means to be overlooked. True, the consequences of an action do not *constitute* its moral character, but they are necessary to be consulted in order to *ascertain* its moral character. The idea of right is unquestionably intuitive, of transcendental origin; but its proper application to practical life is a matter of experience, to be determined by the understanding.[13]

Admit then that slavery is wrong, that it is right to abolish it, it does by no means follow that the citizens of non-slaveholding states have the right to abolish it; nor that the abolition proceedings are commanded by that law of right to which the abolitionists so confidently appeal. A fellow citizen has wronged us. It is right that we should have redress; but it is right that we should seek redress only in conformity to the law of the land. We shall be held justifiable in morals, no more than in law, if we undertake to obtain redress our-

[13] [Ed. Brownson's use of the philosophy of Victor Cousin on intuition and understanding is one of the major differences he has with the so-called 'higher law' abolitionist advocates.]

selves, without reference to the legal method of obtaining it. The abolitionist must do more than prove that slavery is wrong, that it ought to be abolished, and that it is right to abolish it; he must prove first, that *he* has a right to abolish it, and secondly, that he has a right to abolish it in the way he proposes to do—two things we hope he will forthwith undertake to prove, but which we fear he will be able to prove not without difficulty.

We go as strongly for liberty as the abolitionist. We protest with the whole energy of our moral being against the right of any man to hold his brother man in slavery. To the slaveholder, boasting the beauties of the slave system, its happy effects, and the sweet ties it creates between the master and slave, we have no answer, but "Do unto others as you would they should do unto you." When we find the master willing to become, and desirous of becoming a slave, then, and not till then, will we listen to his defense of slavery. Man is born with the right to be free. Liberty is his inalienable right and there is nothing in heaven or on earth to justify one man in depriving another of his rights. We can see, we think we do see, how God overrules slavery for good, and makes it serve to restrain or destroy other evils, which might perhaps lead to consequences still worse than those of Negro slavery itself; but this is in our judgment of the matter no excuse, no palliation of the guilt of those by whose agency slavery was introduced and is perpetuated. On this point we have no controversy with the abolitionist. We sympathize with slavery no more than he does; and we are as far as he would be from appearing as the defender or the apologist of the slaveholder. Slavery is wholly indefensible; it ought to be abolished; it must be abolished; it will be abolished. But does it belong to us, who are citizens of non-slaveholding states, to abolish it? This is the first question we want answered.

To emancipate the slaves, viewed in itself, might be a praiseworthy deed. It were, if it could be done, a good work. But it is not therefore necessarily true that it is a work for us to perform. It is not only necessary to prove the work a good one, but that it is *our* work, before we have proved that we have a right to undertake it. Every man has in the general allotment of Providence his special work. Every community its special mission; and it is each man's duty to ascertain and perform his own work, each community's duty to ascertain and fulfil its own mission. Evil always results from the attempt of any one man to be that for which God and nature have not designed him, and consequently evil must always proceed from the attempt of any one to perform the task assigned another.

The emancipation of the slaves, we say, is not our work. Slavery may be a sin, but it is not ours; and there is no occasion for us to assume the responsibility of other people's sins. We have sins enough of our own, and more than we can answer for; we have more work to perform for freedom here, within the limits of our own territory, than we can perform in many centuries, even should we direct to its performance our exclusive attention and all our energies. Slavery, it may be, is a stain, a disgrace upon the community that tolerates it; but if so, it is not a stain nor a disgrace on non-slaveholding communities. We are not disgraced because Constantinople is a slaveholding city, nor are we because Charleston is a slaveholding city. The states that hold slaves are alone responsible for the institution. If, as they pretend, it be a good and praiseworthy institution, theirs be the glory of maintaining it; if it be, as the abolitionists regard it, a disgraceful, a wicked institution, theirs be the sin and disgrace of perpetuating it. They are of age and are responsible for their own deeds.

The abolitionist considers that it is our duty to labor for the emancipation of the slaves because our nation is a slaveholding nation, and is therefore disgraced in the eyes of foreigners. To foreigners, who reproach us with slavery, all we have to say is, when you have done as much to elevate labor and the laboring classes, as we have, we will hear you; till then hold your peace. To the abolitionists we deny the fact in toto, that we are a slaveholding nation. We are made one nation by the Constitution of the United States, and are one nation no further than that declares us to be so. Now in the sense in which these United States are one people we do not hold slaves. Slavery is not recognized by the Constitution; that is, it in no sense whatever exists by virtue of the Constitution. It is not established by the laws of the Union, nor is it protected by those laws. In our capacity of one people, in the sense in which we are one nation, we have no cognizance of the subject of slavery. We deny therefore that our republic is a slaveholding republic. We deny that it tolerates slavery, and request the abolitionists not to be too ready to assume a reproach to which they are not obnoxious.

But some of the members of the Confederacy hold slaves. Granted. So does Brazil, so does Turkey, so do a great many nations. But the members of the Confederacy that hold slaves, do it not by virtue of constitutional grants, not by virtue of powers conferred on them by their sister states, but by virtue of their state sovereignty, which they did not surrender into the hands of the Union, and which they still retain in all its plenitude, at least so far as this question is concerned.[14] They stand then in regard to this question, as we have shown on a former occasion,[15] precisely as independent nations, and we of course are no more responsible for their deeds, or affected in our national character by their misdeeds, than by those of any independent or foreign community whatever. Let us talk no more then about a slaveholding republic. We are not a slaveholding republic.

We must again point out to our abolitionists, that the Federal Republic is limited to a very few specific purposes. The states, for their mutual convenience, for the general welfare and common defense of the whole, formed themselves into a federal league or Union. In the Constitution is specified the extent to which the states, as free, independent, sovereign nations, consented to merge their state character and sovereignty into one nation. To the extent there specified, we regard the people of the several states as one people, and no further. To the extent there specified, and for the purposes there specified, a citizen of Massachusetts is also a citizen of the United States, and has the same right to concern himself, according to the mode there pointed out, with the affairs of South Carolina that he has with the affairs of Massachusetts. But beyond this extent he has no more right to concern himself with the affairs of any state but the one of which he is specially a citizen, than he has with the affairs of France or China. Our duty, as citizens of the United States, is to observe in good faith the stipulations into which we have entered with our sister states; and so long as the slaveholding states perform towards us all the engagements they have made to us, we have, as citizens of the United States, no fault to find with them.

Now have the slaveholding states ever entered into an engagement to emancipate their slaves? Is it in the bond? When they came into the Union, did they stipulate to abolish slavery? Not at all. They retained that matter in their own hands. What right have we then to insist upon their doing it now? In what capacity do we call upon the Southerner to free his slaves? In our capacity as citizens of the United States? But in that capacity we have no right to meddle with the matter, because slavery is not one of the matters which come under the jurisdiction of the United States. The people of the United States have no legal cognizance of it. In our capacity as citizens of Massachusetts then? But as citizens of Massachusetts, we hold no other

[14] [Ed. Here Brownson sides with John C. Calhoun (1782-1850), United States Senator from South Carolina who supported the state rights doctrine in Congress.]

[15] [Ed. See "Sub-Treasury Bill," *Boston Quarterly Review* 1 (July, 1838): 333-60. See also EW, 3, chapter 21.]

relation with the slaveholder in South Carolina, than we do with the slaveholder in Constantinople. In what capacity then? In our capacity as men and as Christians?

We are far from denying that as men and Christians we have no concern with the slave question. As a man, as a Christian, I have a right to concern myself with whatever affects my brother man wherever he is. But has this concern no limitation? Limitation or not, it is no greater in the case of Southern slavery, than in the case of slavery anywhere else. Our right and our duty to labor for the emancipation of Southern slaves, rest on our general right and duty to labor for the abolition of slavery wherever it exists. Now, before the abolitionist can make out that it is my right and my duty to make any special efforts to effect the emancipation of the slaves in the Southern states, he must show that it is my right and my duty to make special efforts for the abolition of slavery everywhere. Nay, more than this, he must prove that it is my right and my duty to make special efforts for the correction of all abuses of all countries, to abolish every bad or wrong institution of every nation, to remove all national sins of all nations. Can he do this? He can do it only by doing another thing which is yet more difficult. He must prove that every man has the right and the duty to concern himself with the whole conduct, the entire life, of every other man, and that every man has the right and the duty to see that every other man forsakes his sins and does his duty.

It is the duty of Massachusetts to educate all her children; but is it the duty of South Carolina to undertake to compel her to do it? It is the duty of the citizens of this state to abolish the barbarous law that treats poverty as a crime; but is it the duty of the citizens of Georgia to compel us to do it, or to do it for us? The autocrat of the Russias ought to restore Poland to her national independence; but is it our duty to do it for him, or to undertake to force him to do it? England ought to abolish the laws of primogeniture and entail, monarchy, and the hereditary peerage; but is it our duty to make special efforts to induce her to do it? Is that abolition her work, or is it ours? Universal freedom should be established throughout the earth; is it therefore our duty to become propagandists, and band our whole community together into associations for carrying on a war with all nations who have not adopted a republican form of government?

Freedom requires us to recognize in each individual certain rights, and rights which we may no more invade to do the individual good than to do him harm. He must have a certain degree of liberty. That liberty he may abuse; but so long as he does not attack our liberty, we cannot, without sapping all liberty in its very foundation, interfere with him. So of communities. They stand in relation to one another as individuals. So long as any given community respects the rights of all other communities, no other community has any right to interfere with its conduct. Its external relations are just, and its internal affairs, so far as other communities are concerned, it has a right to regulate in its own way. To deny this is to deny its independence, is to strike at its liberty; and to attempt to interfere with its internal policy is to declare war upon it, and must, if it be a spirited community and able to fight for its independence, lead to bloodshed and incalculable sufferings. Peace among the nations of the earth is to be maintained only by each nation's attending to its own concerns, leaving all other nations to regulate their internal policy in their own way. This principle is even more imperative in the case of the states which compose this Republic than in that of nations generally. Our relations are so multiplied, are so intimate, and our intercourse is so frequent and various, that, without the most punctilious respect for the reserved rights of each, perpetual embroilment must result, and our union instead of harmony be a source of perpetual discord. We say, therefore, inasmuch as slavery is an institution over which the slaveholding states have the exclusive jurisdiction, inasmuch as we, as citizens of the United States and of non-slaveholding states, have no concern with it, we are not called upon, whatever may be our opinion of it as an institution, to labor specially for its abolition. We are not called upon to abolish it.

But even admitting we were called upon to abolish it, or to labor for the abolition of slavery wherever it exists, we should still deny that the abolition proceedings are justifiable. They are contrary to the genius of our institutions; they make war upon the relations, which it was intended by our federal system should subsist between the states which compose the Union, and are therefore, as we have said, revolutionary in their character and tendency.

We do not say that to abolish slavery is contrary to the genius of our institutions. The genius of our institutions is liberty, and unquestionably is repugnant to every species of slavery. If the institutions subsist, they must in their gradual unfolding sweep away slavery, and every vestige of man's tyranny over man. But according to our federal system all the internal affairs of the several states are to be managed by the states themselves. When, therefore, the citizens of one state disregard this system, and labor to control the internal affairs of another state, in the manner we have shown the abolitionists do, they are acting in opposition to the American system of government. The citizens of slaveholding states might, if they chose, adopt all the measures our abolitionists do, without being liable to this charge, and perhaps they ought in justice to labor even more zealously than do the abolitionists for the abolition of slavery. The error of the abolitionists consists in concluding from the duty of the citizens of the slaveholding states to their own—of concluding from the fact that it is right for South Carolina, for instance, to labor to emancipate the slaves, it is therefore right for citizens of Massachusetts to do the same. The wrong is not in the end sought, but in the persons who seek it, and the means by which they seek it.

The abolitionists are wrong as to their point of departure. They begin, consciously or unconsciously, by assuming that the people of the United States are one people, not in the restricted sense in which they are so declared by the Constitution, but in all senses, to the fullest extent, as much so as the people of France or England. They regard themselves not as citizens of Massachusetts or of New York, but as citizens of the United States. The division of the territory into separate states, they regard as merely for administrative purposes, or for the convenience of transacting governmental business. They see not and understand not that the division into separate states, is a division, in point of fact and in theory especially, into distinct communities, separate nations, afterwards to be united by a league or compact; but a division altogether analogous to the division of a state for municipal purposes into counties, townships, and parishes. In giving the legal form to any public measure, they indeed recognize the boundaries of the states in like manner as they do the boundaries of a county, a township, or a parish; but in all else, in preparing the measure, in urging its adoption, in the combination and direction of influences which shall lead to or compel its adoption, they know no geographical boundaries, no civil or political divisions. Here is the source of their error. They begin by denying the sovereignty of the states, and consequently the Federal Republic created by the Constitution, and by asserting the system of consolidation, another and altogether different system—a system by which we become one vast centralized republic, adopting the division into states only as a convenient regulation for facilitating the administration of the affairs of government.

We say not that the abolitionists are in general aware of this or that they would knowingly and intentionally do all this. They are probably aware of nothing but a morbid craving after excitement, and the determination, cost what it may, to abolish slavery. But we do say that the doctrine of consolidation, which we have stated, is that which lies at the bottom of their proceedings, and which has influenced them, and led them to adopt the proceedings they have. Had they been in the habit of contemplating the American political system in its true character, had they been in the habit of seeing in the division into states something more than a municipal regulation, than an affair of internal police, had they been accustomed to see in each state a distinct, independent, and sovereign community, in all matters, except the very few specified in the Constitution of the United States, they had never taken those peculiar views of their own relations with the slaveholding communities, which have led them to adopt the measures of which we complain. Anti-slavery men they might have been, but abolitionists they could not have been.

We would acquit the abolitionists also of all wish to change fundamentally the character of our institutions. They are not, at least the honest part of them, politicians; but very simple-minded men and women who crave excitement, and seek it in abolition meetings, and in getting up abolition societies and petitions, instead of seeking it in ballrooms, theaters, or places of fashionable amusement or dissipation. Politics, properly speaking, they abominate, because politics would require them to think, and they wish only to feel. Doubtless some of them are moved by generous sympathies, and a real regard for the well-being of the Negro; but the principal moving cause of their proceedings, after the craving for excitement, and perhaps notoriety, is the feeling that slavery is a national disgrace. Now this feeling, as we have shown, proceeds from a misconception of the real character of our institutions. This feeling can be justified only on the supposition that we are a consolidated republic. Its existence is therefore a proof that, whatever be the conscious motives in the main of the abolitionists, their proceedings strike against our federal system.

Well, what if they do? replies the abolitionist. If federalism, or the doctrine of state sovereignty, which you say is the American system of politics, prohibits us from laboring to free the slave, then down with it. Any system of government, any political relations, which prevent me from laboring to break the yoke of the oppressor and to set the captive free, is a wicked system, and ought to be destroyed. God disowns it, Christ disowns it, and man ought to disown it. If consolidation, if centralization be the order that enables us to free the slave, then give us consolidation, give us centralization. It is the true doctrine. It enables one to plead for the slave. The slave is crushed under his master's foot; the slave is dying; I see nothing but the slave; I hear nothing but the slave's cries for deliverance. Away with your paper barriers, away with your idle prating about state rights; clear the way. Let me run to the slave. Anything that frees the slave is right, is owned by God.

We express here the sentiment and use very nearly the language of the abolitionists. They have no respect for government as such. They indeed are fast adopting the ultra-radical doctrine that all government is founded in usurpation, and is an evil which all true Christians must labor to abolish. They have, at least some of them, nominated Jesus Christ to be president of the United States; as much as to say, in the only practical sense to be given the nomination, that there shall be no president of the United States but an idea, and an idea without any visible embodiment; which is merely contending in other words that there shall be no visible government, no political institutions whatever. They have fixed their minds on a given object, and finding that the political institutions of the country, and the laws of the land are against them, they deny the legitimacy of all laws and of all political institutions. Let them carry their doctrines out, and it is easy to see that a most radical revolution in the institutions of the country must be the result.

Now, we ask, has a revolution become necessary? Is it no longer possible to labor for the progress of humanity in this country, without changing entirely the character of our political institutions? Must we change our federal system, destroy the existing relations between the states and the Union and between the states? Nay, must we destroy all outward, visible government, abolish all laws, and leave the community in the state in which the Jews were, when there "was no king in Israel, and every man did that which was right in his own eyes" [Judg 18:1; 21:25]? We put these questions in soberness, and with a deep feeling of their magnitude. The abolition ranks are full of insane dreamers, and fuller yet of men and women ready to undertake to realize any dream however insane, and at any expense. We ask therefore these questions with solemnity, and with fearful forebodings for our country. We rarely fear; we rarely tremble at the prospect of evil to come. The habitual state of our own mind is that of serene trust in the future; and if in this respect we are thought to have a fault, it is in being too sanguine, in hoping too much. But we confess, the proceedings of the abolitionists, coupled with their vague speculations, and their crude notions, do fill us with lively alarm, and make us apprehend danger to our beloved country. We beg, in the name of God and of man, the abolitionists to pause, and if they love liberty, ask themselves what liberty has, in the long run, to gain by overthrowing the system of government we have established, by effecting a revolution in the very foundation of our federal system?

For ourselves, we have accepted with our whole heart the political system adopted by our fathers. We regard that system as the most brilliant achievement of humanity, a system in which centers all past progress, and which combines the last results of all past civilization. It is the latest birth of time. Humanity has been laboring with it since that morning when the sons of God shouted with joy over the birth of a new world, and we will not willingly see it strangled in its cradle. We take the American political system as our starting-point, as our primitive data, and we repulse whatever is repugnant to it, and accept, demand whatever is essential to its preservation. We take our stand on the idea of our institutions, and labor with all our soul to realize and develop it. As a lover of our race, as the devoted friend of liberty, of the progress of mankind, we feel that we must, in this country, be conservative, not radical. If we demand the elevation of labor and the laboring classes, we do it only in accordance with our institutions and for the purpose of preserving them by removing all discrepancy between their spirit and the social habits and condition of the people on whom they are to act, and to whose keeping they are entrusted. We demand reform only for the purpose of preserving American institutions in their real character; and we can tolerate no changes, no innovations, no alleged improvements not introduced in strict accordance with the relations which do subsist between the states and the Union and between the states themselves. Here is our political creed. More power in the federal government than was given it by the Convention which framed the Constitution would be dangerous to the states, and with less power the federal government would not be able to subsist. We take it then as it is. The fact that any given measure is necessary to preserve it as it is, is a sufficient reason for adopting that measure; the fact that a given measure is opposed to it as it is, and has a tendency to increase or diminish its power, is a sufficient reason for rejecting that measure.

The Constitution then is our touchstone for trying all measures. Not indeed because we have any superstitious reverence for written constitutions, or any overweening attachment to things as they are; but because we have satisfied ourselves by long, patient, and somewhat extensive inquiry, that the preservation of the Constitution is strictly identified with the highest interests of our race. Its destruction were, so far as human foresight can go, an irreparable loss. We would preserve it then, not because it is a Constitution, not because we are averse to changes, nor because we have a dread of revolutions, but because the safety and progress of liberty demand its preservation.

But can efforts in behalf of liberty be repugnant to the spirit of a constitution established avowedly in the interests of liberty? The abolitionists are in pursuit of liberty; liberty is their great idea; liberty is the soul of their movements; liberty is to be the end of their exertions; how then can their proceedings be dangerous to liberty? Very simply. In their character of efforts merely in behalf of liberty, of course they are neither unconstitutional nor dangerous; but they may have another character than that; beside being efforts in behalf of liberty they may be efforts which strike against international law. The abolitionist would free the slave. So far so good. But he would free the slave by forgetting that slavery is an institution under the sole control of a state of which he is not a citizen. Here comes the danger to liberty. Here is a blow struck at the rights of communities, and as dangerous to liberty as a blow struck at the rights of individuals. He would free the slaves by combining the non-slaveholding states against the slaveholding states, by collecting in the non-slaveholding states a force sufficient to control the internal policy of the slaveholding states. Let him do this, and where is the independence of the states? Let him do this, and one part of the Union has the complete control of the other; and when this is done, is not our federal system destroyed? It is possible then to pursue liberty in such a manner that the pursuit shall be in open violation of free institutions, and this is, as we allege, the case with the abolitionists.

But we can pursue the subject no farther at present. We are sorry to be compelled to separate ourselves from the abolitionists. There is something exceedingly unpleasant in being, even in appearance, opposed to the advocates of freedom. We have ever been with the movement party; our own position, the much we have suffered from things as they are, the wounds yet rankling in our heart, together with our own love of excitement, of new things, to say nothing of certain dreams we indulge concerning a golden age that is to be, strongly dispose us to join with the abolitionists, and to rush on in the career they open up to a bold and energetic spirit. There is something too in the very idea of freeing two or three millions of slaves, which, in these mechanical and money-getting times, is quite refreshing and capable of dazzling many an imagination. It addresses itself to some of the strongest propensities of our nature, and gives us apparently an opportunity to indulge a taste for the adventurous and the chivalric. There is something almost intoxicating in the idea of going forth as a bold knight in the cause of humanity, to plead for the wronged and the outraged, to speak for the dumb, and to do valiant battle for the weak and the defenseless. Much that is noble, that is generous, that is godlike, naturally combines itself with such an idea, and enters into the motives of him who goes forth at its bidding. It may be that we have felt something of all this. But self-denial, even in the indulgence of what we call noble impulses, or rather the subordination of our impulses to the clearest and soberest convictions of our understandings, is one of the first laws of morality.[16]

So long as we regarded the abolitionists as merely contending for the right to discuss the subject of slavery, we were with them; we spoke in their behalf, and were willing to be reckoned of their number. Later developments on their side, and a closer examination of the bearings of their movements on the political institutions of this country, into which we have entered, have convinced us that the cause of free discussion is not now, if it ever was, at all involved in their proceedings; that the cause of liberty even, is by no means in their hands; and therefore that we ought to separate from them, and to state clearly and boldly, the reasons which we think should induce all lovers of our common country to combine to stay their progress. It may be too late. We fear it is. The ball has been set in motion. It increases in momentum and velocity with every revolution, and the result we pretend not to be able to foresee. Already is it hazardous to one's reputation in this part of the Union to oppose them; already is it nearly impossible for any political party to succeed unless it can secure their suffrages. They have become a power. It is in vain to deny it. They are not likely to become weaker very soon. We have not, therefore, dared to keep our convictions in regard to them to ourselves. In opposing them, we have had to show as much moral courage as they profess to have shown in opposing slavery. We have not, therefore, spoken from considerations we need be ashamed to avow. We may have spoken in vain. But we have said our word, feebly we own, but in sincerity; and we leave the result to God. We see danger ahead. We tremble for the fate of our republic; there are mighty influences at work against it; the money power is seeking to bind its free spirit with chains of gold, and mistaken philanthropy is fast rending it in twain; associations, sectarian and moral espionage are fast swallowing up individual freedom, and making the individual man but a mere appendage to a huge social machine, with neither mind

[16] [Ed. The argument Brownson uses here against the abolitionists is the same that he will use against Ralph Waldo Emerson's Divinity School Address, which immediately follows this essay. Both Emerson and the abolitionists threatened society and historic Christianity by their over-emphasis upon the ideal and intuition and their under appreciation of the role of understanding. Antinomian tendencies, according to Brownson, were evident in both.]

nor will of his own; but we do not, we will not, despair of the republic. We hope with trembling, nevertheless we hope. The destinies of individuals or of nations are not left to blind chance. There is a providence that rules them, and we will trust that in due time the clouds that lower over us shall break and disperse, and the glorious son of freedom and humanity shine forth in all his noonday splendors. We cannot go back to the night and gloom of the past; the irresistible law of progress does and will bear us onward; and this republic shall yet prove itself the medium through which the human race shall rise to the knowledge and enjoyment of the inalienable rights of man.

In conclusion, we would merely add that in our judgment the first duty of the friends of freedom, of democracy, of progress, is to secure the political institutions established by our fathers. Nothing can come but in its time and its place. There is a method to be followed in taking up and discussing the great questions which concern mankind, or the progress of society. Errors always come from the fact that we take them up in a false order. Our inquiry should be, what is the question for today? Having ascertained the problem for today, we should bend our whole attention to its solution. The answer to the question of today, will of itself lead to the solution of the problem which shall come up tomorrow. The question for today is the currency question—not the most interesting question in itself surely, nor a question of the first magnitude; but it is the first in the order of time. It must be disposed of before we can proceed systematically to the disposition of any other. What will be the question for tomorrow, we ask not. Sufficient for the day is the evil thereof. It will doubtless be a question of magnitude. Great questions are hereafter to be ever expected. Humanity approaches manhood, grows serious, and refuses to trifle. As it regards the slave question, we leave it to those whom it more immediately concerns. If our republic outlive the dangers to which it is now exposed, the gradual unfolding of its spirit will abolish slavery; and we believe slavery will be sooner abolished, that is, the Negro race sooner elevated to the rank of freemen, by leaving the whole matter to time, to the secret but sure workings of Christian democracy, than by any violent or special efforts of abolitionists, even if successful in declaring slavery abolished. Leave the whole matter to the slaveholding states, and in proportion as the Negro advances internally, the legislature will spread over him the shield of the law, and imperceptibly but surely shall he grow into a freeman, if a freeman he can become.

If we would serve him and hasten that day, we shall best do it, not by direct efforts in his behalf, but by a steady development and realization of democratic freedom within the bosom of the non-slaveholding states. Let us correct the evils at our own doors, elevate the free white laborer, and prove by our own practice, and by the state of our own society, that the doctrine of equal rights is not a visionary dream. O we have much to do here at home. The beggar full of sores lies at our own gate. In our own dark streets, blind courts, narrow lanes, damp cellars, unventilated garrets, are human beings more degraded, and suffering keener anguish, and appealing with a more touching pathos to our compassion, and demanding in more imperative tones our succor, than is the case with the most wretched of Southern slaves. O here are objects enough for our humanity. We walk not through the streets of a single Northern city without a bleeding heart. Wash the faces of those children, abolitionists, which meet you in our cities incrusted with filth, clothe their shivering limbs, let in light upon their darkened minds, and warm their young hearts, before it is too late, with the hope of being one day virtuous men and women. Instead of poring over the horrors of slavery, read your police reports, and see your own society as it is. You have work enough for all your philanthropy north of Mason and Dixon's line. Do this work, do it effectually, and you shall aid the cause of oppressed humanity everywhere, and the slave a thousand times more than by your direct efforts for his emancipation.

6.

MR. EMERSON'S *ADDRESS*[1]

Boston Quarterly Review 1 (October 1838): 500-14

This is in some respects a remarkable address, remarkable for its own character and for the place where and the occasion on which it was delivered. It is not often, we fancy, that such an address is delivered by a clergyman in a Divinity College to a class of young men just ready to go forth into the churches as preachers of the gospel of Jesus Christ. Indeed it is not often that a discourse teaching doctrines like the leading doctrines of this, is delivered by a professedly religious man, anywhere or on any occasion.

We are not surprised that this address should have produced some excitement and called forth some severe censures upon its author; for we have long known that there are comparatively few who can hear with calmness the utterance of opinions to which they do not subscribe. Yet we regret to see the abuse which has been heaped upon Mr. Emerson. We ought to learn to tolerate all opinions, to respect every man's right to form and to utter his own opinions whatever they may be. If we regard the opinions as unsound, false, or dangerous, we should meet them calmly, refute them if we can; but be careful to respect, and to treat with all Christian meekness and love, him who entertains them.

There are many things in this address we heartily approve; there is much that we admire and thank the author for having uttered. We like its life and freshness, its freedom and independence, its richness and beauty. But we cannot help regarding its tone as somewhat arrogant, its spirit is quite too censorious and desponding, its philosophy as indigested, and its reasoning as inconclusive. We do not like its mistiness, its vagueness, and its perpetual use of old words in new senses. Its meaning too often escapes us; and we find it next to impossible to seize its dominant doctrine and determine what it is or what it is not. Moreover, it does not appear to us to be all of the same

[1] [Ed. Review of Ralph Waldo Emerson's *An Address Delivered Before the Senior Class in Divinity College, Cambridge, Sunday Evening, 15 July, 1838* (Boston: James Munroe & Co., 1838).]

piece. It is made up of parts borrowed from different and hostile systems, which "baulk and baffle"[2] the author's power to form into a consistent and harmonious whole.

In a moral point of view the leading doctrine of this address, if we have seized it, is not a little objectionable. It is not easy to say what that moral doctrine is; but so far as we can collect it, it is, that the soul possesses certain laws or instincts, obedience to which constitutes its perfection. "The sentiment of virtue is a reverence and delight in the presence of certain divine laws." "The intuition of the moral sentiment is an insight of the perfection of the laws of the soul." These "divine laws" are the "laws of the soul." The moral sentiment results from the perception of these laws, and moral character results from conformity to them. Now this is not, we apprehend, psychologically true. If any man will analyze the moral sentiment as a fact of consciousness, he will find it something more than "an insight of the perfection of the laws of the soul." He will find that it is a sense of obligation. Man feels himself under obligation to obey a law; not the law of his own soul, a law emanating from his soul as lawgiver; but a law above his soul, imposed upon him by a supreme lawgiver, who has a right to command his obedience. He does never feel that he is moral in obeying merely the laws of his own nature, but in obeying the command of a power out of him, above him, and independent on him.

By the laws of the soul, we presume, Mr. Emerson means our instincts. In his Phi Beta Kappa Address, reviewed in this journal for January,[3] he speaks much of the instincts, and bids us "plant ourselves on our instincts, and the huge world will come round to us." The ethical rule he lays down is then, "follow thy instincts," or as he expresses it in the address before us, "obey thyself." Now if we render this rule into the language it will assume in practice, we must say, obey thyself, follow thy instincts, follow thy inclinations, live as thou listest. Strike out the idea of something above man to which he is accountable, make him accountable only to himself, and why shall he not live as he listeth? We see not what restraint can legitimately be

[2] [Ed. The phrase in a modified form comes from Ralph Waldo Emerson's "Divinity School Address." See *The Collected Works of Ralph Waldo Emerson*, general editor, Alfred R. Ferguson, 5 vols. (Boston: The Belknap Press of Harvard University Press, 1971-1994), 1:78, where Emerson asserts that the world is the product of one will, "and whatever opposes that will, is everywhere baulked and baffled, because things are made so, and not otherwise."]

[3] [Ed. "Emerson's Phi Beta Kappa Oration," *Boston Quarterly Review* 1 (January 1838): 106-20.]

imposed upon any of his instincts or propensities. There may then be some doubts whether the command, "obey thyself," be an improvement on the Christian command, "deny thyself."

We presume that when Mr. Emerson tells us to obey ourselves, to obey the laws of our soul, to follow our instincts, he means that we shall be true to our higher nature, that we are to obey our higher instincts, and not our baser propensities. He is himself a pure minded man, and would by no means encourage sensuality. But how shall we determine which are our higher instincts and which are our lower instincts? We do not perceive that he gives us any instructions on this point. Men like him may take the higher instincts to be those which lead us to seek truth and beauty; but men in whom the sensual nature overlays the spiritual, may think differently; and what rule has he for determining which is in the right? He commands us to be ourselves, and sneers at the idea of having "models." We must take none of the wise or good, not even Jesus Christ as a model of what we should be. We are to act out ourselves. Now why is not the sensualist as moral as the spiritualist, providing he acts out himself? Mr. Emerson is a great admirer of Carlyle; and according to Carlyle, the moral man, the true man, is he who acts out himself. A Mirabeau, or a Danton is, under a moral point of view, the equal of a Howard[4] or a Washington, because equally true to himself. Does not this rule confound all moral distinctions, and render moral judgments a "formula," all wise men must "swallow and make away with"?[5]

But suppose we get over this difficulty and determine which are the higher instincts of our nature, those which we must follow in order to perfect our souls, and become, as Mr. Emerson has it, God; still we ask, why are we under obligation to obey these instincts? Because obedience to them will perfect our souls? But why are we bound to perfect our souls? Where there is no sense of obligation, there is no moral sense. We are moral only on the condition that we feel there is something which we *ought* to do. Why ought we to labor for our own perfection? Because it will promote our happiness? But why are we morally bound to seek our own happiness? It may be very desirable to promote our happiness, but it does not follow from that we are morally bound to do it, and we know there are occasions when we should not do it.

[4] [Ed. Comte de Mirabeau (Honoré Gabriel Victor Rigueti, 1749-91) was a politician in the forefront of the French Revolution. Georges Jacques Danton (1759-94) was also a leader of the French Revolution. John Howard (1752-1827) was an American Revolutionary soldier, statesman and politician.]

[5] [Ed. Unable to identify quotation.]

Put the rule, Mr. Emerson lays down, in the best light possible, it proposes nothing higher than our own individual good as the end to be sought. He would tell us to reduce all the jarring elements of our nature to harmony, and produce and maintain perfect order in the soul. Now is this the highest good the reason can conceive? Are all things in the universe to be held subordinate to the individual soul? Shall a man take himself as the center of the universe, and say all things are for his use, and count them of value only as they contribute something to his growth or well-being? This were a deification of the soul with a vengeance. It were nothing but a system of transcendental selfishness. It were pure egotism. According to this, I am everything; all else is nothing, at least nothing except what it derives from the fact that it is something to me.

Now this system of pure egotism, seems to us to run through all Mr. Emerson's writings. We meet it everywhere in his masters, Carlyle and Goethe.[6] He and they may not be quite so grossly selfish as were some of the old sensualist philosophers; they may admit a higher good than the mere gratification of the senses, than mere wealth or fame; but the highest good they recognize is an individual good, the realization of order in their own individual souls. Everything by them is estimated according to its power to contribute to this end. If they mingle with men it is to use them; if they are generous and humane, if they labor to do good to others, it is always as a means, never as an end. Always is the *doing*, whatever it be, to terminate in self. Self, the higher self, it is true, is always the center of gravitation. Now is the man who adopts this moral rule, really a moral man? Does not morality always propose to us an end separate from our own, above our own, and to which our own good is subordinate?

No doubt it is desirable to perfect the individual soul, to realize order in the individual; but the reason, the moment it is developed, discloses a good altogether superior to this. Above the good of the individual, and paramount to it, is the good of the universe, the realization of the good of creation, absolute good. No man can deny that the realization of the good of all beings is something superior to the realization of the good of the individual. Morality always requires us to labor for the highest good we can conceive. The moral law then requires us to seek another good than that of our own souls. The individual lives not for himself alone. His good is but an element, a fragment of the universal good, and is to be sought never as an end,

[6] [Ed. Johann Wolfgang von Goethe (1749-1832)—German poet, dramatist, scientist and court official—was a favorite Romantic poet among the Transcendentalists, especially Emerson.]

but always as a means of realizing absolute good, or universal order. This rule requires the man to forget himself, to go out of himself, and under certain circumstances to deny himself, to sacrifice himself, for a good which does not center in himself. He who forgets himself, who is disinterested and heroic, who sacrifices himself for others, is in the eyes of reason, infinitely superior to the man who merely uses others as the means of promoting his own intellectual and spiritual growth. Mr. Emerson's rule then is defective, inasmuch as it proposes the subordinate as the paramount, and places obligation where we feel it is not. For the present, then, instead of adopting his formula, "obey thyself,"[7] or Carlyle's formula, "act out thyself," we must continue to approve the Christian formula, "deny thyself, and love thy neighbor as thyself."[8]

But passing over this, we cannot understand how it is possible for a man to become virtuous by yielding to his instincts. Virtue is voluntary obedience to a moral law, felt to be obligatory. We are aware of the existence of the law, and we act in reference to it, and intend to obey it. We of course are not passive, but active in the case of virtue. Virtue is always personal. It is our own act. We are in the strictest sense of the word the cause or creator of it. Therefore it is that we judge ourselves worthy of praise when we are virtuous, and of condemnation when we are not virtuous. But in following instinct, we are not active but passive. The causative force at work in our instincts is not our personality, our wills, but an impersonal force, a force *we* are not. Now in yielding to our instincts, as Mr. Emerson advises us, we abdicate our own personality, and from persons become things, as incapable of virtue as the trees of the forest or the stones of the field.

Mr. Emerson, moreover, seems to us to mutilate man, and in his zeal for the instincts to entirely overlook reflection. The instincts are all very well. They give us the force of character we need, but they do not make up the whole man. We have understanding as well as instinct, reflection as well as spontaneity. Now to be true to our nature, to the whole man, the understanding should have its appropriate exercise. Does Mr. Emerson give it this exercise? Does he not rather hold the understanding in light esteem, and labor almost entirely to fix our minds on the fact of primitive intuition as all-sufficient of itself? We do not ask him to reject the instincts, but we ask him to

[7] [Ed. "Obey thyself" is in Ralph Waldo Emerson's "Divinity School Address," in *The Collected Works of Ralph Waldo Emerson*, 1:82.]

[8] [Ed. Brownson could have any number of biblical passages in mind: Lev 19:18; Matt 19:19; 22:39; Mark 12:31; Rom 13:9; Gal 5:14; James 2:8.]

compel them to give an account of themselves. We are willing to follow them; but we must do it designedly, intentionally, after we have proved our moral right to do it, not before. Here is an error in Mr. Emerson's system of no small magnitude. He does not account for the instincts nor legitimate them. He does not prove them to be divine forces or safe guides. In practice, therefore, he is merely reviving the old sentimental systems of morality, systems which may do for the young, the dreamy, or the passionate, but never for a sturdy race of men and women who demand a reason for all they do, for what they approve or disapprove.

Nor are we better satisfied with the theology of this discourse. We cannot agree with Mr. Emerson in his account of the religious sentiment. He confounds the religious sentiment with the moral; but the two sentiments are psychologically distinct. The religious sentiment is a craving to adore, resulting from the soul's intuition of the Holy; the moral sentiment is a sense of obligation resulting from the soul's intuition of a moral law. The moral sentiment leads us up merely to universal order; the religious sentiment leads us up to God, the Father of universal order. Religious ideas always carry us into a region far above that of moral ideas. Religion gives the law to ethics, not ethics to religion. Religion is the communion of the soul with God, morality is merely the *cultus exterior*, the outward worship of God, the expression of the life of God in the soul: as James has it, "pure religion"—external worship, for so should we understand the original—"and undefiled before God and the Father is this, to visit the fatherless and widows in their affliction, and to keep himself unspotted from the world" [James 1:27].

But even admitting the two sentiments are not two but one, identical, we are still dissatisfied with Mr. Emerson's account of the matter. The religious sentiment, according to him, grows out of the soul's insight of the perfection of its own laws. These laws are in fact the soul itself. They are not something distinct from the soul, but its essence. In neglecting them the soul is not itself, in finding them it finds itself, and in living them it is God. This is his doctrine. The soul then in case of the religious sentiment has merely an intuition of itself. Its craving to adore is not a craving to adore something superior to itself. In worshiping, then, the soul does not worship God, a being above man and independent on him, but it worships itself. We must not then speak of worshiping God, but merely of worshiping the soul. Now is this a correct account of the religious sentiment? The religious sentiment is in the bottom of the soul, and it is always a craving of the soul to go out of itself, and fasten itself on an object above itself, free from its own weakness, mutability, and impurity, on a being all-sufficient, all-sufficing, omnipotent, immutable, and all-holy. It results from the fact that we are conscious of not being sufficient for ourselves, that the ground of our being is not in ourselves, and from the need we feel of an Almighty arm on which to lean, a strength foreign to our own, from which we may derive support. Let us be God, let us feel that we need go out of ourselves for nothing, and we are no longer in the condition to be religious; the religious sentiment can no longer find a place in our souls, and we can no more feel a craving to adore than God himself. Nothing is more evident to us than that the religious sentiment springs, on the one hand, solely from a sense of dependence, and on the other hand, from an intuition of an invisible Power, Father, God, on whom we may depend, to whom we may go in our weakness, to whom we may appeal when oppressed, and who is able and willing to succor us. Take away the idea of such a God, declare the soul sufficient for itself, forbid it ever to go out of itself, to look up to a power above it, and religion is out of the question.

If we rightly comprehend Mr. Emerson's views of God, he admits no God but the laws of the soul's perfection. God is in man, not out of him. He is in the soul as the oak is in the acorn. When man fully develops the laws of his nature, realizes the ideal of his nature, he is not, as the Christian would say, god-like, but he is God. The ideal of man's nature is not merely similar in all men, but identical. When all men realize the ideal of their nature, that is, attain to the highest perfection admitted by the laws of their being, then do they all become swallowed up in the one man. There will then no longer be men; all diversity will be lost in unity, and there will be only one man, and that one man will be God. But what and where is God now? Before all men have realized the ideal of their nature, and become swallowed up in the one man, is there really and actually a God? Is there any God but the God Osiris, torn into pieces and scattered up and down through all the earth, which pieces, scattered parts, the weeping Isis must go forth seeking everywhere, and find not without labor and difficulty?[9] Can we be said to have at present anything more than the disjected members of a God, the mere embryo fragments of a God, one day to come forth into the light, to be

[9] [Ed. Osiris was in Egyptian mythology the god and judge of the dead, and lord of the Underworld. Isis was Osiris' sister. She had gathered up the pieces of her brother's body, after he had been killed and cut into pieces, and buried them throughout Egypt.]

gathered up that nothing be lost, and finally molded into one complete and rounded God? So it seems to us, and we confess, therefore, that we can affix no definite meaning to the religious language which Mr. Emerson uses so freely.

Furthermore, we cannot join Mr. Emerson in his worship to the soul. We are disposed to go far in our estimate of the soul's divine capacities; we believe it was created in the image of God, and may bear his moral likeness; but we cannot so exalt it as to call it God. Nor can we take its ideal of its own perfection as God. The soul's conception of God is not God, and if there be no God out of the soul, out of the *me,* to answer to the soul's conception, then is there no God. God as we conceive him is independent on us, and is in no sense affected by our conceptions of him. He is in us, but not us. He dwells in the hearts of the humble and contrite ones, and yet the heaven of heavens cannot contain him. He is the same yesterday, today, and forever. He is above all, the cause and sustainer of all that is, in whom we live and move and have our being. Him we worship, and only him. We dare not worship merely our own soul. Alas, we know our weakness; we feel our sinfulness; we are oppressed with a sense of our unworthiness, and we cannot so sport with the solemnities of religious worship, as to direct them to ourselves, or to anything which does not transcend our own being.

Yet this worship of the soul is part and parcel of the transcendental egotism of which we spoke in commenting on Mr. Emerson's moral doctrines. He and his masters, Carlyle and Goethe, make the individual soul everything, the center of the universe, for whom all exists that does exist; and why then should it not be the supreme object of their affections? Soul-worship, which is only another name for self-worship, or the worship of self, is the necessary consequence of their system, a system well described by Pope in his Essay on Man:

> Ask for what end the heavenly bodies shine,
> Earth for whose use? Pride answers, 'Tis for mine:
> For me, kind nature wakes her genial power,
> Suckles each herb, and spreads out every flower;
> Annual for me, the grape, the rose, renew
> The juice nectarous, and the balmy dew;
> For me, the mine a thousand treasures brings;
> For me, health gushes from a thousand springs:
> Seas roll to waft me, suns to light me rise;
> My footstool earth, my canopy the skies.[10]

[10] [Ed. Alexander Pope, *Essay on Man,* epistle 1, lines 129-40.]

To which we may add,

> While man exclaims, 'See all things for my use!'
> 'See man for mine!' replies a pampered goose:
> And just as short of reason he must fall
> Who thinks all made for one, not one for all.[11]

Mr. Emerson has much to say against preaching a traditional Christ, against preaching what he calls historical Christianity. So far as his object in this is to draw men's minds off from an exclusive attention to the "letter," and to fix them on the "spirit," to prevent them from relying for the matter and evidence of their faith on merely historical documents, and to induce them to reproduce the gospel histories in their own souls, he is not only not censurable but praiseworthy. He is doing a service to the Christian cause. Christianity may be found in the human soul, and reproduced in human experience now, as well as in the days of Jesus. It is in the soul too that we must find the key to the meaning of the Gospels, and in the soul's experience that we must seek the principal evidences of their truth.

But if Mr. Emerson means to sever us from the past, and to intimate that the Christianity of the past has ceased to have any interest for the present generation, and that the knowledge and belief of it are no longer needed for the soul's growth, for its redemption and union with God, we must own we cannot go with him. Christianity results from the development of the laws of the human soul, but from a supernatural, not a natural, development; that is, by the aid of a power above the soul. God has been to the human race both a father and an educator. By a supernatural, not an *un*natural influence, he has, as it has seemed proper to him, called forth our powers, and enabled us to see and comprehend the truths essential to our moral progress. The records of the aid he has at different ages furnished us, and of the truths seen and comprehended at the period when the faculties of the soul were supernaturally exalted, cannot in our judgment be unessential, far less improper, to be dwelt upon by the Christian preacher.

Then again, we cannot dispense with Jesus Christ. As much as some may wish to get rid of him, or to change or improve his character, the world needs him, and needs him in precisely the character in which the Gospels present him. His is the only name whereby men can be saved. He is the father of the modern world, and his is the life we now live, so far as we live any life at all. Shall we then crowd him

[11] [Ed. Ibid., epistle 3, lines 45-48.]

away with the old bards and seers, and regard him and them merely as we do the authors of some old ballads which charmed our forefathers, but which may not be sung in a modern drawing-room? Has his example lost its power, his life its quickening influence, his doctrine its truth? Have we outgrown him as a teacher?

In the Gospels we find the solution of the great problem of man's destiny; and, what is more to our purpose, we find there the middle term by which the creature is connected with the Creator. Man is at an infinite distance from God; and he cannot by his own strength approach God, and become one with him. We cannot see God; we cannot know him; no man hath seen the Father at any time, and no man knoweth the Father, save the Son, and he to whom the Son reveals him.[12] We approach God only through a mediator; we see and know only the Word, which is the mediator between God and men. Does Mr. Emerson mean that the record we have of this Word in the Bible, of this Word, which was made flesh, incarnated in the man Jesus, and dwelt among men and disclosed the grace and truth with which it overflowed, is of no use now in the church, nay, that it is a let and a hindrance? We want that record, which is to us as the testimony of the race, to corroborate the witness within us. One witness is not enough. We have one witness within us, an important witness, too seldom examined; but as important as he is, he is not alone sufficient. We must back up his individual testimony with that of the race. In the gospel records we have the testimony borne by the race to the great truths it most concerns us to know. That testimony, the testimony of history, in conjunction with our own individual experience, gives us all the certainty we ask, and furnishes us a solid ground for an unwavering and active faith. As in philosophy, we demand history as well as psychology, so in theology we ask the historical Christ as well as the psychological Christ. The church in general has erred by giving us only the historical Christ; but let us not now err, by preaching only a psychological Christ.

In dismissing this address, we can only say that we have spoken of it freely, but with no improper feeling to its author. We love bold speculation; we are pleased to find a man who dares tell us what and precisely what he thinks, however unpopular his views may be. We have no disposition to check his utterance, by giving his views a bad name, although we deem them unsound. We love progress, and progress cannot be effected without freedom. Still we wish to see a cer-

[12] [Ed. Brownson refers here to biblical passages like the following: Matt 11:27; Luke 10:22.]

tain sobriety, a certain reserve in all speculations, something like timidity about rushing off into an unknown universe, and some little regret in departing from the faith of our fathers.

Nevertheless, let not the tenor of our remarks be mistaken. Mr. Emerson is the last man in the world we should suspect of conscious hostility to religion and morality. No one can know him or read his productions without feeling a profound respect for the singular purity and uprightness of his character and motives. The great object he is laboring to accomplish is one in which he should receive the hearty cooperation of every American scholar, of every friend of truth, freedom, piety, and virtue. Whatever may be the character of his speculations, whatever may be the moral, philosophical, or theological system which forms the basis of his speculations, his real object is not the inculcation of any new theory on man, nature, or God; but to induce men to think for themselves on all subjects, and to speak from their own full hearts and earnest convictions. His object is to make men scorn to be slaves to routine, to custom, to established creeds, to public opinion, to the great names of this age, of this country, or of any other. He cannot bear the idea that a man comes into the world today with the field of truth monopolized and foreclosed. To every man lies open the whole field of truth, in morals, in politics, in science, in theology, in philosophy. The labors of past ages, the revelations of prophets and bards, the discoveries of the scientific and the philosophic, are not to be regarded as superseding our own exertions and inquiries, as impediments to the free action of our own minds, but merely as helps, as provocations to the freest and fullest spiritual action of which God has made us capable.

This is the real end he has in view, and it is a good end. To call forth the free spirit, to produce the conviction here implied, to provoke men to be men, self-moving, self-subsisting men, not mere puppets, moving but as moved by the reigning mode, the reigning dogma, the reigning school, is a grand and praise-worthy work, and we should reverence and aid, not abuse and hinder him who gives himself up soul and body to its accomplishment. So far as the author of the address before us is true to this object, earnest in executing this work, he has our hearty sympathy, and all the aid we, in our humble sphere, can give him. In laboring for this object, he proves himself worthy of his age and his country, true to religion and to morals. In calling, as he does, upon the literary men of our community, in the silver tones of his rich and eloquent voice, and above all by the quickening influence of his example, to assert and maintain their independence throughout the whole domain of thought, against every species of tyranny that would encroach upon it, he is doing his duty; he is doing a work the effects of which will be felt for good far and wide, long after men shall have forgotten the puerility of his conceits, the affectations of his style, and the unphilosophical character of his speculations. The doctrines he puts forth, the positive instructions, for which he is now censured, will soon be classed where they belong: but the influence of his free spirit, and free utterance, the literature of this country will long feel and hold in grateful remembrance.

7.

AMERICAN LITERATURE[1]

Boston Quarterly Review 2 (January, 1839): 1-26

Mr. Emerson in this oration professes to discuss the subject of Literary Ethics. He speaks of the resources, the subject, and the discipline of the scholar.

The resources of the scholar are proportioned to his confidence in the intellect. They are coextensive with nature and truth. Yet can they never be his, unless claimed with an equal greatness of mind. He must behold with awe the infinitude and impersonality of the intellectual power; learn that it is not his, that it is not any man's; but the soul which made the world; that it is all accessible to him, and he, as its minister, may rightfully hold all things subordinate and answerable to it. He must feel that he stands in the world as its native king; that he may inhale the year as a vapor; and give a new order and scale to the grand events of history. He is the world; and the epochs and heroes of chronology are pictorial images in which his thoughts are told. So must the scholar feel. All things are his, and he is equal to all things, nature and its laws, life and its deeds, the world and its events.

And not only must the scholar feel his right, but he must claim and exercise it. He must assert and maintain his spiritual independence; feel that he is a new man, and that the world into which he comes is not foreclosed; is not mortgaged to the opinions and usages of Europe, Asia, or Egypt. Every man, as to his spiritual independence, comes into a new world, and may roam as freely over it, as if he were the first born of time. Every man is an Adam in the Garden, and may summon all creatures before him, distribute them into their classes, and give them their names. No one is bound to follow the classifications, or to adopt the names given by his predecessors. Creation is born anew with every new-born soul; and each new-born soul may hear the sons of the morning singing with joy over a new created world. In plain terms, the whole field of thought and action are open to the scholar, and he must, to avail himself of his resources,

[1] [Ed. Review of Ralph Waldo Emerson's *An Oration delivered before the Literary Societies of Dartmouth College, July 24, 1838* (Boston: Charles C. Little and James Brown, 1838).]

feel that he comes into the world as free as the first born man; that he is bound by none of the opinions, or usages of those who have preceded him; that he has the right to read all nature with his own eyes; and is in duty bound to form his own creed, his own life-plan, his own system of the universe.

The subject offered to the scholar is as broad as his resources. His subject today is the same that it was yesterday. Nothing has been exhausted; science is yet in its cradle; literature is to be written; and poetry has scarcely chanted its first song. The perpetual admonition of nature to us is, "The world is new, untried. Do not believe the past. I give you the universe a virgin today."

Latin and English poetry sing us ever the praises of nature, and yet poetry has hitherto conversed with only the surface of things. Its chants reveal to us nothing of the handsome things of nature. The poet has not seen and felt for himself. All is yet undescribed, almost unattempted. The man who stands on the seashore, or who rambles in the woods, seems to be the first man that ever stood on the shore, or entered a grove, his sensations and his world are so novel and strange. Nature still awaits her poet, and listens to catch the strains of the voice that shall sing her praises worthily.

Civil history is yet open to the labors of the scholar. The past shall wear a new aspect as each new man of genius looks upon it. Since Niebuhr and Wolf, Roman and Greek history have been written anew.[2] May not a new Niebuhr and Wolf be needed to re-write them? Is the story told, and its lesson fixed forever? Let a man of genius pronounce the name of the Pelasgi,[3] of Athens, of the Etrurian, of the Roman people, and under what new aspect do we instantly behold them. Are there not still new aspects under which they may be seen? Who can say what shall be the new aspect under which the next man of genius shall reveal them? As in poetry and history, so in all other departments. There are few masters or none. Religion is yet to be settled on its fast foundations in the breast of man; and politics, and philosophy, and letters, and art. As yet, we have nothing but tendency and indication.

[2] [Ed. Barthold Georg Niebuhr (1776-1831) was a German historian who became well known for his studies of Roman history, especially his *Römische Geschichte*, which was translated into English. Friedrich August Wolf (1759-1824) was a German classical scholar who had published a number of editions of Greek works and who championed the cause of classical studies.].

[3] [Ed. Brownson may be referring here to the Greek mythological figure Pelasgus, thought to be the first man, a son of Earth who sprang from the soil of Arcadia.]

Such are the resources and the subject of the scholar. The world is his; but he must possess it, by putting himself into harmony with the constitution of things. He must be a solitary, laborious, modest, charitable soul. He must embrace solitude as a bride. He must have his glees and his glooms alone. His own estimate must be measure enough; his own praise reward enough for him. We live in the sun and on the surface of things—a thin, plausible, superficial existence, and talk of muse and prophet, of art and creation. But out of our shallow and frivolous way of life how can greatness ever grow? We must go and be dumb; sit with our hands on our mouths a long Pythagorean lustrum; live in corners, and do chares, and suffer, and weep, and drudge, with eyes and hearts that love the Lord; by silence, seclusion, austerity, pierce deep into the grandeur and secret of our being; and so diving, bring up out of secular darkness the sublimities of the moral constitution. How mean to go blazing, a gaudy butterfly, in fashionable or political saloons, the fool of society, the fool of notoriety, a topic for newspapers, a piece of the street, and forfeiting the real prerogative of the russet coat, the privacy, and the true and warm heart of the citizen?

But we give it up. We cannot analyze one of Mr. Emerson's discourses. He hardly ever has a leading thought, to which all the parts of his discourse are subordinate, which is clearly stated, systematically drawn out, and logically enforced. He is a poet rather than a philosopher—and not always true even to the laws of poetry. He must be read not for a work of art, which shall be perfect as a whole, but for the exquisite beauty of its details; not for any new or striking philosophical views, but for incidental remarks, frequent aphorisms, valuable hints, rich and original imagery and illustration. In all his productions, the decorations strike us more than the temple itself, and the shrine evidently surpasses the god. Nevertheless, he always selects an important topic for his discourses, and furnishes us subjects which well deserve our consideration. This is something.

In reading Mr. Emerson's various productions, and in listening to his lectures, we obtain the impression that he thinks very meanly of the past achievements of the human mind. No poet according to him has ever yet seen the seashore, or entered a grove; and nobody but himself has ever heard the "wild geese scream."[4] As it regards American scholars, they have done nothing to redeem the pledges we

[4] [Ed. The phrase in a modified form comes from Ralph Waldo Emerson's "Literary Ethics." See *The Collected Works of Ralph Waldo Emerson*, general editor, Alfred R. Ferguson, 5 vols. (Boston: The Belknap Press of Harvard University Press, 1971-1994), 1:106.

made the world when we adopted free institutions. American Literature can scarcely be said to have a being. Not that we want men who write very clever books, and make commendable verses which fill up the corner of a newspaper with much respectability, and look very decent in a scrapbook, or lady's album; but of the higher literature, which addresses itself to the higher faculties of the soul, and is the out-speaking and the embodiment of the national life, we have produced nothing worth naming. And worse than all this, we seem to have no adequate conception of what American literature should be, and what it is capable of becoming. Why is this, and what is the remedy?

This is the question which is laboring in his mind, and which he appears to be striving to answer. One of the chief causes, he thinks, is our want of faith in the intellect. Wanting faith in the intellect, we attempt no great intellectual effort, and therefore produce nothing intellectually great. We have no faith that great things may be done, and therefore do not attempt to do great things. The remedy here is to increase and confirm our faith in the intellect, to learn that the intellectual power, which develops itself within us, is the power that made the world, and therefore infinite and inexhaustible.

Another cause is our want of confidence in ourselves. We regard ourselves as born in the dotage of the world, and out of work, except to treasure up in our memories, and mimic as we may in our lives, the sayings and doings of the giants, who lived long ago, when the world was in its prime. Genius has no vocation; poesy has sung her swan-song; philosophy is finished; the sciences are completed; creeds are all determined; opinions made up; miracles ended, and the book of prophecy is closed. Sad creatures are we! Born long ages too late, after all the work cut out by the Almighty for thought, fancy, imagination, genius, is completed! We are doomed to idleness, and by idleness to imbecility. The spiritual nature is useless and must be discharged. We sink our humanity and become mere prudent, calculating animals; content to labor for a little worldly wealth, to fill the belly or clothe the back; to flutter in a saloon, or to catch a breath of empty applause from brainless fellow mortals; to be complaisant and decorous; to provide for a commendable funeral, a showy coffin, and a respectable tombstone.

To remedy this evil, we must cease to look back to learn what has been, around to learn what is, and must look into ourselves to learn what we are, and what we can do. Man is man today as much as he was six thousand years ago; and every man is born with all that constitutes a man, with as rich endowments, and as creative a genius, in this age or country as in any other. Men in the past were great, were heroes. Be it so. Men in the present are also men, and may be great, may be heroes, if they will but act out the divinity that is slumbering in them. Our senses are as acute, our minds as penetrating, our bodies as finely molded and as firmly knit, our limbs as active and as vigorous, and our souls as capable of swelling with noble thoughts, with rich affections, and of burning with as pure, as free, and intense a love for the true, the beautiful, and the good, as theirs who lived in the past, and before whose shadows we prostrate ourselves with such servile devotion. Nature is ever renewed, and is as fresh now, as when beheld by the divine bards of old; and is as open and as beautiful to us, as it was to them. We stand as near to God as did the prophets, who had "open vision" and conversed with him face to face; and we may be inspired, illuminated by his spirit, as well as they were. The whole spiritual world is ours. Truth, beauty, goodness, are not monopolized, foreclosed. God has not disinherited us nor left us no employment. Every man has an indefeasible right to the universe, and may labor in what part of it he pleases; in work which commends itself to his taste and genius; and be his own producer; and in his own way too. He need labor where others have labored, and be their imitators, not unless it be his choice. He may whistle his own tune and sing his own song. Nobody has the right to insist on his obligation to imitate the tone or gestures of others. He may pitch his voice to his own key, and modulate it to his own ear. Plato, Bacon, Cousin, have philosophized; let who will philosophize also, and be a Plato, a Bacon, a Cousin, not by imitating them, but by claiming and maintaining that right to philosophize for oneself, which they claimed. We must assert our spiritual independency, or never shall our minds act freely, and show forth the divine stuff they are made of. And without free, strong, and varied action, no living literature; no original creations; no works of art, worthy of the age, of the country, of man.

This may be true, if understood in strict reference to literature, and what are usually considered the higher walks of art and science; but we are not disposed to regard the American mind as strikingly deficient in originality and independence. We doubt if there ever was a country in which the people had more faith in the intellect, or less of servility to the mind of other ages or other countries. We may not be ready at once to adopt every new notion or new doctrine, which may be set forth in metaphysics, theology, morals, aesthetics; but we are by no means backward in considering and adopting everything, which promises to be an improvement in agriculture, manufactures, the mechanic arts, commerce, and navigation. In these matters we are not wanting in faith in intellect, nor are we slaves to routine, to established usage, to fixed opinions, to the teachings of other ages, other countries, other men. We create for ourselves, and our creations are by no means despicable. The American ship is not a servile copy of a foreign model. The Yankee exercises his own original genius in its construction; and he mans and works it in his own way. The Patent Office may bear witness that we are cunning to seek out many inventions. Our political institutions can hardly be termed a copy, a tradition, a reminiscence. They are original. In whatever direction the American mind is turned, it is self-confiding, original, creative. Hitherto it has been turned almost exclusively in a material direction; to the realization of progress in our external condition; not to the realization of progress in the moral and intellectual sciences. With us, genius has come forth into practical life; instead of the marble statue, it gives us the ship; for a picture, it gives us a mule or jenney; for systems of metaphysics and ethics, it gives us railroads, canals, and steamboats; for the novel or the poem, it furnishes us with an improved system of legislation, ministries to the poor, and universal education; and for an elevated and living literature, it creates an elevated and living people. Genius has come out of the cloister and the university, and creates in the shipyard and the smithy, reasons on change, and sings in the music of the axe, the hammer, and the loom, giving dignity to labor and the empire of the world to the laborer.

Shall we complain of this? Is this all low utilitarianism? Why is it that our minds have been carried away in an outward direction? In this world there is a reason, and usually a pretty good reason, for whatever is. Nothing is arbitrary, or the production of blind chance. It is not by accident that a people at a given epoch is wholly intent on improving its outward condition, all engrossed in useful labors; and at another epoch, equally intent on spiritual progress, and engrossed with the embellishments of life. It is true that we have not, as it concerns high literary matters, that full faith in intellect which may be desirable; and it is true, that in such matters, we depend too much on the taste, criticism, and opinions of others. But what then? Our first and most urgent work in this country was not the creation of an original literature. Give the whole American people that peculiar self-trust and faith in intellect called for in the oration before us, and every man, woman, and child would be soaring into the regions of ideas, or seeking in vain a pathway through the wilds of imagination; the useful arts would be neglected; the fields would lie fallow; commerce would languish; manufactures would fail; silence would reign in the workshops; and nakedness and starvation cover the land. Nature ordains that we provide for the body, before we provide for the soul; that we obtain those things without which life is not possible, before we attempt life's embellishments.

We have a few misgivings about the propriety of this declamation, in which some of our scholars are beginning to indulge, against the utilitarian pursuits of our age and country. We are not quite sure but we ought to be very thankful for these pursuits. Perhaps this business world on which the scholar looks down, is fulfilling a higher mission than it or the scholar dreams of. We can hardly persuade ourselves, that the young man, who has no means of living but by his daily labor, can be applauded for neglecting all useful labor and devoting his whole time to playing the flute or the fiddle. Why not? Music is one of the fine arts, and to play the flute or the fiddle well is an elegant accomplishment; and why not then applaud the young man who devotes himself to it at the expense of his worldly fortunes? What is true of individuals, is true of nations. Let a nation provide for its physical well-being, let it provide for the easy subsistence of all its citizens, before it takes itself to fiddling or flute-playing.

We commenced in this country poor; we had little beside our hands, our wits, and our self-confidence. We had a savage world to subdue, and by our labors a wilderness to convert into a fruitful field. We had this to do also for the *whole* people. In the old world the mass of the people are drudges, and we know not but always must be drudges. There a favored few may study life's embellishments, because the drudges are at hand to furnish them with subsistence. But here, all must be drudges or none; so long as drudgery is necessary, all must drudge; and when a part enter into the paths of elegant literature, the mass must enter. If at any previous epoch in our history, a number of our people sufficiently large to secure success had engaged solely in literary pursuits, and labored exclusively for progress in the spiritual order, they must have imposed an extra amount of drudgery on the rest; for scholars, all spiritual as they would have us believe them, have bodies and stomachs, and require food and raiment, as well as the drudges themselves, and in general of a somewhat superior sort too; they would have established a literary caste, which, when it is a caste, is no better than a sacerdotal caste, or a military caste; divided the community by a broad and distinct line into two classes, of which one would have been regarded as altogether superior to the other. The scholars would have constituted a nobility; they would have glorified themselves, boasted the dignity of their pursuits; and, speaking to the mind and passions of the people, they would have had all things pretty much in their own way. The drudges, marking the leisure and apparent ease of the scholars, their freedom from many of the cares, vexations, and hardships of ordinary life, would have regarded them as a privileged class, a superior order of beings; and in return, they would have looked upon themselves as a doomed race, lying under the curse of God, bound to the dust they cultivated, and fated to live and die mere beasts of burden. Now this would have been at war with the mission of this country. A literary class, as such, we cannot tolerate. They who call for a literary class, and labor diligently to create one, were they not impotent, should be regarded as our worst enemies. Here, no man can safely be exempted from the ordinary duties of practical life. The scholar must be a man of business, and do his own share of the drudgery.

We confess, therefore, that we are beginning, of late, to look favorably on the business habits of our countrymen, and to declaim less and less against their money-getting propensities. It is, in fact, a real cause for gratitude to God, that our whole population has been carried away in a material direction, engaged in the accumulation of material wealth. Not that literature is unimportant, not that progress in the spiritual order is not in the last degree desirable and imperative; but because it is as desirable and as imperative in the case of all men, as in the case of a few; and because it can be possible in the case of all men, only on the condition that all men be placed in such circumstances, as to their physical wants, that with moderate labor they can obtain a respectable subsistence. It was necessary then in the first instance, to cut down and clear away the eternal forest, to break the stubborn glebe, and convert the barren field into a garden, to build up our manufactures, to extend and perfect our commerce, and so to augment and distribute the wealth of the country, that all our citizens should have the requisite independence and leisure for the cultivation of their minds. And this could not have been done, had not our whole people been carried away in a material direction.

It is said that the whole nation has been absorbed in the pursuit of wealth. We admit it, and rejoice that it has been so. It is a proof of the unity of our national life; that we all move together, feel the pulsations of one heart, and engage as one man in whatever is the work for the moment. It is also a proof that we are an earnest race, and that what we attempt, we attempt with our whole heart; that we throw our whole being into our work, and live and move but in it and for it. This is a noble trait of character. It is full of promise. It assures us that whatever the nation undertakes, it shall accomplish; that when it has provided for the most pressing wants of the body, and turned its attention to the creation of a literature, it shall bend its whole soul to it, and create a literature which shall deserve and receive the world's admiration. The very intensity with which we pursue wealth is full of hope. It proves that the pursuit of wealth can be only a temporary pursuit, that we must soon satisfy our material wants, and be ready to engage with similar intenseness in providing for the wants of the soul.

The pursuit of wealth, we are told again, is a low, degrading pursuit, proceeding from a mean and sordid ambition. It can in no sense compare with the elegant and ennobling pursuit of letters. The businessman, counting dollars and cents, and balancing his losses and gains, is a low and servile being compared with the scholar, whose soul is unbound, whose thoughts are free to roam over the universe, to commune with all nature, and to rise to close intimacy with the "first good and first Fair." "The scholar is the favorite of Heaven and Earth, the excellency of his country, the happiest of men. His duties lead him directly into the holy ground, where other men's aspirations only point. His successes are occasions of the purest joy to all men. Eyes is he to the blind; feet is he to the lame."[5] Is there no "optical illusion" in all this? Is there not here, in this estimate of the comparative dignity of literature and business, no want of independence? Is there no slavishness to what we have been taught, to the mind of the past? What occasion is there for the men of letters to scorn the men of business? Is this business world as contemptible as the literary world would fain make us believe? Genius has not hesitated to weave a garland of fadeless flowers around the brows of ancient heroism, and later chivalry, and why should it hesitate to do the same for modern business, since there is many a merchant moved by as heroic and chivalric aspirations, as ever moved an ancient hero or a modern knight? We often suppose that the merchant is moved by mere love of gain, that his ruling motive is avarice; but we are greatly mistaken. The merchant fits out his ships with as lofty feelings, as those with which an ancient monarch led forth his armed followers to make conquests. He loves excitement; he has a taste for the adventurous; and he longs to act a conspicuous part in great events. The great and active man is in him; the soul of the chivalric knight is in him; and it is only in immense business calculations and business enterprises, that the spirit of the age allows him to act out what is in him. It is not

[5] [Ed. Ralph Waldo Emerson, *An Oration Delivered before the Literary Societies of Dartmouth College, July 24, 1838* (Boston: Charles C. Little and James Brown, 1838), 1.]

the littleness, but the greatness, of his soul, that leads him to cover the ocean with his rich "argosies," and to lay every clime under contribution. Now we ask, wherein is this merchant-prince less honorable, less glorious, than the warrior-prince, around whom men of letters love to cluster, and whom they conspire to deify? His enterprises are infinitely more serviceable to humanity.

In all ages of the world, business pursuits have been regarded as ignoble. Kings and military chieftains, tyrants and "man-killers," royal and noble hunters, have passed for the representatives of God on earth; while the honest laborer has been accounted low and vulgar, a menial, a slave. Is not this contempt, which men of letters cast on the men of business, a tradition of the old contempt with which they looked upon all useful labor? Is it not a reminiscence of the times when all useful labor was performed by slaves, or by the ignorant and vulgar; and when the "better sort" lived in idleness and luxury, or engaged only in war or "manly sports?" If so, the business world has not yet succeeded in rendering labor perfectly honorable. The patent of its nobility bears a too recent date; the scholar remembers the time when it was plebeian and accounted vile. But does the scholar well to remember this? Has he a right to look down on the man of business? And is he aiding the cause of humanity by sowing dissensions between those who labor to accumulate wealth for the body, and those who are seeking to create wealth for the soul? The scholar, in fact, ought to be chary of producing a disgust, a loathing for the practical duties of life, or of undervaluing those pursuits without which society and life must fail, or worse than fail. Instead of regarding the material improvements of society, efforts to perfect political institutions, and to increase the physical comforts of the people, as low, sordid, mercenary, he should elevate them to the rank of liberal pursuits. His mission is to ennoble business, and to make drudgery the path to honor, as it is to independence. He may, and he should, point out the abuses into which the business world falls—the errors it commits—the low standard of morals it adopts; but he should also seek to combine business with literature—as we would practice with theory—and make it felt to be not beneath the dignity of the most learned man, the most accomplished scholar, to enter the arena of politics, to cultivate a farm, to manage a shop, to engage in manufactures, or commerce. The business world doubtless has its errors; its morality is of too low an order; its aims are not high enough; many of its practices are injurious to society; many of its members are purely selfish, and fall far below the standard of even its own morality; its politics are short-sighted and selfish, deficient in enlarged views and true policy; but nevertheless the more closely we examine it, the more we see it in all its bearings, the more shall we find in it to approve, and the better satisfied shall we be with the mission it is fulfilling.

Moreover, we believe the charge brought against the American people, of being exclusively devoted to money-getting, of being great lovers of money, is altogether too sweeping. The American people are far, very far, from being supreme lovers of money. They have no disposition to hoard. Not a native born miser can be met with in our whole country. We pursue wealth indeed to a great extent, but not as an end. We pursue it not for its own sake, but as a means; because we crave independence and would possess what wealth alone can purchase. The majority start in life poor, obliged to depend on their own exertions for the means of living. They are obliged, for a time at least, to struggle hard; they are made to feel the evils, the slights, the inconveniences of poverty; the consideration, influence, ease, and pleasures of which it deprives them; and they seek with great earnestness, by all the means in their power, to escape it; to cease to be mere drudges, living and toiling but for the human animal; to gain independence, and a position by which they can take rank as men amongst men, and act a useful and respectable part in the affairs of society. What is there in this to blame? The end is surely honorable and elevated; and the most we can say is, that the means adopted are not the most appropriate, or that some few forget the end in the means. No doubt many among us continue the pursuit of gain, long after the original reasons which induced them to adopt that pursuit have ceased to exist; but they do it not from the mere love of money, but from the force of habit; from the pleasure they find in doing today what they did yesterday; from the excitement, the employment afforded by their business exercises; and because they must, in order to enjoy themselves, do something, and there is nothing else they are fitted to do. Those among us who are most absorbed in money-getting, and who acquire wealth fastest, often spend it faster than they acquire it, proving thus that they value something else more than they do money. There is nothing miserly, sordid, mercenary in the American disposition. We are fond of show and consideration, anxious to be thought well of both at home and abroad, of holding a respectable social rank, and of gathering around us the comforts and elegances of civilized life; and so far as wealth can contribute to this end, we love and seek it; but no farther. The man who seems wholly absorbed in counting dollars and cents, and balancing his losses and gains, may on close inspection be found to be moved by an honorable ambition, and to be contributing not a little to the means of moral and intellectual progress.

This general and absorbing pursuit of wealth, which seems so low and mean to the man of letters, is, moreover, essential to the existence and success of the scholar. A poor people, a people sunk in the depths of poverty, all of whose thoughts and exertions are needed to gain a mere subsistence for the human animal, can never be expected to contribute anything to the cause of letters. Men must be taught to read, and have leisure to read and reflect, before they can either become scholars or the audience of scholars. This instruction and this leisure can be obtained only on the condition that there be a certain independence as to the means of living. The scholar cannot be far in advance of his countrymen, at least not far in advance of the class to which he addresses himself. He never appears alone. He may surpass his brethren; but there will be always many near him, who reach the goal almost as soon as he. He must have competitors. He must have an audience, a public. This is always an indispensable condition of his existence. Give the audience, and the speaker will present himself; the public, and the philosopher will bring forth his theories, the scholar unfold his treasures.

Now in this country the whole people must constitute the audience, the public. The scholar here must speak not to a clique, a coterie, but to the entire nation. The first thing to be done, then, is to make the whole nation a "fit audience." To talk of a "fit audience though few,"[6] betrays an entire ignorance of the age and the country. This is neither the age nor the country for scholars to consult only the tastes of scholars, and to address themselves only to a literary nobility. He who would be an American scholar must address himself to the whole American people; and his own attainments cannot far outrun the capacity of the masses to comprehend and relish his speech. It follows from this, that the first requisite to the scholar's success, in this country, is to make the whole nation a nation of readers, and to secure to the great mass of the people the leisure necessary to attend to the subjects on which the scholar discourses. The mere ability to read, however, is not enough. He who has worked all day with his hands, and sits down at night fatigued with the day's labor, and harassed in mind about the employment of the morrow, can hardly be expected to read and relish the profound and finished compositions of the true scholar. Now this very business world, against which we war, is the most active in teaching all to read, in providing

[6] [Ed. John Milton's *Paradise Lost,* Book VII, line 31.]

the means of universal education. And how, without this general and absorbing devotion to money getting, is the general wealth of the country to be sufficiently augmented to allow the leisure we have determined to be necessary?

We go still further; we say that the general attention to business in this country is itself favorable to the growth of mind, to moral, spiritual progress. We could verify this assertion by history, were we so disposed. But we ask, what can more tax the mind and call forth its powers than the pursuits of commerce? Can the merchant make his calculations, extend his business to all parts of the world, without mental exertion? All industrial employments require more or less of skill and science. The desire to become rich, and quickly rich, stimulates improvements, seeks out inventions, makes perpetual demands on science to abridge the process. Many an ordinary mechanic in our city makes use of a science that a Newton might have been proud to own, and employs a mental power equal to that which discovered the law of gravitation, and determined the laws of the universe. The more intense the desire to accumulate wealth, the more use will be made of science; consequently the more employment will be given to mind, to intellect. The business world is in no sense inferior in active intellect to the world of letters; all the difference is in the application.

Nor is American literature, as it is, to be condemned outright. True, not much is to be said of our regular built books; but we have newspapers. Our newspapers are conducted for the great mass of the people, by men who come out immediately from the bosom of the people, and they of necessity express the sentiments of the people. They constitute, therefore, in the strictest sense of the word, a popular literature. And scattered through our newspapers and popular journals, may be found more fine writing, more true poetry, genuine eloquence, vigorous thought, original and comprehensive views, than can be found in the classics of either France or England. All the elements of the soul by turns are appealed to, and in turn find their expression; all subjects are discussed, and on all sides too; and often with a clearness and depth which leave little to be desired. Your most ordinary newspaper not infrequently throws you off an essay, that it would be impossible to match in the writings of Addison, Steele, or Johnson.[7]

[7] [Ed. Joseph Addison (1672-1719), English essayist and politician, was a distinguished classical scholar and co-founder with Richard Steele of the *Spectator*. Sir Richard Steele (1672-1729), Irish essayist and politician, focused much of his writing on social and moral essays. Samuel Johnson (1709-84), English writer and critic, was well known for his *Dictionary of the English Language* (1755) and his moral essays in *The Rambler* (1750-52).]

The great merit and wide circulation of our newspapers and periodicals are doubtless the cause of the meagerness of our "book" literature. They are a ready channel through which he who thinks can communicate his thoughts to the public; and they therefore supersede the necessity, in some measure, of writing books. They answer the most urgent wants of the people, talk to the people on the topics on which they are thinking, discuss the subjects in which they feel an immediate interest; and therefore lessen the demand for more elaborate productions. At least this is their effect for the moment. But in the end they will increase the demand for more elaborate productions, by calling forth the ability and giving the preliminary information necessary for understanding and relishing them. The newspaper gives us a general view of all matters, and therefore prepares us for a special view of any particular matter. Not to insist then on the newspaper as affording in fact a definitive literature, we cannot fail to perceive that it must end in creating a taste for literature; in preparing a literature; in leading directly to its creation; and that so long as we sustain it, we can by no means be said to be doing nothing for literature.

It may be alleged that our newspaper literature, whatever its excellence, is so scattered, so mixed up with what is impure and noxious, and withal presented in so frail and perishing a form, that it can neither be made available nor preserved. But it is preserved; perhaps not on the shelves of the student's library, but in the hearts and intellects of the people; in the actions it prompts, and in the public measures, the adoption of which it secures. And this is enough. A literature is of no great value any farther than it becomes absorbed into the popular mind, and constitutes an integral part of the life of the people; and a literature which becomes so absorbed, can hardly be said to be unavailable.

But passing over all we have thus far said, admitting all that may be urged against the business pursuits of our countrymen, and the meagerness of American literature; we must still call in question the soundness of the doctrine set forth in Mr. Emerson's oration. This oration teaches us, if we understand it, that the creation of a literature is a thing entirely dependent on the individual will; that a man has nothing to do but to rise up and say, be there produced a literature that shall command the world's homage, and forthwith it shall be. Now in point of fact, few things are less dependent on mere will or arbitrariness than literature. It is the expression and embodiment of the national life. Its character is not determined by this man or that, but by the national spirit. The time and manner of its creation are determined by as necessary and invariable laws, as the motions of the sun, the revolutions of the earth, the growth of a tree, or the blowing of a flower. It is not by accident that this man sings and that one philosophizes; that this song is sung, and this system of philosophy is brought out now and in this country; and that another song is sung and another system of philosophy is broached, at another time and in another country. The thing is predetermined by the spirit of the age and nation. It depended not on Homer alone to sing. He sung because his song was in him and would be uttered. The God moved, and he must needs give forth his oracle. The choice of his subject, and the manner of treating it, depended not alone on his individual will. It was given him by the belief in which he had been brought up, the education which he had received, the spirit, habits, beliefs, prejudices, tastes, cravings of the age and country in which he lived, or for which he sung. Had he been born at the Court of Augustus, or of Louis XIV, he had not sung the wrath of Achilles and prowess of Hector;[8] or if he had, it would have been to listless ears. His song would have taken no hold on the affections, and would have died without an echo. He might even not have been a poet at all.

This notion, which some entertain, that a national literature is the creation of a few great men, is altogether fallacious. Chaucer, Shakespeare, and Milton, Spencer, Pope, and Johnson are not the creators of English literature; but they are themselves the creatures of the spirit of the English nation, and of their times. Bacon, Hobbes, and Locke are not the authors of English philosophy, they are but its interpreters. Great men do not make their age; they are its effect. They doubtless react on their age, and modify its character; but they owe their greatness not to their individuality, but to their harmony with their age, and to their power of embodying the spirit, the reigning views of their age and country. Know the great men of a country, and you know the country; not because the great men make it, but because they embody and interpret it. A great man is merely the glass which concentrates the rays of greatness scattered through the minds and hearts of the people; not the central sun from which they radiate. To obtain an elevated national literature, it is not necessary then

[8] [Ed. References are to the Roman emperor Augustus (63 B.C.–14 A.D., emperor, 31 B.C. to 14 A.D.); Louis XIV (1638-1715), king of France (1643-1715); Achilles, the only mortal son of Peleus, king of the Myrmidones at Phthia in Thessaly, who was the literary hero of Homer's *Iliad* and one of the leading heroes of the Trojan War; Hector was the greatest of the Trojan heroes during the Trojan War who was killed by Achilles. Brownson refers here to the opening line of the *Iliad*.]

to look to great men, or to call for distinguished scholars; but to appeal to the mass, wake up just sentiments, quicken elevated thoughts in them, and direct their attention to great and noble deeds; the literature will follow as a necessary consequence. When a national literature has been quickened in the national mind and heart, the great man is sure to appear as its organ, to give it utterance, form, embodiment. Before then his appearance is impossible.

We find also some difficulty in admitting the notion that the scholar must be a solitary soul, living apart and in himself alone; that he must shun the multitude and mingle never in the crowd, or if he mingle, never as one of the crowd; that to him the thronged mart and the peopled city must be a solitude; that he must commune only with his own thoughts, and study only the mysteries of his own being. We have no faith in this ascetic discipline. Its tendency is to concentrate the scholar entirely within himself, to make him a mere individual, without connections or sympathies with his race; and to make him utter his own individual life, not the life of the nation, much less the universal life of humanity. He who retires into the solitude of his own being, in order to learn to speak, shall never find a companion to whom he can say, "How charming is this solitude!" He who disdains the people shall find the people scorning to be his audience. He who will not sympathize with the people in their sentiments and passions, their joys and sorrows, their hopes and fears, their truths and prejudices, their good and bad, their weal and woe, shall gain no power over the mind or heart of his nation. He may prophesy, but it shall be in an unknown tongue; he may sing, but he shall catch no echo to his song; he may reason, but he shall find his arguments producing no conviction. This is the inflexible decree of God. We can make the people listen to us only so far as we are one of them. When God sent us a Redeemer, he did not make him of the seed of angels, but of the seed of Abraham. He gave him a human nature, made him a partaker of flesh and blood, in like manner as those he was to redeem were partakers of flesh and blood, so that he might be touched with a sense of human infirmities, sympathize with our weakness, and through sympathy redeem us. So he who would move the people, influence them for good or for evil, must have like passions with them; feel as they feel; crave what they crave; and resolve what they resolve. He must be their representative, their impersonation.

He who has no sympathies with the people, and who finds himself without popular influence, may console himself, doubtless, with the reflection that he is wiser than the people; that he is above and in advance of his age; that a few choice minds understand and appreciate him; and that a succeeding generation shall disentomb him, posterity do him justice and dedicate a temple to his memory. Far be it from us to deprive any man of such consolation as this; but for ourselves, if we cannot succeed in commanding to some extent the attention of our own age, we have no hope of succeeding better with a future and more advanced age. He who is neglected by his own age, is more likely to be below his age than above it. We recollect not an instance on record of remarkable posthumous literary fame, in opposition to the decision of the people during the man's life time. Posterity often reverses the judgments our own age renders in our favor; rarely, if ever, the judgments rendered against us. We speak not here of the judgments rendered by professional judges, but by the real, living, beating heart of the people. We, therefore, notwithstanding we have experienced our full share of neglect, derive very little consolation from the hope that a coming age will do us better justice. Alas, it is that "better justice," we most dread. If we have failed to interest our own age, how can we hope to interest the age to come? Is it not as likely to be our fault as that of the age, that we do not reach its heart? We always distrust the extraordinary merits of those who attribute their failures not to their defects, but to their excellences, to the fact that they are above the vulgar herd, and too profound to be comprehended, till the age has advanced and called into exercise greater and more varied intellectual powers. We are disposed to believe that of our scholars the greater part may attribute their failures to the fact that they have drawn their inspirations from books, from the past, from a clique or coterie, and not from the present, not from the really living, moving, toiling and sweating, joying and sorrowing people around them. Did they disdain the people less, did they enter more into the feelings of the people, and regard themselves strictly as of the people, and as setting up for no superiority over them, they would find their success altogether more commensurate with their desires, their productions altogether more creditable to themselves, and deserving of immortality.

Moreover, we doubt whether we show our wisdom in making direct and conscious efforts to create an American literature. Literature cannot come before its time. We cannot obtain the oracle before the Pythoness feels the God.[9] Men must see and feel the truth before they can utter it. There must be a necessity upon them, before they

[9] [Ed. Pythoness was the priestess of the Delphic oracle, or any woman supposed to be possessed of the spirit of prophecy.]

will speak or write, at least before they will speak or write anything worth remembering. Literature is never to be sought as an end. We cannot conceive anything more ridiculous than for the leading minds of a nation to set out consciously, gravely, deliberately, to produce a national literature. A real national literature is always the spontaneous expression of the national life. As is the nation so will be its literature. Men, indeed, create it; not as an end, but as a means. It is never the direct object of their exertions, but a mere incident. Before they create it, they must feel a craving to do something to the accomplishment of which speaking and writing, poetry and eloquence, logic and philosophy are necessary as means. Their souls must be swelling with great thoughts struggling for utterance; haunted by visions of beauty they are burning to realize; their hearts must be wedded to a great and noble cause they are ambitious to make prevail, a far-reaching truth they would set forth, a new moral, religious, or social principle they would bring out and make the basis of actual life, and to the success of which speech, the essay, the treatise, the song are indispensably necessary, before they can create a national literature.

We feel a deep and absorbing interest in this matter of American literature; we would see American scholars in the highest and best sense of the term; and we shall see them, for it is in the destiny of this country to produce them; but they will come not because we seek them, and they will be produced not in consequence of any specific discipline we may prescribe. They will come when there is a work for them to do, and in consequence of the fact that the people are every where struggling to perform that work. How eloquently that man speaks! His words are fitly chosen; his periods are well balanced; his metaphors are appropriate and striking; his tones are sweet and kindling; for he is speaking on a subject in which his soul is absorbed; he has a cause he pleads, an idea he would communicate, a truth he would make men feel, an end he would carry. He is speaking out for truth, for justice, for liberty, for country, for God, for eternity; and humanity opens wide her ears, and her mighty heart listens. So must it be with all men who aspire to contribute to a national literature.

The scholar must have an end to which his scholarship serves as a means. Mr. Emerson and his friends seem to us to forget this. Forgetfulness of this is the reigning vice of Goethe and Carlyle. They bid the scholar make all things subsidiary to himself. He must be an artist, his sole end is to produce a work of art. He must scorn to create for a purpose, to compel his genius to serve, to work for an end beyond the work itself. All this which is designed to dignify art is false, and tends to render art impossible. Did Phidias[10] create but for the purpose of creating a statue? Was he not haunted by a vision of beauty which his soul burned to realize? Had the old Italian masters no end apart from and above that of making pictures? Did Homer sing merely that he might hear the sound of his own voice? Did Herodotus and Thucydides write but for the sake of writing, and Demosthenes and Cicero speak but for the purpose of producing inimitable specimens of art?[11] Never yet has there appeared a noble work of art which came not from the artist's attempt to gain an end separate from that of producing a work of art. Always does the artist seek to affect the minds or the hearts of his like, to move, persuade, convince, please, instruct, or ennoble. To this end he chants a poem, composes a melody, laughs in a comedy, weeps in a tragedy, gives us an oration, a treatise, a picture, a statue, a temple. In all the masterpieces of ancient and modern literature, we see the artist has been in earnest, a real man, filled with an idea, wedded to some great cause, ambitious to gain some end. Always has he found his inspiration in his cause, and his success may always be measured by the magnitude of that cause, and the ardor of his attachment to it.

American scholars we shall have; but only in proportion as the scholar weds himself to American principles, and becomes the interpreter of American life. A national literature, we have said, is the expression of the national life. It is the attempt to embody the great idea, or ideas, on which the nation is founded; and it proceeds from the vigorous and continued efforts of scholars to realize that idea, or those ideas, in practical life. The idea of this nation is that of democratic freedom, the equal rights of all men. No man, however learned he may be, however great in all the senses of greatness, viewed simply as an individual, who does not entertain this great idea, who does not love it, and struggle to realize it in all our social institutions, in our whole practical life, can be a contributor to American literature. We care not how much he may write; how rapid and extensive a sale his works may find; how beautifully in point of style they may be written; how much they may be praised in reviews, or admired in

[10] [Ed. Phidias (ca. 490-430 B.C.) was a famous Greek sculptor.]

[11] [Ed. Herodotus (ca. 484-424 B.C.), "the father of history," was a Greek historian known especially for his multi-volume and lively history of the Persian Wars. Thucydides (ca. 460-401 B. C.) was also a Greek historian especially known for his history of the Peloponnesian wars. Demosthenes (384-322 B.C.) was considered the greatest of the Greek orators. Marcus Tullius Cicero (106-43 B.C.) was a Roman orator, philosopher and statesman who is known as one of the greatest stylists of the Latin language.]

saloons; they shall not live and be placed among the national classics. They have no vitality for the nation, for they meet no great national want, satisfy no national craving.

In order to rear up American scholars, and produce a truly American literature, we would not do as the author of the oration before us, declaim against American literature as it is, against the servility, and want of originality and independence of the American mind; nor would we impose a specific discipline on the aspirants to scholarship. We would talk little about the want of freedom; we would not trouble ourselves at all about literature, as such. We would engage heart and soul in the great American work. We would make all the young men around us see and feel that there is here a great work, a glorious work, to be done. We would show them a work *they* can do, and fire them with the zeal and energy to do it. We would present them a great and kindling cause to espouse; wake up in them a love for their like, make them see a divine worth in every brother man, long to raise up every man to the true position of a man, to secure the complete triumph of the democracy, and to enable every man to comprehend and respect himself, and be a man. If we can succeed in doing this, we can make them true scholars, and scholars who shall do honor to their country, and add glory to humanity. When our educated men acquire faith in democratic institutions, and a love for the Christian doctrine of the brotherhood of the human race, we shall have scholars enough, and a literature which will disclose to the whole world the superiority of freedom over slavery.

Let Mr. Emerson, let all who have the honor of their country or of their race at heart, turn their whole attention to the work of convincing the educated and the fashionable that democracy is worthy of their sincerest homage, and of making them feel the longing to labor in its ennobling cause; and then he and they may cease to be anxious as to the literary results. It will be because a man has felt with the American people, espoused their cause, bound himself to it for life or for death, time or eternity, that he becomes able to adorn American literature; not because he has lived apart, refused "to serve society," held lone reveries, and looked on sunsets, and sunrise. If he speak a word, "posterity shall not willingly let die,"[12] it will not be because he has prepared himself to speak, by a scholastic asceticism, but by loving his countrymen and sympathizing with them.

[12] [Ed. A paraphrase from Milton's *The Reason of Church-government.* See *Complete Prose Works of John Milton*, Vol. 1, 1624-1642, ed. Don M. Wolfe (New Haven: Yale University Press, 1953), 810.]

8.

THE ECLECTIC PHILOSOPHY[1]

Boston Quarterly Review 2 (January, 1839): 27-53

M. Cousin, the principal founder of the Eclectic Philosophy in France, is thought by many in this country to be merely a philosophical dreamer, a fanciful framer of hypotheses, a bold generalizer, without solid judgment, or true science. An impression to this effect was conveyed some months since, in an article in one of our most respectable periodicals, by the teacher of philosophy in the oldest and best endowed university in the country, an article, by the way, which nothing but the youth and inexperience of its author could induce us to pardon.[2] But nothing is more unjust than this impression. M. Cousin is the farthest in the world from being a mere theorizer, or from founding his philosophy, as some allege, on mere *a priori* reasoning. They who censure him for his "eloquent generalizations" give us ample proof that they are ignorant of both the method and the spirit of his philosophy. Would they but attain to a tolerable acquaintance with his writings, they would at once perceive that he is most remarkable for those very qualities which they most strenuously deny him; and we cannot refrain from reminding them that they have no moral right to condemn a man of whom they know comparatively nothing, or to sit in judgment on a system of philosophy which they will not take the pains to comprehend. Understand, and then judge, is an old maxim, and a good one, and sorry are we to find occasion to repeat it.

[1] [Ed. Review of Victor Cousin's *Cours de philosophie professé á la Faculté des Lettres pendant l'année 1818*, ed. Adolphe Garnier (1801-64) (Paris: L. Hachett, 1836). This text, as Brownson indicates toward the end of the article, was not written by Cousin because the style is not Cousin's. It was probably written by Garnier, but the ideas were Cousin's. The book is on the foundation of the absolute ideas of the good, the true, and the beautiful.]

[2] [Ed. Reference is to the Harvard philosopher Francis Bowen (1811-90), a major philosophical critic of the Transcendentalist school of thought and a proponent of Common Sense philosophy. The article Brownson refers to may be: "Locke and the Transcendentalists," *Christian Examiner* 23 (November, 1837): 170-94. On Bowen, see Introduction to EW, 3.]

There is manifested, in a quarter from which we ought to be able to look for better things, a singular pertinacity in confounding M. Cousin with certain persons among ourselves, who, for some reason not known to us, have received the appellation of Transcendentalists. This is altogether unpardonable. If they who persist in doing this know no better, they are deplorably ignorant; if they do know better, we leave it to their own consciences to settle their claims to morality. We assure our readers that M. Cousin has very little in common with those they are in the habit of calling Transcendentalists. He professes no philosophy which transcends experience, unless by experience be understood merely that of the senses; he differs entirely as to his method from the New German philosophy represented by Schelling and Hegel, and on many essential points in the application and results of his method from Kant, the father of the Transcendental Philosophy, with whom we perceive there is a strong disposition to class him.[3] He cannot be classed with Kant nor with any of the Germans. He has all that Germany can give that is worth having, and much which Germany cannot give. Profited much he undoubtedly has by his study of Kant, and by his acquaintance with Schelling and Hegel; but he is the disciple of none of them. He has some things in common with the Scotch school; but he leaves that school at an immeasurable distance behind him.

Nor is it just to assert, as some do, that he is merely reproducing the old Alexandrian philosophy or Neoplatonism. The Alexandrians called themselves Eclectics, and Eclecticism was no doubt in their intention; but they failed utterly in their attempt to realize it. "Their school had the decided and brilliant character of an exclusive school,"[4] and ended in exclusive mysticism, a tendency to which no man, however lynx-eyed he may be, can discover in Cousin. The slightest acquaintance with his writings is sufficient to convince any man, at all

[3] [Ed. Friedrich Wilhelm Joseph Schelling (1775-1854) was a German objective idealist philosopher that clearly influenced Cousin and, through Cousin, Brownson. Georg Wilhelm Friedrich Hegel (1770-1831) was a German idealist philosopher of history who also had a profound impact on Cousin.]

[4] [Ed. I could not locate the exact quotation, but the substance of the judgment is Cousin's. See, e.g., Cousin's *Course of the History of Modern Philosophy*, trans. O. W. Wight, 2 vols. (New York: D. Appleton and Co., 1852), 1:445, where Cousin writes: "the exclusive idealism of the school of Alexandria soon drew it into all the follies of mysticism. Mysticism is the true character of the school of Alexandria, it is that which gives it an elevated and original rank in the history of philosophy." Cousin then refers the reader to his first series of lectures on the history of philosophy, volume 2, lectures 9 and 10, *du Mysticisme*, pp. 109-18. See also *Cours de philosophie . . . pendant 1818*, lectures 9 and 10, pp. 80-100.]

familiar with the Alexandrian philosophy, that Cousin has done quite another thing than to reproduce it. He has given us a faithful account of it; he has criticized it with great judgment, pointed out its vices, and shown us why it failed to realize the Eclecticism to which it aspired.[5] Indeed, he is so far from being a Neoplatonist that he is not even a Platonist; at least he is no more a follower of Plato than he is of Aristotle. He reverences Plato and Aristotle as philosophers by way of eminence; the first as having given birth to philosophic ideas, and the latter as having reduced them to order, and given them their language, which is still the language of philosophy; but properly speaking he is the disciple of neither. He has translated Plato and enabled us to comprehend him;[6] he is devoting much attention to Aristotle, and doing what he can to raise up the Stagyrite from the neglect into which he has fallen, since the ruin of the Scholastic Philosophy. If he himself is remarkable for one thing more than another, it is for the freedom and independence with which he seeks and accepts truth wherever he can find it.

We say again that M. Cousin is not a Transcendentalist as the term appears to be understood in this community. It is not easy to determine what people mean by the term Transcendentalist; but we suppose they mean to designate by it, when they use it as a term of reproach, a man who, in philosophizing, disregards experience and builds on principles obtained not by experience, but by reasoning *a priori*. In this sense, Cousin is no Transcendentalist. Nor indeed was Kant. Kant's method was as truly experimental as Bacon's or Locke's. He starts with the proposition that "all our knowledge begins with experience." (*Dass alle unsere Erkenntniss mit der Erfahrung anfange, daran ist gar kein Zweifel*).[7] But experience is possible only on certain conditions. If the human mind be in its origin a mere blank sheet, as Locke represents it, incapable of furnishing from its own resources any element of experience, we must admit with Hume that no experience is possible, and that every sane philosopher must needs be a

[5] [Ed. Cousin treats the Alexandrian School in *Course of the History*, 444-52.]

[6] [Ed. Cousin started to translate Plato in 1822, a task which he completed in 1840. For one edition of the translation, see *Platon Oeuvres*, trans. Victor Cousin, 13 vols. (Paris, 1840-1846).]

[7] [Ed. This was the first line of the introduction to Immanuel Kant's *The Critique of Pure Reason*. Kant's *Critique* was not translated into English until 1838. See *Critick of Pure Reason*, [trans. Francis Haywood] (London: William Pickering, 1838). Brownson used a German edition of Kant's text as is evident by the language Haywood used to translate the first line: "That all our Cognition begins with Experience, there is not any doubt."]

skeptic.[8] If we admit the possibility of experience, we must admit certain *a priori* conditions of experience; that is, we must admit in the mind, prior to experience, certain inherent qualities, properties, laws, elements, by virtue of which experience is rendered possible. What are these *a priori* conditions, qualities, properties, elements, ideas, forms, categories, or whatever else they may be termed, and without which no experience can take place? This is the problem Kant proposes to solve, and the solution of this problem is what he calls the Transcendental Philosophy: and his attempt at its solution, he calls the Critique of Pure Reason, that is, of the reason considered as abstracted from all the elements it receives from experience. Kant saw very clearly the conclusion to which Hume had been conducted by assuming Locke's point of departure—a conclusion wholly repugnant to the common sense of mankind, and to every man's practical convictions—and he felt that before proceeding farther in the attempt to create a philosophy, it was necessary to make a critique of the pure reason, that is, to ascertain the possibility of experience, and the conditions without which it cannot take place. This he contends had not been done, nor even seriously attempted.

Now, although these *a priori* conditions of experience, these elements which the reason itself furnishes, precede experience, since they are essential to experience—it is experience that develops them, and it is by experience that we ascertain them, separate them from the empirical elements with which they are always connected in the consciousness, and become able to see them by themselves and in themselves. From the fact that they are said to precede in the understanding the fact of experience, we must not infer that we can seize them by *a priori* reasoning. Kant's philosophy, it is admitted, professes to give an account of what is in the reason prior to experience; but it does not profess to give this account before experience has developed the reason, much less without the aid of experience. He seeks by experience, by experiment, by a careful analysis of the facts of consciousness, as they actually present themselves to the eye of the psychological observer, to distinguish the rational elements of those facts, from the empirical elements which they also contain, to trace the non-empirical elements to their source, and to give us their real

[8] [Ed. David Hume (1711-76) was a Scottish philosopher and historian who based his philosophical method on the empiricism of Locke, but by reducing reason to a product of experience he destroyed its claims to sole or universal validity in reaching truth. Because of this he has sometimes been identified as a philosophical skeptic.]

character. His method, therefore is, as we have said, as truly the experimental method as that of Bacon or Locke.

Moreover, Kant's problem was not essentially different from the problem Locke himself undertook, in his own estimation, to solve. Locke saw that before proceeding to discuss the objects of knowledge it was necessary to ascertain the nature and character of that with which we know, namely, the human understanding. "For I thought," says he, "that the first step towards satisfying several inquiries the mind of man was very apt to run into, was to take a survey of our own understandings, examine our own powers, and see to what things they were adapted."[9] But Locke surveyed the understanding, the instrument with which we know what we do know, not in its character of pure understanding, or pure reason, but in its mixed character, in its manifestations, as developed by experience, or as it develops itself by the aid of experience. Abstract from the understanding all the elements, facts, or ideas, furnished it by experience, and according to Locke nothing remains to be surveyed, but a mere *tabula rasa,* a mere blank sheet. Kant, however, proceeded on the ground that after we have abstracted from the understanding everything furnished it by experience, there remains the pure reason itself with certain laws or categories of its own, which it is necessary to ascertain and describe. Locke undertook as well as Kant to give us a critique of the pure understanding; but he immediately came to the conclusion that the pure understanding, that is, the understanding considered in itself, and apart from everything derived from experience, is a mere nullity, and not worth troubling oneself about. He, therefore, confined himself to the understanding in action, as made up by experience. Kant resumes the original problem of Locke, comes to the conclusion that the pure understanding is not a nullity, but a something of considerable value, well deserving to be known, abounding in wealth which may be considered as the inalienable patrimony of the race, and of which it behooves every philosopher to draw up an inventory. Here is all the difference there is, as to their problems, between these two distinguished philosophers. Their method, and even their object, was virtually the same. Locke applied the experimental method to the survey of the understanding, without abstracting the elements furnished it by experience; Kant applied the experimental method to the pure understanding, seeking not to construct a philosophy on *a priori* reasoning, but merely to ascertain the *a priori* conditions of

[9] [Ed. John Locke's *Essay Concerning Human Understanding*, Introduction, paragraph 7, second line.]

knowledge. Both were, in fact, engaged in the same work, as it presented itself from their respective points of observation, and both pursued the same method, observation and induction, in accomplishing it. Kant's philosophy is in many respects incomplete, unsatisfactory; but not because he leaves the path of experience and rushes off into speculation; not because he leaves observation for ratiocination; but because he fails in the application of his method to the phenomena of consciousness, and in the proper classification of the phenomena which a profound psychology detects.

The mistake on this point, in relation to both Kant and Cousin, probably arises from supposing all experience is necessarily the experience of the senses. Cousin and Kant while they admit, and give a large place to empiricism, or the experience of the senses, facts of consciousness introduced, generated, by means of sensation, contend for an experience which transcends sensible experience, and which, though taking places only on occasion of sensible experience, is not generated by it.

"Is there not," says Cousin, in commenting on a disciple of Hegel, "is there not another experience than that of the senses? Above the senses there is in us understanding, reason, intellect, which, on occasion of sensible impressions, the wants and affections which they excite, enters into exercise and discloses to us what the senses cannot attain to; sometimes truths of a very common order, at other times truths of the most elevated order, the most general; for example, the *principles* on which turns the whole metaphysics of Aristotle. Aristotle says positively, that he admits the immediate intuition of first principles. There is here no longer a question of the senses. It is the reason which reveals principles to us spontaneously. But know we not also that reason and its fruitful action by means of which we know? And how know that? Is it not by consciousness and reflection? And do not consciousness and reflection constitute an experience as real as that of the senses? Is not this rational experience which is wholly internal, certain, regular, and fruitful in great results? Will it be said that the knowledge we owe to this internal experience, to consciousness and reflection, contracts a personal and subjective character? I reply that this personal and subjective character is only the covering, not the ground, of consciousness; that the true ground of consciousness is the reason and intelligence attaining to a knowledge of themselves. Will it be denied that there is in human thought an eternal ground, which manifests itself by its subjective side even, as power manifests itself by the act, and the universal by the particular? Will it be pretended that the reason, by virtue of the fact that it manifests itself and acts in us, and we have the consciousness of it, ceases to be reason, that is the essence of things, if, as it is alleged, the essence of things is in thought? Let us leave mere words to the schools, and not waste ourselves in vain formulas. All that we know of any subject whatever, an essence or a thought, we know only by virtue of the fact that we think. All ends in thought in its personal and impersonal character combined; and in this is the firm foundation of our sublimest conceptions and our humblest notions. To study in ourselves this interior development of the intelligence, and verify its laws by mingling as little as possible of our own personality, is to derive truth from its most immediate and surest source.

"This rational experience, combined with sensible experience, furnishes the philosopher all the materials of science.

"To experience also we refer the attentive investigation of common notions, generally diffused, borne witness to in the languages of men, manifested in their actions, and which compose what is called common sense, that is, the universal experience of mankind. Each of our fellow men is our self. The artisan and the shepherd are also men; human nature in all its integrity, the human soul with all its faculties is in them; reason and thought manifest themselves in them, and manifesting themselves in them with order, and according to their own laws, do manifest in them both the nature and the laws of the essence of things. To study our like is to study ourselves; and the experience of common sense is always the necessary control, and frequently even the light and the guide, of our internal experience.

"By the side of the experience of common sense is the experience of genius. Humanity, in acting, in speaking, manifests a system which she herself knows not; but some few men, who have more leisure and reflection than the mass, seek this system, and the essays they make to discover it, transmitted from age to age, form a second experience more precious yet than the first. This experience is called the History of Philosophy.

"These four great species of experiences compose an experimental method, all the parts of which mutually support and enlighten one another. *This method is for me the true one.* Aristotle has suspected it with his *Four Elements,* and has observed it on some points with admirable fidelity and depth. But he no where treats specially of method; he has not perfectly determined it. It is modern philosophy that has for the first time treated of method in itself, and it is to its adoption of the experimental method that it owes its progress."[10]

[10] [Ed. Victor Cousin's *De la Métaphysique d'Aristote* (Paris, 1835), 84-89.]

Surely here is proof enough that Cousin does by no means condemn experience; and we commend this extract to all those who call him a mere speculatist, remarkable only for his eloquent generalizations; who class him as to his method with the New German school, and range those who in this country profess to be his friends with a few speculatists, half mystics and half skeptics, christened Transcendentalists. We commend it especially to the author of the article before alluded to, and trust that he will learn from it to discover a difference where he has heretofore seen only an identity.

Cousin's method, we have now determined, is the experimental method. His method is the method of modern philosophy itself, the only method philosophy has been permitted to follow since Bacon and Descartes.

This method consists of two fundamental movements, analysis and synthesis, or as they are more commonly named, observation and induction. All true science results from a careful and profound analysis of facts, and the induction from facts, properly analyzed, of their principles, their fundamental laws. If the analysis be incomplete, the facts be not properly observed, rightly classed, the induction will be faulty and without scientific value. Everything, therefore, depends on the first movement. Observation must be complete, analysis must exhaust the subject, before we have any right to proceed to our inductions.

The defects of most systems of philosophy, the more frequent errors of philosophers, arise from incomplete analysis, and from proceeding to the induction of principles, of laws, before the facts themselves have been duly observed and experimented upon. They catch a glimpse of a fact here, and a fact there, and forthwith proceed to construct a system. As wise were he who with half a dozen bricks should attempt to reconstruct the walls of Babylon.

The instrument of philosophy is the human intelligence; its field is the human consciousness, that world which each man carries in himself, a world diminutive indeed in the estimation of the unreflecting, but in reality far transcending the bounds of all outward nature.

The first step in philosophizing is to turn the mind in upon itself, upon this interior world of consciousness, and observe, examine with care, patience, and fidelity, its various and fleeting phenomena. The first object is to ascertain what is there. We must not begin by seeking what ought or ought not to be there, what can or cannot be there, how what is there did or did not come there, could or could not come there, but simply what *is* there. We must seek for facts, not theories, for realities, not hypotheses, to know what is, not to uphold or overturn a belief.

The error of Locke and his school, under the head of method, was in proceeding to discuss the origin of our ideas before determining what are our ideas. He begins by an assumption, an hypothesis. He assumes in the outset that there can be no ideas in the consciousness, which have not either been generated by sensation or manufactured by reflection out of materials furnished by sensation. How does he know this? How knows he but when he comes to inquire he shall strike upon an idea, a fact of consciousness which no metaphysical alchemy can transmute into a sensation, and which no Vulcan can forge out of materials furnished by the senses? If he should chance to strike upon such an idea, what shall he do with it? Nay, is he not in great danger of overlooking all such ideas, if such ideas there be, or of falsifying them in his account of them? Would he not have acted altogether more wisely, if he had just ascertained what is in the consciousness, before undertaking to tell how what he guesses to be there came there?

The true philosophical method is to begin with the facts of consciousness and ascertain what they are. The study of the facts of consciousness, the analysis and classification of the interior phenomena, gives us psychology, as the analysis and classification of the facts or phenomena of the human body gives us physiology; or as the analysis and classification of the facts or phenomena of external nature gives us physics or the natural sciences.

The only difference there is between metaphysical science and natural science is in their subject-matter, and the instruments by means of which we make our experiments. In the natural sciences we make experiments, or observe, by means of the external senses; in psychology, since the interior phenomena escape the cognizance of the outward senses, we observe or make experiments by means of that inward sense, or interior light, called consciousness.

That there is an internal order of facts as real and as open to our inspection as the facts of the outward world, no man can doubt. We may doubt as to the origin or the validity of our ideas; we may doubt whether we have the means to determine their origin or their validity; but we can never doubt our competency to determine what are our ideas. For instance, we may dispute how we came by the idea of God, and whether there be or be not in the world of reality anything to respond to our idea; but the fact that we entertain the idea, in case we do entertain it, is a matter that admits of no discussion, and one on which we feel as certain as we do in reference to any fact observed by the outward senses.

There is then an internal order of facts to be observed, and we are capable of observing them. We know as well what is passing in us as we do what is passing without and around us. I know the facts of my consciousness, which I observe by means of an inward sense, as well as I do the facts of outward nature, observed by means of my five senses. I know that I think, believe, disbelieve, what I think, believe, or disbelieve; that I entertain certain notions and reject certain other notions; as well as I know that I see that lamp on my table, and feel in my fingers the pen with which I am writing.

Be there no mistake on this point. We say nothing now of the genesis of our ideas, or of their ontological value. The idea, so far as we are for the present concerned, may or may not have a sensible or a rational origin, may or may not have a value beyond the sphere of the individual consciousness; it may or may not be responded to in the world of reality. All these questions, very important and very proper in their place, we waive now. All we pretend at this moment is that there are phenomena of consciousness, and that we can observe them as steadily and as certainly as we can the phenomena of the external world.

When we have examined, carefully ascertained, what are the facts of consciousness, we may then proceed to the question of the origin of our ideas. If we find, among our ideas, ideas which are unquestionably facts of consciousness, certain ideas which could not have been generated by the senses, we have a right to infer that we have another source of ideas than the senses. If we can trace these ideas to the reason, which is not a creature of sensible experience, for without reason sensible experience would be impossible, then we may say, that the reason is a source of ideas, and that we have rational ideas as well as sensible ideas.

Now Cousin admits, contends, that there is an order of facts in the consciousness which owe their origin to sensation; but he also contends that there are facts in the consciousness, which have another origin than that of the senses. He recognizes in the consciousness three orders of phenomena, which he refers to three fundamental faculties; 1st. Sensibility; 2d. Activity, or will; 3d. Reason, or understanding. To illustrate these, take the example of a man who studies a book of mathematics.

"Assuredly if this man had no eyes he could not see the book, neither the pages nor the letters; he could not comprehend what he could not read. On the other hand, if he would not give his attention, constrain his eyes to read, and his mind to reflect on what he reads, he would be equally far from comprehending the book. But when his eyes are open, when his mind is attentive, is all done? No. He must also comprehend, seize or think he seizes the truth. To seize, to recognize the truth, is a fact which may indeed require various circumstances and conditions; but in itself it is simple, indecomposable, which cannot be reduced to a mere volition, nor to sensation; and must by this consideration have a separate place in a legitimate classification of the facts which fall under the eye of consciousness.

"I speak of consciousness: but consciousness itself, the perception of consciousness, this fundamental and permanent fact, which nearly all systems commit the error of pretending to explain by a single term, which sensualism explains by a sensation become exclusive, without inquiring what renders it exclusive, which M. de Biran[11] explains by the will producing a sensation, his fact, can it take place without the intervention of something else which is neither sensation nor volition, but which perceives them both? To be conscious is to perceive, to recognize, to know. The word itself (*scientia-cum*) says as much. Not merely do I feel, but I know that I feel; not merely do I will, but I know that I will; and this knowing what I feel, and what I will, is precisely what is meant by consciousness. Either is it necessary then to prove that sensation and volition are endowed with the faculty of perceiving, of knowing themselves, or it is necessary to admit a third term, without which the two others would be as if they were not. Consciousness is a triple phenomenon, in which to feel, to will, and to know, serve as the mutual conditions of one another, and in their connection, simultaneousness, and difference, compose the whole intellectual life. Take away *feeling* and there is no longer either occasion or object for the will, and the will ceases to be exerted. Take away the *will* and there is no longer any real activity, me, or personality, percipient agent, or perceptible object. Take away the power of *knowing,* and there can be no perception whatever, no light to disclose what is, feeling, willing, and their relation; consciousness loses its torch and ceases to be.

[11] [Ed. François-Pierre Gonthier de Biran, called Maine de Biran, (1766-1824) was a French philosopher who had during his early career identified himself with the French sensualist and Enlightenment tradition, but gradually moved away from that tradition and after about 1812 began to develop an original spiritualist ontology. Maine de Biran had a considerable influence upon Cousin who edited some of his works.]

"To know is therefore unquestionably a fact, distinct, *sui generis*. To what faculty refer it. Call it understanding, spirit, intellect, reason, no matter which, provided it is understood to be an elementary faculty. It is usually termed the reason."[12]

That the sensibility alone cannot be the source of the facts of consciousness these remarks of M. Cousin sufficiently demonstrate to all familiar enough with psychological matters to comprehend them. Aristotle, who, strange enough, has been sometimes considered as favoring sensualism, states the same thing. He says the senses cannot give us wisdom, that is, knowledge of causes, principles. "Although the senses are the true means of knowing individual things, they do not tell us the *why* of anything. For example, they do not teach us *why* fire is hot, they merely tell us that it *is* hot."[13]

Locke, although his philosophy run into complete sensualism, thought he had contended for another source of ideas than that of sensation. According to him, all our ideas are derived from sensation and reflection. He divides our ideas into two classes, simple and complex, or primary and secondary. Primary ideas come directly from sensation; secondary ideas are produced by the action of the mind or reflection on the primary ideas. Now this indeed makes all ideas in the last analysis come from sensation, for the secondary ideas are merely modifications of the primary. But Locke did not so intend it. He thought he had escaped the sensualism of Hobbes, and obtained a rational origin as well as a sensible origin of ideas.

Locke's error consisted merely in his exposition. His account of the matter was erroneous. His mistake doubtless arose from confounding the occasion with the origin of our ideas; and from regarding what is unquestionably the origin of a *part* of any given fact of consciousness, as the origin of the *whole* of it. He understood perfectly well that before sensible experience there are no facts of consciousness. The sensibility has always been acted upon before we have an idea. Hence no innate ideas. So far Locke was right. The organs of sensation are affected; a sensation is produced; there is a fact of consciousness—an idea. Now as sensation chronologically precedes the idea, he concludes that it is its cause, and does not inquire, whether analysis might not detect in the idea an element or elements which sensation could not furnish, but which must have been furnished by the mind itself. Here is the source of his mistake and that of the sensualists generally.

12 [Ed. Brownson cites *Ouvrage Posthume de M. Maine de Biran*, ed. Victor Cousin (Paris, 1834), Preface de l'Editeur, xxix-xxx.]

13 [Ed. *De la metaphysique d'Aristote*, 124.]

Undoubtedly there can be no idea, no fact of consciousness, in which there is not an element derived from sensation. But is the sensible element the *whole* of the fact? Have we any purely simple ideas? Are not all ideas, is not every fact of consciousness, complex? And into every fact of consciousness does there not enter an element which can by no means have a sensible origin? Now these are the questions the sensualists should ask. But instead of these questions, they ask, have we any ideas or facts of consciousness that are wholly of a rational origin, in which the senses have no share? Unable to find any fact of consciousness in which Sensibility does not intervene, they rashly conclude that all phenomena, and the whole of every phenomenon of consciousness, are derived from sensation.

Every man, we presume it will be admitted, has the idea, conception, or notion of *cause*. The idea of power, of causative force, is unquestionably a fact of human consciousness. We speak of causes, and all our reasonings, and all our actions imply the idea.

Now what is our idea or notion of cause? What do we mean by the term? Invariable antecedence, as Thomas Brown[14] asserts, and as Locke himself also virtually asserts? Interrogate consciousness. The universal belief of mankind is that cause is a something, a power, force, or agency which produces or creates effects. I will to raise my arm; a muscular contraction succeeds; my arm rises. Does the voluntary effort merely precede the muscular contraction and the rising of the arm, or does it produce them? It produces them is the universal answer of consciousness.

The idea of cause, as a fact of consciousness, is the idea of a causative, productive, or creative force, power, or agency. What is the origin of this idea? It has been demonstrated over and over again that the senses can attain only to phenomena; that they do not and cannot give us information of causes. A piece of wax is placed close to the fire; forthwith it is changed from a solid to a fluid. Here is what all our senses take cognizance of; and of course all that we can attain to by sensation. Nevertheless, we all say and believe that the fire melts the wax, causes, produces the change we observe in its state or condition. An angry fellow has struck me a severe blow on my head; a contusion follows, and I suffer acute pain. My senses have noted the phenomena; the raising of his hand; its motion towards my head; its

[14] [Ed. Thomas Brown (1778-1820) was a Scottish Common Sense philosopher who combined an empiricist analysis with a principle of intuitive belief in coming to a knowledge of cause and effect. Cause was "that which immediately precedes any change." His most important work on causality was *Inquiry into the Relation of Cause and Effect* (Edinburgh, 1818).]

contact with my head; the contusion, the pain which have followed; and this is all they have noted; but this is not all that I believe. I connect these several phenomena together in the relation of cause and effect, and pronounce the blow struck, not merely the antecedent, but the cause of what I suffer. I have then the conception of something which the senses do not perceive. They note the simple phenomena only; but I believe an agency, a causative force, which escapes the senses, has been at work in them; and so does everybody. Now this belief is not and cannot be the product of sensation. It may spring up only on the occasion of sensation, of observing the sensible phenomena; but it contains in itself an element not derivable from sensation, and which necessarily transcends sensible experience.

Whence does it originate? We observe the sensible phenomena, and from the data they furnish us we infer it, it may be said. But what is that which infers? And how can we draw out of sensible phenomena that which is not contained in them? Would the mind unconscious of the idea, and unable to furnish it from its own resources, ever dream of inferring it from data which do neither contain it, nor in any way indicate it? If the understanding were previously furnished with the idea, we could easily conceive of its applying it to the relation of the phenomena in question; but we confess that we cannot conceive how an understanding made up of purely sensible elements, as it must be if sensualism be true, can infer a non-sensible idea from merely sensible phenomena. The logic by which it can be done we have not yet learned.

Chronologically we admit sensation precedes the idea of cause; we even admit that without sensation, without sensible experience of some individual case of causation, we should never have had the idea of cause. Never till we have witnessed the phenomena do we conceive of their relation, or of any relation of cause and effect. But as soon as we witness the phenomena, we find and apply the idea. The experience to which we are indebted for the first development of the idea is probably internal experience. We obtain the idea of cause by detecting ourselves in the act of causing. I will, and perceive that my will produces effects; and from this act of willing which is performed in myself, in the bosom of my consciousness, the idea of cause is probably first suggested to me.

But if this be a true account of the historical origin of the idea of cause, it proves that it comes not from sensation, nor from reflection operating on sensible materials. There are in the case of voluntary causation, the me, or personality, willing or making a voluntary effort, and the motion of a part of the body in obedience to the will. I will to raise my arm. Here we must note, 1st, the volition; 2d, the muscular contraction; 3d, the rising of the arm. Now the senses take cognizance of the rising of the arm, and, if you please, of the muscular contraction; but not of the volition, much less of the fact that the volition is the cause of the phenomena succeeding it. The sensation, I am conscious of in this case, is the result of the muscular effort, not of the voluntary effort. How then by sensation alone am I to connect my volition, or more properly myself, with the muscular contraction, and the rising of my arm, as their cause? I am conscious of the fact. I want no reasoning to prove to me that the connection implied does really exist. I cannot for one moment doubt that I am the cause of the phenomena in question. Whence comes this feeling of certainty, this conviction, this conception of myself as a cause? It cannot come from sensation.

Grant that I am a cause, that I do and can produce effects, grant me sensibility, and nothing more; I ask, how am I to know that I am a cause? I am indeed conscious of causing, producing, and I need no argument to prove to me that I am a cause; but I am conscious only by virtue of the fact that I am intelligent as well as causative. Activity of itself does not necessarily imply intelligence. We can easily conceive of a causative force which shall cause, but be unconscious of causing. Beyond the me as a causative force, as we have seen in the extract from Cousin's preface to Maine de Biran, there must be intelligence or reason, in order to render us conscious of our own acts. Were we unconscious beings, we could obtain no idea of cause from the fact that we ourselves cause or produce; for we should take no cognizance, have no conception of our own acts. Mere activity, or power of causing, which is the characteristic element of the me, or personality, of that which we mean when we say *I*, or *me,* does not then alone of itself suggest the idea of cause. It can suggest it only to an intelligent me, or personality. As we said of sensation, so may we say of the Activity. Were we not endowed with the power of causing, producing effects, and did we never exert this power, we probably should never be conscious of the idea of cause; we should never obtain the notion or conception of a causative force; nevertheless, the idea itself, as a fact of consciousness, contains an element which it is as impossible to derive from activity as from sensation.

It may be said that we *feel* ourselves produce; and as the phenomena of feeling are ranged under the head of sensibility, it may be thought that the idea of cause, as obtained from the exertion of the will, is after all obtained from sensation. But we do not, in fact, feel ourselves produce. The feeling, we are conscious of in every creative act we attribute to ourselves, is, as we have said, of the muscular effort, not of the voluntary effort. Moreover, feeling cannot go beyond itself. Grant merely that I am conscious, capable merely of feeling, and of perceiving or knowing that I feel and all I can know is simply my own feelings. The cause, or causes of what I feel must be beyond the range of my conceptions. A blow is struck on my head. I feel the pain it produces. But all I know is simply the pain I feel. In this case, all the multiplied causes around me, and ever acting on me, the external world with all its endless variety, would be reduced to mere sensations, to mere modifications of my sensibility. They could never be regarded by me as out of me, existing independently of me, and causing in me the sensations I am conscious of receiving, and which I am in the habit of ascribing to their action upon my organs of sense.

But even grant that sensibility may attain to causes, we must still demand intelligence as the ground, the indispensable condition of sensibility. In the first place, mere sensation can of itself shape itself into no proposition. There must be the me, the personality, the invariable something we call *our self,* to receive the sensation, and to give unity to the impressions received through the organs of sense. In the second place, and this is the point now under consideration, we must not only have the capacity of receiving sensations, but of knowing them. It is not enough that we feel, but we must know that we feel. Take away the intelligence, the faculty of knowing, which can no more be confounded with the sensibility, or capacity of receiving sensations, than the capacity of receiving sensations can be confounded with the activity, or power of producing effects, and sensibility itself becomes impossible. Intelligence is always at the bottom of sensation. What were pain if unknown? Joy or grief unperceived by the joying or grieving subject? Simple organic impressions, or affections, of which the recipient of them would have no consciousness. Pleasure and pain, joy and grief, if we are unconscious of them, are for us as though they were not. Nay, they are not for us at all. They can exist for us only on the condition that we know as well as feel. We must not only feel them, but know that we feel them. Though both sensibility and activity combine to suggest to us the idea of cause, and are indispensable conditions of its suggestion, neither of them nor both of them can therefore suggest it without the intervention of another element, diverse from them both, and to which they both must look for their light.

This will appear still more conclusive if we remark that we not only have the idea of cause, such as we have described it, that we not only believe ourselves the cause of our own acts, and that certain bodies are the cause of the motions we observe in certain other bodies; but we also have the idea of the principle of causality; we believe that every phenomenon whatever that begins to exist must have a cause. We believe that nothing begins to exist without a cause. Now this belief may or may not be well-founded. This principle may or may not be true. Whether it be or be not is not now the question. What we allege is that we do entertain the principle. It is not in our power to reject it. All languages imply it; all reasoning involves it; the whole juridical action of society is based upon it; and it lies at the bottom of that curiosity which leads us to seek a cause for every phenomenon we observe.

Whence the introduction of this principle into the consciousness? What is its origin? It cannot come from sensation, even admitting sensation is of itself competent to suggest the idea of cause; for sensation at best can suggest only the notion of individual causes, and only of the particular causes of which it has had experience. Suppose the senses really do inform us that the fire melts the wax, give us the idea we have that it is the fire which produces the change we observe in the wax, when brought into contact with it; still, we ask, how is it possible for them to generalize this notion, which is the notion of a concrete, individual cause, into an abstract and universal principle? How from the particular cause, the fact that fire melts wax, go to the universal and necessary principle, that no phenomenon can begin to exist without a cause? Any induction broader than the premises, all logicians will assure us, is illegitimate. The conclusion must be contained in the premises, or it will be without validity. But the general, the universal, the abstract is not contained in the particular, the concrete, and consequently cannot be inferred from it. From the fact that fire melts wax no man would ever dream of inferring that no phenomena can begin to exist but by virtue of a cause.

Inferences from sensibility cannot go beyond the experience of sensibility. Reduce me to simple sensation, leave me only my senses, and whatever power to attain to causes you may claim for the senses, I can obtain a notion of no cause which has not passed under the observation of my senses. Now nobody can pretend that the senses have taken cognizance of all that is; consequently nobody can pretend that the principle, nothing can begin to exist without a cause, is a fact of sensible experience. In order that it should be a fact of sensible experience, we must with our senses have observed all things which exist, all possibilities of existence, and all conditions of existence. We have not done this. The principle of which we speak is not then a fact of sensible experience. Yet it is unquestionably a fact of consciousness. There are facts of consciousness then which cannot be traced to a sensible origin.

Nor can the principle, no phenomenon can begin to exist but by virtue of a cause, be derived from the notion of our own causality. The cause which we ourselves are is always conceived as voluntary and personal. The idea of cause which I obtain from the consciousness of the fact, that I create or produce, is the idea of myself as a cause. It is by no means the conception of cause in general, of any cause, in fact, existing out of the bosom of my own consciousness. Now, how can we pass from this purely individual and personal cause, to general and impersonal causes—to causes which we are not, and which stretch over the whole domain of all actual existence and of all possible existence. From the fact that I know myself to be the cause of my own volitions, by what means am I led to believe that the fire melts the wax, and especially to adopt the principle that every phenomenon, which begins to exist, exists by virtue of some cause?

The idea of cause obtained from the consciousness of our own causative force is merely the idea of ourselves as causes, not the idea of causes out of us, of cause in general. It is of myself as a cause, and only of myself, that I conceive. Now let me transfer this conception of cause to the external world, as I must, if from this conception I am to derive, consciously or unconsciously, all my notions of causality, and the causes, I may fancy I see at work in that external world, must be regarded by me as myself—will be merely myself projected. I am in this case the cause at work there. I create or produce all the phenomena I am accustomed to represent to myself and to others as existing out of me. The sun, moon, and stars, with their light and glory; the earth with its variety; the ocean with its majesty; men and women with their infinitely varied actions and sentiments, with their love which charms and blesses me, their hatred and opposition which grieve and overwhelm me; yea, God himself with the solemn awe of his being, the unsearchable riches of his grace, and the unfathomable depth of his wisdom; what are all these but myself taken as the object of my thoughts and emotions? I am therefore the only existence; I am the universal Creator. I make God, man, and nature. I am all, and in all, and there is only me. To this conclusion we must come, if we have only the conception of our own causality, out of which to form the notion of cause in general. But this conclusion is rejected by common sense, and nobody can entertain it even for a moment, unless system-mad indeed, and system-madness cannot have affected the race. But even if this idea could be entertained, it would not relieve us; because it is not the idea of cause which actually exists in the consciousness. It is not the notion of cause which mankind entertain. Now we are not inquiring what is the true idea of cause, what idea of cause men ought to have, but the idea they really do have, together with its real origin.

The remarks we have thus far made will show, if we have made ourselves understood, that we have the idea of cause; that we conceive of cause always as something which creates, or produces effects; and that this idea, whether it be true or false, cannot be derived from the experience of the senses, nor from the experience of the activity; but must be derived from the intelligence, the reason, or whatever that is in us, by virtue of which we are knowing, as well as feeling and acting beings. It must therefore be an intuition of the reason. It is the reason that sees the relation of cause and effect in the phenomena presented by experience; and the reason that furnishes us the principle, that nothing can begin to exist but by virtue of a cause. If we are correct in this, it must be admitted, that there are facts in the consciousness which have not an empirical origin, but a rational origin.

This conclusion may be established by analyzing several other facts of consciousness. Now it is unquestionably a fact that we entertain the notion of space. We do never conceive of a body as existing, without conceiving of it as existing somewhere. No doubt this conception of the *where* springs up only on the occasion of the presentation of some body occupying space; but does the idea of body not only suggest but originate it? Space is never conceived as a part of body, and we always distinguish it from the body which fills it. Give the body or take it away, the idea of space, once suggested, remains unaffected. Has it a sensible origin? Through which of our senses do we receive it? Can we see it, feel it, hear it, taste it, smell it, touch it? Locke indeed pretends to derive the idea of space from the senses of touch and sight; but as he himself contends the senses of sight and touch can take cognizance of only bodies, from which he carefully distinguishes space, and from which everybody distinguishes it, it is evident that it must come from some other source. That it springs up in the consciousness along with the conception of body, we readily admit. But it cannot be derived from our conception of body because without the conception of space we can form no conception of body. Body, in our conception of it, is always extended; but how conceive of extension without space? Nor does the idea of space come from the activity, that is, it is not a creation of our will. Supposing that we could create the idea by an effort of the will, we should still need to have the conception before we could will to create it. To will always implies a conception of something as the object of the voluntary effort to be put forth. We see more or less clearly what it is that we would create. We do not will we know not what. So then if we could produce the conception by an effort of the will, its origin would not be accounted for. Before we will to have the idea of space, we must have conceived of space. There remains therefore only the reason to be regarded as the source of the conception. The idea of space is an intuition of the reason. The reason furnishes the idea of space on the occasion of the experience of a body occupying space. It is not the senses nor the activity that tell us that body must be somewhere, but the reason. Where does the reason obtain this information, but from its own resources?

The idea of the Infinite is another fact of consciousness, which cannot be introduced into the consciousness by sensation. If we had no experience of finite things, we should doubtless never have been conscious of a conception of the infinite. But the conception of the infinite is not derived from the experience of the finite. Sensible experience—which is all the experience which now concerns us—can give us nothing beyond its own objects, and these objects are all finite, individual, concrete. Multiply these objects into one another as we will, and the product can be at most only the indefinite, never the infinite; the undefined, not the undefinable. Induction can draw from particulars only the particular; for it can draw from them only what is in them. Suppose then the finite is given by sensible experience—a fact we by no means admit, except for the argument's sake—we cannot conclude from that to the infinite, unless the infinite be in the finite. But the finite with the infinite in it is not the finite but the infinite. Either then we have not the idea of the infinite, or all our ideas are not derived from the experience of the senses. But we have the idea, as we may all satisfy ourselves by interrogating our own consciousness. Therefore we have another than an empirical source of ideas. Comes this idea of the infinite from the will? Certainly not; for we must conceive an object before we can will to create it. There remains, then, only the reason as its source. The reason furnishes the idea. It is an intuition of the reason furnished in point of fact, though obscurely perceived, contemporaneously with the idea of the finite.

We pretend not in these examples we have adduced that our demonstration is complete, that our reasoning leaves nothing to be desired. We are indicating a method, rather than constructing a philosophy; and the space to which we have felt ourselves restricted has not permitted us to say all that we could say, much less what probably would be necessary to satisfy our readers. More than all this, we shall have to return upon all the ideas of which we have spoken, in our future numbers, as we proceed in our exposition of the Eclectic Philosophy. All we have thus far attempted is simply to show that Cousin's method is really the experimental method, and to point out what is the order in which the several metaphysical questions should be taken up; and that by taking them up in their proper order, and applying the experimental method faithfully to the study of the facts of consciousness, we shall be led to the conclusion that there are facts of consciousness which have a rational origin, and not, as some pretend, that all our ideas have an exclusively empirical origin.

We have asked two questions: First, What are the facts of consciousness with their actual characters? Second, What is their origin? We have found that though sensibility and activity concur in the generation of the facts of consciousness, yet that without intelligence, or reason, there is no fact of consciousness, and that the ideas of space, the infinite, of cause, and especially the principle that no phenomenon can begin to exist but by virtue of a cause, are pure intuitions of the reason. So much we think we have done; at least pointed out the way by which our readers may easily do so much for themselves. But admitting that we have done all this, we have not touched the main metaphysical question. The great problem remains as yet unsolved. Suppose it granted that we have the idea of cause, the idea of the infinite, the idea of space; suppose these ideas to be facts of consciousness, to possess the characters under which we have spoken of them; and to have the origin we have assigned them; it is still necessary to ask, what is their validity? Is there really any cause to respond to our notion of cause? Is the infinite a reality? This is the ontological question.

Now we all are conscious of entertaining the idea or notion of a God; most men, if not all men, believe in a God. The idea of God is then, we will suppose, a fact of consciousness. Psychologically, then, it is true that there is a God. But this is not enough. Is it ontologically true that there is a God? That is, is there out of us, independent of us, really existing a being which answers to our idea of God? We believe, all men believe, there is an external world. Is this belief well founded? The belief is a fact of consciousness; but is it a chimera, a mere illusion, having nothing in the world of reality to respond to it? Here, it is evident, is a momentous question. It is a question of no less magnitude than what is the validity of human beliefs. It is the question which under some form or other has ever tormented the souls of philosophers; and indeed, not of philosophers only, it torments the souls of all men. Can we answer this question? Vain are all our pretensions to philosophy, if we cannot. I want no philosophy to teach me that I believe in my own existence, in nature, in God—to tell me what are the facts of my consciousness, nor even what is their origin. These are matters I know already, or can easily dispense with knowing. But what is their validity? Am I cheated, duped? Or is there that immense world of being around, beyond, and above me, which is revealed to me by the light of the reason shining in me? I have the idea of God. Is there a God who exists out of me, independent of me, who is not my conception, but the object of my conception? I have the conception of a life beyond this life, an immortal life, for which I hope, in which I believe, and to which, when overburdened with the sorrows of this, I sometimes look forward with inexpressible longings. Is there such a life? I have the conception of duty; I feel that some things I ought to do, and that some things I ought not to do; that I am under a law from which I cannot withdraw myself. Am I deceived? These and such like questions every reflecting man is ever asking himself. The soul grapples with these mighty questions, and experiences her bitterest grief when she feels herself unable to answer them. Can they be answered? This, we say again, is the true metaphysical question; in comparison with this all other questions are insignificant, and have no importance, save as the answer to them paves the way for an answer to this.

Our readers will readily perceive that we have no room now to take up a question of this magnitude. We must therefore postpone it till our next number. In the mean time, we commend to their study the work placed at the head of this article, in which they will find the method of solving this momentous question very clearly pointed out, and, in our judgment, very successfully prosecuted. Its style is not Cousin's, though it is in general clear, forcible, and elegant; but the thought is his, and is characterized by all his admirable analytic power, his rare sagacity in seizing the phenomena of consciousness, and compelling them to disclose their real characteristics and fundamental laws. It is a work, though in some respects incomplete, which we should be glad to see given to the public in an English dress.

Eclecticism—Ontology[15] 2 (April, 1839): 169-87

We proceed now to answer the ontological question started near the conclusion of the paper on the Eclectic Philosophy in our last

[15] [Ed Brownson's continuing review of Victor Cousin's *Cours de philosophie . . . pendant l'année 1818.*]

number; and, since ontology must have its root in psychology, since we must attain to the reality existing out of us, by a careful analysis of the facts which exist within us, we have thought it best to introduce what we have to say in answer to the question proposed, by returning for a few moments upon psychology, which we do by translating some appropriate extracts from the instructive volume before us, the title of which we have for a second time quoted.

"The last century was divided into two great schools—both exclusive, and both incomplete. On one side was the school of Locke, Condillac,[16] and their disciples; on the other that of Reid, Kant, and their adherents. The first considers thought or the human ME simply as a sort of reflex of the material world, incapable in itself of creating anything; the second considers it as drawing all its ideas from itself, constituting the external world by its own intellectual energy. A profounder analysis of the intelligence must lead, we think, to the discovery that the ME is neither the slave of the material world, nor its creator. Independently of sensation, which subjects the ME to the physical world, independently of the will, which renders it master of itself, there exists a *third* element, which has not been sufficiently analyzed and described, and which we may call the world of reason, regarded not as a faculty, but as the rule of our judgments—*reason,* which is neither you nor I nor any one else, but which commands us all—sovereign and absolute truth, which communicates itself to all men, but is the property of no man; in a word, the impersonal reason, which is neither the image of the sensible world, nor the work of my will.

"Locke, the illustrious chief of the school of sensation, gives no place, in the minute analysis he undertakes of all the intellectual facts, to necessary truths, truths which are not objects of sensation. He is indeed distinguished from his successors by the fact that he recognizes not merely ideas of sensation, ideas which come from without, *adventitious,* as Descartes calls them, and which are an effect of the external world, but he also recognizes a ME, a percipient agent, which perceives these ideas, appreciates them, and judges them. He belongs therefore, in some sort, to both schools. But as in his view the ME produces no idea, as it is a simple spectator of the impressions produced by the material world, a strict classification must leave him at the head of the school of sensation. Locke's ME being wholly unproductive, and as it were a sort of echo of the sensible world, is as if it

[16] [Ed. Étienne Bonnot de Condillac (1715-80) was a French philosopher who admired Locke and was instrumental in promoting sensationalism in France.]

were not. For myself, I deny, 1. that this ME can attain to all the ideas which are in the understanding; 2. that it can form a single idea even; 3. that it is capable of obtaining merely the idea of sensation.

"1. Locke's ME cannot attain to all our ideas, for it operates only on sensible, multiple, variable, and relative objects. Now it is an unquestionable fact, that our understanding contains ideas of the infinite, of space, of time, objects which are immaterial, simple, immutable, and absolute; but how deduce the immaterial from the material, unity from multiplicity, the invariable from the variable, the absolute from the relative?

"2. Locke's ME is incapable of thinking. Thought is always indivisible. Let any one descend into his own consciousness, he will be convinced that, in spite of the diversity of objects on which he thinks, the thinking being is ever one, indecomposable; that it is to the same ME that belong the beginning, middle, and end of thought; that it is the center in which all the rays meet. If you will give to thought a material form, that is, express it in a proposition, you will see that all the parts of the proposition are inseparable, and that you can take from it neither the subject nor the attribute without destroying its sense. Now if the ME be merely the counter-part of the sensible world, how can it give to that world the unity which it wants, and which is found in thought? I have the idea of an extent: what is there in this phenomenon? There is, first, the *I*, simple, undivided, and, second, in addition to this, extent, which is composed of a multitude of points. Now, how shall this multitude of points be embraced in its whole, in its totality, by a ME that is not simple?

"3. Locke's ME cannot attain even to the idea of sensation. In fact if it be only a sort of reaction of the sensible impression upon itself, never can this impression, extended, and multiple as it is, rise to the pure and indecomposable unity which is the characteristic of every idea.

"Thus the ME is not merely a reduplication of sensation, which receives the law from abroad without imposing it in return. It is active; it produces; it imposes unity on matter, or rather, on the material impression; it thinks, which is something altogether different from being shaken or moved. It rises to cognitions, which on all sides go beyond the limits of sensible objects.

"Condillac, who introduced Locke into France, went still further than his master. Locke attempted to set up a ME in face of matter, although he exiled it into a corner of the edifice as a useless guest; Condillac, forced by the rigor of deduction, banished it altogether. For the French philosopher the ME is not even contemporary with sensation; it is posterior; that is, it exists still less in his system than in Locke's. According to him [Condillac], men are the dupes of an illusion when they speak of a ME distinct from sensation. What they call the unity of the ME is the aggregate of several sensations; what they call its identity is the sequence of two sensations; and attention is only a sensation prolonged. [What prolongs it?][17] Before the first sensation there is no ME; it begins to exist only with the second sensation, or with the simultaneous occurrence of several sensations. It is an inert and dead element [. . .][18]; or rather, it is not an element, but a sum, a total, a collection, which can have no existence aside from the units which compose it. What then do all ideas which go beyond the reach of sensation become? Mere words, according to Condillac. Without language, he says, men would never acquire general ideas, abstract ideas, nor, in fine, distinct and clear ideas. It is not the mind that generalizes, abstracts; it is language that is charged with this labor. So the highest mechanism of the intelligence is only a grammar without a grammarian!

"The successors of Condillac [in France] have separated into two schools. Some, admiring the elegance and unity of the monument erected by their master, labor merely to polish it, and decorate it with the prestige of fine language. Others have attempted to restore to the ME the initiative of which Condillac had despoiled it. This had been to restore to the ME its existence, for the ME consists only in liberty. But in separating attention from sensation, they have not marked sufficiently the character of liberty, which constitutes attention. They have, moreover, confounded desire with the will. Desire springs up by necessity. I am not free to desire or not to desire. They have not, therefore, reinstalled the ME; they have not marked it with the sign which chiefly distinguishes it from the external world, that is, of liberty.

"The school of sensation has thus overlooked or misconceived two important elements which, in our view, are discovered in the analysis of thought; 1. the ME itself, without which there can be no thought; and, 2. necessary truth, which not more than the ME can be a product of sensation, or a sensation transformed."[19] . . . .

"We have given in our last lecture the history of a school to which the analysis of thought discloses only a single element, that of sensation, and which imposes upon itself the obligation of supporting, on

[17] [Ed. The question was inserted by Brownson.]

[18] [Ed. Brownson left out the following: "qui ne prend jamais l'initiative."]

[19] [Ed. *Cours de philosophie*, 15-20. Brownson had wrongly listed pages 6-20.]

this narrow basis, the whole structure of human cognitions. We have sought to demonstrate that the analysis of this school is incomplete. Sensation being only the reflex of the external world, and that world being multiple, sensation will also be multiple, from which it will be impossible to make a single thought come forth in all its integrity. Indeed, first, among our thoughts are some which are marked with another character than that of multiplicity; for example, the ideas of time and space are not formed from the collection of places and moments which we have felt: time and space are unities, or if it be preferred, simple totalities, which will suffer no dismemberment, and which are in reality undivided and indivisible. We may call these ideas absolute ideas, for they relate to no particular space, to no particular time, but to an absolute space, and to an absolute time; that is to say, independent, immutable, partaking in no sense of the relative or the transient. Sensation, on the contrary, is relative, variable, and multiple, and it is impossible to obtain the absolute, the immutable, unity, from these. Secondly, the humblest of all thoughts, thought taken at its lowest level, conceals unity. If we examine what we are conscious of in ourselves, we shall perceive that every fact of consciousness is *one,* that every thought is indivisible. If from psychology we pass to grammar, if we contemplate thought in the proposition which represents it, we are struck again by the unity and indivisibility of the proposition. Now, how shall sensation, which is multiple, generate this indecomposable unity, which is at the bottom of every thought? According to this school, the interior world is all absorbed in the outward; the ME is only a sensation rendered more vivid; or sensations bound together by an abstract and unreal bond; there is no center, no seat even for sensation itself; all thought is henceforth impossible.

"We pass now to the opposite school, the school which attempts to reestablish the ME in all its reality, but which, pushing the reaction even to excess, absorbs in its turn the NOT-ME in the ME. This school finds unquestionable proofs of the existence of the ME, not merely in the faculty of knowing, but also in that of self-determining, that is, in the understanding and in liberty. The intelligence ceases to be a merely verbal bond between intellectual facts, the will to be a mere collection of desires; both become integral and constituent elements of the human ME, or rather the ME itself considered in two different applications. We demonstrate neither the existence of the intellectual force nor that of the will; both are revealed to us by the immediate intuitions of consciousness. The reality of liberty has been oftener attacked than that of the intelligence; and yet the first is as much an object of the immediate view of the soul as is the second. [. . .][20] I produce a movement; I know that it is the ME that produces it; I give myself a sensation, I know that it is the ME which does it. I have the double perception of the effect and of the productive force; I know that I produce this effect, because I will it, and can refrain from willing to produce it, if I please. In vain you demand proofs of liberty from argumentation. This would give you a belief, not a knowledge of your liberty. When we say that liberty is the power of producing an effect, we do not mean that the effect must be a material one. The outward world may resist man, he is nevertheless free, only the effect in this case is purely spiritual—a volition, and man is reduced to internal freedom.

"The ME thus reestablished by the unity of the intellectual power and by liberty, can the new school obtain from it all that which the first school found it impossible to obtain from sensation? Can it make it produce the absolute, that is, those principles or axioms which preside over metaphysics, mathematics, morality, &c., such as the following; every phenomenon which begins to exist implies a cause; the whole is equal to the sum of the parts; reason should govern the passions,—principles which are regarded not as mere opinions, but as the expressions of the eternal reason, of immutable truth? Montesquieu has asserted that laws in their broadest signification are the necessary relations derived from the nature of things.[21] This illustrious philosopher has not said that laws are derived from the human ME; because in fact man does not institute necessary laws; he perceives them, acknowledges them, but does not create them. They have, then, an existence real and independent of him; in a word, they are absolute.

"Let us inquire, therefore, if the ME can generate the absolute. It can do so only in two ways. Either it will suppose it by virtue of its liberty, as a creative force; or it will suppose it in spite of itself, through the necessity of the forms in which it shall itself be imprisoned. In this last case the ME will be divided, for example, into sensibility and understanding. It will experience a sensation, and by virtue of cer-

[20] [Ed. Brownson left out the following: "Voici le fait de la liberté, tel qu'il nous est naïvement offert par la conscience:"]

[21] [Ed. Charles-Louis de Secondat, Baron de Montesquieu (1689-1755) was a French philosopher and political theorist who supported constitutional government along the British model. *De l'Esprit des lois* (1748) was his masterpiece of political philosophy, emphasizing the concrete circumstances in which freedom and law are realized in governing a people. See Book 1, chap. 2, for Montesquieu's treatment of laws deriving from the nature of things.]

tain *laws of the* ME, *or forms of the sensibility*, it will place this sensation in time and space. It will be the same with the reason; it will be able to act only under certain conditions, certain laws, which will be called, if you please, categories, and which will force it to consider all things under the point of view of cause and effect, of substance and mode, of unity and multiplicity. It is by these forms that we admit existences; by the category of substance, that we conceive of the soul and of matter, and by the category of cause, that we rise to God. But these forms being constituent laws of human nature, mere forms of the ME, they are *mine*, personal, subjective. We can, therefore, by their aid, conclude nothing of the absolute; truth becomes relative; I am under the yoke of an inward and personal necessity; I become a slave to myself; and unable to rise from the reason. You already see that we can legitimately deduce the absolute from the ME no more than we can from the physical world or from sensation. But after having in vain essayed to ground the absolute on forms imposed upon the human understanding, some members of this school have gone still further, and loosed the ME from the cords with which they had at first bound it, allowed it to suppose freely and at its own pleasure, the existence of the external world. Thus they have withdrawn the ME from the necessity which enchained it, and instead of representing it as forced to acknowledge existences, they have even dared pretend that it derives all truths from its own resources, and have also affirmed it to be the power that creates the world. The ME gives birth to absolute principles, and these absolute principles give birth to the external world. For example, the ME supposes the principle of causality; the principle of causality supposes God; therefore it is the ME that supposes God. Let us follow and shrink from no consequences. If the ME, in supposing absolute principles, supposes external existences, external existences are only the ME itself, and all existences are nothing but the different positions of the ME; so that we arrive at this formula, the ME equals ALL, ALL equals the ME. It only remains for us now to give the names to which the two systems we have just exposed are attached. The first belongs to Reid and Kant. Reid, embarrassed by the reasonings of Berkeley[22] and David Hume against the existence of the exterior world, establishes a certain number of laws of the understanding which he furnishes to the human ME as an escort, and which he calls beliefs, or principles of common

[22] [Ed. George Berkeley (1685-1753) was an Irish empiricist philosopher and bishop of the Anglican Church who developed an idealist metaphysical system to safeguard against skepticism.]

sense. The illustrious Kant undertook a work of the same kind, but with more rigor and method than the Scotch thinker; he attempted to render an exact account of what he calls the subjective forms of the intelligence.

"The second system is that of Fichte,[23] a disciple of Kant; still more rigorous than his master, whose system he simplified, as Condillac had simplified the doctrine of Locke. He retrenched the forms imposed by the philosopher of Koenigsberg on the human ME, declared it free from all trammels and the benevolent creator of the NOT-ME; and as there remained in the system of Condillac only sensation without consciousness, so there remained in the doctrine of Fichte only consciousness without sensation: and on one side, as on the other, absolute and independent truth was sacrificed. It is for the restoration of this essential element of human thought that the philosophy of our times must labor."[24]

"The two schools which divide the eighteenth century recognize in thought only a single element, the one sensation, the other the human ME. They impose upon themselves, therefore, the necessity of deriving all human cognitions from this single origin, and of making certainty repose on this single foundation. An incomplete analysis has conducted these two schools to an erroneous system. To construct the mind with sensation or with liberty, is to destroy the intellectual life, which is nothing but the opposition of activity and sensation. We may apply to intellectual life the definition given to organic life—a longer or shorter struggle of the internal force against external forces. In order that this struggle should cease, it would be necessary either that the ME should triumph over nature, which were to destroy the physical world, or that it should abandon the struggle, which were to destroy its activity. Man is at first only a physiological being [. . .];[25] his movements are those of material nature; but one day he reacts: it is then that he has cognizance of external nature. He is agitated for a long time in the bosom of the universe without knowing it; the world is no more for him than it is for a plant; but when he sets himself at work to move himself by his own movement, he supposes himself and opposes nature. Thus the ME exists only by combat; it is the opposition of the ME and of nature that forms the beginning of [intellectual] life.

[23] [Ed. Johann Gottlieb Fichte (1762-1814) was a German subjective idealist philosopher who tried to overcome what he perceived to be an inherent dualism in Kant, emphasizing the ego as the starting point of philosophy.]

[24] [Ed. *Cours de philosophie*, 21-27.]

[25] [Ed. Brownson left out the following: "il vit long-temps de la vie du monde."]

"But these two elements are not yet sufficient. Beyond the ME and physical nature there lies a third world, which we have called the *absolute,* that of immaterial and necessary truth, which contains the general principles of all the sciences. We have seen that this world had perished in one school and the other of the eighteenth century; in order to establish its existence, it is sufficient to bring forth to the light a single absolute truth. Be it, for example, the following axiom, every quality supposes a subject; we ask if anyone doubts this truth, and what would all human sciences become if it should be questioned? In morality can this principle be contested, namely, reason ought to govern the passions? We cannot enumerate here the principles of all the sciences; it would be to perform the work of a whole course in a single lecture; we content ourselves for the present with establishing the existence of a third element, which has been misconceived by both the schools of the eighteenth century. I lay down this axiom, reason ought to govern the passions. If no one contests it, I say here is an element which can be generated neither by the ME nor by sensation. To what origin, then, shall we refer it?

"The ME is active. It manifests itself, or rather, it exists only by activity. But this ME, free and creative, does not create the absolute, it opposes it. It is a fact; I do not explain, I merely describe. Can it be believed that these axioms sustain the same relations with the ME as do the movements of which it is the cause? If it be I who make these axioms, they are mine, and I can unmake them, suspend them, change, annihilate them. However, it is manifest that I am unable to strike them a single blow. Nevertheless I recognize that the absolute is not derived from physical nature, nor from sensation. It is neither pleasure nor pain; it is not an impression which I undergo, as I do joy or grief. I arrive then at this result, namely, what is called truth is in me, but is not ME. The error of Kant was in representing the sovereign reason and human reason as equal one to the other. Truth is independent of man; as sensibility places man in relation with the physical world, so another faculty places him in communication with truths which depend neither on the physical world, nor on the ME, and this faculty we may call the reason.

"There are then, in man, three general faculties: the first is activity, which is the foundation of thought, the resting place, without which man would vanish from himself, and reenter into nature and necessity. But although the ME is active, it is affected by the laws of the external world; it suffers and enjoys, without having itself provoked its joys or its sufferings. This is a necessity which wounds its pride, but from which it cannot withdraw itself. Sensibility is therefore also one of the faculties of the ME. In fine, beyond activity and sensibility, it possesses also reason, by which it attains to a world which it confounds neither with itself nor with the sensible world, and which makes its appearance in man, but which is not man. That which constitutes the human ME is activity. Let anyone examine himself at the moment a lively sensation is produced in him, and he will find that there is a perception only on condition of a reaction of the ME, and that perception ends the moment in which activity ends. We then, to avail myself of a just but common expression, know not what we do. Activity is the ground of the ME; and on this ground are designed sensation and reason, the one conducting to physical nature, the other revealing immaterial truth."[26]

There are some who object to this psychological analysis; and we ourselves objected to it, until we had attempted to write a refutation of it. Cousin makes the reason objective, and therefore by the very fact of its appearing in us, suppose the objective. But in order to make the reason objective, some have thought that he has been forced to give an inaccurate definition of personality. He makes the ME, or personality, consist in liberty or activity. Now, if we were not intelligent should we be persons? Does not the common sense of mankind make reason or intelligence an essential element of personality? If not, why do we regard those who are deprived of reason as irresponsible?

But this is not the main difficulty. M. Cousin, in making the reason objective, seems to deprive us of the power of knowing. The reason, he says, is objective—that is, exterior to our personality. We, as *persons,* then, are not intelligent. Now how can a non-intelligent personality come into relation with objective intelligence? If there be no intelligence in the ME, how is it to avail itself of the intelligence which lies outside of it? The sun may shine never so brightly, but if there be no light in us, we cannot behold it. Grant the reason is objective, that it contains all truth, and that it can reveal itself spontaneously, yet it can reveal itself only to intelligence. If it be objective, and, as Cousin says, the only source of intelligence, then there is no intelligence in us to receive its revelations, and it must be to us as if it were not.

It is possible that M. Cousin has not been quite so explicit on this point as was desirable; but while he has treated the reason as objective, he has been careful to designate it as one of the three fundamental faculties of the human ME, and there can be no question

[26] [Ed. *Cours de philosophie,* 28-32.]

that he regards the reason as an integral element of human nature, as much so as the activity itself. It is true that he makes activity the characteristic of the ME, or personality, not because the reason is not necessary to constitute us persons, but because in the activity there is nothing which necessarily goes out of the sphere of personality; while there is that in it which is, if we may so speak, the central essence of personality. The reason, while it is an integral element of human nature, and therefore presenting a subjective side, always extends beyond the sphere of personality, and presents an objective side. The reason is in us, one of our faculties, an element of our being, and we may, to a certain extent, use or not use it; but in its developments it is always governed by laws not of our enacting, obeys a power which we are not, and therefore necessarily involves objective existence.

Perhaps it would not be amiss to divide the reason into objective reason and subjective reason. By the objective reason we may understand the eternal reason, the immaterial world, the world of necessary truth which overshadows us, underlies us, and constitutes the ground of our intelligence—identical with the Logos of the Apostle and the Greek Fathers, the "inner Light"of the Quakers,[27] the word of God which was in the beginning with God, by which all things were made that were made, which inspired the ancient prophets, was made flesh, incarnated in Jesus, and is adored by the church as the second person in the Holy Trinity.[28] This view, perhaps, if carried out, would go far to legitimate the belief of the church in the Divine Sonship of Jesus, and to convince those who arraign the doctrine of the Trinity, that they are as unphilosophical as they are anti-orthodox.[29] In this sense reason is not mine, nor any man's. It is impersonal and absolute: and this is what the Quakers have felt, when they have relied on it as an authoritative teacher, and yet denied that they set up their own reason as the criterion of truth.

[27] [Ed. Brownson probably gained his knowledge of the Quakers from George Bancroft's (1800-1891) *History of the Colonization of the United States*, vol. 2 (Boston: Little Brown and Co., 1837), chapter 16, "The People Called Quakers in the United States." Bancroft's chapter was an encomium to freedom and the inner life, which were grounds for a democratic egalitarianism that was for Bancroft, and for Brownson, a key to American genius. Bancroft was a historian, diplomat, and Transcendentalist-like Jacksonian Democratic politician who was active in Massachusetts party politics.]

[28] [Ed. Reference here is to John 1:1-14.]

[29] [Ed. These references to the Trinity demonstrate something of Brownson's initial movement toward a more orthodox Christian view of God. Cousin's Alexandrian views were, perhaps, leading him in this direction.]

By the subjective reason we may understand—not as many do, mere reasoning, drawing inferences, which is a particular mode of exercising the reason—but our general faculty of knowing, that by virtue of which we are intelligent beings, capable of intelligence. This is the sense in which the word is understood when we use it to designate one of our faculties. But we apprehend that a careful analysis of the facts of consciousness would go far to identify this subjective reason with the objective reason; so far at least as to prove that our reason must be in immediate relation with the impersonal reason, that it is, in fact, as it has been called, "a fragment of the universal reason."[30] If so, the reason is at once objective and subjective, and the distinction we have marked is of less importance than it might at first view appear. But be this as it may, even the reason taken exclusively as a faculty of the human soul, and made as subjective as this fact can make it, involves objectivity, implies something which lies out of the sphere of personality. If we can be certain of anything, it is of the fact that our intelligence, in its development, is subject to a power aside from us, which we are not, and from which we cannot withdraw it. Though it be one of our faculties, the eye of our soul, we cannot determine what it shall see, nor what it shall not see. We see what we can, not what we will, believe what our reason reports as true, not what we will to believe. We see a phenomenon begin to exist, and we cannot but believe that it has a cause; we see a man carried away into deplorable excesses by the lawlessness of his passions, and we cannot but believe that he ought to submit his passions to the wholesome restraints of reason. There is then, in the fact of intelligence, the presence of something which we are not, which enchains our intelligence, which necessitates us, which is above us, and overwhelms us with its weight. This something which controls our reason, gives the law to our intelligence, must needs be out of us. That which can enchain, necessitate us, cannot but be exterior to our personality. The fact then, that we find our intelligence subjected to, and obeying, a foreign power, is conclusive proof of objective existence. The fact of intelligence then supposes the objective. We must then either deny the intelligence altogether, or admit the existence of something out of the sphere of our personality.

But to deny the intelligence altogether is no easy matter. It needs some intelligence to deny all intelligence. He who says he knows

[30] [Ed. One source of this idea is in Cousin's *Introduction to the History of Philosophy*, trans. Henning Gotfried Linberg (Boston: Hilliard, Gray, Little, and Wilkins, 1832), 128-29.]

nothing, yet assumes to know that he says that he knows nothing; he who really believes that he knows nothing, yet assumes to know that he so believes. He who doubts all things, doubts not that he doubts, or that he knows what it is to doubt. No man doubts, or can doubt, that he exists, for in doubting his existence he must affirm it. He who doubts affirms, of necessity, the existence of the doubter. No man doubts the intuitions of consciousness. Every man within a given sphere admits, and cannot but admit, the reality of intelligence. Every man, then, is *forced* to admit the existence of something out of himself. The fact, that he is *forced* to do it, is the best possible proof that he ought to do it; for that which forces must needs be other than that which is forced.

The reason, or our faculty of intelligence, being proved by its own revelations to be governed by a law not derived from our personality, carries us necessarily out of the sphere of the subjective into that of the objective. By detecting in the fact of intelligence the presence of an element which escapes our control, and which determines our judgments, we obtain the objective by a process at once simple and legitimate. The discovery of a legitimate method of passing from the subjective to the objective has, from the birth of philosophy, been the great problem with every metaphysician. The imperishable glory of having made the discovery belongs, so far as our knowledge extends, to M. Victor Cousin. In making it, he has done more for metaphysics than Harvey[31] did for physiology by the discovery of the circulation of the blood, or Newton for natural science by the discovery of the law of gravitation. We may assume for metaphysics henceforth the character of a positive science, and forever silence those who would regard it as conjectural in its basis, and useless or bewildering in its results. If there be any who would speak sneeringly of Cousin, call him fanciful or superficial, represent him as a mere "hasher up of German metaphysics," or as misled by an "optical illusion," we would point them to this method of passing from the sphere of personality into an objective world, and ask who has ever made a discovery of equal importance in metaphysical science; and if he, who has made it, does not deserve well of humanity, and to be held in lasting remembrance?

Yet in speaking thus of Cousin we do not forget that he has had predecessors, and that these predecessors have also a claim upon our gratitude. Reid detected an element of necessity in the fact of intelli-

[31] [Ed. William Harvey (1578-1657) was the English physician who discovered the circulation of blood.]

gence. He perceived that we are led to a belief in the objective, not by argument, by reasoning, but by common sense, by certain first principles of belief, constituent principles of human nature, as he calls them, which irresistibly compel us to believe in the existence of the material world and in that of the spiritual world. But not perceiving that personality consists eminently in liberty, and that whatever binds it or lays it under a necessity, must needs be outside of it, he represented these first principles, the necessity which controls our beliefs, as subjective, as inherent in the ME, and therefore personal. Being personal they could not conduct legitimately to the impersonal and objective. Reid was therefore condemned to turn forever in the sphere of his own consciousness, and never could succeed in refuting Hume and Berkeley, or in reestablishing the worlds they overthrew.

Kant, again, detected an element of necessity in the fact of intelligence, which he described under the denominations of forms of the sensibility and laws of the understanding, or categories, compelling us, on the one hand, to place every sensation in time and space, and on the other hand, to view every cognition under the relation of cause and effect, or substance and accident. But he regarded these forms and categories as subjective and personal. By their aid he could only proceed so far as to be able to say that we are, by the laws of our nature, necessitated to believe in the objective, but never so far as to attain to the objective legitimately. His error was precisely that of Reid. He failed to perceive that the characteristic of the ME, of personality, is liberty, and therefore, if necessitated, it must needs be by a force exterior to itself.

Fichte detected this error of Reid and Kant, discovered that a personality which is not free is no personality at all, and that it can be bound, necessitated, by nothing inherent in itself. But he was so intent on establishing the freedom of the ME, that he overlooked the fact that the decisions of the understanding are governed by laws not derived nor derivable from our personality. He therefore found himself unable to come out of the ME, and sunk into complete egoism. The ME became to him the universe, the objective became merely the ME projected, taking itself as the object of its own perceptions. Maine de Biran also recognized the fact that personality resides in liberty, and to the demonstration of this fact devoted his philosophical life. But being solely intent on maintaining this position, he, like Fichte, overlooked the element of necessity present in every fact of intelligence, and fell virtually, like him, into complete egoism.

These four great men prepared the way for Cousin, and facilitated his important discovery: Reid and Kant by showing that belief is determined by necessary laws, Fichte and Maine de Biran by demonstrating that the characteristic of personality, of the ME is liberty, and therefore that nothing which shall necessitate it can be inherent in it. This was much, and enough to entitle them to the profound respect and gratitude of every philosophical inquirer. Yet it was little more than amassing gold and silver and other materials for building the temple. A Solomon was needed to build it. Cousin followed them, classified their facts, admitted with Reid and Kant the element of necessity in the intelligence, and with Fichte and Maine de Biran that the characteristic of personality is liberty, and then drew the natural conclusion. But he saw what none of them did, that if personality consist in liberty, and there yet be in the fact of intelligence an element of necessity which governs it, that element must needs be impersonal and objective. Psychological analysis assured him that there is this element in every fact of intelligence, as we have seen; then the intelligence contains an objective element; then the objective exists; then we can pass legitimately from the subjective to the objective; for the objective is shown by the intelligence in every cognition, and to repose on the same authority with that of any fact of intelligence whatever.[32] This all seems so natural, so easy, and to follow so much as a matter of course, that we are tempted to question the merits of the discoverer. But so it is with all the discoveries of genius. They always seem to be lucky hits. But it may be said in revenge, that it is only genius that is ever favored with such "good luck."

We are now out of the subjective, out of the sphere of personality, the ME, and in the NOT-ME. We have obtained the objective. But can we go no further? If the reason be good authority for one thing out of the ME, why is it not good authority for all that it reveals? We have granted that we know something; but is it not the reason that knows, that perceives, within the sphere within which we admit the fact of intelligence? If we regard the knowledge the reason gives within a certain extent as incontestable, why shall we not regard all knowledge which the same reason gives as equally incontestable? The same reason which assures me that I exist, also assures me that no phenomenon can begin to exist without a cause, that the whole is greater than a part, that reason ought to govern the passions; and why shall I credit it in the one case and not in the others? "Why shall we admit the independence of the reason in one case and not in

[32] [Ed. After reading Pierre Leroux in the early 1840s and Vincenzo Gioberti in the mid 1850s Brownson would deny the possibility of passing from the subjective to the objective. On this see, e.g., "Leroux on Humanity," *Boston Quarterly Review* 5 (July, 1842): 257-322.]

another? Reason is one in all its degrees. We have no right arbitrarily to contract or extend its authority, to say to it, thus far shalt thou go, but no further."

But we cannot pursue our argument better than in the words of Cousin himself. We therefore conclude this paper with the following extract from Cousin's preface to the second edition of his *Fragmens Philosophiques*, which we insert from Mr. Ripley's excellent translation, in his Philosophical Miscellanies.[33]

"As soon as reason is reestablished in its true nature and its rightful independence, we easily recognize the legitimacy of its applications, even when, after having been confined within the sphere of consciousness, they regularly extend beyond that sphere. Reason accordingly arrives at beings as well as phenomena; it reveals to us the world and God with as much authority as our own existence or the least of its modifications; and ontology is no less legitimate than psychology, since it is psychology, which, by enlightening us as to the nature of reason, conducts us itself to ontology.

"Ontology is the science of being. It is the knowledge of our own personal existence, that of the external world, and that of God. It is reason which gives us this threefold knowledge on the same authority with that of the smallest knowledge which we possess; reason, the sole faculty of all knowing, the only principle of certainty, the exclusive standard of the true and the false, of good and evil, which alone can perceive its own mistakes, correct itself when it is deceived, restore itself when it is in error, call itself to account, and pronounce upon itself the sentence of acquittal or of condemnation. And we must not imagine that reason waits for slow developments before it presents to man this threefold knowledge of himself, of the world, and of God; on the contrary, this threefold knowledge is given to us entirely in each of its parts, and even in every fact of consciousness, in the first as well as in the last. It is still psychology which here explains ontology, but a psychology to which only profound reflection can attain.

"Can there be a single fact of consciousness without a certain degree of attention? Let attention be weakened or entirely destroyed, and our thoughts become confused, they are gradually dissipated in obscure reveries, which soon vanish of themselves, and are for us as if

[33] [Ed. See *Philosophical Miscellanies, Translated from the French of Cousin, Jouffroy, and Benjamin Constant*, trans. by George Ripley, 2 vols. (Boston: Hilliard, Gray, & Co., 1838). Brownson had reviewed this text. See chapter 3 of this volume.]

they were not. Even the perceptions of the senses are blunted by want of attention, and degenerate into merely organic impressions. The organ is struck, often perhaps with force; but the mind being elsewhere does not perceive the impression; there is no sensation; there is no consciousness. Attention therefore is the condition of all consciousness.

"Now is not every act of attention more or less voluntary? And is not every voluntary act characterized by the circumstance that we consider ourselves as the cause of it? And is it not this cause whose effects vary while it remains the same itself, is it not this power which is revealed to us only by its acts, but which is distinguished from its acts and which its acts do not exhaust, is it not, I ask, this cause, this force, which we call I, me, our individuality, our personality—that personality of which we never doubt, which we never confound with any other, because we never refer to any other those voluntary acts which give us the inward feeling, the immovable conviction of its reality?

"The me is then revealed to us in the character of cause, of force. But can this force, this cause which we are, do everything which it wishes? Does it meet with no obstacles? It meets with them of all kinds, at every moment. A sense of our feebleness is constantly united with that of our power. A thousand impressions are at all times made upon us; take away attention and they do not come to our consciousness; let attention be applied to them, the phenomenon of sensation begins. Here then, at the same time that I refer the act of attention to myself, as its cause, I cannot, for the same reason, refer to myself the sensation to which attention has been applied; I cannot do this, but I cannot avoid referring it to some cause, to a cause necessarily other than myself, that is to say, to an external cause, and to an external cause whose existence is no less certain to me than my own existence, since the phenomenon which suggests it to me is no less certain than the phenomenon which suggested my own, and both the phenomena are presented to me with each other.

"We have here then two kinds of distinct causes. The one personal, placed in the very center of consciousness, the other external and beyond the sphere of consciousness. The cause which we are is evidently limited, imperfect, finite, since it constantly meets with bounds and obstacles among the variety of causes to which we necessarily refer the phenomena that we do not produce—the phenomena purely affective, and not voluntary. On the other hand, these causes themselves are limited and finite, since we resist them to a certain degree as they resist us, we limit their action as they limit ours, and they also mutually limit each other. It is reason which reveals to us these two kinds of causes. It is reason, which, developing itself in our consciousness and perceiving there at the same time attention and sensation, as soon as these two simultaneous phenomena are perceived, suggests to us immediately two kinds of distinct causes, but correlative and mutually limited, to which they must be referred. But does reason stop with this? By no means. It is a fact, moreover, that as soon as the notion of finite and limited causes is given, we cannot but conceive of a superior cause, infinite and absolute, which is itself the first and last cause of all others. The internal and personal cause and external causes are incontestably causes in relation to their own effects; but the same reason which reveals them to us as causes, reveals them as limited and relative causes, and thus prevents us from stopping with them as causes sufficient to themselves, and compels us to refer them to a supreme cause, which has made them and which sustains them; which is in relation to them what they are in relation to the phenomena that are peculiar to them; and which as it is the cause of all causes, and the being of all beings, is sufficient in itself, and sufficient to reason, which seeks and which finds nothing beyond."[34]

We shall resume this subject in our next number[35] and hope to receive before then a third edition of the *Fragmens Philosophiques*,[36] which M. Cousin has sent us, and in which he has briefly replied to the objections which have been brought against his philosophy in Germany and in Scotland.

[34] [Ed. Ibid., 1: 68-72.]

[35] [Ed. Brownson did not resume this discussion, and after reading Pierre Leroux in the early 1840s he began to criticize Cousin's ontology because Brownson believed it was incorrectly based upon his psychology. According to Brownson's 1840 interpretation, Cousin did not escape the charge of subjectivism that he thought he had discovered in Kant's philosophy and which his own philosophy intended to avoid.]

[36] [Ed. *Fragmens philosophiques*, Third Edition (Paris: Ladrange, 1840). In 1829, the Scottish Common Sense philosopher William Hamilton published a critique of Cousin's philosophy of the absolute in the *Edinburgh Review*. Hamilton opposed Cousin's view that humans had the power of attaining a positive knowledge of the infinite, arguing instead that humans had only a negative knowledge because their knowledge of the absolute comes through that which was conditioned. The unconditioned was inconceivable according to Hamilton.]

9.

NORTON ON THE EVIDENCES OF CHRISTIANITY[1]

Boston Quarterly Review 2 (January, 1839): 86-113

As a contribution to the theological literature of this country, and especially of Cambridge, this work by Mr. Norton deserves to be well spoken of. Not perhaps because it offers much that is absolutely new, or that was not already known to theologians generally; but because it gives us in a condensed, convenient, and readable form the essential views of the respectable Lardner.[2] This in the opinion of all competent judges will be thought to be an important service, and well worth the some fifteen or twenty years' labor which, we learn from the author, has been devoted to its performance.

This volume is taken up with the consideration of the evidences of the genuineness of the four Gospels, and it makes it appear quite evident, we think, that the four Gospels, essentially the same as we now possess them, were in general use among Christians about the close of the second century of our era; and also that if they were not written by the individuals whose names they bear, it is nearly if not quite impossible at this late day to determine by whom they were written. Indeed, he makes it appear almost probable that they were actually written by Matthew, Mark, Luke, and John; and altogether certain that we have no means of proving that such was not the fact.

More than half of the volume is filled with "Additional Notes"; but of their precise value, we are not sufficiently versed in theological and biblical criticism, to be able to speak with any degree of confidence. If we have failed to profit much by their perusal, we presume it is because we are too ignorant of their subject-matter to be able to perceive the new and strong light which they, no doubt, throw on the important and difficult questions they discuss. From the author's

[1] [Ed. Review of Andrews Norton's *The Evidences of the Genuineness of the Gospels*, vol. 1 (Boston: American Stationers' Company, 1837).]

[2] [Ed. Nathaniel Lardner (1684-1768) was a British non-conformist minister who set about to reconcile the discrepancies in the biblical narratives. His work was published in the famous fourteen volume *The Credibility of the Gospel History* (1727-57).]

familiarity with and attention to the writings of a German, Credner[3] by name, a young man, scarcely known in his own country, we infer, that his acquaintance with German theologians is both very extensive and very minute.

When we heard that this work was announced as actually published, we trusted it would wipe out that suspicion of infidelity, which had long been attached to the author in the minds of some of his religious friends, as well as of his religious enemies; but we are sorry to say, that, to a certain extent at least, we have been disappointed. He bears the reputation of being a first-rate logician, and is said to surpass most men in the acuteness and strength of his reasoning powers; consequently, he must know better than others when he has made out his case, and done all that by the nature of his argument he is required to do. It is, therefore, difficult to believe that he himself can be satisfied with the evidences he has adduced, or that he is not well aware that his argument, taken as a whole and in all its force, falls far short of proving the truth of Christianity.

There are persons who believe that the truths of Christianity bear on their face a certain stamp of divinity, which the soul is capable of recognizing; that "the inspiration of the Almighty, which giveth men understanding" [Job 32:8], enables us to see, and know, and be well assured of the great truths of the gospel. To these persons the question of the genuineness of the four Gospels is a matter of comparative indifference. They have in themselves a witness for God, and may know the things whereof they affirm. With these Christianity is not a mere matter of opinion, but of experience; and they can speak of it as of something they know, which they have seen, felt, handled. But the author of the work before us, if we rightly apprehend his views, does not arrange himself with these persons; he does not believe that the truths of Christianity bring with them their own vouchers; nor does he believe that the soul possesses any inherent power of perceiving their truth, and of knowing that they are from God. Christianity with him is an historical fact, to be established by historical evidence alone. "A Christian," he tells us in a recent publication, "believes that Jesus Christ, his divine mission being attested by miraculous displays of God's power, taught us, in the name and upon the authority of God, truths which infinitely concern us." In order to prove Christianity, then, it is necessary to prove that Jesus professed to teach its truths "in the name and upon the authority of

[3] [Ed. Karl August Credner (1797-1857) was a German Lutheran theologian and biblical scholar.]

God," and that "miraculous displays of God's power" attested the fact that he was sent from God for the express purpose of teaching them.[4] The proof of these positions is necessarily in the main historical. If, therefore, the historical proof of these be insufficient, then the truth of Christianity cannot be established.

The truth of Christianity, on the ground now taken, rests on the word of Jesus as an authorized teacher from God; and the fact, that he was an authorized teacher from God, is to be proved by miracles, and by miracles alone. Two questions of some importance now come up: 1. Was the mission of Jesus actually attested by miracles, or did the extraordinary events recorded in the four Gospels actually take place? 2. Admitting these events did take place, do they or can they authenticate the fact that Jesus was sent from God as an authorized teacher of truth, and, therefore, render it absolutely certain that what he taught is true? Both of these questions must be answered in the affirmative before the truth of Christianity can be established; and answered too with as high a degree of certainty as we have in any case whatever—not with vague conjectures, mere probabilities; for it is not the probable truth of Christianity we want made out, but its certain truth.

Now this second question our author passes over in silence. We have found in those of his writings which have come under our notice, no attempt even to prove that miracles are legitimate evidence of the divine mission of the miracle-worker. He assumes that they are, and all his reasoning is based on this assumption. Yet was this an assumption to be lightly or inconsiderately made? It is only on the ground that miracles are a legitimate proof of the divine authority of the miracle-worker, that the genuineness of the four Gospels rises into a matter of much importance. That genuineness is only one link in the chain of evidence by which we establish the fact, that the miracles recorded in them actually took place; but if it should turn out on inquiry that miracles are no proof of the divinity of the mission of the miracle-worker, nothing would be gained by way of evidence of the truth of Christianity, though the genuineness of the gospel history should be established beyond the possibility of doubt. The genuineness of the four Gospels would then become a mere question of historical criticism, interesting no doubt as are all such questions, but by no means of vital importance to religious faith.

It is not for us to say that miracles are not a legitimate proof of the divine authority of Jesus Christ; but that they are so, does not

[4] [Ed. *Boston Daily Advertiser and Patriot*, October 15, 1838.]

appear to us to be a self-evident proposition. Admitting the extraordinary events recorded in the four Gospels actually occurred, how do we know that they were "miraculous displays of God's power?" What is a miracle? If we understand by a miracle—what the word implies—something *wonderful,* then everything which is wonderful is a miracle, and those events recorded in the New Testament, not more so than a thousand others. Everything, on this supposition, is miraculous, which transcends our comprehension, or which we cannot at once arrange under some recognized law. In this case, miracles are merely appeals to our ignorance, and so far as we can see, prove nothing but that ignorance. If we say with others, that a miracle is "something extraordinary," then every extraordinary event is a miracle; and the occurrence of some rare phenomenon during a professed prophet's discourse, would be a good and valid proof of his divine mission. If we say with others, yet, that a miracle is "something done in violation of the laws of nature," we shall be unable to determine whether a given act be or be not miraculous, until we have ascertained the whole of nature, and become certain that the act in question could be done in accordance with no natural law. Now there are few of our race who can pretend to knowledge so extensive as this. We do not believe that even our author's knowledge extends so far. For ourselves, we know but little of this universe in the immensity of which we are lost. We know neither the extent nor the number of the laws of nature. We know not what powers, hitherto concealed from human observation, may yet be discovered in man and in nature. Did we know more, we know not but we should know enough to know that what are usually termed miracles are as normal as the "blowing clover or the falling rain."[5]

But admitting that we can determine what is a miracle, it does not appear, at first sight, how a miracle can prove the divine authority of the miracle-worker. How can it prove that the miracle-worker speaks by the authority of God, and is therefore to be believed? It can do this only on the ground, that no being can work a miracle but by a special grant of power from God for that purpose; and that no one, to whom God grants the power to work a miracle, can possibly misconceive the truth, or assert that which is false. Now, how do we

[5] [Ed. Ralph Waldo Emerson, *An Address, Delivered before the Senior Class, in Divinity College, Cambridge, Sunday evening, 15 July, 1838* (Boston: J. Munroe and Co., 1838). Emerson actually says: "But the word Miracle, as pronounced by Christian churches, gives a false impression; it is a Monster. It is not one with the blowing clover and the falling rain." See reprint in Perry Miller, ed., *The Transcendentalists: An Anthology* (Cambridge, Mass.: Harvard University Press, 1950), 192.]

know that no being can work a miracle, but by a special grant of power from God for that purpose? We say *special* grant of power; for if the miracle be wrought by virtue of the general or ordinary powers which God bestows, it falls of necessity into the same category with any other deed or performance. Say you, no being can work a miracle but by virtue of this special grant of power? It may be so, but how do you know, or how can you prove that it is so? Are you acquainted with the whole range of being; and know you all actually existing orders of beings, superior to man, together with all their powers? You must know much before you can know all this, and consequently, before you can know that no being can work, what you call a miracle, but by a special grant of power from God for that purpose.

Moreover, how do we obtain the conclusion that a man clothed with the power of working miracles must necessarily know and assert the truth? By what dialectic law will you conclude from the miraculousness of my act to the infallibility of my understanding, and to the necessary truth of my assertions? Do you say that God will not confer the power of working miracles, without also conferring intellectual infallibility? And that he will never grant this power to one who will not tell the truth? In other words, do you assume the ground that the power of miracle working is in itself conclusive proof of intellectual infallibility and of perfect veracity? Is this ground defensible? If we may take the New Testament as authority, the fact, of having the power to work miracles is not conclusive proof of a man's veracity. Peter, we are distinctly informed in the third chapter of Acts, performed a notable miracle in healing the lame man;[6] and yet Paul tells us, in the second chapter of his Epistle to the Galatians, that Peter was somewhat blameworthy in his conduct; that he dissembled, and did not walk according to the *uprightness* and *truth* of the gospel.[7] Now, a man, who will deny the uprightness and truth of the gospel in his deeds, and dissemble his own convictions, has not far to go to deny the truth, or to assert falsehood in his words. If it be alleged that the charge, which Paul brings against Peter, is not well founded, it will not help the matter; for in that case Paul would be guilty of falsehood, and yet Paul was a miracle-worker.

Furthermore, it is no rare thing for men, even with the honestest intentions in the world, to assert false doctrines, or at best doctrines that are only partially true. Men do sometimes honestly mistake the truth. Now, if we may take the New Testament and our author for

[6] [Ed. Reference is to Acts 3:1-11.]

[7] [Ed. Reference is to Gal 2:12-14.]

authority, the power of working miracles, we have a right to say, does not necessarily involve intellectual infallibility. Nothing would seem to be more positively asserted in the New Testament than the fact that the apostles had the power of working miracles. Now our author in a work called Statement of Reasons,[8] published in 1833, labors at great length, and with much earnestness, to prove that the apostles, in some instances at least, misconceived the teachings of Jesus. "The conceptions of the Apostle," he says, "respecting our Lord's future coming were erroneous."[9] If an apostle who worked miracles could also err, as is here alleged, the possession of the power to work miracles is not conclusive proof of infallibility. It does not follow then from the fact that Jesus could work miracles that he knew the truth and could assert it, any more than it does that he must necessarily assert it, in case he did know it. Now, if miracles of themselves prove necessarily neither the veracity nor the intellectual infallibility of the miracle-worker, how can they, even admitting them to have been performed, authenticate the mission of Jesus, and so authenticate it as to authorize us to assert positively, without any qualification, that what he taught was taught by the authority of God and is therefore absolutely true? Is this a question which it was right to pass over in silence? The answer to this question is essential to the argument from miracles, and we cannot but hope that if, after the lapse of some fifteen or twenty years more, the author of this work shall see fit to favor the public with another volume, that he will give this question a full and satisfactory answer.

But passing over the difficulties thus far suggested, admitting miracles to be a good and valid proof of the divine mission of the miracle-worker, the question comes up, Did the miracles recorded in the four Gospels actually take place? Our evidence of the truth of Christianity, on the ground assumed, cannot exceed our evidence of the fact that the miracles by which the divine mission of Jesus is said to be authenticated were actually wrought; and our evidences of the fact that these miracles were actually wrought cannot surpass those we have of the genuineness and integrity of the history or histories in which they are recorded. In point of fact, they must fall far short of those; for the genuineness and integrity of a record do not necessarily

[8] [Ed. Brownson refers to Andrews Norton's *A Statement of Reasons for Not Believing the Doctrines of Trinitarians Concerning the Nature of God and the Person of Christ* (Boston: Wells and Lilly, 1819). The text was first published in 1819, but nine further enlarged editions appeared between 1833 and 1877.]

[9] [Ed. Norton, *A Statement of Reasons* (Boston: Hilliard, Gray, and Co., 1833), 300.]

involve its authenticity. Although we should prove the Gospels were written by the individuals to whom they are ascribed, and that we possess them precisely as they were originally written, it would still be a question, whether the events they record ever took place. But setting aside this question, admitting that proof of the genuineness and integrity of the four Gospels is also a proof of their authenticity; it is still true, that our proofs of Christianity can rise no higher than our proofs of the genuineness and integrity of the four Gospels. Aside from the gospel histories, we have no historical records whatever of the miracles ascribed to Jesus; and the truth of these histories rests, so far as the miracles are concerned, on the personal authority of their presumed authors. We can then, to say the least, never have any stronger evidence of the truth of Christianity, than we have that Matthew, Mark, Luke, and John wrote the Gospels ascribed to them, and wrote them essentially the same as we now possess them.

Now is it certain that Matthew, Mark, Luke, and John wrote the Gospels which bear their names, and wrote them essentially as we now possess them? Our author asks this question, and it is his sole object in the volume before us to answer it. He has made out a strong case; we have seldom seen the genuineness and integrity of the four Gospels more satisfactorily made out. The impression the volume produces on our mind is that the probabilities incline to the hypothesis assumed. But this is not certainty, and certainty, moreover, the nature of the case does not admit. The earliest mention of the four Gospels by name even, which has come down to us, is by Irenaeus[10] who flourished about the close of the second century, and consequently nearly a century and a half after the latest of the Gospels must have been written, if we suppose them to have been genuine. Giving all due credit to Irenaeus for honesty and intelligence, his testimony therefore cannot be conclusive, for he had and could have no positive knowledge of the facts he asserts. His testimony merely amounts to the fact that an honest, intelligent bishop and the church, so far as he knew its belief, about the close of the second century, regarded the four Gospels as genuine. This is much, and in all ordinary cases, where mere likelihood was all that was required, it would be sufficient; but in all cases where that degree of certainty is demanded, which every reasonable man demands in respect to his religious faith, it is quite insufficient. Beyond Irenaeus we have no posi-

[10] [Ed. Irenaeus (c. 130-c.200) was one of the first great theologians of the early church, the bishop of Lyons, and an apologist against the gnostics. His *Adversus omnes Haereses* was his principal work.]

tive testimony, and consequently, no absolute historical proof of the genuineness of the four Gospels. Their genuineness can, at best, be only a matter of inference, an hypothesis which offers the readiest, the easiest, and most probable solution of the problem of their authorship. This hypothesis may be true, and we by no means question it, but it nevertheless is an hypothesis, and one which we can never verify. If no one can prove it untrue no one can prove that it is well founded. Grant that it is more likely to be true than false, which is more than many of the ablest theologians of our times will grant, and it merely follows that Christianity is more likely to be true than false. If such and such things be so and so, but whether they are or are not we can never know assuredly, then is Christianity true. Here the truth of Christianity is merely hypothetical, not absolutely established. On our author's own ground, then, conceding him all that he can in any fairness claim for his own argument, he can be only an hypothetical believer in Christianity, which, in our judgment of the matter, is about as good as being no believer at all.

But, unfortunately, there is a heavy drawback upon even this hypothetical Christianity. This volume casts serious suspicions on the integrity of the four Gospels, and renders it not a little uncertain, whether we possess the genuine productions of Matthew, Mark, Luke, and John, even admitting they wrote Gospels, or memoirs of Jesus and his sayings and doings. Mr. Norton contends for the integrity of the four Gospels, and says we possess them essentially the same as they were originally written; but he is far, very far, from admitting this, when he comes to take them up in detail. The liberties he takes with the text are alarming; and he strikes out whole paragraphs, and even whole chapters. He rejects the first two chapters of Matthew's Gospel; renders doubtful the first chapter of Luke's, which he says "has something of a poetical and even fabulous character;"[11] discards, as interpolations, Matthew's account of the conduct of Judas after his betrayal of his Master, and of the rising of the saints at the crucifixion of Jesus. He may have some historical and critical facts to countenance his rejection of the first two chapters of Matthew's Gospel; but we are not aware of any facts which bear him out in his rejection of the other passages he cites, which would not equally justify him in regarding, as an interpolation, any passage of Scripture not to his taste. In calling an interpolation Matthew's account of that extraordinary miracle of the opening of the tombs, of the rising from the dead of the saints, and their walking about in the Holy City and

[11] [Ed. Norton, "Additional Notes," in *Evidences,* liv.]

appearing unto many, he pleads no historical fact, the authority of no recension, of no manuscript. He appears to reject the account solely because he finds it incredible. The miracle is too big for him to swallow. But if he may reject this miracle arbitrarily, simply because it appears to him incredible, why may we not reject the miracle of cursing the fig tree for not bearing fruit out of season; and why may not our temperance friends reject that of turning water into wine at a wedding feast, after the guests had already drunken as much as was probably for their good? Why does he not lay down some canon of criticism, which may guide us; give us some criterion by which we can distinguish real miracles from false miracles, and genuine Scripture from spurious? Much to our sorrow, he lays down no such canon, furnishes no such criterion. He proceeds, so far as we can perceive, arbitrarily, and calls whatever does not comport with his taste or his judgment an interpolation. What right has he to complain of us then, should we strike out all the miracles of the New Testament? Why may not he strike out the miracles of feeding the five thousand, of the extraordinary draught of fishes, of walking on the water, of raising Lazarus from the dead, just as well as those he does strike out? The authority for those he rejects is precisely the same with the authority he has for those he retains. Will he say those he rejects are unreasonable, and therefore to be rejected? Then does he erect his reason into a criterion of truth, and instead of establishing the truth on the authority of miracles, he undertakes to establish it on the authority of his reason, which is a virtual abandonment of his whole ground—a thing which, we apprehend, he is by no means partial to.

If we can have no better foundation for our faith in God, Christ, and immortality, than follows from what we have thus far said—and we have given to what we suppose to be Mr. Norton's argument altogether more weight than we can believe he himself, with his surpassing acuteness and strength of mind, can be understood to give it—we confess we see no good reason for believing religion is anything more than a splendid illusion. We trust, therefore, that we shall be believed, when we say that the extraordinary and comparatively novel ground chosen by him and some of his friends, on which to rest the defense of our holy religion, fills us with deep and unaffected concern. He and they tell us that the truths of Christianity rest not on the authority of the infinite reason, "a portion of which is given unto every man to profit withal" [1 Cor 12:7], and which John assures us "is the true light which enlighteneth every man who comes into the world" [John 1:9], but on the authority of the man Christ Jesus. We are to believe the truths of Christianity, truths which infinitely concern us, solely because they were taught by Jesus Christ who, they tell us, was an authorized teacher from God; and that he was an authorized teacher from God, we can prove by miracles, and by miracles only. Religious truth never springs up spontaneously in the human mind; there is no revelation made from God to the human soul; we can know nothing of religion but what is taught us from abroad, by an individual raised up and specially endowed with wisdom from on high to be our instructor. This individual we must hear and obey, because he speaks by divine authority. The fact that he speaks from divine authority, no man of himself can know. There is no divinity in man to respond to and vouch for the divinity that speaks to him from without. Man has no inward power to recognize the voice of God spoken by the mouth of his inspired messengers. These messengers, when they come to us from God, must bring their credentials, sealed with God's seal; and God's seal is a miracle. Hence the vital importance of miracles. They authenticate the mission of the teacher. Did not the teacher authenticate his mission by working miracles, we, alas for us! could not know whether he came from heaven above or from hell beneath; whether he were a teacher of truth or of falsehood! God has made us all the closures of truth, he proposes to make; and has sent us all the messengers he ever intends to send. How much then depends on the records in which are contained those miracles which authenticated the mission of these past messengers! Deprive us of the record of those miracles, or invalidate the testimony by which the genuineness, integrity, and authenticity of those records are established, and we shall be without God or hope in the world, plunged into midnight darkness, with not the glimmering of one feeble star even to direct us.

Now all the authority we have for saying that the miracles, the sole vouchers for these God-commissioned teachers, were ever wrought, is the record in which they are contained. Admit for one moment that this record has been impaired by the lapse of ages, or corrupted by the hands through which it has passed, and that it has been interpolated; its authority is gone, and all our proof of the fact that miracles were ever wrought, vanishes as the morning mist before the rising sun. Admit further, that this record is confessedly so corrupt that a modern critic may strike out at will any passage that does not comport with his notions and where are we? This question, as it naturally must, appears to have suggested itself to our author. "The objections," he says, "which have been brought against the passages examined may be new to many readers, and a suspicion may arise in their minds, that were other passages in Matthew's Gospel subjected to a like scrutiny, as great difficulties would be found, and their genuineness appear equally questionable. But after many years' acquaintance with this Gospel, as an object of study, *I have not come to such a result.*"[12] This we admit is much; but still we have no absolute surety that, although *he* has not come to such a result, others may not, and not only in reference to this Gospel, but to the others also. He rests the whole religious edifice on the miracles. Having done this, he comes along and strikes out two or three of the more important; his friend Dr. Palfrey,[13] who was reviewed in a former number of this journal,[14] follows and strikes out four or five more; he must pardon us, then, if we are unable to view this proceeding without deep solicitude; for who shall guaranty us that their successors in the Divinity School of Cambridge, or that some other professors of biblical literature, shall not come along and strike out the remainder, and leave the building without any prop or support whatever.

But conceding to historical testimony all that its warmest partisans can claim for it—and we certainly esteem it very highly in its place, and in relation to the ends to which it is adapted—we cannot help remarking, that the condition of the greater part of mankind, as to the evidences of their religious faith, must be anything but enviable, if there be not also another, a more immediate, a more certain, and a more available kind of evidence. The great mass of mankind have no access, and can have no access, to the historical evidence; and very few of our race can aspire to the degree of historical information necessary to appreciate its value. On this point we must be allowed to recommend to those who reject all but historical evidence of Christianity, to study the works of Jonathan Edwards,[15] a writer of whom we presume they have heard, and who, we will take it upon us to say, was one of the most extraordinary men this country ever produced, and one who would do honor to any country and to any age. He was the father of New England theology; and whoever would comprehend that theology must comprehend his writings. On re-

[12] [Ed. Ibid., lxix-lxx.]

[13] [Ed. John Gorham Palfrey (1796-1881) was a Unitarian minister, editor, historian, and professor of biblical literature at Harvard from 1831 to 1839.]

[14] [Ed. Theodore Parker reviewed Palfrey's *Academical Lectures on the Jewish Scriptures and Antiquities* (1838) in "Palfrey on the Pentatuech," *Boston Quarterly Review* 1 (July, 1838): 261-310.]

[15] [Ed. Jonathan Edwards (1703-58) was a Puritan pastor, theologian, and philosopher whose *History of the Work of Redemption* Brownson claimed he had read as a youth. Edwards' *Religious Affections* and his sermon on the Divine Light became for Brownson and others sympathetic to the "movement party" another support for their Transcendentalist religious epistemology.]

curring to his writings, as we have lately done, for the first time since our boyhood, when we read but did not understand him, we have been astonished at the wealth of his intellect, and the depth of his philosophy, and delighted with the rational and spiritual character of his theology. He had grasped some profound and universal truths, which are now almost for the first time finding their true place in our systems of philosophy; and if he still retained many errors as to his theological or metaphysical formulas, his mind stood in the front rank of the master minds of his day. On the point we are considering he says,

"Unless men may come to a reasonable, solid persuasion and conviction of the truth of the gospel, by the internal evidence of it, in the way that has been spoken, viz. by *sight of its glory;* it is impossible that those who are illiterate, and unacquainted with history, should have any thorough and effectual conviction of it at all. They may, without this, see a great deal of probability of it; it may be reasonable for them to give much credit to what learned men and historians tell them; and they may tell them so much, that it may look very probable and rational to them, that the Christian religion is true; and so much, that they would be very unreasonable not to entertain this opinion. But to have a conviction, so clear, and evident, and assuring, as to be sufficient to induce them, with boldness to sell all, confidently and fearlessly to run the venture of the loss of all things, and of enduring the most exquisite and long-continued torments, and to trample the world under foot, and count all things but dung for Christ; *the evidence they can have from history cannot be sufficient.* It is impossible that men who have not something of a general view of the historical world, or the series of history from age to age, should come at the force of arguments for the truth of Christianity, drawn from history, to that degree, as to induce them effectually to venture their all upon it. After all that learned men have said to them, there will remain innumerable doubts on their minds; they will be ready, when pinched with some great trial of their faith, to say, 'How do I know this, or that? How do I know when these histories were written? Learned men tell me these histories were so and so attested in the day of them; but how do I know that there were such attestations then? They tell me there is equal reason to believe these facts as any whatsoever, that are related at such a distance; but how do I know that other facts related of those ages ever were?' Those who have not something of a general view of the series of historical events, and of the state of mankind from age to age, cannot see the clear evidence from history of the truth of facts in distant ages; but there will endless doubts and scruples remain.

"But the gospel was not given only for learned men. There are at least nineteen in twenty, if not ninety-nine in an hundred, of those for whom the Scriptures were written, that are not capable of any certain or effectual conviction of the divine authority of the Scriptures, by such arguments as learned men make use of. If men, who have been brought up in heathenism, must wait for a clear and certain conviction of the truth of Christianity, until they have learning and acquaintance with the histories of politer nations, enough to see clearly the force of such kind of arguments, it will make the evidences of the gospel to them immensely cumbersome, and will render the propagation of the gospel among them infinitely difficult. . . . "We may therefore undoubtedly suppose and conclude, that there *is some sort of evidence* which God has given, that this covenant, and these promises are his, beyond all mere probability; that there are some *grounds of assurance* of it held forth, which, if we were not blind to them, tend to give an higher persuasion, than any *arguing from history, human tradition, &c.,* which the illiterate and unacquainted with history are capable of; yea, that which is GOOD GROUND FOR THE HIGHEST AND MOST PERFECT ASSURANCE THAT MANKIND HAVE IN ANY CASE WHATSOEVER. . . . But it is certain, that such an assurance is not to be attained by the greater part of those who live under the gospel, by arguments fetched from ancient tradition, histories, and monuments.

"And if we come to fact and experience, there is not the least reason to suppose, that one in an hundred of those, who have been sincere Christians, and have had a heart to sell all for Christ, have come by their conviction of the truth of the gospel in this way. If we read over the histories of the many thousands that died martyrs for Christ, since the beginning of the Reformation, and have cheerfully undergone extreme tortures, in a confidence of the truth of the gospel, and consider their circumstances and advantages; how few of them were there, that we can reasonably suppose, ever came by their assured persuasion this way; or indeed, for whom it was possible reasonably to receive so full and strong an assurance, from such arguments! Many of them were weak women and children, and the greater part of them illiterate persons, many of whom had been brought up in popish ignorance and darkness, and were but newly come out of it, and lived and died in times wherein those arguments for the truth of Christianity, from antiquity and history, had been but imperfectly handled. And indeed, it is but very lately that these arguments have been set in a clear and convincing light, even by learned men themselves: *And since it has been done, there never were fewer thorough be-*

lievers among those who have been educated in the true religion; infidelity never prevailed so much, in any age, as in this, where in these arguments are handled to the greatest advantage.

"The true martyrs of Jesus Christ are not those who have only been strong in the opinion that the gospel of Christ is true, but those that have *seen* the truth of it; as the very name of martyrs or witnesses (by which they are called in Scripture) implies. Those are very improperly called witnesses of the truth of anything, who only declare they are very much of opinion that such a thing is true. Those only are proper witnesses, who can, and do testify, that they have seen the truth of the thing they assert. John 3:11: 'We speak that we do know, and testify that we have seen.' John 1:34: 'And I saw, and bare record, that this is the Son of God.' 1 John 4:15: 'And we have seen, and do testify, that the Father sent the Son to be the Savior of the world.' Acts 22:14-15: 'The God of our fathers hath chosen thee, that thou shouldst know his will, and see that Just One, and shouldst hear the voice of his mouth; for thou shalt be his witness unto all men, of what thou hast seen and heard.' But the true martyrs of Jesus Christ are called his witnesses; and *all the saints,* who by their holy practice under great trials, declare that faith, which is the substance of things hoped for, and the evidence of things not seen, are called witnesses (Heb 11:1; 12:1) because by their profession and practice they declare their assurance of the truth and divinity of the gospel, having had the eyes of their minds enlightened to *see* divinity in the gospel, or to behold the unparalleled, ineffably excellent, and truly *divine glory shining in it,* which is altogether distinguishing, *evidential,* and convincing; so that they may truly be said to have *seen* God in it, and to have seen that it is indeed divine; and so can speak in the style of witnesses, and not only say, that they *think* that it is divine, but say, that it *is* divine, giving it in as their testimony, because they have *seen* it to be so. . . .

"There is no true and saving faith, or spiritual conviction of the judgment, of the truth of the gospel, that has nothing in it of this manifestation of its internal evidence in some degree. The gospel of the blessed God does not go abroad begging for its evidence so much as some think; IT HAS ITS HIGHEST AND MOST PROPER EVIDENCE IN ITSELF."[16]

This doctrine, which some few among us are putting forth with so much confidence, with regard to miracles as the sole proof of the

[16] [Ed. Brownson is quoting here from Edwards' *A Treatise Concerning Religious Affections* from *The Works of President Edwards*, ed., Samuel Austin, 8 vols. (Worcester: Isaiah Thomas, 1808), 4:243-48.]

divine mission of Jesus, and therefore, of the truth of Christianity, is, comparatively speaking, a recent innovation. It was unknown to the Fathers, who, we believe, never relied on miracles as the means of authenticating the mission of Jesus, or of establishing the truth of his doctrines. The Reformers discarded it, Luther especially. Edwards, we see, placed no confidence in it. The New England churches, in their doctrine of experimental religion, have uniformly borne their testimony against it. Experimental religion means an inward perception and love of the truths of religion, and obedience to their commands. All who embrace it contend for another source of evidence than that of ancient, recorded miracles. They contend that they can have from their own experience a firm persuasion and a well-grounded assurance of the truths of Christianity. This doctrine of experimental religion is the prevailing doctrine of the American churches. The immense majority of the people in this country, who profess to be Christians, profess to have an inward assurance, direct and immediate from God, of the truth of the Christian religion. And this is what is called "saving faith." All other faith is looked upon as cold, formal, without vitality, and unable to bring the soul into union with God.

That we have another source of evidence than the historical argument drawn from miracles, was taught by President Edwards, in a sermon on the Reality of the Spiritual Light, preached at Northampton, more than a century ago. In that remarkable sermon, he contends with great earnestness and force, that the soul has immediate intuition of the truth and divine excellency of the gospel. He describes the Spiritual Light to be

"A *sense* of the divine excellency of the things revealed in the word of God, and a *conviction* of the truth and reality of them thence arising. This spiritual light consists primarily in the former of those, viz. a real sense and apprehension of the divine excellency of things revealed in the word of God. A spiritual and saving conviction of the truth of these things arises from such a *sight* of their divine excellency and glory; so that this conviction of their truth is an effect and natural consequence of this sight of their divine glory. There is therefore, in this spiritual light, a true sense of the divine and superlative excellency of the things of religion; a real sense of the excellency of God and Jesus Christ, and of the works of redemption, and the ways and works of God revealed in the gospel. There is a divine and superlative glory in these things. He that is spiritually enlightened *truly apprehends and sees it*, or has a sense of it. . . . There arises, from this sense of divine excellency of things contained in the word of God, a *conviction* of the truth and reality of them."[17]

Edwards, it may be urged, did not regard this power of seeing, apprehending the truth and reality of the gospel revelation, as one of the original powers of the soul, but as superinduced upon the soul in the fact of regeneration. But this makes no practical difference. They, who regard it as one of the original powers of the soul, regard it nevertheless as an immediate gift from God. The light, they would say, is in us, but is not us; without it we could have no spiritual vision, but it is not *ours;* it is God's light shining in us. If Edwards should say it shines only in the hearts of the regenerate, they would say, in the hearts of the unregenerate it "shineth in darkness, and the darkness comprehendeth it not" [John 1:5]. Both admit the reality of the Light, the ability to see and know the truth; and, if we find this ability whenever we are disposed to look, what difference does it make, whether it be bestowed then for the first time, or whether it had been always possessed in our unconscious life? We are required to behold "the glory of God in the face of Jesus Christ" [2 Cor 4:6]; and Edwards would contend that all who look may behold it; and the others would say, those who do not look will not see it.

The doctrine opposed to this which is set forth by Edwards, and almost universally embraced by the American churches, is, as we have said, of a comparatively recent date. We are not aware that it ever received any very distinct utterance, nor any firm hold upon any portion of the church, till after the prevalence of Locke's philosophy, of which the author of the work under review is one of the few remaining disciples. Locke was a great and good man, but his philosophy was defective, and altogether unfriendly to religion. It denied the possibility of proving religion by any other arguments than miracles addressed to the outward senses, and in point of fact, it denied even those. Locke reduces man to the capacity of receiving sensations, and the faculty of reflecting on what passes within us. According to him we can have no ideas which do not enter through the senses, or which are not formed by the operations of the mind on ideas received by means of sensation. Consequently, we can have no idea of anything which is not either an object of the senses or an operation of our own minds. Now as the truths of Christianity are confessedly neither objects of the senses nor operations of our own minds, it follows that we can form no idea or conception of what

[17] [Ed. Brownson is quoting "A Divine and Supernatural Light," from *The Works of President Edwards*, ed. Samuel Austen, 8:296-99.]

they are, or what is their worth. Every consistent disciple of Locke must, therefore, conclude with Abner Kneeland and Frances Wright,[18] that as the objects of religion transcend the horizon of human observation, we can decide nothing concerning them; and that the words God, the soul, and the like, are mere words, to which the mind can affix no positive meaning.

That we are right in this statement may be historically verified, and an historical verification must of all others be the most acceptable to our author; indeed, the only kind of verification which we could expect him to regard with any degree of attention. France has for some time been proverbial for her infidelity. Yet France is naturally religious, much more so than the English nation, as her whole history demonstrates. Her natural tendency is to a spiritual philosophy. Descartes, Malebranche,[19] and Cousin are Frenchmen. Her infidelity is an exotic, transplanted from England. All the leading French Infidels, they who did the most to overturn the church and prepare the Reign of Terror were disciples of Locke and Anglo-maniacs. Voltaire was the first, we believe, to introduce Locke into France, where simplified and systematized by the Abbé Condillac, it was immediately professed by all the French philosophers.[20] And what in France was the result of this philosophy? In what did it end, when subjected to the free and vigorous action of the acute and logical mind of the French? It ended, as it must, in the *L'Homme plante,* and *L'Homme machine* of La Metrie, *De l'Esprit* of Helvetius, and *Système de la Nature* of d'Holbach.[21] In a word, it ended in discarding all the objects of religious veneration and belief.

[18] [Ed. Abner Kneeland (1774-1844) was an excommunicated Universalist who had renounced Christianity and eventually became editor of the *Boston Investigator*. Frances (Fanny) Wright (1795-1852) was a utopian socialist, editor of the *Free Enquirer*, and advocate for universal education and the working class.]

[19] [Ed. Nicholas Malebranche (1638-1715) was a French Catholic semi-Cartesian philosopher and theologian known for his doctrine of the vision of God and occasionalism among other things.]

[20] [Ed. Voltaire, the pseudonym of François-Marie Arouet (1694-1778), was a French writer and biting critic of French life. The most famous perhaps of the French philosophes who defended deism. He had a good deal of respect for English institutions and ideas, and helped to promote those ideas in France.]

[21] [Ed. Julien Offray de la Mettrie (1709-51), French physician and philosopher, gained a European reputation for his most famous *L'Homme machine* (1747), which aroused considerable opposition in Holland and France because of its materialistic and atheistic contents; *L'Homme plante* (1748) was equally unorthodox. Claude-Adrien Helvétius (1715-71) was a wealthy French supporter of the philosophical enterprise in France. *De l'Esprit* (1758) was his principal work, which evoked ecclesiastical and ministerial opposition for its dangerous heretical and sub-

And in what else does it, in fact, so far as logic is concerned, end in the mind of our author? Were it not for the miracles addressed to the outward senses, would he admit that we can know anything at all of the truth of the gospel? That we can have any sufficient reason for believing in Jesus Christ as a teacher of truth? In himself, he professes to have no power of knowing whether what a teacher of religion says is true or false. If he believes what the teacher says, it is on the teacher's word, because the teacher says so, and has worked a miracle to prove that he is an authorized teacher. He differs, then, from the French *philosophes* in no respect, save that he credits certain ancient writings to a greater extent than they did.

Moreover, to a consistent follower of Locke's philosophy, a miracle addressed to the outward senses can be no proof that the miracle-worker is from God. Assuming Locke's point of departure, that the mind is a blank sheet, and that all the objects of our knowledge are reducible to objects of sensation and the operations of our own minds, it follows that we can have in ourselves no power of apprehending anything distinct from the operations of our own minds but sensible objects. We can, then, have in ourselves no power of apprehending religious truth, of apprehending the glory of God, the divinity of Christianity, the binding nature of duty; for all these are neither operations of our own minds, nor objects recognizable by the senses. Now, suppose these things to be announced to us in words, even admitting we could comprehend their significance, we could not perceive and know their truth and reality. But suppose, while we are pondering them in our minds, there appears in the center of the blue arch, over our heads, a living form of more than mortal radiance, outshining the sun, as the sun outshines the twinkling stars of night; and straight from that form, in a clear and distinct voice, proceed the words, "I am God, the Creator and upholder of the universe; he who is teaching you is my beloved Son, whom I have commissioned to make known to you my will; hear ye him." And forthwith the form vanishes, darkness succeeds, the rocks rend, the tombs open, and many of the dead start to life. Here is a miracle, apparently as clear and as convincing as could be asked; and what does it prove? The messenger from God must bring his credentials sealed with God's seal, and God's seal is a miracle, it is said. Be it so. But suppose, as

versive opinions. Paul-Henri Thiry, Baron d'Holbach (1723-89) was a German-born philosopher who after his education associated with young French *philosophes* in Paris, becoming the foremost exponent of atheistic materialism, which he methodically articulated in his *Système de la nature* (1770).]

every disciple of Locke must suppose, that we have no *a priori* knowledge of God's seal, that we have never seen it, and have in our possession no fac-simile of it, how are we to recognize it when presented? Does the disciple of Locke claim to be acquainted with God's seal prior to its exhibition? Or is he furnished with a fac-simile of it? Alas, his fac-simile, when he produces it, is according to his own confession, "a piece of white paper."[22] Deny us then, prior to the exhibition, all knowledge of God and divine things, and the miracle can never prove to us that the miracle-worker bears with him the signet of the Almighty. The admission of miracles as a proof is, therefore, a gross inconsequence in a believer in Locke's philosophy.

The system of philosophy embraced by our author is as fatal to all sound morality as it is to religious faith. All sound morality is based on the recognition of a law which we are bound to obey. It is not merely pleasant, useful, or best for us on the whole to obey it; but we are bound to obey it; it is our duty to obey it, whatever may be the consequences to ourselves. Now this law is obviously neither an object of sensation nor an operation of the human mind. The believer in Locke's philosophy can, therefore, have no conception of it, unless he goes out of his system. We find no distinct recognition of this law in the system of Locke. Locke says, "Things are good or evil only in reference to pleasure or pain. That we call good which is apt to cause or increase pleasure, or diminish pain *in us,* or to procure or preserve us the possession of any other good or diminish any evil."[23] Evil is the opposite of all this. Now morality must undoubtedly consist in eschewing evil, and voluntarily seeking good. He, therefore, is the most moral who the most earnestly seeks to diminish his own pain and increase his own pleasure. What this will be, will vary with almost every individual. One thing will please one man, and another thing another. "Hence it was," says Locke, "that the philosophers of old did in vain inquire whether the *summum bonum* consisted in riches, or virtue, bodily delights, or contemplation. And they might have as reasonably disputed whether the best relish were in apples, plums, or nuts."[24] Let the miser then rob and plunder the widow and the orphan to possess himself of the gold he craves, if he find his pleasure in it; let the cruel imbrue their hands in their brother's blood, if it can gratify them; let the sensual indulge in their revelries, drunkenness, and debauchery, if they please. For says Locke again, "if there

[22] [Ed. *An Essay Concerning Human Understanding*, Book 2, Chapter 1, paragraph 2.]

[23] [Ed. Ibid., Book 2, Chapter 20, paragraph 2.]

[24] [Ed. Ibid., Book 2, Chapter 21, paragraph 55.]

be no prospects beyond the grave, the inference is *certainly right,* let us eat, drink, and enjoy what we delight in, for tomorrow we shall die."[25] So also says the author of the work before us, in his review of Mrs. Hemans' poetry in the Christian Examiner for January 1836.[26]

> Sapias, vine liques, et spatio brevi
> Spem longam reseces.
> Quid brevi fortes jaculamur aevo
> Multa?
> Laetus in presens, animus quod ultra est
> Oderit curare, et amara lento
> Temperet risu.[27]

"In the absence of religious faith this is true philosophy. If this life were the limit of our being, its pleasures and pains would be the only objects of our concern." And again, "If all human hopes were limited to this world, it would be folly for any one to act as if he and others were to exist forever."[28]

He who hopes to live forever, we presume, ought to be a man of an elevated and noble character; he should do justly, love mercy, walk humbly; visit the fatherless and the widow in their afflictions; weep ever with those who weep; joy with those who joy; love truth, virtue, goodness; and offer up ever to the Supreme Father the incense of a pure, grateful, loving, and confiding heart. In a word, he must love and reverence truth and justice, and devote himself unreservedly to the highest good of God's creatures, his brethren. But if this life be the limit of our hopes, the *opposite* of all this will be true wisdom. Our author is a wise man; and we cannot but regard it therefore as a truly fortunate circumstance, so far as the best "interests of society" are concerned, that he has hopes which extend beyond this world.

But even these hopes, in a disciple of Locke, are illegitimate. Locke declares positively that a "life beyond the grave" cannot be discovered by the reason,[29] and that it is a mere matter of faith, which

[25] [Ed. Ibid. Locke is paraphrasing here Isa 22:13.]

[26] [Ed. Felicia Dorothea [born Browne] Hemans (1793-1835) was an English poet who was a prolific writer. See "Poetry of Mrs. Hemans," *Christian Examiner* 72 (January 1836): 328-62 for Andrews Norton's review of her work.]

[27] [Ed. Latin for "Be wise, pour out your wine, and contract your hopes within life's narrow compass." "Why in so short a life do we in our bravery aim at so much?" "Joyous during the present hour, the mind should reject all care for what is beyond and temper what is bitter with a gentle smile."]

[28] [Ed. "Poetry of Mrs. Hemans," 337.]

[29] [Ed. Locke makes this argument in his "Reply to the Right Reverend the Lord Bishop of Worcester's Answer to his Second Letter," in *The Works of John Locke*, 10 vols. (London: Thomas Tegg, 1823), 4:476.]

can be made known to us only by an outward revelation, authenticated by miracles addressed to the senses. Our author agrees with him. But this authentication of a revelation, by miracles addressed to the senses, we have demonstrated to be impossible, if Locke's philosophy be true. No man who embraces that philosophy can indulge hopes of a future life, but at the expense of his logical, his systematic consistency. There is great fear, then, that he will lose them, and say, "Let us eat, and drink, and be merry, for tomorrow we shall die."

The system of philosophy on which we are animadverting is no less fatal to political liberty than to religion and morality; and the fact that many generous defenders of freedom in its broadest sense have sometimes embraced it makes nothing against this position; for their defense of freedom was a sublime inconsistency, which does them honor. This philosophy necessarily disinherits the mass. It denies to man all inherent power of attaining to truth. In religion, if religion it admits, it refers us not to what we feel and know in ourselves, but to what was said or done in some remote age, by some special messenger from God; it refers us to some authorized teacher, and commands us to receive our faith on his word, and to adhere to it on peril of damnation. It therefore destroys all free action of the mind, all independent thought, all progress, and all living faith. In politics it must do the same. It cannot found the state on the inherent rights of man; the most it can do is to organize the state for the preservation of such conditions, privileges, and prescriptions, as it can historically verify. "Locke," says, the author of the History of the United States, "deduces government from Noah and Adam, and announces its end to be the security of property."[30] His philosophy, if it decide in favor of freedom, can do it only on the ground of some contract, express or implied, made between the people and their rulers, on coming out of the state of nature into the social state. Its Magna Charta is preserved in the archives of state, not engraven on the heart, and preserved in the very constitution of man. Hence, the notion of a *Contrât Sociale* so famous in French revolutionary history.[31]

The doctrine that truth comes to us from abroad cannot coexist with true liberty. A democracy, in any worthy sense of the term, is

[30] [Ed. Brownson is loosely quoting from George Bancroft's second volume of the *History of the Colonization of the United States*. See the twentieth edition (Boston: Little, Brown, and Co., 1864), 378, where Bancroft asserts: "Locke deduces government from Noah and Adam, rests it upon contract, and announces its end to be the security of property."]

[31] [Ed. The reference here is to Jean-Jacques Rousseau's (1712-78) famous political work of 1762.]

founded only on the belief that "there is a spirit in man, and the inspiration of the Almighty giveth him understanding" [Job 32:8]. If the mass of the people can come to a knowledge and to the evidence of truth only as truth comes to them from a teacher possessing inherent or miraculous powers for discovering and authenticating it, which they do not or may not also possess, democracy is an illusion, a utopian dream; nay, an attempt against nature, to which every wise man should oppose himself. The democrat is not he who only believes in the people's capacity of being taught, and therefore graciously condescends to be their instructor; but he who believes that reason, the light which shines out from God's throne, shines into the heart of every man, and that truth lights her torch in the inner temple of every man's soul, whether patrician or plebeian, a shepherd or a philosopher, a Croesus[32] or a beggar. It is only on the reality of this inner light, and on the fact that it is universal, in all men, and in every man, that you can found a democracy, which shall have a firm basis, and which shall be able to survive the storms of human passions.

But the disciple of Locke denies the reality of this inner light; he denies the teachings and the authority of the universal reason. Truth may, indeed, by a miracle, kindle her torch in one man's mind, once in a thousand generations; but it is only as they borrow their light from him that the mass can ever hope to be illuminated. He may be a central sun from which light may emanate, but they must be opaque and shine not save as he shines upon them. It is folly, therefore, to repose confidence in the people, to entertain any respect for popular decisions. The disciple of Locke may compassionate the people, but he cannot trust them; he may patronize the masses, but he must scout universal suffrage, and labor to concentrate all power in the hands of those he looks upon as the enlightened and respectable few. He distrusts the stability and endurance of our institutions. He thinks we have made a hazardous experiment. The ignorance of the people is so great, the influence of the enlightened and respectable is so small, the passions of the multitude are so brutal, blind, and violent, that it is impossible that the experiment should succeed; and our Republic must ere long fall like Athens or Rome, and a despotism be erected on its ruins. His goodness of heart, his love of humanity may induce him to make no open war upon our institutions, and in some instances, to do what he can to give them a fair trial; but he works against his convictions, and hopes, if he hope at all, against hope.

[32] [Ed. Croesus, the wealthy king of Lydia in the sixth century B.C. The name is generally used to refer to a wealthy person.]

The history of the University, in which our author is or was a professor, together with that of her favorite sons, may tend to confirm this conclusion, to which invincible logic conducts us. That University, we believe, has not of late years been renowned for her reverence for the people, her faith in democratic institutions, or her efforts to establish universal suffrage and equal rights. We have not heard that she takes any peculiar pains to educate her sons in harmony with those free principles which are the just pride of all true Americans. And we do not expect that she will so long as Locke is her textbook in philosophy.[33]

Our limits forbid us to proceed further. We have commented on the method of proving Christianity, adopted by the author of the book before us, as we have thought the cause of Christianity, true morality, and democratic freedom required. We war not with the author. He has the same right to adopt his method of proof that we have ours; but then he must expect that it will be commented on, and rejected even by those who think it insufficient, inconclusive, or too bold and hazardous. We can only add that we have grieved to witness, of late, certain demonstrations of uncharitableness on his part towards some of our friends, and of a determination to check, by the use of hard names, and by severe denunciations, the free action of thought, and the bold utterance of honest opinion. In this he is inexcusable; for it is well known that the brand of heresy is and long has been as deep on him as it can be on any one else; and we presume that were he to recall somewhat of his past history, he would find that he himself has been guilty, if there be guilt in the matter, of the very charges he has recently brought against some of his former pupils and younger brethren in the ministry.[34] Perhaps he may recollect that he was once severely criticized for praising an infidel. He would do well, then, not to fill the newspapers of this city with too many denunciations of a young man who chances to say a good word for the poet Shelley.[35] The only wise course, the only consistent course,

[33] [Ed. Locke's philosophy, especially his metaphysical optimism, was still prominent at Harvard in 1839; however, the Scottish Common Sense Realism of Thomas Reid dominated the philosophy of knowledge and the moral philosophy of Harvard throughout the antebellum period. On this, see Daniel Walker Howe, *The Unitarian Conscience: Harvard Moral Philosophy, 1805-1861* (1970; Middletown, Conn.: Wesleyan University Press, 1988), 36-38.]

[34] [Ed. The reference is to Norton's attack on Emerson's "Divinity School Address" and upon American Transcendentalists in the *Boston Daily Advertiser* (27 August 1838).]

[35] [Ed. Reference is to James Freeman Clarke (1810-88), editor of the *Western Messenger* who had written favorably of the English poet Percy Bysshe Shelley (1792-1822) who some like Norton considered a moral misfit.]

for any man to adopt, who resolves to think for himself, is to respect the right to think for oneself in every other man; and this, too, when that other man comes to conclusions different from his own, as well as when he comes to the same.

For ourselves, we believe the method of proving Christianity, adopted by this theologian, essentially injurious to the cause of pure religion; but believing, as we do, that Christianity is seated in the heart of man, and is as indestructible and as immutable as his nature, we feel assured that it can survive the publication of all such works as the one we have commented upon; and that, long after they shall be forgotten, it will lead us to build the temple, erect the altar, and bring to God our Father a perennial offering of love and duty.

10.

LIEBER'S *POLITICAL ETHICS*[1]

Boston Quarterly Review 2 (January, 1839): 113-93

The object of this work, as indicated by the title and introductory chapters, is to state the principles of morals as applied to politics. This is the branch of political philosophy commonly called the law of nations. Dr. Lieber, however, expressly omits, *for the present,* any allusion to international law; so that it is not very easy to see what is to form the precise subject of the treatise. His remarks on this head are not very clear; but so far as we understand him, his intention is to point out the moral rules by which the individual citizen, whether in or out of office, is to govern himself in his political conduct, so far as it relates to the internal affairs of his own country.

This subject is, however, hardly entered upon in the present volume, which consists of two books, occupied respectively by treatises on *Morals* and on *Politics,* intended as introductory to the treatise on *Political Ethics,* which is to form the main subject of the work. The introductory matter in this arrangement is obviously of a wider and more important character than the principal subject; and we think it would have been more natural to publish the treatises on *Morals* and *Politics* as independent works, than to bring them out as preliminaries to the essay on *Political Ethics.* But a really valuable treatise on either of the former topics would be so important and acceptable, a present to the reading world, that we should not be disposed to find fault with it, under whatever form it might make its appearance.

The treatises on these subjects that occupy the volume before us are far from being entirely without value. They exhibit extensive reading and a generous tone of sentiment. These, we think, are the chief merits. The principles are of the liberal political school and make but little pretensions to originality, excepting, perhaps, in forms of expression, where the innovations are not always of the happiest kind.

[1] [Ed. Review of Francis Lieber's (1800-72) *Manual of Political Ethics, designed chiefly for the use of College and Students at Law*, Part I, (Boston: Charles C. Little and James Brown, 1838). Lieber was born in Berlin, Germany. As a young man he was accused of liberalism and was imprisoned. In 1827, he emigrated to the United States. He was professor of history and political economy at the University of South Carolina (1835-55) when he wrote his manual, which was adopted by Harvard as a textbook.]

There is a great want of the precision of thought, which is indispensable in an elementary work, and of correct taste in style. The language is throughout obscure, confused, and full of foreign idioms, besides unauthorized terms, in many cases avowedly coined by the author. In this particular he adopts the usage of his German countrymen, who coin a new word without scruple, whenever they think they have a new idea. We find no fault with this practice; but then we must remind our author that such innovations can only be justified by complete success; that is, the new word must be coined with so much skill and felicity as to recommend itself at once to the favor of the public. In such cases, which are, however, exceedingly rare, the public receive it gratefully, and adopt it without hesitation. Where a new word is coined without necessity or in a clumsy and unskillful manner, the effect is anything but agreeable. Of this latter unhappy description is a large proportion of Mr. Bentham's[2] coinage, and, we must add, of the new terms, which our author invents or adopts from others. As a single example we may mention the word *Catallactics,* which he adopts, without naming his authority, from Archbishop Whately, as a substitute for *Political Economy.*[3] "*Catallactics,*" he says," is far the best name that has been proposed for Political Economy."[4] This science, even in the most popular aspect in which it can be presented, is but too repulsive to most readers, and, if labeled with this formidable title, would, we fear, remain forever a sealed book to the million. We must say that we very much prefer the commonly received name. *Hamarchy* and *hamacratic,*[5]

[2] [Ed. Jeremy Bentham (1748-1832), English jurist and philosopher, whose writings stimulated the rise of utilitarianism.]

[3] [Ed. Richard Whately (1787-1863), Anglican archbishop of Dublin (1831-63), was in 1829 a professor of political economy at Oxford. He was known for his anti-Erastianism. Whately used the term "political economy" in his introductory lectures at Oxford in 1831, but he admitted he did not like the relatively new term and preferred instead to use the "more descriptive" term Catallactics (i.e. "Science of Exchanges") when treating of a nation's wealth. On this, see his *Introductory Lectures on Political Economy* (London: B. Fellowes, 1831), 6.]

[4] [Ed. *Manual of Political Ethics, designed chiefly for the use of College and Students at Law,* Part I (Boston: Charles C. Little and James Brown, 1838), 1:165. Catallactics, according to Lieber, comes from the Greek work καταλλασσω or διαλλασσω, meaning "not only to exchange, but also to exchange hatred, to *reconcile,* and what reconciles man to man, nation to nation, more powerfully and originally, than the exchange of their produce?" It is an exchange of labor, produce, service, capital and skills.]

[5] [Ed. *Hamarchy,* according to Lieber, is "that polity, which has an organism, an organic life, if I may say so, in which a thousand distinct parts have their independent action, yet are by the general organism united into one whole, into one living system." See ibid., 411.]

which come from the author's own workshop, are to our ears not much better.

The leading defect of the work from which the particular faults adverted to above appear to result is the want of maturity. The materials collected are valuable; the author's reading is really extensive and varied; but in his haste to make a new book out of the stock of information which he has collected, he has not given himself time to digest his facts, or to mature either his thoughts or his style. Hence the vagueness of his language in regard to the very object of his work, which, with a good deal of effort to explain it, he does not make quite clear to others, nor apparently to himself. Hence, too, the confused and outlandish aspect of the style, and the often loose and unsuccessful manner in which he endeavors to state principles, in themselves correct and true, in scientific forms. Dr. Lieber, if we are rightly informed, lectures professionally in one of the southern colleges upon the subjects treated in the present work. He is, therefore, very favorably situated for gradually maturing his conclusions and bringing them to the highest point of clearness and certainty, which he is able to give them, as well as for improving his taste and talent for mere literary composition. We should advise him, as friends, not to publish, at present, the other part of the work, to consider the publication of the first part as *non avenu,* and to go on quietly and steadily for some time to come, reading, talking, thinking, and lecturing, without any view to publication. Whether he would be able, under any circumstances, to give us an original, profound, and complete, in one word, a *standard* work on *Morals* or *Politics* we are rather inclined to doubt. But we are satisfied that by following the course which we have pointed out, he would be able, some eight or ten years hence, to publish a work much more substantially valuable, and much better digested and written than the one before us is, or, when complete, is likely to be.

An immature work, which does not contain the best results which the author is capable of furnishing, is, of course, hardly a fit subject for elaborate and extended criticism. We will merely add a few remarks upon the leading principles laid down respectively in the two divisions of the volume before us.

The treatise on *Morals,* which occupies the first book, is less extensive and complete than that on *Politics.* Our author adopts the theory of a *moral faculty,* by which we recognize the distinction between right and wrong, but does not clearly indicate whether he considers it as belonging to the department of the understanding or the affections. The principle which he lays down as the basis of natural law or morals is as follows: *I am a man: therefore I have a right to be a man.* This principle, if it were true, would form a rather questionable foundation for the superstructure of moral science since the precise question in morals is, what are the rules or laws to which I am subject as a man? Independently of this, the principle is in itself very doubtful, or rather obviously untrue. It is a particular application of the general principle, which forms the groundwork of the philosophy of the *Essay on Man*, "*whatever is, is right.*"[6] I am; therefore I am right. Is this correct and satisfactory reasoning? Is there no such thing as wrong or evil in the world? If there be, how can the mere fact that a thing exists, prove it to be right? If there be not, why take the trouble to write a book upon the distinction between right and wrong? Why could not the worst man in existence prove his *rectitude* in this way, just as well as the best? *I am a thief; therefore I have a right to be a thief.* This is just as strong an argument as the more general proposition, *I am a man; therefore I have a right to be a man;* or the still more universal axiom of Pope and Bolingbroke, *whatever is, is right.*[7]

Were the principle as true, as it is obviously false, it could not be used as the basis of moral philosophy. The law of nature is the system of relations established by the Creator among the individual members of the human race. The rights, belonging to individuals under this system, are the consequences and not the basis of it. I have a right as a father to respect from my children; but the fact that I am a father, is not the basis of this right. My right results from the general law of nature that fathers are entitled to respect from their children, which had its foundation in the will of the Creator. The fact that I am a father, does not establish the law, but merely brings me within its operation. So the President of the United States is entitled by law to receive twenty five thousand dollars a year from the public treasury. The fact that he is President brings him within the operation of the law, but the foundation of his right is the law itself, and this has for its basis the will of the people.

The treatise on *Politics,* which forms the second part of the present volume, is more full, and on the whole more satisfactory, than the one on *Morals,* but is, after all, far from being a thorough and finished work. The author's theory on the origin of society is rather obscure. He very properly rejects the idea of a state of individual

[6] [Ed. Alexander Pope's *Essay on Man*, epistle 1, line 294.]

[7] [Ed. Henry St. John, Viscount Bolingbroke (1678-1715) was a British politician, philosopher, and historian who supported Tory parties in England with his philosophical and political writings.]

independence anterior to the existence of society; but he seems, on the other hand, hardly willing to admit that society is the original condition. On this subject Cicero has expressed himself in the following terms. "Bees do not congregate for the purpose of constructing a honey-comb, but, being by nature gregarious animals, combine their labor in making a comb. And man, even still more, is formed by nature for society, and subsequently, as a member of society, promotes the common good in conjunction with his fellow creatures."[8] This appears to us to be sound doctrine. Our author quotes the passage, and rather peremptorily adds, "neither one or [nor] the other is the case." Now when Cicero says one thing and Dr. Lieber another, we are strongly tempted, not perhaps to apply the *malo errare*,[9] but to suspect that the Doctor labors under a mistake, which seems to be in this case a mistake in regard to his own meaning. The reasons by which he sustains his contradiction of Cicero are curious. "It is true," he says, "that man *is led* to promote the final ends of society, to move towards them, long before he is fully aware of them, but *he is not,* as has been stated, *instinctively gregarious, nor does he join society in consequence of reflection.*"[10] If then neither instinct nor reflection lead him into society, what does? Our author replies in the next sentence: "He is led to *do it* by his nature, physical and intellectual, which gradually unfolds itself with every step of progress he makes."[11] Now we are at a loss to imagine what is meant by the *physical and intellectual nature of man,* as the terms are here used, unless it be *instinct* and *reflection*. To us the two phrases appear to be identical in their signification. Our author, instead of being as he supposes at issue with Cicero, agrees with him exactly; and if he had known his own meaning a little better, might have spared himself the trouble of his somewhat unceremonious contradiction of the illustrious Roman.

Montesquieu treats this point more concisely than Cicero, and with more precision than Dr. Lieber. "I hear much said," he remarks, "about the origin of society. The whole matter lies in a nutshell. Men are born by the side of their parents, and there they stay. This is society and the origin of society."[12]

[8] [Ed. *Manual of Political Ethics,* 1:110. *Cicero De Officiis,* Loeb Classical Library (New York: Macmillan, 1921), Book 1:157, p. 160.]

[9] [Ed. Latin for "I prefer to err."]

[10] [Ed. *Manual of Political Ethics,* 1:110. No italics in original.]

[11] [Ed. Ibid.. No italics in original.]

[12] [Ed. From Montesquieu's letter 95 (94 in French editions) of *Persian and Chinese Letters* (London: M. Walter Dunne, 1901), 178.]

The origin and nature of *property* are treated in the same vague way. Considerable pains are taken to prove that production gives to the producer a property in his product; but the author does not feel that the only delicate question in this matter is *how much* of this product represents the labor of the individual producer and of course belongs to him. The individual is supported by society and his family, for ten, twenty, or, in some cases, thirty years, before he can bring out anything valuable. At this period he begins to produce. This product represents, first, his own labor upon this particular article, and, secondly, the labor of society and of his family, which has been employed upon him, and, as it were, accumulated in his person.

The society, therefore, and the family, of which the individual is a member, have the same right to their proportional share in his product that he has. It is the fruit of their labor as well as of his. Who shall make the distribution? This is done and can only be done by the society. The society, acting through the government, agreeably to general laws, levies, in the first place, upon the individual product, the proportion wanted for social purposes. The amount to be taken in this way is at her discretion. If necessary she takes the whole, and even anticipates in the form of public loans, the whole labor of one or more future generations. Society having taken her share, the rest remains for the use of individuals. But is this remainder distributed at the discretion of the individual producer? By no means. Society again steps in and determines by law the principles on which the distribution shall be made. To a large numerical majority, the married women, and the children of both sexes, she says, "you have no property in the product of your labor; it belongs, after deduction of the amount wanted for the public, to the head of the family." To the heads of families and the men of mature age she says, "The produce of your labor and of that of your family, if you have one, is placed in your hands, to be employed for your and their support, agreeably to fixed laws."

What then becomes of the supposed right of property in the individual to the fruit of his labor? It is apparent that the right of society is throughout *paramount*; that society possesses and exercises, under all forms of government, a discretionary power over the *whole* produce of the labor of its members; levying upon it at discretion, in the first place, the amount wanted for its own use, and then determining at discretion the principles on which the rest shall be held and distributed.

Society is, in short, a great joint-stock concern, possessing of right, and exercising in fact, under all forms of government, the power of disposing, at discretion, of the produce of the labor of all its members.

Property is the power entrusted to individuals by the society, that is, by law, of disposing to a limited extent, in specified forms and for specified purposes, of a part of the produce of their own labor or that of others.

Of all this we find little or nothing in the work of Dr. Lieber. He confines himself, upon this topic, to a labored argument in support of the proposition that individuals have an exclusive right to the produce of their own labor; a proposition undisputed and indisputable in the popular sense, in which it is commonly used, but in any strict and scientific construction of it, about as plausible as it would be to say that the individual operative who puts the last finish to a piece of broadcloth, which has been manufactured by the joint labor of perhaps a hundred workmen, out of materials and by the aid of machinery furnished by the labor of a hundred others, has a just right of property in the whole.

The nature and incidents of *sovereignty* are discussed by Dr. Lieber at considerable length. He defines the term as follows: "Sovereignty is the necessary existence of the state, and that right and power, which necessarily or naturally flow from it."[13] We are free to say that this definition does not seem to us remarkably fortunate. Indeed we greatly doubt whether, if we had read the definition without seeing the word defined, we should readily conjecture what it was. By *Sovereignty* we understand the supreme, that is, *the highest,* or *ultimate power* in the state, which controls all others, and from which all others are derived. Dr. Lieber is rather puzzled to assign the origin of this power. He says,

"If a man were to ask, in earnest, whence does this power flow, he could only be answered by a counter-question, such as, whence do you derive the right of *breathing*? He would answer, 'my existence is the self-evident proof of my right of existence, and in order to exist breathing is absolutely necessary.' The same applies to sovereignty. Absolute necessity gives in all cases sovereign power, namely, that primitive power, which supersedes all other, as it is its source. The crew of a vessel are in a state of mutiny; the captain has been killed; an energetic man among the passengers unites the latter and part of the crew with himself; he seizes the mutinous sailors; there is no possibility of subduing or preventing them in any other way from piratical acts. He tries them with the assistance of his fellow-passengers, and hangs them. He is right; and provided he can prove everything as stated above, he will be justified by any court, which decides according to strict justice and this alone."[14]

[13] [Ed. *Manual of Political Ethics,* 1:248.]

[14] [Ed. Ibid., 249.]

It may be true that the passenger is right, but the case supposed seems to us to be a very strange illustration of the nature and origin of the supreme power in a state. It is evidently a case of exception, and would illustrate more correctly a usurpation of political power under justifiable circumstances. The nature and origin of the supreme power, regularly existing in a state, are better illustrated by the authority of the master of a vessel over his crew and passengers. He derives it from his owners who fitted out the vessel. Societies, in like manner, derive their sovereignty from the power which created them, and established as the law of their nature, that they should have supreme and ultimate power over their members.

The volume closes with remarks on the different forms of government according to the usual divisions. Our author proposes a new division. If we understand him rightly, all states where the principle of government, whether monarchy, aristocracy, or democracy, operates *absolutely,* are to be called *autarchies,* while those, in which the operation of the predominating principle is controlled by other forces, existing within the community, are to take the name of *hamarchies.* England and the United States are, it seems, *hamarchies. Hamarchy* is, in fact, we suspect, little else than our old acquaintance *mixed government* under a new name. We are far from being certain, however, that we correctly apprehend the author's idea; for after laboring very hard through several paragraphs to tell what he means by *autarchy* and *hamarchy,* he leaves us almost as much in the dark as we were before. The nearest approach to a precise definition is the following. "*Hamarchy* is that polity, which has an organized, or organic life, if I may say so, in which a thousand distinct parts have their independent action, yet are by the general organism united into one whole, or into one living system." Again. "In the *autarchy* laws are made by *the power;* in the *hamarchy* they are rather generated; in the *autarchy* the law is absolute, after it has been made; in the *hamarchy* the law modifies itself in the application and operation. The political organism may prevent its action entirely, not by force, but simply because it cannot operate."[15] As we are rather friendly to "the supremacy of the laws," we should, for ourselves, prefer the *autarchy,* in which, it seems, the laws, when fairly made, are absolute, to the *hamarchy* in which their action is prevented, for the very sufficient reason, that they *cannot operate.* Indeed if *hamarchy* be a form of government, in which the laws *cannot operate,* we should question the claim of the United States to the title, for it is an acknowledged

[15] [Ed. Ibid., 411-12.]

fact that the power of the law, as such, is greater in this country, than in any other. At all events, we must say that we prefer the name of *Representative Democracy* to that of *Hamarchy*, as decidedly as we do that of *Political Economy* to *Catallactics*.

We would remark, as a deficiency in the present work, the almost total omission of any notice of the principle of *Representation*, the great modern improvement that has opened a new era in political science. The little that our author says of it appears to us to be erroneous. But this notice has already exceeded the intended limits, and we must bring it at once to a close, reserving what farther we have to say upon the subject for the appearance of the second volume.

3 (April, 1840): 137-66[16]

We noticed in a preceding number at some length the former volume of this work, and we then advised the author, before publishing the remainder, to keep his materials on hand for some years, in order to give a greater degree of maturity to his thoughts and style. We did not much expect that this piece of advice would be acted on, and are therefore not surprised at the early appearance of this large and thick volume.

We still think that the author would have improved his work in both its parts by keeping it longer on the anvil; but there are, nevertheless, defects in it which no amount of labor employed in polishing and maturing would entirely remove. The two leading objections to the work are the foreign air that pervades the language, and the want of any precise and distinct subject.

The language consists substantially of English words put together on the principles of arrangement and construction belonging to the idiom of Germany. The result is a dialect not only inelegant but at times almost comic; an effect entirely at variance with the character of the work. Thus, in quoting from a French dictionary a remark upon the employment of informers by the government, our author does it into English in the following singular style.

"The French dictionary says *ad verbum Mouchard* with much *naïvetè*. Those who have the misfortune to employ these abject persons, *believe to disguise their contemptibleness* by calling them *observers*."[17]

To avoid indulging in a hearty fit of laughter at the perusal of this passage would probably be with most persons in good health, what the execution of the order to slaughter the Protestants on St.

[16] [Ed. Brownson's review of Francis Lieber's *Manual of Political Ethics, designed chiefly for the Use of Colleges and Students at Law*. Part II, *Political Ethics Proper* (Boston: Charles C. Little and James Brown, 1839).]

[17] [Ed. *Manual of Political Ethics*, 2:333. No italics in original.]

Bartholomew's day was to Viscount d'Orthèz: *une chose non faisable*, or as our author has it, an *unfeasible* thing.[18]

In, the same way, in treating the interesting subject of woman, the author throws a comic air over the whole discussion, by employing frequently the German form, *the woman,* instead of the English, *woman's,* or *women.* If he were required to translate Schiller's[19] beautiful little poem, *Die Würde der Frauen,* into English, he would probably render the title, *The Dignity of the Women,* instead of *The Worth of Woman.* The different effect of these forms is easily seen by substituting one for the other in any part of the poem alluded to. Thus, if instead of

> Woman invites him with bliss in her smile,
> To cease from his toil and be happy a while,

we substitute

> *The woman* invites him with bliss in her smile,
> To cease, &c.

the effect changes at once from the serious to the comic.

Again:

> Woman contented in silent repose,
> Enjoys in its beauty life's flower as it blows.

On reading this couplet, the ear is soothed by the harmony of the language, and the imagination gratified by the beauty of the image; the judgment acquiesces in the correctness of the thought. The effect is a quiet, serene satisfaction. Substitute *the woman* for woman in the first line, and every reader, not provided with a diaphragm of adamant, bursts at once into a fit of laughter. So true it is, as Napoleon

[18] [Ed. Ibid., 278-79. Viscount Orthes or Ortez was a commandant at Bayonne when King Charles IX of France (1560-74) or his mother, Catherine de' Medici (1519-89) in 1572 ordered the slaughter of Protestants in the provinces. He refused to carry out the command. The actual quotation from Ortez is not exactly as Brownson has it and Lieber does not use "unfeasible thing" to translate the following passage: "Ainsi eux [i.e., brave soldiers] et moi supplions V. M. d'employer nos bras et nos vies à choses faisables." The quotation could actually read: "Sir, I have found among the inhabitants and the warriors only good citizens, brave soldiers, and not one executioner; thus, they and I together beg your majesty to use our arms and our lives for things that can be done." On this whole episode, see Théodore Agrippa d'Aubigné's *Histoire universale,* book 6, chap. 5; 3.]

[19] [Ed. Johann Christoph Friedrich von Schiller (1759-1805) was a German historian, poet, and playwright who participated in the Romantic movement in Germany. He was famous for writing a number of *Sturm und Drang* ("storm and stress") verse and plays, his *An die Freude* (Ode to Joy) that Beethoven set to music, and his historical drama *Maria Stuart.*]

remarked, that there is only one step from the sublime, and we may add the pathetic, to the ridiculous. *Du sublime au ridicule il n'y a qu'un pas.*

When Frederic the Unique attempted to write French poetry, he took the precaution to put it into the hands of Voltaire for correction before he published it. Voltaire was accustomed to describe the operation, which he performed upon it, under the figure of *washing the king's soiled linen.*[20] The wits of Paris remarked at the time, that Voltaire did not do his work thoroughly, and that he should have passed the royal linen through *two or three more waters.* Dr. Lieber, we believe, submits his lucubrations to a similar process; and if he must publish in a language, which he really does not and probably never will write with either correctness or elegance, he is perfectly right in so doing; but we must in conscience say to him that the literary washerwomen, whom he employs, slight their work at least as much as Voltaire did his, and do not give him his money's worth.

Take for another example the following precious specimen of the Babylonish. In speaking of the employment, by the Pope and the Cardinals, of their family connections, a practice commonly designated under the name of *Nepotism,* Dr. Lieber remarks:

"The crime and plunder which was [were] connected with nepotism, is [are] appalling: state property was alienated and changed into hereditary principalities for the *Nepots.*"[21]

The introduction of railroads has recently enriched our language with the French word *depôt,* which is commonly pronounced with a full enunciation of every letter, so as to form a complete double rhyme with *tea-pot.* We cannot but congratulate our poetical friends upon the acquisition of another new word of precisely the same form which will supply them, if necessary, with materials for a triplet, founded on this most delectable "concord of sweet sounds."[22]

In good earnest, why should not Dr. Lieber either write his works in German, of which he is probably a master, and have them fairly translated into English, or if he prefer writing them in English himself, wait until he has acquired the command of our idiom, which at present he certainly has not, but with a few years more usage probably might have? We entertain no other than the most friendly intentions when we seriously advise him, as we did before, to refrain from, publishing for the present, and give himself more time to mature his thoughts and his language.

[20] [Ed. Reference is to Friedrich der Einzige, i.e., Frederick II, Frederick the Great (1712-86), king of Prussia (1840-86) and an enlightened absolute monarch.]

[21] [Ed. *Manual of Political Ethics*, 2:139.]

[22] [Ed. Shakespeare, *Merchant of Venice*, Act 5, Scene 1.]

So much for the style of the work before us, which in all books, and especially in a book intended chiefly for the use of students in schools and colleges, is a matter of no small importance. Buffon[23] said that *style was the whole man*; meaning probably that a man's style is a complete index to his whole intellectual and moral character. However this may be, and we must own that we do not adopt implicitly this opinion of the eloquent naturalist, we may well say that for popular effect at least, *the style is the whole book.* The soundest reasoning, unless recommended by an agreeable style, fails of effect because it is not read.

The other objection to the present work, which we mentioned at the outset, is of a more substantial character, and lies in this, that it has no precise and well defined subject.

Ethics, as the science of morals—in common parlance, moral philosophy—admits of two great divisions, which treat respectively of the conduct of nations and of that of individuals. The former is commonly called the law of nations, and is what we should naturally expect to find in a work entitled *Political Ethics.* This whole division of ethics, however, our author expressly excludes, reserving it perhaps for a separate treatise. The other division, which prescribes rules for the private conduct of individuals, is of course foreign to the subject. What then remains to occupy these two thick volumes? The author himself seems to have been rather at a loss to solve this question, and has foraged far and wide to collect materials. The first volume, as we have seen in our notice of it, is wholly introductory, and contains two distinct treatises on the great subjects of morals and politics, each much more important in itself than that of *political ethics,* on any natural explanation of the terms, can well be supposed to be. In the second volume, now before us, and which comprehends the principal work, the author seems to have had on his mind, as a subject, the conduct of the individual in matters connected with government. But this is a quite narrow, if not wholly barren field of discussion. The individual, as a member of the community, may act either in a public or a private capacity; may be either in or out of office. In the former case he represents the state, and his conduct is governed by the law of nature and nations; in the latter, he has no concern with the state but to obey the laws. This single phrase, obey the laws, seems to constitute of itself the whole code of political ethics, as the term is explained by our author.

[23] [Ed. George Louis Leclerc, comte de Buffon (1707-88), was a French naturalist and author of the famous *Discours sur le style* (1753), which he delivered on his reception into the French Academy.]

We find, accordingly, as we should expect, that this second volume is made up substantially, like the former, of a series of digressions. Thus we have a succession of chapters on perseverance, moderation, ambition, gratitude, and continence, or, as our author prefers to call it, *continency*. Friendship and love find their place. Education and religion are severally discussed. *The Woman* has a section of her own. All these topics belong to the department of morals. On the other hand, we have a number of chapters which treat of subjects belonging properly to politics or law, such as those on representative government, on war, on the right of instruction, on parties, on the liberty of the press, and on juries. The author endeavors to connect these foreign topics in a loose way with what he proposes as his immediate subject. Thus he begins the chapter on continence by remarking, that "Continency, a virtue demanded by all moral systems and all the purer religions, is an element of great importance under a civil point of view."[24] The development of this text makes up the chapter, which consists of twenty or thirty pages. In the same way ambition, gratitude, friendship, love, and *The Woman*, are brought within the sphere of *Political* ethics. All this shows very clearly the want in the author of a distinct and precise conception of his subject. The two great divisions of ethics, as we have remarked above, prescribe respectively the proper rules of conduct for the individual, considered in a political and in a private capacity. A steady observance of the rules applicable to either of these departments will, no doubt, render the individual more useful in the other. An upright judge will be, as such, a more valuable citizen than he otherwise would have been, because his station will give his good example a wider influence. In the same way a temperate citizen will make, other qualifications being the same, a better judge, general, or ambassador, than a drunkard. But this consideration can have no effect in determining what the rules are that belong respectively to these departments of conduct. The obligation, not to be a drunkard is common to the judge and the general, with all the other citizens. When we inquire into the duties that devolve upon him in his public capacity, or generally when we inquire into the political duties of the citizen, we leave out of view the merely private virtues as foreign to the subject. The dissertations on continency and on the physiology of *the woman*, are as much out of place in the work before us, as they would be in Burn's Justice of

[24] [Ed. *Manual of Political Ethics*, 2:177.]

the Peace, or Vattel's Treatise on the Law of Nature and Nations.[25] On the other hand, the chapters that treat on subjects belonging directly to politics, such as those on the liberty of the press, and on representative government, are still more obviously out of place, all such topics being previously excluded by the author himself in laying out his plan. Thus if all the irrelevant matter were stricken out there would in fact be nothing left in the book.

If the materials with which we are furnished in the present volume were of real value, we should object less than we have done to the form. Unfortunately this is not the case. In this respect, the essential characteristics of the present volume are the same as those of the former one. It evinces extensive reading, but no power of methodical arrangement, or correct, precise, and original thought. It conveys of course no real instruction. We deem it unnecessary to go over the contents in detail, but will advert particularly to one or two of the more important passages.

In noticing the former volume, we pointed out, as an omission in the treatise on politics, the absence of anything like a complete discussion of the great modern invention of *representative government,* and added that, in the little which he had said upon the subject, the author had mistaken its character. In the present volume, where such a discussion is out of place, he has treated the subject in several chapters, adhering to the same erroneous principles which he had professed before. We cannot of course enlarge upon this great topic within the narrow limits now remaining to us, but will add a few remarks upon our author's views.

The system of representative democracy, as exemplified in the political institutions of the United States, has been pronounced by one of the greatest writers and statesmen of modern Europe (M. de Chateaubriand),[26] to be the most brilliant scientific discovery of modern times. The virtue of it lies in reconciling the possibility of free government with the security from foreign conquest and sudden internal commotion that can be enjoyed only in large states. Com-

[25] [Ed. References are to Richard Burn (1709-85), an Anglican clergyman and justice of the peace for Westmorland and Cumberland, as well as chancellor of the diocese of Carlisle. He was author of *The Justice of the Peace and Parish Officer* (1755, and many subsequent editions), and he edited three volumes of *Blackstone.* Emerich de Vattel (1714-67) was a Swiss philosopher and jurist who was famous for his *Droit de gens; ou, Principes de la loi naturelle appliqués á la conduite et aux affaires de nations et de souverains* (1758; trans. *Law of Nations,* 1760).]

[26] [Ed. François René Chateaubriand (1768-1848) was a powerful French Catholic Romantic writer and a politician of the restoration in France.]

munities which govern themselves on the democratic principle, and without the aid of representation, must be very limited in extent, and are of course liable to be swept away by the first invader, or destroyed by any accidental domestic convulsion. Such has been in fact the fate of all the free states of ancient and modern times without exception. Such communities have and can have neither stability nor independence. By the aid of representation, the forms and principles of democracy may be spread over regions of indefinite extent, and sustained by resources which the mightiest neighbors are compelled to respect.

This explanation of the leading idea in the system of representative government, which we suppose to be the one generally received, is too simple to satisfy our author. He treats the subject in the following superior style.

"If we resort to representatives only because we cannot any longer meet in the market ourselves, the whole representative system amounts to nothing more than a *second hand* contrivance; something which may be good enough, and with which we must put up since we cannot any longer have the true and essential thing itself, the ancient, pure, real, and visible market democracy; a political *pis-aller*; something indirect and circuitous."[27]

This is a precious specimen of the figure of speech commonly called *nonsense.* We employ a lever or a pulley to raise a weight which we cannot lift with our hands. Does this prove that levers and pulleys are *second-hand contrivances?* We make use of a telescope to see a distant object which we cannot discern with the unassisted eye. Does this show that the telescope is an optical *pis-aller*?

In pursuing the subject, our author inquires with equal sagacity why, if representative government be a mere substitute for pure democracy, we do not at once reject the former, and return to the latter? Why not split into a number of city-states again?

This is about as wise a question as it would be to ask why, since the telescope is a mere substitute for the naked eye, we do not at once reject the telescope, and return to the simple, unassisted vision. In the same way we might ask why, if forks be a mere substitute for fingers, we do not at once abandon the use of the modern invention, and like the Eastern nations, plunge our five digits at once into the dish? Representative democracy is a great practical improvement on *simple*, or as our author prefers to call it *market*, democracy, so great an improvement that it has been regarded as the most remarkable

[27] [Ed. *Manual of Political Ethics,* 2:488-89.]

modern discovery, not merely in politics, but in science at large. Our author, when informed of this, gravely inquires why, if representative democracy be a mere improvement upon a former system, we do not at once reject it and return to the old and exploded method? Such a question carries of course its own answer, and we may add, its own commentary with it.

As our author rejects the common theory of representative government, we feel some curiosity to know what his views are. Unfortunately his manner of explaining himself on this, as on all other parts of his work, is extremely vague, and he does not succeed in making his ideas at all clear. The nearest approach to a distinct and tangible statement is in the following passage.

"By the representative system, we obtain these two advantages. We restrict the impulse of the mass which is inherent to the mass as such, [. . .] and we avoid the being ruled by one leader as the Athenians in the latter portion of their history always were. We the people, therefore, are not absent from the legislative halls because for local reasons we cannot be there, but because we ought not to be there as people, as mass; for the same reason that in monarchies the king is not allowed to be present in the halls of justice, or as the legislators cannot debate in the presence of the monarch. In both cases the reason is the same. The prince, that is, the power holder, [. . .] must be limited and circumscribed by law," &c.[28]

It is hardly necessary to insist upon the incorrectness of these ideas. So far is the law in a representative or any other government from being intended to restrict the prince, taking, this term as a general name for the law-giving power, that it is the expression of his will. The law is not intended to act at all upon the law-giving power. Its action is upon the individual. In this country the state is not only not restricted by law, but is expressly exempted by the Constitution from liability to any legal process. "We the People" not only have a right "to be in the legislative halls," that is, to make the law which is to govern us in our individual capacity, but we are the only rightful law-giving power. If the community is not to make the law for itself, by whom shall it be made? By some other community? By some one or more privileged families? Or, in Mr. Jefferson's language, have we found angels in the shape of kings to make the law for us?[29]

[28] [Ed. Ibid., 508.]

[29] [Ed. The reference is to Jefferson's first inaugural address, March 4, 1801: "Or have we found angels in the form of kings to govern him?" See *Inaugural addresses of the Presidents of the United States from George Washington 1789 to George Bush 1989* (Washington: United States Government Printing Office, 1989), 15.]

So much for one of the two supposed advantages of a representative government. The other is equally questionable. "We avoid," says the author, "the being ruled by one leader, as the Athenians in the latter portion of their history always were." How does this appear? We see no reason why "one leader" may not exercise a decided preponderance in a representative body, as well as in a purely popular one. Experience is in fact directly opposed to our author's view. There are usually in representative bodies one or more persons exercising precisely the same sort of influence which is exercised by the leaders in a popular assembly. In either case, if there happen to be among these one of a very commanding character, he monopolizes the greater part of the influence, which is more commonly divided in unequal portions among a number. Did not Pitt[30] sway the British House of Commons, and through it the nation, for twenty years in succession, with at least as complete a mastery as Pericles possessed in the assembly of Athens?[31] Did Aristides, Themistocles, Alcibiades, Cymon, or any other popular leader ever reign more despotically over that "fierce democratie" than Mirabeau did over the National Assembly of France?[32]

The great virtue of the representative principle lies in this, that it accomplishes the union, which could never be effected in any other way, between *power* and *liberty*. Liberty in ancient times was wild, turbulent, blood-stained, short-lived, because she was weak. In modern times, and in this country, she is discreet, temperate, humane, healthy, because she is strong. She was weak in ancient times and is at this time weak in Europe because she dwells in *city-states*, or in small rural republics administered on the principle of the *market-democracy*. She is strong in this country, because by the aid of the representative principle, in its double application to the Union and the States, she has been able to comprehend a vast continent under the same

[30] [Ed. William Pitt, the Younger (1759-1806), was British prime minister (1783-1801, 1804-06).]

[31] [Ed. Pericles (c. 493-429 BC) was an Athenian statesman, orator, and general. He was famous for making Athens the political and cultural focus of Greece.]

[32] [Ed. Aristides, called "the just," was a fifth century BC Athenian statesman and general. Themistocles (c. 527-460 BC) was an Athenian military and political leader famous for his victorious battle at Salamis. Alcibiades (450-404 BC) was an Athenian politician and military commander who provoked sharp political antagonisms at Athens that led to Athens' defeat by Sparta in the Peloponnesian War (431-404 BC). Cymon or Cimon (c. 507-449 BC) was an Athenian general and statesman who opposed the policies of Pericles and who contributed to the building up of the Athenian empire following the Greco-Persian wars. Mirabeau has been previously identified.]

democratic system, and thus consolidate a purely popular power, which the mightiest monarchies of Europe have found by experience that it were not safe to trifle with.

When, therefore, our author inquires why, if representation be a mere substitute for pure democracy, we do not at once reject the former, and split up into city-states—we might answer, if it were worth the while to treat such a question seriously, that representation is not only a substitute for pure democracy but a great improvement upon it. We might answer that *city-states* do not and cannot possess either the *security* or the *stability* which are essential to political prosperity, and which can only be enjoyed in large communities. Why is it, we might ask in turn, that our author, a native Prussian, is now reposing in peace under the broad banner of the United States of America? Is it not because our fathers, by employing the representative in connection with the democratic principle, were able to embody the latter in a community *powerful* enough to protect him against the bloodhounds of despotism, which have hunted him like a partridge upon the mountains, through the whole of Europe, and would follow him across the Atlantic if they dared? Why did his countryman, the late lamented Dr. Follen,[33] exchange the market-democracy of Switzerland, that classic land of liberty, for the representative democracy of this country? Read the letter which he addressed to the government of Basil, on his departure. "Because the Republicans of Switzerland, who have protected so many fugitive princes, noblemen, and priests, would not protect him, a republican like themselves, he is compelled to take refuge in the *great asylum of liberty,* the United States of America."[34] The letter is, however, hardly just to Switzerland. She *would* willingly enough have protected her republican guest, if she had had the power. Her weakness, and not her will, consented to his departure. If then we do not in this country "split up into city-states" again, it is for this, among many other good reasons, that we may have the *power* to protect our author and other foreigners, who honor us with their presence, against the diplomatic votes of their excellencies, the ministers of Russia, Prussia, Austria, France, and Spain, who, if our refugees were living in a *city-state* or a *market-democracy*, would very soon get possession of them, in spite

[33] [Ed. Charles Follen (1796-1840), a German professor who emigrated to the United States in 1824, was the first professor of German at Harvard, an ardent abolitionist, a Unitarian preacher, and a friend to many American Transcendentalists.]

[34] [Ed. It is not clear how and where Brownson obtained this letter, but it was later published in part in a memoir of Follen's life. See *The Works of Charles Follen*, 5 vols. (Boston: Hilliard, Gray, and Company, 1841), 1:119.]

of all their learned citations from Wicquefort, Puffendorf, and Grotius.[35]

It is time, however, to close this article. The work before us, such as we have shown it to be, is nevertheless introduced to the public by a strong recommendation, from no less a personage than Chancellor Kent.[36] The facility, with which individuals, who enjoy the general confidence as men of learning and talent, lend their names to promote the circulation of worthless books, is a great and growing mischief, which ought to be corrected. Another recent and very remarkable instance of it is to be found in the testimony, publicly borne, to the merit of Mr. Otis's translation of the Tusculan Questions of Cicero, by President Quincy, the late William Sullivan, and what we should consider as much higher authority, Mr. Prescott and John Quincy Adams.[37] Why should this be? Is it not a fraud upon the public to pass a high encomium upon a book of no value, and thus cheat the people out of their money, by inducing them to buy it, or out of their time, by inducing them to read at least a portion of it; which is our own case in regard to the Tusculans? Are we at liberty to aid and abet others in doing what we have no right to do for ourselves? Is the moral obligation to be sincere and honest less impera-

[35] [Ed. Abraham de Wicquefort (1598-1682) was a Dutch diplomat, political theorist, and long resident of Paris who authored *L'ambassadeur et ses fonctions* (1681) on history and diplomacy. Samuel Pufendorf (1632-94) was the first German professor of natural and international law and author of *De Jure Naturae et Gentium* (1672); Hugo Grotius (1583-1645) was a Dutch jurist and theologian who had had an influence on Pufendorf by his famous *De Jure Belli ac Pacis* (1625).]

[36] [Ed. Chancellor James Kent (1763-1847), a famous New York jurist, was chief justice of the New York Supreme Court (1804-14) and Chancellor of New York (1814-23), the highest juridical position in the state. He is famous for the publication of his four-volume *Commentaries on American Law*, a text that would go through fourteen editions in the nineteenth century. The *Commentaries* transplanted the English common law to America.]

[37] [Ed. The reference is to *The Tusculan Questions of Marcus Tullius Cicero in five books*, translated by George Alexander Otis (1781-1863) (Boston: James B. Dow, 1839). Brownson briefly noticed the piece in *Boston Quarterly Review* 2 (July, 1839): 392, where he noted that the translation was "not so good as we could wish it, but it is on the whole quite respectable, and deserves the thanks of the English student. The work itself is above all praise, as one of the most valued and valuable remains of classic antiquity." Josiah Quincy (1772-1864) was a Federalist congressman, Boston mayor, and president of Harvard University (1829-45). William Sullivan (1774-1839) was a Boston lawyer, Federalist politician, and writer of popular historical works. William Hickling Prescott (1796-1859) was the premier romantic historian of the period whose three-volume *History of the Reign of Ferdinand and Isabella, the Catholic* (1838) won him instant fame. I was unable to locate where these authors and John Quincy Adams reviewed and endorsed Otis' work.]

tive in the book-selling business than in others? Dr. Warren[38] would think himself dishonored by endorsing a quack medicine. Why should Mr. Adams endorse a quack translation of Cicero; or Chancellor Kent a quack treatise on *Political Ethics*?

[38] [Ed. Brownson is probably referring to John Collins Warren (1778-1856), a Boston surgeon and professor of anatomy and surgery at Harvard Medical School (1809-45), which his father, John Warren, had founded.]

11.

PROSPECTS OF THE DEMOCRACY[1]

Boston Quarterly Review 2 (January, 1839): 123-36

In all countries where there is life, where thought is active, and has scope to manifest itself in some degree, the community is divided into two parties more or less equal in numbers and strength. One party may be termed the stationary party, the party whose object is to retain things as they are, or to recall the order that is passing away; the other party may be termed the movement party, the party whose leading object is always to develop and improve the existing order, or to introduce a new, and, as it hopes, a better order. The members of the first named party are usually that portion of the community whom the existing order, whatever it may be, most favors, or who hope the most from things as they are; and consequently of those who have, or fancy they have, the most to lose by a change: the members of the last named party are, in general, those on whom the burden of the existing order chiefly falls; who suffer the evils of things as they are, and of course, of those who have the most room to hope that a change will better their condition.

They whom the existing order of things most favors are in most countries the few; they whom it favors the least are the many. The interest, then, sought to be promoted by the stationary party, is necessarily the interest of the few in contradistinction to that of the many. Its object is always to secure or increase the special advantages of the few over the many. It is therefore always the party of privilege, the aristocratic party. The movement party is the opposite of the stationary party. Its object is to diminish the privileges enjoyed by the few and to introduce as great a degree of equality as is practicable among all the members of the community. It is therefore the party of equality, and consequently, the Democratic party. The war which is ever carried on between these two parties, whatever the name it may bear, or the forms it may assume, is always, at bottom, a war of EQUALITY AGAINST PRIVILEGE.

[1] [Ed. The running title was preceded by the following title of this article: "Political Parties—Their Prospects—The Lesson Taught us by the Results of Late Elections."]

These two parties may be found in every country in Christendom; and in every country in Christendom does the war of equality against privilege rage with more or less fierceness, and with prospects of an issue more or less favorable to the movement or Democratic party. Here, as well as in all other Christian countries, does this fearful war rage; and perhaps never with more fierceness than at this present moment. But equality is stronger here than elsewhere; it has gained here more than anywhere else, has achieved more brilliant and decisive victories, and conquered a larger extent of territory. It therefore comes to the battle with high hopes, and with great confidence in its own strength, and the terror its name inspires. Nevertheless it can count on no easy victory. Privilege exists here, has existed here from the origin of our government, and will exist much longer. Its forces are numerous, well disciplined, well furnished, and liberally paid; and they promise to do effectual service in its cause.

These two parties have always existed here and they showed themselves very distinctly in the Convention which framed the Federal Constitution. The party of privilege, the aristocratic party, feeling themselves in the position to wield the power of the government, and of course to wield it in their own favor, asked for a strong government, one capable of holding the people in awe, in check, in submission. The party of equality, the Democratic party, on the other hand, distrustful of governments, in consequence of having suffered from their abuses, demanded a weak government and a strong people; so that the few, by seizing its reins, should not be able to make the government trample on the rights and the interests of the many. The party of equality triumphed, so far as the organization to be given to the federal government was concerned.

This triumph threatened to be fatal to the party of the few. Equality was proclaimed, and the death warrant of privilege was signed. The partisans of privilege took the alarm, and resolved, come what might, to save its life and prolong its reign. But how was this to be done? Not openly, avowedly, directly; but covertly, indirectly, while professing and appearing unto the party of the many to be laboring for the good of the whole people. They must, while seeming to yield to the popular voice, gain possession of the government, and place themselves in a position to control its measures.

This, after all, was not so difficult as it seemed. Governments cannot operate without funds; consequently, they who can control its funds, or the sources whence it obtains them, can control its action. By connecting the fiscal concerns of government intimately with the business operations of the country, they who have the control of those operations, necessarily control the government.

Consequently, the first effort of the aristocratic party, after their defeat in the Convention, was to bring about this connection. This they did, first, by funding the national debt, and making thereby a portion of the capitalists the creditors of the government; and secondly, by chartering a National Bank, and making it the depository of the government funds, which were to be used as the basis of loans to business men. The party of privilege became, as a matter of course, the purchasers of government stock, and the owners of the Bank; they became, therefore, the creditors of the government, and through the bank, sustained by government funds, the creditors of the whole trading community, and through the trading community, of nearly the whole population; and therefore able to exercise over both government and people the all but absolute control, which the creditor exercises over the debtor. With this control the aristocratic party cared little for the democratic forms of government the people in their simplicity had adopted; nay, they became partial to those forms, for under them they could carry their measures into effect without suspicion, and make it believed that they were approved and carried into effect by the people themselves.

This was the system early devised and adopted to defeat the people, and prolong the reign of privilege. We say not that it was wholly framed before hand, "with malice prepense," nor that all who supported it foresaw all its bearings. It was doubtless adopted in most cases instinctively, because the interests of those by whom it was adopted led to it; and because some whom a portion of the people respected supported it. Be this as it may, such was the system, briefly given, adopted by Hamilton,[2] who thought altogether more of guarding governments against the turbulence of the mob than the people against the tyranny of governments. Such was the system sustained by the old Federal party, and such, too, is the system, unless we are grossly deceived, sustained by its veritable successor, the modern Whig party. Hence the importance of the Currency question; hence the bearings of the Independent Treasury Bill.[3] The Whig party, at least,

[2] [Ed. Alexander Hamilton (1755?-1804) was an American Federalist political leader who was largely responsible for the ratification of the United States Constitution and the establishment of a strong central government. As the first Secretary of the Treasury, he organized American fiscal policy and helped create credit for the United States at home and abroad.]

[3] [Ed. After President Andrew Jackson separated federal funds from the United States Bank, President Martin Van Buren supported a bill to establish an indepen-

"their leaders," wish to retain the government in the hands of the party of privilege; and they are well aware that they can do this only by a National Bank, which shall centralize the money power, and give it unity of aim and effort. The Democratic party, the real Democratic party, we mean, whatever its name, wish for an Independent Treasury, because it is the only treasury known to the Constitution, and because they would emancipate the government from the fatal thrall of the creditor influence, and enable it to feel and obey the impulse of the popular will.

Here is the great question which now divides the country: Independent Treasury, and a government free to follow the democratic will, or a National Bank, and a government and people under the dominion of the party of privilege. The question is one of magnitude, of immense bearings; altogether more so than that which induced our fathers to take up arms against the mother country. There is a deeper principle involved in the question now at issue than in that of the duty of "three pence a pound on tea," which our fathers refused to pay. If we had failed in our effort to resist foreign taxation, we should have been externally enslaved; but if we fail in our effort to resist the rechartering of a National Bank, and to secure the Independent Treasury, we become enslaved both externally and internally. The recharter of a National Bank is a regular installation of the money power, as the hereditary sovereign of this country, who cannot henceforth be dethroned without one of those social convulsions of which we have had an example in the French Revolution.

Well, what is the prospect? What will be the issue of this fearful and protracted war of equality against privilege? Which party will win the day? As yet neither party has won. The battles thus far fought have been very nearly drawn battles, and both parties have felt it necessary to retire and recruit their forces. What will be the issue, we know not; though we have no fears but the right in the long run will triumph. The difficulty of foreseeing the immediate result arises from the great confusion of parties. On the side of privilege are whole battalions who belong to the army of equality; while more than one division of the army of equality is led on by a chief,[4] whose only

dent governmental treasury as a way of divorcing the government from the banks, thereby maintaining the independence of the government from control of the banks. On the Independent Treasury Bill, see Arthur M. Schlesinger, Jr. *The Age of Jackson* (Boston: Little, Brown and Co., 1945), 227-41; 250-52; 265.]

[4] [Ed. The "chief" is President Martin Van Buren. Brownson is more than likely referring to the conservative Bank Democrats as the one battalion that belongs in the party of privilege.]

appropriate place is in the ranks of the army of privilege. This confusion is disastrous. Were the opposing parties fairly drawn out, were there no democrats fighting for privilege, and no aristocrats pretending to fight for equality, the contest would not be doubtful. If all true Whigs, according to the present meaning of the term, were on one side, and all true Democrats on the other, were the line, which separates the two parties by which the country is now divided, drawn accurately between the partisans of privilege and the friends of equality, there would be no engagement; the Independent Treasury would be at once established, and the project for a National Bank abandoned in despair. For, there can be no question that the great mass of the people of this country are thoroughly democratic, and that they have the moral power to make every needed sacrifice for the triumph of democracy. No measure, clearly seen to be anti-democratic, can stand the least possible chance of succeeding. No party, not believed to be democratic, can rise even to respectable minority.

Of this our late elections have afforded us ample proof. We do not in this respect refer to the successes of the Democratic party, so called; for in fact neither party has gained much to boast of; though the Democratic party has gained somewhat since 1837; but we refer to the claims which both parties set up. The Whig party, which, whether right or wrong, we have been in the habit of regarding as the legitimate heir of the old Federal party, modified merely to meet the new questions which have come up, has not been willing to rest its claims on the fact of its being the continuation of that party; but it has called itself democratic, and challenged success on the ground of being more democratic than the Democratic party itself. Why has it done this, if not from the conviction that democracy is the dominant faith of the country, and that all open and avowed opposition to it must be unavailing? In doing this, has it not said that its success must be proportionate to the belief it can produce that it is the real Democratic party? That to conquer it must steal the democratic thunder, and swear that it is Whig property? If so, it is well; it is a proof that the American people are sound at the core, and that nothing is necessary to carry any measure but to make it be seen to be a truly democratic measure.

The course pursued by the Democratic party, so called, for the last year, has also testified clearly to the same point. We could say something against the party which has called itself democratic, were we so disposed; especially in the State of New York, where it has been twice so severely rebuked. The failures of that party have been entirely owing to itself. A party really democratic is in harmony with the dominant sentiment of the American people, and must be invincible. But the party which has borne the name has not always been true to the principle. Confident in its numbers, its organization, and the prestige of its name, it has taken too little care to be really and truly democratic in its principles. It had too little respect, at least, the men who for a long time gave it its tone, had too little respect for the equality recognized by our institutions, and which the people were craving to see realized. In this fact must we look for the cause of the reverses which it has experienced. No party ever fails or loses ground unless by its own fault; and there is no greater folly, not to say injustice, than for one party to attribute its ill success to the intrigues of another. Let a party be true to the dominant idea of its country, and its success is as certain as the revolutions of the earth. When it deserts that idea, when it loses sight of the principle which makes the life of its country, and depends on something else for success, it fails, and deservedly fails. We are free to confess that the party, calling itself democratic, had, to some extent, at least, lost sight of the democratic principle; it had imbibed some of the doctrines, and adopted the practices, of the party of privilege. And severely, and justly too, has it been rebuked. But, and this is the point, it bids fair to profit by its rebukes, and henceforth to be in fact, as well as in name, the Democratic party.

The failures of the administration party, not its successes, are to us the encouraging facts we witness. We say not this because we would see that party driven from power, nor because we have any apprehensions that it will be; but because we believe that party had in many places become exceedingly corrupt. The time has not long gone by, since it was more than the reputation of a member of that party was worth, to be bold and uncompromising in the advocacy of true democratic measures and doctrines. We have not forgotten the manner in which it received, some years ago, the very proposition for an Independent Treasury which it now puts forth; nor have we forgotten a certain proclamation, which, for its strong centralizing doctrines, surpassed even what the boldest leaders of the old Federal party would have dared put forth under similar circumstances; nor the demoralizing doctrine unblushingly avowed on the floor of the United States Senate, that "to the victor belong the spoils"; nor the reception which was given to the really democratic doctrines proposed by the workingmen, doctrines which are now, in substance, the creed of the party. We have not forgotten these things; but we do not bring them against the party as it now is; we refer to them merely for the purpose of showing that the failures the party has experienced were not uncaused nor unmerited. The party needed to be checked, to be made aware that it would be permitted to possess power, only on the condition of being thoroughly democratic. Its failures were a needed discipline; its reverses, as in the case of individuals, were necessary to purify its heart, and by purifying to fortify it, to throw it back on first principles, and compel it, as it hoped for success, to place itself in harmony with the great democratic idea which constitutes the life of the country. And it *has* fallen back on first principles; it *has* revived the old party lines, and brought on virtually the same controversy as that of '98. It has done this, and already we see the good effects of it; already do we see its strength increase, and its prospects of success brighten; and if it will but remain true to the creed it now avows, it must soon have the great body of the confederacy with it.

The true, we say not the nominal, Democratic party, always relies with a firm faith on principle. It is conscious of its own rectitude, that its cause is the cause of truth and justice; and it knows the people are with it; that the prayers of all good men the world over are for it; and that heaven, with all its omnipotence, stands pledged to give it success. In prosperity it is not elated; in adversity it does not despond; but ever keeps on the even tenor of its way with a serene brow and a tranquil pulse. It confides too firmly in the power of truth and justice to ever resort to artifice for its success. Calmly, but distinctly, it proclaims its great doctrines, which are always the intuitions of the universal reason, and doubts not that in due time those doctrines will embody themselves in institutions, and diffuse their fragrance over the whole earth.

Into perfect harmony with this true Democratic party, we think we see the Democratic party, so called, now coming, and therefore do we hope. If it puts forth the doctrines it now does, and adheres to them in its practice, as we have reason to believe it will, it must secure the cooperation of every man who has democratic sympathies and hopes. As it presents itself to us today, it is the true movement party of the country, forming the advanced guard of the grand army of progress now displaying its plumes throughout the civilized world, and promising not to lay down its arms till man everywhere is free, and the true kingdom of God is established on the earth. It is the party of liberty, of humanity, and as such must commend itself to every friend of his race. If it fulfil its present promises, it will realize a truly democratic society; enlist religion, art, science, literature, philosophy, on its side, and prove to the world that man can be really great and good only where the people are sovereign.

The result of late elections and the present aspect of parties, teach us forcibly the necessity of adhering to the great principles which lie at the foundation of our institutions. Our present embarrassments, so far as concerns federal politics, arise from the fact that the Republican party which came into power with Mr. Jefferson, soon lost sight of the principles of the Federal Constitution, and gradually came to adopt the principles avowed by the party over which it had triumphed. At the close of the war all the tendencies of the Republican party were to the centralizing doctrines of the Federal party. The amalgamation of the two parties, which followed soon after, was brought about not by the fact that Federalists became Republicans, but by the fact that Republicans became Federalists. Here is the source of our difficulties, difficulties which can be surmounted only by going back to the principles of '98, and, in federal politics, planting ourselves firmly on the doctrine of state rights.[5] We must revive TRUE FEDERALISM, and recall the federal government to the few specific objects for which the states in their sovereign capacity instituted it. Let this be done by the Democratic party, and every old Jeffersonian Republican, every young man who comprehends the theory of the federal government, must and will rally to its support. If it does not do this, it will fail, and justly.

In the states themselves, the party must become really and truly democratic. It must go for the whole people; against all monopolies; against all exclusive privileges; against all aristocratic measures; and in favor of mild and equal laws; in favor of equal rights; in favor of education, literature, art, and philosophy. It must plant itself on the primitive fact that all men are born essentially equal, and that there is something divine in every man. It must be ever on the side of freedom, sympathize with the oppressed, with all who are struggling for their rights. It must be high-toned and moral; confiding in the people, and still more in the immortal vigor of truth and justice.

Then its triumph, though it may not be today, nor tomorrow, is certain; and its triumph will be a blessing to the country, to the world.

But in order to succeed, the Democratic party must bear in mind that its hopes of success should rest on the fact that it rallies around a principle which is planted deep in the human heart, and in the triumph of which entire humanity is interested. The masses are moved only by great and everlasting principles, which touch every individual of the race. Parties, merely as parties, are nothing to the masses; indi-

[5] [Ed. Brownson is clearly following the lead of Senator John C. Calhoun of South Carolina in supporting state rights.]

viduals, as simple individuals, are nothing to them. A Clay, a Webster, a Van Buren, a Calhoun, are nothing to them, any further than they are the impersonations of great principles. Show them that this or that man embodies in himself the cause of the millions, that in raising him to office the cause of the millions is secured, and then as the representative of a cause does he become of importance; and it is only then that he ceases to be an object of indifference. No matter how great or how worthy a man is, viewed simply as an individual, the masses will not sustain him, and ought not to sustain him, unless he represents their cause. This is seen in literature as well as in politics. What has not been said to depreciate Byron![6] His character has been depicted in the most unfavorable light possible; and critics and reviewers have pronounced his poems destructive of all that is dear to man and society; they have dwelt long and often on the immoralities of which he was guilty; and yet he is *the* Poet of the age; everybody reads him; the millions clasp him to their heart, for they recognize in him the poet of humanity; they hear him speaking out for man, for freedom, and declaring in tones that thrill through their inmost souls,

> And I will war, at least in words (and—should
> My chance so happen—deeds) with all who war
> With thought; and thought's foes by far most rude,
> Tyrants and sycophants have been and are.
> I know not who may conquer: If I could
> Have such a prescience, it should be no bar
> To this my plain, sworn, downright detestation
> Of every despotism in every nation.[7]

And they claim him as one of themselves, cherish him as the apple of their eye, and defend him as it were with their lives against every adversary who would rise up against him. On the other hand, with all the advantage of private and personal worth, with all the puffing and blowing, and heaving and tugging of critics and reviewers, nothing can be made of Wordsworth. The people do not hear his voice nor follow him. Though he sings of "Beggars," "Wagoners," and "Idiot Boys,"[8] and in the simplest strains, his song fetches no echo from the

[6] [Ed. George Gordon, Sixth Baron Byron of Rochdale (1788-1824), an English poet of Scottish ancestry, was a champion of political liberty. He created the so-called "Byronic hero." He was also known for his liberty with respect to sexual relationships.]

[7] [Ed. George Gordon Byron, *Don Juan*, canto 9, stanza 24.]

[8] [Ed. Brownson is referring here to William Wordsworth's (1770-1850) "The Old Cumberland Beggar" (*Lyrical Ballads*, 1800), "The Wagoner" or "Benjamin

universal heart of humanity. He impersonates no cause; at least, he impersonates not the cause which is dear to the millions. Ever must he live or die as the poet of the lakes, and experience the fate of the local and temporary objects he sings. In accordance with the same law, a Webster, with his almost superhuman talents, can wake no response to his appeals. The people do not hear him, do not follow him, because they do not recognize him as an impersonation of their cause. A Jackson, again, carries the people with him. When he speaks there comes an echo from all parts of the republic. Notwithstanding all that is said against him, notwithstanding the virulent assaults upon his moral and personal character, upon his intellect, upon his acquirements, upon his public acts, he secures the masses, because in supporting him they feel they are securing the triumph of their own cause. And if Mr. Van Buren fail in his administration, it will be because he fails to identify himself in the minds of the people with the popular cause. Let him be really and truly the representative of that cause, and no power on earth can prevent his reelection.

The contest for men is insignificant. Individuals are nothing, causes are everything; and the man who would stand at the head of his country must be the impersonation of his country's cause. Parties, as such, again, are nothing, causes everything. Let the standard of the masses be raised, the banner of equality be unfurled, and distinctly seen to wave over the camp of any given party, and the masses shall rally around that standard, joyously enrol themselves under that banner. Let there then be no thought about men, none about parties, but let the whole energy of the soul be given to causes. Seize the right cause, and doubt not the right party will gather round you with the right man at its head. Ideas are omnipotent; bring out the true idea, it will choose its leader, and organize its party. If the Democratic party, so called, adhere to the democratic idea, if it continue to show that it has in its keeping a sacred cause, a cause dear to humanity, and which ought to prevail, it may rest assured of complete success, for the world is under the government of justice, not of iniquity.

If it is asked again, which of the two parties that now divide the country will succeed? We answer, we know not. But truth and justice reign, and they have decreed that this shall be the land of freedom; and the party which best represents the cause of freedom will triumph. The party which best represents this cause is, in our judg-

the Wagoner" (1819), and "The Idiot Boy" (*Lyrical Ballads*, 1798). On Brownson's evaluation of Wordsworth's poetry, see chapter 12 below, and "Wordsworth's Poems," *Boston Quarterly Review* 2 (April, 1839): 137-68.]

ment, at the present moment, the party which calls itself democratic. Since it has fallen back on first principles, it has come into harmony with the mighty spirit of freedom now agitating the world; and we doubt not its ultimate success. Through it now speaks the voice of eternal principle, which is the voice of the people; and the voice of the people is the voice of God; and when God speaks, who dare deny that he will be heard and obeyed?

12.

WORDSWORTH'S POEMS[1]

Boston Quarterly Review 2 (April, 1839): 137-68

This is not the latest edition of the poetical works of William Wordsworth that has appeared either in England or in this country; but it is the latest which happens to be in our possession, and it is the one from which we shall make such extracts as we may see proper to introduce in the course of our remarks.

In proceeding to offer some considerations on the merits of William Wordsworth as a poet, we find ourselves in a sad predicament, or, as the worthy Captain Truck would say, "in a category." Our brethren of the reviewing tribe seem to have conspired to elevate the said William Wordsworth to the throne of English Poesy, and we are in danger of suffering decapitation if we do not go with them, and pretty sure of being hung as traitors to the legitimate sovereign if we do. We hardly know what course to take. But, inasmuch as we are by nature strongly attached to legitimacy, and by education and habit not a little averse to innovations, rebellions, revolutions, and all such like matters, we believe we shall adhere to the old dynasty, and die, if die we must, in defense of the established line of succession. This, upon the whole, is the safest course, and the one to which a scrupulous conscience the most easily reconciles itself. We do not, it is true, object absolutely to being hung; but if we must be hung, we choose it should be with a good conscience, and in the full assurance of the rectitude of our cause. The rebel, the man who seeks to overturn the settled order of things, and to introduce a new and untried order, can rarely have this good conscience, this full assurance. He wars against the sovereign he was taught and accustomed in childhood to love, reverence, and obey; and he meets not his fate without some inward questionings, some unpleasant misgivings. There is a wide difference between dying as a rebel, as a revolutionist, and dying as the advocate of legitimacy. In the first case the man dies in a strange land, away from all the associations dear to the heart, in the midst of strangers,

[1] [Ed. Review of William Wordsworth's *The Poetical Works of William Wordsworth*, 4 vols. (London, 1832).]

looking only on strange faces, and listening only to strange tongues; in the last case the man dies at home, beneath the paternal roof, in the midst of old familiar friends, beholding old familiar faces, and hearing old familiar voices, which recall for him his earliest and sweetest life. We would die at home, beneath that same blue sky on which we gazed with the freshness of our young hearts, and in that humble but never forgotten cottage in which our eyes first opened to the light. So the heretic, however he wanders, whatever strange countries he visits, strange connections he forms, returns at last to the church of his forefathers, and reposes on that soft maternal bosom on which his infant head was pillowed. We cannot prove false to our first love; and our latest offering shall be laid on the same altar which received our first and best.

Doubtless we shall be told that Wordsworth is the true poetical sovereign, and that, as the advocates of legitimacy, we ought to own his sway, and yield him our heart's homage. But this is the point in dispute. Is Wordsworth the real sovereign of English Poesy? Is he a true poet? Who is a true poet? What is poetry?

The question, what is poetry, is not easily answered, and especially by one who, like ourselves, is to be regarded as destitute of the poetic temperament, as a sort of incarnation of prose. Nevertheless we will try to answer it and answer it for the understanding, though we fail to answer it for the heart.

In justice to ourselves, we must premise that we undertake to answer the question, what is poetry, not without some scruples of conscience. Poetry is something to be felt, not defined. It appears to us almost an act of sacrilege, to attempt to analyze it and determine its essence. Who would apply the rule and dividers, or the dissecting knife to that loved face which beams upon his heart, which goes with him whithersoever he goes, and is to him the visible embodiment of his soul's ideal of the beautiful. When the true poet chants, we do never ask ourselves, is this poetry? We listen, and it occurs not to us to ask, why we are pleased; why now we melt with tenderness; why now we frown with indignation; why now we are fired with love, with devotion; and why now we kindle, nerve our souls for deeds of lofty daring, and rush to the battlefield, the dungeon, the scaffold, the cross, for justice, for liberty, for country, for man, for God? We are in the hands of the poet as clay in the hands of the potter; or rather we are the living lyre, whose strings he sweeps with a bold hand, and from which he discourses his divine harmonies, and soul subduing melodies. He who claims to be a poet, and yet cannot make his claims felt, is no true poet; his song may be divine-like, but it is not divine. It is in the absence of the miracle-worker, not in his presence, that we question the reality of the miracle.

Nevertheless, after the poet's strain has died into a distant echo, and we are left to recover from the spell with which he bound us, and to exercise with some degree of calmness the reflective powers with which we are endowed, to enter into ourselves, and analyze our spiritual nature, we may possibly approach the source of the emotions of which we have been conscious, and obtain some clue to the answer to the question, what is poetry?

All the facts of consciousness, or phenomena of that world we carry in ourselves, are of a complex nature, but a profound psychology arranges them under three fundamental faculties, which, though never acting separately, are yet radically distinct. These three faculties, after Cousin, and some others, we term the reason or intellect, sensibility or capacity of feeling, and the activity, or power of willing. Man is a being capable of *knowing*, *feeling*, and *willing*. Reason or intellect is his only source of light, that by virtue of which he sees all he does see, and knows all that he does know.

Reason is both personal and impersonal, spontaneous and reflective. It sometimes acts by virtue of its own inherent energy, independently of our volitions, and instead of being subjected to them, it subjects them to itself, and compels us to receive and obey its laws. Sometimes, however, it acts only as we will to exercise it, and on such subjects only as we choose. In this last case it is personal, and is called reflection. In the other case it is impersonal, and is called spontaneity, or in ordinary language, inspiration.

The spontaneous reason, or spontaneity, expresses itself in various manners. Sometimes it utters itself by means of harmonies and melodies, and its utterance is called music; sometimes by means of forms and colors, and its utterance is sculpture and painting; sometimes by construction, in the Doric column, and the Gothic minster, and its utterance is architecture; sometimes in words, and then its utterance is poetry. We do not mean by this that every utterance of spontaneity by means of words, language, is poetry. The ordinary utterances of spontaneity, though akin to poetry, are not poetry. There is poetry only where spontaneity so utters itself as to move the sensibility. Poetry always excites, always kindles, and when it is genuine and of a lofty kind, it affects the sensibility in the most powerful manner, and produces that spiritual state called enthusiasm.

Spontaneity is the divine in man. It is the voice of the universal reason, or Word of God, uttering itself in us. It is in immediate relation with God, and consequently with the primal source of truth, beauty, and goodness. It reveals to us truth, beauty, goodness, which are but different phases of absolute being—God. When these are revealed to the soul, when by spontaneity we are enabled to look through the veil of sense, and behold, as it were, the infinite God face to face, we are conscious of a shudder, not of fear, but of awe and delight. A thrill of inexpressible pleasure runs through us, and our whole souls, and even our bodies become instinct with life and enjoyment. This shudder, this delight, this pleasure, this enjoyment, feeling, is the poetic sentiment. When it is quickened by a distinct consideration of the Absolute as God, the Father, the Creator, the Protector, the Preserver, or the Sovereign, we call it the religious sentiment, or devotion, which we seek to express in prayers, praises, and the various forms of religious worship. When we express it without any conscious reference to the Divinity as such, we call it poetry.

Now any expression of the spontaneous reason which does not quicken the feeling, the sentiment here described, which does not make the soul shudder, thrill—which does not produce more or less of enthusiasm, is not poetry, whatever use may be made of rhyme or measured language. He who shudders not before the infinite, dimly or clearly revealed to his soul, before the beautiful or the good which unveils itself to his spiritual vision, is no poet. The spontaneous reason is in all men, and reveals to all men, every day of their lives, the infinite, the true, the beautiful, the good; but all men are not poets, because the revelation of which we speak does not excite emotion, does not move the sensibility in all men, and produce enthusiasm.

A man who can stand before the infinite unawed, behold God unmoved, and contemplate in nature or in man the truth, beauty, goodness which are in them, is no poet, however clear and comprehensive may be his views. If he can retain a perfect self-mastery, and disport himself at his ease, he may be a philosopher, a very extraordinary man, but not a poet. He masters the God that moves within him, instead of being mastered by him, and utters his own word, not God's word. So also the calm utterance of the inward revelations, their cool statement, which leaves the hearer wholly self-possessed, quiet, unagitated, is not poetry.

The poet is always a seer; and it is worthy of note that the common sense of mankind, which makes languages, frequently calls the poet and seer, or prophet, by the same name. Thus in Latin *vates* is either a prophet or a poet. The poet is not, strictly speaking, a *maker,* as the Greek name implies. He does not create—he finds; hence, poetry has with justice been made to consist chiefly in *invention,* in discovering, in seeing, finding, that which ordinary men heed not, see not, or do not imagine to exist. He catches glimpses more or less perfect of the infinite reality, which lies back of the phenomena observed by the senses, or which shines out through them, whether under the aspect of truth, beauty, or goodness; and his sensibility is agitated, his soul takes fire, and he utters what he sees in words that burn, in tones which make those who hear him feel as he feels, burn as he burns. This he may do, because the spontaneous reason, by means of which he obtains the glimpses which fill his soul with so much joy, is in all men, and thus lays the foundation of a secret but entire sympathy between him and them, making them capable of recognizing the infinite he recognizes, and of joining their voices with his in sublime chorus to the God of truth, beauty, goodness.

The poet, we have said, is a seer. He is a spectator. He stands before the spiritual universe, and merely sees what is before him. He does not make that universe; nay, he has not sought to behold it. It has risen in its majesty, or in its loveliness before him. He does not seek his song; it comes to him. It is given him. He is, to a certain extent, a passive, though not an unmoved recipient of it. To this fact he always bears witness. It is not he that sings, it is his muse.

Musa, mihi causas memora.[2]

Apollo or some God inspires him. The power he feels, the beauty he sees, he cannot ascribe to himself. The song he sings is a mystery unto himself, and he feels that it must have been given him from abroad, from above. A spirit glows within him, a mind agitates him, which he feels is not his spirit, is not his mind, but the mind of his mind, the spirit of his spirit, the soul of his soul. In this he is right. The spontaneous reason, spontaneity, from which his song proceeds, is, we have said, the divine in man, and it acts without being put into action by the human will. We may, by effort, by discipline, place ourselves in relation with it, bring ourselves within the sphere of its action; but it is impersonal, and divine; it is the spirit of God, a portion of which is given unto all men, the logos (reason) which John assures us enlightens every man who comes into the world.[3]

It follows from the view now taken, that there is always truth in poetry. Of all known modes of utterance poetry is one of the truest; for it is the voice of the spontaneous reason, the word of God, which is in immediate relation with truth. It is truer than philosophy. For

[2] [Ed. Latin for "Muse, relate to me the causes," from Virgil's *Aeneid* 1:8. I would like to thank Stephen Beall of Marquette University's Classics department for locating this text for me.]

[3] [Ed. Reference is to John 1:9, a favorite biblical passage for Brownson since his early twenties.]

in poetry God speaks; whereas in philosophy it is only man that speaks. The reflective reason which gives us philosophy is personal, subject to all the infirmities of the flesh, short-sighted, and exclusive; but the spontaneous reason, of which poetry is one of the modes of utterance, is impersonal, broad, universal, embracing, as it were, the whole infinitude of truth. Hence the confidence mankind have universally reposed in their sacred prophets, in the inspired chants of their divine bards, and the distrust they have pretty uniformly manifested for the speculations of philosophers. In trusting the bard, they have felt that they were relying on divine authority; but in trusting the philosopher, that they were confiding in a merely human authority.

Poetry, if it be poetry, is always inspired. It is inspiration, clothing itself with words. And inspiration is never referred to ourselves; we always refer it to God.

"In inspiration," says Cousin, "we are simple spectators. We are not actors, or at best our action consists in being conscious of what is taking place. This doubtless is activity, but not a premeditated, voluntary, and personal activity. The characteristic of inspiration is enthusiasm; it is accompanied by that strong emotion which forces the soul out of its ordinary and subaltern state, and calls into action the sublime and divine part of its nature:

Est Deus in nobis, agitante calescimus illo.[4]

And indeed man in the marvelous fact of inspiration and enthusiasm, unable to refer to himself the pure and primitive affirmation, which it is, refers it to God, and calls it revelation. Is the human race wrong? When man, conscious of his own feeble share in inspiration, refers to God the truths which he has not made, and by which he is subjugated, is he deceived? No, assuredly. For what is God? He is, I have said, thought in itself, absolute thought with its fundamental movements—the eternal reason, substance, and cause of the truths man perceives. When therefore man refers to God the truth which he can neither refer to himself nor to the external world, he refers it to that to which he ought to refer it, and the absolute affirmation of truth without reflection, inspiration, enthusiasm, is a real revelation. This is the reason why, in the infancy of civilization, he, who possesses the wonderful gift of inspiration in a higher degree than his brethren, is regarded by them as the confidant and interpreter of God. He is it for others because he is it for himself; and he is it for

[4] [Ed. Latin for "There is a god in us; when he stirs us, we grow warm." From Ovid, *Fasti* 6.5. I would like to thank Stephen Beall of Marquette University's Classics department for identifying this passage for me.]

himself, because he is it, in fact, in a philosophical sense. Here is the sacred origin of prophecies, pontificates, and religions.

"Remark also a peculiar effect of the phenomenon of inspiration. When pressed by the vivid and rapid intuition of truth, and transported by inspiration and enthusiasm, man attempts to utter in words what is passing within him, he can do it only in words which have the same character as the phenomenon itself. Hence the necessary form, the language of inspiration, is poetry, and the primitive word is a hymn."[5]

The poetic sentiment in its essence is not distinguishable from the religious sentiment. Either is that affection of the sensibility we are conscious of, when by inspiration, spontaneous revelations, we catch some glimpses of the truth, beauty, or goodness of God, that is, of God himself. Religion and art are identical. Every work of art is a sacrifice to God; and every sacrifice to God is a work of art. Poetry, music, sculpture, painting—all, no less than what are usually termed religious rites and ceremonies, proceed from the same intuition of the true, the beautiful, the good, and are the homage the soul pays to the living God. All tend to proclaim the glory of God, and to develop and perfect the human soul. In the service of God's house, the soul seeks to utter the revelations made to it by the spirit of God; in every work of art, whatever its form, it seeks to do the same. Every genuine artist is a priest of the Most High God.

Poetry, as well as every other branch of art, then, is religious. Poetry is never an infidel. Its essence is a boundless faith in the Infinite. As dies out of the soul this boundless faith, so sinks the soul's power to produce poetry or even to relish it. Poetry affirms; it does not deny. Whoso would deny God, must do it in prose; he cannot do it in song. Atheism cannot be set to music. Every poet, so far forth as he is a poet, is devout; and every truly devout man is more or less of a poet, and chants rather than speaks the prayers and praises he addresses to the Deity. Who ever uttered his devotional feelings in sober prose, or sung his unbelief? Voltaire was a poet, and some may allege, also, an infidel; but he is a devout believer whenever he sings, and his loftiest and truest poetry is found in those passages in which he approaches nearest the Christian faith, and utters the religious sentiment.

Poetry is also moral. Immorality has no power to wake the lyre and call forth its soul-subduing melodies. We have heard of the song

[5] [Ed. *Introduction à l'histoire de la philosophie*. (Paris: Pichon and Didier, 1828), 6: 11-13. In the original footnote Brownson notes: "The whole lecture may be read in this connection with pleasure and profit."]

of Moses and the Lamb; we have not heard of the song of the devil and his angels. There are no harps in hell. The poet cannot sing the false, the licentious, the low, the mean, the harmful. His soul kindles only in view of the true, the beautiful, the good, the lofty, the ennobling, the grand, the sublime. His song enlarges, purifies, strengthens, and exalts. He may not always, indeed, be pure in heart or upright in conduct, but just so far as he leaves the path of virtue, does he lose his inspiration, and cease to be a poet. Those passages, we sometimes come across in the writings of what are termed licentious poets, which seem to have a vicious tendency to throw ridicule on the moral virtues, and which make good men weep and the chaste blush, are not poetry, any more than the Anteros of the Greeks was Eros,[6] the true God of love. They are wretched prose. Art is divine and nothing that is not of God can inspire the artist. The moment he loses sight of the Godlike, his productions become mean and contemptible.

And yet the true poem is by no means merely the sermon or homily "done into meter." God is the universal life, life itself, as his name, I AM, implies. All life, all being is from God, and he is in all life, all being. He is all that is. The universe with its endless variations is but "the varied God."[7] In all outward nature and in man there are truth, beauty, goodness; and truth, beauty, goodness are, as we have said, but different aspects of the indwelling, all-creating, all-sustaining God—a truth beautifully expressed by our American poet in his Forest Hymn:

> But thou art here—thou fill'st
> The solitude. Thou art in the soft winds
> That run along the summit of these trees
> In music; thou art in the cooler breath,
> That from the inmost darkness of the place
> Comes, scarcely felt; the barky trunks, the ground,
> The fresh moist ground, are all instinct with thee.[8]

In all that exists there is a living reality, which we may contemplate under the threefold aspect of the true, the beautiful, and the good, and which quickens thought, love, and devotion. This living reality, wherever seen, under whatever aspect beheld, is God. Our

[6] [Ed. In Greek mythology Anteros was the son of Aphrodite and Ares, and the brother of Eros.]

[7] [Ed. From the Scottish poet James Thompson's (1700-48) "A Hymn," in *The Seasons* (1728), line 2.]

[8] [Ed. Quotation from William Cullen Bryant's (1794-1878), American Romantic poet and editor of the *New York Evening Post*, "A Forest Hymn," lines 39-45.]

senses do not attain to this reality; they see only the appearance, the outward fact, which is but its shallow. Yet the soul may pierce the fact, go behind the appearance, and stand face to face with that which makes the fact, which casts the shadow. Then do all things live; all nature breathes, has a feeling and a voice.

> How often we forget all time, when lone,
> Admiring nature's universal throne,
> Her woods, her wilds, her waters, the intense
> Reply of hers to our intelligence.
> Live not the stars and mountains? Are the waves
> Without a spirit? Are the dropping caves
> Without a feeling in their silent tears?
> No, no: they woo and clasp us to their spheres,
> Dissolve this clog and clod of clay before
> Its hour, and merge our souls in the great shore.[9]

God is not merely in words and definitions. He is everywhere, and manifests himself in an infinite variety of forms. If blest with spiritual vision, we may see him in the starry heavens, in the foaming ocean, in the green earth, in the placid lake, the murmuring rill, the bubbling fountain, and humble violet that blooms in modesty beneath the hedge; in the planting of the infant colony, the growth of the state, the overthrow of the empire. It is God that delivers the children of Israel from Egyptian bondage, leads them through the wilderness, gives them a code of laws, drives out the heathen before them, and plants them in a "land flowing with milk and honey." It is God that conducts our pilgrim fathers, lands them on Plymouth Rock, sustains them in their war with the elements and their savage brethren, cuts down the forest before them, increases them to a mighty people, and erects them into a free state. God is in all events, from the death of the monarch on his throne, to the fall of the lonely sparrow. He is all and in all. He

> Warms in the sun, refreshes in the breeze,
> Glows in the stars, and blossoms in the trees;
> Lives through all life, extends through all extent,
> Spreads undivided, operates unspent;
> Breathes in our soul, informs our mortal part,
> As full, as perfect in a hair as heart;

[9] [Ed. George Gordon Byron (1788-1824), *The Island, or, Christian and His Comrades* (1823), canto 2, xvi, lines 382-97. See *The Poetical Works of Byron*, Cambridge Edition, rev. by Robert F. Gleckner (Boston: Houghton Mifflin, 1975), 424.]

As full, as perfect in vile man that mourns,
As the rapt seraph that adores and burns.
To him no high, no low, no great, no small,
He fills, he bounds, connects, and equals all.[10]

Religion is confined to no one manifestation of the Deity. The truly devout soul contemplates him in all his works, in the sacred chants of bards and prophets, in the woody dell, the opening flower, the waving grain, the golden sunset, the lengthening shadows of evening, the hues of the rainbow, the music of birds, the sublimity of the heavens, the majesty of the ocean, the roar of thunder, the fearful blast of the tempest, or the still loftier majesty of man, and higher sublimity of moral nature. Consequently, the range of the poet is as boundless as the Infinite, and the variations of his song may be as numerous as the various aspects under which the infinite God manifests himself to the soul of man.

It is of no consequence, then, what particular object, amidst the innumerable objects of the universe, the poet selects, the subject of his song is always the Infinite—that boundless world of being, of truth, love, goodness, beauty, which lies back of the world of sense, and is ever, as it were, peering through it. Whether he select the forest, the sun, the moon, the stars, the sea, the flower, the landscape, the generous sentiment, the lofty deed, the noble daring, the self-sacrifice, the humble affections of everyday life, the romantic passions of youth, the restless longings of a soul ill at ease, or the burning thirst to know, to pierce through the veil of sense, to explore the universe of mystery which lies round, about, and within us, and compel the mighty Unknown to surrender his secret, it is always the indwelling God he seeks, to whom he prefers his petitions, and whose praises he sings. The strong emotion he feels is always the result of his intuition in all these of something more than appears—truer, better, more beautiful, more permanent, more Godlike. He who sings heroic deeds, sings God, for there is something of God in every act of true heroism; wherefore hero worship is not necessarily idolatry. He who sings liberty, sings God, for God is the essence of freedom, his law is the perfect law of liberty, and we approach him in proportion as we become free.

These remarks will suffice to show that in denying poetry to all that is irreligious and immoral, we do by no means advance a narrow and exclusive theory. The theory we put forth is broad enough to embrace every imaginable species of poetry. Poetry, according to this

[10] [Ed. Alexander Pope, *Essay on Man*, epistle 1, lines 271-80.]

theory, may be lyric, epic, dramatic, descriptive, narrative, didactic, idyllic, elegiac, or what not, only it must ever be the spontaneous utterance of the voice of truth, beauty, goodness, which fill the universe, are the ground of its being, and, as we have said, but varying aspects of the infinite, the living God.

We may now define poetry to be that branch of art, which seeks to express in words the revelations of God made to the soul by the spontaneous reason, or spontaneity, which is, as we have said, the divine in man. These revelations in some degree are made to all men, but to the poet they come with more vividness and power, and are always accompanied by an inward shudder, a strong affection of the sensibility, which is usually termed enthusiasm. The poet lives; he kindles, he burns; and he kindles the souls of all who listen to his inspired chant, and makes them burn as he burns. This effect on others he is able to produce, because he addresses in them that same spontaneity which is active within himself, and gives them glimpses of that same God by whom he himself is so deeply moved and agitated.

With these preliminary remarks on the nature of poetry, too extended we fear for the patience of our readers, and yet too brief for their subject, we proceed to an examination of the poetical works of William Wordsworth, and to ascertain, if we can, the poetical rank to which they are entitled.

That these works do not deserve the highest poetical rank is evident from their great want of popularity. Wordsworth, we readily admit, is at present quite a favorite with reviewers, and most of our contemporaries in this country and in England have taken him under their especial protection; but still he is not popular. The circle of his admirers may be select, and highly cultivated, but it is not large. Notwithstanding his boasted simplicity and naturalness, it requires an artificial taste to relish him. The great mass of the reading public appear to hold him in no high esteem. This is especially true in this country, where only two moderate editions of his works, if we have been rightly informed, have as yet been called for.[11] Now this is altogether against him. The popular voice is the only authority to which we may appeal in matters of poetry, or any of the fine arts. The few may be deceived, misled by their own speculations, disposed to applaud because their own idiosyncrasies are flattered, or to condemn

[11] [Ed. Brownson may be referring to *The Poetical Works of William Wordsworth* (New York: Hurst, 1835) and (New Haven: Peck and Newton, 1836). He may also be thinking of Henry Reed's (1808-54) edition, *The Complete Poetical Works of William Wordsworth* (Philadelphia: J. Kay, Jr. and brother; Boston: J. Munroe and Co., 1837).]

because they are not flattered. The many approve only that which is common to human nature, which is general, adapted to the race. To say of a poet that he is unpopular, is about the same as to say that he is no poet at all. The philosopher may, indeed must, to a certain extent, be unpopular. He deals with problems of which only a few, comparatively speaking, have any distinct conception, and which can be solved only by long study and patient reflection, for which few have a taste, and to which not many will submit. It is therefore nothing against a philosopher that he is not popular. The people taken at large are not philosophers, and have little or no craving for philosophy. The people crave poetry and religion, and to say of either that it does not commend itself to the common soul, that the "common people do not receive it gladly," is to say that it is false.

Spontaneity, we have repeatedly said, is in all men, and the same in all men. When therefore spontaneity speaks, it finds that in all men which is prepared, in various degrees doubtless, to recognize it, and welcome its song. When I am the organ through which it speaks, I am responded to by all who hear my voice. Genius, which is only another name for spontaneity, is always popular. Who ever heard of an unpopular genius? When he whom God inspires speaks, all humanity listens; the people are astonished; they feel that he teaches with authority, not as the Scribes, for his word is with power. Just so is it with every true genius. The Scribes and Pharisees, the chief priests and elders, the interested few, may close their ears, cry out against him, persecute, imprison, impale, or crucify him; but this is never because he is unpopular, but because he is popular, because they dread his influence with the people, and fear that his authority may undermine their dominion. Martyrs to religion, truth, justice, liberty, country, fall not by the hands of the people, but by those of the people's masters. These sheepskin and goatskin clad prophets that wander the earth alone, live apart in the desert, the mountain, or the cave, of whom it is said the world is not worthy, want not sympathy with the people, or power to touch the popular heart, and carry the people along with them; but an interested few, fearing the changes they may produce, the revolutions their God inspired words may generate, interpose between them and the people, or exile them from their brethren. Genius is essentially democratic; his voice is always music to the democracy, and only they who love not the democracy, or have a private end to gain, ever dream of stifling his voice. This accounts for what has but too often been his fate. But wherever his word has free course to run and be glorified, wherever it can meet the ear of the people, it vivifies the mass, and becomes the people's law, it may be, for a thousand centuries.

Now Wordsworth has had no obstacle to his popularity, but of his own creating. The people's masters have not opposed him. He has had free access to the people, and yet is he not popular. Why is it that long ere this, he has not caught an echo to his song from the depths of the human heart? Why, but because he is wanting in some of the essentials of a true poet? To us the voice he utters is the voice of William Wordsworth, not the voice of God, and his word is not a living, nor a life-imparting word. It does not come to us with authority. It does not take possession of our souls, and carry us away captive. We must give him our attention; he does not take it. We have rarely met an author who required so much discipline on the part of his readers. He does not take us up where he finds us, and carry us into the state in which we can relish him; but we must, by suppressing all our ordinary emotions, and sinking ourselves into a state of as complete negativeness as is compatible with a strong effort of the will, bring ourselves into his mode, into harmony with his fancies. Now this we might consent to do in case of a scientific work, addressed avowedly and intentionally to the pure intellect, but not in case of poetry, which is addressed to the sensibility, as well as to the intellect, and is designed to kindle, exalt, and enrapture us. It is taxing our good nature altogether too much.

Wordsworth aims to be simple and natural. He aims well. Good taste always delights in simplicity and naturalness, and no work of art is deserving any attention in which they are wanting. But in aiming to be simple, Wordsworth not infrequently becomes silly. His story of the Idiot Boy[12] is a proof of this, and almost justifies the well-known satire of Byron.

> Next comes the dull disciple of thy school,
> That mild apostate from poetic rule,
> The simple Wordsworth, framer of a lay
> As soft as evening in his favorite May;
> Who warns his friend 'to shake off toil and trouble,
> And quit his books for fear of growing double';
> Who, both by precept and example, shows
> That prose is verse, and verse is merely prose,
> Convincing all, by demonstration plain,
> Poetic souls delight in prose insane;
> And Christmas stories, tortured into rhyme,
> Contain the essence of the true sublime:

[12] [Ed. *Idiot Boy* (1798).]

> Thus when he tells the Tale of Betty Foy,
> The idiot mother of 'an idiot boy';
> A moon-struck, silly lad who lost his way,
> And, like his bard, confounded night with day;
> So close on each pathetic part he dwells,
> And each adventure so sublimely tells,
> That all, who view the 'idiot in his glory,'
> Conceive the bard the hero of his story.[13]

We cannot quote the tale, but will select a specimen or two.

> And Betty's most especial charge
> Was, 'Johnny! Johnny! mind that you
> Come home again, nor stop at all,
> Come home again, whate'er befall,
> My Johnny, do, I pray you do.
> . . . .
> Burr, burr—now Johnny's lips they burr,
> As loud as any mill, or near it;
> Meek as a lamb the Pony moves,
> And Johnny makes the noise he loves,
> And Betty listens, glad to hear it.
> . . . .
> And Susan is growing worse and worse,
> And Betty is in a sad *quandary*;
> And then there is nobody to say
> If she must go, or she must stay!
> She's in a sad *quandary*.[14]

These specimens have been selected at random. No doubt the poem contains many more such, and which the poet must have been in "a sad quandary" to have written. We select a few choice stanzas from a piece entitled "Anecdotes for Fathers." The poet addresses his little son.

> 'Now tell me, had you rather be,'
> I said, and took him by the arm,
> 'On Kilve's smooth shore, by the green sea,
> Than here at Liswyn farm?'
> In careless mood he looked at me,
> While still I held him by the arm,

[13] [Ed. The "thy" of "thy school" is a reference to Robert Southey (1774-1843), an English poet. For the reference see George Gordon Byron, *English Bards and Scotch Reviewers: A Satire* (London: James Cawthorn, 1809), lines 175-95.]

[14] [Ed. *The Poetical Works of William Wordsworth* (1832), 1: 160-64. "The Idiot Boy" (1798), lines 57-61; 98-101; 167-171.]

And said, 'At Kilve I'd rather be
Than here at Liswyn farm.'
'Now little Edward, say why so:
My little Edward, tell me why.'
I cannot tell, I do not know.
'Why this is strange,' said I.
. . . .
O dearest, dearest boy!
My heart For better lore would seldom yearn,
Could I but teach the hundredth part
Of what from thee I learn.[15]

But here is poetry with a vengeance, as well as a moral lesson every lazy urchin trudging unwillingly to school will joy to learn, and to practice.

Up! up! my friend, and quit your books,
Or surely you'll grow double:
Up! up! my friend, and clear your looks;
Why all this toil and trouble?
. . . .
Books! 'tis a dull and endless strife!
Come hear the woodland Linnet,
How sweet his music! On my life,
There's more of wisdom in it.[16]

Certainly, more than in such prattle as this, and the music we own is much sweeter to our ears. For once we agree with the Bard.

All this, together with much more like it in the volumes before us, we shall be told is simple and natural. Simple it may be, but not in the sense in which the admirers of simplicity would have us understand it. It may be natural, but we fear in the sense in which individuals, who have the misfortune to be born without reason, are sometimes called *naturals*. Wordsworth does not seem to us capable of being simple without approaching the silly. He loses his dignity the moment he attempts to place himself at ease, and enter into familiar chat. His naturalness is altogether too near akin to that attained in Dutch paintings—a copy rather than a reproduction of nature. The nature represented by the true artist is never the nature

[15] [Ed. *The Poetical Works* (1832), 1: 16, 17. "Anecdote For Fathers" (1798), lines 29-40, 57-60.]

[16] [Ed. *The Poetical Works* (1832), 3: 206, 207. "The Tables Turned" (1798), lines 1-4, 9-12.]

of the senses, but a higher and truer nature—the ideal, of which that of the senses is but a mere type or shadow. An actual landscape merely copied, were the production of an artisan, not of an artist. It is not the actual landscape that a Salvator Rosa or Claude Lorrain paints, but the ideal landscape, the higher, truer, and more beautiful landscape, which the artist finds in his soul, and to which the outward serves him but as an index.[17] He who represents only what everybody sees and feels in nature is not an artist. His copies are nought, because nature herself is before us. Fidelity to nature in the poet is fidelity to that higher truth, which lies back of the outward, and which is visible to the soul only in its moments of inspiration. We say not that Wordsworth never attains to this higher truth, for sometimes we think he does, and to a degree to which few poets ever attain; but in general he does not. His nature is bald and naked. Notwithstanding his spiritual philosophy, he does not spiritualize nature. He leaves it cold and material, uninviting and uninspiring.

Wordsworth's poems, again, rarely strike us as genuine effusions of spontaneity. They seem, in a majority of cases, to be mere creations of reflection. They appear to have been first meditated and molded in prose, and then done by laborious effort into verse. They wear their poetic garb as something which may be put on or off at the pleasure of their author, not as an integral part of themselves. They may, therefore, be very good sense, very good philosophy, but they are not poetry. The most we can say of them is that they are very successful imitations of poetry. The thoughts they contain could be expressed with equal naturalness, vividness, and force in prose. The poetic dress is by no means essential; and wherever it is not essential, we hold it to be objectionable.

The appropriate language of powerful inspiration, of spontaneity, is poetry; and when spontaneity is active in us, we cannot avoid the use of a poetical diction, even if we would. The natural language of reflection is prose. When we reflect, we suppress passion, we calm ourselves, and aim to leave the pure intellect undisturbed, and to remove everything which would tend to distract it. We are cool, clear, logical, precise, and require a language possessing the same characteristics. He, therefore, who attempts to express the spontaneous inspirations, which the spirit of God breathes into his soul, in the cold and precise language of prose, or the results of reflection in the burn-

[17] [Ed. Salvator Rosa (1615-73) was an Italian painter famous for landscapes of wild and savage scenes. Claude Lorrain (1600-82) was a French landscape painter known for his classical and biblical themes.]

ing words of poetry, offends correct taste, and sins against nature. Of this sin against nature Wordsworth appears to us to be frequently guilty. We take his great poem, called "The Excursion."[18] This poem, we cheerfully own, contains many beautiful passages, which were worthy of the greatest poets; but, taken as a whole, it is a philosophy rather than a poem. Its leading design appears to be to solve the great problems which relate to the destiny of man, society, and nature. These are great and sublime problems, and are well deserving all the attention the profoundest philosopher can give them. But the solution which Wordsworth proposes, if solution it can be called, has evidently not been obtained by inspiration. It has not flashed upon his soul like lightning from heaven. The spirit of God has not descended and rested on him, as on the apostles, in "cloven tongues of fire" [Acts 2:3]. It has been obtained by reflection, by study, in a word, by philosophizing. Its natural language then is prose, not verse; and, in point of fact, it must have existed in prose before it was turned into meter. The meter is to us, therefore, an incumbrance, a hindrance. The work is addressed to the reflective reason, is intended mainly to teach us certain doctrines, and all propriety calls aloud for the natural language of reflection.

We have heard this production praised beyond all measure; we can only say that we have found it a very dull performance, and have never been able, notwithstanding repeated trials, to read the whole of it. But aside from this real or supposed dulness, the work does not satisfy us. The author makes a reflection, or throws out a thought, and when we look to see him point out its bearings, and show its systematic relations, we find him prattling about golden sunsets, gilded tree tops, quiet lakes, sequestered paths, sloping hills, and mountain cliffs. His peddler, into whose mouth he puts his philosophy, such as it is, never wins our hearts or satisfies our understandings. He is, no doubt, a very wise peddler, and we sometimes think that he might furnish us something valuable if he would; but, alas! he is ever a peddler, true to his early habits. His delight is to wander from cottage to cottage, and consequently he provides himself only with such light wares, as are not so heavy as to exhaust his strength, and which answer by no means the purpose for which he recommends them. In short, the peddler has too much reflection to be a poet, and not enough to be a philosopher.

Moreover, the poem bears no evidence of having been written because the author felt himself constrained to write it. He did not

[18] [Ed. Wordsworth's *The Excursion* (1814) was a long dramatic poem in nine books, which was generally not well received.]

undertake it because it was rending his bosom, and must be uttered. It was not a "burden" to his heart as were their sacred songs to the hearts of the divine bards of old. In retiring to the lakes, Wordsworth thought it was his duty to undertake to construct a literary work that should live. He accordingly took a survey of his own powers, in order to ascertain for what he was by nature and education best fitted. This survey convinced him that he was best qualified to sing the sublimest of all subjects, and therefore he resolved to sing it. Having thus resolved, he very deliberately cast about him to see what he knew of the matter, and could say about it. Here is no burning with unquenchable desire to utter a word which is given him to utter. Nothing forces him out of his quiescent state. He is ever as calm as the unruffled lake sleeping beneath the moonbeams on a gentle summer evening. Nor does he look to God for inspiration, for the light which is to guide him into all truth, but to his own powers. These are to solve the mighty problems with which he proposes to grapple. He takes it upon himself to lash Pegasus[19] into a divine rage, and make him frisk about among the stars. Now no man, who sets out in this way, need ever hope to attain to immortality. No man sings well unless his song be given him, in acceptable numbers unless they come, as it were, of their own accord. The poet must feel a hand upon him not his own, a power above him forcing him to sing; his song must press heavily upon his heart, giving him no rest by day or by night till it be sung. No word shall sound out forever, but the word of God. All that is of man shall die. Providence sports with the creations of mortals, and delights to lay the monuments of their pride in the dust. We may build with greatest pains, lay the foundations deep, rear the summits high, and flatter ourselves that our structures shall stand; but the breath of the Lord passes them by, and we look in vain to find the places where they stood. "Vanity of vanities, all is vanity" [Eccles 1:2; 12:8]; and there is not a greater vanity beneath the sun, than man's hope of being able to "construct a literary work, or any other work, that shall live."[20] Let man discipline his soul, let him aim well, and aim high, for this is his duty; but let him do the work that is given him to do, utter the word given him to utter, and utter it in the very tones in which it comes to his own heart, and concern himself no

[19] [Ed. In Greek mythology Pegasus was the immortal winged horse who carried the thunder and lightening of Zeus. In Roman times Pegasus became a symbol of immortality.]

[20] [Ed. A paraphrase of William Wordsworth's Preface to "The Excursion," second paragraph. Wordsworth wrote only: "construct a literary work that will live."]

more about it. If it be of God it will sound out through eternity, and fetch its echos from the depths of the Infinite; if it be of man, however much he may have prized it, however great the pains he may have taken to utter it in the strains of the immortals, it shall die in the breath that made it.

Wordsworth's great defect is not his want of intellect, nor his want of poetic sensibility, for he possesses both in a high degree; but the fact that he frames all his poems in accordance with a theory. We say not that his theory is false, for in the main it may be true; but no man can write poetry according to a theory. Genius spurns all fetters, all systems of philosophy, and makes and follows his own rules. From the practice of genius, we are to learn the laws of genius. We, critics and system-makers, have no right to attempt to frame a code of laws for his observance. Our glory is to take our law from him, and interpret it faithfully. But Wordsworth, as the theorizer, has attempted to legislate for Wordsworth, as the poet, and hence his failure. Whenever he loses sight of his theory, and abandons himself to the workings of spontaneity, he sings a true song. Would that this were not so seldom!

In the history of our race poetry precedes systems of philosophy. The primitive word is a poem, the last word is a system. So is it with the individual. Spontaneity precedes reflection. Spontaneity gives us all the truth we ever have, but it gives it us enveloped in mystic though enchanting folds. So long as we are satisfied with truth in this envelope, we are satisfied with poetry. But one day it comes into our head to ask the poet what he means. We wish to have the truth he has taught us developed, stript of its mystic folds, laid bare to our gaze, nay, dissected for our better understanding of it. We begin to philosophize, to reflect, to analyze, reason, compare, draw inferences, in a word, form theories, construct systems. In our systems truth is developed, drawn out in distinct propositions, rendered clear, precise, intelligible. After we have done this, why seek to reenvelope truth, why seek to plunge it back into the primitive confusion, where, though all is seen, nothing is seen clearly? Are we wrong in saying this is what Wordsworth does seek to do? He has begun by framing a system, by constructing a philosophy—such as it is—and then he has sought to poetize it. This is an inversion of the order of nature, and it renders Wordsworth the most unnatural of poets. In this we see his great defect, and the cause of his failure.

We are inclined to believe that those who admire Wordsworth, admire him more for his supposed philosophy than for his poetry. They, who have outgrown the material, the soulless philosophy of the last century, and turned their minds inward to seek a more spiritual and living philosophy, seem to themselves to find in Wordsworth a congenial soul. They find after the great events and intense activity which closed the last century, and the echo of which hath not yet died away, something attractive in his gentle spirit, in his quiet smile, and kindly feeling for all animate and inanimate nature. Wearied with the pomp of kings and artificial strut of kinglets, too often and for too long a time the theme of the poet's chant, they have joyed to meet a brother who has an eye for the unpretending objects of nature, and a heart to sympathize with the humble and unobtrusive emotions of ordinary and everyday life. Here we confess we sympathize with Wordsworth as fully as the warmest of his admirers. We find much in his philosophy to approve, much in his quiet and gentle spirit to love, much in his tenderness to all that live and breathe for which we bless him. But all this is said of him as a man, not as a poet. There is many a man we love, whom we would clasp to our "heart of hearts," on whose lips we hang with intense delight, whose words are to us as "apples of gold set in pictures of silver" [Prov 25:11], who nevertheless is no poet.

With the present century commenced a reaction against the stirring and revolutionary spirit of the last. After violent action a season of rest, if not of exhaustion, must follow. This season of exhaustion, or of rest, Wordsworth represents. His song, so far forth as it is a song, is a sort of lullaby, a

Hush, my dear, lie still and slumber.[21]

The virtues he sings are mainly the passive virtues. The minds of many, doubtless, have been turned by the reaction of which we speak to regard these virtues with new favor. Disappointed in its hopes for social progress, saddened and disheartened by the failure of so many projects for advancing man's earthly weal, wearied with the "pomp and circumstance of war,"[22] the soul at the commencement of the present century turned away from active pursuits, came to the conclusion that the only cure for the ills of life is to bear them, and therefore, that the passive virtues are the most Godlike. To the soul in this state Wordsworth is doubtless an acceptable poet. But the passive virtues, after all, are not the highest, nor those best fitted for song. Man was made for action, and the universal sentiment of the race awards the highest rank to the active virtues. He who chants the

[21] [Ed. Isaac Watts' (1674-1748) "A Cradle Hymn," line 1.]

[22] [Ed. Shakespeare's *Othello*, Act 3, scene 3: "pomp and circumstance of glorious war."]

quiet scenes of nature, the gentle affections of the heart, may have listeners, but only at a certain age and in a certain mood of mind; but he who chants the active virtues, though displayed in war, in acts from which the soul shrinks with horror, is sure of the race for his audience and his chorus. Man pants for action, and delights in the strife, the effort, the struggle. The sailor lives in the tempest, but dies in the calm; the old soldier, as he catches the sound of "the ear-piercing fife,"[23] and martial drum, draws himself up, takes a measured step, and longs to rush to the charge again. Sweeter to him than music of "Woodland Linnets"[24] is the volley of musketry, or the thunder of artillery; and dearer by far is the battle ground on which hero grapples with hero, than "flower-enameled meads."[25] And this is right. Life is a warfare, and demands perpetual battle, a warfare in which there is much undoubtedly to be borne, but in which there is still more to be done. Well is it, then, that we are so made that we can delight in action, and joy to behold it as does the war-horse the battle which he snuffs from afar.

The shrine at which Wordsworth worships is innocence. Hence his love and reverence of childhood, which he regards as the type of innocence. Innocence is unquestionably an inoffensive Deity, but it is a negative one. It consists in the absence of sin, not in the presence of virtue. Its value may be learned from the fact that idiots are sometimes termed *Innocents.* We are poor creatures if we are only innocent. The servant who received the one talent, for aught that appears, was innocent. He put his talent to no bad use, but preserved it safe and sound for his master. Nevertheless, he was condemned as a "wicked and slothful servant" [Matt 25:26]. We must have positive virtue in order to recommend us to the favor of God. The praises of innocence, then, are inferior to the praises of virtue, and the worship of innocence is not necessarily the worship of the Most High.

Nor are we sure that childhood is a perfect type of innocence. We confess we cannot join in this baby-worship, which Wordsworth is said to have instituted, and which is becoming somewhat fashion-

[23] [Ed. Shakespeare's *Othello*, Act 3, scene 3.]

[24] [Ed. The reference is to Wordsworth's "The Tables Turned" (1798), line 10 of the following:

Books! 'tis a dull and endless strife:
come, hear the woodland linnet,
How sweet his music on my life,
There's more of wisdom in it.]

[25] [Ed. From William Godwin's *Imogen: A Pastoral Romance: From the Ancient British* (1784), Book 1.]

able among ourselves. "God is a jealous God, visiting the iniquities of the fathers upon the children to the third and fourth generations" [Deut 5:9]. It is a fact well attested by experience that the corruptions of parents descend to their children; and who dare say that the corruptions of Adam's nature, by his transgression, have not passed upon all his posterity?[26] We confess that we have some misgivings about this doctrine of the immaculate holiness of all children, which seems to be put forth by some with as much confidence as if it were a doctrine of revelation. Children are unquestionably born with corrupted natures, and they rarely sooner begin to act than we see some of the fruits of corruption. We must have holy parents in order to have holy children. When parents no longer have a fallen or corrupted nature, then it may be contended that children are born pure and incorrupt.

We also dissent from the doctrine of the superior wisdom of childhood, which Wordsworth hints, and which has some advocates in our own city and country.[27] We love childhood; it joys our heart to witness the child's cherub smile; when overwhelmed with a sense of our own sinfulness, of our shortcomings, or grieved with the shortcomings of others, we sometimes look back with regret to the comparative innocency of childhood, and sigh for that sweet period of life which is gone to return never; but we cannot admit, without some important qualifications, the doctrine we suppose to be implied in the following.

Our birth is but a sleep and a forgetting:
The Soul that rises with us, our life's Star,
Hath had elsewhere its setting,
And cometh from afar:
Not in entire forgetfulness,
And not in utter nakedness,
But trailing clouds of glory do we come
From God, who is our home:
Heaven lies about us in our infancy!
Shades of the prison-house begin to close
Upon the growing Boy,
But He beholds the light, and whence it flows,
He sees it in his joy;

[26] [Ed. This question will eventually turn into an assertion of the doctrine of original sin, a position that will separate Brownson from his Unitarian and Transcendentalist friends. For a clear sign of the change, see "The Mission of Jesus," *Christian World* 1 (January 7, 1843): 2.]

[27] [Ed. Reference is to Amos Bronson Alcott.]

The Youth, who daily farther from the East
Must travel, still is Nature's Priest,
And by the vision splendid
Is on his way attended:
At length the Man perceives it die away,
And fade into the light of common day.[28]

We are not yet prepared to admit the Platonic doctrine that to learn is but to remember, and that all knowledge is a reminiscence. The child is born with all the capacities of the man, but with them undeveloped. The oak may be said to be in the acorn, for its germ is there; but without light and warmth, earth and moisture, with all the acorns in the world, we cannot rear an oak. All does not come from within; something must come from without.[29] The germ is in the child, but when that germ is unfolded into the man, it will be found to contain something it did not in the child. As the child's capacities are unfolded, its knowledge and wisdom increase; and we must continue to believe, that, other things, as say the phrenologists, being equal, hoary age is wiser than "muling and puking"[30] infancy.

Some among us approve Wordsworth because he selects the subjects of his poems from humble life, and because he makes a peddler the mouth piece of his philosophy. In this it is said that he does homage to the democratic tendencies of the age. There may be something in this, much there certainly would be if he were really inspired by these subjects. Saving the case of the Idiot Boy, and which we ought to except, because idiots may be found in high life as well as in low life, we do not recollect an instance where he writes under the influence of real inspiration, when the subject is a humble one, unless it be when recording the worth and giving vent to his sad grief for the loss of his good dog Touser, if Touser be the name.[31] His selection of subjects from humble life always appeared to us a sort of condescension on his part for which no democrat need thank him. However, we like the following, which proves that the author does sometimes utter a thought worth preserving.

Our life is turned
Out of her course, wherever Man is made

[28] [Ed. Wordsworth's "Ode: Intimations of Immortality from Recollections of Childhood" (1803-06), lines 59-77.]

[29] [Ed. This idea of development from outside the self will become a much more consistent theme in Brownson's work after he reads Pierre Leroux in the early 1840s.]

[30] [Ed. Shakespeare, *As You Like It*, Act 2, Scene 7, line 144: "At first the infant, mewling and puking in the nurse's arms."]

[31] [Ed. Reference may be to Wordsworth's "To the Memory of the Same Dog" (1805).]

An offering, or a sacrifice, or a tool,
Or implement, a passive thing employed
As a brute mean, without acknowledgment
Of common right or interest in the end;
Used or abused, as selfishness may prompt.
Say, what can follow for a rational Soul
Perverted thus, but weakness in all good,
And strength in evil? Hence an after-call
For chastisement, and custody, and bonds,
And oft-times death, avenger of the past,
And sole guardian in whose hands we dare
Entrust the future. Not for these sad issues
Was Man created; but to obey the law
Of life, and hope, and action. And 'tis known
That when we stand upon our native soil
Unelbowed by such objects as oppress
Our active powers, those powers themselves become
Strong to subvert our noxious qualities:
They sweep distemper from the busy day,
And make the Chalice of the big round Year
Run o'er with gladness; whence the being moves
In beauty through the world; and all who see
Bless him, rejoicing in his neighborhood.[32]

But notwithstanding this, we have little faith in Wordsworth's democracy. He is a kind-hearted man, that would hurt no living thing, and who shudders to see a single human being suffer. So far, so good. But he has no faith in anything like social equality. He compassionates the poor, and would give the beggar an "awmous"; but measures which would prevent begging, which would place the means of a comfortable subsistence in the hands of all men, so that there should be no poor, he apparently contemplates not without horror. A man is not necessarily inclined to democracy because he sings wagoners, peddlers, and beggars, any more than he is necessarily inclined to aristocracy because he brushes his coat, and maintains his personal dignity and independence. Aristocracy may be found clad in rags, scarcely less often than in embroidery. True democracy compassionates the poor no more than it does the rich. It reverences all men, and seeks to put all men into possession of their native, inalienable rights. It rarely gives alms, except to relieve present suffering; it discovers no beauty in the beggar, and cannot pause to idealize him. It loathes the beggar,

[32] [Ed. *Poetical Works*, 4:305.]

though it loves the man, and seeks to convert him into an independent man, able to live without begging.

Wordsworth sings beggars, we admit, and shows very clearly that a man who begs is not to be despised; but does he ever fire our souls with a desire so to perfect our social system, that beggary shall not be one of its fruits? A Wordsworthian society without beggars, or such feeble old paupers as Simon Lee, would be shorn of all its poetic beauty. Herein lies the defect we discover in his democracy. He would lead us to love all men, but always in the condition in which we find them. This is to us the height of aristocracy. Aristocracy always delights in giving alms, in doing something *for* the poor and needy; but it never delights in taking measures to prevent there being any poor and needy, or to enable the poor and needy to work out their own salvation. Democracy, on the other hand, attempts to do little *for* the people. It believes the people do not need so many dry nurses as it has been thought; it believes the people, if their kind masters will let them alone, are fully competent to take care of themselves. It labors therefore to remove oppression, to take off the restraints which have been imposed upon their natural liberty, and to leave them free to employ their own limbs in procuring the means of their own well-being. Aristocracy gives alms to the poor, and nurses them as dependents; democracy proclaims their rights as men, and seeks to secure to them their possession. Aristocracy, with much kindness of look and voice, seeks to relieve the hunger of today; democracy seeks, often with a stern look and a harsh voice, to lay down principles and establish an order of things which shall relieve the hunger of all coming time. Good Henry the Fourth of France,[33] in the benevolence of his heart, wished he could put a chicken into the pot of every man in his kingdom; democracy would so arrange matters that every man in its kingdom shall have it in his power to boil a chicken whenever he pleases. We have seen nothing in Wordsworth to induce us to believe that his feeling towards the poor differs essentially from that of good king Henri Quatre.

The tendency of a man's soul is usually to be ascertained by the party with which he arranges himself. Wordsworth goes with the high Tory party of his country, and opposes, as much as a man of his inertness can, the efforts of the friends of freedom. During the wars created by the French Revolution all his sympathies and all his powers were consecrated to the defense of the tyrants. His odes and his

[33] [Ed. Henry IV (1553-1610) was a French Protestant who became Catholic four years after he became king of France (1589).]

sonnets, blasphemously inscribed to liberty, were in praise of those who fought for old abuses, never in praise of those who sided with the people. If he loves the people and desires their freedom, he has taken an odd way of showing it. We are aware that the French Revolution is a bugbear to many; but we dare be known among those who see in it a great, though terrible, effort of humanity to gain possession of those rights which Christianity had taught her to regard as her inalienable patrimony, and to cherish as the apple of her eye, and we can own no man as a friend to his God, to his race, or to his country, who sided with those who took up arms against it, and sought to perpetuate old wrongs, time-hallowed oppressions. He must repent of his doings in sackcloth and ashes, with deep humility, with all the marks of sincere contrition, acknowledge his error, before we can believe the love of liberty lives in his heart. That Revolution had doubtless its excesses, but it needs no apology. Its apology stands in the fact that it has been. Its excesses will be forgotten much sooner than the excesses, the proscriptions, the murders, the soul-destroying tyrannies, of kings and aristocracies. The day will come when humanity shall regard the chapter which records that Revolution as the brightest in her history. We should be the most shameless of all the world, citizens as we are of a country which owes its national existence to a Revolution, whose institutions are based on the very principles of liberty and equality, which France sought, but sought in vain, yet not wholly in vain, to make the basis of her own, did we not sympathize with the French Revolution, and pity the blindness of a Wordsworth, who could not see that the cause of humanity was in it.

But we can continue our remarks no further. We say in conclusion, that we regard Wordsworth as endowed by nature with a fine poetic temperament, and respectable talents, which he has assiduously cultivated. He has a reflective as well as a dreamy turn of mind, though his mind has but a limited horizon, and is full of narrow and local prejudices, as is unfortunately the case with most Englishmen. We regard him as the Cowley[34] of the nineteenth century, though on this point we will not insist, for we are not very familiar with Cowley's works. As the poet of external nature, he is inferior to our own Bryant.[35] We have read nothing of his that pleases us so much as Bryant's "Death of the Flowers," and we would by no means ex-

[34] [Ed. Reference is probably to Abraham Cowley (1618-67), an English poet known especially for his *Pindarique Odes* (1656).]

[35] [Ed. William Cullen Bryant (1794-1878) was a lawyer who became a poet, and then became the co-owner and editor of the *New York Evening Post* in 1829.]

change "The Ages" for "The Excursion."[36] Wordsworth is gentle and amiable, but he wants vigor, force of soul. We should like him altogether better were he made of sterner stuff, were he more robust and manly. But enough. There are moods of mind when we can read some of his pieces without any extraordinary effort. He does not address himself to the broad, universal soul of the race, but there will always be individuals and coteries to admire him.

[36] [Ed. "Death of the Flowers" (1825) about the death of Byrant's beloved sister who died at the age of twenty-two. "The Ages" (1821) was Byrant's longest poem, stating his own philosophy of life; it was delivered as the Phi Beta Kappa poem at Harvard's commencement.]

13.

FOREIGN STANDARD LITERATURE[1]

Boston Quarterly Review 2 (April, 1839): 187-205

When we first meditated this article, we designed to discuss the literary merits of Goethe and Schiller, and to form an estimate of their relative greatness. With this design, we began to study anew the principal works of these illustrious writers. But as we went on with the productions of Goethe, we felt every day an increasing sense of our inability to measure his height, and construct a *Mecanique Celeste*,[2] from the various and conflicting phenomena observed in his writings. What seemed single stars at first, appeared double and treble on a second examination, and were at last found to be constellations. The reader of Goethe is often surprised to see that a song or story, which at first appeared only a clever monument of the author's rythming skill, is really covered all over with hieroglyphics, which are full of deep significance. The first attempt, therefore, was speedily abandoned.

It is difficult to form an estimate of the character of Goethe. He is so "many-sided," that "you never know where to find him." At one time, you find him recommending action and practical life. He counsels men to take a part in the doing and driving of the world. But when French cannon thunder at the gates of Weimar, the first poet of Germany, that "many-sided man," fearful lest his mind should be disturbed, sits down to study Chinese. Now he seems cool, indifferent to the great interests of humanity, and again he is filled with the love of man. He seems to have followed an Epicurean plan of life. The words of an old writer would have served him for a motto: "Come on, therefore, let us enjoy the good things that are present, and let us speedily use the creatures like as in youth. Let us fill ourselves with costly wine and ointments, and let no flower of the spring pass by us. Let us cover ourselves with rosebuds before they be withered. Let

[1] [Ed. Review of *Specimens of Foreign Standard Literature*, edited by George Ripley, vol. 3 (Boston: Hilliard, Gray & Company, 1839).]

[2] [Ed. Probably a reference to Pierre Simon, Marquis de Laplace's (1749-1827) massive five-volume *Mécanique céleste* (1799-1825), a landmark in applying mathematical knowledge to physical astronomy.]

none of us go without his part of our voluptuousness. Let us leave tokens of our joyfulness in every place" [Wisd 2:6-9], for "our life is short and tedious, and in the death of man there is no remedy" [Wisd 2:1].

But whatever was his character as a man, his power as a writer is unrivaled among the moderns, and his claims to immortal renown uncontested. He goes silently up to take his place among the fixed stars of creation. His works pass "into the ages," to shine with perennial brilliancy. His faults as a man detract nothing from the artistic value of his works. An amateur would be censured for his folly, if he should refuse to admire a painting of Adrien Braur,[3] because that artist was the most licentious of profligates.

All true lovers of poetry will gratefully welcome the little volume Mr. Dwight[4] and his friends have prepared from these great masters of German Art. The pieces selected from Goethe are perhaps the best specimens of his style; many of them are masterpieces—models in this department of art; perhaps they are the most favorable that could be selected, though we are far from believing, with Mr. Dwight, that they are all which would be valuable to the English reader. Some of these little pieces will not, at first sight, commend themselves to the general reader of English poetry. That merit must be very shallow which can be seen through at a single glance. The German Lyrics, and especially Goethe's, differ essentially from the productions of the great masters of the divine art among us. English poetry overflows with thought. Its thoughtfulness is its most striking trait. It is profound. Metaphysical treatises pass for good, genuine English poetry when translated into verse. Homilies have been "done into meter," and pass current as lyrics, odes, and songs. Compare the sonnets of Shakespeare, Milton, and Wordsworth—in many respects their most remarkable productions—with the best sonnets of any other nation, and the difference in thoughtfulness will immediately appear. The former are thoughts chiseled in cold marble, or rather they are huge crystals, that have silently elaborated themselves, and speak of wondrous power that "lives and works unseen."[5]

[3] [Ed. Reference may be to Adriaen Brouwer (ca. 1606-38), a Flemish genre painter who helped to establish the "low life" school of Dutch painting.]

[4] [Ed. John Sullivan Dwight (1813-93) was at the time a Transcendentalist Unitarian minister in Northampton, Massachusetts. He selected and translated the works of Goethe and Schiller for volume 3 of *Specimens of Foreign Standard Literature*. He later became a music critic and president of the Harvard Musical Association.]

[5] [Ed. Unable to identify quotation.]

English poetry is full of energy; there is a majesty in its march. Its images are bold and distinct. Our lyric poetry, partakes of the same character. The English mind is fully portrayed therein. It is based on good sound common sense, and seldom rises far above the actual. Even our songs have little of that light, cloudy, dream-like, evanescent substance which forms the material of so many German songs. Our songs are simple; no man can mistake their meaning; the allusions are generally broad hints. You see the thread on which the pearls are strung.

The German song is quite different; it is filled rather with profound sentiments than profound thoughts. Yet sometimes vast meaning is condensed in a few words. It is complicated, allusive, full of dark hints, "nods and becks and wreathed smiles."[6] Goethe's songs, in particular, are often bewitchingly vague, all their meaning does not come forth at once. The English song is a tree. You see its trunk, its branches, its leaves. You learn the blossom from the bough, and the fruit from the blossom. The only mystery is, "How has it grown?" The German song is a cloud. You cannot define its shape. By looking at one phase, you learn nothing of the next; for one side may be dark, and the other all covered with rainbow light. It is in a perpetual change, and often "overflows with terrible beauty."[7] Like the cloud that Hamlet gazed on, it takes all the forms of the observer's fancy.[8] This vagueness is peculiar to the songs of the Germans, and this people have a prescriptive right to be shadowy, for the legend says, with deep truth, that while the French had the land, and the English the sea, the Germans had the clouds, for their inheritance.[9] But there is a simple freshness in German poetry, especially in lyric composition. There is no imitation of hackneyed models; no "troubling of the mind" of Goethe and Schiller towards Orpheus and Petrarch,[10] or any of the canonized oracles of song. A Teutonic spirit clothes itself *in its own* Teutonic dress.

[6] [Ed. John Milton's *L'Allegro*, line 25.]

[7] [Ed. Ralph Waldo Emerson's, "Literary Ethics," in *The Collected Works of Ralph Waldo Emerson*, general editor, Alfred R. Ferguson, 5 vols. (Cambridge, Massachusetts: The Belknap Press of Harvard University Press, 1971-1994), 1:100.

[8] [Ed. Hamlet's clouds is a reference to Shakespeare's *Hamlet*, Act 3, scene 2.]

[9] [Ed. One source of the legend is from the Baroness Madame de Staël-Holstein who attributes it to Jean Paul Richter in her *De l'Allemagne* (1808-1810), chp. 2, "Of the Manners and Character of the Germans," *Germany*, trans. O. W. Wight (London, 1883).]

[10] [Ed. Orpheus, son of Apollo and a Muse, was the quintessential mythical singer whose song had more than human power. Francesco Petrarch (1304-74) was an Italian humanist scholar, poet, and author of the *De viris illustribus* (1338-39, rev. 1341-43). The text was repeatedly translated into English and was much read in the United States as in England.]

The high hymn of German bards,
—in its own fulness swelling,
From the heart's own depths out-welling,
Spurns restraint, nor rule regards.[11]

The careless reader will perhaps sometimes pass over the beautiful little pieces of Goethe, not discovering what deep meaning lies under them. But the true poetic Argus[12] will be at no loss to penetrate their depths.

Goethe's songs have been carefully arranged by the translator, and wrought into a beautiful mosaic, thus affording a more correct delineation of the artist's character than most biographies would furnish. You see how he thought, and how he felt; what he aspired after, and what he reached. As he was an Epicurean, so his songs are the songs of this world. The different periods of his life are distinctly marked in these pieces, and the careful reader will readily refer one song to his fiery youth; another to his philosophic manhood, when he had "a generous view of life," and still others to a period of more mature wisdom "when he was too old to sin," as some one has said.

These translations are not all by the same hand. Mr. Dwight has been favored with the assistance of Mr. Frothingham, Mr. Bancroft, Mr. Clarke, Miss Fuller, Mr. Channing, Mr. Hedge, Mr. Haven, Mr. Brooks, and Mr. Cranch.[13] The different writers necessarily translate in different spirits, and in obedience to different theories of art. But it is certainly remarkable that ten different persons should be found in New England able to produce such fine translations as are contained in the present specimens. But the book must be suffered to

[11] [Ed. *Specimens* 3:333.]

[12] [Ed. In Greek mythology Argos was the son of Zeus and the Argive Niobe. He was a giant with a hundred eyes who was killed by Hermes and then his eyes were put in the peacock's tail.]

[13] [Ed. The references are to Nathaniel Langdon Frothingham (1793-1870), Unitarian minister of the First Unitarian Church of Boston; George Bancroft, previously identified in this volume; James Freeman Clarke (1810-99), Unitarian minister in Louisville, KY, and member of the Transcendentalist Club; Sarah Margaret Fuller (1810-50), a leading Transcendentalist feminist intellectual; William Henry Channing (1810-84), Unitarian minister in Cincinnati and editor of the Transcendentalist *Western Messenger* (1839); Frederic Henry Hedge (1805-90), Unitarian minister in Bangor, Maine, and founder and charter member of the Transcendentalist Club; G. W. Haven could not be identified; Charles Timothy Brooks (1813-83), Unitarian minister of Newport, Rhode Island, and a Transcendentalist poet; and Christopher Pearse Cranch (1813-92), Unitarian minister with Clarke in the Ohio Valley, editor of the *Western Messenger* (1827-39), Transcendentalist poet and landscape painter.]

speak for itself. The "November Song" has a cheerless title, which it does not merit:

The Archer!—not the ancient one,
Within whose cheerless Sign
Winters the far-retreating Sun,
And seems but half to shine;
The Archer boy! to him the song,
Who 'mid the roses plays,
And hears and aims, nor aimeth long,
But hits the heart always.
Through him the winter evenings lend,
So hateful else, and bare,
To us full many a worthy friend,
And many a lady fair.
And hence forth shall the charming child
I' the starry heavens be set,
And, rising, setting, clear and mild,
Shoot twinkles at us yet.[14]

The following, with the scriptural title of "Vanitas vanitatum vanitas," is a good disclosure of the author's philosophy of life:

I've set my heart upon nothing, you see;
Hurrah!
And so the world goes well with me.
Hurrah!
And who has a mind to be fellow of mine,
Why, let him take hold and help me drain
These mouldy lees of wine.
I set my heart at first upon wealth;
Hurrah!
And bartered away my peace and health;
But, ah!
The slippery change went about like air,
And when I had clutched me a handful here,
Away it went there.
set my heart upon woman next;
Hurrah!
For her sweet sake was oft perplexed;
But, ah!
The False one looked for a daintier lot,

[14] [Ed. *Specimens*, 19.]

The Constant one wearied me out and out,
The Best was not easily got.
I set my heart upon travels grand,
Hurrah!
And spurned our plain old Fatherland;
But, ah!
Nought seemed to be just the thing it should,
Most comfortless beds and indifferent food,
My tastes misunderstood.
I set my heart upon sounding fame;
Hurrah!
And, lo! I'm eclipsed by some upstart's name;
And, ah!
When in public life I loomed quite high,
The folks that passed me would look awry:
Their very worst friend was I.
And then I set my heart upon war.
Hurrah!
We gained some battles with eclat.
Hurrah!
We troubled the foe with sword and flame,
(And some of our friends fared quite the same)
I lost a leg for fame.
Now I've set my heart upon nothing, you see;
Hurrah!
And the whole wide world belongs to me.
Hurrah!
The feast begins to run low, no doubt;
But at the old cask we'll have one good bout.
Come, drink the lees all out![15]

Goethe's connection with Lili,[16] which did not ripen into marriage, gave occasion to some exquisite little poems. The following extract from some lines addressed to a Golden Heart, received from her, and worn round his neck, is a good specimen.

The bird may burst the silken chain which bound him,
Flying to the green home, which fits him best;
But, ah! he bears the prisoner's badge around him,

[15] [Ed. Ibid., 51.]

[16] [Ed. In 1775 Goethe was briefly engaged to Lili Schönemann, a young woman of high social standing in Frankfurt.]

Still by the piece about his neck distressed.
He ne'er can breathe his free, wild notes again;
They're stifled by the pressure of his chain.[17]

Here it may be well to speak of Mr. Dwight's principles of translation. He says—

"Only such of them are given, as have, from time to time, interested the translator, and such as he could translate in the hours when they have most filled his fancy and spoken to his experience. This has been the only principle of selection. Many a time he has turned them over, attracted only by a significant look, a promising glimpse of a meaning, in here and there one; and often has a song, several times dismissed with a look of irrecognition, revealed itself afterwards, in all its beauty, by the merest accident, when some mood or circumstance has thrown him into the right point of view, or when some fresh experience, grave or trifling, has recalled the song as its fittest word. On this fact he founds whatever confidence he has that these translations are in any degree successful. Full justice to the original could not be done. A song is but a breath. It came out whole, just as it is, as much a mystery to the poet as to any one. Its dress cannot be torn away from its substance; the rhythm, the tones, the coloring, the imagery, the very length or shortness of it, are determined by a sort of inward necessity—that nicer instinct, by which the soul, in all its genuine productions, instantly chooses out of nature whatever will serve it for a language. A song is a feeling which has found utterance in a beautiful form, and satisfied itself. The form is not the container of the spirit of a song; the form is thoroughly instinct with the spirit, and, in fact, grew out of it. The spirit, therefore, or essence of a lyric piece cannot be transfused out of one form into another. Imitation always fails, and would, even if it were possible to effect an exact literal copy. The translator's only hope, then, is to reproduce, to reoriginate, to repeat, as near as may be, in himself the very experience in which the song first had its birth. Let not this ideal of translation be deemed a boast of what has been realized in the present case: it is a simple confession of inability."[18]

Is not this the only true theory of translation? How can a lyric be adequately rendered into a new language, unless the translator is stirred by the same spirit which moved the author, and reproduces the same form? In most instances Mr. Dwight has come nearer his ideal than his modesty has permitted him to confess. Some of the versions seem

[17] [Ed. *Specimens*, 31.]
[18] [Ed. Ibid., 361, 362.]

to have sprung out of the original at the command of a magician. Others, however, are not so well executed. But two or three, to our judgment, are improvements upon the originals. One of these is "restless love," which almost defies translation. Sometimes, however, the version falls far below the original; this fault is not always to be ascribed to the haste, or carelessness of the translator, but to the fact that the spirit and form of a lyric cannot be separated, and the English language will not take the requisite form, or supply the necessary words. Some of Goethe's songs are so Teutonic, they will not admit of *Anglification.* One of the most pleasing translations in the book, "The Minstrel," p. 62, is far inferior to the original, for this reason: the spirit of the piece is well preserved in the rendering, but the capital charm of the original consists in the language; the beautiful adaptation of the sound to the sense. Mr. Dwight has given us the sense without the sound. But in this he has merely failed to accomplish an impossibility. The original has an exquisite imitative melody, which it would be unfair to ask of a translation. The first four lines of the fifth stanza are beautiful in the version.

I sing but as the wood-bird sings,
That dwells in shady tree;
The song that from my light heart springs
Is rich reward for me.[19]

Excepting a slight imperfection in the second line, this verse is exceedingly well translated. But to our ear, the first line in the German has the clear warble of the black-bird in its changing notes.

Ich singe wieder Vogel sings
Der in dem Zweigen wohnet,
Das Lied das aus der Kehle springt,
Ist Lohn der reichlich lohnet.

But in the general way the translation is surprisingly well done. High as Mr. Dwight has placed his ideal, he has uniformly approached nearer to it than he could reasonably expect. The same is to be said of the pieces from the other writers, who have honored this book with their contributions. It is rare that a judicious critic will find occasion for censure. The following specimen shows the fidelity with which the original is adhered to. We give Mr. Dwight's version and our own literal one beside it.

[19] [Ed. Ibid., 63.]

TO THE MOON.

FREE VERSION.

Fillest hill and vale again,
Still, with softening light!
Loosest from the world's cold chain
All my soul tonight!
Spreadest round me, far and nigh,
Soothingly, thy smile;
From thee, as from friendship's eye,
Sorrow shrinks the while.
Every echo thrills my heart—
Glad and gloomy mood.
Joy and sorrow both have part
In my solitude.
River, river, glide along!
I am sad, alas!
Fleeting things are love and song,
Even so they pass!
I have had and I have lost
What I long for yet;
Ah! why will we, to our cost,
Simple joys forget?
River, river, glide along,
Without stop or stay!
Murmur, whisper, to my song
In melodious play,
Whether on a winter's night,
Rise thy swollen floods,
Or in spring thou hast delight
Watering the young buds.
Happy he, who, hating none,
Leaves the world's dull noise,
And, with trusty friend alone,
Quietly enjoys
What, forever unexpressed,
Hid from common sight,
Through the mazes of the breast
Softly steals by night![20]

LITERAL VERSION.

Fillest again bush and vale
Still with mist-splendor,
At last settest free once more
My soul entirely.
Widen'st over my meadows,
Softening, thy glance,
Like the eye of a friend, mild
On my destiny.
My heart feels every echo
Of gay and sad time;
It walks betwixt Joy and Pain
In the solitude.
Flow on, flow on, lovely stream,
I shall ne'er be glad;
Thus Sport and love must away,
And Fidelity.
Once, indeed, I possessed
What is so precious,
That man, to his sorrow,
Never forgets it.
Rush, River, along the vale,
Without stop or rest;
Rush, and whisper to my song
Melodious notes,
When thou in the winter night,
Raging, overflowest,
Or in spring's splendor
Waterest young shoots.
Happy he, who from the world,
Without hate, shuts himself;
Holds a friend to his bosom,
And with him enjoys
Whatever unknown by men
Or not conceived of,
Thro' the labyrinth of the breast
Wanders in the night.

[20] [Ed. Ibid., 32, 33.]

There is a pleasing family picture, called "For life."[21] The plan is quite simple; a wedded pair are together looking out of their cottage to see the blessings the "warm spring rain has brought." The storm is swelling in the blue and misty distance, but love dwells with them. They look, very naturally, to the little grove of trees—sober as the cares of man and wife, with violets, like youthful love, at their feet. They think of the times when they, two bashful lovers, stole thither to gather the first flowers of spring. Two emblematic doves fly thither at the same moment. The aged pair speak of their marriage, when new moons rejoiced in chorus, when a *new* sun arose, and *new* life began. They speak of their children, and add that this is the anniversary of their wedding:

> Still, still to love we listen,
> While years are gliding on;
> And now we go to christen
> Our grand-child and our son.[22]

The English reader will naturally be reminded of a similar piece in our tongue, "John Anderson my Jo, John."[23] Each is characteristic of its own nation. The latter proceeded from a grave, thoughtful, forecasting people, and its last stanza would do well at the end of a sermon; yet it is perfectly natural in the mouth of a religious woman, even in a song.

Goethe's Ballads will, perhaps, be more popular amongst us than his songs. The "Fisher" has long been a favorite in Germany. It is difficult to preserve the dreamy character of the original, in a translation, but in general it is quite well done:

> The water rolled, the water swelled;
> A fisher sat thereby,
> And quietly his angle held;
> Chilled to his heart was he.
> The water in dreamy motion kept,
> As he sat in dreamy mood;
> A wave hove up—and a damsel stepped,
> All dripping, from the flood.
> She sang to him, she spake to him:
> 'Why wilt thou lure away
> My sweet brood by thy human art

[21] [Ed. Ibid., 37.]
[22] [Ed. Ibid., 40.]
[23] [Ed. From Robert Burns' (1759-96) "John Anderson, my Jo," line 1.]

To the deadly light of day?
Ah! knewest thou how light of heart
The little fishes live,
Thou wouldst come down, all as thou art,
And thy true life receive.
Bathes not the sun with all his skies?
Bathes not the moon by night,
To breathe my dew awhile, and rise
All smiling doubly bright?
And tempt thee not the deep, deep skies,
Here spread in watery blue?
And tempt thee not shine own dark eyes
Down through th'eternal dew?'
The water rolled, the water swelled;
It wetted his bare feet;
A something through his bosom thrilled;
He seemed his love to meet.
She spake to him, she sang to him;
With him 't was quickly o'er:
Half drew she him, half sank he in,
And never was seen more.[24]

In one or two instances, Mr. Dwight gives us two versions; one literal, and his own; the other free, and from the pen of Mr. Bancroft:

MY GODDESS.

LITERAL VERSION.

Which of the Deities
Shall we give the palm to?
With none dispute I;
Yet would I give it
To that ever-changeable,
Ever-youthful,
Singular child of Jove,
His darling daughter, Fantasy.[25]

FREE VERSION.

Who, of Heaven's immortal train,
Shall the highest prize obtain?
Strife I would with all give o'er,
But there's one I'll aye adore,
Ever new and ever changing,
Thro' the paths of marvel ranging,
Dearest in her father's eye,
Jove's own darling Fantasy.[26]

[24] [Ed. *Specimens*, 67, 68.]
[25] [Ed. Ibid., 94.]
[26] [Ed. Ibid., 97.]

Gretchen's Song is a pretty little piece:

My peace is hence,
    My heart is lone,
My rest is for aye
    And ever gone.

The following shows to what the author aspired:

Ah! that the true creative Soul
    Through all my sense were ringing,
Like pieces ready for the flower,
    From out my senses springing.[27]

We would gladly multiply extracts, but have only space for Mr. Dwight's definition of a Philistine:

"The word 'Philistine' (*Philister*) was originally a cant term, among the students in the German universities, for a townsman, a shopkeeper. In its more extended use, it describes the narrow, positive character, made up of common places and conventionalisms, who is a perpetual contradiction in the way of a poetic nature, like Goethe's, wishing to live widely and genially 'in the Whole, the good, the Fair,' extemporizing life, culling the fresh flowers of the moment in its own fulness of activity, exploring all regions of thought and poetry and love, resolutely *ignoring* the hackneyed falsehood which timid spirits have turned life into; spurning the poor complacency of settled maxims and set aims, which make it seem as if the soul's limits had all been tried, and experience had settled beforehand for each new comer *what life is.* This may seem to be making many words of a definition. But a true definition of a 'Philistine' would be an exhibition, by contrast, of the most characteristic and instructive phase in which Goethe presented himself to the world; it would show, embodied in a word, all which it was the first article of his creed to shun. He would find *what life was* for himself. He would *be,* and not let himself be molded into a tame creature of views, purposes, habits, and manners, which, however successfully caught and worn, would only belie his own real nature, and could have no root within him. He wished to begin life afresh, and not take it at second hand, living by pattern and on purpose, with painful fidelity, as too many do, consulting the past to find out what is in them. He had unbounded faith in himself, which, practically rendered, means this: Let a man only be himself, and he will be the best which he can be; and which,

[27] [Ed. Ibid., 124]

practically tried, continually surprises him with the discovery that nothing is too much to hope to him that is faithful to his hope; that the ideal is the real, and that the large presumptions of childhood are the genuine oracles, and that immortality, peace, one-ness with God, are more substantial verities, and are nearer than most theologies have made them. Hence, all *Philisterey* was his especial annoyance; all canting moralities, which distrust nature, and do not fortify and save, but only impoverish and unman the soul; all *systems* in theology, philosophy, taste, which foreclose the illimitable, ever-fresh and trackless fields of thought; all narrow criticism, at war with individuality; all life-plans which voluntarily include drudgery, low or high, as such; all yoking of the soul's Pegasus into the vulgar plough of self-enslaving thrift; all toleration of conventionalisms and utilities, except as knacks or conveniences, in the free realm of poetry, and pure literature, and art, where, to work with an eye to consequences, to popular effect, to established formulas, or admired patterns, is at best but clever manufacturing, not creating from the life. His genius would be true to itself. But *Philisterey*—the 'knowingness' of the world—does not trust the honesty of genius—must hamper it with all the vulgar pledges and securities that it will not go wrong."[28]

Schiller was an antipode to Goethe. He was full of lofty aspirations. He was less a poet than his illustrious rival, but we fancy he was more a man. But it is needless to speak of his character or merits, while Carlyle's life of him is before the public.[29] We will give a few specimens.

The following is smooth and liquid. It is a most perfect translation:

INDIAN DEATH SONG.

On the mat he's sitting there:
See! he sits upright,
With the same look that he ware
When he saw the light.
But where now the hand's clinched weight?
Where the breath he drew,
That to the Great Spirit late
Forth the pipe-smoke blew?
Where the eyes, that, falcon-keen,
Marked the rein-deer pass,
By the dew upon the green,
Where with beasts of chase each wood,
Where with birds each tree,
Where with fish is every flood
Stocked full pleasantly.
He above with spirits feeds;
We, alone and dim,
Left to celebrate his deeds,
And to bury him.
Bring the last sad offerings hither!
Chant the death lament!
All inter with him together,

[28] [Ed. Ibid., 376-78.]

[29] [Ed. *The Life of Friedrich Schiller* (London: Printed for Taylor & Hessey, 1825; Boston: Carter, Hendee, 1833).]

By the waving grass?
These the limbs, that, unconfined,
Bounded through the snow,
Like the stag that's twenty-tyned,
Like the mountain roe!
These the arms, that, stout and tense,
Did the bong-string twang!
See, the life is parted hence!
See, how loose they hang!
Well for him! he's gone his ways
Where are no more snows;
Where the fields are decked with maize,
That unplanted grows;
That can him content.
'Neath his head the hatchet hide,
That he swung so strong;
And the bear's ham set beside,
For the way is long;
Then the knife, sharp let it be,
That from foeman's crown,
Quick, with dexterous cuts but three,
Skin and tuft brought down;
Paints, to smear his frame about,
Set within his hand,
That he redly may shine out
In the spirits' land.[30]

He sings of the dignity of Woman in a fine strain:

Honored be Woman! To her it is given
To twine with our life the bright roses of heaven;
'Tis hers to be weaving affection's sweet bond;
Beneath the chaste veil she loves to retire,
And nourish in silence the holy fire,
That burns in a bosom faithful and fond.
Far beyond truth's simple dwelling
Man's wild spirit loves to sweep;
And his heart is ever swelling,
Tossed on passion's stormy deep.
To the distant good aspiring,
There is still no peace for him;
Through the very stars, untiring,
He pursues his dazzling dream.
But Woman's mild glance, like a charm, overtakes him,
And from his visions of wandering wakes him,
Warning him back to the present to flee.
In the mother's still cot her enjoyment
Finds she in modest and quiet employment;
Faithful daughter of nature is she.[31]

The author's own character is well delineated in the following lines:

LIGHT AND WARMTH.

The world the generous spirit meets,
Free-hearted, nought concealing;
Trusting to find in all he greets
His own o'erflowing feeling;

[30] [Ed. *Specimens*, 234, 235.]
[31] [Ed. Ibid., 329.]

Pledging, with honest fervor warm,
  To truth the aid of his true arm.
But men are selfish, mean, and small,
  He fails not long of seeing;
The worldly throng are eager all
  To seek their own well-being.
Sullen and cold he stands apart,
  And love is frozen in his heart.
Alas! Truth's brightest beaming ray
  Too oft no heat diffuses;
He's blest, who, with experience gray,
  No youthful ardor loses.
Wouldst thou attain thy highest good,
  Blend warmth of heart with wisdom shrewd.[32]

Schiller's pieces are good expressions of the aspirings of the human soul. We are never satisfied with what is attained. On Mount Carmel we sigh after Zion; on Zion we languish for Eden; and when that is reached, we aspire to heaven. Thus, an ideal, when realized, becomes the foundation of other ideals, still higher and more beautiful; as fast as our dreams become life, they send up other dreams that haunt us like a passion. This feeling of dissatisfaction, so common in Schiller, and so rare in Goethe, expresses itself in the "Pilgrims," from which the following extract is made:

THE PILGRIM.

"Life's first beams were bright around me,
  When I left my father's cot,
Breaking every tie that bound me
  To that dear and hallowed spot!

Childish hopes and youthful pleasures!
  Freely I renounced them all;
Went in quest of nobler treasures,
  Trusting to a higher call.

For to me a voice had spoken,
  And a Spirit seemed to say,
Wander forth; the path is broken;
  Yonder, eastward lies thy way.

Rest not till a golden portal
  Thou hast reached; there enter in;
And what thou hast prized as mortal,
  There, immortal life shall win!"[33]

We would gladly notice some of the larger pieces, in particular, the "Song of the Bell," "The Walk," "Ideals," "Hero and Leander," with several others. But we have only time for a few words on the "Artists," a work which displays the profoundness of Schiller's mind

[32] [Ed. Ibid., 342.]
[33] [Ed. Ibid., 226.]

better than any other single piece he has produced. This poem is a philosophy and a history of art. It commences by extolling the beauty and dignity of man, bids him remember the hand that found him an orphan in his tears, and taught him lofty duties in his play. The bee and the silkworm are man's superiors in skill and industry; all high spirits share knowledge with him; but he alone has art:

Only through Beauty's Morning-gate
wouldst thou to Knowledge penetrate.
The mind, to face truth's higher glances,
Must swim some time in Beauty's trances.
    The heavenly harping of the Muses,
Whose sweetest trembling through thee rings,
    A higher life into thy soul infuses,
And wings it upward to the Soul of Things.
The truth, which had for centuries to wait,
    The truth, which reason had grown old to find,
Lay in the symbol of the Fair and Great,
    Felt from the first by every child-like mind.
'T was Virtue's beauty made her honored so:
    A finer instinct shrunk back, when it saw
    The ugliness of sin, ere Solon wrote the law,
Forcing the plant unwillingly to grow.
Long ere the thinker's intellect severe
    The notion of eternal space could win,
Who ever gazed up at yon starry sphere,
    That did not feel it prophesied within?[34]

Truth, under the name of Urania, takes the form of beauty, to please the infant eye of man, and win him to her. When he is driven out of paradise, she accompanies him, guiding him to virtue. The poet then speaks of the well-being of those who are blessed by doing the holy work of truth. The wild man took little notice of nature as she flew past him. But art followed close behind her, and traced her form. Then nature yielded to art. The plastic power awoke in the rude bosom; nature confided her riddle to inquisitive man. He reproduced her works, in architecture, sculpture, and unending song.

The choosing of a lily or a rose,
    With skilful choice into a nosegay bound,
So the first form of Art from Nature rose;

[34] [Ed. Ibid., 208.]

Then nosegays into wreaths were wound,
And so a second loftier Art began
From the creative hand of man.
The child of beauty, all complete alone,
From your still-shaping hand goes forth,
But to a new idea must yield the crown,
As soon as realized on earth.
The column must proportion's law obey,
And to the sister group its graces lend;
The hero in the host of heroes blend,
And Homer's harp begins the Epic lay.[35]

The barbarians were enraptured at these works. The song of Orpheus made heroes, even of them.[36] Then the soul breathed a freer air. Manhood shone on the brow, and thought came forth to assert its right. Thus man stood forth:

Upon his cheek there bloomed a smile;
His voice's soul-full play the while
In melody flowed forth;
His moist eye swam with feelings fond;
And Grace and Humor, in harmonious bond,
To every word gave worth.[37]

Next art matures her works, and strives after higher ideals. Man carries art with him, wherever he goes:

The boundaries of Knowledge disappear;
The soul
Sets farther forward Nature's goal,
And speeds her on her dim career.

Man is reconciled with destiny and clothes her in graceful forms. Poetry shimmers over our barren life, like the evening red over the field. At last the goddess, who hitherto had pleased man, conducted him, and wakened his higher life, under the guise of beauty, throws off her veil, and stands before him as simple truth. He is astonished,

[35] [Ed. Ibid., 212.]

[36] [Ed. The song of Orpheus refers to Orpheus' song in Hades after the death of Eurydice, his new wife who had died and gone to Hades. Orpheus descended to Hades and sang so magnificently that Hades allowed her to return if Orpheus promised not to look back when leading her up. He failed the test and lost her forever.]

[37] [Ed. *Specimens*, 213.]

like Telemachus,[38] at finding his companion was a god. He concludes in a noble strain:

> On bold wing seek a loftier sphere,
> Above your narrow time-career,
> That on your mirror clear may dawn
> From far the coming century's morn.
> O'er all the thousand winding ways
>   Of rich Variety
> Meet ye at last with glad embrace
>   Round the high throne of Unity!
> As into seven softer hues
>   Shivers the silvery beam of light;
> As all the seven rainbow hues
>   Run back into the dazzling white;
> So round the swimming eyes of youth
>   With all your glancing witcheries play;
> So flow into one bond of truth,
>   Into one stream of perfect Day.[39]

It now remains to say a few words more upon the manner in which these translations have been executed. Sometimes we find additions made to the original; somtimes a thought is omitted from it. Occasionally we notice an imperfect rhythm; or a halting verse. Such are the following: "Oh happy ye, of millions the few."[40] "Leander" and "arrow" are made to rhyme together, p. 266; "toward" and "coward" are "unequally yoked."[41] Some verses are not melodious; e.g., "My sweet brood by thy human art," in the third line of the second stanza in "The Fisher." "On faith's sunny mountain, wave, Floating far," &c.,[42] is another instance. Expressions of doubtful propriety are sometimes fixed upon the translator. Such as "Ideal and rarity;"[43] "wisest" is used for the wisest thought.[44] But we only mention these slight blemishes, which can easily be amended in the next edition, which is already called for.

[38] [Ed. Telemachus was the son of Odysseus and Penelope in Homer's *Odyssey*, where he develops from a timid to a very resourceful and self-reliant young man.]

[39] [Ed. *Specimens*, 223.]

[40] [Ed. Ibid., 210.]

[41] [Ed. Ibid., 298.]

[42] [Ed. Ibid., 205.]

[43] [Ed. Ibid., 18.]

[44] [Ed. Ibid., 214.]

It is unnecessary to say anything in commendation of the whole work. It praises itself. Schiller will, perhaps, please at the first reading, more extensively than Goethe. Some will always prefer him. His genius took a loftier flight than Goethe's. But its excursions were not so wide. Goethe was a broad, Schiller a high man. But perhaps the true poetical reader will finally prefer the exquisite delicacy and consummate skill of the latter, to the warm love and lofty aspirations of the former.

14.

PRETENSIONS OF PHRENOLOGY[1]

Boston Quarterly Review 2 (April, 1839): 205-29

Phrenology, properly speaking, is a physiology of the brain; and, as such, an interesting and useful branch of science. Considered solely in this light, we are disposed to think favorably of it, indeed, to believe it. But phrenologists pretend that it is something more than this. They claim for it the high merit of being a philosophy of the human mind, and the only sound philosophy of the human mind ever set forth. Mr. Combe recommends it on the ground of its throwing a flood of light on the philosophy of mind; and we heard him declare positively that, if it be not true, mental philosophy cannot be understood. The American Phrenological Journal[2] grounds the utility of phrenology, in part, on the assumed fact that it forms the basis of a more correct system of mental philosophy than has hitherto been embraced. We are, therefore, called upon to examine its pretensions, not merely as an account of the functions of the brain, but as a system of metaphysics; and an examination of it, in this respect, will probably be acceptable to the majority of our readers.

Phrenology, as defined by its advocates, treats of the manifestations of mind, and of the physiological conditions under which they take place; but it is all embraced in the four following facts or principles: 1. The brain is the organ of the mind; 2. The brain is a congeries of organs, and each individual organ serves to manifest a special faculty of the mind; 3. The strength of a faculty, *caeteris paribus*,[3] is proportioned to the size of the organ; 4. The size of the organ, and therefore, with the above qualification, the strength of the faculty may be ascertained by examining the external head. As these four

[1] [Ed. Review of George Combe's (1788-1858) *A System of Phrenology* (Boston: Marsh, Capen, and Lyon, 1835). Combe was a Scottish educational and moral reformer who helped to popularize, especially among some American Transcendentalists, the idea of phrenology which he himself had obtained from the Viennese physician Franz Joseph Gall (1758-1828) and the German physician Johann Christoph Spurzheim (1776-1832). In 1837 and 1838 Combe lectured in the United States to spread his ideas.]

[2] [Ed. The *American Phrenological Journal* was published from 1839 to 1848.]

[3] [Ed. Latin for "other things being equal."]

facts or principles embrace the whole of phrenology, nothing can be claimed as phrenology which does not come within their scope. We accept these four facts or principles, and all that necessarily grows out of them. We, therefore, concede to phrenologists their whole science. We controvert, at present, none of their facts. But though we make this concession, which is all that they can in conscience ask of us, we are by no means prepared to admit the inferences by which they erect it into a complete system of mental philosophy.

Phrenologists offer us an enumeration and classification of the primitive tendencies—faculties, they call them—of human nature. This enumeration they consider as nearly complete, and this classification as just. On this ground, and on this alone, must they found their pretensions as metaphysicians. But we ask them, 1st. If their account of the primitive faculties of human nature be the true account? 2d. Admitting it is, does it take in the whole of mental science? And 3d. Admitting it does take in the whole of mental science, is it obtained by means of phrenological principles instead of the method adopted by metaphysicians in general? These three questions are pertinent, and we regret that we do not find phrenologists giving them that distinct consideration their importance demands.

We proceed to consider the last question first. Admitting the phrenologist's account of the primitive faculties of human nature is the true one, we ask how has he obtained it. Grant his psychology; how has he constructed it? Has he done it by means of his phrenological facts, or by simply noting the facts he is conscious of in himself?

The simple fact that a phrenologist is able to give, and does give, us a true account of the faculties of the human soul, is not necessarily a proof that this account is involved in, or that it grows out of the four phrenological principles we have enumerated. It is not, then, a proof that this account has any necessary connection with phrenology. A shoemaker may chance to construct a true system of astronomy, but it does not follow from this that astronomy is a branch of shoemaking, or that it can be successfully prosecuted by none but shoemakers. Before the phrenologist can claim his psychology as a part of phrenology, he must show that it can be arrived at only by means of his four phrenological principles; and that, if these be denied, its truth cannot be maintained.

The phrenologist has counted some thirty or forty primitive faculties of human nature, *located,* named, and described them. We will, for our purposes, take but one of these, that of benevolence. Two things are to be considered: 1. The faculty of benevolence; 2. The cerebral organ by which it is manifested. We presume the phrenologist does not intend to confound the faculty with the organ. We do not confound the sense of sight with the eye. The faculty of benevolence is psychical, the organ physical. Now, does a knowledge of the organ afford any clue to the nature and character of the faculty of benevolence? Certainly not. Knowledge of the fact, then, that each special faculty of human nature has its appropriate cerebral organ, together with manipulation of that organ, cannot lead to a knowledge of the faculty. What aid, then, do we derive from phrenology in constructing our psychology?

How, we ask, does the phrenologist come to the knowledge of the fact that benevolence is one of the primitive faculties of human nature? Will he say, here is a cerebral organ for benevolence, therefore there must be a faculty of benevolence? With his leave, this is not sound logic. When he declares this or that portion of brain the organ of benevolence, he assumes the existence of the faculty of benevolence. How can he say this portion of brain is consecrated to benevolence, if he be ignorant of the fact that there is such a faculty as benevolence? Man has an organ for veneration, therefore veneration is a primitive faculty of human nature. But how know that this is an organ of veneration before we know that man venerates, and venerates by means of this portion of the cerebrum?

We confess we cannot see how the phrenologist obtains his psychology by means of his phrenological principles. He does not pretend that the organs are distinctly marked on the brain. There are no cerebral marks by which he can tell where benevolence ends and veneration begins. The number of the organs cannot be ascertained so as in return to aid in determining the number of faculties. This is evident from the fact that phrenologists do not agree in their enumeration of one or the other; some reckoning more faculties and organs, and others fewer. The portion of brain, which Spurzheim and Combe devote to ideality, others devote to ideality and sublimity, thus dividing what was regarded as one organ into two, and making two primitive faculties out of what was at first pronounced to be but one. It is evident from this that the examination of the skull can no more determine the number of our primitive faculties than it can their nature and character. We ask again, then, what light does phrenology throw on psychology?

The phrenologist must determine the number and character of our primitive faculties independently of his craniology, or not determine them at all. How, then, does he determine their number and character? We presume by analyzing his own consciousness. Mr. Combe declared in his lectures that a man destitute of conscientiousness would be incapable of conceiving moral distinctions. He differed with Dr. Spurzheim as to a particular faculty and claimed superior authority for his own opinion because the organ of the faculty in question was large on his head, and almost totally deficient on Dr. Spurzheim's. Phrenologists, then, resort to consciousness. They turn their eyes in upon themselves, and analyze the facts of the mental world. But this is the way all psychologists do, and ever have done. Phrenologists then, as psychologists, have nothing peculiar in their method. Their psychology, then, is not obtained by their phrenological principles, but by the usual process. If any one doubts this, let him ask if a phrenologist would feel himself warranted in denying the existence of a faculty he should be conscious of possessing, and which he should see manifested in the lives of others, merely because he could find no organ for it? We do not believe he would. We conclude this part of the subject, then, by saying that, admitting that the phrenologist has accurately enumerated and rightly classed the faculties of human nature, he has not done it by virtue of his phrenology, but by virtue of his superior psychological analysis.

But we go farther. We deny both the completeness and the justness of the phrenological psychology. Dr. Spurzheim and George Combe enumerate and describe thirty-five faculties, and speak of two more which are considered doubtful, or not fully settled. But what they call faculties, are evidently nothing but instinctive laws or tendencies of human nature, and not at all deserving the name of *faculty*. We accept the number and character of these tendencies, as given by phrenologists, but they by no means exhaust the consciousness.

These tendencies are all instinctive; they are blind cravings, and the causality at work in them is not our personality. We are separate from them, and either obey them or control them. The faculties proper, those powers by which we control our instincts, are not accounted for by phrenologists. Memory is unquestionably a faculty of the human soul, but the phrenologist has no organ for it. He virtually denies memory. True he says each faculty remembers, that eventuality remembers events, individuality remembers individual facts, causality remembers causes, comparison relations, and so on through the whole list. But does he not see that this is all aside the mark? It is not this or that faculty that remembers, but *we* remember. What he alleges merely explains why it is that we remember some things rather than others; but it says nothing of why we remember at all. Memory is twofold. Sometimes the past comes up of its own accord, sometimes it comes up only as we recall it. Now, how, if we have no faculty of memory, are we able to recall the past?

Sensibility is another faculty of which phrenologists give a very unsatisfactory account. The feelings they speak of are merely modes or variations of sensibility, not the capacity of feeling itself. Endowed as I am with the capacity of feeling, I can easily understand that with the brain large in the region of benevolence, I shall have that modification of sensibility strong; or if small in the region devoted to self-esteem, I shall not be proud. But this does not explain the capacity of feeling, nor give it a cerebral organ. There is no organ for sensibility; there are simply organs for its modes.

The same difficulty occurs in relation to the faculty of *knowing*, intelligence, or reason. We know well what phrenologists say on this subject; we know that they have devoted to the intellect the anterior lobe of the brain, or at least the larger portion of it; and that they speak of perceptive faculties and reflective faculties; but wherefore we understand not. If true to their own system, they must pronounce the intellectual faculties, as they call them, instincts, desires, cravings, as well as the propensities and sentiments. Comparison, in their account of the matter, is nothing but a craving to know relations, causality to know causes, individuality to know individual facts. The cerebral organ of causality, with all deference to George Combe, we must suggest, does not take cognizance of causes; it is merely the organ by which the man manifests his desire to know causes. Similar remarks may be made of all the intellectual faculties, as they are called. They do not constitute the knowing faculty, but are merely its modes, and simply account for the fact that all kinds of knowledge are not acquired by all men with equal facility. To know, is the same, whether it be of causes, relations, facts, tunes, times, colors, or events. It is a general power, which, if we choose, will be directed to an investigation of causes, of ideas, of beauty, of religion, as causality, comparison, ideality, or veneration is the larger organ on the head. But the fact that it is directed to one class of facts rather than another, in consequence of cerebral development, can by no means destroy its unity, or make it not a faculty of the human soul. The phrenologists, in rejecting it, appear to us to make out but a very defective psychology.

The *will*, or personality, is also denied by phrenologists. We mean not to say that they have banished the word, but the thing. Benevolence does this, causality does that, is their way of speaking. The man, the person, does nothing. There is no unity. Phrenologists even labor to disprove all unity of consciousness; and Dr. Spurzheim introduces a man crazy on one side of his head, but sane on the other, to prove the fact of double consciousness. One can hardly refrain from adding that a man resorting to such testimony for such a purpose must needs be crazy, not on one side of his head only, but on both sides.

One while, the phrenologists confound will with desire; another while, with a decision of the understanding, and generally, with the circumstances which influence it. Each faculty is said to will its appropriate objects. Here by will they mean desire. When the intellect perceives that a certain group of organs ought to be obeyed, there is a will to obey them. Here will is taken for a decision of the understanding. If a group of organs giving a determinate character be predominant, there is a will to follow them. Here will is confounded with both desire and the circumstances which influence us. Are men, who can commit mistakes like these, philosophers?

The will, we have shown elsewhere,[4] is the ME, the personality, the power of acting, not the mere capacity of receiving an action. The causality at work in the will is always the person, the ME, myself. It is the power of self-determination. Take away the will, and you destroy personality. The will is always free. Indeed it is identical with freedom. A necessary will, or a will that is not free, is a solecism. But desire is not free. It does not spring up because I will it. It takes place independently of my personality. The causality at work in it, then, is not mine. If, then, there be no will but desire, there is no will at all; then there is no personality, then we reenter into nature and necessity, and fatalism is truth. The same remarks may be made on the decision of the understanding. I cannot control the decisions of my understanding. I see as I can, not as I will. The decisions of the understanding are controlled by a power which I am not. They are necessary, not free. If we confound the will with them, we destroy it, efface personality, and reduce man to a thing, at best, to an animal. We reside eminently in our power of acting, and this power of acting is what we mean by the will as a faculty of human nature.

Now, we are conscious of possessing this power. We do not seek to prove it, for we know it as immediately and as positively as we know that we exist. Our judgments may decide one way, but we can resolve to go another. Desire may prompt us to one deed, but we can will to do another. Every man knows this, for every man repeats the experiment every day of his life. It is true, I may be overpowered by my appetites, my desires, my passions, and led into sin; nevertheless I retain ever the power of willing to resist. This power may not always manifest itself in outward acts, but it exists and manifests itself

[4] [Ed. See, in particular, "The Eclectic Philosophy," and "Eclecticism—Ontology," *Boston Quarterly Review* 2 (January, 1839): 27-53; (April, 1839): 169-87. The articles are republished in this volume; see chapter 8.]

internally in the sphere of consciousness. A strong man may hold me to the ground so that I cannot rise; but though I cannot rise, I can will to rise. Here, then, is a faculty or power which I unquestionably possess, or rather which is myself, of which phrenologists take no account. We can find no recognition of it in their psychology. By what authority, then, do they say that they have constructed a complete psychology? Here is the man himself, of which they take no account, and for which they find no place.

"The knowing and reflecting faculties," says Mr. Combe,[5] "are subject to the will, or rather constitute will themselves." In his Lectures he told us repeatedly that will is seated in the anterior lobe of the brain, and is identical with intellect. Consequently the power of perceiving is identical with the power of willing, and to know is simply to resolve! This may be true philosophy, and deserving the vote of thanks and piece of plate from Bostonians, which Mr. Combe received for it; but we confess that it is a philosophy which we are not yet prepared to embrace. We pretend not, however, to refute it; for he who can see no difference between knowing a thing, and resolving to do or not to do a thing, though he win not conviction, must needs be unanswerable.

What, again, do phrenologists mean by calling causality and comparison *reflective* faculties? Have they analyzed reflection? In reflection there is both intelligence and will. We will to reflect. In every act of reflection we turn the mind in upon itself. But phrenologists deny will, they deny activity, freedom; how, then, can they admit reflection? And moreover, what are causality and comparison but simple tendencies to inquire into causes and relations? They do not, of themselves, take cognizance of causes and relations, otherwise every man who has them large would be sure to have an extensive knowledge of causes and relations, without having ever inquired, which is not the fact. But suppose causality knows causes, and comparison knows relations, we should like to know if they reflect in knowing these, any more than individuality does in knowing facts, or time in knowing dates? Admit they do, how does the phrenologist know the fact? How does he learn that causality is a *reflective* faculty, and individuality a simple *knowing* faculty?

Again, phrenologists boast much of phrenology as harmonizing with Christianity. Now, one of the plainest injunctions of Christianity is that of self-denial. We should like to see the phrenologist explain, on his principles, the doctrine of self-denial. He recognizes no self, no ME, but some thirty or forty faculties having no common

[5] [Ed. *A System of Phrenology*, 467.]

spiritual center. What to him, then, will be self-denial? To deny oneself, we presume he will say, is to give predominance to the moral and religious sentiments over the lower or animal propensities. But two questions in reference to this answer: 1. What is that which gives the predominance to the moral and religious sentiments? and 2. Is this predominance really a self-denial? Are not the moral and religious sentiments as much parts of *self,* in the view of phrenologists, as the propensities themselves? Why is it, then, any more self-denial to bring the propensities into subjection to the sentiments, than it would be to bring the sentiments into subjection to the propensities?

But what is it that brings the one into subjection to the other? What is this which exerts this power? Is it the ME, the personality, activity, liberty, which is not the tendencies, but their subject, their common center? Is it, in a word, the will? Why have phrenologists then neglected to describe it, to give us an account of it? And why do they give us such an account of the will as necessarily excludes it? Will they say, as George Combe does, that it is the intellect? Well, what directs the intellect to that end? A power which we are, or which is objective to us? If objective to us, as they imply in all they say, then it is not we that subject our propensities to our moral and religious sentiments, but something else. Then we do not deny ourselves, and cannot. Then the Christian duty of self-denial is impracticable.

Once more—Christianity teaches the doctrine of accountability; how will the phrenologist make this doctrine harmonize with his philosophy? Mr. Combe took up this subject in his lectures; but his mode of treating it struck us at the time as peculiarly vague and inconclusive. Christianity represents man as placed under a law which he is morally obliged to obey, and which he has the power to obey or not to obey. We believe every man's conscience bears witness to the truth of this Christian doctrine; all languages imply it and all systems of morality and jurisprudence are based upon it. But if a man be the slave of his instincts, if he be not free to control them, to will the right, though they would lead him to pursue the wrong, it is obvious that he is not accountable for his actions, and therefore is not a subject of moral discipline. Phrenologists say the character of the man will be good, if the moral and religious sentiments and intellect predominate, and bad if the animal propensities predominate. The question which naturally arises is, has a man with large organs for the animal propensities, and small organs for the moral and religious sentiments and intellect, the power to be a strictly moral and upright man? Or has a man with an organization the reverse of this, the power to be a bad man? If not, then the man is controlled by an exterior force; his acts are not, strictly speaking, his acts, but the acts of the force at work in his instinctive tendencies. If then you make him accountable, you make him accountable for deeds not his own. I am responsible only for my own deeds. What is done in me, but not by me, is no more my doing than what is done in a man of whom I never heard, and with whom I have no relation. How then can I be responsible? Indeed does not phrenological psychology destroy all responsibility?

This is a grave question, and as such Mr. Combe gave it a grave, but we are sorry to say, not an explicit answer. The cautiousness so characteristic of his nation seemed all the while to be predominant. He did not say, man has the power in question, nor that he has it not. He evaded the real question at issue, and introduced another, which was but remotely related to it. He asked, what do we mean by responsibility? Responsibility to whom? To God? Do we mean by the question to ask whether God will have a right to punish us or not? Phrenology has nothing to do with such questions. Phrenology does not profess to answer theological questions, although one of its chief recommendations in the minds of many is the aid it brings to scriptural exegesis.[6] We leave the question of responsibleness to God, and ask again, to whom are we responsible? To society? But the question he should have asked was not to whom we are responsible, nor to what we are responsible, but, if our characters are determined by our cerebral development, can we be accountable at all? Yet this question, for reasons best known to himself, he did not choose to ask or answer. He considered merely our responsibleness to society, that is, the right of society to punish us. He placed before us the casts of three heads, one decidedly bad, one middling, and one decidedly good. The first question is to determine who are responsible. Now, persons with heads like this, showing us the cast of the villain, are not responsible. You see, here are large propensities, feeble sentiments, and deficient intellect. Such a man should be treated as a *moral patient,* and asylums should be built, in which all persons with heads organized in this way, should be confined. Then again, showing us the middling head, is this man responsible? You see the propensities are large, the moral and religious sentiments rather small, though the intellect is considerable. Persons with heads organized in this manner will do very well, if kept out of the way of temptation; but if tempted, they will assuredly fall. But here is a different head. Persons with heads like this are proof against temptation, and maintain their

[6] [Ed. How phrenology aids scriptural exegesis is not clear, but Brownson might be referring to Combe's view of the "faculty of language." See *A System of Phrenology*, 419-33]

integrity amidst all circumstances. Persons of this class are responsible. You see here moderate propensities, large moral and religious sentiments to perceive the right, and large intellect to will it. If such a person does not do right, he has no excuse.

But we wished Mr. Combe to tell us whether this man, with the good head, had the power to neglect his duty—whether he did right by the force of instinct, or by voluntary striving. We wished to know whether there be in man a power or faculty by which he controls his instinctive tendencies, and directs them to the fulfilment of the moral law, or by which he can, if he choose, direct them to the breach of the moral law. If man has not this power, he is not a moral being, and the accountability spoken of in the Christian revelation is unfounded. Phrenology, then, instead of being in harmony with Christianity, would be directly opposed to it. If there be such a power, phrenologists have not given us a true philosophy of man, because they have failed to recognize and describe it.

If the phrenological psychology be admitted, virtue is indeed, as Brutus said, "an empty name." In none of the phrenological lectures we have heard, in none of the phrenological books we have read, have we found anything on which virtue can be based. We can conceive how a man, on phrenological principles, may be good or bad, in the sense in which we say a good or bad knife, but we cannot conceive it possible for one to be virtuous or sinful. Virtue is my own act; it springs from my will, and can spring from no other. No power can compel me to be virtuous; for the deeds I do through compulsion, I do not, but the power that compels me, and therefore they are not mine, and however good they may be, they are not virtuous.

Now, in the primitive instincts of my nature, *I* do not act. In relation to these primitive tendencies, which the phrenologists call faculties, I am passive, and hence they are termed *passions.* The active force in them is not my ME, my personality, but a force foreign to it. Admitting, then, that all these tendencies are good, and that all which is done through their impulsive force is in harmony with the law of God, it does not follow that I am virtuous. The sun and stars obey God's law, but are they virtuous? Not at all. Because they are not persons, are not active but passive, and revolve in obedience to God's law only because a power foreign to them makes them so revolve. The analogy holds good in man. When I find myself in harmony with the law of God, by the force of my instinctive tendencies, I am there by no act of mine, and consequently have no claim to virtue. This distinction between virtue and goodness, our phrenologists seem not to have made. Goodness is conformity to the will of the Creator;

virtue is the voluntary striving after that conformity. I may be forced to conform, and therefore forced into goodness; but I cannot be forced to will to conform, therefore cannot be forced into virtue. Now, what I do in obedience to my instinctive tendencies, I am forced to do as much as if the impelling power were outside of my body; consequently, though forced to conform by my instincts, I am only good, not virtuous, unless I have also willed to conform. Phrenologists seem always satisfied when the conformity is obtained, although in obtaining it, they annihilate the man. They do not regard it as essential that we should will that conformity, therefore do not regard virtue itself as essential; and as they do not give us this power of willing, they represent virtue as impossible.

But waiving all this, we must tell our phrenological friends, that psychology does not embrace the whole of philosophy. Their views of mental science are low and narrow, and make them physicians rather than metaphysicians. They seem to imagine that mental philosophy is merely a sort of natural history of the mind—that when they have enumerated and described the primitive tendencies or laws of human nature their work is done. But we must assure them that the mental philosopher has other and more important matters than these to settle, and which, in our judgment, phrenology does not in the least aid him to settle. There is the somewhat important question of the criterion of truth or ground of certainty. We should like to know what light phrenology throws on this question. Does it give us any clue to its answer? Phrenologists assert many things as true; how do they know that what they assert is true? How do they know that the authority on which they rely, and to which they appeal, is legitimate and safe? How do they determine that all human knowledge is not dream, or that our faculties are to be trusted? They may tell us that phrenology does not ask these questions, and that it should not be called upon to answer them. Be it so. But these are philosophical questions, and if they do not bring them within the scope of phrenology, what right have they to call phrenology a system of mental philosophy? Does it afford the basis of an answer to these questions? Not at all. Then it does not embrace the whole of philosophy.

Men generally believe in something existing outside of them; but some philosophers contend that we cannot pass, by any legitimate process, from the world within us to a world outside of us. We do not expect our phrenological readers, generally, will comprehend the problem here implied, for they do not seem to possess the capacity of distinguishing between the ME and the NOT-ME; but still, we trust some of them will understand what we mean, when we say that a few men have questioned the existence of an external world; have, like Berkeley, regarded it as a picture stamped by God on the retina of the mind, or, like Fichte, as the ME projected, taken as the object of itself. Now, what light has the phrenologist to throw on this question? Are these philosophers right; or shall we continue to believe, with the great mass of mankind, that there is a real world existing outside of us, and independent of us? How, out of the four phrenological principles we have enumerated, shall we extract an answer to this question? If phrenology cannot answer it, how can its friends call it a system, or the basis of a system, of mental philosophy?

Mr. Combe touches in his book upon this question, but unfortunately he does not give it that direct and explicit answer which its importance seems to demand. He says Berkeley denied the external world, because he could see no necessary connection between the conception or idea of it, which is a mental affection, and its existence. But instead of informing us whether Berkeley was right or not, or showing us how phrenology enables us to solve the problem, he merely undertakes to tell us how we can explain, on phrenological principles, the fact that Berkeley denied an external world, and also the fact that Reid asserted it. "Individuality, aided by the other perceptive powers, in virtue of its constitution, perceives the external world, and produces an intuitive belief in its existence. But Berkeley employed the faculty of causality to discover *why* this perception is followed by belief; and as causality could give no account of the matter, and could see no necessary connection between the mental affection, called perception, and the existence of external nature, he denied the latter."[7] This, translated into the language of mortals, means, we suppose, that Berkeley denied the existence of external nature because he could discover no reason for asserting it. This is a very satisfactory reason, no doubt, why Berkeley denied the existence of an external world, but Mr. Combe must pardon us, if we cannot accept it as a satisfactory answer to the question, whether Berkeley was justified in his denial or not.

There are two other points in this answer deserving attention. "Individuality, aided by the other perceptive powers, in virtue of its constitution, perceives the external world, and produces an intuitive belief in its existence." Translated, as we have said, into the language of mortals, this means, we suppose, that we perceive an external world, or by the constitution of our nature, are led irresistibly to believe in its existence. This is the doctrine of Reid, advanced in reply to Hume

[7] [Ed. *A System of Phrenology*, 453-54.]

and Berkeley. It is not, then, necessarily, a phrenological doctrine. But this is of no consequence. Does phrenology throw any additional light on it, or give to it any additional certainty? Is our belief in an external world made more rational or philosophical, by saying that "Individuality, by virtue of its constitution, perceives the external world, and produces an intuitive belief in its existence," than it was when we said with Reid, we are irresistibly led, by the constitution of our nature, to believe in an external world?

Again—how does Mr. Combe know that individuality does actually perceive an external world? The perception, we suppose he will admit with Berkeley, is a mental affection; how, then, by the aid of phrenology, pass from the mental affection, the idea, to the object? We wish he would tell us what principle or fact phrenology has disclosed, which enables him to do this. We cannot see that he has advanced at all on Berkeley, or obtained any means of legitimating our faith in an external world. Phrenology appears to us to leave this question where it found it.

This answer of his also implies that we cannot legitimate belief in the objective. He says that causality can assign no reason why we should believe in the existence of external nature—that is, we have no other ground for asserting that existence than that we believe it because it is our nature to believe it. Hume and Berkeley both said as much. Phrenology, then, so far from legitimating the universal belief of mankind in an external world, either leaves that matter untouched, or, according to its greatest living expounder, tells us that we cannot legitimate it. We should like to know wherein phrenology decides that we can *not* pass legitimately from the subjective to the objective?

The friends of phrenology boast its value in settling the great problems of natural theology. Some of them go so far as to say that it puts the question of the existence of God at rest. If it be a complete system of mental philosophy, it ought to do this. Let us see, then, if it does it. Mr. Combe attempts, in his book, to show that it does; but he merely shows us why some men believe in God, and why others do not. Men on whose heads the organ of causality is large, believe in God—those on whose heads it is small, do not. Now this, in point of fact, is not true. Abner Kneeland has large causality, and the Abbé Paris[8] was almost entirely deficient in it. Hume had large causality, and Reid, according to Mr. Combe, had small causality. But let this pass. Suppose Mr. Combe

[8] [Ed. Abbé Matthew Paris (c. 1199-1259) was a Benedictine monk of St. Albans in England, and the medieval chronicler of the famous *Chronica Majora*, a history of the world from creation to 1259.]

is right, his remark no more proves the legitimacy of theism than it does of atheism; and the argument which he introduces after this remark, and which he represents as always silencing atheists, is nothing but the old argument from design, which is inconclusive, unless we have first established the existence of a designer. But be it ever so conclusive, it derives no additional force from phrenology.

But phrenologists profess also to find a proof of the existence of God in the sentiment of veneration. "Destructiveness is implanted in the mind, and animals exist around us to be killed for our nourishment; adhesiveness and Philoprogenitiveness are given, and friends and children are provided, on whom they may be exercised; benevolence is conferred on us, and the poor and unhappy, on whom it may shed its soft influence, are every where present with us; in like manner, the instinctive tendency to worship is implanted in the mind, and, conformably to these analogies of nature, we may reasonably infer that a God exists whom we may adore."[9] That is, man is disposed to venerate, *therefore* there is a God for him to venerate. Supposing you had first proved a God, who has implanted in us the tendency to venerate, you might then take the existence of the tendency as a proof that it is God's will that we should venerate him; but that the tendency, of itself, supposes God, is more than we can conceive. The logic, by which we conclude from the existence of the tendency to the object, is, we presume, peculiarly phrenological.

But the evidence of a God to be derived from this source is taken away by the very persons who adduce it. "Man," says Dr. Gall, "adores everything, fire, water, earth, thunder, lightning, meteors, grasshoppers, crickets."[10] The existence of the fact that man worships is, then, according to phrenologists themselves, no better evidence of the existence of God, than it is that God, if he exists, is a cricket or a grasshopper. After this, we hope they will cease to boast of the new light their science throws on the fundamental truths of natural theology.

But passing over this; phrenologists have only told us what we all knew before, that men have a disposition to venerate, to adore. All have admitted this. The only question in dispute is, is there a God to be adored? This question phrenologists leave where it was before. They have merely, by pointing out an organ of veneration, led people to reflect, perhaps, more on the fact that man is naturally religious than they otherwise would have done; but whether religion is grounded in truth, or whether it be an illusion, is a question they have not answered, nor increased our means of answering.

[9] [Ed. *A System of Phrenology*, 261.]

[10] [Ed. The concept but not the exact quotation is in Ibid., 263.]

One great object of philosophy is to demonstrate the fact that man is a moral being, that there is above him a law he ought to obey, and that he is in the way of his duty when he obeys it, and sinful when he disobeys. That man is under such a law is the universal sentiment of the race, as the universal presence of conscience testifies. But some men have questioned this law, in fact denied its reality. This has led others to seek to establish it. Now, if phrenology be a complete system of philosophy, it must settle this question. Does it do it? So say the phrenologists. How does it do it? Why, there is on man's head an organ of conscientiousness, and those who have it large are disposed to be honest, upright, moral; and those who have it very small are incapable of perceiving moral distinctions. We will not laugh at this answer, for we suppose it is given in good faith; but, taking it in its most favorable light, we must ask what it amounts to? Simply to the fact that men are so organized, or so constituted, that they do believe in moral distinctions. Is this belief well founded? Is there that moral world actually existing, which it implies? Here is a question our phrenological friends do not answer. Can they answer it?

The immortality of the soul is another philosophical question, and one which philosophy ought to settle. Does phrenology throw any light on this question? Not at all. It professes to leave this, and all similar questions, by the way. Very well. We do not ask it to answer them, only we say, if it does not, it takes in but a small part of what we understand by the philosophy of the human mind; and therefore its friends should not claim for it the high merit of being the foundation of all correct mental science. We do not complain of phrenology, because it does not do more, but of its friends for representing it as being more than it is.

Mr. Combe speaks of phrenology as exalting the dignity of human nature. It teaches, he said, in his Lectures, that all our faculties are in themselves good, and given by our Creator for useful purposes, and that they become the occasion of evil only when abused. Phrenologists teach this, we admit, and perhaps to recommend their science; but how they deduce this from their phrenological principles is to us a mystery. It is a conclusion to which they doubtless arrive by reasoning from certain notions of justice which they entertain; but do they derive those notions from phrenological facts or from sources in no sense dependent on the truth or falsity of phrenology?

Phrenologists speak of the moral and religious sentiments as the *higher* nature of man. Is this because their organs are located on the upper part of the head? They say the moral and religious sentiments *ought* to govern the propensities. We admit it; but will they tell us how they verify this fact by phrenology? Is there anything to be discovered by manipulation to establish it? Or do they establish it by consulting the revelations of consciousness, just as all philosophers do? But Mr. Combe ridicules the idea of knowing anything of the mind by the study of consciousness. "The human mind," he says, "in this world, cannot, by itself, be an object of philosophical investigation."[11] The mind, then, cannot investigate itself, thought cannot be an object of thought, and we can never turn our minds in upon themselves and study the facts of consciousness! This, we confess, is a novel view of the matter, and one which, we presume, no mental philosopher ever suspected before Gall, Spurzheim, and George Combe.

But enough. We wish our readers to distinctly understand that we make no war upon phrenology, when restricted to its legitimate sphere. As a physiological account of the brain, a treatise on its functions, and as enabling us to explain the causes of the differences we meet within individual character, we believe it, and value it. Within these limits, within which Gall usually confined it, it is, as we have said, a useful and interesting branch of science. The mischief of it lies in attempting, as Spurzheim and Combe do, to make it a system of mental philosophy, which it is not and never can be. The fundamental principles of phrenology are easily reconcilable with a sound spiritual philosophy, and on some future occasion we may attempt to show this. The objections we have brought forward, do not bear against those principles, but against the doctrines phrenologists profess to derive from them. We war, then, not against the science, but against what its friends have superinduced upon it, or alleged it to be.

They, who oppose phrenology by controverting its physiological facts, do not seem to us to act very wisely. Mr. Combe's Lectures, we confess, tended to weaken our faith in the reality of those facts, and to induce us to class phrenology with the other humbugs of the day; but our own observations have been somewhat extended, and we are satisfied that the phrenologists have really made some physiological discoveries not altogether worthless; and their assertion of a connection between the instinctive tendencies of our nature, and cerebral organization, has led to a kind of observation on the different traits of individual character, which has enlarged our stock of materials for a natural history of man. They have, also, made many valuable observations on education, and the means of preserving a sound mind in a sound body; and induced many to turn their attention to the study of mental science, who, but for them might never have done it. This is considerable; enough to give them an honorable rank among

[11] [Ed. Ibid., 6.]

the benefactors of their race,—and a rank they should be permitted peaceably to enjoy, unless they claim one altogether higher, and to which no man of any tolerable acquaintance with mental science can believe them entitled.

Admitting all the facts phrenologists allege, all that legitimately belongs to their science, we contend that it throws no light on the great problems of mental philosophy. In relation to all those problems, we stand unaffected by the discoveries of Gall and Spurzheim; and had phrenologists clearly perceived the nature of those problems, they would never have dared to put forth the claims they have, and which we have contested. Phrenology is a physical, not a metaphysical science, and all it can, with any propriety, pretend to do, is to point out and describe the physiological conditions to which, in this mode of being, the mental affections are subjected. This it has, to some extent, done; but this does not amount to so much as they imagine. In doing it, they do not approach the boundaries of metaphysical science, and therefore we have felt it necessary to show them that they claim for it more than it is or can be.

We are grateful to all laborers in the field of science, and to every man who discovers a new law or a new fact. But we confess we are a little impatient with arrogant pretensions. Let the discoverer of the new law, or the new fact, describe it to us, and claim the merit that is his due; but let him not fancy his merit must needs be so great as to sink out of sight the merit of everybody else. We could bear with our phrenological friends altogether better, were they not perpetually addressing us, as if all wisdom was born with Gall and Spurzheim. To believe them, before these two German empirics Plato and Aristotle, Bacon and Descartes, Leibniz and Locke, Reid and Kant, sink into insignificance. Now, this is more than we can bear. "Great men lived before Agamemnon,"[12] and we believe there were philosophers, before Gall and Spurzheim set out with a cabinet of skulls on their wanderings from Vienna. It is because phrenologists lose sight of this fact, and would fain make it believed that nothing can be known of the human mind, but by means of their four principles, that we have deemed it necessary to rebuke them. We hope they will bear our reproof with the meekness of philosophers.

We honor the man who has the courage to proclaim a new doctrine, one which he honestly believes, and which he knows is in op-

[12] [Ed. The phrase comes from Quintus Horatius Flaccus (65-8 B.C.), Roman poet, *Od.* IV, ix: "Vixere fortes ante Agamemnon." Verse is paraphrased in George Gordon Byron's *Don Juan*, 1:5: "Brave men were living before Agamemnon."]

position to the habitual faith of his age and country; but we always distrust both the capacity and the attainments of him, who can see nothing to venerate in his forefathers, and who bows not before the wisdom of antiquity. Progress there may be, and there is; but no one man can advance far on his predecessors, never so far that they shall sensibly diminish in the distance. These arrogant reformers with the tithe of an idea, who speak to us as if they had outgrown all the past, and grasped and made present the whole future, are generally persons who, having advanced on their own infancy, imagine therefore, that they have advanced on the whole world. But the more we do really advance, the more shall we be struck with the greatness of those who went before us, and the more sincere and deep will be our reverence for antiquity. The darkness we ascribe to remote ages is often the darkness of our own minds, and the ignorance we complain of in others may be only the reflex of our own. Progress we should labor for, progress we should delight in, but we should beware of underrating those who have placed us in the world. "There were giants in those days" [Gen 6:4].

Phrenologists must attribute the ridicule and opposition they have encountered to themselves. Their method of propagating their science, their character of itinerant lecturers, and their habit of manipulating heads, likening their science so much, in its usages and effects, to the science of palmistry, together with their uncouth terminology, and the absurd statements which they are continually making, betraying at once their ignorance and simplicity, can hardly be expected not to excite a smile of pleasantry, or of contempt, in every man of ordinary discernment and information. But if they will betake themselves to their cabinets, and study their science in the modest, unpretending manner physiologists in general do, instead of perambulating the country, manipulating skulls at so much a piece, or treating their science in a way that encourages the ignorant and designing to do it, they will find the public ceasing to oppose them and gratefully accepting the fruits of their labors. Let them lay aside their pretensions as system-makers, reformers, revolutionists, and throw into the common mass the facts or principles they discover, and suffer them to go for what they are worth, and, in common with all studious men, they will contribute something to the well-being of the race, and deserve well of humanity.

15.

OUR INDIAN POLICY

Boston Quarterly Review 2 (April, 1839): 229-59

Within the last few years, the subject of our Indian relations has assumed an importance wholly unfelt at any former period of our history. To a great extent individual as well as national feeling has undergone a decided change. Instead of meditating, or attempting, as formerly, a speedy extinction of the entire aboriginal population of the country, the most laudable and philanthropic efforts are now put forth for its preservation and improvement. Individuals, acting in concert with various societies, appropriately organized under the sanction of the general government, are laboring with great energy and zeal to advance the moral and intellectual condition of this most singular variety of the human race.[1] What may be done, only the future can make known with absolute certainty. What has been done, is matter of history. That nearly all efforts, thus far, for the improvement and civilization of our Indian neighbors, have failed, is by no means surprising, when the condition and character of the race are considered.

The North American Indian has traits of character that greatly distinguish him from every other class belonging to the human family. Wherever met with, whether under the genial influences of a southern sun, or among the snow-clad hills of the icy north, whether sporting upon the waters of the upper lakes, or chasing the buffalo over the vast prairies of the "far west," he is, with slight shades of difference, the same careless, improvident being, living on without an effort to improve his condition, or seemingly caring for the fate of those who shall succeed him. The North American Indian lives for the present. To him the past calls up little or nothing worth remembering. The future presents few bright or ennobling anticipations.

[1] [Ed. For background on this assertion, see Francis Paul Prucha, "Thomas L. McKenney and the New York Indian Board," *Mississippi Valley Historical Review* 48 (March 1962): 625-55; idem, *American Indian Policy in the Formative Years* (Cambridge: Harvard University Press, 1962), 51-65, 213-49; *Cherokee Removal: The "William Penn" Essays and Other Writings. By Jeremiah Evarts*, edited with introduction by Francis Paul Prucha (Knoxville: University of Tennessee Press, 1981).]

What has been, may be again; but whether a worse or a better fate awaits him, does not for a moment disturb his habitual stoicism. Regardless of consequences, he follows the momentary impulses of his wayward soul, hating even unto death, or liking to the verge of his own destruction. With him, revenge for an injury, either real or imaginary, is certain and terrible. Years may intervene, kind words and kinder offices may pass between him and his intended victim, but nothing can obliterate the remembrance of a wrong received; blood is the only balm; he drinks, and becomes himself again. Hunger will not tame, cold will not rouse him. He endures both with scarcely an effort for relief, or dissipates, at a sitting, the fruits of a successful chase, against the clearest probability that his wants for the morrow will then be supplied. Improvidence is his birthright, and privation his companion. He glories in the one, and disregards the admonitions of the other. He would not exchange his hut for a palace, nor his wild domain for a cultivated empire. And yet, the North American Indian is not without many of the higher and nobler attributes of the human soul. He is patient under the severest privation, hospitable to all who meet him on terms of friendship and equality; mindful of favors received, and magnanimous according to his own interpretation of personal honor. The sufferings of death he holds in contempt, and redeems the faith of a promise, even at the expense of his own life. With the hungry he will divide his last morsel, and into the sanctity of his hut receive the wanderer and the outcast. If his hates are terrible, his likes are not less strong and enduring. He is rarely the first aggressor, and as rarely deserts a personal benefactor. If the good of his clan seems to require the sacrifice, he will die without a murmur. He will take the life of another, without scruple, when the same necessity apparently demands it.

Such was the North American Indian when the Anglo-Saxon first set foot upon his wilderness empire. Such he now is, where not debased by the vices of civilization. Two hundred years ago, he was lord and master of a mighty continent. Today, he is but a tenant at will, begging a patch of earth in which to lay his bones.

With the landing of the white man, commenced the declension of aboriginal supremacy in the new world. The greater numerical strength of the wandering tribes, was no match for the well-trained, highly cultivated intruders, who sought a home and a habitation at their side. They saw the disparity existing between themselves and the new comers, but felt no inferiority, till it was too late to oppose a destiny which their apathy and ignorance had rendered inevitable. When physical force would have availed, they were quiescent; when they did resort to it, the hour for success had forever passed away. The emigrants had secured a footing. The small, scattered bands of Anglo-Saxon origin—which, a few years before, had begged corn of their Indian neighbors, for immediate subsistence—had become a powerful people, rich in everything but the luxuries of the old world. The splendid war talents of an Opechancanough and a Phillip[2] failed them in the hour of their greatest need; and they, who, a few years before, could have easily annihilated the intruders, perished in successive struggles, only inglorious because they were unsuccessful.

The right of discoverers and emigrants to appropriate exclusively to their own use, large portions of the territory, occupied at the time by the aboriginal race, has been often debated, and the decisions of the question are scarcely less numerous than the individuals who have attempted its equitable adjudication. At present, it is rather a speculative, than a practical question. The die is cast. We are now in possession of the soil. The original occupants have either melted, or are melting away, before the tide of civilization and improvement. The extinct tribe; the primitive forest; the deer, the bear, and the wolf; the unbroken sod; the wild glen, and the unobstructed waterfall, will not again spring into existence at our bidding. These races and things are passing away. We may lament, but can we stay the destiny which threatens them? With the indigenous race, unquestionably lies the abstract right of ownership. This was generally acknowledged, in theory at least, though by no means always heeded in practice. Large portions of territory were often acquired by conquest, but much larger by purchase or gift. That the intruders often drove bargains more advantageous to themselves, than beneficial to the original occupants, is indeed more than probable. They were the superior race. They saw more clearly, and farther into futurity, and understood better the vast resources of the earth, than the uncultivated tribes with whom they contracted. It was then, as now; the enlightened Caucasian was more than a match for the wandering savage. The former is far-sighted, the latter content with the fulness of the present moment. The one labors for himself, and for all coming time; the other seeks only his own good—his own gratification. It is, also, in the order of God's providence that the earth shall be subdued,

[2] [Ed. Opechancanough was the Pamunkey Indian chief who led a war party against Virginia settlers in 1622 and 1644, massacring great numbers of them. Phillip was a young Wampanoag sachem who led an uprising against New England frontier communities, producing what has become known as King Philip's War (1675-76). Both leaders were eventually killed by the settlers.]

shall be peopled by a *progressive* race. The vast capacities of the human soul cannot be expanded and perfected among wandering tribes of naked, starving barbarians. Mind is to triumph over matter. The physical must yield to the intellectual man.

"Shall," said John Quincy Adams, in an address in commemoration of the landing of the Pilgrims, at Plymouth, delivered in 1802, "shall the liberal bounties of Providence to the race of man be monopolized by one of a thousand for whom they were created? Shall the exuberant bosom of the common mother, amply adequate to the nourishment of millions, be claimed exclusively by a few hundreds of her offspring? Shall the lordly savage not only disdain the virtues and enjoyments of civilization himself, but shall he control the civilization of the world? Shall he forbid the wilderness to blossom like the rose? Shall he forbid the oaks of the forest to fall before the axe of industry, and rise again, transformed into the habitations of ease and elegance? Shall he doom an immense region of the globe to perpetual desolation, and to hear the howling of the tiger and the wolf silence forever the voice of human gladness? Shall the hills and valleys, which a beneficent God has formed to teem with the life of innumerable multitudes, be condemned to everlasting barrenness? Shall the mighty rivers, poured out by the hands of nature, as channels of communication between numerous nations, roll their waters in sullen silence and eternal solitude to the deep? Have hundreds of commodious harbors, a thousand leagues of coast, and a boundless ocean, been spread in front of this land, and shall every purpose of utility to which they could apply, be prohibited by the tenant of the woods? No, generous philanthropists! Heaven has not thus placed at irreconcilable strife its moral laws with its physical creation!"[3]

We would not be understood as advocating the monstrous doctrine, that, because the American Indian will not, at once, cultivate and improve the soil, he ought, therefore, to be hunted down and swept from the face of the earth. God forbid that we should thus feel towards any of the children of men, however degraded, however lowly sunk in the scale of humanity. We have better thoughts, and higher hopes. We would make him a new being. We would mold him to a new destiny; not under the lash, nor at the point of the bayonet, but

[3] [Ed. See Adams, *An Oration Delivered at Plymouth December 22, 1802, at the Anniversary Commemorative of the First Landing of Our Ancestors at that Place* (Boston: Russell and Cutler, 1802). Later Adams acknowledged that he used this argument at Ghent in 1814-15 when he was trying to work the treaty with England. On this, see "Ecce Iterum," in *The Writings of John Quincy Adams*, ed. Worthington Chauncey Ford, 7 vols. (New York: Macmillan Co., 1914), 3:11.]

by a course of treatment suited to his peculiar nature, to his peculiar wants. That he has been often cheated, oppressed, insulted, by individuals, and sometimes by governments, none, acquainted with the history of his wretchedness for the last two hundred years, will have the hardihood to deny. Our offers of mercy have often followed our infliction of outrage and wrong. His good has been consulted too often, only after our robbery of his home, his country, his self-respect. We have too often reduced him to dependence and beggary; held him up as an object of scorn; treated him as an outcast, driven him from the haunts of his childhood, and from the graves of his kindred. Much of this treatment, undoubtedly, resulted from circumstances over which neither party had any control. The two races differ as widely as two varieties of the same species can well be imagined to differ. The one is cultivated, laborious, and highly progressive; the other ignorant, idle, and stationary. They have few things in common but their animal wants, and these being sought after in opposite modes, the existence of the two becomes incompatible in the same community. In this state of things, mutual wrong begets mutual strife, and previous aggression was forgotten in subsequent outrage. Unconditional submission, or entire extermination, became the end and aim of the two races, and while the contest was raging, humanity was dumb, or only spoke in inaudible whispers.

From the first moment of discovery, our connection with the Indian race has been one of trial and perplexity. The assumption, on the part of discoverers, to right of soil, necessarily implied, in some sense, the right of jurisdiction over it; and with the exercise of this right, arose the first great difficulties between the two races. It was not, at first, within the scope of an Indian mind to conceive it possible that a few hundreds of poor men and women would ever become either troublesome or dangerous neighbors; and more difficult was it for him to conceive it possible that the illimitable forests through which he was wont to range in pursuit of game would ever disappear before the hand of industry. He had nothing with which to compare such a result. He felt, therefore, at first, no great reluctance at parting with small portions of territory, for the exclusive use and benefit of the soliciting emigrants. But when these hundreds became thousands, when the demands for additional concessions of territory were, from time to time, repeated, the Indian could not fail to see that every successive grant was circumscribing, more and more, his own accustomed range, and farther restricting his own necessary means of subsistence. He became alarmed, and appealed sometimes to the hatchet, at others, to the humanity of the intruders, for that justice which fate or fortune seemed to deny him. Attempts, amicably to adjust differences between the two races, early led to the practice of treating with the Indians, as with other foreign, independent powers, modified by certain rights, asserted by the whites, and sanctioned by the practice of every nation under like or similar circumstances. The most important of these rights was a right in the soil, arising from discovery. This right is recognized by all civilized nations, and enforced whenever and wherever settlements are made on lands, over which barbarians merely range in pursuit of game. Judge Marshall says:

"All the nations of Europe, who have acquired territory on this continent, have asserted in themselves, and have recognized in others, the exclusive right of the discoverer to appropriate the lands occupied by the Indians."[4]

And in 8th Wheaton, it is observed:

"Discovery gave title to the government by whose subjects, or by whose authority, it was made, against all other European governments, which title might be consummated by possession."[5]

Judge Story remarks:

"It may be asked, what was the effect of this principle of discovery, in respect to the right of the natives themselves? In the view of Europeans, it created a peculiar relation between themselves and the aboriginal inhabitants. The latter were admitted to possess a present right of occupancy, or use in the soil, which was subordinate to the ultimate dominion of the discoverer. . . . But, notwithstanding this occupancy, the European discoverers claimed and exercised the right to grant the soil, while yet in the possession of the natives, subject, however, to their right of occupancy; and the title so granted was universally admitted to convey a sufficient title in the soil to the grantees in perfect dominion."[6]

Judge McLean says:

"At no time has the sovereignty of the country been recognized as existing in the Indians, but they have always been admitted to possess many of the attributes of sovereignty. . . . Their right of occu-

[4] [Ed. *Johnson v. McIntosh*, 8 Wheaton 584 (March 10, 1823).]

[5] [Ed. Ibid., 573.]

[6] [Ed. Joseph Story (1779-1845) was an American jurist from Massachusetts and an associate justice of the Supreme Court (1812-45). For quotation see Story's *Commentaries on the Constitution of the United States* (1833), in *Joseph Story: Commentaries on the Constitution of the United States*, reprint with Introduction by Ronald D. Rotunda and John E. Nowak (Durham, North Carolina: Carolina Academic Press, 1987), 6, 7.]

pancy has never been questioned, but the fee in the soil has been considered in the government."[7]

Chancellor Kent says:

"This assumed but qualified dominion over the Indian tribes, regarding them as enjoying no higher title to the soil than that founded on simple occupancy, and to be incompetent to transfer their title to any other power than the government which claims the jurisdiction of their territory by right of discovery, arose, in a great degree, from the necessity of the case. . . . It is established by numerous compacts, treaties, laws, and ordinances, and founded in immemorial usage. The country has been colonized and settled, and it is now held by that title. It is the law of the land, and no court of justice can permit the right to be disturbed by speculative reasonings or abstract rights."[8]

At the Treaty of Ghent, in 1815, between the United States and Great Britain, the British Government endeavored so to frame a portion of the treaty relating to the Indian tribes, as to recognize them as independent nations. This, the American ministers objected to, and, among other things, say:

"The United States claim, of right, with respect to all European nations, and particularly with respect to Great Britain, the entire sovereignty over the whole territory, and all the persons embraced within the boundaries of their dominions. . . . With respect to her, and all other foreign nations, they are parts of a whole, of which the United States are sole and absolute sovereigns."[9]

These extracts are important. They show us the extent of jurisdiction claimed and exercised by the United States over the Indian tribes, and the right of the aborigines, independent of the United States. The right claimed and exercised is one thing, its abstract justice another. But, as Chancellor Kent observes, the system "arose, in a great degree, from the necessity of the case," and cannot now be disturbed. It is the settled law of the land, and our dealings with the native tribes must conform to it. Whether a better system could have been adopted, it is now idle to inquire. Time and wisdom have given it their sanction, and nothing short of revolution can change it. But

[7] [Ed. John McLean (1785-1861) was an associate justice of the Supreme Court (1829-61). For quotation, see *Worcester v. The State of Georgia*, 6 Peters 580 (January, 1832).]

[8] [Ed. See Chancellor James Kent's *Commentaries on American Law*, fifth edition, 4 vols. (New York: Printed for the Author, 1844), 3:257, 258.]

[9] [Ed. The quotation is not from the Treaty of Ghent. On negotiations at Ghent, see Bradford Perkins, *Castlereagh and Adams: England and the United States, 1812-1823* (Berkeley: University of California Press, 1964), 81-127. Unable to identify quotation.]

this assumed right of holding the Indians as dependents, and treating them as such, did not originate with the government of the United States. The colonial authorities exercised it long before any national form of government was conceived of in the new world. In fact, the practice is as old as the oldest of the Anglo-Saxon settlements on the continent. The colonial assembly of Massachusetts, in 1633, enacted that *only* the lands improved and inhabited by the Indians, should belong to them; and that all other "lands and plantations shall be accounted the *just* right of the English."[10] Virginia, in 1658, asserted and exercised the same power over the Indian territory, within her colonial limits. In 1663, the colony of Rhode Island extended her jurisdiction over the Indian tribes, as well as all the lands within the boundaries of her royal charter, by forbidding "any person or persons to purchase any lands or islands within the colony, of or from the native Indians, upon the penalty of forfeiting all such lands or islands, so purchased, to the colony."[11] And in 1696, it was enacted by the same colonial assembly, that no Indians or Negroes, bond or free, should be out after nine o'clock, without a certificate from some white inhabitant, "responsible for their good conduct."[12] In 1672, the colonial legislature of Connecticut enacted, "That no Indian or Indians shall, at any time, powow, or perform outward worship, to false gods, or to the Devil, within this colony, on pain of forfeiting the sum of *five pounds* to the public treasury, for every time any Indian or Indians shall be convicted of performing the same."[13] The same act also provides, that if any Indian shall murder a white man, he shall suffer death, *under the laws of the Colony.* In addition to all this, one of the commands of the famous code, known as the "blue laws," is in the following words:

"The inhabitants of this colony are commanded to abstain from all *cheating,* and are enjoined to pursue the strictest integrity and honesty in all their dealings—*except with the Indians.*"[14]

[10] [Ed. *Laws of the Colonial and State Governments Relating to Indians and Indian Affairs, from 1633 to 1831 Inclusive* (Washington City: Thompson and Romans, 1832), 9-10.]

[11] [Ed. Ibid., 52-53.]

[12] [Ed. Ibid., 53-54.]

[13] [Ed. The quotation is not exactly as it is in the original. Brownson has changed the word order, inserted some words, and substituted some words, but the substance is the same as the original. See *The Book of the General Laws for the People within the Jurisdiction of Conecticut* [sic] (Cambridge: Samual Green, 1673), 34; reprint in *The Earliest Laws of the New Haven and Connecticut Colonies, 1639-1673,* ed. John D. Cushing (Wilmington, Delaware: Michael Glazier, 1977), 108.]

[14] [Ed. Unable to identify quotation.]

At this day we may smile, if we will, at the *morality* contained in this enactment, but in one sense it was rather honorable to the old law-makers in the land of "steady habits" than otherwise. They dared to express, by implication, what every other colony practiced without the sanction of law!

In 1717, the Legislature of Connecticut enacted "that no title to any lands in this colony can accrue by any purchase made of Indians, on *pretence* of their being native proprietors thereof, without the allowance and approbation of this assembly."[15] In 1700, the colony of Pennsylvania enacted, "That if any person presume to buy any lands of any natives within the limits of this Province and territories, without lease from the proprietors thereof, every such bargain of purchase shall be void and of no effect."[16] And so early as 1710, Maryland extended her jurisdiction over the whole Indian territory within her colonial limits. North Carolina did the same in 1715; New Hampshire in 1716, and South Carolina in 1739. The enactments of these last enumerated colonies were couched in nearly the same language, lands were not to be purchased of the Indians, except by the king of Great Britain, or the colonial governments.

We have been thus particular, perhaps tedious, because the facts, which the above quotations disclose, are important to a just understanding of what we propose further to say on this subject. It is clearly seen that, anterior to the Revolution, all the colonies above enumerated assumed the right of subjecting, to their own independent legislation, the Indian tribes within their respective limits. The *justice* of this assumption we do not propose to discuss. The practice under it was universal, and if an error, it was as an error common to all the independent communities then known to assemble under any form of government, within the limits of the present United States. It is not pretended that the aborigines were not *permitted* to regulate their own internal affairs, in their own way, when, by so doing, they did not interfere with the general sovereignty of the whites. They were so permitted, and the numerous treaties, bargains, and compacts made with them, show conclusively, that, to some extent, they were regarded as independent nations; but it is plain they were only so considered, while pursuing a course not in conflict with the power, pride, or interest of their civilized neighbors. The true state of this question, setting aside the justice of the assumption, was very fairly stated

[15] [Ed. *Laws of the Colonial and State Governments Relating to Indians*, 41.]

[16] [Ed. The law was passed on November 27, 1700. *The Statutes at Large of Pennsylvania from 1682 to 1801*, ed. James T. Mitchell and Henry Flanders, 16 vols. (Harrisburg, 1896-19ll), 2:18.]

by Mr. Stuart, British Superintendent of Indian Affairs, in a speech delivered at Mobile, in 1763. Addressing himself to the Indians then present, Mr. Stuart says:

"I inform you that it is the king's order to all his governors and subjects, to treat the Indians with justice and humanity, and to forbear all encroachments on the territories allotted to them; accordingly, all individuals are prohibited from purchasing any of your lands; *but, as you know that as your white brethren cannot feed you when you visit them, unless you give them land to plant, it is expected that you will cede lands to the king for that purpose.*"[17]

This, it must be admitted, was a *cheap* mode of procuring lands. The people were prohibited from *purchasing,* but then it was expected the Indians would cede all that might be asked for, in order merely, that when on a visit to their *generous* neighbors, these "poor Indians" should not starve to death! It shows, however, what was the practice of the English nation with their red brethren, in relation to this subject. Like our colonial fathers, they were for securing any quantity of land needed, at the cheapest possible rate; and if falsehood was found a better coin than a string of beads, there seems to have been no difficulty in procuring any amount of this irredeemable currency, even among a people proverbial for their reverence of holy things! We would not, however, be too severe upon our venerable fathers. We would permit them, with Chancellor Kent, to take shelter under "the necessity of the case," and quietly to rest in their graves until the resurrection.

But it is time to turn our attention to the character and extent of our relations with the Indians within the limits of the United States since the establishment of our national form of government. If, during this period, the results of our efforts have not been so successful as were desired and expected, we have, at least, the satisfaction of knowing that, as a nation, our intercourse with them has been marked by honest desires, noble aims, and generous feelings. No former government ever attempted so much. From the moment of its organization to the present time, the whole policy of the United States, in relation to the aboriginal population of the country, bears the living impress of Christian philanthropy, and lofty devotion to the interests

[17] [Ed. Scottish born John Stuart (1718-79) was a businessman and resident of Charleston, South Carolina. He served as Indian agent from 1763 to 1775 and was during that period a leading light on frontier controversies in the South. On the Mobile Congress with the Indians, see John Richard Alden, *John Stuart and the Southern Colonial Frontier* (Ann Arbor: University of Michigan Press, 1944), 200-202. Unable to identify the quotation.]

and welfare of this most unfortunate people. From a report made by Mr. Leake,[18] Chairman of the Committee on Indian Affairs, in the Senate of the United States, April 5, 1820, we gather the following facts: From 1775 to 1786, our Indian relations were regulated by the agencies of Commissioners, who executed, under the direction of Congress, such arrangements as were, from time to time, deemed best by that body to be adopted, and pursued such a course of policy as was thought best calculated to promote the peace of the frontiers, and the welfare of the Indians. Originally, the Indians were divided into three departments: the northern, middle, and southern. Five Commissioners were appointed for the southern department, and two for the middle and northern. On the 20th of April, 1776, it was resolved by Congress, "that no traders ought to go into the Indian country without license from the agent in the department, and that care be taken by him to prevent exorbitant prices for goods being exacted from the Indians."[19] Measures were adopted, also, in the same year, though on a limited scale, for the introduction, amongst some of the tribes, of civilization and Christianity; and the acts of those earlier times are characterized with kindness, and a solicitude for the welfare of the Indians.

In 1786, Congress passed an ordinance for the regulation of Indian affairs.[20] Two departments only were authorized, the northern and southern; and to each of these was attached a superintendent, with appropriate powers to attend to the execution of such regulations as Congress should, from time to time, adopt. Under this new system, none but citizens of the United States were permitted to reside among the Indian nations, within the territory of the United States, and none to trade with them, without first having obtained a license therefor. The details of this ordinance were numerous and rigid, and yet, it by no means answered the designs of the government. All manner of frauds were practiced under it, notwithstanding its apparent salutary precautions; and, in 1796, a new act of organization was passed, and an appropriation of one hundred and fifty

[18] [Ed. Walter Leake (1762-1825) was a United States senator from Mississippi (1817-21) and the governor of Mississippi (1822-25). His four-page report from the Senate Committee on Indian Affairs is in *Senate Document* No. 105, 16 Congress, 1 session, serial 27.]

[19] [Ed. See *Journals of the Continental Congress, 1774-1789*, edited by Worthington Chauncey Ford, et al., 34 vols. (Washington: Government Printing Office, 1904-37), 4: 318. Hereafter *JCC*. Brownson has the date wrong. It should be April 29, 1776.]

[20] [Ed. "An Ordinance for the Regulation of Indian Affairs," August 7, 1786, *American State Papers, Indian Affairs*, 1:14. See also *JCC*, October 11, 1786, 31: 767-68.]

thousand dollars made to carry it into effect.[21] The system provided for supplying the Indians with all necessary and useful articles, at such rates as would preserve the capital from diminution. In 1806, a superintendent of Indian trade was authorized to be appointed, and the capital of the system increased to two hundred and sixty thousand dollars. In 1811, the capital was increased to three hundred thousand dollars, and upwards of nineteen thousand dollars annually appropriated to defray current expenses.

From the above facts, it will be seen how promptly the government of the United States undertook, after its organization, the improvement of the Indian tribes within its territorial limits. Whatever outrages individuals or small political communities may have been guilty of, previous to the establishment of our present constitutional form of government, not a solitary act of oppression towards the indigenous tribes can be traced to any enactments emanating from the Congress of the United States. At the very commencement of open hostilities between the mother country and the American colonies, the provisional government of the Republic promptly took measures to prevent the Indian tribes from embarking on either side in the then approaching contest. On the 30th of June, 1775, Congress resolved,

"That the Committee of Indian Affairs do prepare proper talks to the several tribes of Indians, for engaging the continuance of their friendship to us, and *neutrality* in our present unhappy dispute with Great Britain."[22]

On the 17th of July following, it was farther resolved,

"That it should be recommended to the Commissioners of the northern department, to employ Mr. Kirkland among the Indians of the Six Nations, in order to secure their friendship, and to continue them in a state of *neutrality* with respect to the present controversy between Great Britain and the Colonies."[23]

In 1776, other resolves on the subject of our Indian relations were passed, among which we find the following:

"Resolved, That a friendly commerce between the people of the United Colonies and the Indians, and the propagation of the gospel, and the cultivation of the civil arts, among the latter, may produce many and inestimable advantages to both, and that the commission-

[21] [Ed. On the trading houses, see 1 *United States Statutes at Large* 452-53.]

[22] [Ed. *JCC* 2:123.]

[23] [Ed. Ibid. 2:187. July 18, not July 17, 1776. The reference is to Samuel Kirkland (1741-1808), a Congregational missionary to the Iroquois Indians and an Indian agent for the United States government after 1774.]

ers for Indian affairs be desired to consider of proper places, in their respective departments, for the residence of ministers and schoolmasters, and report the same to Congress."[24]

We see here, even at this early period of our national existence, our patriot fathers devising means to send among the scattered tribes the arts of civilization and religious instruction. We challenge any Englishman, or any admirer of *English* philanthropy, to show that the British Parliament, during its whole intercourse with the Indian race, from the first peopling of the country to the commencement of the Revolutionary War, attempted so much for their welfare as was proposed in the three resolves above quoted; and this was done, it must be recollected, in the midst of troubles threatening the very existence of those most conspicuous in this great work of Christian philanthropy. It is truly disgusting to read the taunts and strictures of British reviewers and English travelers on the subject of our treatment of the Indian race. A rebuke from those who, during nearly a century and a half, had it in their power, at least to *attempt* something for the improvement of this people, yet did nothing but cheat, rob, and employ them to fight the enemies of England, would be galling and insupportable, were it not for the unblushing falsehood and base hypocrisy, which, in every instance, accompany their ridiculous charges. If any people on earth have maltreated and degraded the Indian population of North America, it is the English. They have, at all times, and without scruple, used them as whips with which to scourge their own enemies; and when the work of vengeance was over, when their own ends were attained, they cast them off, broken in spirit, naked and sick, with the same indifference that an old musket is discarded by the same people. We have no hesitation in saying that the British government is justly chargeable with much of the misery endured by the Indian race, from 1775 to the present moment. It was the British government which opposed their neutrality in the war of the Revolution; it was the same government which led them into the field against the Americans in 1812; and it was the British government, through her well paid agents, which kindled up, and kept alive in their benighted souls, that feeling of deep hostility, against which we have been compelled to war from time to time during the last twenty years.

On the other hand, it has been the invariable practice of the American government, if possible, to persuade the Indian tribes to stand aloof, in all contests between ourselves and other independent

[24] [Ed. February 5, 1776, *JCC* 4:111.]

powers. The Indian commissioners, at the commencement of the Revolution, were instructed to use their best exertions to dissuade the Indians from taking any part in the expected contest between the two countries. Previous to the rupture of 1812, the same instructions were given to the commissioners, and the same exertions used to induce them to observe a neutral attitude. Our want of success in the attempt is no reproach to us. Had our exertions been promptly seconded by the agents of the British government, the result, in all human probability, would have been most fortunate for thousands of the Indian race, who took part in the two contests referred to. They had nothing to gain, even had the English succeeded. As it was, they lost everything but the anxious wishes of the American government still to render them a happy and a prosperous people. For this purpose, the plan of intercourse, already noticed, was pursued with all the energy and care which the importance of the subject, and the hopes of the benevolent, seemed to demand. No expense, on the part of the government, was suffered to arrest or check the entire operation of the system. Some of the best talent of the country was engaged in carrying it forward; and, for a time, strong hopes were entertained that the philanthropic efforts of the government would be successful. Many, however, from the commencement, entertained strong doubts as to the feasibility of improving the aboriginal race, while they were surrounded by, and in immediate contact with, a people in everything their superiors. Besides, their political and civil condition was not well defined. The states, it is true, on the adoption of the Constitution, relinquished their control over the Indian tribes within their respective limits, except inconsiderable remnants in the older states; still there were grounds for differences of opinion as to the extent of the control contemplated in this grant of power. The important question, whether they were to be regarded as *foreign* nations, and treated with as such, seems never to have been clearly settled. Unpleasant collisions between some of the states and the indigenous tribes within their territorial limits, were greatly feared, and, in fact, have since occurred; and above all, it was clearly seen, that whatever merits the then existing system of intercourse possessed, it lacked the essential one of elevating and improving the condition of the race. Under its operation, tribe after tribe gradually dwindled away; and it became apparent that some other course must be adopted, would we preserve a remnant of this once powerful people. Impressed with this idea, Mr. Crawford, Secretary of War, in 1816, in a report on our Indian affairs, observed:

"If the system already devised has not produced all the effects which were expected from it, new experiments ought to be made. When every effort to introduce among them (the Indians) ideas of separate property, as well in things real as personal, shall fail, let *intermarriages* between them and the whites be encouraged by the government. This cannot fail to preserve the race, with the modifications necessary to the enjoyment of civil liberty and social happiness."[25]

This idea was not original with Mr. Crawford. Patrick Henry, years before this, advocated the same plan, and more recently, Mr. Bouldin, of Virginia,[26] referred to it, in the Congress of the United States, in terms of approbation. Whatever merits it possesses on the score of humanity, there are objections to it so serious as to prevent its adoption on a scale sufficiently extensive to effect the object proposed. We have, indeed, no objections to the amalgamation of individuals in this way, providing the thing be brought about in obedience to the high behests of the blind god; but to grant a bounty for the ingress of a mixed posterity at the moral and intellectual expense of a race able and willing to people the republic, without resort to foreign competition, is a proposition too revolting to be entertained for a single moment. Could it be effected, the result would be, to all intents and purposes, extermination. The Indian race, greatly inferior in numbers when compared with the Anglo-American, would, in a few centuries, be entirely swallowed up in the dominant party, and every distinctive mark of its original character nearly obliterated. The resulting compound from a union of races so unlike, would be a class, probably, not materially better than the present aboriginal population. We had better, therefore, grapple with the savage as he is, than encounter a race, of the exact character of which, in the mass, we have no precise conceptions.

The failure of the system of 1786, subsequently several times modified, but still remaining essentially the same, suggested the necessity of adopting some other plan for the preservation of the In-

[25] [Ed. William Harris Crawford (1772-1834) was a United States senator from Georgia, a presidential cabinet member, and presidential candidate. In 1815 President James Madison appointed him secretary of war. As secretary he had charge of the country's Indian affairs. For the quotation, see Crawford's March 14, 1816, report to the United States Senate, *American State Papers, Indian Affairs*, 2:28. No italics in original.]

[26] [Ed. Brownson may be referring to James Wood Bouldin (1792-1854), a United States representative from Virginia (1834-39) or to his brother Thomas Tyler Bouldin (1781-1834) who preceded his brother James in the House of Representatives (1829-34).]

dian race. That of collecting the remaining tribes upon a territory, secured to them and their posterity forever, seemed to promise the fairest hopes of success. The idea was first suggested by Mr. Jefferson, and subsequently entertained and developed to some extent by several succeeding administrations. The plan, however, was not fully laid before the people, till the commencement of General Jackson's administration in 1829. The war of 1812, and the troubles with the Indian tribes for some years after growing out of that contest prevented the federal government from carrying into operation its humane intention of securing a home and a country to the scattered remnants of the Indian race. Something, however, was done during the administrations of Mr. Monroe and Mr. Adams. The plan of removal was much agitated and very generally approved. In 1826, the "*project* of a bill for the preservation and civilization of the Indian tribes within the United States" was, at the request of the Committee of Indian Affairs, furnished by Mr. Barbour, then Secretary of War.[27] The following are the main features of the bill, as stated in the Congressional journals of that day:

"First. The country west of the Mississippi, and beyond the states and Territories, and so much on the east of the Mississippi as lies west of lakes Huron and Michigan, is to be set apart for their exclusive abode.

"Secondly. Their removal by individuals, in contradistinction to tribes.

"Thirdly. A Territorial government to be maintained by the United States.

"Fourthly. If circumstances shall eventually justify it, the extinction of tribes, and their amalgamation into one mass, and a distribution of property among the individuals.

"Fifthly. It leaves the condition of those that remain unaltered."[28]

Though there appears to have been no decisive action on this *projected* bill, it did something. It called public attention to a subject every moment growing more important, because becoming more difficult of adjudication. It was clearly seen that within the limits of the United States the Indian race would find as an independent people

[27] [James Barbour (1775-1842), a wealthy Virginia planter, was a United States senator from Virginia (1814-25). In 1825 President John Quincy Adams appointed him secretary of war, a position he resigned in 1828. For the plan, see Barbour's report to the United States House of Representatives, February 21, 1826, in *American State Papers, Indian Affairs* 2:646. See also Francis Paul Prucha, *The Great Father*, 188-89.]

[28] [Ed. Ibid., 2:648.]

no permanent resting place. Removal or annihilation were the only alternatives. The former, probably, would have been at once agreed on, but for a violent civil collision, which, about this time, occurred between the State of Georgia and the Cherokee tribe of Indians, residing within the limits of that State. We feel bound to refer to the principal facts connected with this celebrated controversy, because they do not appear to be generally understood, and because it is due to the State of Georgia, as well as to the Federal government, that no erroneous impressions remain in the public mind, injuriously affecting the good faith and honest intentions of either.

By reference to the ancient records of Georgia, it appears that, in 1763, her limits were defined to extend from the Savannah to the St. Mary's, and inland, from the 31st to the 35th degrees of north latitude, and from the Atlantic Ocean to the Mississippi. On the revision of her constitution, in 1798, a provision was inserted, authorizing the cession of a large portion of her territory to the United States, and the boundary was indicated beyond which such cession might be made. Four years after this, viz. in 1802, a compact was entered into between the United States and the State of Georgia, and the lands, beyond the limits defined in the new constitution, agreeably to stipulations contained in this compact, were made over to the United States. The amount of territory conveyed somewhat exceeded one hundred thousand square miles, now embraced in the States of Alabama and Mississippi. In consideration of this cession, the general government stipulated to pay to the State of Georgia the sum of $1,250,000, and, what was of more importance to her, it was agreed,

"*That the United States should, at their own expense, extinguish, for the use of Georgia, as early as the same can be peaceably obtained, on reasonable terms, the Indian title to lands within the State of Georgia.*"[29]

With the right of the parties to enter into such a compact we have nothing to do. It was in strict accordance with the practice of the times, and had the sanction of numerous precedents under all governments which had preceded that of the United States. It was no more an assumption than was the planting of the first European foot, without leave, upon the soil of the new world. When the compact was entered into, it became binding on the parties making it. And as the United States entered at once into all the enjoyments secured by its provisions, Georgia, in turn, had a right to expect an early com-

[29] [Ed. See the compact of 1802 in Clarence E. Carter, ed., *The Territorial Papers of the United States*, 26 vols. (Washington: Government Printing Office, 1934-1962), 5:142-46.]

pliance with its stipulations on the part of the general government. In whatever light, therefore, we may regard the question of abstract right, it was one, in the language of Chancellor Kent, not "to be disturbed by speculative reasonings." Interruptions, however, in our friendly intercourse with foreign nations, occurred soon after the stipulations referred to were agreed upon and signed by the contracting parties, which prevented the United States from fulfilling her part of the agreement with the State of Georgia. In the mean time, the Cherokees were making considerable advances in civilization, and becoming more and more attached to the land of their fathers. A large fragment of their tribe, it is true, those most strongly attached to the hunter state, had availed itself of the offers of the government, and removed to the west bank of the Mississippi; but the majority was for permanently establishing itself within the limits of the State of Georgia. Accordingly, in the summer of 1827, a council of delegates, chosen by the Cherokee nation, met and adopted a constitution, in which they declared themselves to be a "*permanent, independent sovereignty.*"[30] The amount of territory, over which the new constitution claimed jurisdiction, exceeded four and a half million acres. Here was a government within a government, *imperium in imperio*, a condition or state of things not to be tolerated for a single moment. Georgia was either entitled to her whole territory, or none at all. The treaty of 1783 declared her, in common with the other twelve colonies, a free, sovereign, and independent state. The compact of 1802, had defined her territorial limits, and the Constitution of the United States declares that "*no new state shall be formed or erected within the jurisdiction of any other state.*"[31] Previous to the adoption of the Cherokee constitution, the right of temporary occupancy was never denied by Georgia to the Indians within her borders. In the celebrated Cherokee case, Samuel A. Worcester *vs.* The State of Georgia, Judge McLean says:

"The exercise of the power of self-government, by the Indians within a state, is undoubtedly contemplated to be *temporary.* This is shown by the settled policy of the government, in the extinguishment of their title, and *especially by the compact with the State of Georgia.* It is a question not of abstract right, but of public policy. I do not mean to say that the same moral rule, which should regulate the affairs of private life, should not be regarded by communities or na-

[30] [Ed. For the Cherokee Constitution, see *House Document*, No. 91, 23 Congress, 2 session, serial 273, pp. 10-19.]

[31] [Ed. US Const., Art 4, sec. 3.1]

tions. But, a sound national policy does require that the Indian tribes within our states should exchange their territories, upon equitable principles, or eventually consent to become amalgamated in our political communities."[32]

The State of Georgia, taking precisely this view of the question, felt herself bound, after the last great movement of the Cherokees, referred to above, to extend her jurisdiction over her whole territory including that portion occupied by the Indians. This brought the two powers in direct collision, and produced a legislative and judicial warfare, which only ended with the treaty of 1835.[33]

In the year 1831, the Cherokee nation appeared in the Supreme Court of the United States, and moved for a writ of injunction to restrain the State of Georgia from the execution of certain laws of that State, which, as alleged, went to annihilate the Cherokees as a political society. This application was made to the court on the assumption that the Cherokees were a *foreign* nation. After a careful examination of the question, Chief Justice Marshall delivered the opinion of the court as follows:

"The Court has bestowed its best attention on this question, and, after mature deliberation, the majority is of opinion that an Indian tribe or nation, within the United States, is not a *foreign* state, in the sense of the Constitution, and cannot maintain an action in the courts of the United States."[34]

Again, says the Chief Justice:

"The bill requires us to control the legislation of Georgia, and to restrain the execution of its physical force. The propriety of such an interposition, by the Court, may be well questioned. It savors too much of exercise of political power, to be within the province of the Judicial Department."[35]

The motion for an injunction was denied. This decision *legally* settled one question; "an Indian tribe or nation, within the United States, is not a *foreign* nation, in the sense of the Constitution." The Chief Justice elsewhere denominates them "*Domestic dependent nations*," a definition, to the correctness of which, we believe, all will readily subscribe. In deciding that an Indian tribe was not a *foreign*

[32] [Ed. *Worcester v. Georgia*, 6 Peters 593 (March 3, 1832). There were no italics in the original.]

[33] [Ed. For the treaty, see Charles J. Kappler, comp., *Indian Affairs: Laws and Treaties*, 5 vols. (Washington: Government Printing Office, 1904-1941), 2:439-49.]

[34] [Ed. *Cherokee Nation v. Georgia*, 5 Peters 20 (March 18, 1831).]

[35] [Ed. Ibid.]

nation, the Chief Justice also decided that the Supreme Court had not jurisdiction of the case; yet, unaccountable as it may seem, one year after, this same Court, in the case of Samuel A. Worcester *vs.* The State of Georgia, claimed jurisdiction, and undertook "to control the legislation of Georgia." We are aware of the fine spun distinction attempted to be drawn between the two cases, and the immense amount of special pleading, resorted to by the Court, to sustain itself in the exercise of this new power; but we frankly confess ourselves wholly unable to understand the validity of the distinction, or the justice of the decision. Worcester was imprisoned for residing, contrary to an express law of Georgia, within the limits of the Cherokee country. When the case, upon a writ of error, came before the United States Court, this Court claimed jurisdiction. In 1831, it totally refused to interfere with the legislation of Georgia, on the ground that the Indians were not a foreign nation, within the meaning of the Constitution; and further, that such interposition would "savor too much of exercise of political power." The Court decided against the State of Georgia, but the latter disregarded the mandate which followed, and Worcester remained in prison till liberated upon his compliance with certain terms offered him on the day of his incarceration. Thus ended the "celebrated Cherokee Case."

That the power exercised by Georgia was legitimate, can hardly admit of question. She did, as we have shown, only what every other original state had done before her. General Jackson, in his first message to Congress, referring to the condition of things then existing in relation to this subject, says:

"Georgia became a member of the confederacy which eventuated in our federal union, as a sovereign state, always asserting her claim to, certain limits; which, having been originally defined in her colonial charter, and subsequently recognized in the treaty of peace, she has ever since continued to enjoy, except as they have been circumscribed by her own voluntary transfer of a portion of her territory to the United States, in the articles of cession of 1802. Alabama was admitted into the union on the same footing with the original states, with boundaries which were prescribed by Congress. There is no constitutional, conventional, or legal provision, which allows them less power over the Indians within their borders, than is possessed by Maine or New York. Would the people of Maine permit the Penobscot tribe to erect an independent government within their state? . . . Would the people of New York permit each remnant of the Six Nations within her borders to declare itself an independent people under the protection of the United States? Could the Indians establish a separate republic on each of their reservations in Ohio? And if they were so disposed, would it be the duty of the general government to protect them in the attempt?"[36]

Up to this time, our relations with the Indian tribes had not been made a party question. A feeling of commiseration for the condition of the aboriginal race was general; and all classes, without distinction of party, manifested the most honorable solicitude for their fate. But when General Jackson, in the message from which we have already quoted, urged the justice and necessity of their removal to a territory west of the Mississippi, the question was at once seized on by his political opponents, and for a time every obstacle thrown in the way of its execution, that ingenuity or party malice could devise. The treaty made with the Cherokees in 1835, stipulating for their removal, was pronounced a fraud, and a powerful party in which was included some of the most gifted orators of the day,[37] manifested a zeal in their opposition to the project, worthy of a better cause. But the energy and personal popularity of the President overcame all difficulties. The plan was finally agreed to, and the means for effecting it secured by legislative enactments, not less just to the Indian tribes than honorable to the General Government.

What, then, under the present system, are the prospects of the aboriginal race? Can it survive the changes which its new condition imposes, or will it continue to dwindle away, and finally vanish from the face of the earth? To the philanthropist this question is intensely interesting, but it is one in the present condition of things to which no perfectly satisfactory answer can be given. We confess our hopes are strong. We have seen something of the Indian, know something of his capabilities, and have reflected much on his singular nature. In the midst of the Anglo-American race he cannot exist. All history shows that while living in the bosom of a civilized community, he will rather adopt its vices than imbibe its virtues. It seems to be a settled principle of our earthly being, that no two distinct varieties of the human family, the one a superior and the other an inferior race, can exist on terms of equality in the same community. The inferior caste will either pass into a state of menial servitude, or be exterminated by their more enlightened neighbors. This position, if true, we are aware, may affect more than one variety of the race of man at present existing within the limits of the United States. It is not our purpose, however, to discuss the full extent of its bearing in this place.

[36] [Ed. Jackson's address to Congress, December 8, 1829, in Fred L. Israel, ed., *State of the Union Messages*, 3 vols. (New York: Chelsea House, 1966): 1:308-10.]

[37] [Ed. One of those orators was Ralph Waldo Emerson. On this see, chapter 1, n. 2.]

If it be applicable to the race under consideration, it is sufficient. We reject entirely the opinion of Don Juan Galindo, contained in the last published volume of the American Antiquarian Society, that "the American Indian has arrived at a decrepit old age," and "is now in the last centuries of his existence";[38] we regard the idea in the light rather of an ingenious conceit than a sober truth. Since the discovery of the continent, the Indian race has been denied every fair facility of permanent improvement. In making this statement, we are not unmindful of the labors of Eliot, Williams,[39] and other Christian philanthropists, who devoted their lives to the cause of holiness among the wandering tribes of the forest. But what could they do when the demon of avarice was stalking over the earth, incessantly demanding more land, and always selecting that patch pressed at the moment by the foot of a red skin? We gave them no resting place. How then could they become civilized? Under existing circumstances, would we preserve our Indian neighbors, they must be schooled in the arts of civilization beyond the limits of the present United States. There, under a system of education such as their peculiar character may require, and a code of laws adapted to the new condition in which they are placed, it is more than probable they will emerge from their present state of ignorance and degradation, and take rank with their present enlightened benefactors. There is nothing utopian in this supposition. Other portions of the human race, now among the most enlightened on the face of the earth, have undergone changes not less surprising than those we suppose may happen to the Indian race. Under like, or similar, circumstances, what has been, may be again.

In conclusion, let us glance at their new home, and their present condition, as exhibited in late reports from the commissioner of our Indian Affairs.[40] The country selected for the future residence of this

[38] [Ed. Don Juan Galindo (d. 1840) was an Irish-born Catholic of Spanish descent who emigrated to Guatemala in 1827. He became a colonel in the army and was later made a proprietor of the Province of Peten (he called himself governor). In 1835, he sent an article on Central American Indian ruins to the president of the American Antiquarian Society, which the president published as "A Description of the Ruins of Copan, in Central America," *Transactions and Collections of the American Antiquarian Society*, volume 2 (Cambridge: Printed for the Society at the University Press, 1836): 543-50, the quotation is on page 546.]

[39] [Ed. Brownson is referring to John Eliot (1604-90), a Puritan missionary to the Indians who developed towns of "praying Indians" in New England, and perhaps to Eleazar Williams (1789?-1858), a missionary of the Protestant Episcopal Church who served Indians in upstate New York and in northern Wisconsin.]

[40] [Ed. "Report of the Commissioner of Indian Affairs," November 25, 1838, in *Senate Document* No. 1, 25 Congress, 3 session, serial 338, pp. 440-56.]

people lies west of the Mississippi, and beyond the limits of any state or territory. It is about six hundred miles long from north to south, extending from the Missouri to Red Rivers, and running westwardly as far as the country is habitable, which is estimated to be something over two hundred miles. The soil is represented as being fertile, the country well watered, and the climate healthy. Upon this territory, there were, on the 1st of November, 1838, 81,082 emigrant Indians, and 26,482 more are under treaty stipulations to remove in due time. In this statement is included the 18,000 Cherokees who were then on their way to join their kindred in their new country. Those, who have not watched the progress of this system, will be astonished at the advances already made by some of the tribes west of the Mississippi. To begin with the Creeks, who are settled in the immediate vicinity of Fort Gibson.[41] This tribe numbers between eighteen and twenty thousand, and, according to the statement of the acting superintendent of the Western Territory, made in December, 1837:

"They dwell in good, comfortable farm houses, have fine gardens, orchards, and raise forty to fifty thousand bushels of corn more than what is sufficient for their own consumption. They furnish large quantities to the commissariat at Fort Gibson annually, and contributed greatly in supplying the late emigrants. They raise, also, more stock than is necessary for their own use, and carry on a considerable trade with the garrison in grain, stock, vegetables, poultry, eggs, fruit, &c. There are several traders located among them, to furnish their wants, which are as many and various as those of the most comfortable livers of our own citizens. Two of these traders are natives, who do a considerable business, selling eighteen or twenty thousand dollars worth of goods annually."[42]

This is cheering; but let us look at the Cherokees. We will quote from the same agent:

"The number of farms in this nation is estimated at between *ten and eleven hundred.* There are no Cherokees who follow the chase for a living; the nation is divided into farmers, traders, stock-raisers, and laborers. The produce of the farms is corn, oats, potatoes of both kinds, beans, peas, pumpkins, and melons. The great profit of the Cherokee farmer is his corn, his horses, his cattle, and his hogs. Some of the Cherokees have taken and fulfilled contracts for the garrison at

[41] [Ed. Fort Gibson was established in April 1824 near the confluence of the Arkansas and Neosho rivers in present-day eastern Oklahoma.]

[42] [Ed. Report of the Commissioner of Indian Affairs, Carey A. Harris, December 1, 1837, enclosing "Report of the Acting Superintendent of the Western Territory, " *Senate Document*, No. 1, 25 Congress, 2 session, serial 314, p. 539.]

Fort Gibson, and for subsisting emigrant Indians, to the amount of forty to sixty thousand dollars, without purchasing any articles except in the Indian country. [. . .] At the grand saline on the river Neosho, forty miles above Fort Gibson, they are making eighty bushels of excellent salt per day, for five days in the week; but the manufacture is carried on at considerable expense for labor, fuel, hauling, &c. [. . .] There are several native traders doing very good business in the nation; one of them is doing an extensive business, *and owns a fine steamboat, that plies between New Orleans and the Cherokee nation.*"[43]

It is further added, "The greater portion of the Cherokees [west are farmers,] have good and comfortable houses, and live, many of them, as well and as genteel, and, in a pecuniary point of view, will compare with the better class of farmers in the states."[44]

This is still more cheering; but let us turn to the Choctaws. We quote from the report of William Armstrong, agent at the Choctaw station, made in December, 1838:

"The Choctaws are governed by a written constitution and laws; they meet annually in their general council on the first Monday of October. The nation is composed of three districts, each district electing ten counselors, by the qualified voters of each district—they[45] being every male twenty-one years and upward[s] of age. They have but the representative body, the three chiefs sitting with the veto power upon all laws passed by the council, which, however, when passed by two-thirds becomes a law. They have judges appointed, and officers to enforce the laws, by a jury chosen in the ordinary way. They have, to a great extent, modeled their laws after some of our states, and generally their laws are executed. There is no enforcement for the collection of debts, and whatever trading is done upon credit rests upon the honor of the debtor to pay; and, in most instances, contracts entered into are punctually paid. The Choctaws have passed some wholesome laws against the introduction of spirituous liquor into their country. [. . . .] A large and commodious council house for the nation has just been completed, and occupied,[46] for the first time this year, by the council. The room in which the council meets is large and spacious, sufficiently [so] for the accommodation of all the members, and a railing round, with seats for spectators. There is a

[43] [Ed. Ibid. 540. No italics in original. In the second ellipsis the following sentence was left out: "In the hands of a skilful [*sic*] capitalist, it would be a source of great wealth."]

[44] [Ed. Ibid. 545.]

[45] [Ed. Brownson added "they."]

[46] [Ed. Brownson inserted "occupied" for "used" in the original.]

separate room adjoining, for each of the three districts, in which their committees meet. They usually remain in council from ten to twenty days[;] elect a president and secretary; the strictest order prevails; everything is recorded; and, in fact,[47] it would hardly be credited,[48] but [such is the fact,] in few deliberative bodies is more order and propriety observed."[49]

Are these facts generally known? We doubt it very much. We doubt whether one in fifty of the American people are aware of the fact that we have an Indian population rapidly improving in all the arts of civilization, and growing rich in the good things of this world. We might make many other selections from these reports, equally favorable to the advancement of the aboriginal race; but it is unnecessary. We must, however, say something of their advantages for school education. As all the schools, however, are not within the territory set apart for the residence of the Indians, but scattered over various parts of the country at present occupied by the tribes, we will throw into a tabular form the results of the highly interesting statements which accompanied the last report from the Indian Department:

STATE OF THE SCHOOLS.[50]

Superintendency	No. of Teachers.	No. of pupils.	No. of tribes instructed.
Acting Superintendency of Michigan,	13	149	5
Superintendency of Wisconsin,	20	431	13
Superintendency of St. Louis,	9	74	6
Acting do. of the Western Territory,	9	227	6
Missionary School, Choctaw Nation,	5	123	6
do. do. Cherokee Nation,	3	158	6
Totals, ...	59	1,162	

This is well, but it is not all. The Choctaw Academy is in successful operation, and is a school of great importance to the Indian race. It is under most excellent regulations, and has already turned out many useful men. The following table presents its condition in December, 1838:

47 [Ed. Brownson inserted "in fact."]

48 [Ed. Brownson substituted "credited" for "believed" in the original.]

49 [Ed. Report of William Armstrong in *Senate Document*, No. 1, 25 Congress, 3 session, serial 338, pp. 509-10.]

50 [Ed. This is a compilation of statistics in the "Report of the Commissioner of Indian Affairs," November 25, 1838, in *Senate Document* No. 1, 25 Congress, 3 session, serial 338, pp. 476-79.]

CHOCTAW ACADEMY[51]

Tribes.	Pupils.
Choctaws,	60
Pottawatamies,	21
Quapaws,	2
Miamies,	3
Seminoles,	6
Creeks,	7
Winnebagoes,	9
Cherokees,	14
Chickasaws,	18
Chippewas and Ottawas,	11
Total	151

All these schools are more or less under the control of different religious denominations, and most of them have some funds set apart for their support. They are all, unquestionably, doing substantial good, and ought to receive more efficient aid from the United States.

We would say no hard things against those who are zealously laboring to spread the truths of Christianity among the Indian tribes west of the Mississippi. Their motives entirely forbid severity of remark. But we cannot help thinking that all direct efforts to teach them the peculiar doctrines of Christianity are misplaced, if not absolutely injurious. Can a people, whose thoughts rarely extend beyond the immediate gratification of the senses, be led to embrace doctrines so spiritual and ennobling, without much previous preparation in the arts of civilization, and the laws which regulate society? It seems to us, the agriculturist, the mechanic, and the schoolmaster, are the true pioneers in the great work of Indian civilization. The red man will hold to the religion of his fathers to the last moment. It is seated deep in the dark recesses of his soul, and will there remain, till forced away by the power of mental cultivation. Teach the Indian how to live *honestly* in this world, and he will soon teach himself how to be happy in that which is to come.

Again, we repeat, our hopes are strong, that the North American Indian will yet emerge from his present state of ignorance and barbarism. But we would caution all against expecting too much, and that suddenly. The race has been stationary for centuries. Its peculiar habits and modes of thought are not, therefore, to be broken up and changed in a day. We must expect frequent disappointments, for we

[51] [Ed. Ibid., 478.]

have a wayward being to instruct; but perseverance, kindness, and prompt assistance, free from all expectations of pecuniary reward, will, we cannot help thinking, enable us, at last, to triumph, and the Indian to rejoice in a new career of usefulness and glory. Let his fetters of prejudice and superstition be broken; let the bright, glowing rays of science once penetrate the mental gloom in which the intellect of the Indian is now buried, and a new fountain will be opened, whence will flow living, undying streams of thought, growing broader and deeper through all coming time.

There are several other interesting topics connected with this subject, which it was originally our intention to discuss; but the great, perhaps unreasonable, length to which we have already carried our inquiries, admonishes us that we cannot, at present, in justice, longer trespass on the patience of our readers.

16.

BULWER'S NOVELS[1]

Boston Quarterly Review 2 (July 1839): 265-97

In a short notice which we took, sometime since, of "Ernest Maltravers,"[2] we stated that, on the appearance of the sequel to that work, we would attempt to form an estimate of the general merits of Mr. Bulwer as an author and a novelist. We proceed now to redeem our promise; and we do it the more willingly because we entertain a more favorable opinion of his literary productions than that entertained by several of our contemporaries.

Of Mr. Bulwer's private character we know only what we can infer from his works. Some reports to his prejudice have reached us; but we have lived too long to be in haste to credit reports against an author, who apparently speaks from his own convictions, and, to a certain extent at least, makes war upon commonly received opinions and conventional usages. The good we hear of such an author it is safe to believe, but not the evil. The necessity he imposes upon the men of routine, the good easy men of the world, of vindicating their traditionary creeds, and legitimating their blind practices, readily accounts for the stories which may be told against him, without the gratuitous supposition of their truth.

Mr. Bulwer, like most men of vigor and activity of mind enough to form opinions for themselves, is somewhat of a heretic, and, therefore, inevitably exposed to the universal fate of heretics—misconception and misrepresentation. Still, a knowledge of his private history is not essential to the just estimation of his books. Books, if worth

[1] [Ed. Sir Edward George Earle Bulwer-Lytton (1803-73), First Baron Lytton, was a popular English novelist, playwright, essayist, poet and politician. The running title for Brownson's essay was "Bulwer's Novels—Their Moral Tendency not dangerous." Earlier Brownson had reviewed "Bulwer's Works" for the *Boston Reformer* 3 (1836), a copy of which is located in Brownson's Paper, microfilm roll # 10, which contains a Notebook of clippings from the *Boston Reformer*.]

[2] [Ed. *Ernest Maltravers* (1837) is the first of a two-part novel, the second being *Alice* (1838). For Brownson's very positive first review of *Ernest Maltravers. By the author of "Pelham"* 2 vols. (New York: Harper and Brothers, 1837), see *Boston Quarterly Review* 1 (January, 1838): 121-23.]

considering at all, have a character independent of that of their author. Truth is truth, by whomsoever uttered; and a good moral lesson does not necessarily lose its savor because he who gives it may, perchance, turn out to be no saint. The worth of a book consists in the spirit it breathes, the lesson it inculcates, the influence it is fitted to exert; and if these be unexceptionable in themselves, the character of the author, whatever it may be, cannot impair their value.

Moreover, if these be unexceptionable, the real character of the author cannot be very reprehensible. If the book breathe a pure and elevating spirit, quicken our holier instincts, and fire us with new zeal and courage to attempt a useful and honorable part in life, no biographer in the world, let his array of facts be what it may, can make us believe the author was not a frequent and devout worshiper at the shrine of virtue. A man's outward actions are but his shadows, shortening or lengthening as the sun rises or declines; they are determined, to a great extent, by foreign influences, over which he has no control, and, therefore, are no sure index to his real character. His real character lies beneath the surface, consists in his internal workings, his hopes, fears, struggles, aims, aspirations, ideals, and these the author invariably stamps upon his book.

Nor does it comport with our ideas of consistency to condemn Mr. Bulwer's works merely on the ground of the alleged sins of their author, so long as we approve the works of other authors, who are at least no better than he is said to be. Scott[3] would hardly come off clear if tried by rigid orthodox rules; and yet it is lawful to read and laud his productions. Even clergymen read them and recommend them from the pulpit. Goethe, too, is in tolerable repute. Pious young ladies write his biography, and, with charming *naïveté* ask for more information concerning his marriage. And yet Goethe was but an indifferent saint. He was a confirmed sensualist, and a disbeliever in nearly all that the world upholds as religion. He held him to be the truly wise man who needed no assistance from God or the devil in the conduct of life; and he considered it nobody's business how many of the young and beautiful he seduced and abandoned to infamy, wretchedness, despair, and death, if he but succeeded in "acting out himself," and securing his own gratification. Surely, if we regard such a man as Goethe as a religious man, as a sort of second Messiah, as some among us do, we ought not to be very loud in our condemnation of Sir Edward Lytton Bulwer.

[3] [Ed. Sir Walter Scott (1771-1832) was a Scottish poet and novelist who developed the genre of the historical novel.]

But, waiving the personal character of the author, we proceed at once to his works. These are his best biographies and these are all that concern us. Through these he exerts an influence on this country, for good or for evil, and of these, therefore, instead of him, we should seek to form a correct estimate.

As mere works of art, we have not much to say of Mr. Bulwer's novels. We are neither artists, nor qualified to judge of the niceties of art. We know when and why a work pleases us, but not whether the artist has observed all the rules of the schools or not, whether we are pleased according to rule or against rule. We love art in all its branches; but we approve no work, whatever artistic skill it may display, unless its moral tendency be unexceptionable. Genius and talent are to us worthy of reverence only when employed in a holy cause and directed to noble ends. Moreover, we are in the habit of questioning the artistic merit of all works which have an immoral tendency. A work of art, it strikes us, should be addressed to man's whole nature, and so fill the soul, that no want shall be felt in its presence. The moral sense is an integral element of the soul, and how, then, can a work possess artistical perfection, which does not satisfy our moral sense, or rather, which outrages it? Such a work is marked by a serious defect; it leaves the beholder conscious of a want it does not meet. It is not broad enough for the soul, and it proves its author must have been only the fraction of a man.

Let it not, however, be inferred from this, that we would have every work of art constructed with express reference to some special dogma, or to some special moral lesson. We have no great respect for what are usually termed religious novels, of which "Thornton Abbey," "Coelebs in Search of a Wife," " Dunallen," " The Lady of the Manor,"are tolerable specimens.[4] They are to us very uninteresting productions; we seldom read more of them than we can help. Whoever undertakes to write a work for the express purpose of conveying a special lesson, a special moral, almost invariably fetters his genius,

[4] [Ed. John Satchel, *Thornton Abbey: A Series of Letters on Religious Subjects* (Philadelphia: Johnson and Warner, 1811); Hannah More (1745-1833), a playwright and religious writer, published *Coelebs in search of a wife* (1809); Grace Kennedy (1782-1825), *Dunallen; Or, Know What You Judge: A Story* (London: Horton, Morrison, and Woodward, 1800?); Mary Butt Sherwood (1775-1851), an evangelical Protestant author of numerous religious novels, including *The Lady of the Manor: being a Series of Conversations on the Subject of Confirmation: Intended for the Use of the Middle and Higher Run of Young Females* (Philadelphia: Towar, J and M. M. Hogan, 1831). The American Sunday School Union published some of Sherwood's novels; in fact, its first publication was her *Little Henry and His Bearer* (1817).]

abandons his natural freedom, and with it all grace of motion. His movements become stiff, constrained, and awkward. Be the cravings of nature what they may, all things must bend to the special moral to be brought out, and that moral, too, is everywhere before us, meeting us at every turn. It is *toujours pedrix*,[5] a good dish, no doubt, but, like all good dishes, apt to cloy if served up too often, both in season and out of season. Such a proceeding is also unnatural, for nature nowhere teaches a special moral, but merely makes her various productions conspire to a moral end. It must, too, in general, be a failure. The offspring, if they come to anything at all, which they rarely do, are the huge, ill-shapen beasts of Oriental mythology, not the chaste, harmonious, and graceful creations of Grecian genius. All we ask of the artist, and this we do ask of him, is that he create with a moral purpose, with reference to a moral effect. The love of moral beauty must fill his soul, inspire his undertaking, and pervade his works as an informing spirit. His productions will then have a moral effect, a moral tendency, though there be no special moral tacked on to the end, as in Aesop's Fables.

With this view of art, we must, if we are not mistaken, deny the highest artistic merit to such a writer, for example, as Goethe. We speak with reserve of this distinguished German, for we know him mainly through the representations of others, never having studied his works for ourselves. But so far as we can form an estimate of him from the representations of his professed admirers, we regard him as deficient on the moral side of art. He was not without a sort of reverential feeling for nature, and perhaps for some of the household virtues so common to the Germans; but we never find him creating at the command of high moral instincts. He does not appear to work because his soul is full of love to God and man, and because he feels that all the faculties God has given him should be consecrated to the service of his race. We find in him no pure love of humanity, no unquenchable thirst for a purer and better social state, no throbbing of the heart, no intense longing to stand by the weak, to raise up the low, and bring down the high. Nothing of all this wells up from the depths of his soul, and streams out in the rich melodies of his song. He sings to ease himself, to permit the effervescence of passion to escape, and to recover self-possession for the enjoyment of his pleasures. His songs do not kindle us, exalt us, enlarge our ideals, and make us stronger and more courageous in the cause of virtue; and, therefore, in our judgment, fall short of the highest artistical merit.

[5] [Ed. "*toujour perdrix*" (Brownson has misspelled the term) is French for "always partridges, or always the same thing over again."]

On the same ground, too, we must question the high artistical merit of Sir Walter Scott. Scott's works, be praised as they have been and are, have never satisfied us as moral productions. Nor does he himself come up to our ideal of a moral man. He has no remarkable love of moral beauty, and no abiding sense of his duty to devote his gifts to the good of mankind. No picture of high moral excellence has ever come forth from his studio. His loftiest ideals are but one degree above the common-place, and never does he address his works to the higher elements of the human soul. His characters, it is true, are chiefly taken from actual life, and this may in part excuse him; but he does not select the best which even actual life could furnish. He never selects the real heroes or seers of humanity, nor attempts the portrait of a man of high aspirings, of lofty aims, haunted day and night by visions of a greater good to be wrought out for his country or for his race, and which will not let him rest till he has done all in his power to realize them. There are no Wat Tylers, Jack Cades, Van Arteveldts, Rienzis, Sydneys, Hampdens, Vanes, Miltons, among his offspring.[6] The creator of the Dalgetties, the Marmions, the Quentin Durwards, the Fair services, the Varneys, and the Ned Christians, had no fellowship with these stern lovers of justice, who lived but to resist the tyrant, to lighten the load of the heavy laden, and to enable the oppressed to stand up in the image of their Maker, and look forth in joy upon a world made beautiful by the presence of universal love.[7] He beheld no beauty or comeliness in them that he should desire them, or point them out to the love and reverence of mankind.

[6] [Ed. Wat Tyler (d. 1381) was the principal leader of the Peasants' revolt against the poll tax in England. Jack Cade (d. 1450) was the Irish-born leader of the revolt known as Cade's rebellion against King Henry VI of England in 1450. Brownson could be referring to either Jacob van Artevelde (c. 1295-1345) or to his son Philip (1340-82), both of whom led unsuccessful revolts in Ghent, Flanders (now Belgium). Cola di Rienzo (Rienzi) (c. 1313-54) was a popular Roman leader who overthrew the corrupt aristocracy and instituted reforms. John Hampden (1594-1643) was the English political leader of the revolutionary movement against King Charles I. Sir Henry Vane (1613-62) was an English Puritan statesman, a one-time governor of Massachusetts colony, and a strong supporter of the Parliamentary cause against the king during the English Civil War of the mid 1640s. The English poet John Milton (1608-74) was an ardent participant in the English Civil War.]

[7] [Ed. The references are to various characters in Scott's historical novels and narrative poems: Dugald Dalgetty from *A Legend of Montrose* (1831), Marmion from *Marmion* (1808), Quentin Durward from *Quentin Durward* (1823), Andrew Fairservice from *Rob Roy* (1817), Richard Varney from *Kenilworth* (1821), and Edward Christian from *Peveril of the Peak* (1823).]

True morality is somewhat higher than Scott was in the habit of looking. It is not merely respectability, decency, good feeling, hospitality, vulgar loyalty, and the absence of envy as an author; nor does it stop merely with what are termed the private and domestic virtues. It goes out of self, out of the family circle, and embraces universal man. Pure in motive, lofty in purpose, firm in resolve, it espouses the cause of the weak, takes its stand with the wronged, shelters the friendless, speaks for the dumb, raises up the downtrodden, deposes the tyrant, unbars the prison-door, recalls the exile, and establishes the reign of justice and freedom throughout the earth. Works, which reveal to us nothing of this Christian morality, which kindle in us no desire to possess it, nor strengthen us to do its bidding, are not merely defective in a moral point of view, but also in an artistical point of view. They fail in accomplishing the legitimate purposes of art. In the works of the old masters, unless we have been misinformed, there are proofs that the artist has communed with a beauty, a worth, not of this world. The study of those works tends to enlarge our ideals, to give us glimpses of something purer and more elevated than has yet been attained, to exalt our sentiments, to purify our affections, to create in us inexpressible longings for what we have not, and to make us consecrate ourselves to the glorious work of regenerating the world. This should be the tendency and aim of art. Do we perceive anything of this aim and this tendency in the writings of Sir Walter Scott? Is he true to that higher morality, the possession of which makes us brothers of Jesus and sons of God? Not at all. The perusal of his works has no tendency to make us wiser or better; it furnishes us no food for reflection; clears up no dark passage in human life or in human nature; and does nothing to kindle within us that philanthropy which would do and dare anything and everything to augment the sum of human well-being. In these works, the ordinary is made to suffice us; and we are taught, virtually, that if we have an old baronial castle, a long pedigree, some pieces of old armor to hang up in the hall, a fine horse, and choice hounds for the chase, old books, and plenty of old wine for convivial parties, and in which to pledge the king and some "faire ladie," we need be under no apprehension for this world, nor for that which is to come.

Now, we are far from pretending that Mr. Bulwer satisfies us on this moral side of art; we are free to own that he does not realize our ideal, but he does it more fully than the majority of popular authors with whom we are conversant. He seems to us to write with a moral purpose, seriously and honestly, for a moral end. He always seems to us earnestly enlisted on the side of humanity, and firmly resolved that his works shall not only be amusing, but instructive, kindling our moral instincts, and disposing us to make our lives worth something to the world. If so, we must acquit him, in a moral point of view, at least so far as aims are in question; nay, we must honor him.

But we shall, probably, be told, that the morality, he actually inculcates, is of a low and debasing sort. We have been so told till we are weary of hearing it. Honor to the brave old Athenian who ostracized Aristides[8] because he was tired of hearing him called the just! We sympathize most heartily with his feeling; and, applying it to the opposite case, we can never hear a man perpetually called immoral, but we have an invincible inclination to maintain that he is moral. Let the odds be against a man, and he may call us his friend, and count upon our taking up the cudgels in his behalf. Since the world has turned against our friend Emerson, and set to praising a feeble, though well-meant, performance, in the shape of a Sermon on the Personality of the Deity,[9] supposed to be directed against him, we heartily repent of having appeared among his opponents. We were as much out of our place as Saul was among the prophets. Heavens! Only think of the Boston Quarterly Review joining with grave doctors and learned professors to write down a man who has the boldness to speak from his own convictions, from his own free soul! It was a great mistake on our part, and one which, alas! we perceived not till it was too late.[10] Honor to every man who speaks from his own mind, whatever be his word. He is an iconoclast, a servant of the true God, even though it be a left-handed one.

Now as to this declamation against the immoral tendency of Mr. Bulwer's novels, let it be observed that it proceeds mainly from the Scribes and Pharisees, chief priests and elders of the people—a very suspicious source! For, is it not on record, that the Scribes and Pharisees, chief priests and elders of the people, formerly committed the

[8] [Ed. Aristides, called the just, was an Athenian military and political leader of the fifth century B.C.]

[9] [Ed. Henry Ware, Jr. (1794-1843), *Personality of the Deity. A Sermon, preached in the Chapel of Harvard University, September 23, 1838* (Boston: J. Munroe and Co., 1838). Ware's father, Henry Ware (1764-1845), was the center of the great Unitarian controversy of 1805 when he was appointed Hollis Professor of Divinity at Harvard. In the early years of the controversy, Ware senior was a leader in defense of Unitarianism. Ware junior's *Personality* opposed the theology of Emerson's "Divinity School Address." He maintained that religious faith and moral virtue depended upon a conception of a personal God, which he believed Emerson had rejected.]

[10] [Ed. Brownson is referring here of course to his reviews of Emerson's "Divinity School Address," which are in this volume, chapters 1 and 6.]

egregious mistake of regarding one Jesus of Nazareth as an immoral man; of calling him a glutton, a drunkard, a blasphemer, a pestilent fellow, and of finally crucifying him between two thieves? And who will be our guaranty, that they are one whit wiser today than they were two thousand years ago? Their opinions, therefore, can be of no weight with a wise man. They have no time to devote to the study of moral doctrines; it is enough for them to keep up their respectability. Their doctrines, if they have any, can serve the inquirer after truth only by showing him what truth is not.

Some persons, however, not exactly of this class, have questioned the moral tendency of these novels; and their questioning demands attention, and deserves to be treated with respect. But we would ask them, if they have thoroughly studied these works? Have they done anything more than to read them as interesting stories or amusing tales? Have they examined their moral bearing, looked through society, ascertained its actual sins, and the remedies demanded? Have they duly considered the influence these novels are fitted to have in expelling our actual sins? A book may be very useful, indispensable, in checking or removing a certain class of sins, which actually prevail, although it should be a dangerous book in a community where those sins were unknown; as a drug, which would cause instant death if administered to a person in perfect health, may be a most valuable medicine in restoring the system which is diseased. We must be thoroughly acquainted with the diseases which affect society, as well as with what would be perfect social health, before we can pronounce definitely concerning the tendency of this or that publication. Now have these persons, who condemn Bulwer's novels, become thoroughly acquainted with the social system, in its diseased manifestations as well as in its healthy manifestations, and ascertained by actual experiment what medicines are necessary to restore health, as well as what treatment is necessary to preserve it? If not, their judgment need not be taken as final.

But, be the tendency of these novels what it may, we ask what English novelist of our times gives us novels of a better moral tendency? What novelist surpasses Bulwer in the homage which he pays to that morality which seeks the public good, which calls upon all public men to form opinions for themselves, to ascertain on what principles the public good is based, and to adhere to those principles, through good report and through evil? There are none of his contemporaries, we are acquainted with, in whom we find so deep a cast of reflection, so generous a tone of sentiment, so tender a concern for human well being, so frequent reference to the fact that we live not for ourselves alone, and that we are to find our own good only in seeking that of others. He, who surpasses all his countrymen, though he attain not to the highest ideal, should receive some mercy at our hands. Among Bulwer's contemporaries in his own country, we can find no one to be placed before him, unless it be Thomas Carlyle. We have a strong love for Carlyle. We like him for his hearty hatred of cant and formulas; for his indomitable love of independence; his rich imagination; his poetic sensibility; his tenderness and pathos; his wit and humor; his broad and generous sympathies; his worship of the genuine, and his detestation of the seeming; and—for his wonderful facility in the use of the English language. Taking the world as it is, we think his writings likely to have a healing influence, and therefore are we glad to see them circulate: but we cannot rank him above Bulwer, nor even so high. All his best thoughts may be found in Bulwer who is free from that in him which we do not like. Carlyle's views, taken in themselves, without any special reference to the dominant tendencies of the age, are far from being unexceptionable. His morality, notwithstanding its transcendental garb, is of the school of Goethe, and may be summed up in the formula, "Act out Thyself"; and his philosophy, if philosophy he have, is not much better than Hume's. It ends, like Hume's, in skepticism, albeit by following a different route. In his "Sartor Resartus" he says many fine things, sometimes in a fantastic, sometimes in a surpassingly beautiful manner—fine things, which make one think he sympathizes with the untitled and hard-handed many, and is ready to devote himself, soul and body, to their cause; but he has no faith in efforts to meliorate society, and he sneers at him who would labor for "the progress of the species."[11] He weeps over the wrongs of humanity and mocks at all efforts to right them. He bids us work, but assures us our working will come to nought; he detests the old social garment, but bids us beware of attempting to weave a new one. Now he is a furious Jacobin, and now a staunch conservative. We hardly know what to make of him. We feel and own his power; we imagine him original and profound; and yet, when we have divested his thoughts of the unwonted garb in which he has clothed them, they almost always turn out to be our old acquaintances. But, be this as it may, the man who could find it in his heart to turn the French Revolution into burlesque, and to play the Merry-Andrew amid the dissolution of the old feudal and

[11] [Ed. Carlyle uses this expression several times in his *The French Revolution*, Volume 1, Book 2, Chapter 1; Chapter 4; and Chapter 7. See *Centenary Edition. The Works of Thomas Carlyle*, 30 vols. (London: Chapman and Hall, 1896), 2:31; 2:40; 2:53.]

Catholic world, and over the well-meant, but not always wisely-directed, efforts of the French people to construct a new and better world, can never, with us, rank as a truly moral man.[12]

Bulwer may want Carlyle's power, his wit, his humor, his pathos, his transcendentalism; but he surpasses him in plain common sense, and in the healthiness of the tone of his writings. He has a firmer faith in virtue, in man, and in the utility of efforts to advance society. We never find him sneering at honest efforts to promote the welfare of mankind; he does not deify man, and then mock him, because he does not act the god becomingly. He everywhere inculcates the lesson of charity and mutual tolerance; he takes man as he finds him, a being of clay as well as of spirit, liable to fall as well as able to rise, possessing freedom of will, indeed, but subject to a thousand influences pressing in upon him from without, which he can neither resist nor divert; and with all these imperfections clinging to him, he shows that he loves and respects him, and that we too should love and respect him, and the more instead of the less because of his imperfections. Is not this a correct view of man, and is not the moral to be extracted from it a healthy one?

In giving this general estimate of the moral bearing of these novels, we of course except Falkland,[13] the earliest of Mr. Bulwer's prose publications, because it was a production of his youth, and he himself has since publicly objected to it, as unsound in its philosophy and false in its coloring of life. It belongs to the school of Werter and Childe Harold[14]—a dark, desponding, sentimental school, of most unhealthy influence,—and as the author has shown no attachment to that school in his subsequent publications, we should be unfair critics, were we to take this work into the account in making up our estimate of his general merits.

In Pelham,[15] the work by which the author first became known to any extent in this country, and the first of his works in which the bent of his genius, his moral and political tendencies, became decidedly manifest, he has been said to teach a low and debasing moral. Mr. Henry Pelham is so respectable, has so many attractions, so much

[12] [Ed. Thomas Carlyle's *The French Revolution* (1837) was widely read and commented upon in the United States. As an example, see William Henry Channing's anonymous and favorable review: "Carlyle's French Revolution," *Boston Quarterly Review* 1 (October, 1838): 407-17.]

[13] [Ed. *Falkland* (1827) was hardly a novel, but a series of sentimental letters.]

[14] [Ed. References are to Frederick Reynolds' (1764-1841) *Werter* (1785) and George Gordon Byron's *Childe Harold* (1816).]

[15] [Ed. *Pelham* (1828).]

real worth, notwithstanding his dandyism and devotion to pleasure, that our good folks, simple souls! imagine it was the author's design to commend dandyism and devotion to pleasure as essential elements in the character of a gentleman. But the real design of the author has been, we take it, to show us that a young man, thrown into the vortex of fashionable dissipation, surrounded by dissolute companions, beset on every hand by temptations to sin, may gradually brighten his character, attain to much useful knowledge of men and things, acquire just notions of public virtue, and become a man of solid worth for the soundness of his understanding, the strength of his attachments, and the firmness with which he adheres to the principles on which he has convinced himself the public good is based. The author would teach us that we may pass for men of fashion, men of the world, without becoming lost to all sense of right and wrong, or indifferent to the welfare of our friends, our country, or mankind. He intended Henry Pelham for a satire on the race of dandies of the epoch in which the work was written; but should even the dandies of our day mistake him for the model of a gentleman, and attempt to imitate him, their morals would probably be mended rather than injured. Many, too, who abuse Mr. Henry Pelham most shamefully, might very advantageously take lessons of him in both private morals and public.

None of the author's works have been more rudely assailed than Paul Clifford.[16] In this work, we are gravely told by grave moralists,

[16] [Ed. *Paul Clifford* (1830). As a young man Brownson had given the work a favorable review in the *Genesee Republican and Herald of Reform* 1 (August 18, 1830): 4, which he edited. In part, he wrote: "I know not when I have read anything which interested me more or pleased me better than Paul Clifford; by the author of Pelham, Deveraux, etc. It is seldom I read a novel that I do not find in it much more to condemn than to approve. I dislike the deceptive views novels present of life, their mischievous influence on the unchastened imagination of youth, the sickish sentimentalism they encourage, or equally sickish romantic cast they give to the mind. Youth is sufficiently prone to exaggerate without the aid of the novelist—sufficiently prone to leave reality to ramble in ideal worlds without being farther seduced by the fascinating scenes and glowing descriptions of the writers of fiction. But, notwithstanding my objections to novels in general, I am well please with Paul Clifford. Not that it is liable to no objections, for there are parts which are subject to very heavy ones. But it has more real excellence, it has better passages, traces of a deeper and more sound philosophy, more just sentiment, and well timed observations on popular institutions than we recollect to have met with in any other of the fashionable productions of this most prolific age. There is a richness in its scenes that we have seldom seen equaled in any other writer, a deep and thrilling interest in the plot and incidents that must make the pulse of the coldest reader beat quick. Among the various scenes there are none which strike me more

the author recommends highway robbery; or, in other words, that he paints the robber in such fascinating colors, and surrounds his profession with so many attractions, that we are made to feel an almost irresistible inclination to take the road. There is no reasoning against this statement because they who make it doubtless know the best what they feel; and all we can do is, when we travel abroad, to see that our pistols are in proper order. Still, we cannot help thinking, that this love of the robber's life must be inherent in the hearts of these people, rather than produced by Mr. Bulwer's descriptions; for we have never found them creating in us any disposition to become highwaymen; they have rather produced in us a firm resolution to do what we can so to perfect the social state, that robbery shall not be one of its fruits. In his history of Paul Clifford and his associates, the author has shown us, what he intended, that many of the depravities of individual character are due to the depravities of that social state in which the character is formed. Paul Clifford has no innate love of vice; nay, he is naturally well inclined, and has an honorable ambition to obtain his living by a useful and just calling. He does not become a highwayman from choice, nay, not without repugnance; but through the force of circumstances with which he is surrounded, and which he cannot control. He is corrupted and made a robber by influences which he had not the innate power to resist, and no man who sees him can help regarding him as more sinned against than sinning; in other words, as a victim of an imperfect, a corrupt social state. We are led by the author to transfer our indignation from Paul to the social state, which abandoned him to the corrupting influences which operated his fall; and, instead of seeking to chastise the victim, we are led to labor for the regeneration of society itself. This is an important moral, and the one which will require many such novels as Paul Clifford to teach effectually.

An excellent divine of this city, a friend of ours, said to us one day, "We have not yet learned the responsibility of society to indi-

forcibly, or which better show the skill, the power of the writer than the trial scene, which I find selected to my hands from the *Free Enquirer*.

Clifford is accused of highway robbery, and the crime is satisfactorily proved against him. He is called upon for his defense.

The face and aspect, even the attitude, of the prisoner, were well fitted to heighten the effect which would naturally have been created by any man under the same fearful doom. He stood at the very front of the bar, and his tall and noble figure was drawn up to its full height; a glow of excitement spread itself gradually over the features at all times striking, and lighted an eye naturally eloquent, and to which various emotions, at that time, gave a more than commonly deep and impressive expression." Then follows a selection from the trial scene.]

viduals. We talk much of the responsibility of individuals to society, but we forget that society is bound to protect all her children. I was sometime since dining with a distinguished Judge of the King's Bench, in London. The conversation turned, as you may well imagine, on the condition of the poor. I said to the Judge,

"Sir, did you observe those poor children, ragged and incrusted with filth, which you passed today in driving from your house to Westminster Hall?"

"No, I observed none."

"Yet you must have passed some hundreds."

"It is very likely; but it did not occur to me to observe them."

"And what must be the fate of these poor children?"

"Some of them will die of disease, some may emigrate, and some I shall probably hang."

"What means can they have of obtaining an honest and honorable living?"

"I am sure I do not know."

"Is there any alternative for them but to beg, to steal, or to starve?"

"I presume not."

"And have you considered their condition, ascertained their wants, and done what you could to avert the evils to which they are exposed?"

"Not at all. I have been otherwise engaged."

"Let me tell you, then, sir, that I would rather take my stand, at the Day of Judgment, with those you will *hang*, than with yourself."

"Sir, do you intend to insult me?"

"By no means. I would simply assure you that I regard those you will doom to be hung, as less guilty than yourself. God has given you talents, education, wealth, and a commanding position in society, and yet you can pass daily, unnoticed, hundreds of young beings, who, as they grow up, must necessarily beg, steal, or starve. You do not see them; you do not think of their wretched condition; you do nothing to save them from that crime on which you may hereafter sit in judgment; and am I to regard them as guilty and you as innocent, you who might, had you put forth your hand, have saved them from falling victims to a corrupt and corrupting social organization?"

The zeal of our friend, the divine, perhaps transported him too far; but he read the judge a sound lecture, and one which we would repeat in thunder tones, if we could, to the very soul of every man placed in a position from which he can act on society. Still, we would spare the judge, by including him as well as those he hangs, among the victims of society in its present defective organization. The rich man, the man of talents and education, occupying an honorable and important post in society, who can forget the poor and exposed, fail to observe the thousands growing up for the prison or the gallows, and refuse to labor day and night to save them from the doom which must await them, is, of all the victims of society, the one most sincerely to be pitied, and whose hard lot is the one least of all to be envied.

We shall have occasion to resume this subject before we close; we merely add now that Paul Clifford can recommend the robber's life to no one not already inclined to lead it; and it seems to us more likely to arrest a tendency to become highwaymen than any homily which could be read from the pulpit. It is worthy of note, that if you will but admit to those who are at war with society, that they have some little justice on their side, they are disarmed of their hostile feelings, and ready to lead peaceful and honest lives. This much Paul Clifford does for men who, like him, have been debarred from honest and honorable pursuits. The work, however, is designed not for robbers, at least not for bold highwaymen, but for the people at large. It was written to urge forward a social reform, which the author believed to be necessary, and it teaches a similar moral to that of "Caleb Williams,"[17] only in a more agreeable manner, and with a more happy effect on the nerves and temper of the reader.

In Ernest Maltravers, which has also been censured, the author has taken a higher and broader aim than in any of his previous works. His design has been to give us a general picture of the philosophy of life, and he has brought to the execution of his task a maturity of intellect, an amount of information, a familiar acquaintance with the more secret operations of the human soul, and a depth and truth of pathos, that even his warmest admirers were hardly prepared to expect. It is decidedly the ablest, the most original, the sincerest, and the most finished of his productions, and the one which will perhaps contribute the most to his ultimate fame. Ernest Maltravers is a young man of lofty genius, brilliant acquirements, noble enthusiasm, generous, and even virtuous feelings and aims. The world is bright before him; well-born and rich, what shall hinder him from running a noble career, and achieving an honorable and a lasting fame? He is ambitious, but ambitious mainly of being worthy of himself, of pre-

[17] [Ed. Brownson is referring to William Godwin's (1756-1836) *The Adventures of Caleb Williams* (1794), which called for a number of social reforms. In his youth Brownson had been influenced by Godwin's *Enquiry Concerning Political Justice* (Second Edition, 1798), as he indicated in his autobiography. See *Works*, 5:50-56.]

serving his heart and his character unsullied. But Ernest Maltravers is a man, and, like all men, subject to the infirmities of the flesh. He is not, therefore, to go through life without his trials, his conflicts, his defeats. He shall fall; what is noblest in his nature and most enviable in his condition, shall betray him, and his vices, as it were, shall grow out of his virtues; shame, grief, remorse, shall sink him deeper yet. Disappointment shall discourage him; the lessons of the worldly, acquaintance with the hypocrisies of the world, shall sicken him of life, incrust his heart, make him withdraw himself from mankind, and despair of himself and of society. But he shall not fall utterly. The same causes, his very errors and vices, aided by his own reflections and intercourse with those who have forgiven the world, shall, in the end, work out his reformation, rekindle in his heart the flame of his early love, restore to him his native vigor and hopefulness, and prepare him to be a wiser and better man for his fall. Such is the author's conception, under its moral aspect, and we do not hesitate to pronounce it a conception formed in the very spirit of the Christian religion, as well as in a high school of art, and indicating no ordinary insight into the motives of human conduct, and the influence of the passions, of both good and evil, virtue and vice, sin and shame, joy and grief, in the formation of character.

Superficial moralists may allege that the moral of the character would have been more perfect, had Ernest Maltravers been carried through the world without ever succumbing to temptation, or falling into a single error; but we cannot think so. It would have been the easiest thing in the world for the author to have so represented him; but he would then have been an unnatural character, and adapted to no purpose whatever. It is his failures that redeem him. We are not among those who think meanly of human nature, of man's capacity for an enlarged and generous virtue; but we confess that we have found nothing in experience of actual life, or in our philosophizing on the powers of the human soul, to warrant us in believing, that any man can ever so live and so act as never to need repentance and pardon. Gladly would we believe otherwise if we could; for, of all humiliation, that, which comes from a consciousness of our own guilt, is the most intolerable. But innocence, joined with great abilities, the most judicious education, and the most virtuous intentions, is no shield against temptation, and cannot preserve a man scathless through the fiery furnace he is doomed to pass. No man has any right to presume, that, in his own strength, he can go through the world without sinning. Even his confidence in himself, his consciousness of his own innocence, and his determination to maintain his character free from vice or crime, shall, in the absence of all other causes, effect his downfall. We know not why it should be so; but it is not in man that walketh, to direct his steps, and such is the constitution of this world, that the proudest must some day find occasion to exclaim with the publican, "God be merciful to me a sinner" [Luke 18:13]!

Some persons think that it would be possible so to bring up our children that they should never lose the innocence of childhood.[18] We do not believe it. The garden of childhood is lovely, and in it grow the trees pleasant to the sight; the tree of life grows there; but, also, in the midst, grows the tree of the knowledge of good and evil; and, alas! we pluck its fruit ere it occurs to us to eat of the tree of life, and our fall and expulsion become inevitable. We know this doctrine is a sad one, that it is painful to think, that, do what we will to keep the garden and dress it, we shall be driven forth to wander, guilty, heart-broken vagabonds, over the wide waste of life alone, till God's Son, on his errand of mercy to seek and save the lost, calls us back as penitents, pardons us, and ushers us into that celestial paradise of which the earthly was but a type!

Wisdom and virtue spring from the divine depths of sorrow, and sorrow comes from sin. They grow only as watered by the tears which flow not till a consciousness of wrongdoing has opened their sluices. Poor man, in the pride of his innocency, would that his father should give him his portion of his goods, and permit him to go forth and seek his fortune for himself. Vain fool! He will spend his substance with harlots and in riotous living, and see himself reduced to the necessity of begging of the swine a share of the husks they eat. No man can, before trial, obtain the strength necessary to triumph. It is only in the trial, in the struggle with the world, the flesh, and the devil, that his spiritual strength is developed; and not till he is scarred all over with a thousand defeats, does he become able to conquer. So it has been, and so we fear it always will be. We reach heaven by passing through the devil's territory. If there be another road, we have not discovered it.

Still, education is not in vain. The poor wretch, eating or begging to eat husks with the swine, *remembers* that there was bread enough in his father's house; and this remembrance acts as one of the principal causes in effecting his return. So shall the memory of childhood's innocency, and the wise lessons then taught us, awaken in us, in our humiliation, a desire to return, to recover from our degradation, and shall suggest to us the means. The seeds which are

[18] [Ed. Reference here is to Amos Bronson Alcott.]

sown will indeed lie long embedded in the human heart; but when the storms of passion shall have passed over it, when the tears of deep sorrow shall have watered it, by the genial warmth of heaven they shall spring up and bear the rich and delicious fruits of wisdom and virtue. We may, then, give our children the best education we can, but the unskillful navigator will capsize the boat or run it aground, till experience has taught him how to manage it. The instructions we give may abridge, may render efficient, but they will not supersede, the severe lessons which are learned only in the bitter school of experience.

But, to leave this train of thought, we are inclined to approve these works of Bulwer for the very reasons for which they are usually condemned. It is a remarkable feature of the popular writers of our times, that they portray almost entirely the characters of individuals generally regarded as reprobates, and that they portray them with many amiable qualities, represent them as performing many noble and disinterested acts, and rarely fail to enlist our sympathies in their behalf. This is thought to be an evidence of the corruptions of the age, of the low standard of morals adopted, and many good men and women mourn over it as an indication of a general dissolution of society, and of the impending fate of Sodom and Gomorrah; but we look upon it as a proof of the increasing morality of the age, of the secret, but sure working of Christianity, and of the more extended and salutary manifestation of its divine spirit. It is to us one of the encouraging signs of the times. The literary productions, in which villains appear and demand our respect, engage our sympathy, and, to some extent, even our admiration, do not, in our judgment, teach a false or a dangerous morality.

If Christianity be distinguished from all other religions by any one feature, it is certainly by the estimate it forms of the guilty, and the manner in which it commands us to treat them. It commands us to love and respect even the sinner. This is its crowning glory. Its followers may not as yet have comprehended the full import of this command, nor observed it either in their feelings or their actions; but the binding nature of God's commands is not impaired by men's ignorance and disobedience. Respect for the sinful, we grant, has not been a prominent feature of even professed Christians; but it is not the less a Christian duty on that account. God loves them, and commends his love to them; for Saint Paul assures us that God commended his love towards us, in that while we were yet sinners, Christ died for us.[19] The whole mission of Jesus was a mission of love to the

[19] [Ed. Rom 5:8.]

ungodly; and that none might be left to reject this mission, or to condemn the wicked, God hath included us *all* under sin, that he might have mercy upon all. Jesus always preferred the publicans and sinners to the Scribes and Pharisees, and assured the religious and conventionally moral of his age that publicans and harlots should go into the kingdom of heaven sooner than they.[20]

Christianity also teaches us never to despair of a fellow being. According to it, there is hope for the very chief of sinners. Jesus has bowels for the most depraved, the most hardened, and permits, nay, invites, the "vilest sinner to return."[21] Is there no significance in all this? Was there no meaning in his permission of "a woman that was a sinner,"[22] to wash his feet, and anoint them with oil? Meant he nothing, when he bade the adulteress "go and sin no more" [John 8:11], and rebuked her accusers, by bidding him who was without sin to cast the first stone? Meant he nothing, when he told the thief crucified with him on the cross, "this day shalt thou be with me in paradise" [Luke 23:43]? To us there is meaning in all this. It teaches us exceeding tenderness to the sinner, that no moral pollution can wholly obliterate the original brightness of the soul, or authorize us to believe that nothing good remains. We should abhor the sin, but never the sinner.

Mankind have not generally adopted this principle. They have generally thought it necessary to be exceedingly angry at the wicked, that is, at those they have regarded as the wicked; to manifest a sort of righteous horror at their presence; to treat them with contempt and ignominy; to pursue them with chains, imprisonment, and death. They have borrowed the armor of hell to fight the battles of heaven with. But, in point of fact, nothing is more unjust, or more impolitic even, than this. The sinner is a man, and his reformation is that which should be aimed at. There is joy in heaven with the angels of God over the sinner that repenteth. All good spirits rejoice with joy unspeakable when the sin-sick soul is restored to health.

Now, if we would reform the sinner, we must begin by recognizing in him something worth reforming. We must feel that he is still a man and a brother; that, though he may have erred and fallen, he is still a glorious nature, and is worth redeeming. He will never be reformed by angry denunciation, by being condemned, and declared to retain nothing good or commendable. He is never reformed by

[20] [Ed. Matt 21:31.]

[21] [Ed. Isaac Watts, Hymn 88: "vilest sinner may return."]

[22] [Ed. A reference to Luke 7:37-38.]

having his sins spread out before him. We do him no good by exhibiting before him his deep and loathsome depravity, and assuring him how hateful he is to all good men and angels. The exhibition will only aggravate his horror of himself, and drive him to desperation. Just in proportion as we cause him to lose his self-respect, and to despair of our respect for him, do we endanger or retard his return to virtue. But this is a lesson we shall never learn to practice so long as we retain our old notions concerning those we pronounce the guilty. Now, this lesson modern literature is teaching us, unconsciously on the part of its authors, it may be, and not perhaps in the clearest and most direct manner, we admit; but still in the only manner in which it can be taught, things being as they are; this lesson, we say, modern literature is teaching us by the exhibition it makes of the reprobate, the good it shows in them, and the sympathy it enlists in their behalf. Its tendency, then, so far from being irreligious and immoral, as many good people fear, is highly moral, and encouraging to the Christian philanthropist.

No man loves sin for its own sake; no man does wrong for the love of wrong-doing. Every man, in the exercise of his better nature, loves virtue, and yields it a heartfelt homage. That he does not practice it, is owing not entirely to his corrupt volitions, but to his ignorance, to the wrong bias which was early given to his propensities, to the customs of society, to the influence of his condition, to factitious social arrangements, to various circumstances, which overpower his weakness, hinder his good resolutions from ripening into deeds, prevent him from doing the good that he would do, and compel him to do the evil that he would not.[23]

In the worst of mankind, there are exhaustless stores of goodness, generous sympathy, disinterestedness, craving after moral excellence; in the most abandoned, there is ever raging a fierce conflict between good and evil, a terrible struggle between the flesh and the spirit, between conscience and inclination, the sense of duty and the love of pleasure; and even in them the good triumphs oftener than the bad, the spirit reins more habitually than the flesh. Now, when we see a fellow being torn by these contending principles, worn out and disheartened by a sense of the frequent defeats of the better nature, it is our duty to fly to his relief, and to aid him to subdue the enemies he has to contend against. But we do never relieve him, we never encourage and strengthen him, by fierce looks and angry gestures, by denunciation and wrath. He stands not so much in need of

[23] [Ed. Rom 7:14f.]

reproof, as of hope and moral strength, of remorse, not so much as of solace and refreshment. He is pained and mortified by a sense of his own failures, loathes himself, and would fain fly from his own company. Nothing in this case will do him good but that which tends to calm his irritated spirit, to reconcile him to himself, to make him feel that he is not clean gone in iniquity, that it is not all over with him yet, that another effort, and he may succeed, rise from his fallen estate, and gain a standing among the virtuous and the good.

The world comprehends little of all this struggle. It has anger and reproach for the wrong-doer; it turns away with loathing from the fallen; and leaves the wretched to die. It reaches not forth the hand to raise the fallen brother; says not, rise, and be of good cheer. Ah! it is a hard and difficult lesson to learn that of kindness to the sinner, respect for the outcast, and few have ever learned it. None ever learned it perfectly save Jesus of Nazareth, for none but he ever knew the full worth of even a guilty soul; the severe struggles to which the sinner is exposed, the temptations he has to withstand, the thousand obstacles he has to overcome. And none, but he, ever showed proper respect for sinners; and he did show it, when, in the death agony, he exclaimed, "Father, forgive them, for they know not what they do" [Luke 23:34]!

Modern literature may not directly tend to enforce this lesson; but it springs from the secret though sure working of the great Christian principle which involves it. It proves that the age is taking broader and more generous views of man and men, and is exploding the old doctrine of condign punishment, and the old dream that one sin corrupts the whole man, and renders him henceforth incapable of a holy feeling, a reasonable thought, or a virtuous action.

Mr. Bulwer has finely illustrated this last in his Eugene Aram,[24] a work which teaches, to us, a most salutary moral truth, but one which we have seen no notice taken of. Eugene is a scholar, full of generous dreams, of kind feelings, and laudable ambition; but he coolly, deliberately, without any provocation, commits a murder, and that too for a paltry sum of money. One can frame something of an excuse for him who, in hot blood, murders a man who has deeply injured him, who is his bitter enemy; but what excuse can we frame for him who murders a man, who has not injured him, with whom he has no cause of quarrel, and merely for the sake of money? According to all our ordinary modes of judging, he must be a cold-hearted reprobate, and from whom it would be madness to hope for anything good. But

[24] [Ed. *Eugene Aram* (1832).]

Eugene not only commits a murder of this sort; he not only possesses himself of the fruits of robbery and murder, but he never repents of the deed, never feels any remorse for the act. What a hardened wretch! Yet Eugene was one of the kindest-hearted of men. His life was, even after the murder, singularly moral, and his heart was alive to everything beautiful and good. He loved all nature, and indulged no hatred to the human race. He did not become cold, morose, misanthropic, and imagine that, because he had wronged mankind, mankind were grossly depraved. He would injure no human being, no living thing; he would turn aside his foot that he might not crush the worm. What is the moral of all this, but that one misdeed, of however black a character, does by no means argue a depraved soul, or indicate that the heart is a soil in which no virtues can grow? This, to us, is the moral of Eugene Aram, whether we take him in his true character, or as represented by Bulwer in his novel; and it is the moral which every man may extract from his own experience of himself, and of life in general.

Taking this fact into view, there is little danger of dressing up those whom society generally pronounces the wicked in too fascinating colors. Society cannot be made to believe them better than they really are, or be led to pay them more respect than they deserve. Who would be induced to murder, by being taught to contemplate Eugene Aram as a worthy man, a man of extraordinary talents, of vast erudition, and commanding genius, as filled with the love of virtue, overflowing with kindness, notwithstanding the fact of his having been a murderer? Who would turn pirate, because Cleveland, in Scott's novel, is shown, notwithstanding his piratical character, able to engage and retain the devoted love of the high-minded and virtuous Minna? If we know anything of the human heart, the study of these characters must have an entirely opposite effect. The striking contrast between the real worth of the man, and the meanness or wickedness of the act or pursuit, brings home to us in the most forcible manner possible the hatefulness of sin. We do not hate sin when we see it in such a character as Lumley Ferrers, because it seems to us to be in perfect harmony with his soul, a matter of course. We detest the man, not his acts, viewed separately from himself. But sin in an Ernest Maltravers becomes to us exceedingly hateful; it affects us in the most painful manner; it is a spot on what were else unsullied beauty; it mars what were else exact proportion; and hides that sweet loveliness we would adore. It is only when the great, the beautiful, the gifted, the good sin, that we do really see the exceeding sinfulness of sin; for it is only then that it appears so much out of place that we can, as it were, abstract it from the sinner, and contemplate it in itself, and see it in its own hideousness. We have, then, no fears of the world's being corrupted by the exhibition of the sinner in a light too favorable, in a dress too fascinating.

What we have thus far said, however, needs one qualification. It is strictly true in respect to those generally regarded as sinners, but not true in respect to that class of sinners, and a numerous class it is, too, which society is not sufficiently advanced to regard as sinners. The fact is, those, whom we usually brand as reprobates, are not so much worse than we, who assume to be the virtuous part of the community, as we commonly imagine. We keep within conventional rules, we do not outrage the public conscience; but in the sight of God we may be more guilty than those whom we subject to our penal justice. Our deeds are tolerated; our characters, therefore, may be decked out in robes which shall deceive the young and unsuspecting. Suppose a moralist in the times of our Savior had chosen his hero from among the Scribes and Pharisees, made him the impersonation of the class from which he was taken, and sought to make him pass for the *beau ideal* of the moral, religious, and social virtues, his influence would have been grossly immoral, because he would have given a false morality, and yet have found that in the manners and customs of his age, in the public conscience, which would have sustained him, and given efficiency to his representations. Conservatives may represent vice in dangerous colors, because what they represent is not by the more respectable portion of society regarded as vice, but as virtue. The radical, or he who is at odds with society as it is, can rarely do this. He cannot be a corrupter of public morals by his too favorable representations of vice, for he has society with its main force armed against him, and ready to expose the least deviation, on his part, from the strictest morality. A Scott may dress vice in too favorable colors, and do harm, not a Godwin; because the vice Scott will embellish is the vice the popular voice has not yet condemned; but should a Godwin embellish a vice, it would be an unpopular one, and therefore one without any general influence. Scott, in fact, does corrupt public morals; he does it by the too amiable light in which he depicts the old cavaliers, and the odium he casts upon the Puritans, the Covenanters, the old Whigs, and the advocates of liberty and social progress in general. In all countries, and in all ages, history proves that the tendency to order is much stronger and more universal than the tendency to liberty, and that mankind are much more disposed to submit to the evils they are acquainted with, than, by attempting to remove them, to run the risk of others they know not of. They, then, who seek to spread a halo around the past, to make men quiet under the existing order of things, ready and staunch to uphold the monstrous injustice which is daily practiced, and strong and bold only in suppressing all efforts to obtain a redress of grievances, are the immoral writers, the really dangerous writers, because they commend only what it is popular to commend, and are sure to be sustained by those who profit most by the wrongs which should be righted. They are false prophets, prophesying peace, peace, when there is no peace, and should be no peace; for all peace, so long as injustice obtains, is both impracticable and criminal.

But, in order to justify the general tenor of our remarks, it must be admitted, that individuals are not alone responsible for the acts for which they are condemned. We hold that society herself is responsible for not a little of the wrong she condemns and punishes. Man is passive as well as active; and he is acted upon by society, and corrupted by it, as well as it is acted upon and corrupted by him; and he is undoubtedly much oftener the victim than the criminal. This is the moral we extract from Paul Clifford; and it is one that society must learn and observe, before she will have any right to pursue with much severity those whom she is pleased to denominate offenders.

This great truth that individuals are not alone responsible for their acts that society shares the responsibility with them has not received that place in our moral and criminal codes which its importance demands. Robert Owen[25] caught a glimpse of it, but only on one side. He recognized man's passivity, but failed to perceive his activity. He saw that an artificial and improperly organized society was not merely the effect of individual depravity, but also a cause; that circumstances had much influence in the formation of our characters, and therefore he inferred that our characters are formed altogether by circumstances, without any cooperation of our own. We are, therefore, wholly creatures of circumstances, and in order to make us what we ought to be, nothing is necessary but to surround us with the proper circumstances. Hence, his new scheme of society, and his attempt to induce us to live in parallelograms. His dream was a beautiful one and has not been altogether fruitless; but its realization was impracticable because it made no allowance for individual activity;

[25] [Ed. In his youth, Brownson had been influenced by the Welsh social and educational reformer, Robert Owen (1771-1858), had read his famous *New View of Society* (1813), and called him an environmentalist because of Owen's emphasis upon the social environment as a primary force in shaping character and moral decisions. On Brownson's early association with Owen, see EW 1:23.]

because it recognized only a part of human nature; and, more especially, because it needed for its introduction, the virtue which, according to its own principles, could be obtained only by its successful operation.

The Saint-Simonians[26] in France also obtained a glimpse of the great truth we are speaking of, and proposed a reconstruction of society on a basis altogether new. Of all world-reformers, world-makers, these Saint-Simonians are, in our judgment, entitled to the highest rank. They were profound students of man and society, and, so far as we can see, they overlooked no element of human nature. They recognized the community element, for which Mr. Owen contended, and also the individual element, which is recognized by existing society, and made one the limit of the other. They acknowledged, too, the religious nature of man, which Mr. Owen denied, and gave to religion the highest rank. Their object was to devise a social scheme, which, avoiding the false principles of present society, should allow man ample scope for the full development of all his faculties, his whole nature, in the order intended by the Creator. But, though they formed the body of Adam, and molded his features according to the most approved lines of beauty, they could not breathe into his nostrils the breath of life. There was wanting the elemental fire, which could be struck out only after the body had become a living soul. So, their scheme, like many others, fell to pieces; but the ideas concerning man and society, which they put forth, are not dead, and will not die; but, modified by time and experience, they will exert a mighty influence on the future of our race.

Society, as it is at present organized, causes no small share of the depravity we lament and punish in individuals; but all schemes for destroying it, and constructing a new one in its place, will prove abortive, however wisely or prudently they may be devised: for this plain reason, that *the social state of any given epoch is never an arbitrary creation*. It grows out of the elements of human nature, and is permanently modified only as those elements themselves are modified. A new social state, constructed according to the true theory of man in the abstract, would soon fail, even could it be introduced, because it would find no support in the actual intelligence, habits, customs, associations, and affections of the people. We have always listened with great respect to all who have been disposed to tell us their plans for regenerating society, and often with gratitude; but we

[26] [Ed. On Brownson's association with the Saint-Simonians, see EW 1:33; 2:10-11, 18, 320, 434.]

have never had any faith in the practicability of any scheme, which did not assume society as it is, as its point of departure. God forbid that we should cling with any superstitious fondness to the old social garment. We see as clearly, perhaps, as most men, its numerous rents, and, above all, its awkward and inconvenient fashion. We would modify existing society, and as radically as any one; but we must take it as it is to begin with, and find in its actual constitution the law of our proceeding; reform, not destroy; develop, instead of creating. And this we would do, gradually indeed, but still as rapidly as possible, till we brought the social state into complete harmony, not merely with the human nature which we see developed today, but with that human nature which lies deep within the possible, and whose majesty and loveliness none but a few enthusiasts, a few prophets and seers, have as yet dreamed of.

But, while we confess to our own want of faith in any scheme of social reform which proposes to remodel society altogether, or which proposes any modifications of existing society faster than may be warranted by a more full development of human nature, we hold it of great importance that the defects of the existing social organization should be pointed out, and its influence in the formation of individual character strenuously insisted upon. All books which draw our attention to this subject, whatever the special doctrines they teach, have a value. For the more we look at it, the less angry shall we be at offenders, and the more forcibly shall we be struck with the fact that they are to a great extent but the victims of an order of things of which we, who regard ourselves as the virtuous, are the strenuous supporters, and which, if we would, we could easily so modify as greatly to diminish the number of victims. We like Paul Clifford because it exposes, in a masterly manner, the hypocrisies of society, and draws our attention to corrupting social influences, teaches us to forgive even the robber, to see the man beneath the highwayman's disguise, and to look upon him as receiving greater wrong than he commits. In a word, it reminds us that, if we would be true moralists, we must seek to reform society not less than individuals.

We have thus far spoken of Mr. Bulwer's novels in their moral character and tendency. We should be glad to say something more of their purely literary merits but for this we have left ourselves no space.

In conceiving and drawing characters, Bulwer holds a high rank, though not the highest. In what concerns the external man, he does not compare with Scott; but in what concerns the internal man, in detecting and describing the secret springs of action, the subtler workings of the human heart, the struggles of passion, the conflicts of the spirit and the flesh, he immeasurably surpasses him. His characters are in general faithful to nature, but they appear to be made up by laborious effort, and not spontaneous creations, as is the case with the productions of true genius. We regard Mr. Bulwer, therefore, more as a man of talent than of genius.

Bulwer's mind is rather philosophical than poetical. He has made several attempts at poetry, and though he has not wholly failed, we cannot regard him as a genuine poet. As a philosopher, if reference be had to the higher philosophy, to metaphysics, properly so called, he has no great merit. He has perceived many of the great problems of human nature, and he shows himself somewhat accustomed to psychological analysis, but he does not appear to have attained to any clear and systematic views. There is still much doubt, much confusion in his own mind, and not a little in his writings. He evidently rejects gross materialism, but whether he has been able to attain to a legitimate spiritualism, does not appear. He seems to have embraced phrenology, which is somewhat better than sensualism, we admit; but, as we have heretofore attempted to prove, by no means a complete philosophy of man.[27]

As a moralist, we have defended him so far as the actual tendency of his works is concerned. His system of morality we have not ascertained. He is not a Hobbist,[28] nor an advocate for the selfish scheme. His aim in his works has not been to construct an ethical system, but to induce his countrymen to labor more earnestly for the public good. He does not make the public good, we presume, the criterion of virtue in general, but merely the end which governments, politicians, the statesman, should always seek; by which every law, every measure, every act of a public or private man, which bears upon the public, should be tested. He concerns himself mainly with that branch of morals, which treats of the duties of individuals to society, and of society to individuals. In this branch of morals, we apprehend, he is right in making the public good the rule.

His object, in all his works, is the improvement of masses of men rather than the creation of individual excellence. This may not at all times indicate the highest moral purpose, but in the actual state of things, when the moralists of the church confine themselves almost

[27] [Ed. See Brownson's "Pretensions of Phrenology," *Boston Quarterly Review* 2 (April, 1839): 205-29. See also chapter 14 in this volume.]

[28] [Ed. On Thomas Hobbes (1588-1679), British philosopher, see EW 2:291. Brownson will describe Hobbism in chapter 20 in this volume as the rule of morality that holds that one should avoid pain and seek pleasure. See page 440.

exclusively to the promotion of private and domestic virtue, regarding men almost solely in their individual and domestic relations, it can hardly imply any want of high moral feeling, to represent private and domestic virtue as worthless, if it leave the millions to suffer all the evils of ignorance, vice, poverty, and tyranny. He not only does this, but he addresses himself to the higher classes of his countrymen, the rich, the well born, the educated, the talented, who are wasting themselves on trifles, suffering from satiety, and seeking in vain for successful methods of making time hang less heavy on their hands; and he labors to convince them that there is a PUBLIC for them to regard, a PEOPLE to whom they may speak, whose good they may consult, which they can promote, and that in seeking to promote the public good, the good of the people, they shall find their own good. This, we take it, is not a bad moral, and one which every wise man must wish to see enforced.

In conclusion, we have only to add, that, in our estimation, Mr. Bulwer's works are chiefly valuable for the bearing, they have on the great controversies of the day. They have been produced in the midst of a revolution, and to some of the various phases of that revolution, they all directly or indirectly relate. They have been written, we say, in the midst of a revolution. It is so. A revolution has been and is going on throughout all Christendom. In all Christendom, there is war between the aristocratic element and the democratic element of society. A word has been uttered; the people have heard it, and feel an unwonted fire burn within them. The untitled, the unprivileged many begin to feel that they were not made merely to be used by the titled and privileged few. "We too are men," say they; "and, by heaven, we will be treated as men." They and the few are at war. Every day does the war rage wider and more fiercely. Now, in this fearful but glorious war, we find Bulwer on the right side, fighting, with what skill and bravery are in him, for the PEOPLE. He is for the many and against the few. We greet him, therefore, as a fellow soldier in the army of humanity, and are ready to fight side by side with him in the cause of the democracy.

Other soldiers there may be in this same cause wiser and better than he, braver and more disinterested; but, as to that, we inquire not. Every man on the democratic side is our brother in arms, and as such is welcome. His friends we hold to be our friends, and his enemies to be our enemies. And should we not? Should not all who espouse the people's cause, all who dare speak out for man, ever catch a cheering response from the warm heart of young America, freedom's fairest daughter? Yes. On ye, who war for freedom in the old world;

ye, who would raise man from the thraldom of kings, nobilities, and hierarchies; ye, who dare to live or dare to die that ye may work out a greater good for the human race—on to the battle! The fresh young heart of America leaps to behold you; her sympathies and prayers are with you; and her free voice shall guard your fame, and swell the notes of your triumph!

17.

THE KINGDOM OF GOD[1]

Boston Quarterly Review 2 (July, 1839): 326-50

The phrase, kingdom of God, and its corresponding phrase, kingdom of heaven, may be taken in two senses: 1. As designating the place or state of the blest after death; and, 2. That new order of things, which Jesus was sent to introduce and establish on the earth, and which men have attempted to realize by means of the church.

With the kingdom of God in the first sense, we have no great concernment. We know, and, while in the body, can know, but little of the world to come. We may make a thousand conjectures, devise a thousand schemes in relation to it, but all we can affirm with any tolerable degree of certainty is, that we shall live again, and be happy or miserable as we are good or evil in that new state of being.

Christianity is degraded when its chief value is made to consist in teaching us how to die. God is not the God of the dead, but of the living. No man is or can be a true Christian, whose thoughts are always brooding over the tomb, and the destiny which awaits him beyond it. Sufficient to the day is the evil thereof. We should do our duty in this world, where our Creator has placed us, and leave our future life in the hands of God, where it belongs. Whoso prepares himself to live, need be under no apprehension, that he shall not be prepared to die.

Christianity teaches us how to die, I admit; but it is to die as Jesus did, as the apostles did, in the righteous cause, martyrs to truth, to justice, to love, to man, to God. It enables us to die in the blessed hope of a glorious uprising; but of the glorious uprising of the cause for which we have struggled, suffered, and now die, rather than of our individual selves. It is pleasant to die in the hope of a resurrection of the soul, and of its ascension to the Father; but, to a rightly constituted mind, it is pleasanter yet to die in the hope, that, though overborne now, crucified, buried in the new tomb hewn from the rock, and guarded with armed soldiery, the cause for which we have

[1] [Ed. The following was the full title of this essay: "The Kingdom of God—*not meat and drink, but righteousness, and peace, and joy in the Holy Ghost*" (Rom 14:17).]

lived, and which is dearer to us than life, is not lost forever; that the third day shall dawn, when it shall burst the cerements of the grave, uprise, clothed in shining garments, and, with a face as the lightning, triumphing over death and hell, and leading captivity itself captive. This is the death for which Christianity would prepare us, and this the glorious uprising, with the sweet hope of which, it would cheer and sustain us in poverty and humiliation, in exile, in the dungeon, on the scaffold, or on the cross.

The Apostle, then, when he said "the kingdom of God is not meat and drink, but righteousness and peace, and joy in the Holy Ghost" [Rom 14:17], did not, we may presume, understand by the phrase, kingdom of God, the place or state of the blest after death. He was not speaking of another world, of the condition of the soul hereafter, nor of the means of securing everlasting happiness. He must have used the phrase, then, to designate that new order, or the principles of that new order, of things, which Jesus was sent to establish on the earth.

This new order of things, called sometimes the gospel kingdom, the kingdom of heaven on earth, is termed the kingdom of God, because God is its founder, the authority which obtains in it, and for whose glory it is established. The ordering, arranging, controlling of everything in this kingdom, was to be in harmony with the divine will, and effected by the divine efficacy. It was, therefore, with strict propriety, denominated the kingdom of God.

This kingdom of God, this new order of things, was to be established on the earth. It was said of Jesus,

> He shall not fail, nor become weary,
> Until he have established laws in the earth,
> And distant nations shall wait for his instructions.[2]

The angels that announced his birth to the shepherds professed to bring "glad tidings" to the earth, and the heavenly host, in their sublime chorus, shouted "peace on earth and good will to men," as well as "glory to God in the highest." Though a divine, a heavenly kingdom, it was, then, to be built up in the world, and for men and women while in the flesh.

But this kingdom, though destined to be built up on the earth, was not of the earth, and must needs be diverse from all earthly kingdoms. Jesus said, "My kingdom is not of this world" [John 18:36]. "Render unto Caesar the things which are Caesar's, and unto God the things which are God's" [Matt 22:21]. But, if this order of things

[2] [Ed. This quotation appears to be a conflation of Isa 40:28 and Isa 42:4.]

be rightly regarded as a kingdom; if it is to be a kingdom on the earth, and yet diverse from all earthly kingdoms, what can it be, but a new association, a new society, distinct from the civil society or the state, organized in a peculiar manner, with peculiar laws, institutions, ordinances, duties of its own? A kingdom of God in a more refined and spiritual sense could not be clearly comprehended or appreciated by the mass of the people in the times of Jesus and his apostles. The kingdom of God on earth was, therefore, made to consist in a new organization of the human race, the formation of a new society, separate and distinct from the general society of mankind, and from the civil society or the state—the formation of a spiritual, a religious corporation, in one word, the outward, visible church.

This outward, visible society, the church, must have its ordinances and duties, obedience to which shall constitute the purity and worth of its members; and these must, from the nature of the case, be diverse from those enjoined by the state. For, should the church enjoin the same duties as the state, it would be only a reduplication of the state, or the state under another name. But the state embraces, as far as a corporation can do it, the whole of man's moral and social duties. Whatever the church enjoins, then, must be distinct from these. It has, therefore, uniformly taught, that a man, failing in the discharge of his duties churchward, will be eternally damned, though faithful in the discharge of every duty as a man and a citizen, or member of the body politic.

Salvation is possible only to the true Christian. The true Christian is a subject of God's kingdom. God's kingdom is the church. Therefore, salvation is impossible to those who remain without the pale of the church. He, who comes within the pale of the church but fails to demean himself as a worthy member is no better than those who remain without. None can be saved even by joining the church, if not obedient to its ordinances and faithful in the discharge of the duties it imposes. It follows, then, that salvation can be attained only by faithfully observing the ordinances and duties of the church. It follows, then, again, that by as much as salvation in the world to come is more desirable than mere earthly well being, by as much as heaven is preferable to hell, by so much are the ordinances of the church superior to the ordinances of the state; by so much is a faithful and conscientious observance of the rites and ceremonies of the church to be preferred to a faithful and conscientious discharge of our moral and social duties.

Now, what are these rites and ceremonies, these ordinances, duties, insisted on by the church, and the observance of which constitutes our perfection in the eyes of the religious society? Waiving what is peculiar to individual churches, or special communions, and taking only what is common to all sections of the religious society, we may answer, that he, who professes a certain creed; is baptized; comes at stated periods to the communion; refrains from all labor, and, in some countries, from all amusement or recreation, on one day in seven; says his prayers, with or without bead-roll or book; attends regularly certain gatherings together of his neighbors on the first day of the week or oftener; contributes liberally towards defraying the expenses of the religious society; and, if the father of a family, teaches his children the infinite importance of all this, and brings them up to the conscientious observance of all this, is a perfect man churchward, and, according to the true theory of the church, an heir of salvation, of an inheritance that fadeth not away, eternal and incorruptible in the heavens.

Here, stripped of the poetic and mystic garb in which it is usually presented, is all that the church, in its distinctive character, imposes or exacts. I say not that the church insists upon nothing more, but this is all that it insists upon in its character of a society separate and distinct from civil society; all that it superadds to our moral and social duties; all it enjoins, not so far forth as it is one with the state, but so far forth as it is diverse from the state. The worth of the church must consist, not in what it has or may have in common with other institutions, but in what it has peculiar to itself. What I have enumerated, constitutes, substantially, its peculiarity, the matters wherein it is different from the state, and which justify it in saying that it is not a kingdom of this world. These matters constitute its essence as a distinct corporation, and are all that render its separate existence necessary. Whatever else it may insist upon we could discharge, without assuming any relation which we did not bear as men and citizens before the church was instituted.

Now, I will not say that these matters have no value. Many people have a world of tender associations clustering around them, and could not abandon them without much self-denial; but I must say, that, to make the kingdom of God consist in them, is very much like making it consist in meat and drink; and I must be pardoned if I cannot see, in the founding of a kingdom, of which these are all that distinguish it, any extraordinary proofs of the wisdom and goodness of God; if, indeed, I feel that a kingdom, which has nothing else to recommend it, was not worth the trouble of founding, was not worthy of Jesus, and is not worthy of us.

I speak not against the ordinances of the church. I am aware of the respect which is due to the church, and that trifles, when it enjoins them, cease to be trifles, and become matters of deep significance. I am aware, also, that there are many people who have no way of subduing their fear of the devil but by a most punctilious observance of church rites and ceremonies, and I am willing that they should have rites and ceremonies, and as many as they please. I am not the man to ask them to neglect them, or to intimate that they ought to neglect them; but in reverencing so profoundly, as they do, meats and drinks, I do insist that they should reverence for themselves, and not for others; that they should not dare assert in the face and eyes of Jesus and his apostles, that these meats and drinks are the kingdom of God. In the kingdom of God circumcision availeth nothing, nor uncircumcision, but a pure heart. The true Christian, the true citizen of the commonwealth of Jesus, and subject of the kingdom of God, suffers no man to judge him in respect to meats and drinks, new moons, Sabbath days, or holidays. He values himself never on the possession of that righteousness, which comes from fidelity to the church. He knows that except his righteousness exceed that of the Scribes and Pharisees, he can in no wise enter into the kingdom of heaven, or come under the reign of God. For him the handwriting of ordinances has been declared insufficient, and blotted out. Freed from the beggarly elements of a ceremonial law, he will not entangle himself again in the yoke of bondage; having begun in the spirit, in truth, justice, love, he will not be so foolish as to believe that baptism and the Lord's supper can perfect him.[3]

The kingdom of God must be but an insignificant affair if it be not something altogether different from an outward, visible, religious society, called the church, or even the principles which serve as the basis of such a society, or of the duties it enjoins. A drug, bad in itself, may do good by expelling a disease which is worse; and so the church has done good, and perhaps was a useful, as it was an inevitable institution. But in the actual state of things, it is a chief obstacle to the extension and up building of God's kingdom on the earth. It could have been no part of the original design of Jesus to found it, and if he has tolerated it, it has been as Moses tolerated divorce, on account of the intractableness of men's hearts, not because it was intrinsically good, fitted to be a definitive institution for mankind.[4]

[3] [Ed. Brownson's views of the ordinances or sacraments will change over the next few years. The more his mind moves toward the objective, philosophically speaking, the more he begins to place value and efficacy upon the sacraments.]

[4] [Ed. Brownson places the same value on the church as he does on the sacraments, and the importance of the church changes as he begins to emphasize more clearly the value of the objective in his philosophy.]

There was nothing in the preaching nor in the life and manners of Jesus that indicated the necessity of forming for the realization of the kingdom of God, a peculiar society, distinct from the state and the general society of mankind. He never separated himself from his countrymen. He mingled with them as a brother and as a fellow citizen. No outward observance distinguished him. He affected no singularity or eccentricity. He ate, drank, dressed like the rest of his countrymen; attended their festivals, their merry-makings, their weddings, and their funerals. To all outward appearance, he was a simple, unostentatious Jew, distinguished solely by the purity, worth, and sublimity of his life and conversation. His divine sonship manifested itself only in the fact that he possessed truth and love without measure, and that these reigned in him with absolute authority. As were these divine principles in Jesus, so should be the kingdom of God in the world.

The kingdom of God is an invisible kingdom, the dominion of godly influences and divine principles. Whatever partakes of the power of God, must be invisible save in its effects. God himself is invisible. He is the unseen efficacy, the invisible life, of which we and nature are but the manifestation. *"Mundus universus nihil aliud est, quam Deus explicatus,"* says an old author.[5] The universe is nothing else but God expressed. We see around us visible nature, the sun, the moon, stars, land, water, trees, plants, flowers, animals; but these are only parts of the shadow of the unseen God. They are not ultimates, nor sufficient for themselves. They depend on something which they are not, and are subjected to a law which is over them. This something on which they depend, this law to which they are subjected, is that which men term nature, but, in reality, it is God. We look into what we call the moral world, and there again we see a variety of facts, but they are no more ultimates than the facts of external nature; no more sufficient for themselves, and have the same need of something which they are not, on which to depend, and are subjected to a law which is over them. This something, this law, is the spiritual face of the Deity, or God as expressed by the spiritual world.

Men are apt to regard these two manifestations of the Deity somewhat in the light of a manifestation of two different orders of life or being; but a sublime philosophy identifies them, and proves that it is one and the same life which flows through the natural world, and the moral. Spirit and matter are but the two faces of the self-living life,

[5] [Ed. Latin for "The entire universe is nothing other than God explicated." Unable to identify quotation.]

from whom all life proceeds, and who is called by us God, or the GOOD. Spiritualism and materialism, when we have risen to the true conception of the Christian faith, are swallowed up in the unity of absolute life. But people generally stop, and must stop, far below this sublime height. We are rarely able to trace all the streams back to their primitive source, and unify them in the exhaustless fountain of the divinity.

We therefore take each stream to be complete in itself; think and speak of it as manifested by a particular class of facts, without undertaking to trace it to its source. Thus we go into the external world to study its phenomena, and we name all the forces we find at work there, not according to their nature and origin, but according to the special facts they respectively present. Hence, we speak of gravitation, magnetism, electricity, contraction, expansion, as separate and independent powers or causes, although each class of facts, which we have observed, is produced by the direct agency of God, by the divine efficacy itself. The terms we use serve merely to designate the divine efficacy, viewed simply as the cause of these several classes of facts. These facts we see; the cause, the power, which reigns in them, we do not see; but that cause, however variously it may be named, is one, and is God.

We do the same in the moral world. We isolate the powers we find there, regard them as independencies, and name them according to their respective effects. Thus we speak of truth, justice, beauty, love, without reflecting that the efficacy we recognize in these is the divine efficacy, and that truth, justice, beauty, love, are only so many different terms for designating the Deity, contemplated solely as the principle of certain phenomena of the moral world. But here, as in outward nature, the dominion of God is silent, invisible, save in the facts which express it. It is not an outward, visible dominion. "The wind bloweth where it listeth, and thou hearest the sound thereof, but canst not tell whence it cometh, nor whither it goeth" [John 3:8]. So is the dominion of God.

Now since, owing to our imperfection, we are under a sort of necessity of viewing the Deity, if I may so speak, in parts, and these parts themselves, to a great extent, as wholes, we shall best understand the kingdom of God, by declaring it to be the dominion of those principles which we term godlike or divine. The dominion of moral principle is in the last analysis the dominion of God. The reign of moral principles, then, is the reign of God. These principles may be variously named, but I include them all under the terms, truth and love. The efficacy we name truth and love is the divine efficacy. The empire of truth and love, then, is the empire of God.

I touch here a point of some importance. People do not, generally speaking, admit that truth and love are God manifest, or God viewed under a spiritual aspect. They deny that truth and love, wherever found, are one with God. They thus deny, did they but know it, that God manifests himself in the flesh or in the world. And here is that denial of what is called the doctrine of the Trinity, which is regarded as the virtual denial of Christianity itself, and the most fatal heresy into which men can fall. The doctrine of the Trinity has been contended for more earnestly than any other doctrine the church has ever put forth. The church has never been able to treat those who deny the Trinity as Christians. The denial of this doctrine has been almost universally felt to be a rejection of Christianity. This feeling has been just, and is that which, more than anything else, redeems the church from utter reprobation. But, notwithstanding this, the church has never comprehended the deep significance of the symbol it has adopted and contended for. It has worshiped the symbol; and even while prostrating itself in devout adoration before it, it has anathematized the Idea, disowned the God it should have seen through it. Truth and love have been isolated from their sources, and, though admitted to be very respectable, they have been denied to be the Eternal God. Jesus is a worthy man, and deserving of sincere respect, but is not God; love is a good and sweet influence, and much to be desired, but not God. So have men felt, and so feel they still. Hence, they are unable to identify the kingdom of God with the kingdom of truth and love. Though these reign supreme, something more is thought to be requisite to constitute the veritable kingdom of God. Here is the grand error of the church.

John assures us that the Word, which was made flesh, was in the beginning with God, and was God.[6] And what was the Word, but truth, truth eternal, immutable, and universal. "I am," says Jesus, "the way, the TRUTH, and the life" [John 14:6]. "I and my Father are one" [John 10:30]; for, "I proceed forth and come from the Father"[7] What can more clearly establish the identity of truth with God, their absolute oneness? "He that dwelleth in love dwelleth in God, and God in him, for God is love" [1 John 4:16]. What more do we ask to convince us of the identity of love with God, of their absolute oneness? If truth and love be one with God, then should we honor

[6] [Ed. John 1:1, 14.]
[7] [Ed. Brownson is perhaps paraphrasing John 8:42.]

them even as we honor God, and honoring them is honoring God. "The time shall come," says Jesus, "when men will honor the Son even as they honor the Father" [John 16:4]; and truly, because the Son is one with the Father, is the Infinite God, as manifest, under a moral aspect, to human beings. If, again, truth and love be one with God, their dominion must be the dominion of God, and the kingdom of God resolves itself into the kingdom of truth and love, and must be built up just in proportion as truth and love come to exert their legitimate empire over men's minds and hearts.

We know God but as he reveals himself. No man knoweth the Father save the Son and he to whom the Son reveals him.[8] It is in the face of his Son, his manifestation, that we behold his glory. Admit that the glory we see in the face of the Son is the glory of God, then it follows that we can see and know the glory of God; so, also, admit that truth and love are God manifest, God revealed, we then can know God and comprehend the principles of his kingdom. Deny that truth and love are God, deny their absolute oneness with God, and we cease to have any clear conceptions of God. The word God becomes an empty name, and his kingdom a dream. This is wherefore it is necessary to insist on the identity of truth and love with God. We know something of these; consequently, when we are told that the kingdom of God consists in the reign of these, we comprehend what is meant. But if we are told, that Jesus Christ came to found the kingdom of God; that we must labor for the upbuilding of that kingdom; and are not told at the same time that this means laboring to build up the kingdom of truth and love, we can understand nothing of what is said to us, nor of what is the work we are called upon to perform; and, therefore, shall be as likely to labor against God as for him or with him. In Jesus Christ, God descends to men, manifests himself to their apprehension; in declaring the kingdom of God to be the empire of truth and love, we bring it down to men's intellectual capacities, enable them at all times to recognize it, and to labor understandingly for it.

At first sight, some persons, who shall take in but a part of my meaning, may imagine that the doctrine here set forth is very generally believed, and may wonder where I have lived, that I have judged it necessary to maintain so elaborately a point which no Christian will dispute; but, if I am not much mistaken, the members of the religious society are far from generally admitting that the kingdom of God is nothing more nor less than the reign of the great moral principles I have pointed out. Religious people do, by no means,

[8] [Ed. Luke 10:22.]

take so high and so rational a view of that order of things, which it was the purpose of the mission of Jesus to establish. They are now in very nearly the same situation they were in at the time of Jesus and his apostles. They preach the law of works, by the deeds of which can no flesh be justified. They do not measure the growth of God's kingdom by the progress of truth and love; nor do they estimate the Christian worth of a man by his pure love for all God's creatures, the earnestness with which he seeks for truth, the boldness and energy with which he utters it, and the fidelity with which he obeys it. Something more is demanded, infinitely more important than all this. Certain meats and drinks are insisted on as the indispensable condition of salvation. It is thought to be altogether more *religious,* to be faithful to the church, than it is to be faithful to our own honest convictions and the dictates of our own consciences. We may seek with the greatest pains for truth, and make it the business of our lives to discover and promulgate it; we may seek the welfare of our race with a pure and warm heart, with a love that never tires, which shrinks from no obstacles, is discouraged by no difficulties, and appalled by no dangers, and yet be doomed by religious people to the nethermost hell, if we chance to fail in our respect to the church, or if we show the least disgust at the miserable mummery it would make pass for the worship of God. So far, in point of fact, are religious people from admitting the great doctrine I am laboring to bring out, that I shall be much surprised if they do not term me an infidel, and regard me as an enemy to both God and man, for asserting it. Is there, then, no need of reiterating the doctrine of the Apostle, that "the kingdom of God is not meat and drink, but righteousness, and peace, and joy in the Holy Ghost"?

It is not my wont to look upon the dark side of things; and I generally seek, in men and institutions, the good rather than the evil, for I take no pleasure in convicting those of folly or error who are linked to me by a common nature, and whose lot is bound up with my own, and which—be it what it may—I am willing to share; but I confess I am weary of this heartless worship to God with which men seek to purchase his favor and the eternal bliss of heaven. I look around me for relief, for something which rational and immortal beings may with propriety offer to their Creator, and which he may deign to accept; but I look in vain. Where is the man, believing himself and by others admitted to be a Christian, who places the worship of God in a heart alive to the wants and well being of humanity, in sincere love of truth, firm adherence to lofty principle, and in untiring philanthropic efforts? Where is he? Among the clergy, studiously shunning to say aught that may startle the consciences of respectable sinners, and afraid of uttering the truth in earnest, in that tone of deep sincerity which would indicate that they believe it, and feel that it ought to be obeyed, lest, perchance, they be thought to violate good taste, and detract from the dignity and decorum of the pulpit? Among the men of profligate lives, base feelings, and groveling propensities, calling themselves Christians, and flattering themselves that all will be well with them, because, forsooth, they belong to the church, and "pay tithes of anise, cummin, and mint" [Matt 23:23]?

The world lieth in wickedness. Man, vulture-like, preys upon man. Great social wrongs obtain. The immense majority of the human race are slaves, "hewers of wood and drawers of water" [Josh 9:21] to the few; chained down in abject poverty, and, what is worse, in hopeless ignorance, doomed to vegetate and die, without one glimpse of the noble capacities with which God created them, and the kindling destiny for which he made them. Armed soldiery are everywhere ready to fly, wherever the people are beginning to feel the workings of a higher nature, in order to suppress every effort the struggling peasant, wronged for countless ages, may make in behalf of liberty and the imprescriptible rights of man. The friends of progress are jeered, neglected, or persecuted; the advocates of new views of truth, views in which is contained the future destiny of our race, men of pure hearts, free and energetic minds, are treated as the enemies of God and society; laws are enacted which tend to perpetuate factitious distinctions and hoary abuses; government, almost everywhere, is made an instrument of oppression, strengthening the strong and abandoning the weak. And what are they doing who claim to be the exclusive subjects of God's kingdom? Mourning, it may be, over a breach of the Sabbath; settling a disputed point in Hebrew geography; ascertaining how much falsehood it is necessary to uphold in order to keep the lower classes in submission; kindling fanatical excitements, which shall spread over the land and leave moral desolation in their train; robbing the poor sempstress or the poor housemaid to obtain the means of sending out tracts and missionaries to convert the heathen to creeds, which have long since ceased to find believers among the intelligent at home; going to the temples to thank God that they have been plucked as brands from the burning, and are now holier than others; saying their prayers; singing psalms; damning infidels and heretics; at best, "straining at a gnat and swallowing a camel" [Matt 23:24].

The world lieth in wickedness; and what is the church doing? Flattering the sinner with vain promises, and lulling his conscience asleep, or awakening it to that which is not sin; feeding us with manna, whereof a man may eat and die, not with the bread of life, which comes down from heaven, and whereof if a man eat he shall live forever; baptizing us with water, it may be, but not with the spirit, not with the Holy Ghost and with fire; for truth, giving us unintelligible creeds; for love to God and man, sectarian zeal and blind devotion to the church; for a true, a spiritual righteousness, a superstitious reverence for cant phrases, unmeaning rites and ceremonies, which deaden the heart, stultify the intellect, and enervate the hands. Is there, then, no need of insisting upon the great truth, that the kingdom of God is not meat and drink, but the reign of holy principles, the absolute dominion of truth and love? There is need; and well were it for the human race, would God raise us up another Luther to denounce dead works, and proclaim salvation by faith alone; another John Knox, to wield the battle-axe of the Lord, to attack the old rotten church, and let in daylight through the roofs of the old temples desecrated by a heartless and idolatrous worship; new and bold reformers, who will speak out to the slumbering conscience of Christendom, and, like the staunch old German monk, not fear to throw their inkstands in the devil's face, and send his satanic majesty back howling to hell.[9]

Truth does not reign, nay, its right to reign is denied. Grave divines, and most learned doctors, ask for a higher sovereign than truth, and will not allow truth to act even as vice-sovereign, till various signs and wonders have verified its commission. They ask for miracles to authorize them to call goodness goodness, and love love; and, such is the grossness of their minds, that they can see the verification which they needlessly ask for, only in the strong wind, the fire, the earthquake, or in some marvelous display of power over outward nature. They see no God in an act of heroism, of self-sacrifice, of disinter-

[9] [Ed. The reference here is to Martin Luther's so-called "Patmos" experience at Wartburg in 1521. In his *Table Talks* in *Luther's Works*, ed. and trans. by Theodore G. Tappert, general ed., Helmut T. Lehmann, 55 vols. (Philadelphia: Fortress Press, 1967), 54:280, Luther refers to his battles with the devil. The reference to Luther's throwing his inkwell at the devil is apparently part of a local German oral tradition. I am indebted to Professor Kenneth Hagen for this information. For one source of this tradition, see Heinrich Heine (1797-1856), *Religion and Philosophy in Germany: A Fragment*, trans. by John Snodgrass (1882; rpt. Albany, New York: State University of New York Press, 1986), 37, a text which Brownson had definitely read in its first French edition, *De l'Allemagne* (1833). Heine reported: "On the Wartburg, where he [Luther] translated the New Testament, he was so much disturbed by the devil that he threw the inkstand at his head. The devil has ever since that day had a great dread of ink, and a still greater dread of printing-ink."]

ested love; hear no God in the still small voice which speaks to the heart, subdues the soul, and brings tears to the eyes. They see no God in the love Jesus had for man, stronger than death; no divinity in his life of self-denial, of continued sacrifice for the redemption of man; no truth in the generous lessons he inculcated, in the sublime doctrine he taught of God, of man, the human soul and its destiny, and of which his life was a lucid commentary; and, like the wicked and adulterous Jews of old, they demand a sign, a wonder, a miracle, to prove that that doctrine is truth; that it is authoritative, legitimate, and that they may venture to receive it under their protection, and insist on its being obeyed. Is there a worse infidelity than this? A more fatal blindness than this, which prevents them from seeing that truth is truth the world over, that truth everywhere is the word of God, which was in the beginning with God, which was God, and is God, and therefore possessing a native and inherent right to absolute dominion?

Even these same grave divines and most learned doctors deny not only the authority of truth, but they deny the Holy Ghost. They seem not to have heard even so much as that there is a Holy Ghost. Jesus promised to send us the comforter, who should be ever with us, console us by his presence, and lead us into all truth.[10] But they disown the comforter; and when we tell them Jesus has been as good as his word, that the comforter has come, that he abides with us, bringing to our remembrance the words of Jesus, and unfolding to our hearts and understandings their deep significance, they stare at us in utter surprise and amazement; and no sooner do they recover themselves a little than they denounce us as the setters forth of strange gods, than they look upon us as mad and in need of physic and good regimen, or as desperately wicked and in need of stripes, bonds, and imprisonment. We are told flatly that what we allege cannot be true; that the Holy Ghost we speak of is mere carnal reason, which to follow is death, spiritual and eternal, and that Jesus never promised to send us the comforter, who should lead us into all truth; that he merely promised him to some dozen men or more who lived a long while since, and that we have nothing to do but to learn what he led those dozen men or more to record for our instruction; to yield that the assent of our understandings and the homage of our obedience. Well was it said, "Grieve not the Holy Spirit, lest he depart from you" [Eph 4:30].

[10] [Ed. John 16:12-14.]

The scribe, well instructed, is grateful for all past records of the revelations of God to man, and he studies them with the docility of the child, and the reasoning powers of the man. He is everyday more and more penetrated with a sense of their inestimable value, and of the necessity of becoming familiar with the deep meaning they contain. But he has learned that God's revelations, however made, have a like character; that they are all the revelations of the same God, and contain far more than meets the eye of the careless observer. Nature has her secrets, which no eye has ever yet detected, and the "written word" conceals truths, which no human intelligence has grasped, of which no one has, as yet, the faintest conception. The universe round, about, above, and within us, is written all over with hieroglyphs, full of deep significance. By-gone ages have spelt out and interpreted a few, as best they could; but are there no more to be spelt out and interpreted? Is there nothing but empty space beyond that narrow horizon which bounds our vision, or has the human mind attained its ultimate limits?

In this same universe of which we have learned so little, and of which, with all the knowledge we have inherited from our fathers, we know so little, there lie embedded, like seeds in the earth, truths of which the past had no foresight, no forefeeling, and in which are folded up the future destinies of our race; but where is the seer who may behold them, or who, if beholding them, may, even in this age of boasted light and liberality, when it is pretended the kingdom of God is established on the earth, point them out to the ardent seeker, urge the necessity of attempting their cultivation, or rejoice in their development and growth, without being denounced—as was Jesus—as a blasphemer, as an enemy to truth and righteousness, by the very persons who are loudest in praise of Jesus, in magnifying his name, and making honorable mention of his life, deeds, sufferings, and death for the redemption of man? And where shall we find even now a community in which a man may live according to the eternal truth and fitness of things, regarding all things as they are intrinsically good or evil, without reference to conventional creeds and usages, and not be laughed at, doomed to neglect, to poverty, to beggary, to starvation, or to be prosecuted as a criminal? And where, again, is there a community, in which there are not multitudes passing for good Christians, nay, believing themselves good Christians, who patronize every popular scheme of piety and benevolence, and yet who believe doctrines they never broach, uphold, in word and deed, doctrines they inwardly abhor, and leave him who comes to them, in the name of Jesus, with the very doctrines they believe and secretly rejoice to see prosper, to tread, as did his master, the winepress alone; men who speak not, act not as they believe, lest they lose reputation, their position in society, or, like the Son of Man, have not where to lay their heads? So long as this is the case, who will have the hardihood to assert that the church is identical with that new order of things which Jesus came to institute, that it is generally admitted that the kingdom of God is the simple moral dominion of truth and love, that the Holy Ghost is a reality, and the Comforter promised us is actually in the world, abiding with us, and both able and willing to lead us into all truth?

The great doctrine I wish to bring out and establish is that the kingdom of God is neither more nor less than what we mean by the moral dominion of truth and love; and, therefore, in order that we may be true subjects of that kingdom, truth and love must be supreme within us, inspire all our undertakings, authorize all our deeds and shape our whole lives. This is the great, the central truth of Christianity, around which all its minor truths cluster, towards which all its teachings and influences tend, and in which they find their unity. This is the great truth, hitherto but dimly seen, and scarcely conceived of by the great mass of professed Christians, which it is of the utmost urgency that we bring out and insist upon, if we desire to promote the growth of God's kingdom, either in ourselves or in the world. Religion suffers more than any of us can easily imagine from the obscurity in which this truth is left. Not a few in this age, and they not the least enlightened nor the least well disposed, have outgrown the old forms in which religion has been clothed, become incapable of perceiving any intrinsic vitality or power in what the church urges as the essence of divine worship; and, confounding as they do, but as they should not, the Christianity of Christ with the Christianity of the church, suspect everything which bears, or can be supposed to bear, the name of religion, and who must soon forego faith in God, in man, in virtue, in goodness, become hostile or indifferent to all spiritual matters, sink down into a debasing sensualism, cease to regard the noble faculties with which they are created, the lofty destiny to which they have a right to aspire, and seek to fill up the void in their hearts, or to save themselves from the weariness which comes over them, by sensual indulgence or the vain pursuit of worldly wealth or honors. Man without religion is a wretched animal. He has nothing to exalt his sentiments, refine his affections, or to create within him that burning enthusiasm, without which he can neither effect his own good nor that of his race. It is to the want of this enthusiasm, this moral exaltation, which only religion produces, that we must attribute that unfruitfulness we deplore in so many fine and highly cultivated minds in every community. Even among the ministers of religion, I grieve to say, we find many who spend their lives in utter unprofitableness. They preach to us, indeed, but their discourses are barren, written without warmth or vigor, and delivered in a lifeless manner and a listless tone. They are not deficient in natural endowments; their motives, so far as they have motives, are not bad; their manners in private life are amiable; their conversation is sometimes even instructive, and always entertaining: but their ministry makes no impression; it passes away and leaves no trace behind, save the sorrow of a few friends, who had looked for something better. They are men without a future. Wanting faith, they want employment. They see nothing to be done, nothing they can do; and feeling their inability to accomplish anything, if they chance to undertake something, it is necessarily with so much doubt and misgiving, so much feebleness and indifference, that utter failure is the inevitable result. I never see one of these ministers of religion, but I am touched with a profound sadness. Angels are they, dismissed from paradise, and doomed to eternal idleness. Why shall so much private worth, so many brilliant talents, so many rich acquisitions, lie waste forever, and yield no fruit for their possessor, nor for the world? The evil is a great one, and can be removed but by making it undeniably evident that religion appeals to man's whole nature, and has employment for the intellect and the moral sense, as well as for the affections purely pious; but by frankly admitting and earnestly contending that we promote religion and build up the empire of God, just in proportion as we discover and promulgate truth, obey truth, and promote good will from man to man. It is a fearful infidelity, this to which I allude, and I know no way to cure it but by bringing out the great truth for which I contend, and making it seen and felt that the kingdom of God is no separate and foreign kingdom, but connected with all that we know, feel, and crave of truth and love, in some one or all of their manifold relations with the human soul, human thought, human duty, and human life.

Assuming the kingdom of God to be what I have asserted, we can easily understand what we must do in order to build it up on the earth. We must seek for the truth, truth under all its aspects, in all its relations, as for hid treasure; and, having found it, we must value it as the pearl of great price, hold it fast, and suffer neither angels, nor principalities, nor life, nor death, nor things present, nor things to come, nor any other creature, to separate us from it. To do this, may require us to dissent from the world and from the church even; to forego all the pleasures of friendship and society; to stand alone in the midst of those we love; to be pointed at as singular, mad, or depraved, by those to whom our hearts yearn, and for whom we would willingly die; but what then? Shall we suffer such things to move us? Let us rather remember that Jesus was once a stranger in the world; that he stood alone in the multitude; that of the people none were with him, not one responded to the warm affection of his heart; not one understood his purpose, appreciated his motives, or did justice to his disinterestedness and self-sacrifice; that he went about doing good, lightening the load of the weary and heavy laden, healing the sick, comforting the mourner, opening the eyes of the blind, unstopping deaf ears, and making the dumb sing and the lame leap, when he himself had not even where to lay his head.[11]

Nor is it enough to uphold truth in general. It is necessary to seek out and adhere firmly to the particular truth most needed by our own age and country; and this is always the truth which has not yet risen to empire, the truth which is the least popular, the least understood, in behalf of which the fewest voices are heard, and, therefore, the truth which it is the most dangerous to assert. There is no merit in echoing the truth which everybody shouts, and which, for the reason that everybody shouts it, must needs be exerting all its legitimate influence. In this world, all things change their forms. The watchword of yesterday is not the watchword of today. Once it was a cross, a self-denial, a self-sacrifice, to enrol one's self among the followers of Jesus; for, once, not many mighty men, not many noble, not many rich and honored owned him for their master; but now it is fashionable, and accounted honorable even to join the church and profess Christianity. The cross, the self-denial, self-sacrifice is now, therefore, in standing aloof from the church, in maintaining individual independence, and bringing up and insisting on those truths the church neglects. Truth in itself is immutable, but its aspects are perpetually shifting; and, in this sense, even truth may be said to change. The truth which reigns today is not the truth which must reign tomorrow. Great and glorious as may be the actual sovereign, he shall give way to a successor. Instead, then, of basking in the sunshine of the court, and seeking to share its largesses, we must go among the carpenters, the blacksmiths, and fishermen, and find out him that is born to be king, though lying in a manger, bind ourselves to his cause, follow him in his humiliation, and share his poverty and reproach. We must seek out the neglected truth, the truth which

[11] [Matt. 8:20; Luke 9:58.]

nobody sees, or which nobody speaks well of, and wed ourselves to it, for better or for worse, live and labor, or suffer and die for it, till it be raised to empire and glory.

This principle will lead us always to take our stand with the weak, to aid those who need aid, and not to do as the world, which seeks always to be on the side of the strong, and to aid those who are abundantly able to aid themselves. The Christian will rarely be found on the side of power. His post is always the post of danger, never that of safety. He leaves the "better sort," who, we have been told, on high authority, are not dependent on Divine Providence for support, and espouses the cause of the poor and friendless. He does not wait till that cause has become popular before he espouses it; but he weds himself to it when it is in the lowest repute, when the rich, the great, the fashionable, the learned, despise it and load it with reproach, call an enemy to God and society him who dares speak well of it. They who have no one to speak for them, to plead their cause, who cannot speak for themselves, who are commanded to be silent in their own behalf on pain of being branded as incendiaries, and punished as malefactors, are they who for him are the people of God, whose cause is the cause of truth and love, which he must espouse, and for which he must dare to live or dare to die. In all revolutionary struggles, he takes sides with the unprivileged many, the great unwashed, as somebody calls them, and braves the wrath of kings, nobilities, and hierarchies. When the interested few, who fatten on the sweat and blood of their brethren, and ride rough-shod over human rights and human affections in a moment of panic, cry out "ORDER," "RIGHTS OF PROPERTY," he cries out, in still louder tones, "LIBERTY," "RIGHTS OF MAN!" and in tones, too, which fetch their echoes from afar, ring on the oppressor's heart as a summons from God to judgment, and in the souls of the wronged, the enslaved, the downtrodden, as the jubilee-shout of deliverance. The cause of the suffering sons of toil, who from time immemorial have been made mere drudges, debarred from all the sweets of existence, and doomed to be brutes, as the price of being governed, of being kept in order, and from cutting one another's throats, save at their keepers' pleasure, is for him the cause of God; and to blaspheme that cause or its friends is to blaspheme the Holy Ghost, to commit the unpardonable sin; and to wish to impede its progress, or to embarrass the operations of its friends, is to wish to impede the progress of the eternal God, and to retain the earth under the accursed dominion of the devil and his angels.

The kingdom of God, it follows from what I have said, is identical with no special society, no outward, visible corporation, with no church creed or usage. It lies back and above all forms of faith and worship, in the soul itself, and is a power within us, which renders whatever comes forth from us pure and holy.

This great truth must be brought out and insisted upon; it will check bigotry and intolerance, exchange sectarian wrangling for an honest and earnest pursuit after truth, put down speculative infidelity, not by showing that no truth but religious truth is to be accepted, but that all truth, of whatever name or tendency, is religious; by showing that no man, who believes in truth and love, is or can be an atheist, whatever he may call himself or be called by others; and that every man, who loves his neighbor as himself, seeks earnestly for the truth, and obeys the truth so far as he sees it, is a Christian, in the only worthy sense of the term, whether he be called Jew or pagan, Mahometan or infidel. The dispute about forms of worship will end because when it is understood that the kingdom of God consists in truth and love, all that passes or can pass for external worship will be seen to be without intrinsic value, and to be worthy of regard, only so far forth, as it exalts the sentiments, purifies the affections, and collects a moral force in the soul, which shall make it ready and able to do the biddings of truth and love, without fear or favor. Let the great doctrine I have contended for be brought out and firmly established, and the church, really universal, will be built up, not by bringing all men into a special society called the church, but by diffusing truth and love through all hearts, and making them the basis of the state and of all social institutions. The state will then be holy, religious, because it will be organized and administered in accordance with the immutable truth of things, the will of God, and the nature and wants of man. This is the grand result contemplated in the mission of Jesus; and this is the grand result for which all the saints pray, which all God's prophets predict, and for which all who love God and man labor without ceasing.

18.

UNITARIANISM AND TRINITARIANISM[1]

Boston Quarterly Review 2 (July, 1839): 378-85

We are far from proposing to review this valuable little tract put forth by the American Unitarian Association; we have quoted its title merely as a text, not very appropriate perhaps, for some few remarks, which we are about to offer on Unitarianism and Trinitarianism.

Unitarianism, in the form in which it has heretofore existed in this country, as the creed of a distinct denomination, we suppose it is no offence to say, is virtually if not literally dead. Its hold on the affections of the religious community is relaxed, and its power to excite attention has pretty much passed away. It ceases to excite controversy, and we much doubt whether there can be found a single man among its professed friends, with sufficient life and courage to undertake its defense, should it be seriously attacked. Scarcely a congregation in this Commonwealth takes pleasure in hearing its peculiar doctrines dwelt upon; and it is a principle among Unitarian clergymen, rarely departed from, that its peculiarities are hardly proper subjects for pulpit exercises. No books appear in its defense or elucidation. Unitarian papers and periodicals contain little Unitarianism. The elaborate works put forth, some time since, on biblical criticism, by Professors Norton and Palfrey, two distinguished Unitarians, have taken no hold on the community; and though severely attacked, have found no one to step forward in their defense. The Divinity School at Cambridge is going down. Professor Palfrey has retired from it in disgust, and taken his leave of the ministry. An old fashioned Unitarian, if appointed to succeed him, will hardly be able to sustain himself; to appoint one of the new school, would be a virtual abandonment of Unitarianism. Mr. Norton, one of the ablest men the Unitarians in this country have ever been able to boast, and,

[1] [Ed. Review of James Walker's (1794-1874) *Unitarianism Vindicated Against the Charge of Skeptical Tendencies* (Boston: James Munroe & Co., 1839). Walker was minister of the Unitarian Church in Charlestown, Massachusetts (1818-39), editor of *The Christian Examiner* (1831-39), and Alford Professor of Natural Religion and Moral Philosophy at Harvard (1839-53), before becoming president of Harvard (1853-60). As editor, Walker had published some of Brownson's significant essays and those of other budding young Transcendentalists.]

in his way, one of the honestest, and most earnest, has publicly declared, that there is no longer a Unitarian body extant among us.[2] We may therefore assume that what the founders of the Unitarian denomination understood by Unitarianism has gone the way of all the earth.

This result was inevitable. Unitarianism was mainly a negative system, a protest against certain forms of faith, which had ceased to satisfy the intellectual wants of the times. But no system of negation can long satisfy any community. Religion shrinks from negations. It affirms; its essence is a boundless faith; and it withers and dies when it ceases to affirm. As a positive system, Unitarianism was too meager. Its great doctrine, the Unity of God, it asserted in common with all Trinitarians, and even with Jews and Mahometans. This doctrine is a truth, a great truth, but it is a truth, which has, in the actual state of Christendom, very little direct bearing on practical life. It is not a truth, which has much power to kindle the affections, and send us forth to labor with enthusiasm in the cause of either God or man. Unitarianism, as such, had in itself no germ of reorganization, and therefore could not serve as the nucleus of a new moral and religious world. Consequently, when its work of denial was done, it had nothing to do, but to die.

But now Unitarianism is no more, what shall we do? Shall we throw ourselves into the arms of trinitarians, and embrace the old symbols of faith, against which we have carried on a vigorous war for so many years? Not at all. For, we apprehend, that if the truth were told, trinitarianism would be found to be as dead as Unitarianism. The fact is, there is at this moment no authentic religious symbol in the country; and we look for a general dissolution of the old religious world, and the creation of a new heaven and a new earth, wherein shall dwell righteousness.

God has spoken to us. His Word contains all truth; and none of us need ever hope to get beyond the truth contained in the revelation he has made. But we do not take in at once the full import of his Word. Nay, we never shall take in all its deep significance. We shall study it through eternal ages, and still be ever finding something new in it. We, however, take in what we can. What we comprehend of it at a given epoch, we embody in institutes, creeds, confessions, catechisms. These, which we call symbols of faith, at the epoch of their adoption are to us true expressions of the Word of God. At that

[2] [Ed. See Norton's article in the *Boston Daily Advertiser and Patriot*, October 15, 1838.]

epoch, to question them is to question the Word of God; to deny them is to deny the truth. They are the truth for that epoch, all the truth it can understand, and nothing but the truth.

But the human race is not stationary. Not individuals only advance; the race itself advances. It becomes able to take in more truth than is embodied in the old symbols, and, consequently, must reject them, and seek new and more expressive symbols.

The symbols, which reigned at first in this country, were those of the Calvinistic church, a church to which much reverence is due. In these symbols was embodied, at the time of their adoption, the Word of God as perfectly as it was then comprehended. Much of the deep meaning of that Word was represented by the Thirty-Nine Articles, the Westminster Confession, and the Saybrook Platform.[3] These symbols represented the views of the then advanced party of mankind. But they did not take in all truth. Several elements were left out. Some of these neglected elements were brought up by the Arminians. The Arminians had less truth, and less essential truth, than the Calvinists, but they had some elements of truth which the Calvinists had not.

The Unitarians, in this country, were the lineal descendants of the Arminians. They seized upon certain elements of truth, which the dominant churches neglected. We do not think the Unitarians had so rich a faith as the Calvinists. The truths they seized upon were fewer in number, and, in our judgment, less weighty than those of the Calvinists. Were we obliged to be either a Unitarian or a Calvinist, with our present views, we should unhesitatingly prefer to be a Calvinist.[4] But though the Calvinistic church may be supposed to have more truth than the Unitarian, still the Unitarian has certain elements of truth, which are essential to the completeness of religious faith, and with which humanity cannot well dispense.

What is now needed is a wise Eclecticism, by which the essential elements of all the old systems shall be selected, and, in connection with the new elements which the progress of the race has developed,

[3] [Ed. The Thirty-Nine Articles (1563) of the faith were established after a long history of development to guide the Church of England. The Westminster Confession (ratified 1648) was established to clarify the profession of Presbyterian doctrine. The Saybrook (Connecticut) Platform (1708) was a declaration of ecclesiastical discipline for the Congregational Church that broke somewhat from the tradition of strict Congregational polity.]

[4] [Ed. Such an assertion may have been an exaggeration, which was not unusual for Brownson, but it reveals his growing dissatisfaction with Unitarianism, and reflected an eclecticism that he applied to religion and theology.]

be molded into one systematic and harmonious whole. The great work now to be done is to analyze all systems, find out what each contains that is true, disengage it from the symbolic forms in which it has hitherto been expressed, and present it to humanity in the current language of today.

Our objection to the trinitarian or orthodox church is that it will not permit us to undertake this analysis. The orthodox, as they are called, tell us that we must take their symbols as we find them, and that we must not presume to translate them, to interpret them. They would chain us down to the letter which killeth, and prevent us from embracing the truth in what are today spiritual and living forms. For ourselves, we could put up with their symbols, because we think we have ascertained their significance; but we know that the mass of both orthodox and heterodox Christians, do not look beyond the symbol to the idea it should represent. They stick fast in the letter and are compelled to remain without spiritual life. Now, if we were only permitted to translate these symbols, that is, to translate into what is now the vernacular tongue of humanity the ideas, which they represent to those who comprehend them, the mass would see and embrace the truth, and be sanctified by its free and energetic workings. But this the orthodox will neither do nor suffer to be done. The fault we charge them with is that of worshiping the symbol instead of the idea, the image instead of the reality, which is idolatry, and of rejecting what may be termed the liberal element. This is a serious charge, we admit; but it is gravely made, and we fear but too easily sustained.

We cannot, then, go with the orthodox, the trinitarians. We prefer rather to act with the party which *was* Unitarian, but which *is* now enlarging its views and taking in not only the truth which Unitarians brought up, but which is also to be found concealed under the symbols of the orthodox church. With them there is freedom. They acknowledge the rights of the mind, and, though some of them are a little contracted in their notions of liberty, taken as a whole they are free enough. They are the movement party in theology, and as such are commended to every believer in progress. But we love this party, not because it is Unitarian, or said to be Unitarian; we approve it not for any of its actual dogmas, but for its liberality, because it is the LIBERAL PARTY. Its actual faith even now is meager enough, although it is immensely richer than it was a few years ago; but it does allow a man to think for himself, and even to utter his thoughts, without dragging him before an ecclesiastical tribunal; nay, without imposing any more restraint than, perhaps, is needed to make him weigh well what he is about to utter. Could we say this of our trinitarian brethren; would they accept the element of freedom, acknowledge the rights of the mind, and suffer us to give a free but conscientious version of their symbols into language, which men now-a-days speak and understand, we should be most happy to be of their number, for at bottom we apprehend that we embrace all their doctrines. But this is what they will not do. We cannot, then, go with them, for we go where freedom goes, and find our home only where "the perfect law of liberty" [James 1:25] has its seat.

The party called Unitarian, we have said, is the movement party. It is a progressive party. Its faith today is much changed from what it was fifteen years ago, and we believe it is likely to change yet more. It is taking in, everyday, new elements of truth. It has accepted, not indeed the democratic element in its fulness, but it has accepted that of philanthropy, as manifested by its ministry to the poor. This ministry to the poor, in its actual state, is not worth much; but it will lead to an investigation of social wrongs and social sufferings, and finally to a thorough social reform. They are fast accepting the philosophic element, and will contribute much to the introduction and spread of a more worthy philosophy of the human mind than has ever heretofore obtained in this country. This is promised in the recent appointment of Dr. Walker professor of moral and intellectual philosophy in Cambridge University, and in the adoption of Cousin's Psychology as a text-book, to accompany Locke.[5] They are evidently approaching the orthodox. That is, they are reproducing in their own minds, under appropriate forms, the great spiritual facts, which lie under the orthodox symbols; and from having been cold materialists, on the very verge of infidelity, they will, in a few years, become remarkable as evangelical Christians, and that too in the most worthy sense of the term.

Under every one of the orthodox symbols there lies an important truth. To most men the symbol fails, at the present time, to express this truth. The symbol hides the truth. But as soon as we have reproduced that truth in our own minds, by the free action of our reason, we easily detect it under the symbol. The symbol of the Trinity covers a great truth, a vital truth; but trinitarians themselves do not see it; Unitarians have not seen it. But as soon as they have felt in themselves the need of that truth, they will discover it. And when they discover it, they will see that they may embrace it without aban-

[5] [Ed. The reference here is to Caleb S. Henry's (1840-88) translation of Victor Cousin's *Elements of Psychology: Included in a Critical Examination of Locke's Essay on the Human Understanding* (Hartford: Cooke and Co., 1834)

doning the views they previously entertained. They will then accept the doctrine of the Trinity, translate it into the language of the reflective reason, show its consistency with the unity of God, and thus lay the foundation for a strict union between them and trinitarians. The truth of each will be accepted, and a new creed will be formed, better than the old creed of either party, because reconciling and embodying the peculiar views of each. This done, the orthodox will be obliged to abandon their old symbols, which they will readily consent to do; because they will then see that they may give up their symbols without giving up any idea which they have valued. There will then be new symbols, adapted to the new epoch in the development of truth, and the new religious world will be constituted, and it will be said again, "See how these Christians love one another" [John 13:35]!

This is the result to which we look, and for which we strive with what skill and strength we can. We have ceased—we speak personally—to deny, and have commenced an examination, an analysis of all the symbols of the churches, not to reject them, nor even to modify them, but to comprehend them. We already see, or seem to see, the elements of the new world, and believe we could, had we space and room, even write its catechism. But enough of this. When Unitarians and trinitarians become able to understand one another, they will find that they are brothers. And so will it be with all contending sectarians. All that is needed to produce harmony is for each sect to comprehend its own truth, and the truth put forth by every other sect. Each sect has an element of truth. Would we be wise, we must ascertain and accept the elements of each.

19.

EDUCATION OF THE PEOPLE[1]

Boston Quarterly Review 2 (October 1839): 393-434

We can hardly be expected at this late day, in this ancient Commonwealth especially, to go into any labored argument in favor of popular education, either as a matter of right, or as the only firm foundation of a free government. For ourselves, we hold that every child, born into a community, is born with as good a natural right to the best education that community can furnish, as he is to a share of the common air of heaven, or the common light of the sun. We hold also that the community, which neglects to provide the best education it can for all its children, whether male or female, black or white, rich or poor, bond or free, forfeits its right to punish the offender. We hold, moreover, that a popular government unsupported by popular education is a baseless fabric.

But, while we bear our unequivocal testimony in favor of universal education, and assert the duty of every community to provide the best education in its power for all its children, we are very far from regarding everything which passes or may pass under the name of education, as something to be approved and never condemned. Education may be bad as well as good, a curse as well as a blessing; and in general its quality is a matter of even more importance than its quantity. Educated, in some sense, all our children are, and will be, whether we will or not. Education, such as it is, is ever going on. Our children are educated in the streets, by the influence of their associates, in the fields and on the hill sides, by the influences of surrounding scenery and overshadowing skies, in the bosom of the family, by the love and gentleness, or wrath and fretfulness of parents, by the passions or affections they see manifested, the conversations to which they listen, and above all by the general pursuits, habits, and moral tone of the community. In all these are school rooms and school masters, sending forth scholars educated for good or for evil, or what is more likely, for a little of both. The real question for

[1] [Ed. Review of *Second Annual Report of the Board of Education, together with the Second Annual Report of the Secretary of the Board* (Boston: Dutton & Wentworth, 1839).]

us to ask is not, Shall our children be educated? But, to what end shall they be educated, and by what means? What is the kind of education needed, and how shall it be furnished?

As to the quality of the education to be furnished, we apprehend our community, like most other communities, has no very clear or worthy conceptions. Education, in that sense in which it deserves the grave consideration and the earnest efforts of the community, is something more than the mere ability to read, write, and cipher; and something more too than what is commonly meant by moral and intellectual culture. It is properly defined, the fitting of the individual man for fulfilling his destiny, of attaining to the end, accomplishing the purposes, for which God hath made him. The system of education, which doth not take my child from the cradle, and train him up to go forth into the world a man, in the deep significance of that term, to comprehend the end for which he was made, and the surest and speediest means of attaining to it, is defective, and can never answer the legitimate purposes of education.

We suppose it will be generally admitted that man has an end, that he was created for a purpose. This has always been believed. It is implied in the first question of the catechism: "What is the chief end of man?"[2] Man's worth, perfection, is in exact proportion to the steadiness and success with which he pursues this end. Education is properly that which discloses to him this end, and prepares him to pursue it, points out to him the road he must take, and furnishes him with provisions and strength for his journey.

This end is twofold, corresponding to man's twofold nature, individual and social. Man has a destiny as an individual and also a destiny as a social being, as a member of society, and in this country as a member of the body politic. Education divides itself therefore into two branches; 1st, that which answers the question, what is my destiny as an individual, and fits me for attaining it; and 2dly, that which answers the question, what is the destiny of society, and fits me to cooperate in its attainment.

As an individual I am something more than the farmer, the shoemaker, the blacksmith, the lawyer, the physician, or the clergyman. Back of my professional character, there lies the man, that which I possess in common with all my species, and which is the universal and permanent ground of my being as a man. This education must reach, call forth, and direct, as well as my professional pursuit. Individual education is divided then into general education and special,

[2] [Ed. Reference is to the *Westminster Shorter Catechism* (1647).]

my education as a man, and my education as a doctor, lawyer, minister, artisan, artist, agriculturist, or merchant.

Special education appears to be that which we at present are most anxious to make provision for. Few people think of anything beyond it. The popular doctrine, we believe, is that we should be educated in special reference to what is to be our place in society and our pursuit in life. We think more of education as a means of fitting us for a livelihood than for anything else. The tendency has long been to sink the man in what are merely his accidents, to qualify him for a profession or pursuit, rather than to be a man. Special education has no doubt its place, and its utility, which must by no means be thought lightly of. In a community where hereditary distinctions obtain, where professions and pursuits are transmitted from father to son, it must ever be the main branch of education. In India, the son of a Brahmin should be educated to be a Brahmin, because he can there, according to the established order of society, be a Brahmin and nothing else. The son of one of the warrior caste requires to be educated as a warrior, and nothing else. So of the children of the other castes. For in Indian society there are no men; humanity is not admitted; a common nature is not recognized; therefore a general education as men, the education of humanity, is inadmissible. But in our community it is different. Here professions and pursuits are merely the accidents of individual life. Behind them we recognize humanity as paramount to them all. Here man, in theory at least, is man, not the mere artisan, farmer, trader, or learned professor. Professions and pursuits may be changed according to judgment, will, or caprice, as circumstances permit, or render necessary or advisable. Consequently here we want an education for that which is permanent in man, which contemplates him as back of all the accidents of life, and which shall be equally valuable to him, whatever be the mutations which go on around him, the means he may choose or be compelled to adopt to obtain a livelihood.

General education, which some may term the culture of the soul, which we choose to term the education of humanity, we regard as the first and most important branch of education. This is the education which fits us for our destiny, to attain our end as simple human beings. But in order to impart this education, or in order to educate our children in reference to this destiny or end, we must know what is our destiny or end as human beings. The character of the education will depend almost entirely on the view we take of man's destiny, on the answer we give to the question, "What is the chief end of man?"

If we look upon man as a mere child of earth, born of the dust, and returning to the dust again, possessing no lofty and deathless energies to be called forth and set at work, the education we shall seek to furnish must of necessity be essentially different from what we should seek to give, did we believe man was created in the image of God, immortal, endowed with a moral nature, made capable of endless growth in knowledge and love, and destined one day to stand higher in the scale of being than the tallest archangel now stands. If we believe man accomplishes his destiny on this earth, in the narrow compass of this transitory life, then for this world only shall we seek to educate our children; but if we believe that this world is but the cradle, in which our infancy is rocked, this life but our entrance into existence, but the beginning of a life never to end, that the faculties, the germs of which make their first appearance here, are to be developed elsewhere, and the destiny begun in time is to find its completion in the fulness of eternity, then for eternity, for eternal existence, and everlasting growth must we educate our children.

Now what is that which answers the question, what is the destiny of man? What is the chief end of man? With here and there one it may be philosophy; but with mankind at large, it is religion. Religion is the solution to man's soul of the problem of his destiny, the answer he gives, or rather which is given him, to those solemn questions which do ever and anon rise within him; What am I? Whence came I? Whither do I go? How came I here? Why am I here? What is the purpose of this frail existence? This life of trial and sorrow? These are questions which all men at some period of their lives are forced to ask. A thousand incidents occur to force these questions upon our attention. Our life here is not a calm and unbroken stream, bearing its undisturbed course onward into the great ocean of being. All things around us change. Nothing is permanent. The flowers fade and disappear; the grass withers and dies; the fashion of this world passeth away. We everywhere encounter enemies to our peace, obstacles to our enjoyment; perpetually are our desires thwarted, our plans defeated, our hopes blasted. We are wounded often in the tenderest part of our nature, our purest and holiest affections are sported with; we love and find no return; we love and are beloved, and yet must not embrace the one we love; we are disappointed in those to whom we have given our hearts; our friends on whom we leaned pass away, and we are without prop or support; those we love suffer, and we cannot relieve them; these and ten thousand other things force us to pause in our career, throw us back upon ourselves, and raise within us the problem of our destiny.[3] When this problem is once started, we suffer the deepest sorrow till we find its solution. We weep much that no man is found able to open the book. Religion is the solution of the problem, the Lion of the tribe of Judah, that prevails to open the book and to loose the seals thereof.[4] Hence its value, and the reason why men cling to it with such tenacity, and hold him their worst enemy who would arraign it. The love and reverence men have for Christianity grow out of this fact that it solves for them this problem, which is so torturing in its nature, and gives them a clear view of the destiny which God has assigned them. Hence, too, the impotence of all those who war against religion, and the folly of all those who fear such warring may be successful. So long as there is sorrow or aught to cause sorrow in this world, so long as man meets with obstacles to his instincts, and is interrupted in his march to his destiny, so long there will, there must be religion. There are but few moments in one's life when he is prosperous enough, successful enough, strong enough, happy enough, to dispense with religion. The human heart is a fountain of tears, and from the innermost being of whomsoever lives, sorrow is ever welling up. They are fools who say,

> O happiness! our being's end and aim.[5]

Man, in this life at least, has nothing to do with happiness, and, were he wise, he would cease to trouble himself with its vain pursuit. Let him seek to fulfil the purpose of his being, and he may find at times solace and refreshment. But the word *happiness* should have as little place in our vocabulary as it has in our hearts. Man has a destiny, an end he should seek to gain, and religion is the answer to the question, what is this end, this destiny? According to the principles we have laid down, then, education, to be complete, to be what it ought to be, must be religious. An education which is not religious is a solemn mockery. Those, who would exclude religion from educa-

[3] For an able and eloquent discussion of this subject, see Jouffroy. *Melangé Philosophique*, p. 423, et seq. *Du Problème de la Destinée humaine*. The substance of this interesting article may be found in Mr. Ripley's introductory notice to his translations from Jouffroy, in his Philosophical Miscellanies, a work of which we have heretofore spoken in terms of high, but not too high, commendation. [Ed. Brownson is referring to *Philosophical Miscellanies, Translated from the French of Cousin, Jouffroy, and Benjamin Constant*, trans. by George Ripley, 2 vols. (Boston: Hilliard, Gray, & Co., 1838), reviewed in this volume. See chapter 3.]

[4] [Ed. The reference is to Rev 5:3-5.]

[5] [Ed. See Alexander Pope's *Essay on Man*, epistle 4, line 1.]

tion, are not yet in the condition to be teachers; long years yet do they need to remain in the primary school.

Man is also a social being, and needs an education corresponding to his social nature. He is not a mere individual. He stands not alone. "It is not good for man to be alone" [Gen 2:8], said his Creator, and brought forth from his side Eve, blooming in beauty, blushing with charms, full of tenderness and love, to break the solitude, clothe the dusty earth with soft verdure, give the flowers of paradise their varied hues and sweet fragrance. In Eve Adam found the complement of his being, and rose to manhood. He, who has not loved, who has not felt that love which melts two human beings into one, and of the twain makes one flesh, has not yet attained to manhood. He has perceived none of the deep mysteries of his being; of the immortality of the affections he has conceived nothing; and the infinite fulness of his nature lies shrouded in deep night. It is not till one loves, that he receives intimations of a higher nature, of the wonderful capacities with which he is created, is raised from himself, and permitted to see and taste something of that fulness from the bosom of which the universe proceeded, and in whose embrace it reposes. It is then that he begins to attain to manhood. He is then a child no longer. He is alone no longer. He belongs now to the universe and has a place in it. Love unites him to Eve and Eve to him, and from all-creating love springs the family, and from the family society, crowned by the state. Love makes him a man and multiplies his relations and ties without number, links the first man to the youngest child of the latest generation, and gathers and cements all individuals, however scattered over the face of the globe, sleeping beneath the earth, or riding in sun-chariots through the heavens, into one round, compact, and indissoluble whole. Thus love gives each individual an interest in the whole, a part and a lot in all, and what is better yet, a work. Proceeding from love, made capable of loving with a love that can triumph over time and all its mutations, over pain, sickness, sorrow, death, and the grave, and bloom in immortal beauty when all else has become withered and dry, man has a social nature, is a social being, and needs a social education.

Other problems now come up. What is the mission of the family? What is the mission of the state? What is the destiny of society, of the human race itself? Great problems are these, weighty, and no doubt of difficult solution. But how give man a proper social education without solving these weighty problems? That deserves not the name of a social education, which leaves untouched the problem of society, the destiny of the race. And the social education must needs vary precisely as vary our solutions of this problem. In Russia they solve this problem in their fashion. Society has there for its object, the accomplishment of the will and the manifestation of the glory of the autocrat. Hence, the Russian children are carefully instructed in their duty to the emperor, carefully taught, by authority, that they and all they may possess are his, and that they must love him in their hearts, and honor him as their God. In Austria the problem is solved much in the same way, and so also in Prussia. Absolutism has its solution, and educates accordingly; liberalism has also its solution, and its corresponding education.

In this country we do not solve the problem as they do in Russia, Austria, and Prussia. We deny that it is the end of society to manifest the glory and accomplish the will of the emperor, or even of the state. Here society does not exist for the government, but the government exists as an agent of society. The mission of the government is to aid society in working out its destiny. The education then approved in Russia, Austria, or Prussia, cannot be approved here. Which solution is the true one, ours, or the one given by absolutism?

Again. What is the destiny of society? Has it attained its perfection? Is its organization perfect? Does it give free scope to man's whole social nature, and bring out all his social instincts? Shall we labor to keep it precisely where it is? Prevent it from going backward or forward? Or is society imperfect as it is? Is it progressive in its nature? Is there room to hope for a more perfect arrangement for man's social instincts? Is it our privilege to hope that the evils we now see and deplore may be at length lessened if not removed; and is it our duty to labor to realize that social ideal which haunts the souls of the prophets and seers of humanity? Here are questions of immense magnitude, which the educator should be able to answer, and which in some way every social educator does answer.

Still other questions are involved in these; on which element should society be based, the aristocratic element, or the democratic? If the aristocratic element be the true foundation of social order, then should our schools be under the control of the aristocracy, be aristocratic in their basis and superstructure, and be nurseries of the aristocratic principle. But, if the democratic element be the true basis of society, then should the social education give the democratic solution of the problem, create a love for democracy, and discountenance every aristocratic tendency. It should, also, not only accept the democratic element, but disclose the means by which it may insure the victory, and make all other social elements subordinate to itself. It must, then, touch the nature and organization of the state, determine the mission of government, and the measures it must adopt in order to secure or advance the democracy. It rushes into the midst of politics, then, and decides on national banks and sub-treasuries. An education, which does not go thus far, is incomplete, and insufficient for our social wants.

Education, then, must be religious and social, or political. Neither religion nor politics can be excluded. Indeed, all education that is worth anything is either religious or political, and fits us for discharging our duties, either as simple human beings, or as members of society.

If, then, we are to have in the Commonwealth a system of popular education, which shall answer the legitimate purposes of education, we must have a system which shall embrace both religion and politics. Religion and politics do, in fact, embrace all the interests and concernments of human beings in all their multiplied relations. Nothing can concern me as a man, as an individual, or as a member of society, which cannot be arranged under one or the other. That education, then, which does not embrace either, must be worthless, because in no sense fitting us for performing our part, either as men or as citizens.

Assuming now the absolute necessity of religious and political education, and the worthlessness of every other kind of education, when taken alone, the great and the practical question becomes, how is this education to be provided? In what schools and under what schoolmasters?

We have looked into the reports before us, with the hope of finding an answer to this question; but here, as everywhere else in this world, we have been doomed to disappointment. The great problem education is to work out, the end we have stated education should always contemplate, the honorable board, and its learned and eloquent secretary,[6] seem never to have conceived of. We find no leading idea, no enlarged views, no comprehensive measures; nothing, in fact, to inspire us with the least confidence in the board, or its labors, as a means of aiding us to an education worthy of a free and Christian Commonwealth. That the board does, indeed, propose to advance the cause of education, we do not deny. It proposes, for this purpose, two measures; 1st, improvements in the methods of teaching, and 2dly, the establishment of normal schools, or schools for teachers. The first measure is, doubtless, well enough, as far as it

[6] [Ed. The reference here is to the Unitarian educational reformer Horace Mann (1796-1859), the first secretary of the Massachusetts' board of education. Brownson did not believe, as Mann did, that it was realistically possible to provide a non-sectarian approach to education.]

goes. The machinery of teaching, if we may so speak, should be perfected, and the best possible methods of imparting knowledge found out and adopted. But, however perfect may be our machinery for teaching, it will amount to little, unless we have somewhat to teach, and also somewhat to teach, which is worth the teaching. The normal schools, which the board proposes to establish, will do nothing to impart such an education as we contend for. The most we can hope from them is some little aid to teachers in the methods of teaching. Beyond improving the mechanism of education, they will be powerless, or mischievous.

Schools for teachers require in their turn teachers, as well as any other class of schools. Who, then, are to be the teachers in these normal schools? What is to be taught in them? Religion and politics? What religion, what politics? These teachers must either have some religious and political faith, or none. If they have none, they are mere negations, and therefore unfit to be entrusted with the education of the educators of our children. If they have a religious and a political faith, they will have one which only a part of the community hold to be true. If the teachers in these schools are Unitarians, will trinitarians accept their scholars as educators? Suppose they are Calvinists, will Universalists, Methodists, Unitarians, and Quakers be content to install their pupils as instructors in common schools?

But the board assure us Christianity shall be insisted on so far, and only so far, as it is common to all sects. This, if it mean anything, means nothing at all. All, who attempt to proceed on the principle here laid down, will find their Christianity ending in nothingness. Much may be taught in general, but nothing in particular. No sect will be satisfied; all sects will be dissatisfied. For, it is not enough that my children are not educated in a belief contrary to my own; I would have them educated to believe what I hold to be important truth; and I always hold that to be important truth, wherein I differ from others. A faith which embraces generalities only is little better than no faith at all. Nor is this all. There is, in fact, no common ground between all the various religious denominations in this country, on which an educator may plant himself. The difference between a Unitarian and a Calvinist is fundamental. They start from different premises. Their difference does not consist in the fact that they come to different conclusions, but that they adopt different starting points. The gospel of Jesus Christ is "another gospel," as expounded by the one, from what it is as expounded by the other. No Calvinist can teach Christianity, if he be honest, so as to satisfy a conscientious and earnest Unitarian. No Unitarian, if he be an earnest and conscientious Unitarian, can discourse on religion so as to satisfy a trinitarian. The solution of the problem of human destiny given by the one is not that given by the other. The one embraces a philosophy which the other rejects.

If we come into politics, we encounter the same difficulty. What doctrines on the destiny of society will these normal schools inculcate? If any, in this Commonwealth, at present, they must be Whig doctrines, for none but Whigs can be professors in these schools. Now the Whig doctrines on society are directly hostile to the democratic doctrines. Whiggism is but another name for Hobbism. It is based on materialism, and is atheistical in its logical tendencies. That all Whigs are aware of this, we do by no means assert; that any of them are, is by no means probable; but this alters not the fact. Whiggism denies the internal light; it denies that there is a spirit in man, and the inspiration of the Almighty giveth him understanding.[7] In religion, the Whig must depend upon the uncertain ground of history and criticism; in politics also, upon history and criticism. In neither does he recognize in man the criterion of truth, the universal reason, whereof each man is made a partaker, the ultimate authority in all matters pertaining to religion and politics. In his creed all is imposed, nothing is generated; all comes to us from abroad, nothing from within. Hence his reverence for antiquity, his regard for precedents, and his distrust of the people. Now, we need hardly say, that all this is directly contrary to the faith of the democrat. Democracy is based on the fundamental truth that there is an element of the supernatural in every man, placing him in relation with universal and absolute truth; that there is a true light, which enlighteneth every man that cometh into the world; that a portion of the spirit of God is given unto every man to profit withal. Democracy rests, therefore, on spiritualism, and is of necessity a believer in God and in Christ. Nothing but spiritualism has the requisite unity and universality to meet the wants of the masses. Now, whoever teaches one of these systems, must of necessity offend the advocates of the other. I am a Democrat. Can I entrust my children to the care of those who are to me virtually atheists? All ideas are connected. The Whig educator may, indeed, refrain from teaching my children the importance of Whig measures, but he cannot refrain from teaching them the Whig philosophy. Imbue them with this philosophy and they are secured to the Whig party, to the Whig cause. Establish, then, your Whig Board of Education; place on it a single Democrat to save appear-

[7] [Ed. Reference is to Job 32:8, one of Brownson's favorite biblical passages.]

ances; enable this board to establish normal schools, and through them to educate all the children of the Commonwealth; authorize them to publish common school libraries, to select all the books used in school, and thus to determine all the doctrines which our children shall imbibe, and what will be the result? We have then given to some half a dozen Whigs, the responsible office of forming the political faith and conscience of the whole community. We have done all that can be done to give Whiggism a self-perpetuating power; all that we can do to make a community of practical infidels. Are we prepared for this result?

The truth is, we have, in the establishment of this Board of Education, undertaken to imitate despotic Prussia, without considering the immense distance between the two countries. The craft of the king of Prussia is altogether more admirable than his love of the people. He has seen, what European kings are beginning to see, and what the French Revolution has made quite evident, that the people will have education, and that they cannot much longer be kept in submission to their masters by brute force. "The schoolmaster is abroad," and cannot be sent home again. What, then, remains for absolute kings? Simply to shake hands with the schoolmaster. They must enlist the schoolmaster in their cause. In order to do this effectually, they must have the forming of the schoolmaster, make him their stipendiary, and prohibit him from teaching aught, except what they dictate. Hence, the Prussian system of education, a skillful attempt of absolutism to steal the march on liberalism, to fight liberalism with its own weapons.

Let it be borne in mind that in Prussia the whole business of education is lodged in the hands of government. The government establishes the schools in which it prepares the teachers; it determines both the methods of teaching, and the matters taught. It commissions all teachers and suffers no one to engage in teaching without authority from itself. Who sees not then that all the teachers will be the pliant tools of the government and that the whole tendency of the education given will be to make the Prussians obedient subjects of Frederic the king?[8] Who sees not that education in Prussia is supported merely as the most efficient arm of the police, and fostered merely for the purpose of keeping out revolutionary, or what is the same thing, liberal ideas?

[8] [Ed. The reference is to Frederick William III (1770-1840), king of Prussia (1797-1840) who supported the forces of conservatism after being defeated by Napoleon and after the Treaty of Vienna (1815).]

Let us glance at what is actually taught in these much admired Prussian schools, and we shall find confirmation still stronger, if possible, of what we assert. What, then, does Frederic William allow his dear subjects to be taught? First and foremost, the catechisms of the two established churches, that is, the catechism of the Lutheran Church to the children of Lutherans, and that of the Catholic Church to the children of Catholics. Then they are taught the private and domestic virtues, and their duty to their lord the king. Have they lessons on the rights of man, their duties to the public, and the duty of governments to the people? Let an imprudent schoolmaster but broach these topics, and how long, think ye, he would be permitted to teach? Let a teacher or let the parents of the children taught but introduce into a school a book not designated by the government, especially a book which should agitate somewhat profoundly the great problems of the destiny of man and of society, and would the government, think ye, acquiesce? No; the whole system of Prussian education, which is well adapted in many respects to form the Prussian youth to the love and practice of the several duties of private and domestic life, is mainly designed to implant despotism in the intellect and the heart, to forestall the craving of freedom, and to make man, born to be free, to stand up a man amongst men in the image of his Maker, contented to be a slave, and a supporter of absolutism on principle.

And this is the system of education, in principle, which the fathers of our Commonwealth are seeking to establish here. They have taken advantage of the alleged deficiency of good teachers to demand what they choose to call normal schools. In default of good common school libraries, they have undertaken to prepare a series of publications, which they will at first take the liberty to recommend, and which afterwards they may ask of the legislature authority to enjoin. They assume the authority now to recommend the proper books to be studied, and soon they will try for authority to dictate. As soon as they can get their normal schools into successful operation, they will so arrange it, if they can, that no public school shall be permitted to employ a teacher who has not graduated at a normal school. Then all liberty of instruction, the evil so complained of in France, and which was not among the least of the causes which brought about the revolution of 1830, will be felt here in all its force. Adieu then to republicanism, to social progress.

A government system of education in Prussia is not inconsistent with the theory of Prussian society; for there all wisdom is supposed to be lodged in the government. But the thing is wholly inadmissible here; not because the government may be in the hands of Whigs or Democrats, but because, according to our theory, the people are supposed to be wiser than the government. Here, the people do not look to the government for light, for instruction, but the government looks to the people. The people give the law to the government. To entrust, then, the government with the power of determining the education which our children shall receive is entrusting our servant with the power to be our master. This fundamental difference between the two countries, we apprehend, has been overlooked by the Board of Education, and its supporters. In a free government, there can be no teaching by authority, and all attempts to teach by authority are so many blows struck at its freedom. We may as well have a religion established by law, as a system of education, and the government educate and appoint the pastors of our churches as well as the instructors of our children.

This is not all. The theory of our institutions rests on the progressive nature of man and society. Our institutions everywhere recognize the principle of progress. In most, if not all other countries, progress involves revolution. Here it is the established order, and we have made constitutional provisions for improvement. All our state constitutions contain provisions for amendment, when the people come to judge amendments necessary. In fact, we regard the end of society to advance. There is always a future before us, a good, not yet reached, to be attained. Hence, to be true to our theory, we must be always looking ahead, struggling to advance. To this end should all our systems of education, whether devised for the district school, the academy, the college, the university, directly or indirectly tend; but to this end they cannot tend if left to the management of the government.

Introduce now a system of normal schools, under the supervision of a government board of education. These schools must have professors. But who will these professors be? They must be popular men; men of reputation, not men who have the good of the people at heart, and are known only by their fidelity to popular interests, but men who are generally regarded as safe; in whom the mass of the active members of the community have confidence. But on what condition does a man come into this category of popular men? Simply on the condition that he represent, to a certain extent, the opinions now dominant. A man, who represents the past, is not a popular man, nor is he who represents the future, but he who represents the present. The man who has the misfortune to think in advance of his contemporaries, and to crave a good for humanity beyond that already attained, is necessarily unpopular. If he venture to translate his thoughts into words, and his cravings into deeds, he will be called hard names, deemed an enemy to God and man, or a well-intentioned dreamer, who, whatever be thought of his intellect or motives, is never to be trusted. Men, who have faith in the future, whose mental vision sweeps a broader than the vulgar horizon, whose souls burn to raise up the low, to break the fetters of the captive, to open the prison doors to those that are bound, to preach glad tidings to the poor, hope to the desponding, consolation to the sorrowing, and life to the dead, must always count, whatever the hold they may take on men's higher nature, on being distrusted, and, to no inconsiderable degree, discarded by their own age. They cannot but be misinterpreted. They must pass for what they are not, and would abhor to be. They cannot, therefore, become professors in normal schools, unless it be by accident, and if by accident they become professors, they will be forthwith silenced or dismissed; a fact of which Professor Cousin is an eminent witness.[9] What theological seminary would have selected Jesus, Paul, or John, in their lifetime, for a professor of theology? Nay, what board of education on earth would make the editor of the Boston Quarterly Review a professor in a normal school?

In order to be popular one must uphold things as they are, disturb the world with no new views, and alarm no private interest by uttering the insurrectionary word, reform. He must merely echo the sentiments and opinions he finds in vogue; and he who can echo these the loudest, the most distinctly, and in the most agreeable voice, is sure to be the most popular man, for a time. Men of this stamp do never trouble their age; they are never agitators, and there is no danger that they will stir up any popular commotion; they are the men to be on boards of education, professors in colleges, constables, mayors, members of legislative assemblies, presidents, and parish clerks. Such men look for in colleges, and, therefore, look rarely to colleges for reforms or reformers. Colleges, as a general rule, are the last place to which you should look for new ideas, or inspiration to devote one's self to the cause of spiritual and social progress. If one can survive his college life, and come forth into the world with a free mind, an open heart, and power to do the work of a man for his fellow men, he must possess originally a nature of noble constitution, and

[9] [Ed. Reference is to Victor Cousin's (1792-1867) 1821 dismissal from the faculty of literature at the Sorbonne (where he taught since 1814) because of his political liberalism. He returned to lecture at the school in 1828, receiving a warm response from large numbers of students who attended his classes on the history of philosophy.]

rare endowments. New ideas are placed in the world by those whom the world knows not, or disowns. Reforms come from the obscure and the unheeded, or from the jeered and the persecuted; a crucified peasant and his fishermen followers; not from the men of reputation, and respectability. The weak things of this world are chosen to confound the mighty, and foolish things to bring to nought the wisdom of the wise.[10]

In consequence of this invariable law of Providence, the men who can be placed at the head of these normal schools, if established, will not be men who represent the true idea of our institutions, or who will prepare their pupils to come forth educators of our children for the accomplishment of the real destiny of American society. Their teachings and influences, so far as they amount to anything, will be far from such as are needed. They will not make their pupils living men, bold to conceive and strong to effect a good as yet unrealized. They will be instant in season and out of season, to teach them to respect and preserve what is, to caution them against the licentiousness of the people, the turbulence and brutality of the mob, the dangers of anarchy, and even of liberty; but they will rarely seek to imbue them with a love of liberty, to admonish them to resist the first encroachments of tyranny, to stand fast in their freedom, and to feel always that it is nobler to die, nay, nobler to kill, than to live a slave. They will but echo the sentiments of that portion of the community, on whom they are the more immediately dependent, and they will approve no reform, no step onward, till it has been already achieved in the soul of the community.

We confess, therefore, that we cannot look for much to meet the educational wants of the community, from the favorite measures of the Massachusetts Board of Education. In the view of this respectable board, education is merely a branch of general police, and schoolmasters are only a better sort of constables. The board would promote education, they would even make it universal, because they esteem it the most effectual means possible of checking pauperism and crime, and making the rich secure in their possessions. Education has, therefore, a certain utility which may be told in solid cash saved to the Commonwealth. This being the leading idea, the most comprehensive view which the board seem to take of education, what more should be expected from their labors, than such modifications and improvements as will render it more efficient as an arm of general police? More, we confess, we do not look for from their exer-

[10] [Ed. Reference is to 1 Cor 1:27.]

tions. The board is not composed of men likely to attempt more, and if it were composed of other men, with far other, and more elevated and comprehensive views, more could not be effected. Boards of trade may do something, but boards of education and boards of religion are worthy of our respect, only in proportion to their imbecility. To educate a human being to be a man, to fulfil his destiny, to attain the end for which God made him, is not a matter which can, in the nature of things, come within the jurisdiction of a board, however judiciously it may be constituted.

Nevertheless, the board may, perhaps, do something. There is room to hope that it will do something to improve the construction of school-houses, and to collect the material facts concerning the state of education as it now is; and, judging from the accompanying report of its accomplished secretary, it may also effect some progress in the methods of teaching our children to spell. This will be considerable, and will deserve gratitude and reward. But, notwithstanding this, we must still adhere to our opinion that the board will do nought to increase or improve the facilities which already exist for acquiring an education, in the only sense in which education is of much value; because of education in this sense it has no conception, and no power to labor for it, even if it had the conception. No system of education, no system of schools, which can be instituted and sustained by government, can be adequate to the educational wants of the community. Nothing desirable in matters of education, beyond what relates to the finances of the schools, comes within the province of the legislature. More than this the legislature should not attempt; more than this the friends of education should not ask. Let the legislature provide ample funds for the support of as many schools as are needed for the best education possible of all the children of the community, and there let it stop. The selection of teachers, the choice of studies, and of books to be read or studied, all that pertains to the methods of teaching, and the matters to be taught or learned, are best left to the school district. In these matters, the district should be paramount to the state. The evils we have alluded to are in some degree inseparable from all possible systems of education, which are capable of being put into practice; but they will be best avoided by placing the individual school under the control of a community composed merely of the number of families having children to be educated in it.

For ourselves, we adopt the democratic principle in its fullest extent; but we believe that federalism—we use the word in its etymological sense—is the method by which its beneficial working is best to be secured. The individual state, as well as the Union, should be a confederacy of distinct communities. Our idea of the true form of a republican government for this country is, 1st, that the few material interests common to all parts of the whole country should be confided to a general congress, composed of delegates from all the states; 2dly, that the class of interests, under these, common to the largest extent of territory, should be confided to a state congress, composed of delegates from counties; 3dly, the next more general class of interests under these, should be confided to a county government, composed of delegates from the several townships, or wards; 4thly, the next most general class to a township or ward government, composed of delegates from the several districts of the town or ward; 5thly, the remaining interests, which may be subjected to governmental action, should be confided to all the citizens of the district, which should always be of size sufficient to maintain a grammar school. This is nothing but the actual idea of our government, freed from its exceptions and anomalies, and would require no new divisions to be introduced. Our legislature, in this Commonwealth, is composed of delegates from corporations, or communities, and we hope the hand of innovation will never succeed in giving it a different basis. We would, if we could, revive the old practice of each corporation's paying its own delegates; and we think it would have been an improvement in the Constitution of the United States, if the members of Congress, instead of receiving their pay from the federal Treasury, had been left to receive it from their respective states.

Now, to the smallest of these divisions, corresponding to our present school districts, among other matters, we would confide the whole subject—with the exception heretofore made—of common school education. This exception relates to the finances; but we would make even this exception as narrow as possible. The more exclusively the whole matter of the school is brought under the control of the families specially interested in it, the more efficient will the school be. If the town manage part of it, and the state a part of it, the district will be very likely to be remiss in managing its part, and so in fact no part, in the end, will be well managed. This results from a common principle. Where responsibility is divided, there is always a greater or less want of fidelity in its discharge. Wherever there is a power to be exercised, there should always be a concentration of it in as few hands as possible; and, to counterbalance the centralizing tendency of this, the community should be so divided into sub-communities that the power should in fact affect but a small number, and matters should be so arranged that this small number should be able to obtain speedy redress if wronged. We would have as little government as possible;

but where we must have government, we would have it lodged in few hands, and empowered to speak in a tone of absolute authority. Experience, we think, bears ample testimony to the soundness of this principle. At any rate, experience proves that when the powers of the school district were greater and the interference of the state and the township were less than now, the common school was altogether better than it is at present. In this view of the case, we regard the Board of Education as an unwise establishment. It is a measure designed to reduce yet lower the powers and responsibilities of school districts, to deprive them of their rights, and to bring the whole matter of education under the control of one central government, controlling it in the nature of the case for the children of others, not for their own. In the district, we manage the school for our own children, but the Board of Education have no children in the district school. They are removed to a great distance from it by the fewness of their number, and the populousness of the community for which they act, and can never take the deep interest of parents in each individual school, and, therefore, must want that which has thus far given to the common school its charm and its efficiency. To confide our common schools to the board is like taking the children from their parents, and entrusting them to strangers. I want no board of Education to dictate to me concerning the education of my children, and cannot every father say the same? But the board owes its origin to the warm interest which our community takes in the subject of education, and it is supported, because it is thought that it may give more efficiency to our common school system, and elevate its character. Well will it be for us, if we discover our mistake before it is too late, before we have parted with that system of common schools, which we hold as one of the richest of the legacies left us by our pilgrim fathers.

But, having disposed of the Board of Education, and its secretary, it is time to return to the question, how is the education we have described to be furnished, in what schools, and under what schoolmasters? This question is a grave one and deserves a more extended answer than we have the space or the ability to give it. We can do little more than throw out a few loose hints, which, perhaps, may not be without result.

In the first place, we remark that the education we contend for, as may be guessed from what has already been said, we do not look for from any system of government schools. Government is not in this country, and cannot be, the educator of the people. In education, as in religion, we must rely mainly on the voluntary system. If this be an evil, it is an evil inseparable from our form of government.

Government here must be restricted to material interests and forbidden to concern itself with what belongs to the spiritual culture of the community. It has of right no control over our opinions, literary, moral, political, philosophical, or religious. Its province is to reflect, not to lead, nor to create the general will. It, therefore, must not be installed the educator of the people.

In the second place, we would also remark that education in the sense in which we have commended it can be only approached not perfectly realized. To impart an education answering to the idea we entertain of it, we should need a knowledge far surpassing what mortals can attain to, and resources which superior beings, and only superior beings, can be supposed to possess. But this should not discourage us. If we could not take in an ideal beyond what is actualized, if we had no powers of conception, which outrun our powers of execution, we should not be progressive beings. Our life consists in struggling after the unattained, and even the unattainable. The artist attains to excellence, not so much by realizing his ideal, as by struggling to realize an ideal which he cannot. The greatest excellence of a work of art does not lie so much in what it actually embodies, as in its dim revelations of a beauty or a worth the artist struggled after, saw in his soul, but could not seize, embody in his song, transfer to the canvas, or breathe over the marble. So all greatness is enhanced by the conception it always gives of a greater yet beyond, which does not appear. In accordance with this law, in all our doing, we should have an ideal which is above and beyond all that we can do, an ideal, which haunts us day and night, forbidding us to be satisfied with anything achieved, and compelling us to be ever putting ourselves forth in new and stronger efforts. Grant, then, that the education we contend for cannot be wholly realized. Still, by effort, we of this generation can realize somewhat, which will be so much stock in advance for our successors, who, in their turn, may realize somewhat more.

No system of schools which can be devised can supply this education because there can be no more knowledge and wisdom embodied in schools, than is already in the community, and because chiefly, the education which our schools can furnish, in their best organization, is the smallest part of the education we do and must receive. The influences which go out from the school room are weak in comparison with the general influences of society, of nature, and of Providence, which are constantly acting upon us. Shut up your schoolhouses, and in all essential matters your children would grow up about the same, they would were they open. This is a consideration which it is not wise to overlook. No matter what your schools are, the characters of your children will be determined by that intangible, invisible, indescribable, but very real personage, called the spirit of the age.

But, pass over all this. If there be education, there must needs be educators. The character of the educators will determine the character of the education. The greatest care, then, belongs to educators, our greatest concernment must be to seek out or rear up well qualified teachers. This, we suppose, is the conviction of all those, who are interested in normal schools. Hence their efforts and contributions to their establishment. Yet, not in normal schools are we to look for educators, since it may be as difficult to find good teachers for normal schools as for any other schools, and since school teachers, in the technical sense, are by no means the real educators of the community.

The real educators of the young are the grown-up generation. The rising generation will always receive as good, as thorough an education as the actual generation is prepared to give, and no better. The great work, then, which needs to be done in order to advance education, is to qualify the actual generation for imparting a more complete and finished education to its successor, that is to say, educate not the young, but the grown-up generation. This educating of the grown-up generation is what we mean by the EDUCATION OF THE PEOPLE. Society at large must be regarded as a vast normal school, in which the whole active, doing, and driving generation of the day are pupils, qualifying themselves to educate the young. Our question now changes its aspect, and becomes, how, by what means, may the education of the grown-up generation be advanced? It will be seen from this form of the question that we regard the improvement of the adult as the means of advancing the child, rather than the education of the child as the means of advancing the adult. We shall probably be told that in this we put the cart before the horse; but we respectfully suggest whether it be not possible that they who may be disposed to tell us so have not made the slight mistake of deeming the horse a cart, and the cart a horse? Verily, to our eyes, their horse looks to us as much like a cart, as Lord Peter's shoulder of mutton did like a twopenny brown loaf to his hungry brothers, whom he had invited to dinner.[11]

[11] [Ed. From Jonathan Swift's *A Tale of a Tub*. See *The Prose Works of Jonathan Swift*, ed. Herbert Davis, vol. 1 (Oxford: Shakespeare Head Press, 1939), 72-74.]

What, then, are the means at our disposal for educating the grown-up generation? We can specify but a few, and as in duty bound, both professionally and otherwise, we begin with the clergy, who are really, did they but know it, *ex officio* educators of the people. The true idea of the Christian ministry is that of an institution, designed expressly for the education of the people, and it is to the profound sentiment which mankind have of the vast importance of an institution for this purpose that the Christian ministry is indebted for its origin and support. To the education of the people this ministry in all lands has contributed not a little. Faults, doubtless, the clergy have had, faults they doubtless still have, but there is as little justice as religion in the general condemnation of them, indulged in by but too many of our professed liberals. If the clergy have been less successful educators of the people than they might have been, it has in some measure been owing to two mistakes, into which they have fallen, in regard to the nature of the clerical office. Affected by reminiscences of Jewish and Pagan priesthoods, the Christian clergy have too often regarded themselves as priests, standing as mediators between God and men. They have felt that it was their peculiar province to offer up prayers and supplications in behalf of the people, and to make intercession for them with the common Father of all. But they should have borne in mind that there is but one mediator between God and men, Jesus Christ, who gave himself a ransom for all, and, therefore, that no man has any occasion to seek a priest to mediate between him and the Father, to offer up prayers for him in a particular place because it is now proper for all men to pray themselves wherever they may be, or whatever their profession, "lifting up holy hands without wrath, or doubting" [1 Tim 2:8]. Also should they have borne in mind that a priest, to present the offerings of the people, and to superintend the sacrifice, has become unnecessary, since Christ has appeared to put away sin by the sacrifice of himself as a sin-offering. No priest is now needed to enter into the Holy of Holies to obtain judgment for the people because one is our High Priest, even Jesus Christ the righteous, who hath entered into the Holy of Holies, not made with hands, but into the heavens themselves, and seated himself at the right hand of the Majesty on high, where he ever liveth to make intercession for us. When the veil of the temple was rent in twain, and the Holy of Holies laid open to the gaze of the multitude, when Jesus exclaimed, "It is finished" [John 19:30], bowed his head, and gave up the ghost, as a sin-offering for humanity, sufficient for all time, and for every man, the old priestly office was abolished. Henceforth, if any man sinned, he was not to go to his priest with a lamb, a he-goat, or with fruits and flowers, but to bear in mind that his advocate with the Father is he, who gave himself to death that he might be the propitiation for the sins of the whole world. The Christian clergy have not always kept this distinctly in view. They have at times felt that they were priests, to a certain extent, in the old sense of the word. Hence a chief cause of the errors they have committed and of the opposition they have in modern times encountered.

Another mistake into which the clergy have fallen and which grows out of the one already mentioned is that of supposing it their province not merely to discourse on the destiny of man, but to discourse on it dogmatically, to insist on it, that their solution of the problem of human destiny shall be taken as final, as the only true solution, and that another cannot be entertained, nor even sought after without sin. The clergyman has, in fact, no authority to preach beyond that which his teachings carry in themselves. He speaks to men, who, if they be his equals in intelligence, have the same right to command him that he has to command them. When he placed himself in a high pulpit, above the people, from which he was to command the people what to believe, he forgot his true position, and encroached on the prerogative of Jesus. He assumed to be lord and master, where he was in truth only a brother, and should have wished only to be a servant. Much evil has resulted from this assumption. But the assumption has now become ridiculous. Knowledge is no longer the exclusive possession of the clergy; their monopoly has been broken up; and it is no rare thing to find their superiors, even in theological matters, in the ranks of the laity. The day for authoritative teaching is gone by. Instead of enjoining and enforcing, the clergy, willingly or not, must hereafter labor to explain and convince. They have no longer any anathemas to fulminate; their quiver is exhausted of its thunderbolts, and their heads can no longer bear the triple crown. They must henceforth speak as men to their equals, and subject what they utter to the free action of reason, which all men possess in common.

Correcting these two mistakes, the clergy may contribute much to the education of the people. Freed from these two false notions, the Christian ministry will survive all the mutations of time, all changes in men's creeds, social institutions, and arrangements. There is a deep and permanent necessity for its continuance, in the nature of man and the will of Providence. No institution can ever wholly supersede it, or take its place. It must last as long as man lasts. Let the clergy, then, understand their mission. They are set apart as special educators of the people. They should, then, study attentively the nature of man and society, and arrive as nearly as they can at the true solution of the problem of both.

Some, we are aware, will start at our doctrine, and ask us, if we would have clergymen meddle with politics. They will tell us that clergymen belong to the kingdom of God, that their kingdom is not of this world, and that, therefore, they should keep clear of the field of politics. This is more specious than solid. All man's duties are intimately connected, and there is, and there can be, no such separation between religion and politics, as the doctrine opposed to ours implies. Religion and politics run perpetually into one another. A religion which neglects man's social weal, is defective in the extreme; and politics separated from religion are not only defective, but mischievous, degenerating of necessity into Machiavelism. Politics, rightly understood, are nothing but the great principles of Christianity applied to our social relations and arrangements, and are, therefore, as much within the legitimate province of the clergyman, as are the private and domestic virtues. On neither politics nor religion do we ask of the clergy dogmatic instructions, for they are but men, and often as ignorant as the rest of us of the true solution of the problem of our destiny. What we ask of them is that they direct our minds to the problem of society, as well as to that of the salvation of the individual, and that they enter in their public communications into its free and full discussion. This they ought to do, did they contemplate only the salvation of the individual in the world after death. The sinner is saved only by being redeemed from all sin, and we know no reason why sins against society should not be as impassable barriers to salvation, as sins against the church, or against individuals. Man's whole nature must be developed and perfected, in order to fit him for heaven, and the social element is as much an element, as essential an element of his nature, as the religious. All error is more or less prejudicial, and we know not why error in relation to the problem of the destiny of society should be thought less prejudicial to the growth and perfection of the soul than error in relation to the destiny of man, as an individual, or simple human being. We say, then, let the pulpit be opened to all subjects of general and permanent interest. Let it speak a free, bold, and earnest voice, and not fear to grapple with the weightiest problems, only let it speak to free men, or to men who have, at least, the right to be free men.

We are aware of the usual objection made to the interference of clergymen in political matters. He may give offence, may disturb the harmony of his parish, and diminish his means of usefulness. Be it so. We are never afraid of giving offence. They, whom the free, bold, and earnest utterance of one's honest convictions on any subject of importance can offend, deserve to be offended, and it would be criminal to please them. The harmony of a parish, which would be disturbed by the kind of preaching we demand, ought to be disturbed, for it is a deceitful harmony. Peace is a good thing, but justice is better. We would rather have war, and war to the knife, than a hollow peace, founded on the sacrifice of truth, or duty. Suppose, then, that the kind of preaching we call for should disturb, should agitate, nay, should to some extent call forth angry feelings, better so than the present deadness of our churches. Give us the noise and contention of life, rather than the peace and silence of the charnel-house. Men live in the storm, in the tempest, where they must put forth all their efforts, and use all their wits to keep above water, not in the calm, rocking on a tideless and rotting ocean. Whoso would live and be a man, should joy to snuff the battle from afar, and leap to rush in where blows fall thickest and fall heaviest. Nothing is so much to be dreaded as that calm, respectable state, which our respectable clergy contend for. Be cold or be hot, not lukewarm, lest the Almighty spue thee out of his mouth.[12] Let the clergy, then, preach on politics. If they give offence, they may be sure that they have preached on the subject they should. If they stir up commotion, let them "thank God and take courage," for they have at length found out one subject, at least, in which their congregations take an interest.

Next to the pulpit, in this country, as a means of educating the people, we mention the Lyceum, under which general term we include, not only the associations called lyceums, but the popular lectures, scientific or otherwise, which are beginning to be so frequent, and so fashionable.[13] The lyceum is as yet in its infancy. We cannot say much for its actual performances thus far; but it possesses a capacity, which, when fully developed, will make it an institution of immense power. It has grown up from the feeling of the age and country of the necessity of greater exertions for the education of the people, and to the education of the people, we believe it destined to contribute not a little.

The lyceum has hitherto done not much because it has discussed topics too remotely connected with life, its hopes and affections, tri-

[12] [Ed. A reference to Rev 3:15-16.]

[13] [Ed. On the lyceum movement, see Cecil B. Hayes, *The American Lyceum; Its History and Contribution to Education* (Washington, D.C.: United States Government Printing Office, 1932).]

als and duties. It has dealt with facts, rather than with ideas, with physical science, rather than with moral and intellectual philosophy. Facts gratify to a certain extent our curiosity, and fill our memories, but taken disjoined from the principles which unite and enlighten them, they make us no wiser, nor more knowing. There are deeper wants in most men than curiosity, and somewhat beside the memory to be filled. Ideas interest the people more than mere facts, and appeal to far deeper and more enduring wants. Whoso would take a firm hold of the popular heart, must speak on great and everlasting principles, which lie at the foundation of all science, and which come into play in every day life. You may please a popular audience by a lecture on bugs, or fishes, by a description of St. Peter's, or York Minster, by the details of the battle of Agincourt or Poitiers,[14] by discourses on chemistry, astronomy, geology, electricity, but you please them only for a moment. You give them a few facts to be remembered, not great principles, to be used. You have gratified curiosity, but you have furnished few materials for thought. You have not awakened the mind and set it at work.

There is a great mistake in our age and country on this subject, growing very naturally out of our infidel tendencies. We believe in matter, not in mind; in mechanics, but not in ethics; in geology and chemistry, but not in religion. Hence, the paramount attention we pay to the natural sciences, and our sneers at metaphysics. But, in truth, the natural sciences are little worth without the moral and intellectual. Be never so thoroughly master of all the physical sciences, and you are a fool in all that really concerns men, if you are instructed in nothing else. Religion and politics are the two great concernments of human beings, and in relation to these we are not necessarily instructed at all by the study of physical science. The study of nature, we are sometimes told, tends to make us religious; "an undevout astronomer," some fool has said, "is mad"; just as though there was anything more in the heavenly bodies to convince us of the being of a God, than in the grass that springs up under our feet, or the flowers that bloom along our path. The man who already believes in God will, no doubt, become more devout by the study of astronomy; but he, who goes to that study without a belief in God, will, however far he may push his researches, find only confirmation

[14] [Ed. The battle of Agincourt (1415) was one of the decisive battles of the Hundred Years War (1337-1453) when King Henry V of England defeated King Charles VI of France. In the battle of Poitiers (1356), also decisive in the Hundred Years War, Edward of England, the Black Prince, defeated John II of France.]

of his atheism, and say, in the end, with Lalande, "*Je n'ai jamais vu Dieu au bout de mes lunettes.*"[15] In herself, nature is mute and uninstructive. She is to us very much what we make her, and the voice she utters is but the voice we give her. To the religious, she is of a religious tendency; to the unbeliever, she is a teacher of infidelity. The wisdom you call hers is your own projected, and the beauty you ascribe her is the beauty of your own souls. Strike out the beauty within you, and you shall see none in the starry heavens, none in those sweet flowers you love so well; none in those distant mountains, with their harmonious outlines, nor in the tranquil ocean, sleeping so gently beneath the moon beams which play upon its unruffled bosom. Without the beauty which our own souls project, all nature were to us but an huge, ill-shapen, drab-colored jumble of earth, stones, and water. It is the spirit of God that breathes out from the soul over the weltering chaos, which brings light out of darkness, order out of confusion, and beauty out of deformity. Nor does the study of the natural sciences tend in the least to solve the political problem. The men whose lives are spent in poring over outward nature are not the men who will feel the deepest interest in the destiny of society. Was there not an ancient mathematician, who was found quietly solving some mathematical problem, while the enemy were battering down the walls of his native city, and butchering or leading captive his countrymen? Tyrants have no dread of the physical sciences. When your Napoleons remodel French Institutes, they preserve the classes devoted to natural science, and exclude only the class devoted to moral and political science; exile your De Staels, but patronize your Cuviers.[16] They have no dread of the facts of external nature. The disclosure of these facts throws no dangerous light on the worth of the soul, and the rights of man. It tells the people nothing of their wrongs, nothing of the manner in which they have been cheated, nor that they are re-

[15] [Ed. French for "I have never seen God at the end of my telescope." Joseph Jérôme Lefrançais de Lalande (1732-1807) was a French astronomer.]

[16] [Ed. Madame de Staël, whose proper name was Anne Louise Germaine Necker, Baroness of Staël-Holstein (1766-1817), was a writer whose Paris salon became a center for much political discussion. In 1803 she was forced to leave France because of her political views. She visited Germany returning to France periodically. Her most famous work was *De L'Allemagne* (On Germany), introducing many to the German Romantics and idealists. Georges Léopold Chrétien Frédéric Dagobert, Baron Cuvier, (1769-1832) was an anatomist at the College de France, famous for establishing the sciences of palaeontology and comparative anatomy. He received many political favors for his work. He was made Chancellor of the University of Paris after 1815, admitted into the cabinet by Louis XVIII, and under Louis-Philippe made a peer of France.]

garded by the government only as a sort of tax-paying animals, useful in proportion to the amount of taxes they pay with the least drawback in police expenditures for the purpose of keeping them in order. People may dig into the bowels of the earth, they may speculate on the revolutions of the globe, and seek to reconstruct from a few fossil remains the huge animals of an earlier time. This shakes no throne, changes no dynasty, and makes no absolute monarch feel insecure. But let them once become busy with the problem of society, let them once attempt to investigate the foundations of the actually existing society, and to search into the manner in which the world is governed, and for whose benefit, and forthwith the tyrant turns pale, absolute kings stand aghast, hierarchies give way, nobilities fall, and there is heard a sound as the "crack of doom." The people indignant rise, and swear that they are, and will be men; and wo to whomsoever dare gainsay them.

The physical sciences may be studied under any form of society and they can adapt themselves to the service of the tyrant as well as the father of the people. They necessarily involve no social revolution. But with ideas the case stands different. The study of the moral and intellectual sciences, necessarily brings up the great religious and social problems, and acts directly on existing social relations. All who fear the people and distrust the democracy, encourage them as little as possible. To this fact we supposed it was owing that our Cambridge University was for so many years without a professor in the moral and political sciences; and it is not one of the least encouraging signs of the times that it has finally been forced to fill the long vacant chair, and with a man, too, from whom the public may hope somewhat.[17] It proves that a confidence in the people, and in popular institutions, is beginning to find its way into old Harvard. Who can henceforth doubt the triumph of democracy?

Whoever would act on the masses, produce changes for good or for evil, must deal, not with facts merely, but with ideas, and the profounder and the more universal the ideas he puts forth, the greater shall be his power, the more wide and lasting his influence. Whoso has an idea is always a king and a priest. Ideas work all the revolutions which affect the moral and political world. One day in an humble town of a mountainous district in Lesser Asia, an obscure carpenter's

[17] [Ed. Brownson is referring here to James Walker (1794-1874). The position in moral philosophy was vacant for nine years. In 1830 Levi Hedge (1766-1844) retired as Alford chair of moral philosophy at Harvard; he was not replaced until 1839 when Walker was appointed to the Alford chair. On this, see Howe, *Unitarian Conscience*, 13-14.]

son stands up in the synagogue, and reads, "The spirit of the Lord is upon me, because he hath anointed me to preach the gospel to the poor; he hath sent me to heal the broken-hearted, to preach deliverance to captives, and recovering of sight to the blind, to set at liberty them that are bruised, to preach the acceptable year of the Lord" [Luke 4:18], and the veil of the temple is rent, idols and idol-worships pass away, and the whole moral and political world is changed. Whence this result? The carpenter's son uttered an idea, and that idea has made the world after its own image. An obscure Wittenberg monk, possessed with an idea, is more than a match for the whole religious and political organization of his epoch. Possessed of an idea, a few pilgrims, landing on Plymouth Rock, are able to found an empire, and ensure liberty to the world. Ideas are the sovereigns of the universe. Whoso would educate the people must do them homage. The Lyceum must represent this truth. Its lectures and discussions should be on subjects connected with what is deepest, and most enduring in human nature. When they shall be so, it will not only add to its interest and popularity, but become one of the most efficient agents desirable in the education of the people. But, it must put away its childish tricks. It must become serious and manly. It must aim higher, and strike deeper. Instead of wasting its strength on questions, such as, which is the more useful element to man, fire or water, it must bend all its energies to the solution of the problem of human destiny—to the questions, what is my destiny as a man? What is the destiny of society? And how may I best fulfil my own destiny, and contribute to the fulfilment of the destiny of society?

One more agent in the education of the people, and only one more, we have space to mention. This agent is the press, by which we mean mainly the periodical press, newspapers, magazines, and reviews. In this sense, the press in modern times has become a power, a sort of "fourth estate," and the most efficient agent in our possession for acting on the opinions of the people. It has, in a great measure, superseded the stage, and to some extent even the pulpit. Whoever has a doctrine to advance, or a measure to carry, writes, or causes to be written, a leading article in a daily, or an essay in a quarterly. The increasing number of periodicals, their ever-widening circulation, owing to the constantly increasing number of readers, make, and must make for a long time to come, the periodical press, or *journalism,* if you please, the first object of consideration with all who take any interest in the opinions entertained and acted on by the people.

The press must, undoubtedly, to a great extent reflect public opinion, collect and utter what is already believed and cherished by the public. But it may do more. It has the capacity to be a leader of public opinion, in some degree to originate it, to correct and elevate it. How great this capacity is, it is impossible to say. We have no means of measuring it. But that it exists, cannot be doubted. The great value of the press, as an educator of the people, depends almost entirely on the proper unfolding and exercise of this capacity. The mischief, or inefficiency of the press, hitherto, has consisted in its attempt to follow rather than lead public opinion. Editors have inquired WHAT IS, rather than, WHAT OUGHT TO BE? In this inquiry, too, they have consulted a few individuals, just around them, instead of taking enlarged and comprehensive views of the whole community; and have, therefore, given out as public opinion, what, in fact, was only the opinion of a coterie, a faction, or a few noisy partisans, or sectarians. In this way it happens, often that party papers do by no means express the real sentiments of their party. Your party paper, again, instead of speaking out honestly what its editor holds to be true or desirable, utters only what the same editor, or his advisers, have concluded to be what the party will be most likely to approve. "That is a noble measure," said one day a distinguished Senator in the State of New York, to the present writer, "and if adopted would be attended with the most beneficial results." "Will you support it in your place, as Senator?" said we. "If it is a measure of my party, I will," was the reply. This is the principle on which party politicians and party editors too often act. The Independent Treasury scheme was originally a Whig measure, and then it was opposed by the opposing party. It is now advocated by the Democratic party, and all the Whigs oppose it, and in most cases, we apprehend, simply because it is not *now* a measure of *their* party. In this way the press fails, on the one hand, to lead public opinion, and on the other even to reflect it.

It will easily be seen from these remarks that we look upon its want of freedom and independence, as the chief cause of the inefficiency of the press as an educator of the people. We call our press free, but, in truth, the press is very little, if any, more free in this country, than it is in the monarchical countries of Europe. There is here a censorship of the press, hardly less paralyzing than that established by Austria and Prussia. The government, to be sure, lets it alone, but in the absence of governmental restraint each man erects himself into a censor, and if the paper utters an opinion he does not like, he forthwith stops his subscription. The publisher, therefore, finds very soon that he must either pocket his independence, and echo the popular dogma, whatever it may be, or quit publishing, or starve. There is hardly a civilized country on earth, whose literature is so tame and servile as ours has been. Our reviews, in general, take as much pains to avoid the utterance of any new or leading idea, as they would, were they published under the immediate supervision of the Spanish Inquisition, or the Ottoman Porte. Even our favorite North American[18] refuses to utter the truth, when the truth is not of the sort to please its erudite editor. The honest and enlightened contributor to its pages must submit to a censorship altogether more humiliating than would be exacted by a European despot. This the Italian exile, who has fled from Austrian tyranny to enjoy life and freedom in America, can bear witness to, for he has been prohibited from telling the truth, and made to tell what is not true, and what he does not believe to be true. Sorry are we to say such things of the American press, but he is not always the worst patriot, who tells his countrymen of their faults.

If we pass from our periodical press to our regular built books, we shall find still deeper cause to blush and hang our heads. Scarcely a book has ever issued from the American press that breathes anything like the free spirit we find in French literature, or even in that of Germany. The Anglo-Saxon mind is free enough in what relates to material interests, free enough in all practical matters, but in what relates to the region of ideas, to the higher departments of thought, it is a skeptic, or a slave. Scarcely shall you find a single English or American statesman that has not a most holy horror of abstract principles, a most prudent detestation of "abstract right." Listen in the Parliament of Great Britain, or in the Congress of the United States, for the free utterance of great principles, or to the attempt to determine the worth of certain measures by considering them in the light of first principles, and you shall listen in vain. The Anglo-Saxon mind conceives nothing of first principles, has no acquaintance with ideas, no faith in mind, and faith only in steam-ships and rail-ways. At least, this has been its predominant character since the "glorious Revolution" of 1688.

This same trait of character appears in our literature. We can easily account for it and are very far from declaiming against it, or about it. Still it prevents our literature from being what it ought to be. It shows us wherein we are defective, and wherein we should seek to amend. What American writers want is thought, free, deep, earnest thought. This they will not have until they learn to speak out

[18] [Ed. Brownson did not hide his disdain for the *North American Review* (1815-1940), perhaps the most important review in the United States, but Brownson thought it represented the aristocratic element in American society.]

freely what is in them. Man is man, here as well as elsewhere. There is nothing in our heavens, nothing in our lakes and rivers, our mountains and plains, the earth, on which we stand, the scenery, amidst which we are reared, or the food on which we feed, to hinder us from attaining to as lordly a stature of mind or body here as elsewhere. Let man here dare be a man, and a man he shall be, worthy to be the model-man of all ages and countries. He has had here the courage to free himself from kings, nobilities, and hierarchies. Why, then, shall he not have the courage to speak out the rich thoughts the Divinity sends him, to tell without apology or misgiving what comes to him as truth? Shall I be thought the less of if I tell my honest convictions? Shall I feed the worse? Be clad in a coarser garb? What then? Am I nothing but what the opinion of others, my food, and my clothing make me? Am I not a man, and not the less a man, whatever be my environment? Shall I bend to popular prejudice? Shall I be false to my own soul, false to all that is true within me, that I may he thought the better of, feed on costlier viands, or wear a finer coat? No. Let me be cast out from the society of men; let me wander the earth in sheepskins, or in goat-skins; let me dwell alone on the mountain, or in caverns; let me beg, let me starve sooner. When God gave me a manly nature, he bid me be true to it; when he gave me reason, he bid me listen to its oracles, and when he gave me a social nature, and linked me by ties sweet as heaven to my kind, he bid me be true to whatever I should be honestly convinced would be for their good, and let me die, nay, let me sink into eternal torture, sooner than be false to the trust committed to me. This, it strikes us, is the only language becoming a man. Talk not to me of my party or my sect, talk not to me of reputation or of wealth; these are nothing; they can follow me only to the tomb. They cannot make me amends for having been false to my God. They will not quench the eternal fire, which must scorch the tongue which has uttered falsehood, or refused to utter the truth. He, who shrinks from free thought and free speech, is the most abject of slaves, is not a man but a pitiable thing, unworthy of heaven, and too imbecile for hell.

Still, we apprehend that the American press is needlessly chary of free speech. There is, after all, something in even the Anglo-Saxon that looks with contempt on the mental slave, and which leaps to behold the brave spirit that snaps his fetters and stands up a free man. Policy, interest, craft, may say what they deem expedient against the man who utters new thoughts, unpopular truths in free, bold, and manly tones; but the universal heart of humanity does him homage, and even they, who are loudest in their censures, do inwardly reverence him. This is as true in this country as in any other; for even the Anglo Saxon is a man, and the character we have given of his mind is only accidental and temporary. His mind was freer and richer once, and will be again. Nay; even now, all unconsciously, lie concealed within it the nobler elements, which constituted a Milton, a Sidney, and a Hampden. There is good stuff after all in the Anglo-Saxon mind, and whoso dare use it shall be crowned priest and king. There is not so much danger in speaking freely in this country as the conductors of our press apprehend. Our own Review is a proof of it. We say nothing by way of boasting, but this journal has spoken freely, and boldly, and strongly, on subjects of the greatest delicacy. It has uttered, without apology, as unpopular opinions as a man can utter in this country. And what has been the result? So far as the Review has been commended at all, it has been for the very qualities in which we contend the American press is most deficient. What reputation the editor has secured to himself, he has secured by means of the independence, the freedom, and boldness, which have characterized his discussions. The editor, in fact, instead of losing reputation by the course he has pursued in this Review, is almost wholly indebted to it for what little literary reputation may be allowed him. We regard this as a proof that a man may speak out honestly and fearlessly what is in him, without losing reputation, or endangering his success as a writer. In fact, the American public are prepared for discussions altogether freer than the conductors of the press seem to imagine.

Let the American press but assert its freedom, and enter freely and fully into all the great questions we have raised, and it will do not a little to advance the education of the people. It must be free; it must address itself to the mind of the community, and labor incessantly to quicken thought, and direct it to the solution of the problem of human destiny. It must not dogmatize, must not seek to establish a creed, but to throw what light it can on all questions of interest to man or society, to elicit discussion, and induce the people to find out truth for themselves. It will be well also for the people to bear in mind, that, if they are to have the advantages of a free press, they must tolerate great latitude of discussion that they must not withhold their support from a periodical because it now and then puts forth an heterodox opinion. Perhaps the periodical's heterodoxy, upon closer examination, may turn out to be wholesome orthodoxy. Who knows? "Prove all things; hold fast that which is good" [1 Thess 5:21].

These are some of the means which we possess for educating the people. Let these be judiciously and faithfully employed, and it will matter but little what the schools are. The most that can be asked of our schools is simply instruction in the art of reading and writing, and in the positive sciences. To them we may look for instruction, but never should we rely on them for education. The community can never be educated in schools, technically so called; they can be educated only by the free action of mind on mind. Whatever means we have for bringing mind to act on mind, so many means we have for educating the people. Let every man do what is in him to employ these means judiciously and effectively.

20.

DEMOCRACY AND REFORM[1]

Boston Quarterly Review 2 (October, 1839): 478-517

The first pamphlet on our list is a tract issued by a society for social reform in the city of New York, of which society we know nothing, and have no wish to know anything. We do not see any call for social reform societies. There are already so many associations for religious, social, and philanthropic objects that we can rarely find an individual with a sense of individual independence and responsibility. The pamphlet, however is respectable. We know nothing personally of its author, Mr. Townsend, but his address speaks well for his talent, acquirements, and philanthropic feelings. His views strike us as being in general just and well-timed.

The second pamphlet enumerated is from the pen of a young clergyman of great promise, and is written, for the most part, with rare beauty and power. It clearly defines and ably sustains the democratic principle. It, however, shuns all allusion to what may be considered democratic measures, and democratic men. Mr. Osgood, as a clergyman, may think that he is not required to take a very decided party stand, but he seems to recommend on principle all wise and good men to keep as much aloof from party as possible. He appears to adopt for his motto, "principles—not measures, nor men."

The third pamphlet is from a plain, self-made democrat, who makes no pretensions to literary culture. But his Address is written with great clearness and force, and is an eloquent and able vindication of the principles and measures of the Democratic party. Mr.

[1] [Ed. Review of Robert Townsend's *An Inquiry into the Cause of Social Evil; with its Remedy. A Inaugural Address. Delivered July 8, 1839* (New York, 1839); Samuel Osgood's *An Oration, delivered on the 4th of July, 1839* (Nashua: Allen Beard, 1839); Seth J. Thomas' *An Address, delivered before the Democratic Citizens of Plymouth County, Mass., at East Abington, July 4, 1839* (Boston: Beals & Greene, 1839); and John P. Tarbell's *An Oration, delivered before the Democratic Citizens of the North part of Middlesex County, at Groton, July 4, 1839* (Lowell: Abijah Watson, 1839). Townsend (c.1807-43) was a member of Tammany Society in New York and as a house carpenter he became actively involved in the Workingmen's party after the 1829 elections. Osgood (1812-80) was a Unitarian minister and Transcendentalist who edited the *Western Messenger* for 1836 and 1837. Thomas (1785-1859) was a Connecticut clock manufacturer who supported the cause of workingmen. I was unable to identify Tarbell.]

Thomas possesses a strong mind, is a sound logician, and is fitted to be a popular political writer.

Mr. Tarbell's oration is also a defense of the democratic principles and measures. It is sound in its doctrine, and in some passages genuinely eloquent. Mr. Tarbell is a young man who somewhat distinguished himself last winter as a member of our General Court. As a writer he wants practice. His oration smacks too much of the strained, the affected style, for which Fourth of July orations have been but too remarkable. He will do much more honor to himself by cherishing a severer taste, and adopting a simpler style of oratory. Homer, we have heard it said, was not less remarkable for simplicity, than for sublimity. Our American writers are too apt to get on stilts, which makes them appear rather awkward. The truly great man goes calmly to his work, is always self-possessed, always unaffected, and able to breathe an air of repose, of quiet dignity over all his productions.

All these pamphlets show that their authors belong to the movement party and that they are looking forward with the eye of hope to great and important changes in man's social condition; and what has pleased us even more than this is the fact that whatever meliorations of society they may anticipate or struggle for, they evidently expect them from the more perfect application of Christian principles to man's social and political relations. They all apparently cherish the conviction that democracy is nothing but the political application of Christianity; and not one of them seems to dream of hitching the car of reform on to that of infidelity. This to us is a cheering fact, a proof that our social reformers are beginning to take juster views of religion, and that the friends of religion are beginning to feel more deeply that their faith requires them to labor for man's earthly well-being.

Some ten or twelve years ago, there were indications that the cause of social reform in this country would be connected with that of disbelief in the gospel. The attention of the American people was first seriously called to the defects of all existing social organizations, and to the importance and duty of laboring for social progress, by Robert Owen, his son Robert Dale Owen, Miss Frances Wright, and others, whose shallow philosophy was represented in the "Free Enquirer," and the "Lectures on Knowledge."[2] The Owens and Miss

[2] [Ed. Robert Owen (1771-1858) promoted social utopian communities at Nashoba, Tennessee and New Harmony in Indiana, and his son Robert Dale Owen (1801-77), was co-editor of the *Free Enquirer* with Frances Wright and like her supported radical ideas on the education of children, on marriage, and on the rights of workingmen, believing that the ills of society were caused by the institutions of property, marriage, and religion.]

Wright produced a profound sensation; they quickened many a young heart, and recalled enthusiasm to many an old man, who had fondly dreamed that his labors for this world were over. They were the immediate occasion of the workingmen's movements, which took place in various parts of the country, cheering some and alarming others; and they have contributed not a little to that general examination into the actual state of American society, which has been for some time going on amongst us. This is the good side of their influence. But unhappily, these generous and philanthropic foreigners had no just appreciation of the gospel, and assigned no place to religion in the new order of things they sought to bring about. They considered religion, even in its purity, a vulgar superstition, they looked upon it as favoring priestcraft and tyranny, and as hostile to all exertions for the improvement of society. They wished to brush it out of the way, recall men from the contemplation of another world, compel them to limit their hopes and affections to the narrow compass of this life, so that their attention should not be distracted from their earthly dwelling, and so that they might be left free to labor for its embellishment. The world, said they, lies waste; society is infested with noxious weeds, overgrown with thistles and brambles, because men have neglected this world for another. They must, therefore, leave the world after death, cease to be amused with dreams of paradise, or alarmed by dreams of tophet,[3] and think only of making the earth the abode of peace, love, and happiness.

This was their doctrine and there was apparently some danger that it would spread further than the safety of the commonwealth would permit. The Owens and Miss Wright did not oppose religion on its own account. They disdained to concern themselves with so vulgar a subject. It became worthy of their opposition, only inasmuch as it appeared to them to be an impediment to the social progress they were desirous of realizing. But, there were others amongst us, who were opposed to what they called religion, on its own account. They were infidels rather than social reformers. They believed in disbelief, and had a creed to propagate. Such were the late leader of the Free Enquirers in this city and his more prominent friends.[4] These men saw the strong democratic tendency of the American people, and fancied that if they could bring about a union between infidelity

[3] [Ed. In the Old Testament, tophet was a place in the Valley of Hinnom, near Jerusalem, where the Jews were said to sacrifice their children to Moloch. The place was later used for burning refuse. Figuratively, it refers to a place of endless perdition.]

[4] [Ed. Brownson is more than likely referring to Abner Kneeland.]

and radical democracy, they should be able, by means of the popularity of the democracy, to make infidelity triumph. Here was a deep laid scheme; and there were many things, which seemed to favor its success. Most of the champions of the people in the old world had been, and were at war with religious establishments; the French democrats, with La Fayette at their head, were claimed to a man to be infidels. In our own country, the father of American democracy, Thomas Jefferson, was looked upon as an unbeliever; Washington's orthodoxy was said to be questionable; the elder Adams was at best a heretic, and Franklin, in early life, an infidel, and there was no proof that he had ever changed his opinions. Add to this, the clergy, especially the clergy of New England and of the more influential sects, were pretty generally found on the side against the democracy. They had opposed Jefferson, they had opposed Madison and the War, and were at best indifferent to the subject of social progress. From these facts, it was not worse logic than often obtains to infer, on the one hand, that, to be thorough-going democrats, we must be infidels, and on the other hand, to be thorough-going Christians, we must uphold social abuses.

But happily the dark cloud has passed or is now passing away. The reformers are now pretty generally coming to the conclusion that infidelity is a mere negative force, and can effect no solid, enduring reform; and that Christianity, originally taught by a carpenter's son, and, under the providence of God, propagated by fishermen and tent-makers, declaring all men equal in the sight of God, and, therefore, equal to one another, so far from tending to uphold social abuses, commands us, with all the authority of God, to labor for the elevation of the masses, and permits us to hope for heaven only on the ground that we have fed the hungry, given drink to the thirsty, clothed the naked, visited the sick, and unloosed the captive. Christianity is the very creed of the reformer; its spirit is the spirit of reform itself; and the unbelievers who are laboring for a reform, are unconsciously obeying it.

We consider this a great gain. It is a result that we have been many years laboring, apparently almost alone, to bring about, and we can but rejoice that in this direction our labors are no longer needed. By understanding that the social reformer, the friend of the "largest liberty," may also be the truest and most pious Christian, we do away with an antagonism, which has heretofore been injurious to both religion and social progress. We effect by this a union from which we may look for the noblest offspring. We bring the whole force of the religious sentiment, the strongest sentiment in our nature, and the source, or the ally of all our generous and disinterested affections—we bring the whole force of this sentiment, and the whole authority of the church, to strengthen the reformer; while we bring the whole force of our love of freedom, our desire to perfect social institutions, of the whole democratic movement of the age, to the aid of religion and the church. It is, in fact, a sort of realization of the atonement, a bringing together, if we may so speak, of God and man. It unites the instinct of a Deity with the instinct of humanity, and gives us the God-man, in whom is redemption from all sin.

The reconciliation between Christians and reformers is now virtually effected. Religion is taking a social direction, and reform is becoming spiritual. On the side of progress, and especially social progress, we see the most advanced philosophy of the age, and the noblest creations of literature. Philosophy, literature, art, religion, all with us, are enlisting in the service of the democracy. This is well. It is encouraging to the true philanthropist. But, there is a still further reconciliation, which we wish to see brought about. We wish to see the union consummated between the reformers and the Democratic party, so called. We contend and it is the purpose of this article to prove that it is the interest and the duty of the friends of progress, in whatever direction, to unite cordially with the Democratic party, so called, and to give it all the support in their power. The ends they have in view, so far as they are practicable, will be obtained by so doing, and they can obtain them by no other method.

It is not pretended by anybody that all who are contending for the progress of humanity act with the Democratic party. There is among us a large number of educated and intelligent men, who have outgrown the old-fashioned Federalism, in which they were reared. These men now take broad and generous views of human nature; they have protested against old forms, against conventionalisms and factitious distinctions, which make enemies of brethren; they have seen the necessity, and believe in the practicability of great social meliorations; but they cannot bring themselves to cooperate with the Democratic party. They have been accustomed, from their earliest life, to look upon it as made up of a disorderly rabble, led on by unprincipled demagogues, and they cannot stoop to enter its ranks. They like the democratic principles, claim to be thorough-going democrats themselves, and would be much hurt, should we deny them the democratic name; they even like, and some of them profess to approve, the more prominent and leading measures of the Democratic party; but then the democratic men, the men, what pureminded, philanthropic, enlightened, disinterested Christian and patriot can associate with them? A difficult question no doubt to answer. But, we apprehend, a little more intimate acquaintance with the democratic men, would soften this repugnance somewhat. Furthermore, with the most profound respect for these men, we must suggest that their democratic progress has not been quite so great as they fancy. The Democratic party embraces the majority of the people of the United States. To complain of the party as these men do, is but saying that the majority of the people of the United States are unworthy to be the party associates of a man of respectability. This is not very complimentary, and we suspect they who say so still retain a considerable portion of the leaven of the Pharisees, of which they would do well to get rid as soon as possible. And lastly, if the Democratic party is composed of such a worthless rabble, there is but so much the greater necessity that these good and wise men should enter its ranks, so that it may have some virtue whereof to boast. If all good men keep aloof from the party, is it possible that it should be composed entirely of good men and true?

We are aware that we have many excellent men among us, who entertain a most lively repugnance to party, and party action. We ourselves, without claiming either matchless wisdom or immaculate virtue, have all our life long declaimed against party. But a little practical acquaintance with the affairs of the world, and some reflection on the laws which control the action of society, have finally convinced us that whatever be our aversion to party, parties are inevitable, and will be till all men become perfect, or until a uniformity of opinion is brought about by means of absolute despotism. Doubtless, no man should seek party for party's sake; but whoso would take a part with his fellowmen in the management of what concerns the public good, must act with a party, unless he fancies himself capable of constituting, in himself alone, a party strong enough to cope with all existing parties.

Parties are not arbitrary creations. They are called forth and sustained by higher laws than any of human enactment. They are inseparable from the imperfect development of humanity, and will ever be a source of complaint to those who think more of the end to be gained, than of the power which is created in struggling to gain an end. It was the will of Providence to make man an imperfect being, to give him his point of departure in weakness and ignorance. As an indemnity for this, he gave him the capacity for illimitable progress. Parties grow, on the one hand, out of this imperfection, and on the other, out of the unfolding of this capacity. Society, in its various institutions, is but the reflex of human nature. Contemplated at any given epoch, it merely marks the point to which the progress of humanity has attained. It must, therefore, at any given epoch, fall just as far short of perfection, as human nature at that epoch falls short of its complete development. A portion of every community will be more alive to this imperfection than the rest, and also more confident in the power of human nature to advance. These will constitute a movement party, or party of the future; the rest of the community, either satisfied with things as they are, or destitute of faith in man's power of progress, will constitute the stationary or stand-still party. In some epochs, in some countries, the first of these parties will be in a feeble minority; in others, it will be in a majority, as it is at present in this country. The first of these parties with us is called the Democratic party, the other is denominated the Whig party. These two parties have existed among us from the first settlement of our country; and analogous parties may be found in every country that possesses freedom enough to allow of any mental activity. We must accept them, or abandon our freedom.

The Democratic party is, no doubt, an imperfect embodiment of the great idea of progress. Nobody pretends that it is faultless. It would be saying not a little for the American people, to say that the majority of them constitute a party, which has not a single fault. It would also be virtually saying that we have no further progress to make that we have realized the idea of our institutions, finished our work, and have nothing before us, but to die. The Democratic party, doubtless, partakes of all the faults of the country, and shares in all the imperfections which belong to our stage in the general progress of humanity; but it represents what is most advanced in our condition. Its virtues are always the living virtues of the times, and its intelligence that which reaches farthest into the future and which is to be for the longest time to come the dominant intelligence. The virtues of its enemies will be always the virtues which were most in repute yesterday, and its intelligence that which was novel, and truly admirable in our fathers.

But our friends, with whom we are at this moment engaged, doubt much of this, and tell us that, although they do not like to be enrolled in the stand-still party, or, if you please, the party of yesterday, they cannot consent to join the Democratic party. It is too coarse, too vulgar. It wants refinement, elevation, high moral aims, and disinterested affections. Let us have, say they, a third party, composed of virtuous and enlightened men, who will labor for the public good, without any reference to their own interest. This is very fine. Who would not like to be a member of such a party? But on what principle shall we call forth such a party? What shall be its watch-word, its rallying cry? You can call forth a third party only when there is some great and pressing interest, which the two existing parties neglect. Is there such an interest in this country? If so, what is it? If this interest relate to progress, then it is an interest for the Democratic party to take up, and if that party has not yet taken it up, what should be the inference, but that the country is not yet prepared to act upon it? If it be an interest opposed to progress, there is already your stand-still party, your Whig party, to espouse it. If the question concern merely its discussion, it can be discussed in the bosom of that existing party, whose general principles embrace it, and it will not cost more time or trouble to bring that party, as a party, to act on it, than it will to raise up a new party, sufficiently large to act on it with effect.

Moreover, we wish to be informed whence we are to obtain all these excellent men, who are to make up our third party. If the third party be but a minority, it will not be able to accomplish much. If the two parties now existing are so corrupt as to render a third necessary, whence can we obtain good men enow to constitute a party, which shall embrace a majority of the people of the United States? We are speaking to reformers, who, of course, wish their third party to be a party of progress. Its recruits, then, must be taken from the Democratic party, as the members of the Whig party are not in favor of progress. So, if your third party rise to a majority, it will be little else than the present Democratic party under a new name. Will a change of name change its character? Judging from what we know of our Whig friends, who have had considerable experience in this matter of changing names, we should infer not.

A few years ago there was organized amongst us what was called the Workingmen's party. We know something of that party for we were among its earliest friends and supporters, and have made some sacrifices for it. So far as it raised up certain questions for discussion, and so far as it called the attention of our countrymen more immediately to the interests and rights of labor, it was not without its results. But, where is the party now? Has it failed because its leaders betrayed it, because the American people have reprobated its doctrines, or because there was not virtue and intelligence enough in the laboring classes to sustain it? Not at all. No party is or ever can be betrayed by its leaders, if it have a living principle for its basis. When a Benedict Arnold undertakes to betray the cause of American liberty, he merely betrays himself, and obtains everlasting infamy. Your Washingtons always arrive in time to prevent the threatened mischief, and to disconcert all the plans of the traitor. The cause of American liberty goes on, conquering and to conquer, for it contains in itself the seminal principle of victory. Nor have the American people reprobated the doctrines put forth by the workingmen. So far as these doctrines were applicable to our present stage of development, they have been accepted, and do now constitute an integral portion of the democratic creed, as we may learn from the nickname, loco foco,[5] given to the democracy by their enemies. Nor have the workingmen failed for the want of sufficient virtue and intelligence to sustain a party. They yield to no portion of our population in either. It is no rare thing to find an ordinary mechanic able to refute Mr. Webster's "Great Speech" on the currency question.[6] The true cause of failure should be sought in the fact that there was no general and permanent demand for such a party. The population, which could be enlisted in such a party, were not numerous enough to make it sufficiently powerful to accomplish anything. Its doctrines, so far as they were true and immediately practicable, were parallel with those of the Democratic party. The few social abuses which gave rise to the party were of a local nature, and were scarcely felt out of our cities and large towns. Few, therefore, could be drawn into the party, except journeyman mechanics, and, in fact, but a small portion of these. But, could all these have been enlisted, they would have constituted but a feeble minority, compared with the whole population of the country. The great body of the agricultural population was not to be enlisted. These constituted the main portion of the Democratic party, so called. They were democrats, but democrats in the sense in which the party itself was democratic. They had not outgrown their party, and could not outgrow it; for being, as it were, the party itself, that must needs advance just in proportion as they advanced. The agricultural population, therefore, could see no necessity of separating from the Democratic party for the purpose of uniting with the journeymen mechanics of the towns. If they approved the measures contended for by the mechanics, they could support them without leaving their party, or deserting the principles, which constituted its basis. Here is the true

[5] [Ed. Loco foco was the name given to radical democrats of New York City because at a meeting in 1835 they used locofoco matches to light candles for their meeting when conservatives in the group turned off the gas that had lighted Tammany Hall.]

[6] [Ed. Brownson is referring to Daniel Webster's (1782-1852) *Mr. Webster's Speech on the Currency, and on the New Plan for Collecting and Keeping the Public Moneys. Delivered in the Senate of the United States, September 28, 1837* (Washington: Printed by Gales and Seaton, 1837).]

cause of the failure of the Workingmen's party, as a party. Similar causes will always be found to check the growth of every third party which comes up. Its doctrines and measures must needs be, in this country, parallel with those of one or the other of the two existing parties, with which they will very soon become coincident. The workingmen are now an integral portion of the Democratic party if they did but know it, and a separate party organization is out of the question.

The reformers, then, whether we mean the workingmen, or the other class of whom we have spoken, must see, it strikes us, the utter inutility and impracticability of attempting to raise up a third party. A third party is not wanted. Nothing can be gained by means of such a party, which cannot be gained just as well without it. And, moreover, it is utterly impossible to raise up such a party that shall last for any length of time, or be powerful enough to effect anything. The proper course is for both of these classes to join and support one or the other of the two existing parties.

We are addressing ourselves to reformers, to men, who profess to believe in progress, and to be desirous of laboring in the holy cause of social melioration. Can they hesitate, which party to join, when the alternative is to join one or the other of the two existing parties? We have no disposition to speak disparagingly of the Whig party. In that party are many men whom we are proud to reckon among our personal friends. We freely acknowledge that it embodies much talent, and not a little private worth. But every party, if it be worth considering, has a set of principles, which it must develop, and which it is compelled, by the laws of Providence, to push to their last consequences. These principles are stronger than individuals. They carry away individuals in spite of themselves. There is an invincible logic, which conquers the stubbornest will. He, who refuses to go where the principles of his party lead, is inevitably left by the way, and he, who steps before his party to arrest its onward career, is swept away by a resistless current, or trampled in the dust by a thousand feet. To judge of a party, you need not to inquire what are the private virtues of the individuals which compose it, but, what are the principles on which it is founded, the idea around which it rallies, and which it is its mission to realize. This idea, nakedly presented, may be repudiated by a large portion of the party, few of the party may comprehend it, or will its realization; nevertheless, they must all obey it, and nearly all will ultimately adopt its last consequences.

The idea of the Whig party in this country is of yesterday, not of today, far less of tomorrow. The party is the anti-progress party. Its doctrines were doctrines of progress once, but they are not now. They were proper, once, to be supported, and were the doctrines of the movement party. In the progress of humanity, there was a period, when it was necessary to bring up the interests of what may be termed commercial capital, against landed capital, which was almost exclusively possessed by an hereditary and titled nobility. Then the Whig party was the party of progress; and where it is still necessary to break down an aristocracy founded on the rights of birth and the sword, and monopolizing the greater part of the soil, the Whig party is even now the party of progress, because its principles are the proper antagonist of the principles of such an aristocracy. Hence, in England, in 1688, and subsequently, the true friends of progress sided with the Whigs, because the Whigs were against the old hereditary, landed aristocracy of the kingdom. They supported the Bank, the Funds, the Merchants, and the East India Company. But their doctrines were tolerable only for a time, only so long as it was necessary to humble the landed or military aristocracy.

Now this state of things has never existed with us, and never can exist here. The English nobleman, or rather the old feudal baron is represented in this country, it is true, but he is represented by the American farmer, whose estate is so cut up and parceled out among his brother barons that he no longer possesses any undue preponderance in the commonwealth. The capital invested in the soil has with us not even its legitimate share of influence. The commercial capital, the capital employed in business operations, is the preponderating power. To give it additional weight, is, therefore, to war against the true interests of humanity. The party, which labors to do this, is not, and cannot be, in this country, the party of progress. But the leading idea of the Whig party is the preponderance of commercial capital. As the old English Whigs supported the Bank of England, so they support the Bank of the United States; as the old English Whigs supported the merchants, corporations, funding systems, so our American Whigs support the same. The American Whigs possess the larger portion of the commercial capital of the country, and they contend that, therefore, they ought to control the government of the country. They ask, with the celebrated Addison, in his "Whig-Examiner,"[7] is there anything more reasonable, than that they, who have

[7] [Ed. Joseph Addison (1672-1719), English essayist and poet, was editor of the *Whig Examiner* in 1712 and also of *The Spectator*, originally issued from March 1, 1711 to December 6, 1712, and June 18 to December 20, 1714. For a reprint, see *The Spectator*, 10 vols. (Boston: Hastings, Etheredge and Bliss, 1809-10).]

all the riches of the nation in their possession, or that they, who have already *engrossed* all our riches, should have the management of our public treasure, and the direction of our fleets and armies?" This question might be very proper if our work were to put down an aristocracy founded on birth and the sword, like the old feudal aristocracy; but it indicates the worst possible system, here, where our work is to raise up man, and give him the preeminence over money.

The Whig party also is a foreign party, and anti-American in its principles. Its policy and movements are necessarily controlled, not by a regard to true American interests, but by a regard to the interests of the "credit system," which the party is wedded to, of which the Bank of England is the common center, and whose ramifications extend to all parts of the globe. By commerce and manufactures, by their various business operations which are carried on mainly by means of credits, they are intimately connected with this system, and virtually enslaved by it. We should be asking more than our knowledge of the weakness of human nature warrants, were we to ask them, in case of collision between this "credit system" and their country, to be faithful to the latter. Where a man's treasure is, there will be his heart also.[8] Their treasure is in the "credit system," the principal seat of which is not in this country; consequently their hearts are abroad, rather than at home. So long as the "credit system" is controlled by foreign nations, or in other words, so long as our country is not the first commercial nation of the world, support of the system must be incompatible with patriotism. England is, at present, the ruling commercial nation; she controls the credit system, so far as it can be controlled; and consequently controls all who are dependent on it. In case of collision between this country and Great Britain, during the existence of the "credit system," we must always look to see all true Whigs sustaining Great Britain, as its grand supporter, although her "cannon should be battering down the walls of our Capitol," resolving that it is unbecoming a moral and religious people to rejoice at American victories over her armies, and singing Te Deums,[9] whenever her mercenaries succeed in suppressing the democratic movements of the Old World. We must expect them to do this, for the system they have espoused will compel them to do it; and they will do it spontaneously, religiously, with the feeling that in so doing they are honoring God, and serving man. Whiggism with us is, there-

[8] [Matt. 6:21; Luke 12:34.]

[9] [Ed. *Te Deum* is a famous early Christian Latin hymn to God the Father and the Son. The origins of the hymn are obscure, but its use was already prescribed in the Rule of St. Benedict in the early sixth century.]

fore, incompatible with patriotism. The Whig virtually expatriates himself, or rather, forswearing the land of his birth, adopts the "credit system" as his country, makes it his home, in it erects his altar, and places his household gods. When that system coincides with American principles, he is an American; when they do not, he is an Englishman, a Frenchman, a Chinaman, or one of that nation with whose interests for the time being they chance to be coincident.

Mr. Biddle,[10] who is not altogether destitute of patriotic feelings, had, we apprehend, a glimpse of this fact, and hence his efforts to transfer the seat of the credit system from London to Philadelphia. He probably dreamed of making the American merchants, through the Bank of the United States, all that English merchants now are through the Bank of England. This was a lofty ambition, only a single remove from the sublime. All that was wanting for its complete success was that this country should stand first in the scale of commercial nations, a rank it unfortunately does not hold, and will not, for some considerable time to come. So long as this country is only a second or third-rate commercial nation, it cannot be the principal seat of the "credit system." So long as it retains its present position in relation to Great Britain, a Bank of the United States can only be a branch of the Bank of England. The Bank of England, as the great center of the credit system of the world, can, at any moment it chooses, ruin the credit of American merchants, and crush our whole banking system, as past experience fully demonstrates. By the intimate connection, which has heretofore existed between the fiscal concerns of our government, and the general business of banking, we have, government and all, been virtually under the control of Great Britain. Hence, the reason why, whenever we have demanded justice of Great Britain, we have uniformly armed our business men against our own government. The war, which we have been carrying on against the banking system for the last ten years, has been really a war for national independence, and General Jackson, in warring against the Bank, was fighting in the same cause in which he fought at New Orleans, and against the same enemy. It was therefore that the people, by an unerring instinct, selected him, the hero of New Orleans, to be their chief in the new campaigns, of which they had a forefeeling.

The Whig party is also the anti-Christian party. We mean not by this that all Whigs reject Christianity, but that Whiggism embraces certain principles, which the party are developing, and which they will, if

[10] [Ed. Nicholas Biddle (1786-1844) from Philadelphia was government director of the Second Bank of the United States and then president of that bank in 1822.]

they meet with no counteracting force from without, push to their last results; and that these principles do necessarily involve the rejection of our holy religion, and can end in nothing short of infidelity and universal skepticism. This is ascertained from the Whig doctrines on the origin and nature of government, on the origin of ideas, and on the grounds of faith.

The Christian doctrine is that government is of divine origin and rests for its legitimacy on the authority of God. This, we take it, is the meaning of that famous passage of St. Paul, "the powers that be are ordained of God" [Rom 13:1]. The Apostle, we apprehend, was not so much intent on asserting the divine appointment of the then or any actually ruling magistrates, as on asserting the divine institution of government itself, as the foundation of the virtue of loyalty, which he was enforcing. According to Christianity, man is bound to obey no authority, but that of God; consequently, he can owe allegiance to no earthly government, unless it be of divine ordination. Either, then, give up the duty of obedience, and consequently, all government, or assert that government is of divine origin. It is oppression, it is rank tyranny, to compel me to obey my fellowman. To this as a Christian I will not submit, for I have but one master, and he is in heaven. Consequently all governments resting on human authority are illegitimate, are usurpations; their acts are not, and cannot be, laws; and, therefore, they can never have the right to demand, much less to coerce, obedience.

On this ground, which, if we rightly comprehend it, is that of the most perfect freedom, the whole Christian church has ever taken its stand. The Catholic Church has always taught the princes that they have no right to reign in their own name, but that they must reign as the servants, the deputies of God. Bossuet thundered in the ears of the "Grand Monarque" himself that kings reign only by the authority which they receive from God, and are as much bound to obey God, as the meanest of their subjects.[11] King James, in his Remonstrance for the Right of Kings, is merely defending the divine right of civil government against the exclusive claims of the Pope in favor of the church.[12] He would merely show that kings receive their crowns from as high and as sacred a source as the bishops do their miters. The great idea which was in the minds of the advocates of the

[11] [Ed. Jacques Bénigne Bossuet (1627-1704) was a French Catholic bishop of Meaux (1681). Brownson may be referring to the bishop's well known position on the divine right of kings or specifically to Bossuet's *Art of Governing* (1709), a classic statement on the divine right of kings theory.]

[12] [Ed. Brownson is referring to James I (1566-1625), king of England (1603-25), who like Bossuet, was well known for his defense of the divine right of kings in his *The True Law of Free Monarchies* (1598) and *Basilikon Doron* (1599).]

divine right of kings, and of passive obedience, who fill so much space in the history of England during the seventeenth century and the first part of the eighteenth, was that mere human authority is not obligatory on man, that allegiance to a king is due only on the ground that he is the representative of the will of God. They dared not declare the king's will the law, and teach men that they were bound to obey it. The king was to be obeyed only as the lieutenant of the Almighty; consequently God only was in reality acknowledged as the sovereign. This, at the moment, was supposed to favor the doctrine of absolutism, and to clothe the tyrant with divine authority. In this sense it was urged. It was, no doubt, urged against subjects, in favor of kings; but who sees not that it may be urged with equal force against kings, in favor of the people? Government is of divine appointment; and because it is of divine appointment, you are bound to obey it; therefore, obey the king. Stop there, if you please. We admit your premises, but deny your conclusion. We believe government is a divine ordinance, and that we are bound to obey God; but prove to us that the king is God's lieutenant, that God speaks through him, for this is not quite so clear to us. But be this as it may, that civil government is of divine origin, and is, for this reason, and this reason alone, obligatory, endowed with the right to exact obedience, is the great idea, which lies at the bottom of the doctrines of the divine right of kings and passive obedience, and of their apparent antipodes, the Fifth Monarchy men in England, Samuel Gorton, Roger Williams, and others, in our early colonial days, and the Non-Resistants and No-Government men of our own times.[13] This doctrine,

[13] [Ed. The "Fifth Monarchy Men" were a seventeenth century radical British sect whose members aimed to bring in the Fifth Monarchy of Daniel 2:44, but after unsuccessful revolts in 1657 and 1661 the leaders were executed and the sect died out. Samuel Gorton (c. 1592-1677) was a British born radical who came to Massachusetts and whose heterodoxy, religious and political, got him in trouble with authorities there. Roger Williams (c. 1603-83) was the founder of Rhode Island and a primary advocate of religious liberty against the prevailing notions of church-state relations. By non-resistants Brownson is probably referring to the New England Non-Resistance Society, founded 20 September 1838, which was a radical Christian pacifist society whose members pledged conscientious objection to military service, no service in offices that executed penal law, no voting for politicians whose authority derived from physical force, no capital punishment, and non-violent resistance to civil laws that were unjust or unchristian. William Lloyd Garrison was a prime mover behind the establishment of the society. The no-government men were more than likely radical abolitionists and others who were beginning to speak of obedience to the inner higher law over the status quo laws of the state. Many of the radical abolitionists were also members of the Non-Resistance Society.]

however it may have been perverted to the purposes of tyranny, or anarchy, is in fact the only solid and enduring ground, on which government can be established, for it is the only ground, on which the legitimacy of government can be maintained, and disloyalty made a crime *in foro conscientia.*[14] It is also the only ground on which freedom can be safely rested; for freedom consists, not in the absence of restraint, but in being subjected to no restraint but the will of God.

Let no one start at the doctrine we here put forth. We all feel that the word of God is our supreme law. This word is truth, is justice, is love, whatever we conceive of the highest. How it has been or may be uttered, we do not now inquire. Whether it has pealed in thunders from heaven upon the ears of startled humanity, and been caught up and recorded in a book, or whether it has sounded out in that voice, which comes to us from all nature, declaring its wondrous beauty and harmony, and revealing the law by which it is governed, or whether it has been whispered to the soul in its moments of quiet, in the still small voice of conscience; or whether it has been, as we believe, uttered in all these ways, is foreign to our present purpose. God is the Creator of the universe, he is its sovereign, and his word, whether speaking through hierarchies, monarchies, aristocracies, democracies, inspired prophets, or the reason with which we are endowed, is our supreme law, and obedience to this, and this alone, is freedom. No man feels that he is oppressed because he is bound to conform to truth, to obey justice, to be holy; and to conform to truth, to obey justice, to be holy, is precisely what is meant, if we understand ourselves, by obedience to the will of God.

Now Whiggism denies the divine origin of government. It gives it a human origin, and founds it on contract, a bargain, wherein it is stipulated by the magistrates, of the first party that they will rule, govern, command the people, and by the people, of the second party that they will consent to be ruled, governed, and commanded by the aforesaid magistrates of the first party. The idea of a contract, whatever may be its terms, evidently assigns to government a human origin, and admits no authority above that of man. Government demands loyalty, but loyalty is due only to that which is above us. How, then, can we be loyal towards a government, which is the work of our own hands, and which originates in a bargain, which we ourselves have made?

This doctrine of the mere human origin of government was introduced into England by Hobbes, if we remember aright, and it was

[14] [Ed. Latin for "before the tribunal of conscience."]

taken up and enlarged upon by John Locke, the apostle and philosopher of Whiggism. Hobbes regarded man merely as susceptible of pain and pleasure, and assigned him no other rule of morality than that of seeking the last and avoiding the first. He talks of a state of nature, prior to the institution of civil society, in which all men are equal; and which, in consequence of this equality among men, is a state of war. The design of civil society is to put an end to this war, and maintain a state of peace. As war is the greatest of evils, so peace is the greatest of blessings, and cannot be purchased at too high a price. Mankind become convinced of this, and institute civil government, and surrender to it all their natural rights, clothe it with absolute power that it may preserve them thenceforth in a state of peace. Locke's idea is similar. He contends, with Hobbes, for a state of nature, regards it as a state of war, and supposes that men, by a voluntary and deliberate act, instituted civil government. In instituting this government, he supposes the people gave up a certain portion of their rights to government that they might enjoy the rest in peace and safety. He is less liberal to government than Hobbes, for he does not allow the surrender of *all* our rights, only in fact as many as are necessary to clothe the government with the requisite power to fulfil its functions. But government, according to him, has no authority, but what is derived from the terms of the original bargain. Its rights are merely the rights of individuals, voluntarily surrendered to it. This makes it of mere human authority. Obedience to government, then, is obedience to a human power. According to this theory, I am obliged to obey man, which is slavery, instead of God, as Christianity teaches, which is freedom.

But in their doctrine on the origin of ideas, the Whig party are still further removed from Christianity. Christianity requires a belief in a supersensual world, a world of reality, which lies back of the world of merely sensible forms and logical deductions. By the senses, we look out upon the material world; but if we have no eye by which we can look in upon the world of reason, and take cognizance of God and duty, Christianity has for us no certain ground of evidence, and its truth is in no way perceptible. The world, it professes to reveal, it does not reveal, because there is nothing in us, which can perceive it. The Christian, talking to us of his spiritual world, is as one talking of colors to a man born blind.

Now, what is the Whig doctrine on the origin of ideas? Hobbes and Locke are here again our authority. They are the politicians of the Whigs, and their politics grow out of their metaphysics. Hobbes assigns man two faculties, force and cognition. The cognitive faculty is merely sensation; for he admits no source of knowledge but the senses. Hence his nominalism, his denial of the reality of all abstract ideas. General, universal, eternal, infinite, are in his philosophy mere words, which serve to abridge discourse, but which name no realities. Locke's doctrine is but a modification of the same. Locke allows two sources of knowledge, sensation and reflection. From sensation we derive all our primary ideas, on which reflection subsequently acts. Through the senses we receive notices of the external world merely. Reflection adds to these notices simply a knowledge of the mind's own operations. According to Locke, therefore, we can take cognizance of no existences, but those of the external world, and ourselves. We can, then, have no knowledge of the world Christianity professes to reveal. That world is neither ourselves, nor the external world. Nor can it be a deduction of logic from either. Logic can deduce from the data furnished it, only what those data contain. External nature and ourselves are evidently both finite. They, then, neither of them, nor both of them, contain the infinite. Then the infinite cannot be deduced from them. Then, for us, the infinite does not exist. Then Christianity, as a professed revelation of the infinite, can receive no faith from us.

This is the inevitable result, if we start with Hobbes and Locke. Hobbes was aware of this, and scarcely disguises it. Locke, who was a man of some religious feeling, and never disposed to push matters to extremes, does not appear to have perceived it. He was a religious man, and professed faith in Christianity; but he pared his faith down to the smallest point compatible with any faith at all. He disrobed our religion of all its mysteries; and in endeavoring to show it *reasonable,* endeavored to make it, as he had government, a mere human authority; for in his philosophy reason is human, not the word of God, "which was in the beginning, which was with God, and which was God" [John 1:1]. He admitted another life, but asserted that we can have no proof of it, but an outward revelation, authenticated by miracles addressed to the senses; and, though he did not assert the materiality of the soul, he thought it not unreasonable to suppose that God might confer on matter the power of thinking. Virtue with him was an empty name; pleasure the supreme good; and in his "Private Thoughts," he declares that the end, a man should always have in view, is the promotion of his own happiness.[15]

[15] [Ed. The reference is to Locke's *Essay Concerning Human Understanding,* Book 1, chapter 3, section 11.]

The consequences of this doctrine of Locke have been none of the best. On this point, Shaftesbury,[16] his friend and pupil, and also, under other relations, an eminent Whig, is good authority. "Although I honor infinitely," he says, "the other writings of Locke, whom I knew, and for whose sincere faith in Christianity I can answer, I am, nevertheless, forced to confess that he took the same route that Hobbes did, and that he has been followed by Tindal,[17] and other free thinkers of our times. It was Locke himself who struck the fatal blow, for the known character of Hobbes, and his slavish principles, by discrediting his philosophy, deprived it of its poison. But Locke struck the very basis of the edifice, *banished all order and all virtue from the world, placed out of nature ideas* which are intimately blended with those of the Divinity itself, and asserted that they had no foundation in the human mind."[18] In England, we know Locke has produced Tindal, Toland, Collins, Chubbs, Morgan, Mandeville, Woolston, Hume, Hartley, Dodwell, Darwin, Priestley, Belsham; in France, Voltaire, Condillac, Diderot, Helvetius, D'Holbach, Volney, and many others of nearly equal notoriety; and in this country, Norton and Palfrey.[19] Some of these, it is true, have professed, and no doubt en-

[16] [Ed. Anthony Ashley Cooper, Third Earl of Shaftesbury (1671-1713), was a deist politician and essayist whose most famous work was *Characteristicks of Men, Manners, Opinions, Times* (3 vols., 1711).]

[17] [Ed. Matthew Tindal (1655-1733) was a leading British deist whose *Christianity as old as the Creation, or the Gospel a Republication of the Religion of Nature* (1730) Brownson had read as a young man.]

[18] [Ed. This is a paraphrase of a passage from a letter written by Shaftesbury. See *The Life, Unpublished Letters, and Philosophical Regimen of Anthony, Earl of Shaftesbury*, ed. Benjamin Rand (New York: The MacMillan Co., 1900) Facsimile reprint, University Microfilms, Ann Arbor, MI, 1973, "To Michael Ainsworth (June 3rd, 1709)," 403.]

[19] [Ed. John Toland (1670-1722) was an Irish deist who lived in England and published *Christianity not Mysterious* (1696). Anthony Collins (1676-1729) was also a British deist who supported English freethinking in his famous *A Discourse of Freethinking* (1713). Thomas Chubb (1679-1747) was likewise a British deist, many of whose published works were read in colonial America, where Jonathan Edwards attacked his doctrine of free will. Brownson may be referring to the Welch deist Thomas Morgan (d. 1743) or to his son Sir Thomas Charles Morgan (1783-1843), both of whom tried to popularize deist ideas. Bernard Mandeville (1670-1733) was a British satirist most famous for his *The Fable of the Bees* (1723), describing all virtues as forms of selfishness. Thomas Woolston (1670-1733) was a British deist who attacked the Christian doctrines of the Virgin Birth and the Resurrection. David Hartley (1705-57) was a British philosopher, physician and psychologist who developed a theory of the association of sensations with sets of ideas. Henry Dodwell (d. 1784) was a British deist who achieved some fame with his *Christianity not Founded on Argument* (1742). The Darwin Brownson is referring to is probably Charles Darwin's grandfather Erasmus Darwin (1731-1802), an English phy-

tertained, a sort of faith in Christianity, and several of them, by virtue of one of those sublime inconsistencies, which do so much honor to human nature, have been generous defenders of liberty; but they have all denied us all intuition of a spiritual world, and most of them have questioned, or denied all existences, but such as fall under the senses. According to them all, we can have no certain knowledge of the truth of Christianity. Of what we are not certain we must doubt. Consequently, we must always doubt the truth of Christianity. We find this conclusion expressed in still stronger terms by an eminent ex-professor in the Theological School of Cambridge University, a firm adherent of Locke's philosophy, and as good authority as can be desired on its actual tendency. Mr. Norton, the gentleman of whom we speak, says, in his late publication, entitled "The Latest Form of Infidelity," "To the demand for certainty, let it come from whom it may, I answer that I know of no absolute certainty, beyond the limit of momentary consciousness, a certainty that vanishes the instant it exists, and is lost in the regions of metaphysical doubt. . . . There can be no intuition, no direct perception of the truth of Christianity."[20] This is strong language, plain and unequivocal; and it exhibits, we must needs think, not merely the "latest," but also a very old "form of Infidelity." There can be no direct perception of the truth of Christianity. There can, it seems, be no certainty, but that of momentary consciousness. Mr. Norton has not had even a momentary consciousness of the fact of the divine mission of Jesus; and if he could have had such a consciousness at any period of his life, it would have "vanished the instant it existed, and been lost in the regions of metaphysical doubt." But we have, and can have, no absolute certainty. Then all inquiry concerning the evidence of any subject resolves itself into a balancing of probabilities. Nay, how can we be sure that this or that is probable, if there be no certainty for us? If we say there

sician and poet. Thomas Belsham (1750-1829) was a British Unitarian who took over the pulpit of the Unitarian Joseph Priestley (1733-1804) when Priestley wentto the United States. Denis Diderot (1713-84) was a French Encyclopaedist and deist who gradually gave up belief in a deity. Constantin François Chasseboeuf, Comte de Volney (1757-1820) was a French deist, geographer, historian, social scientist and politician whose *Les Ruines, ou méditations sur les révolutions des empires* (1791) Brownson had read as a young man. Hume, Voltaire, Helvétius, d'Holbach, Norton and Palfrey were previously identified.]

[20] [Ed. Brownson is referring to Norton's *A Discourse on the Latest Form of Infidelity; delivered at the Request of the "Association of the Alumni of the Cambridge Theological School," on the 19th of July, 1839* (Cambridge, Mass.: John Owen, 1839; rpt. Port Washington, New York: Kennikat Press, 1971), 30, 32.]

can be no absolute certainty, we must accept universal skepticism, and go so far as even to

> Doubt, if it doubt itself be doubting.[21]

This anti-Christian character of the party in question will show itself, perhaps, still more clearly, if we advert to its doctrine on the grounds of faith. The Christian doctrine on the grounds of religious faith is that man, unassisted by the inspiration of the Almighty, is incapable of discovering the objects of religious faith; but, with the assistance of divine inspiration, which, to a certain extent, is vouchsafed to all men, he is able to perceive and know the objects, the spiritual realities of that world which Christianity professes to reveal. The soul has an eye, which looks in upon that world, by means of which it sees and knows it, as certainly as it knows the sensations produced in it by means of the objects of sense. The church implies this in its doctrine of experimental religion. It teaches us that, in experimental religion, we see and know the truth of Christianity. We do not merely believe the simple fact that there is a spiritual world, but we become acquainted with it, know it, even better than we know the world of sense. Ask the true Christian, if Christianity be true, and he answers, it is true, and he knows it is true, because he *feels* it is true. Hence it is that we are exhorted in Scripture, not merely to believe there is a God, but to make ourselves acquainted with him, and be at peace, and are assured that it is life eternal to know the only true God, and Jesus Christ, whom he hath sent. When the soul perceives the truths of religion, it knows them, and at once recognizes them as truths. It asks not for arguments to prove them. It has the witness within itself. There is a divinity within that receives the message which God sends, responds to it, and vouches for its truth. This we regard as the Christian doctrine, and it is, in substance, what has been the prevailing doctrine of the church, from its birth down to our own times.

But the party we are speaking of adopting Locke's philosophy, which denies that the human mind can take cognizance of any existences but those of the outward world and itself, necessarily denies that we can take any cognizance of the objects of religious faith. Those objects we cannot be acquainted with; they cannot even by Omnipotence be revealed to us, because we are endowed with no capacity to

[21] [Ed. The actual quotation, "doubt that doubt itself be doubting," is from George Gordon Byron's (1788-1824) *Don Juan* (1823), Canto ix, Stanza 17, Line 136, in *Lord Byron: The Complete Poetical Works*, ed. Jerome J. McGann, vol. 5 (Oxford: Clarendon, 1986).]

perceive them. Divine revelation does not make them known to us; it merely assures us that off in a world, of which we know nothing, such objects do really exist. The fact of their existence we cannot judge of, and we must take it solely on the authority of him who reports it. The credibility of the reporter becomes, therefore, the question. If he be worthy of credit, then we may believe that the spiritual world is a reality; if he be not worthy of credit, then we have no evidence of the existence of a world transcending the world of the senses and that of our own minds. By what means can the credibility of the reporter be established? By miracles addressed to the senses. The divine authority of him, whom God commissioned to speak to us in his name, Mr. Norton assures us, can be attested only by miraculous displays of his power. Miracles, if they occurred every day, would cease to be miracles, as we learn from the erudite Dr. Palfrey. Consequently, they can occur only at distant intervals. The great mass of mankind cannot, therefore, be eye-witnesses of miracles, and must depend on the record, which may be made of them. They can have no evidence of their actual occurrence, but the evidence of history, written or unwritten. But, of the truth of the history, as things go, they cannot judge. The generality of men must, then, rely on the testimony of the few scholars, who have leisure and means to investigate the proofs of its genuineness and authenticity. The fact of the occurrence of the miracles, by which we establish the authority of the reporter, whose authority must, in turn, establish the fact that off in the vast unknown, there is a spiritual world, in which we should believe, but whether it really exists, or not, we can never know, must be taken by the generality, on the authority of a few learned men. According to Mr. Norton, in his "Latest Form of Infidelity," already quoted, the condition of faith in Christianity, for the great mass of mankind, is "trust in the capacity and honesty of others." We must rely on the knowledge of others, which reliance "*may be called belief on trust, or belief on authority.*" [22]

This, it will be seen at once, leaves Christianity, for the great mass of mankind, a very doubtful matter; for who will assure us that these privileged few, this learned caste, are not themselves deceived, or at least deceivers? May not these scholars have an interest in deceiving us? Do they not derive rank, consideration, and wealth, from inducing us to believe what they tell us? And do they not, by inducing us to believe them, really become our masters? Let the people once entertain a suspicion of this sort, and you will need an inquisi-

[22] [Ed. Norton, *The Latest Form of Infidelity*, 58.]

tion, dungeons, fire, and sword, to maintain even a decent outward regard to religion. On the other hand, this doctrine of belief on authority, if once admitted, strikes at the root of all free faith in God, all voluntary obedience to his command; perpetuates the worst features of Catholicism, establishes a sacerdotal caste, and plunges the human race into the gloomiest and most debasing of all servitudes. It is essentially a skeptical doctrine, and strikes at the root of all faith. They, who support it, fear that the human mind, if left to its own free and honest action, would reject all religion, and they, therefore, seek to keep up religion by means of coercion. It is this doctrine, which has done and is doing so much mischief to the church. The worst of all heresies is that, which strikes out from the human soul the capacity to see and know God.[23]

But we cannot pursue this train of remark further. What we have thus far said, applies not we readily own, to all the individuals who belong to the Whig party. We have described the party, not according to the actual characters of its members, but according to the principle, which lies at the bottom of its reasoning, and its measures. We have seized the ultimate doctrine of the party, and pointed out the results, to which it must inevitably come, in the development of its idea, providing it meets, as we have said, with no counteracting force from without. Viewed as the opposite of the Democratic party, in the light of its own peculiar, fundamental principle, it is the anti-progress party, the anti-American party, and the anti-Christian party. Its complete triumph would be fatal to the progress of the race, to the development of American institutions, and to the continuance of the Christian religion. This fact shows at once that so long as there is an overruling Providence, there can be no ground to apprehend its success. It will always fail. Yesterday never returns. When yesterday becomes today, or today tomorrow, the Whigs will come into power throughout the United States, but not till then. The friends of progress, of reform, men whose faces are on the front side of their heads, and whose hearts are in the future, and whose souls leap up to meet the good that is to be, we are sure cannot, for one moment, dream of uniting their fortunes with those of the Whigs. Nothing remains for them, then, but to unite with the Democratic party, so called, and through that labor to carry the race forward to its destiny.

[23] [Ed. In his early Catholic period, i.e. from about 1845 to 1850, Brownson supported a form of this doctrine of credibility, trying to establish evidentiary foundations for the credibility of the Catholic Church; see, as an example of this approach, "The Church Against No-Church," *Brownson Quarterly Review* 7 (April,1845): 137-94.]

The Democratic party is the American party. That party is the American party which gathers round the idea, which it is the mission of American institutions to realize. The idea, which lies at the bottom of our institutions, is the supremacy of man. Here is to be established and developed not the sovereignty of the sacerdocy, not the sovereignty of the city or state, not the sovereignty of the king, not the sovereignty of the noble few, the high born, not that of the rich, nor yet that of estates, or corporations, but the sovereignty of man. Here man is not made for the state, but the state is instituted for man. The order of civilization, which it is ours to develop, is an order of civilization, in which things are subordinate, and subservient to humanity. Humanity, in all its integrity, is in every individual man. Then every individual man is to be raised to empire, so that all shall be, in the language of Scripture, "kings and priests." This is the American idea. This idea in the political world is translated by universal suffrage, that is, the equal right of every man to his voice in the choice of political agents, and through them, in the laws, which shall be enacted, or governmental measures, which shall be adopted. Now, is not the Democratic party the acknowledged universal suffrage party? From the first, it has regarded suffrage as a right belonging to every man, by virtue of his human nature, and it has contended that the people, taken individually, have not only the right, but, taken collectively, will exercise it judiciously, ultimately in accordance with the public good, and universal reason. The Whig party waives the question of right, contends that the people are not sufficiently enlightened to be *entrusted* with universal suffrage, and that we ought to educate them before we allow them the *privilege* of voting.

The Democratic party is also the patriotic party. It is the party jealous of national honor. The Whig party, composed in the main of business men, whose idea is property, not man, are insensible to national honor, when its maintenance requires the sacrifice of the facilities of trade or commerce. In their estimation, the national honor is well enough, when they are making large profits, and is endangered only when their chances of gain seem to be diminished. Hence it is that every measure taken to maintain the honor of the nation, or to enhance its real prosperity, has been taken by the Democratic party, amidst the most violent, and all but treasonable hostility of the Whigs. The democracy purchased Louisiana, and thus secured to trade the Mississippi, to agriculture an immense territory of unrivaled fertility, and to free institutions many millions of supporters. The democracy declared and sustained the war against Great Britain, in which we vindicated our national honor, and asserted the freedom of the seas.

And during its continuance, the Whig party were plotting treason with the enemy, refusing all support to the government of their country, and cutting off, as far as they could, its supplies. It was the democracy also that compelled France, much against the will of the opposition, to do us tardy justice for its spoliations of our commerce.

The Democratic party is the party of liberty. This is involved in the fact that it is the American party. The idea of this country is, we have said, the supremacy of man. This supremacy is attained only by the broadest freedom. The American idea, under another aspect, then, is that of liberty. The truly American party always rallies around the quickening idea of liberty. No man can have the hardihood to pretend that liberty is the idea, the Whigs are struggling to bring out. The Whig party is not particularly anxious to sustain or extend liberty, even according to its own account. Its sole objects, taken as its own witness, are the preservation of the Union of the states, and the support of the credit system. In this, it is true to itself. It is the business party of the country, and it is, and must be true to its idea. The Union of the states was, and is desirable, almost solely on account of the interests of trade and commerce. It facilitates trade between the different states, and gives us an imposing aspect, which favors our foreign commerce. Take away the aid, which the Union of the states gives to trade and commerce, and the Whigs would estimate its value somewhat below par. Their cry about the preservation of the Union, does not, then, proceed from their anxiety to maintain freedom, but to preserve certain advantages to trade. It is in relation to its bearing on business operations that they wish to sustain the credit system. So that their dominant idea, according to their own showing, is the preservation or increase of facilities for business operations. They pursue business, of course, for the purpose of accumulating property. So in the last analysis the dominant idea of the Whigs is not MAN, but PROPERTY; and the contest between them and the democracy was rightly declared by Mr. Benton to be a contest between MAN and MONEY.[24]

As the Whig party is the party seeking to give predominance not to the idea of freedom, but to the idea of property, the protection of which Locke declares to be the end of government, it follows, that the Democratic party is the party of freedom, or else we have no such party in this country. Its history proves that it is. In all controversies, it takes the side of liberty. In the convention which framed the fed-

[24] [Ed. Thomas Hart Benton (1782-1858) was United States Senator of Missouri (1821-51) who led the fight in the United States Senate against a national bank. Like Brownson, he was a hard-money man and supported Martin Van Buren during the presidential race of 1840.]

eral Constitution, it opposed centralism, and defended state rights. In the conventions which have framed our state constitutions, it has always favored those clauses, which leave the most liberty to the people, and best protect the rights of the individual. In the great struggle between the aristocratic and democratic elements of European society, which broke out in the French Revolution, and which has been continued, with various success, even to our own times, it has always sympathized with the people, and rejoiced in their successes. Its sympathies were with France, so long as France represented the democracy; while the Whigs, or Federalists, sympathized with England, as the representative of the aristocracy. In the late unsuccessful struggle of the Canadians for independence, the Democratic party has been true to its idea of liberty.[25] It has given them its sympathies and its prayers, and trusts yet to see the Canadas a free and independent nation. The day of emancipation yet lingers, but it will come, and we shall have a great and noble people for our northern neighbor.

The Democratic party has always been faithful to freedom of mind and conscience, the basis of all freedom. It has always opposed everything even approaching a religious establishment, and contended that man's intercourse with his Maker should be free and voluntary. It has opposed all test laws and uniformly frowned upon every effort to molest a man for his opinions. It inserted in the federal Constitution the amendments, which forbid Congress to establish a religion, or to pass any law prohibiting freedom of speech, or of the press. It opposed the elder Adams and his party, because, in their Alien and Sedition Laws, they proved themselves the enemies of free thought, and free utterance;[26] and it raised Thomas Jefferson to the presidential chair, because he was the unflinching friend of freedom of mind. It has always said, with Milton, "Let truth and falsehood grapple. Who ever knew truth put to the worse in free and open encounter? Her confuting is the best and surest suppressing."[27]

[25] [Ed. Brownson is referring to the Papineau-Mackenzie Rebellion of 1837 in which Louis Joseph Papineau (1786-1871), French-Canadian political leader, and William Lyon Mackenzie (1795-1861), journalist and political insurgent of Ontario, joined forces and decided on an armed rebellion against British control in order to establish a republican form of government in Canada. The rebels were decisively beaten in December of 1837.]

[26] [Ed. Brownson is referring to the Alien and Sedition Acts of 1798, passed by Congress under President John Adams' term. One of those acts, passed on July 14, imposed severe penalties on those who criticized the government and thereby condemned "any false, scandalous and malicious writing."]

[27] [Ed. John Milton, *Areopagitica* (1644). See the *Complete Prose Works of John Milton*, ed. Douglas Bush, et al., 5 vols. (New Haven: Yale University Press, 1959), 2:561. Milton's first line reads "Let her" (meaning "truth"), and he has "wors" for Brownson's "worse." The *Areopagitica* was Milton's celebrated defense of the freedom of the press.]

The Democratic party is the Christian party. Christianity is a revelation of God's mercy to man. It is always on the side of freedom and humanity. It addresses man as endowed with the capacity to judge of himself what is or is not right. Democracy is based on the fact that man does really possess this capacity. Christianity, by addressing itself to all men, necessarily recognizes this capacity in every man; democracy, by defending universal suffrage, does the same. Christianity values man for his simple humanity, not for his trappings, the accidents of birth, wealth, or position; so does democracy. Christianity, aside from its design to fit the individual for communion with the blest after death, seeks to introduce a new order of things on the earth, to exalt the humble, abash the proud, to establish the reign of justice, and enable every man to "sit under his own vine and fig tree, with none to molest or make afraid" [Mic 4:4]; and, who knows not that this is the aim and tendency of the Democratic party?

Christianity recognizes God as the only rightful sovereign and regards all government not founded by him as usurpation. Man is bound to obey God, and God only. Therefore, it commands us to call no man master on earth, for one is our master in heaven. Translated into the language of politics, this teaches us that government is legitimate, and laws are obligatory only as they represent the will of God, that is, the decrees of eternal and immutable justice. Is not this the doctrine of the Democratic party? Jefferson, a good authority on this point, says, "the will of the majority must govern, but in order to govern rightfully, it must be just."[28] The orations and addresses named at the head of this article, as well as several others now lying before us, delivered by democrats on the last anniversary of our independence, with one accord, assert the supremacy of justice; and the whole party adopts the definition of democracy, given in a lecture by the historian of the United States; "Democracy is Eternal Justice ruling through the People."[29] Justice is the political name of God. The reign of justice is the reign of God; and in defining democracy to be Eternal Justice ruling through the people, we identify the doctrine of the Democratic party with the doctrine of the New Testament, namely, that government is of divine ordination, and in all legitimate governments God is king.

[28] [Ed. Unable to identify the quotation. The concept is evident throughout Jefferson's works.]

[29] [Ed. Unable to identify the exact quotation. The concept itself, though, is evident in a number of George Bancroft's works, including *An Oration Delivered before the Democracy of Springfield and Neighboring Towns, July 4, 1836* (Springfield: George and Charles Merriam, 1836).]

The idea of justice, in all its length and breadth, is undoubtedly in every man; but it exists in the individual mixed up with much, which belongs to the individual, rather than to the race. The individual, therefore, cannot be a safe interpreter of justice. For the voice of eternal justice he may mistake the voice of his own passions or interests. We must, therefore, listen to the voice of the race. The race can agree only in that which is universal, invariable, and eternal, only in justice and truth. Hence, the unanimous assent of the race is justly regarded as the highest evidence of truth.[30] In order, then, to make as near an approach as possible to the decrees of eternal justice, we must place the government, not in the hands of one man, not in the hands of a few men, nor in the hands of a class, corporation, or estate, but in the hands of the whole people, whose voice will always be our best representative of the voice of the race, and whose decisions are the nearest approximation a nation can make to the decisions of justice itself. Rightly, then, is democracy defined eternal justice ruling through the people. Rightly, too, is the Democratic party termed the Christian party, since it, like Christianity, acknowledges God alone as the rightful sovereign, and labors incessantly to wrest the government from the hands of individuals, classes, castes, estates, corporations, and to place it in the hands of the whole people, in their character of simple human beings, so that justice may reign on the earth.

The Democratic party is the party of progress. This is involved in what has already been said. A party gathers round an idea, or principle, which is its life, its soul. That idea it can never abandon, and live; nor can it ever receive a new idea without losing its identity. If left to itself, it will unfold, exhaust its idea; and having done this, it dies. Thus, English Whiggism, having exhausted its original idea,

[30] [Ed. This sounds very much like the traditionalism of the early Félicité Robert de Lamennais (1782-1854), seeking certitude or the only criterion of truth in the "*sens commun*" or general reason of the human race. Brownson knew something of Lamennais' views but whether or not he had read his *Essai sur l'indifférence en matière de religion* (1818) is unclear. If he had read this early Lamennais essay he certainly would not have agreed with him that toleration was an evil, nor would he have agreed entirely with the idea that the individual is dependent upon the community (or human race) for a knowledge of the truth. At this time Brownson had a much more progressive or developmental view of revelation than did the early Lamennais. Nonetheless, Brownson had a sympathy for universal consent as a criterion for truth that was analogous to that of Lamennais. More than likely Brownson received his knowledge of French traditionalism from Cousin who had argued against it in his second edition of *Fragmens philosophiques* (Paris: Ladrange, 1833).]

having found its euthanasia, in the Reform Bill,[31] has gone the way of all the earth, and is suffered to lie in state still, merely because neither Tories nor Radicals are prepared to assume the responsibility of heirs, and give it burial. The Whigs in this country are demonstrating the same law. The idea, around which they gather, is offensive to a majority of the American people. This the more discerning of our Whig friends perceive, and, therefore, they would fain change the doctrines of the party. They have even tried to make it pass for the Democratic party. Vain efforts! They may change its name, receive into its ranks many, who once thought themselves republicans, and submit to be led on by men, who once enjoyed the confidence of the democracy; but nothing can change its character; its identity remains; and your Lincolns, Seldens, Duanes, Verplancks, Tallmages, and Riveses,[32] who generously undertake to give it a democratic aspect, can change nothing in its principles or direction, but are themselves swept away by its resistless current,

> To that bourne, whence no traveller returns.[33]

The idea of the Whig party is one, which cannot, in this country, rise to empire, because it is not broad enough to comprehend the work which God has given us to do. Always, therefore, will it be in the minor-

[31] [Ed. Brownson is referring to the British Parliament's Reform Act of 1832, which extended the vote, previously the preserve of the landed class, to the more prosperous middle classes. Some like Lord John Russell thought the reform would render further reforms superfluous, and hence he was tagged "Finality Jack."]

[32] [Ed. Brownson is most likely referring to the following: Levi Lincoln (1782-1868) was governor of Massachusetts (1825-34), a United States Whig Representative from Massachusetts (1834-41), and a political leader who had helped transform "right wing Jeffersonianism into the National Republican party" (on this, see, Arthur Schlesinger, Jr., *The Age of Jackson*, 144); I was unable to identify Selden; William J. Duane (1780-1865), a secretary of the Treasury under President Jackson who was fired by Jackson because he refused to go along with the decision to withdraw federal funds from the National Bank; Gulian Crommelin Verplanck (1786-1870), a United States Representative from New York who had been a Federalist but became a Whig after having lost confidence in President Jackson and Jacksonian Democracy; Nathaniel Pitcher Tallmadge (1795-1864), a conservative Democratic Senator from New York (1833-44) who opposed many Jacksonian Democratic policies, especially on a National Bank, and eventually sided with Whigs on many economic issues; William Cabell Rives (1793-1868), a United States Senator from Virginia (1832-34; 1836-45) who initially had supported the Jacksonian position on a National Bank but in the late 1830s opposed President Martin Van Buren's subtreasury plan, siding to some extent with other conservative Democrats and Whigs. Brownson saw all of these men as political turncoats.]

[33] [Ed. Percy Bysshe Shelley, *An Address to the People on the Death of Princess Charlotte* (1817), paragraph 3.]

ity, or if not absolutely in the minority, so torn by intestine divisions, and so destitute of "available" leaders that it must uniformly fail of success.

The Democratic party is governed by the same law. It can receive no new idea and it must share the fortunes of the idea with which it originally started. But there is a difference between the two parties. The Whig party gathered around an idea, which is of a limited and transient nature; the Democratic party rallied round an idea, which is universal, immutable, and eternal. The Whig seized upon one of the accidents of humanity, the democrat upon humanity itself. The democrat planted himself in the center of the vast globe of humanity, the Whig placed himself on the circumference, where he hangs as a foreign substance, and from which he must be thrown the moment the globe revolves. The great idea of the Democratic party is, as we have shown, under one aspect, the supremacy of man over his accidents, under another aspect, the reign of eternal justice. The two aspects are, in fact, one and the same. The mission of the Democratic party is to unfold the great idea of justice, and reduce it to practice in all man's social and political relations. It stands, therefore, not as the representative of a fraction of the race, but of the race itself, and, therefore, like the race, it is immortal. This great idea of justice the party is destined to realize. From this work it cannot withdraw itself, even if it would. Its leaders may be false to it, and seek to betray it; but it leaves them by the way, and with or without new leaders, continues its march. No matter how high a rank a man may have held in its estimation, the moment he proves false to the mission of the party, he is left, though leaving him be like plucking out a right eye, or cutting off a right hand. Nothing from within can betray it or divert it from its onward course. Many of the most active members of the Whig party were once in its ranks, but it has not missed them. It is never in want of a man competent to lead on its forces, nor of an "available" candidate for its suffrages. A panic may now and then occur, and produce a momentary confusion, but it instantly recovers itself, reestablishes order, and takes up its line of march, ready to grapple with any force it may meet.

Now as the party, according to the general laws of party, must go on unfolding its idea, and as that idea is universal and all-comprehensive, we say truly that it is the party of progress. Justice is its idea, and this idea it must unfold, and this idea in its unfolding must reach all the reforms the friends of progress can desire. Progress is simply the better and fuller application of justice to our social and political relations. All the progress, which in the very nature of things now can be, must come from the unfolding of the idea which constitutes the life and soul of the Democratic party. Then as friends of progress you should support that party, and contribute what you can to help it onward in the development and application of its general principles.

Are you contending for universal education? What principle will establish a true system of universal education, but that which declares the supremacy of man over money, and recognizes man in all his integrity in every individual man? Are you the advocate of the rights of woman? How will you succeed but by appealing to the great principle of the democracy that right is paramount to might? Are you a non-resistant, a peaceman? What means have you to compass your ends, but by aiding the democracy to introduce the rule of justice into all public affairs? Are you an advocate for the workingman, anxious to secure to honest industry its due reward, and to the laborer his true social position? You must do it by means of that party which struggles to raise up universal humanity, to abolish all privilege, and to place the government in the hands of MAN, instead of MONEY. Are you an abolitionist, and would you free the slave? What party puts forth general principles which in their gradual unfolding must break every unjust bond, and set every captive free? The day of emancipation is not yet. It were useless to emancipate the slave today because we should be merely changing the form not the substance of his slavery. But the Democratic party puts forth principles, which must in the end abolish slavery, and do it too at the very day, the very hour, when it can be done with advantage to the cause of freedom, of justice. Slavery is doomed; man will not always tyrannize over man. There are causes at work, which will free the slave, and free him too with the consent and to the joy of his master. Let these causes work on, and do not murmur because their full effects are not realized today. God doubtless could have made the world in one day, but we are told that he chose to employ six days in creating it. The seed is not sown and the corn harvested the same day. Be sure that you have principles in operation that will effect your work, and you may retain your composure. The Democratic party embraces the idea of universal freedom to universal man, and it will realize this idea, just as fast as we can urge onward the general progress of humanity, and no faster.

We have now given some of the reasons why reformers should sustain the Democratic party. That party embraces the general principles of liberty, of progress, which include within them, as the oak is included in the acorn, all possible reforms. It represents today, in this Western world, entire humanity, and as such has a right to demand the hearty cooperation of every true friend of his race. We see many and essential reforms, for which we have labored, and still labor, which it has not yet taken up; but we see that, following its principles, obeying the high laws to which in God's providence it is subjected, it must and will take them up in due time, and in due order. Today it is engaged in rescuing the government from the grasp of associated wealth, which it will do by adopting the Independent Treasury Bill, and causing the revenues of the country to be collected and disbursed in gold and silver. When it has effected this, it will proceed to reform the banking system as it exists in the states. In what way it will reform the system, as the moment for acting has not yet come, it is not wholly agreed. Whether it will do it, by abolishing all banks and returning to an exclusively metallic currency, as is the wish of some, or by instituting a system of free banking, as is the wish of a still greater number, or by devising a new scheme based upon a combination of the elements of free banking with what may be termed government banking, as we ourselves should propose, it is at this moment impossible to determine; but be it as it may, the party will dispose of the question in that way which shall best advance the cause of individual freedom and national prosperity. This question disposed of, the party will proceed to reform the judiciary, and to revise our criminal code. Then it will proceed to other reforms which perhaps have not yet been dreamed of save by a few visionaries, who would gain nothing but a smile of compassion were they to tell their dreams. Where it will stop we know not; for we are not able to set bounds to the spirit of improvement, or to say where the progress of the race is to be arrested. We speak not as the seer, but as the philosopher, who, from the causes he sees in operation, and which he understands, infers the effects which must inevitably follow, unless God changes the order of his providence. The reforms which the party effects in legislation, the principles which it infuses into public institutions, will gradually pass into social life, form our manners, our morals, and determine our social relations and intercourse.

Sinking now the editor and speaking in my own name I may say, here is my view of the Democratic party, and here are my reasons for enrolling myself among its members. I have formed this view not hastily, nor without considerable reflection; I have adopted it only as I have been compelled by my general principles of politics, religion, and philosophy. I have never been a partisan. I have, it is true, always been a democrat. I sucked in democracy with my mother's milk; I imbibed a feeling and a love of independence, as I roamed a child over the Green Hills, or clambered up the scarped rocks, or plunged in the dark forests of my early home. I could not have been a Green Mountain Boy, bred in a mountain home, in what may one day be regarded as the Switzerland of America, without cherishing a free spirit, and becoming the friend of the "largest liberty." I have always been found on the side of freedom in its widest signification. To my love of it I have given years of intense study, sacrificed ease, sometimes reputation, pecuniary independence, and professional success. But, except on rare occasions, I have never acted with the Democratic party so called. I have had many prejudices against it, and against its prominent members. I have thought it too intent on office, on maintaining itself as a party, and too indifferent to the progress and application of free principles. It may readily be believed, then, that I have not given in my adhesion, so unequivocally, without having been compelled by, what have seemed to me, cogent reasons. These reasons are given to some extent in this article. They are to me weighty and sufficient. They may be carped at, they may be denied; but I must give up all the confidence I have hitherto placed in religion or philosophy, before I can believe they can be successfully refuted. I am therefore compelled, not merely to declare myself a Democrat, but a Democrat, if you will, in a party sense. I take my stand with the Democratic party. Its fortunes, whatever they may be, I am content to share. If I can in any way aid it onward and assist it in carrying out its principles, my ambition and my conscience will be satisfied. I say this in no partisan spirit, but in obedience to those broad principles of freedom, to which, with or without success, my life has thus far been devoted. I do this because I am required to do it by my love of freedom and of man, because through this party, and this party only, can be carried out into all the relations of life those great principles of justice, on which the institutions of this country are based. Through this party it is possible to reach humanity; with it is bound up the cause of freedom in this country, on this continent, and throughout the world.

INDEX OF BIBLICAL REFERENCES

INDEX OF NAMES AND SUBJECTS

B

C

D

E

F

H

M

N

Q

R

T